D1754121

Joseph Jung
From Schweizerische Kreditanstalt to Credit Suisse Group

Joseph Jung

From Schweizerische Kreditanstalt to Credit Suisse Group
The History of a Bank

NZZ Verlag

© 2000, Credit Suisse Group, Zurich
Verlag Neue Zürcher Zeitung, Zurich

Translated by James Knight, Leamington Spa, from the original German 'Von der Schweizerischen Kreditanstalt zur Credit Suisse Group. Eine Bankengeschichte', which was first published in May 2000

Proof reading: Martin Trachsler, Alfred Schaufelberger, Edgar Haberthür, Alison Lopez
Design: Heinz Egli
Layout: Markus Fasnacht, Robert Ohmayer
Charts: Roger Turin, Nassenwil ZH
Printing: NZZ Fretz AG, Schlieren
Binding: Buchbinderei Burkhardt AG, Mönchaltorf
ISBN 3-85823-891-0
Printed in Switzerland

Contents

Foreword by Rainer E. Gut 9
Introduction 11

Part One: Events   13

A historical overview of Switzerland as a banking center 15
A late start, but now a leading international banking center 16
From the 18th century to 1914: entering the modern era 17
    The Golden Age of private banks in the 18th century 17
    New banks emerge: from Bank Leu (1775) to the savings banks (Sparkassen)
    and joint-stock banks (Aktienbanken) 18
    After 1848: commercial banks, issuing banks and co-operative banks battle it out 23
    Consolidation, diversification and the first mergers up to 1914 29
From 1914 to the present day: advancement despite setbacks 34
    Ups and downs for the major banks and cantonal banks 34
    The post-1945 boom: a surging economy and the expansion of foreign operations 37
    Deregulation and liberalization: new structures emerge in the 1980s and 1990s 39

**Schweizerische Kreditanstalt: from a Zurich commercial and industrial bank
to a global financial services company** 43
SKA's first years in the context of Swiss economic history 44
    Conflicts between cantonal and global perspectives 44
    Regional, national and business motives 44
    SKA's foundation in 1856: Swiss money for Swiss railways 47
1856–1914: growing pains 49
    Trial and error instead of strategy 49
    Railways, shares and factories 51
    Competition or co-operation? 68
1914–1945: conflicts, crises and credit 69
    First World War provides a harsh test 70
    Uncertain inter-war years 71
    Business interests during the Second World War: caught between adapting
    to political circumstances and protecting customers' interests 77
1945–1976: reticence and stagnation 91
    Losing ground: SKA in competition with the other major banks 91
    Fewer risks in domestic business 92
    Hesitant moves into international markets 95
1977–1996: restructuring and growth 97
    A new dynamic 97
    Restructurings 98
    Expansion in Switzerland and abroad 102
From CS Holding to Credit Suisse Group 105

Part Two: Strategic Pillars	111

The core Swiss market 113
The 1970s: SKA at a crossroads 114
    The need for a new beginning 114
    Deposit business 116
    Mortgage business 119
    Branches 121
    Underwriting business 124
The 1990s: breakthrough 129
    Increasing pressure to restructure 129
    The first coup: the takeover of Bank Leu 131
    Riding to the rescue: the acquisition of EKO Bank Olten 136
    'The opportunity of the century': union with SVB 137
    An ideal complement: the acquisition of Neue Aargauer Bank 142
A restructured Swiss core market 144
    Market leader in savings and investments 144
    Attempted alliance between CS Holding and SBG 149

Global investment banking 155
Expansion in the global arena 156
    Hesitant steps up to the end of the 1950s 157
    Acceleration in the 1960s and 1970s 159
    Conditions change and expansion explodes at the end of the 1970s 160
    The 1990s: tapping into new markets 167
From White Weld to Credit Suisse First Boston 172
    The beginnings 172
    The Eurobond market 172
    Alliance with First Boston 182
    Geographical and cultural differences 188
    New opportunities and risks 192
    Big Three or Big Four? 199

Allfinanz 209
Cooperation between a bank and an insurer in the 19th century:
    Schweizerische Kreditanstalt/Rentenanstalt 211
Financial services in the 20th century 218
    The USA leads the way 218
    Customers' attitude to investment 220
    Allfinanz activities in Switzerland 221
Allfinanz at SKA 223
    On the way to CS Life 223
    Dynamic development 225
Merger between Winterthur and Credit Suisse Group 227
    Integration and new prospects 228
    Focusing on strengths in European Allfinanz 229
    Personal Financial Services (PFS) 231

Part Three: A New Paradigm 233

Mentalities and images 235
The Chiasso Affair. 245
Testing times for the Swiss banking industry 287
The social profile of executive board members 301
Human resources management 315
Organizational and management structure. 327
Optimization as a constant of SKA's culture 339
From agreements and protectionism to competition 357
Marketing and communication. 373

Outlook and review: the financial services industry in flux 405
By Lukas Mühlemann

Appendices 411

Timeline 412
Members of the executive board of Schweizerische Kreditanstalt (1856–1996) 414
List of tables 418
List of charts 419
Glossary of abbreviations. 420
Notes 422
Sources and bibliography 439
Picture credits. 445
Acknowledgements 446

Foreword

We are used to seeing company histories published to coincide with anniversaries. The purpose of such histories is clear: only if the past has been documented and dealt with can the celebrations decently begin. It has been, and still is, a matter of little importance in these cases that alongside the genuine reappraisals, much of the real story is left out or rewritten. In recent years, we Swiss banks have seen only too clearly where such a cavalier approach to history can lead. The debate about dormant accounts has forced us to confront a past which is not familiar from our own history books, and which for a long time we simply did not want to acknowledge.

A good reason for bringing this book out now, therefore, is precisely that we do not have an anniversary to celebrate, meaning that we can look back at our history with a somewhat more objective, and occasionally self-critical, eye. The point is not to indulge in the luxury of hindsight and criticize from a safe distance those events and decisions which can now be seen to have been wrong or inadequate. It is all too easy to find fault with all the things that could have been done much better, and in so doing to ignore the historical circumstances. However, I believe that a genuine engagement with our own history can help us to cope better with the present and to approach the challenges of the future with more composure.

Another reason why now is a good time for this book to appear, I believe, is because the banks, and indeed the whole financial services industry, find themselves in the middle of a dramatic process of change – a process which is by no means over. This change is calling into question things that only a few years ago seemed unshakable, forcing us to make a careful appraisal of where we have come from and where we are going. We do not just want to be swept along by rapidly changing operating conditions, but want to be in a position where we can look forward and realize our own aims with true conviction. A better understanding of our own history can only help.

The historian Joseph Jung has resisted the temptation to rewrite history. However, with characteristic persistence, he has reassessed the various events and phases of our story and put them into a wider context. His work is carefully backed up by numerous sources, by intensive archive study and, above all, by a large number of conversations with contemporary witnesses. The result is a clear portrayal of events, of successes and failures, of great foresight and of undistinguished short-termism. All of these things can be found in the history of Schweizerische Kreditanstalt, and thus of today's Credit Suisse Group. I am very grateful to Joseph Jung for all he has done.

What else remains to be said? Certainly it is worth acknowledging that the development of a company is determined not only by well thought-through strategies and long-term planning, but also by the practical actions of all its employees. This book is thus also dedicated to those of you that have helped to write the real history of SKA. What also remains is the example of the people – Alfred Escher foremost among them – who with courage, a willingness to take risks and with entrepreneurial vision have charted the course of Schweizerische Kreditanstalt since 1856. Everyone whose decision-making and commitment are currently helping to secure a successful future for Credit Suisse Group owes a debt of gratitude to these people.

Zurich, March 2000

Rainer E. Gut
Chairman of the Board of Directors
of Credit Suisse Group

Introduction

If one of a company's principal strategic aims is to ensure sustained corporate development, that company needs to review its own history. Nowadays, a considered approach to business has to include an acknowledgement of historical responsibility; and historical responsibility can only be taken on by corporations that know their history. It was the recognition of this fact that in 1996 prompted the executive board of Schweizerische Kreditanstalt to give me, a historian, the following mandate:

- To view and order the documents in the bank's archives and to organize them using professional techniques into a new central corporate archive.
- Thereafter to prepare a history of the bank during the Second World War, and subsequently an overall history of Credit Suisse.

This mandate, which in the wake of the restructuring that was to follow shortly afterwards was extended to include the new Credit Suisse Group, was prompted by two fundamental considerations. Firstly, the bank's directors and executives were adamant that they wanted to actively tackle the questions – old ones and ones which were only then beginning to emerge – surrounding the Second World War, and thus to draw up a definitive account of the period. Secondly, there was a desire to assemble the relevant sources so as to facilitate the production of subsequent monographs on individual institutions and companies within the Credit Suisse Group.

As soon as the research required by this mandate was begun, it became clear that a wider perspective was required before real work on the specific history of the bank could be contemplated. The fact that there was no systematic literature on key aspects of Swiss banking history left no alternative but to open up the narrowly defined corporate history to include the national and international context that helped to determine that history. In the light of this consideration, at the beginning of May 1998, the chairman of the board of directors and the executive board of Credit Suisse Group approved a research concept, the initial results of which were to be summarized in an introductory study of the bank's strategic development. Starting with Schweizerische Kreditanstalt (SKA), this study should at the same time trace the bank's development into CS Holding and into today's Credit Suisse Group, and highlight the significance of the individual companies involved in this process of development.

This work is essentially historical, but results from a broad interdisciplinary collaboration. Consequently, the view it takes ranges between the perspectives of economic history, cultural history, psychological history (in the sense of prevailing mentalities), and social history. These different perspectives determine not only the content, but also the structure of the book.

The results of the research are divided into three sections:

- The first section explores the relevant historical events and the connections between them.
- The second section looks at the three strategic pillars which have underpinned the development of Schweizerische Kreditanstalt since the 1970s, and which constitute the guiding lights for Credit Suisse Group: the core Swiss market, global investment banking and Allfinanz.
- The third section is devoted to the process which, after the Chiasso Affair of 1977, transformed the conservative, elitist Zurich bank into a modern, dynamic Swiss bank, and which laid the foundations for the metamorphosis of Schweizerische Kreditanstalt into the international financial services conglomerate, Credit Suisse Group.

Because of this structure, some events are inevitably mentioned more than once in the book so that they can be examined and interpreted from different historical perspectives.

From the beginning, the research project was dependent on original sources. Without such texts as the minutes from the various management meetings and the annual reports, this book could never have been written. However, the fact that the corporate archive was being restructured in parallel with the preparation of this corporate history allowed me to refer to a wealth of material previously unseen by researchers. This includes, for example, records from the accounting and legal departments, as well as strategy papers and correspondence. A special mention should be given to the oral history that I was able to use: the large number of conversations I had with former and current personnel from the different hierarchical levels of the various banks provided a wealth of important information.

The fact that such a study has been written 'internally' will inevitably attract questions about its impartiality. Can a company history written by the company itself fulfill the methodological requirements of genuine academic study? If scientific rigor is the absolute criterion for the quality of a historical study, it should not matter whether the research is done within or outside the company. The goal of all research must be to get as close as possible to the actual events and to the historical truth. A key prerequisite for achieving this goal is to have all the necessary sources at one's disposal. In the case of this book, the creation of Credit Suisse Group's central corporate archive provided just such a wealth of sources. A second and no less important prerequisite for any academic enterprise is that it be unconstrained by any personal or corporate interests. This prerequisite was also met in full.

I would like to thank Rainer E. Gut, chairman of the board of directors of Credit Suisse Group, for granting me this indispensable freedom, and also for the opportunity to publish the results of my research in this form.

Zurich, January 2000   Joseph Jung

Part One: Events

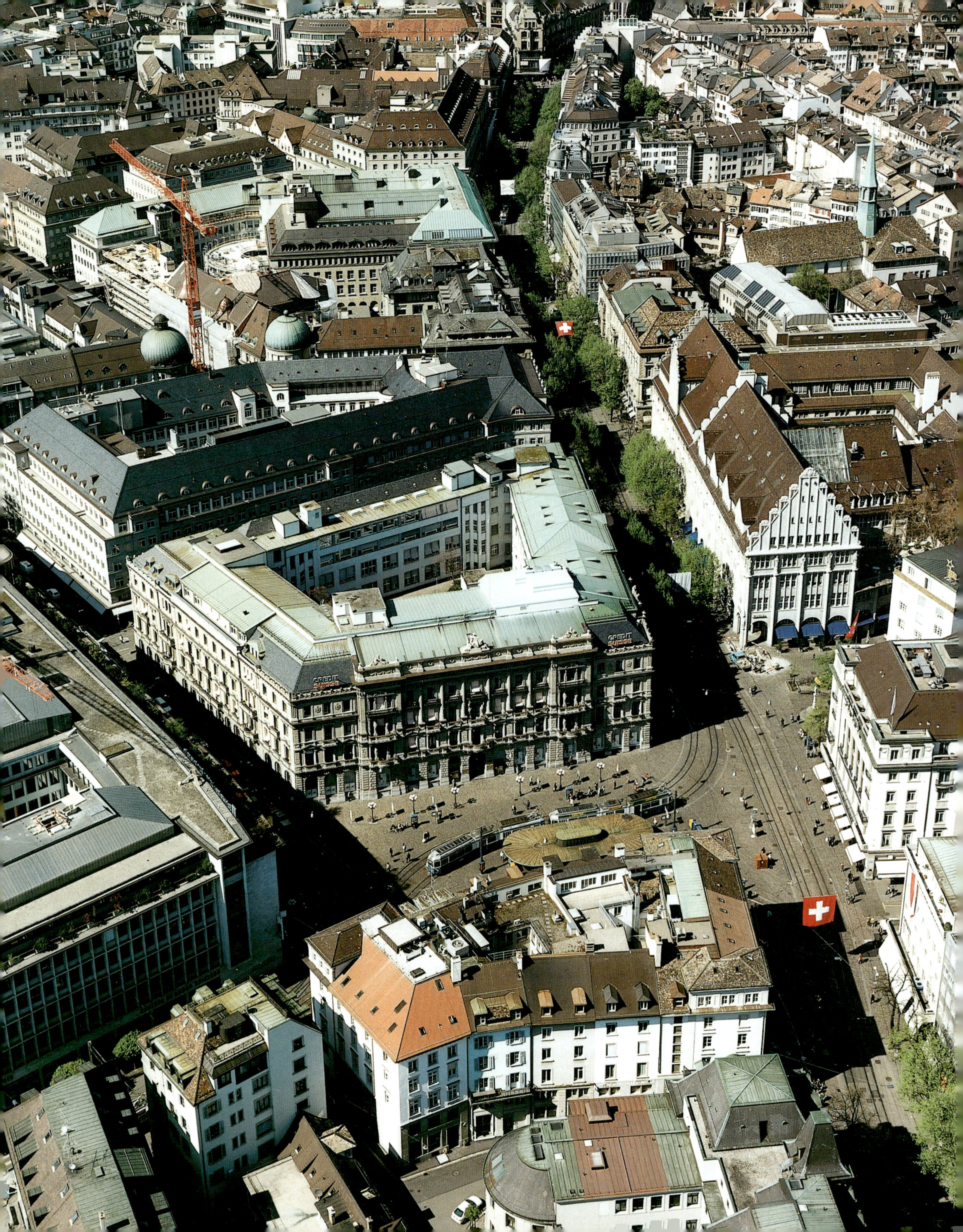
CREDIT
SUISSE

A historical overview of Switzerland as a banking center

The process of development that eventually created Switzerland's modern banking system began in the middle of the 18th century. Previously, banking had been dominated by so-called 'Stadtwechsel' (city exchequers) and private banks, which concentrated on very specific banking disciplines. Then, in an initial growth phase, new types of institution, such as savings banks and mortgage banks, emerged. In a second phase – from the 1830s onwards – these were joined by cantonal banks and commercial banks organized as joint-stock companies (Aktiengesellschaften). Influenced by what was going on abroad, larger commercial banks began to spring up in all parts of the country from 1853 onwards; these included what were to become the major Swiss banks. The wave of new bank start-ups between the middle of the 19th century and 1880 was followed by a period of slower growth. Then the establishment of the Swiss National Bank in 1905 led to the first reduction in the number of Swiss banking institutions.

The period between 1914 and 1945 brought two world wars, an economic boom and an economic crisis. By the end of the Second World War only five of the original eight major banks remained. In the 1960s, Switzerland grew to become one of the leading international centers of banking and finance. Around 1990, a phase of deregulation and concentration began, and another shake-up in the Swiss banking industry cut the number of major banks still further until only two were left. However, these two – Credit Suisse Group and UBS – have grown in size and strength and, as internationally active banks, are well equipped to tackle the challenges of the future

Aerial view of Zurich's Paradeplatz looking towards the main railway station. Photo taken in 1998.

A late start, but now a leading international banking center

The beginnings: measured, considered, modest.

As long as Switzerland was structured as a federation of states, there could be no question of a unified Swiss banking system. Banks were very much rooted in their local communities. Despite this, they were quick to engage in international business, though as a rule this was restricted to asset management for the European nobility and collaboration in the commercial business of the original federated cantons. Even after the structures of the Swiss Confederation were thoroughly overhauled in 1848, a lot of banking business went on in the same old way. Any ideas, innovations and new ways of thinking tended to come to Switzerland from abroad and were then carefully adapted to Swiss conditions.

While many major banks, the Midland Bank in the United Kingdom or Crédit Lyonnais in France for instance, had already transformed themselves into national institutions, the Swiss commercial banks remained in the hands of local elites for a long time.[1] Interestingly, the initiative to develop a Swiss banking and insurance industry, the drive to open up the country through the construction of railways, and the move towards industrialization in general came not from the public but from the private sector.

The emergence of the major banks in the second half of the 19th century did not grant the Swiss automatic entry to the premier league of international finance, since even these new institutions were still predominantly focused on the domestic market. At the start of the 20th century the Swiss financial center grew in stature thanks to more intensive co-operation with other countries, and to a process of concentration that focused the financial industry's strengths more effectively. The crisis that broke out in 1930 brought this boom period to a premature end and forced the Swiss banks to redirect their energies back to the domestic market. Finally, during the economic boom that followed the Second World War, the Swiss financial center embarked upon the upward march that would for a time make it the third most important financial hub in the world.

The development of an internationally significant financial industry was made possible by the fact that from the beginning of the 20th century, the individual Swiss financial centers started to grow closer together. This meant that the qualities that had already set Switzerland apart could come fully into play. Most important of all was the stability that assured people that operating conditions in Switzerland could be relied upon. The country's far-sighted political solution to the challenges presented by its heterogeneous linguistic and cultural mix created the atmosphere of confidence without which no financial center could develop.

After the Second World War ended and the Cold War began, Switzerland, with its banking secrecy and liberal tax regime, proved to be an ideal destination for international capital. After some delay, the banking sector also began to look for business beyond Switzerland's borders. In an attempt to win new markets in other countries, the major banks took the decision to develop an international network of branches and representative offices.

What made Switzerland attractive as a financial center?

- Neutral status recognized under international law since 1815
- No involvement in military conflict since the federal state was established in 1848
- Democratic tradition
- Stable economic and political conditions thanks to well-functioning cooperation between a consensus government and a parliament dominated by conservative moderates
- Plentiful supply of capital, thanks not least to the high savings rate
- Social stability
- Multilingual society
- Banking secrecy
- Liberal tax regime

Contribution made by banks to GDP (1998)

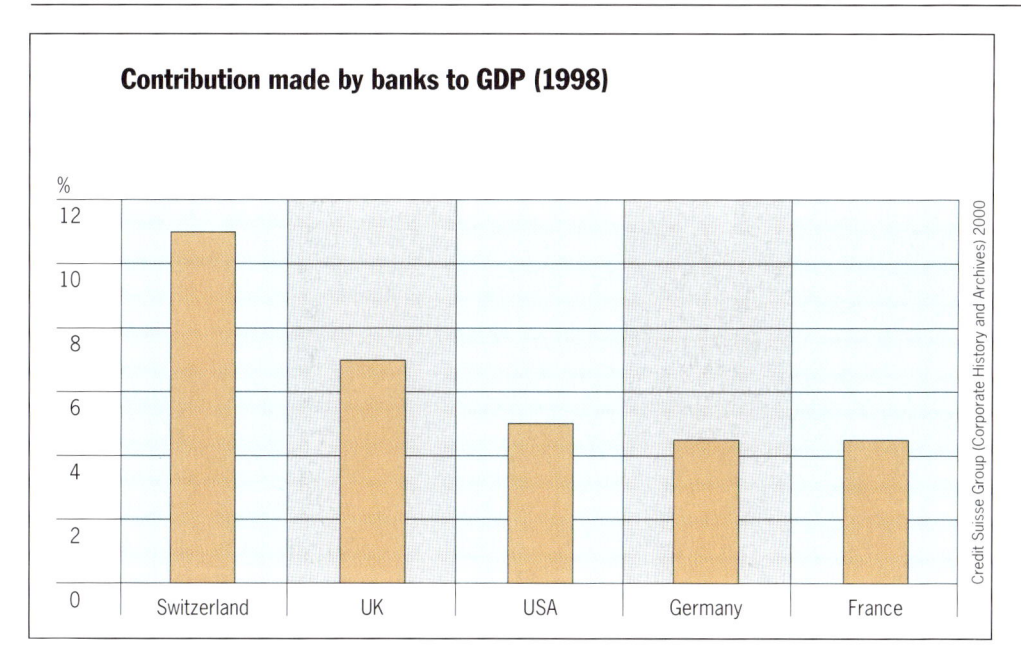

Country	%
Switzerland	~11.5
UK	~7
USA	~5.5
Germany	~5
France	~5

Credit Suisse Group (Corporate History and Archives) 2000

Today, in an increasingly globalized world, where national boundaries are becoming irrelevant – especially from an economic perspective – the two remaining major Swiss banks have managed to break out of the confines of their domestic markets and to integrate other corporate cultures. At the same time, however, they have safeguarded their Swiss identity.[2]

From the 18th century to 1914: entering the modern era

The Golden Age of private banks in the 18th century

During the 18th century, a time of Absolutism, the ruling houses that controlled all sectors of the European economy for their own purposes, found that they needed a great deal more capital. As a result, investment activity in Europe became more intense, creating ideal conditions for the rise of private and commercial banking institutions.[3]

In Switzerland, the public sector banks – known as Stadtwechsel (city exchequers) – that had grown out of the public exchange offices in the late middle ages, lost ground to the private banks and increasingly had to content themselves with small-scale lending on a local basis.[4] In Zurich and Basel, guild legislation restricted economic development and made it difficult for the nascent financial industry to take off properly, but in Geneva the private banks had already enjoyed one Golden Age under Ludwig XIV. In fact most of the many Swiss bankers and financial operators who worked in Paris and elsewhere in the 18th and the beginning of the 19th century came from Geneva.[5]

On the whole, the Swiss private banks of the time only had loose ties to the Swiss domestic economy. Most of them did manage a considerable amount of

Bank Leu's ledger book contained details of loans to various members of the European nobility, such as the one to Empress Maria Theresia in 1758: 'WE Maria Theresia, Empress of Rome by GOD's grace, [...] hereby publicly declare on behalf of Ourselves, Our heirs and successors in the empire that [we] have petitioned [...for] a cash loan of thirty thousand guilders from Leu & Co.'

Swiss private assets alongside the portfolios of their major foreign clients, but they tended to invest these assets abroad. Other private banks maintained close contact with the commercial houses to which they owed their establishment, often operating more in the manner of mercantile institutions than banks, which is why they can be accurately referred to as 'marchands-banquiers', or merchant bankers.[6] The private banks concentrated primarily on asset management, but were also involved in real estate business, and in the inter-regional and international bill discounting and payment transactions conducted by Swiss companies. During the 19th century, the Genevan banking houses focused mainly on equity and bond issues in France, Italy and Austria, especially for canal building and mining companies. Meanwhile, Basel bankers were putting most of their investors' capital into the Alsatian textile industry. Until the middle of the 19th century, the small number of St. Gallen-based financial institutions – such as the oldest surviving private bank, Wegelin & Co. – and the Zurich banking houses relied heavily on the industries which they had originally run: textiles and haulage.

New banks emerge: from Bank Leu (1775) to the savings banks (Sparkassen) and joint-stock banks (Aktienbanken)

The great exception to the general rule in the Swiss banking scene of the 18th century was Bank Leu & Co., by far the oldest of the institutions that were to become the major Swiss banks. As Switzerland became a capital-exporting

A historical overview of Switzerland as a banking center

Johann Jakob Leu (1689–1768), Mayor of Zurich and compiler of the *Helvetisches Lexikon*, was a driving force behind the establishment of Leu & Co. in 1755. Leu – which grew out of the Zürcher Zinskommission (Zurich Interest Commission) – was Switzerland's first 'modern' bank. In 1990 it was integrated into CS Holding.

Unknown artist. Johann Jakob Leu. Around 1750. Oil on canvas. Credit Suisse Group Collection.

country in the 18th century, the governments of the original Swiss cantons not only invested large sums of their own money abroad, but also encouraged the export of private capital. In 1755, an independent organization named after Johann Jakob Leu, the incumbent Treasurer of Zurich, was created to handle transactions by the 'Interest Commission' of Canton Zurich, a purely governmental institution which itself had been set up in 1747. In this way, the first 'modern' Swiss bank was brought to life.[7]

On the assets side, Leu & Co. concentrated on purchasing foreign debt paper (issued by sovereign and private borrowers) and collecting the annual interest due on these bonds. Its liability-side business focused on issuing its own interest-bearing paper, known as 'Rathausobligationen' ('town hall bonds'), which were bought up by Zurich-based investors. Leu & Co.'s purpose was to encourage capital exports in order to curb the surplus of capital available in Zurich and to stabilize interest rates in the city and surrounding countryside.

The first private savings banks

In 1835 there were 11,886 savings bank books open in the Canton of Zurich, containing deposits of Sfr 2,153,600. Thirty-four years later, there were 84,584 savings books accounting for Sfr 19,039,026 (cf. Ermatinger, *Kapital*, p. 52).

Partly due to the influence of new socio-political and revolutionary ideas from the United Kingdom and France, the final quarter of the 18th century saw a first manifestation of the predilection for saving that has remained a Swiss characteristic ever since. As the Swiss Confederation grappled with political upheaval, savings banks were established to provide farmers, craftsmen and tradespeople with an opportunity to invest their money. The first groundswell of new local bank openings extended up to about 1815 – early by European comparison – and covered all of the larger Swiss towns. In Zurich, for example, the Sparkasse der Stadt Zürich, the oldest savings bank still operating at the end of the 20th century, was founded in 1805.[8] Another 100 or so savings banks were established throughout the rest of Switzerland between 1815 and 1830 on the back of the boom in rural cottage industries.[9] Far from being modern banking institutions, however, these savings banks simply managed the savings of homeworkers and craftsmen. Their lending activity was restricted almost exclusively to mortgage business.[10]

The savings bank movement suffered its first setback during the depression of the late 1840s, though a decade later a third, slightly more modest wave of bank start-ups occurred. These new institutions tended to be factory savings banks set up by the new industrial concerns. Since the existing savings banks were still not really banks in the narrower sense, the Swiss banking system continued to lag behind developments in other countries.

The first joint-stock banks and cantonal banks

In 1835, a brochure published by Orell Füssli & Co. called for the establishment of joint-stock banks ('Aktienbanken'): 'Is it not about time that we found out whether Switzerland too might have a use for banks? […] The public will examine the case and decide. If it thinks that banks are worthwhile, banks will be established; if they prove to be useful, they will thrive, endure and multiply; if the conditions are right, they will be of use throughout Switzerland.'[11] As it hap-

The articles of incorporation of Zinstragende Ersparniskasse Aarau, dated 14 March 1812: 'We the undersigned hereby publicly announce and declare: that in view of the common benefit that would be derived from a general savings bank for the people of Canton Aargau, the establishment of which was approved by the Society for the Culture of the Fatherland on 8th February 1812; and with the intention of promoting the establishment of such a savings bank and providing the members of such a bank with the requisite protection against loss for their deposits, but also to increase the public's confidence in the institution itself, we have decided to guarantee and stand security for the institution, up to the sums entered next to our signatures below.'

Zinstragende Ersparniskasse Aarau, known from 1864 as Allgemeine Aargauische Ersparniskasse, was absorbed by Neue Aargauer Bank (NAB) in 1989. In autumn 1994 NAB was taken over by CS Holding.

A share issued by Bank in Zürich on 1 July 1855. Bank in Zürich, founded in 1836, along with Bank in St. Gallen (1837) and Bank in Basel (1845), was part of the first wave of new private joint-stock banks in Switzerland. In 1907 it was taken over by SKA. Shown in 1:2.8 scale.

pened, there was not long to wait before banks were indeed established. Private consortiums searching for suitable ways of countering the inadequate money supply of the time formed the first Swiss note-issuing banks in the mould of similar banks already to be found in other countries. Bank in Zürich (1836), Bank in St. Gallen (1837) and Bank in Basel (1845) thus became the first joint-stock banks in Switzerland, their objective being to satisfy the demand for means of payment – i.e. notes, coins and bills of exchange. As the private sector founded these new institutions, various cantons, primarily the rural ones, were starting to establish state-controlled savings banks and mortgage banks in order to provide financial security for existing institutions and more effectively to achieve the social aims set out during the country's 'Regenerationszeit' (the period of regeneration between 1830 and 1848 when the liberal movement began to overcome the forces of conservatism and pave the way for the creation of the modern Swiss state). These state-run institutions in turn laid the foundations for the earliest cantonal banks, i.e. the cantonal banks of Bern (1834) and Vaud (1846), which were created as public-sector note-issuing banks. However none of these new types of bank made much progress until the currency reform of 1852 and the subsequent boom in railway construction.[12] The bill discounting business practiced by the new banks was primarily a means of financing long-distance trade and was of little use to local commerce. Until 1852, therefore, the need for paper money and the confidence placed in such tender was minimal.

Swiss banking in the first half of the 19th century was thus based on two separate systems. On the one hand, the rural and parts of the urban banking system were rooted in regional networks, within which borrowers and creditors knew each other and shared the same expectations with regard to risk and return. The other system – dominated by private bankers and the city-based elites – focused on international business, and consisted of larger institutions that concentrated on the longer-term investment needs of their clients.[13] In 1848, the Swiss banking industry comprised 45 to 50 private banks, 150 savings banks, five public-sector or quasi-public-sector cantonal banks[14], a land mortgage bank and nine local banks. It thus reflected the political and economic structures that prevailed in the country in the first half of the century.

*After 1848: commercial banks, issuing banks
and co-operative banks battle it out*

The foundation of the Swiss federal state brought profound change to the country's political, economic and social structures. Fuelled by the cotton industry and blossoming international free trade, the Swiss economy experienced an undreamt-of boom. At the same time it was becoming increasingly clear that the new demands placed on the money and capital markets were simply too much for the existing systems to cope with: the private banks might have managed money accumulated in Switzerland, but these funds were only rarely made available to Swiss business. The early Swiss industrialists had thus far made little use of external finance, so the tradition-bound private banks saw no reason to change their business practices to accommodate the changing demands of the Swiss corporate sector. What is more, industrialization was throwing up new types of risk that the banks found hard to appraise, and that they were thus not prepared to take on. Neither the savings banks that emerged at the beginning of the 19th century nor the first issuing banks established sometime later were any better equipped to cover the industrial sector's growing demand for capital. The issuing banks, for example, refused to grant large-scale unsecured loans.

As industrialization progressed, the vacuum left between elitist private bankers and co-operative banking institutions became ever more evident. On the one hand, the supply of capital was decreasing: for years manufacturing industry had developed mainly by means of self-finance and had little spare capital for investment elsewhere. On the other hand, there was a massive demand for credit for railway construction. Then, in 1852, a decision by the Federal Council 'to leave the construction and operation of the railways to the cantons and to the private sector' changed everything.[15] In order to secure the required capital, two financing instruments were introduced into Switzerland for the first time: the bearer share and the bond issue. Their entrance onto the scene also paved the way for the creation of Switzerland's stock markets.[16]

Crédit Mobilier as archetype

Encouraged by the desire to avoid the 'monopolistic' influence of 'high finance' (particularly the Rothschilds), and to appeal to the large-number of moderately wealthy potential customers, the idea of a large joint-stock bank was made reality in 1852 when Crédit Mobilier was founded in France. Crédit Mobilier was the archetypal company start-ups and underwriting bank, holding the shares issued by newly created industrial or transportation companies long

Until 1848, demand for credit – especially from the public sector – was minimal.

Crédit Mobilier → 47

Development of the major Swiss banks (1755–1998)

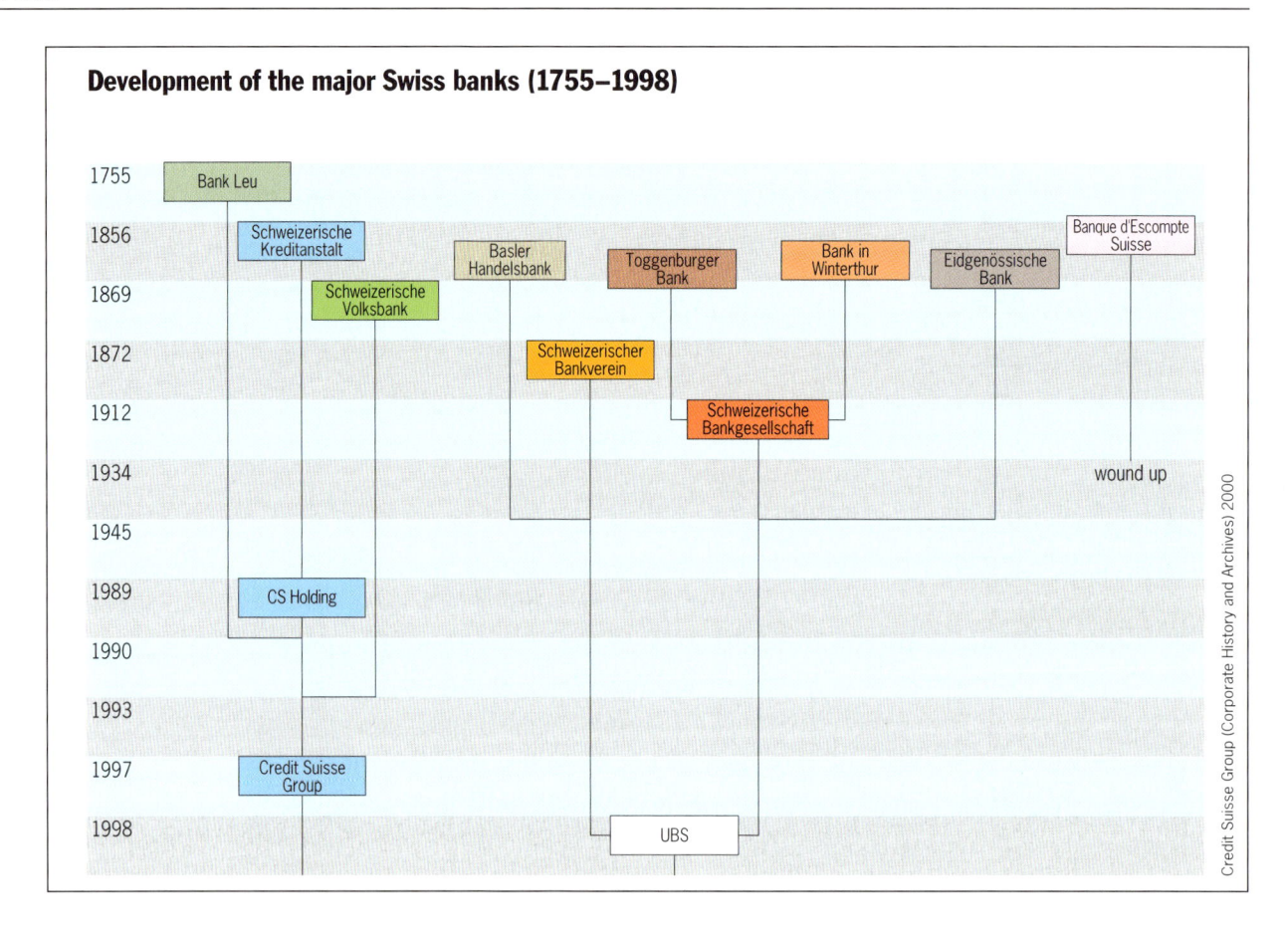

1755	Bank Leu						
1856		Schweizerische Kreditanstalt	Basler Handelsbank	Toggenburger Bank	Bank in Winterthur	Eidgenössische Bank	Banque d'Escompte Suisse
1869		Schweizerische Volksbank					
1872			Schweizerischer Bankverein				
1912				Schweizerische Bankgesellschaft			
1934							wound up
1945							
1989		CS Holding					
1990							
1993							
1997		Credit Suisse Group					
1998				UBS			

Credit Suisse Group (Corporate History and Archives) 2000

enough to ensure a favorable placement with investors. The earnings so generated made further start-ups possible. Alongside the securities trading and bond issuing that served to finance the railways and general industrial development, the similar banks that were subsequently set up all over Europe often engaged in precious metal business, the hypothecation of goods, bills and other discounting business, endorsements, lending, deposit-taking and collections. In Switzerland, six banks were founded that borrowed heavily from the Crédit Mobilier model:

Alfred Escher → 46

- In 1856 Schweizerische Kreditanstalt (SKA) was established in Zurich on the initiative of Alfred Escher, initially with fifty percent German backing. As Switzerland's first commercial bank it was able to face up to the foreign (primarily French) competition in the contest to finance the Swiss railway network.

Railway financing → 51

- Bank in Winterthur was set up in 1862 against a background of economic and political differences between the neighboring towns of Winterthur and Zurich. Bank in Winterthur quickly developed beyond its original interests in warehousing business to become a Crédit Mobilier-like institution, thus strengthening the significance of the Zurich region as a banking center.

Start-ups and participations → 55

- At the end of 1862, a group of private bankers, working together with various Basel-based trading houses and Zurich's SKA, established Basler Handelsbank. Almost from its inception this institution, which was allied to SKA

A historical overview of Switzerland as a banking center

Banking in Geneva in the 19th century

At the start of the 19th century, Geneva's private banks did very well out of the rise of industry, particularly the watchmaking industry.[17] When the 'Regenerationszeit' began in 1830, some of the cantonal governments began to look a little unsteady. Geneva too was rocked by the emergence of the radical movement. Soon after the political coup of 1846 and his entry into Geneva's new radical government, the politician James Fazy started to develop innovative ideas about how to bring an end to the power and privileges of the old-established private banks. In 1848 he not only founded one of the first mortgage banks (Caisse Hypothécaire), but also a cantonal bank – though soon to be privatized – with the right to issue bank notes: Banque de Genève. Two of the other banks he set up, Caisse d'Escompte de Genève in 1849 (which was the first Swiss full-service bank to be created in the image of France's Crédit Mobilier) and Banque Générale Suisse de Crédit International Mobilier et Foncier in 1853, collapsed only a few years after they opened for business. Nevertheless, Fazy did succeed in weakening the hold of the Genevan private banks, at least temporarily. Conservative circles reacted to the upstart competition by forming syndicates, which in line with the old traditions concentrated mainly on foreign projects, or by creating new banks themselves.[18] One of these new banks was Comptoir d'Escompte de Genève, set up in 1855. This bank was later to become one of the majors and, as Banque d'Escompte Suisse, it finally came to grief in 1934. Not least because of their international clientele, the traditional private bankers were ultimately able to hold out well against competition from the joint-stock banks. The creation of the Bourse de Genève, recognized by law in 1857, and thus the oldest stock exchange in Switzerland, prompted a vigorous trade in securities – initially foreign ones. The money markets remained heavily influenced by the foreign interests of Geneva's banks and investors. Fall-out from the Franco-Prussian War in particular caused large volumes of foreign money to flow into the city. The surge in the creation of new finance companies towards the end of the century embraced Geneva too. The private banks especially were involved in many of these start-ups, including those of Association Financière (1872) – which expanded in 1890 to become Union Financière de Genève and which eventually developed into an investment trust with numerous holdings[19] – and Société Financière Franco-Suisse (1892), which helped to finance the railways.

The head office of the Genevan private bank Lombard Odier & Cie, Rue de la Corraterie 11. Founded in 1798, the bank has been at this address since 1857.

The head office of the Genevan private bank Pictet & Cie, Boulevard Georges-Favon 29. The bank, established in 1805 under the name of Candolle, Mallet & Cie, moved into this new building in 1975.

The head office of the Genevan private bank Gonet & Cie, Boulevard du Théâtre 6. Founded in 1842 as a trading and transportation company, since 1852 the institution has concentrated mainly on banking business.

through a co-operation agreement in its early days, had to struggle against repeated business problems.

- In Bern a consortium centered around Jakob Stämpfli, a retired Federal Councillor and opponent of Escher, went into business with two Parisian banks to establish Eidgenössische Bank. Eidgenössische Bank, which had set itself the goal of becoming number one amongst the Swiss issuing banks, and also to compete with SKA for the position of Switzerland's biggest commercial bank, moved its head office to Zurich in 1892.
- Finally, Banque Générale Suisse de Crédit International Mobilier et Foncier (1853–1869) and Deutsch-Schweizerische Kreditbank (1856–1888) were created in Geneva and St. Gallen respectively. These two banks enjoyed initial success, but soon fell into serious difficulties and disappeared from view.

All of the banks set up in the image of Crédit Mobilier were in the front line when it came to driving forward the second phase of industrialization in Switzerland: the development of infrastructure and big industry.

'People's banks' versus 'elitist banks'

> While it was becoming more and more difficult for farmers, craftsmen and small businessmen to obtain loans at reasonable rates of interest, their need for investment was growing in parallel to that of high finance and industry. The outbreak of the 'property loan crisis' in 1863 brought the problem out into the open.

Although the massive increase in demand for capital from the railways, and later from the insurance companies and big industry, triggered imports of capital from abroad, lending was left primarily to the domestic market.

The supply of capital in Switzerland shifted as the banks increasingly sought profit on the securities market, and in the second half of the century a relative shortage of credit became apparent. Exacerbated by the new commercial banks' reluctance to invest in long-term mortgage loans, this led to a rise in interest rates. Farmers, tradespeople and small-scale industrialists, who were suffering from the restrictions placed on their investment opportunities, complained that the big banks' unsound speculative activity and increasingly expensive loans would ruin the country's small businesses.

On the political front, these problems prompted the emergence of the democratic movement in opposition to the existing, increasingly conservative liberal elite. Particularly in the 1860s, the ideas and political successes of this movement led to the creation of a large number of new (semi-)public-sector local and medium-sized banks, as well as to the emergence of co-operatively organized savings and loans institutions. By contrast with the 'elitist banks' these smaller institutions took care of the regular payments needs of the medium-sized and small businesses that made up local and regional economies. They also facilitated the use of savings and deposits for mortgage and lending business at favorable interest rates. Some of these banks, originally conceived as non-profit-making associations, gradually developed into major, profit-making businesses.[20] The best example of this trend is Volksbank in Bern, founded in 1869. By building up a branch network and diversifying its business widely, the erstwhile craftsman's bank soon became a national organization, which from 1881 officially became known as Schweizerische Volksbank (Swiss Volksbank).

Minutes of the constitutive meeting of Volksbank in Bern of 2 April 1869: 'Mr. Arnold Lang, co-editor of the *Tages-Post*, opened the meeting by noting that the preparatory work completed to date for the establishment of Volksbank, which was dedicated to producing a draft set of articles that are now in print, had been accomplished by the Allgemeine Arbeiter-Gesellschaft, but that today's meeting, as soon as it had been constituted, would take the whole matter to another stage, to the extent that further activity was now the preserve of today's general meeting for the establishment of Volksbank, and that the Arbeiter-Gesellschaft should regard itself as having been discharged. [...]'

Volksbank in Bern, later to become Schweizerische Volksbank (SVB), was created out of the 'Allgemeine Arbeitergesellschaft der Stadt Bern' along the lines of the German lending societies. Membership was not restricted to the working classes, however, but extended to other parts of society too. SVB was integrated into CS Holding in 1993.

Despite its rapid growth, the SVB remained at heart a bank for the middle class and for small and medium-sized businesses.

The second wave of cantonal bank start-ups (eight banks established between 1858 and 1878) was also associated with problems surrounding Switzerland's 'property loan crisis' and the emergence of the democratic movement. The cantonal banks' main aim, as state-run discounting and issuing organizations, was to encourage regional economic activity, to alleviate the marked shortage of funds in commercial banking business and to represent cantonal interests vigorously to the federal government.

A new phenomenon that surfaced at this time was the mortgage bank. In the 19th century, the spread of fire insurance, the dismantling of city walls and the boom in residential construction all led to the creation of an urban market for loans secured on land and property. The first blossoming of this market was brought to a halt in the 1850s when creditors pushed through cantonal debt maturity legislation that caused long-term mortgage notes to be reassigned as short-to-medium-term securities. It was decided that this situation should be sorted out by an organization made up of banks, preferably under public-sector control; as a consequence, by the end of the 1860s, 14 large-scale mortgage banks had been established.

In the 1860s, all of these different types of banks – especially the joint stock banks[21] – were caught up in a huge wave of new start-ups reminiscent of the one that had gripped the savings bank movement in the early 19th century. In addition to the 60 or so savings institutions that were set up between 1850 and 1880, 28 new banking organizations were created between 1851 and 1860, another 71 between 1861 and 1870, and another 40 between 1871 and 1880. This exponential growth in the banking industry matched the decisive drive towards industrialization in Switzerland almost step for step.

Proliferation of bank notes

Intensive discussions about the possibility of a central note-issuing bank only started after 1870 when the federal constitution was revised. As a result, the number of regional issuing banks increased still further in the period after 1848.

Before long, competition between all these issuing banks, often operating in very small geographical areas, took on an almost grotesque form: 'In an attempt to disrupt the banknote business of Bank für Graubünden [in 1863], senior managers at Graubündner Kantonalbank came up with the clever idea of collecting as many of Bank für Graubünden's banknotes as possible and then presenting these on bloc for redemption – and what is more to do this at a time that could be assumed to be particularly inconvenient for Bank für Graubünden.'[22] In 1864, some of the biggest issuing banks tried to bring their narrow areas of influence together into two 'currency blocs'. The notes of one bloc were not to be accepted as legal tender in the other. One of these groups was headed by Eidgenössische Bank in Zurich, and the other by Bank in Zürich and Bank in Basel.[23] This meant that in practical terms, Switzerland had returned to the situation that

A banknote issued by Bank in Luzern in 1877. Shown in 1:1.6 scale.

prevailed prior to 1848. However, the enshrining of a national unit of currency in the federal constitution helped to counter these problems and gradually created the conditions for the integration and standardization of the banknotes being produced. Nevertheless, the number of issuing banks continued to increase until by 1880 there were 36.[24] Finally, the banking law of 1881 laid down a set of rules for the issuing of banknotes. For over fifty years, these rules remained the only Swiss-wide legal provisions that circumscribed private-sector banking.[25]

Consolidation, diversification and the first mergers up to 1914

At the beginning of the 1880s, the expansion in lending by the banking industry had caught up with the demand overhang, and the capital market entered a phase of saturation. Competitive pressure increased and many of the institutions originally founded as specialist banks were transformed into full-service banks. This trend was just as evident amongst the cantonal banks, which by 1880 constituted the strongest banking group in the country. The business policies appropriate to the new conditions entailed a more cautious approach to risk. The large commercial banks reduced their often speculative, high-loss equity stakes, built up their current account businesses, and soon began to add mortgage lending to their range of credit products. Apart from SVB and Bank Leu, however, the big institutions regarded mortgage lending as merely a complementary strand to their industrial and commercial financing work, which is why they tended to pursue mortgage business through a separate subsidiary company or through a property loan bank over which they had control. For example, St. Gallische Hypothekarkasse – founded in 1864 – acted as a feeder to Bank in St. Gallen, only gaining greater operational freedom after the Bank in St. Gallen merged with SKA in 1907. Similarly Hypothekarbank Zürich (1896) came under the control of SKA in 1903.[26]

Elektrowatt → 61, 106

Finance companies and Raiffeisen banks

Two more, completely different types of financial institution came into being towards the end of the 19th century: finance companies and Raiffeisen banks (rural credit banks). The first finance companies were created in the late 1870s, initially to help fund the railway industry. Apart from the fact that they sometimes called themselves 'banks', these institutions actually had little in common with the traditional banking houses. These so-called 'Eisenbahnbanken' (railway banks) – such as Schweizerische Eisenbahnbank, which operated in Basel between 1879 and 1886 – supplied capital to a railway company by purchasing railway shares and simultaneously selling their own shares or bonds to other banks. This helped to circumvent the problems caused by the strong fluctuations to which shares in railways were prone: thanks to their liquidity, the railway banks were able to keep the price of their own shares stable.[27] This model, whereby the finance companies acted as a buffer between banks and industrial concerns, was subsequently adopted by the electricity industry too.

From 1887, the first co-operatives in Switzerland to follow the example of the German Friedrich Wilhelm Raiffeisen were established in Canton Bern. From 1899, this new form of incorporation inspired small-scale farmers to set up a large number of Raiffeisen banks within a short space of time. Raiffeisen banks worked on the principle that the sums deposited in a municipality could only be made available as loans to inhabitants of that same municipality.[28] In 1902, the Raiffeisen banks joined together to form the 'Verband schweizerischer Darlehenskassen (System Raiffeisen)' ['Association of Swiss Lending Banks (Raiffeisen System)'], which soon took over the role of central bank for all the member institutions.

The last great wave of bank start-ups
and the creation of the Swiss National Bank

The rise of the electricity industry and of tourism, which expanded with the railways and the increased construction of hotels, set off a renewed wave of investment in the 1890s. This brought an end to the temporary phase of consolidation that had afflicted savings banks since the 1880s, and local banks since the 1890s.[29] Despite the odd crisis and stock market crash, and despite the disappearance of some of the old-established institutions (in 1890/91, for example, the Kreditbank Winterthur and the Bodenkreditanstalt Bern had to file for bankruptcy[30]), the period between 1895 and 1910 marked the final great wave of new bank start-ups. These years saw the creation of another 55 local banks, 17 savings banks, 22 private banks, 12 other banks, and over 20 quasi-bank finance companies[31], such as Bank für elektrische Unternehmungen founded in 1895. In 1895/96, Schweizerischer Bankverein (Swiss Bank Corporation) was formed from the merger of Basler Bankverein (founded in 1872), Zürcher Bankverein (1889), Basler Depositenbank (1881), and Schweizerische Unionbank in St. Gallen (1888).

From 1880 onwards, the number of issuing banks started to go down again as the circulation of banknotes increasingly fell under the control of the cantonal

Banking in Zurich in the 19th century

Zurich did not become a center for banking until relatively late. In fact it wasn't until the middle of the 19th century that banking business assumed 'a pervasive and dominant significance throughout business life' in the city.[32] Initially the leading institution on the banking scene was Bank Leu & Co., founded in 1755. After a period of crisis and reorganization between 1790 and 1803, Bank Leu gradually shifted its business focus to the domestic market, in the process becoming one of Europe's first mortgage banks.[33] In 1854 the bank was transformed into a state-controlled joint-stock company (Aktiengesellschaft), but then was privatized in 1869 in advance of the creation of the Zürcher Kantonalbank. Thereafter, Bank Leu turned increasingly to short-term commercial lending and securities and syndication operations, though it continued to pursue mortgage business as well.

Unlike Basel and Geneva, Zurich was home to only a few old-established private banks: the big companies active in the silk and cotton trade were well endowed with their own capital. Furthermore, they wanted to invest their large holdings of foreign assets without outside help and they also preferred to carry out their monetary transactions themselves.[34] In 1837, the city's newly published companies' register (Ragionenbuch) listed four companies which engaged in banking and discounting business alongside trading or silk manufacturing operations, but only one pure banking institution.[35] The fact that the private banks of Geneva and Basel prevented or delayed the development of joint-stock banks in those cities played a key role in Zurich's growth into the premier Swiss banking center. Many private banks preferred not to use debt capital and so left credit business to other institutions. However, the establishment of Bank in Zürich, Switzerland's oldest joint-stock bank, in 1836 failed to make a significant contribution to the emergence of Zurich as a banking hub. According to the new bank's articles of association, it was set up to handle a wide range of banking business, but in practice it was unable to fulfill this promise. On the one hand it had insufficient appeal for the export-oriented manufacturing and trading firms; on the other it was unable to extend its business operations geographically owing to the different legal regimes that prevailed in the different cantons.

In the wake of the foundation of the Swiss federal state, Zurich – thanks not least to the efforts of Alfred Escher – gradually began to catch up with the two older financial centers, Geneva and Basel. SKA, brought into being in 1856, practiced a more cautious business policy and was thus less prone to crisis than Geneva's Banque Générale Suisse, which had to be wound up in 1869. 1870 saw the creation of the Zürcher Kantonalbank, a typical product of the democratic movement and another key player on the Zurich banking scene. In terms of securities trading, Zurich caught up with the existing stock exchanges in Basel and Geneva in 1876 when the Effektenbörsenverein (Securities Exchange Association) was founded.[36]

Bank in Zürich, founded in 1836, was the first private joint-stock bank in Switzerland. The office building on Bahnhofstrasse, built by Georg Lasius in 1872/73 in the style of the Italian Renaissance, is the oldest purpose-built bank building in Zurich. Photographed around 1895.

The head office of Schweizerische Kreditanstalt (SKA) on Zurich's Paradeplatz. Photographed around 1900.

Number of each different type of bank (1800–1945)
(excl. Raiffeisen banks, private banks, foreign banks, finance companies)

— Savings banks — Local banks — Property loan banks
— Cantonal banks — Major banks

Conventions → 360
Underwriting cartel → 124

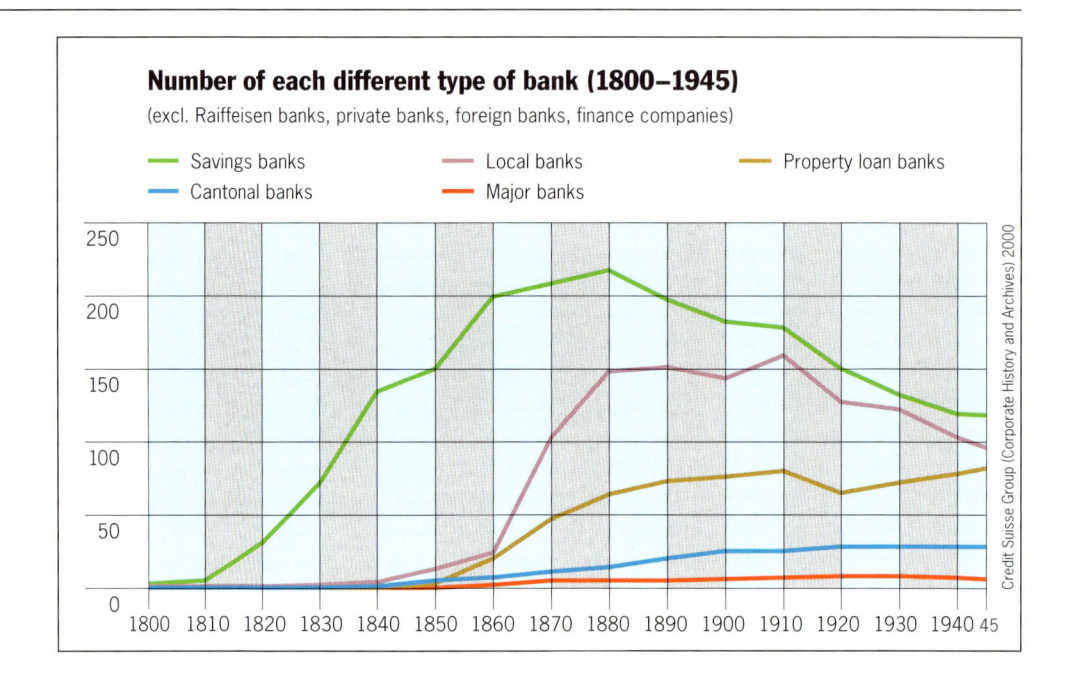

banks, some of which were working very closely together. After various attempts, and a long political wrangle, as part of which the federal government was finally given the exclusive right to issue bank notes in 1891, the Swiss National Bank was able to open its doors for business in 1907. Even during the preliminary discussions about a central bank, the banks reacted to the prospect of government intervention by setting up a system of corporate self regulation which led to the establishment of the issuing cartel (Emissionskartell) in 1897, the Association of Swiss Cantonal Banks (Verband Schweizerischer Kantonalbanken) in 1907, and the Swiss Bankers' Association (Schweizerische Bankiervereinigung) in 1912.[37]

Critical mass:
mergers at the beginning of the 20th century

In 1908 the total number of banking institutions in Switzerland had risen to its peak of 454, after which the growth trajectory leveled off.[38] The structure of the banking industry was lop-sided in that there were too many small institutions of modest financial strength. The banks had failed to keep pace with the needs of a pioneering, capital-intensive industrial sector. Once again the pendulum swung towards concentration and consolidation, encouraged by the formation of the first banking syndicates and the centralization of banknote issuing business. The phenomena of mergers and acquisitions became widespread in the Swiss banking sector; corporate expansion was no longer a matter of internal growth alone. Between 1906 and 1916 about 40 banks were absorbed by larger competitors, with 29 small and medium-sized banks swallowed up in the years between 1911 and 1914 alone.[39] The most important merger during this period was the one in 1912 between Bank in Winterthur and Toggenburger Bank, which was very strong in mortgage business, to form Schweizerische Bankgesellschaft, or SBG (Union Bank of Switzerland, or UBS). The major banks swallowed up issuing banks and local and medium-sized banks, while the savings and loan banks tended to team up with the cantonal institutions.

Three factors intensified the process of concentration in the Swiss banking industry: the financial crisis which had originated in the USA and spread to envelope Europe, the high standards set by the SNB for the quality of bills submitted for discounting, and the removal of the issuing banks' right to print banknotes in 1910. Between 1910 and 1914 it was open season on banks. Particularly in Cantons Bern, Zurich and Ticino[40] a host of commercial banks, lending banks and savings banks collapsed. In the years of economic euphoria prior to the First World War, banks in Switzerland were hampered by insufficient liquidity, inadequate risk diversification, and not least by bank managers who had become high-handed and who did not have a feel for the high-risk business environment. An enquiry by the Federal Department of Economic Affairs confirmed that between 1910 and 1914, about 60 Swiss banks disappeared from view.[41]

The opening up of their first municipal deposit counters extended the appeal of the major banks to customers with moderate assets. In addition, from 1905 onwards, as the industry consolidated and the banks diversified their business, individual institutions also expanded their market positions by building up branch networks – though it has to be said that they did this much later than the leading British, German and French institutions.[42] In any case, the most important banks in Switzerland could not really be compared with the big foreign banking houses. By international standards they were 'actually only large regional banks'.[43] In 1914, the total assets of SBV, the largest Swiss bank, did not amount to even a quarter of the assets held on the balance sheets of the big banks in Britain, Germany and France.[44] Unlike the French deposit-taking banks, the Swiss 'major banks' tended to be involved in areas of business that in France would be handled by the large provincial banking houses.[45]

In the years prior to the First World War, the Swiss financial center had already grown together into a unified whole. As a result it was able to gain international stature.

Development of European major banks compared to SKA (1900–1990)

	Barclays			Deutsche Bank			Crédit Lyonnais			SKA		
	Total assets (Sfr m)	Domestic branches*	Head-count	Total assets (Sfr m)	Domestic branches*	Head-count	Total assets (Sfr m)	Domestic branches*	Head-count	Total assets (Sfr m)	Domestic branches*	Head-count
1900	963	265	1 166	804	20	2 063	1 700	187	10 015	165	1	212
1910	1 365	488	1 990	2 654	73	5 816	2 495	273	15 390	409	8	773
1920	9 669	1794	11 931	2 292	223	17 808	2 215	349	19 913	967	20	1 892
1930	12 966	2403	19 121	6 059	494	20 051	3 078	964	23 500	1 785	26	2 167
1940	12 911	2085	23 382	9 370	489	20 605	2 364	n.a.	18 896	1 190	28	2 309
1950	23 283	2234	30 325	–	–	–	3 807	1325	21 352	2 265	29	2 393
1960	32 217	2450	42 923	11 619	410	19 106	11 360	1650	23 502	4 918	35	3 021
1970	73 788	3215	81 801	37 090	1001	30 764	42 176	1931	36 040	28 032	79	6 535
1980	144 678	2991	116 000	96 009	1139	39 242	140 176	n.a.	45 892	63 475	155	11 589
1990	333 171	2606	116 800	219 184	1257	52 271	289 981	2303	42 775	125 767	209	16 098

* Branches and deposit counters

From 1914 to the present day: advancement despite setbacks

Ups and downs for the major banks and cantonal banks

The outbreak of the First World War brought a liquidity crisis for the banks, though capital exports in the years to follow had an overall positive effect on the Swiss banking industry.[46] The process of concentration continued up to about 1938, with the major banks and cantonal banks gaining financial strength at the expense of smaller institutions. The wave of mergers peaked in the years between 1918 and 1922, during which time a total of 30 banks were taken over, and in most cases converted into one or more branch offices of the acquiring bank.[47] At the start of the 1920s, Switzerland still had a dense network of banks compared to other countries, with one bank branch for roughly every 2,200 inhabitants. At the same time in Britain, for example, each branch served an average constituency of 5,130 inhabitants.[48]

The economic crisis of the 1930s led to yet another round of bankruptcies and takeovers in the banking sector. As a result, the number of banks (not including private banks) fell from 393 in 1918 to 343 in 1938.[49] Despite trailing the major banks in terms of takeovers, the cantonal banks, which benefited

In 1919 the catchment area of SVB, which was organized into co-operative groups, extended from Lake Geneva to Lake Constance.

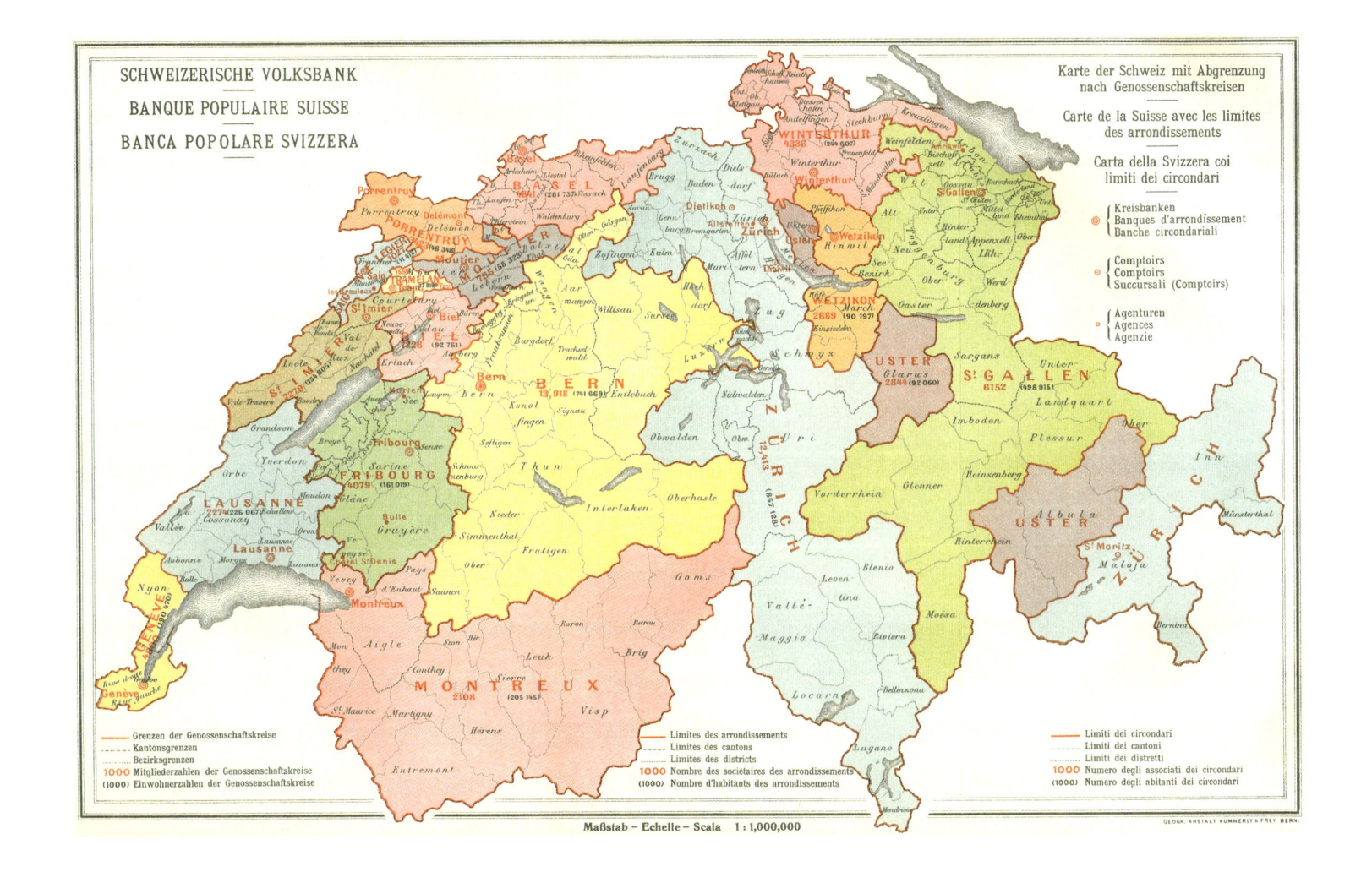

from a government guarantee, remained the strongest group during the years between the wars, and accounted for the greater part of Swiss banking business. The major banks had vigorously pursued business in other countries during the 1920s and were consequently hit harder by the international economic crisis, sustaining heavy losses. They were particularly unfortunate with regard to their investments in Germany and Central Europe, where foreign exchange controls devalued a large proportion of the assets belonging to the Swiss banks.

The ebb and flow of the major banks' fortunes was reflected in the size of their aggregated total assets. Between 1914 and 1930, the total assets of all the major banks rose from Sfr 2.5 billion to Sfr 8.6 billion, but by 1938 they had fallen back down to Sfr 4.5 billion. By contrast the cantonal banks were able to increase their aggregate total assets over the same period from Sfr 3.6 billion (1914) to Sfr 7.5 billion (1930), and then to Sfr 8.1 billion (1938).[51] The economic ups and downs of the 1920s and 1930s confirmed that the performance of the major banks and the cantonal banks could be diametrically opposed to one another in times of boom and crisis.

An analysis of the mergers and acquisitions that took place between 1918 and 1938 reveals two principal trends:
- The major banks accounted for 29 acquisitions, thus playing a more significant role than the cantonal banks, which only acquired nine institutions.
- The main targets for acquisition were smaller banks in Western Switzerland.

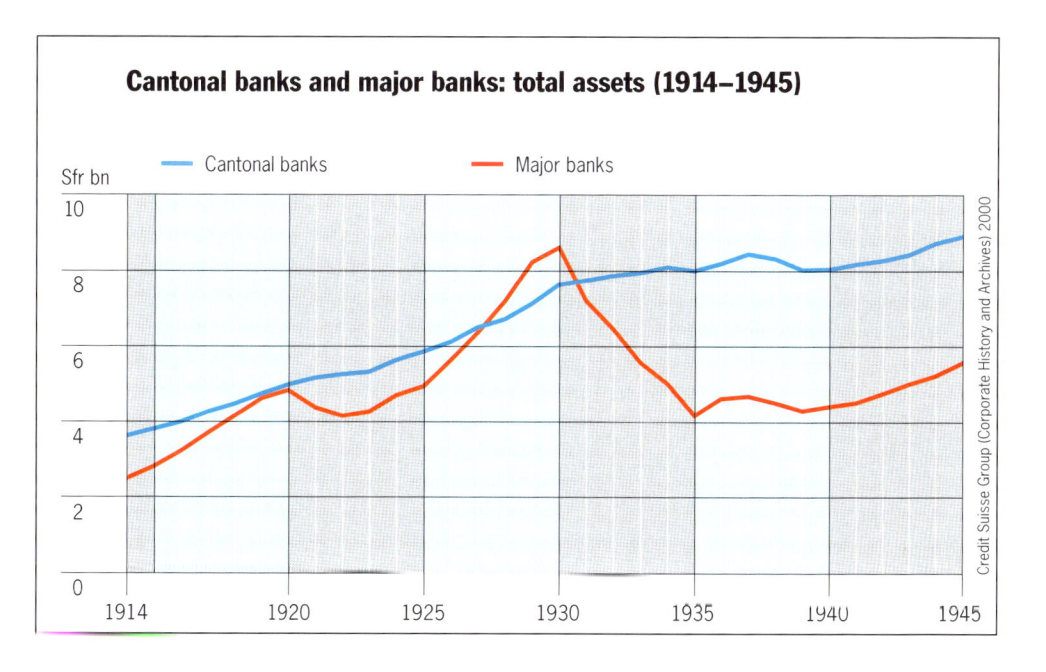

Cantonal banks and major banks: total assets (1914–1945)

Credit Suisse Group (Corporate History and Archives) 2000

What is meant by a 'major bank'?

In its first set of banking statistics, compiled for the years 1906–1913, the SNB used the term 'Grossbank' to describe the commercial banks that had joined the Swiss banking cartel. These banks towered above all the other Swiss commercial banks in terms of the size of their equity and debt capital and the intensity of their national and international business relations. Since then, the term 'Grossbank', usually translated as 'major bank', has been used to describe the country's biggest commercial banks (which at that time numbered eight).[50]

The biggest casualty of the crisis-riven 1930s was Banque d'Escompte Suisse. In the mid-1920s, under the name Comptoir d'Escompte de Genève, this bank had grown to become the only major bank based in Western Switzerland, with branches in seven Swiss towns. The bank's illiquidity was caused primarily by the international banking crisis, which triggered a series of payment moratoriums by over-indebted foreign countries, transfer difficulties and, finally, heavy withdrawals of money. Despite the financial help provided by the federal government, Banque d'Escompte Suisse was forced to close down in 1934.

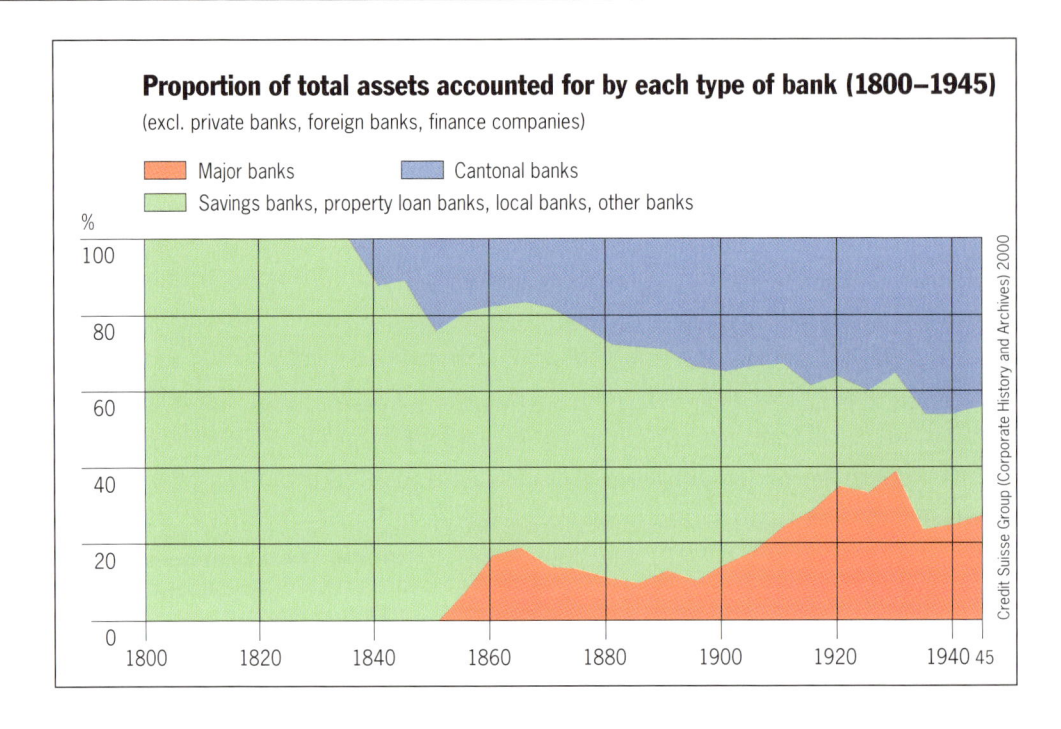

Proportion of total assets accounted for by each type of bank (1800–1945)
(excl. private banks, foreign banks, finance companies)

- Major banks
- Cantonal banks
- Savings banks, property loan banks, local banks, other banks

Credit Suisse Group (Corporate History and Archives) 2000

On 5 December 1933 the National Council discussed the reorganization of the ailing SVB. The speaker of the special commission noted that it would be necessary 'to keep the special character of SVB in mind. [...] Between 1869 and 1930 the bank experienced significant development and far-reaching structural change. Its large number of branches, through which many different types of business were conducted, made the Volksbank into a bank for the "Mittelstand" [the middle classes and small and medium-sized businesses], and this is a quality that it retains to this day. Only because of the size of its total assets has it become known as one of the major banks.' On 8 December 1933 the Federal Council approved the purchase of a Sfr 100 million stake in the co-operative stock of SVB.

Pictured below: Extract from the minutes of the National Council Meeting of 5 December 1933.

Vormittagssitzung vom 5. Dez. 1933.
Séance du 5 décembre 1933 (matin).

Vorsitz — Présidence: Hr. *Huber*.

3033. Schweiz. Volksbank. Bundeshilfe.
Banque populaire suisse. Participation financière de la Confédération.

Botschaft und Beschlussentwurf vom 29. November 1933 (Bundesblatt II, Seite 801). — Message et projet d'arrêté du 29 novembre 1933 (Feuille fédérale II, page 809).

Antrag der Kommission.
Eintreten.

Proposition de la commission.
Passer à la discussion des articles.

In the same year, the economic crisis and the difficulties it caused prompted the passing of the Swiss Banking Law. The Law contained various measures, most of which aimed to protect banks and their customers:

- Capital export controls
- Liquidity rules
- Regulations on extension of maturities, debt moratoria and receivership proceedings for banks
- Definition and scope of banking secrecy
- Introduction of compulsory bank auditing by an independent auditor

The Banking Law was instrumental in saving another bank that had been hit by crisis: SVB. However, it was not enough to prevent the SVB losing the position it had earned by the end of the 1920s as the leading major bank. SKA and SBV were the only major banks to survive this difficult period without government aid or a reduction in share capital. Both institutions were able to pay for their write-offs of around Sfr 150–200 million by releasing unallocated reserves. Job losses were also avoided. In 1939/40, SKA and SBV took a step that was to prove significant in the long term when, prompted by the political situation in Europe and the very attractive business prospects in the USA, they each opened a branch in New York. SBV had already opened an office in London in 1898, but the New York agency was SKA's first-ever foreign branch.

Banking in Basel in the 19th century

At the beginning of the 19th century, a whole raft of firms in Basel, at that time Switzerland's biggest business center, were combining trading and transportation operations with banking. Some of these companies went on to become pure private banks. In 1840, Basel had 16 banking houses, double the number located in Zurich. Alongside the private banks, various other banking institutions were established in the first half of the century, including in 1845 Bank in Basel, at that time one of the leading Swiss banknote-issuing institutions. After 1848, Basel began to stagnate as a banking center, and it seemed that the city might miss out on the developments occurring in Zurich and Geneva. The reasons for this lay in political events abroad – the European crisis of 1848 hit Basel particularly hard – and in the cautious response of many of the city's private bankers to the signals sent out by the creation of Crédit Mobilier. Over-reliance on American securities was also a problem. The private bankers now felt compelled to enter into closer co-operation with each other. Merian, Riggenbach, Speyr and others formed a consortium (the Bank-Verein of 1854) in order to share underwriting risk and to facilitate the management of larger business transactions. In 1863 this group, helped by a Zurich private bank, even tried to establish a joint-stock bank in Zurich, a plan that failed mainly due to opposition from SKA and other competitors. Following the war of 1870/71, as foreign financiers prepared to set up a bank in Basel, the loose Bank-Verein consortium turned itself into Basler Bankverein (founded on 12 February 1872). After further mergers with other banks, in 1895/96 this institution became Schweizerischer Bankverein (known internationally as Swiss Bank Corporation). In 1863, another grouping (La Roche, Lüscher, Dreyfus and others), which came together rather later, founded Basler Handelsbank with the help of some Basel trading companies and Zurich's SKA. The Basel Stock Exchange opened for business in 1876 and in 1899, relatively late compared with the rest of Switzerland, Basler Kantonalbank was established.[52]

Basler Handelsbank was founded on 29 December 1862. Only two years later it needed more office space and so purchased the pictured premises 'Zum Schilthof'. In 1945 Basler Handelsbank was taken over by Schweizerischer Bankverein.

The former head office of Schweizerischer Bankverein at the corner of Aeschenvorstadt/ St.-Alban-Graben in Basel.

The post-1945 boom: a surging economy and the expansion of foreign operations

In 1945, SBG's takeover of Eidgenössische Bank and SBV's acquisition of Basler Handelsbank removed two further major banks from the scene. Both Eidgenössische Bank and Basler Handelsbank had been forced to write off most of their blocked foreign holdings, especially those in the Third Reich, leaving them in a hopeless situation when the Second World War came to an end. Of the eight major Swiss banks operating in 1918, only five now remained.

Between 1945 and the present day, the Swiss banking sector has undergone various overlapping and interlinked trends:

- The increasing importance of Swiss banking to the Swiss economy
- A continuing process of concentration combined with structural change, progressive liberalization, and the growing influence of the shareholder-value approach
- A marked expansion of the major banks' activities abroad

Restructuring → 129

Growth of foreign operations → 167

- The major banks' increased interest in retail business (and their consequent development into full-service, or 'universal' banks)
- Constant adaptation and development of the product range, together with an increase in the different distribution channels used, plus the continuous integration of new financial services (e.g. Allfinanz)
- Revolutionary technological change

Allfinanz → 210
IT → 349

The increasing importance of international business

The first two decades after the Second World War saw the major banks build up their branch networks by acquiring existing banks or setting up completely new offices. Regions that had previously been ignored, such as Canton Valais, now had access to high-performance banks that were much better able to meet their customers' changing needs than the small local institutions.

The pecking order amongst the three biggest Swiss banks changed again when SBG (or UBS, to give it its international name) became the largest and best capitalized of the three thanks to its merger with the finance company Interhandel in 1966.

In the mid-1960s, the total assets of all Swiss banks exceeded the country's gross domestic product for the first time ever.[53] Furthermore, the combined total assets of the major banks overtook that of the cantonal banks. The key factor behind this development was the growth of international business. During the post-war period, domestic Swiss operations were a much higher priority than efforts to expand abroad. Then, from about 1965 onwards, the major banks significantly strengthened their commitment to business outside the home market. The re-introduction of fixed exchange rates between the major Western currencies in 1958, and the formation of numerous multinational companies, all of which required a wide range of financing services, helped to fuel the almost meteoric rise of the Euromarkets and greatly increased the importance of international banking.[54] The major Swiss banks intensified their involvement in money market business, but also in international securities business, which in other countries tended to be the preserve of specialist institutions. Finally, and rather late in the day, they started to build up their networks of international branch offices. By 1968 the three biggest major banks were deriving almost two-thirds of their revenue from outside Switzerland.[55]

Eurobond market → 172

As a counterpoint to the Swiss majors' increasing commitment to international business, more and more foreign banks began to arrive in Switzerland. Nonetheless, in the years between 1965 and 1970 alone, the major Swiss banks were able to expand their share of the overall domestic banking market from 33% to 45%, mainly thanks to their targeted entry into retail business.[56] They started to diversify their risk exposure more widely, and confirmed the full-service nature of their business by integrating new financial disciplines (such as leasing), and by expanding their gold and foreign exchange trading operations. Despite this growth at home and abroad, the major Swiss banks were still rather insignificant players by international comparison: even in 1973 the total assets of each of the three biggest banks in each of seven key industrialized nations were greater than those of SBG, at that time the largest bank in Switzerland. In fact SBG was only ranked 47th by size amongst the world's banks.[57]

At this point, the major Swiss banks entered into a race to open up branches in the domestic market – a race that was not slowed very much even by the two agreements to 'manage growth' that were in effect between 1971 and 1977, and between 1980 and 1983. Five hundred and fifty banks were already operating in Switzerland by 1977 (including private banks and finance companies), 74 more than in 1945.[58] The number of branches maintained by the major banks had risen from 182 in 1945 to 733 in 1977.[59] With 1,311 inhabitants per branch, Switzerland had the highest density of banks in the industrialized world.[60]

Deregulation and liberalization:
new structures emerge in the 1980s and 1990s

In the mid 1980s, the Swiss National Bank began to relax the barriers to foreign capital that had long been used to protect the Swiss franc. They also liberalized the rules on exporting capital. The ossified structures that prevailed in the domestic banking sector also had to be revitalized. Until this point, covenants between the financial institutions, many of them concluded in the belief that the interests of the state were being served, had made it impossible to rationalize the great number of different banks in the Swiss economy. In 1989/90, however, Switzerland's banking cartel was dissolved – not primarily as a result of international pressure, but because of the realization by the Swiss themselves that unfettered competition had to be encouraged.

Until the start of the 1990s, the major banks continued to account for a relatively stable 48-50% of the total assets of all banks in Switzerland – about twice

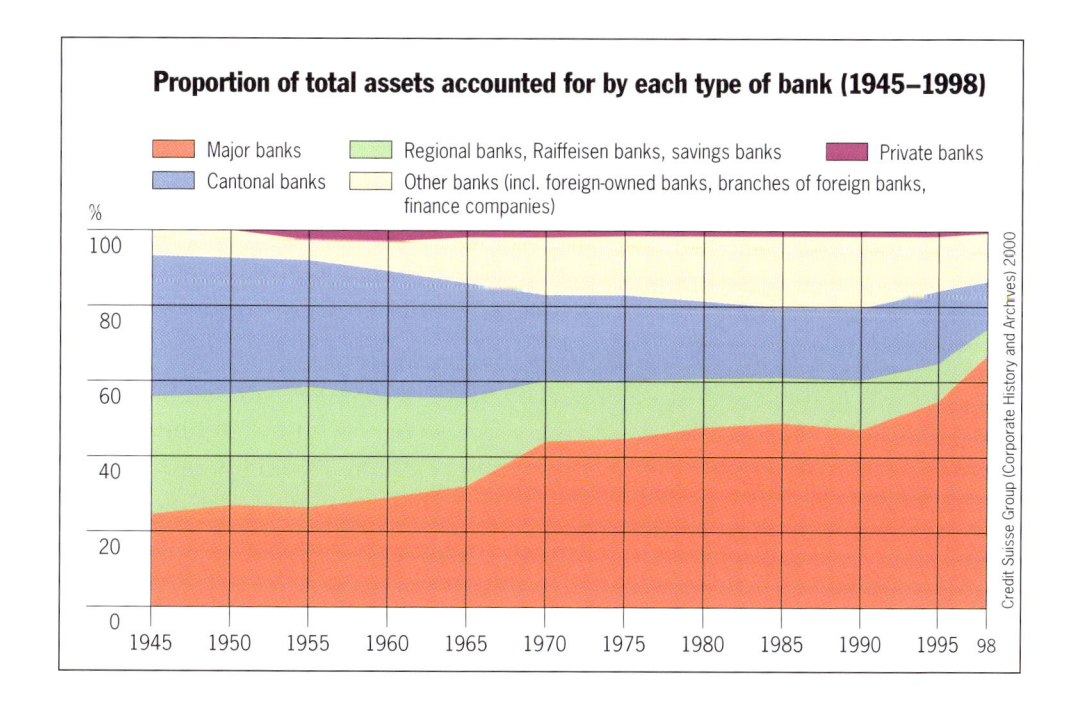

Proportion of total assets accounted for by each type of bank (1945–1998)

- Major banks
- Cantonal banks
- Regional banks, Raiffeisen banks, savings banks
- Other banks (incl. foreign-owned banks, branches of foreign banks, finance companies)
- Private banks

Credit Suisse Group (Corporate History and Archives) 2000

the proportion they boasted at the end of the Second World War. The cantonal banks' proportion remained at about 20% while that of the regional banks, Raiffeisen banks and savings banks fell to 9.3% by the mid-1990s – only about a third of the share they held in 1945.[61]

Initially, the number of banking institutions continued to rise, not least because of all the newly established foreign banks and finance companies arriving in Switzerland. There were 550 banks in 1977, but by 1990 this number had risen to a peak of 625 (including private banks and finance companies). By contrast, the number of independent private banks had declined from 73 in 1950 to 22 in 1990.[62] Finally, the number of branches maintained by the major banks had reached 969. The growth of the banking sector in Canton Ticino was particularly dynamic, and by 1990 the region had replaced Basel as the third biggest Swiss financial center, with 58 banks.[63]

Once the agreements concluded by the Swiss Bankers' Association had been abolished, there was nothing standing in the way of a further bout of structural adjustment and deregulation: CS Holding's acquisition of Bank Leu (1990) and the collapse of the Spar- and Leihkasse Thun (1991) ushered in a major phase of restructuring, over the course of which many smaller banks (such as EKO Bank of Olten, which was taken over and liquidated by CS Holding in 1992), but also a few of the bigger banks, had to close down or seek refuge with another institution. At the end of 1998 there were only 375 banks left in Switzerland, a fall – fueled by a persistent real estate crisis – of 250 since 1990.[64] The disappearance of so many banks, and the downsizing of branch networks, inevitably had an effect on banking density in Switzerland. Having peaked at a level of one branch per 853 people in 1991, the ratio had gradually fallen back to one for every 1,015 people by the end of 1997.[65] For the first time in decades, the banking sector found itself confronted with the prospect of job cuts. By 1990 the number of people working for banks throughout Switzerland had reached a peak of 121,352; by the end of 1998 this figure had fallen to 107,000.[66]

Even the large institutions, which continued to make great strides internationally, were caught up in the wave of restructuring. In addition, various cantonal banks had to be restructured or even privatized:

- Berner Kantonalbank (created by a merger between the Kantonalbank von Bern and the Hypothekarkasse des Kantons Bern – a private-sector joint-stock company since 1998)
- Solothurner Kantonalbank (privatized and taken over by SBV in 1995; new name: SoBa)
- Banque Cantonale de Genève (taken over by Banque Hypothécaire du Canton de Genève and converted into a semi-private joint-stock company)
- Banque Cantonale Vaudoise (merged with Crédit Foncier in 1995, also converted into a semi-private joint-stock company)
- Appenzell-Ausserrhodische Kantonalbank (acquired by SBG in 1996)

Rescue action → 136

The number of major banks also continued to decrease. After acquiring Bank Leu in 1990, in 1993 CS Holding took over the beleaguered SVB, thus becoming the market leader in Swiss retail business. Five years later came the surprise merger between SBV and SBG to form the new UBS AG. The net result was that by the end of the 20th century, only two major Swiss banks remained, Credit Suisse Group and UBS. These two now also enjoy a leading position in the international arena: measured in terms of stock market capitalization, by mid-1999 UBS and Credit Suisse Group were the third and fourth biggest banks in Europe.[67]

Bank Leu takeover → 131

SVB takeover → 137

SBV/SBG merger → 151

Credit Suisse Group's main premises on Paradeplatz.
The building – a milestone in Swiss banking architecture – was constructed between 1873 and 1876 by the star architect of the time, Jakob Friedrich Wanner (1830–1903). Alfred Escher declared that the building's appearance 'would be as much of an embellishment and an ornament to Zurich as the city's singularly attractive railway station'. Photo 1998.

Schweizerische Kreditanstalt: from a Zurich commercial and industrial bank to a global financial services company

Alfred Escher founded Schweizerische Kreditanstalt (SKA) in 1856 as a 'credit engine' to push forward the expansion of the railway network and the industrialization of Switzerland. The bank soon developed from a start-ups bank into a commercial and industrial bank, expanding its activities in lending and deposit-taking business, as well as its involvement with the electricity industry. For fifty years, SKA conducted regional, national and international operations from its head office on Paradeplatz, Zurich. Then, in 1905 it started to build a domestic branch network, and became more attractive to middle-class customers by opening a series of deposit counters. Unlike other major banks, SKA withstood the repeated crises of the period prior to 1945, and successfully defended its position as one of Switzerland's two largest banks.

This position became increasingly precarious in the years after the Second World War. As its rivals became more dynamic and tackled the challenges of rapid modernization, SKA remained committed to an over-cautious business policy, and as a result lost ground to the competition. Forced to act quickly by the Chiasso Affair of 1977, new figures in the bank's senior management committed themselves wholeheartedly to the revitalization of SKA. In particular by taking a stake in the investment bank First Boston, SKA was able to decisively strengthen its position in international business in the mid-1980s. Thanks to a series of strategic takeovers and mergers over the following decade, SKA for a time enjoyed the position of Switzerland's biggest retail bank. In 1996/97 CS Holding, originally founded in 1982 as a sister company to SKA, was transformed into Credit Suisse Group, which further consolidated its global significance as an Allfinanz conglomerate through its merger with Winterthur Insurance.

SKA's first years in the context of Swiss economic history

Conflicts between cantonal and global perspectives

In 1850, Switzerland stood at a crossroads. If it did not join up with the international railway network it was threatened with isolation. An inadequate transportation infrastructure would have serious consequences for Swiss business, science and academia. Furthermore, the businessmen and inexperienced bankers of Switzerland were not used to thinking and acting with the national picture in mind. Their outlook had always been cantonal or conversely, if their business involved trading, global.[68]

The close personal relationships that tied together the key politicians and businesspeople of the new federal state made it easier to overcome these problems within a reasonably short period of time. Alfred Escher, venture capitalist and infrastructure policymaker, embraced both national and corporate interests in exemplary fashion and it was not least thanks to his efforts that Switzerland achieved unity and stability as a state, and that it managed to achieve a degree of integration with the rest of Europe before it was too late.

Within the financial sector, the recently created large insurance companies were the first to reorient their business activities away from the regional and towards the national and international, using agencies to create the required distribution networks. The new commercial banks, by contrast, continued to find themselves caught between the two stools of regional and global business; 'Swiss' business only slowly moved to the forefront of their thinking. This ambivalence was less pronounced at SKA than elsewhere in the banking sector. The very name of German speaking Switzerland's first commercial bank emphasized the fact that it was an emphatically Swiss organization. (Schweizerische Kreditanstalt translates as 'Swiss Credit Institution', though for many years the bank has been known internationally as 'Credit Suisse'). At the same time, SKA's other priorities right from the start were its regional business and trade throughout the world.[69]

Regional, national and business motives

The young SKA's leaning towards Zurich and the Northeast Switzerland region was clearly reflected in the make-up of its first management bodies. Nonetheless the bank also defended Swiss national interests – especially in the railway industry – against the influence of foreign banks. Over the decades, national and business motives progressively became more important than regional interests. When in 1885, for example, discussions were held about a project to build the Simplon railway line, SKA's board of directors decided not to take account of the fact that Northeastern Switzerland was against the plan. The bank was also willing to nurture its profitable relations with banks in Geneva and Basel, and with the major Parisian bank Comptoir d'Escompte.[70] By underwriting public debt, SKA, as well as promoting business relations with the federal authorities,

'From all sides the railways move ever closer to Switzerland. The question of how they are all to be brought together is already the subject of vigorous debate; plans are being made which would see them going round Switzerland. The danger is that Switzerland will thus be completely bypassed, condemning it to a sorry future of solitude within Europe.' Alfred Escher in 1849 as the 30-year-old President of the National Council (taken from Gagliardi, Escher, p. 145).

SKA as a driving force behind the Swiss economy.

Front cover of the catalogue for the 1994 'Alfred Escher' exhibition shown at the 'le point' gallery in SKA's head office building in Zurich.

became increasingly involved in matters of national interest. In 1857, for example, the bank agreed to underwrite a tranche of the bond issued by the federal government to fund the mobilization of troops in Neuchâtel; and in 1870/71, SKA took part in a bond issued to finance the defense of the Swiss border against French incursion. Over and above this nationally oriented activity, from the end of the 1870s onwards, the bank was also involved in a growing number of bond issues by the cantons and municipalities. SKA took part in 11 cantonal or municipal bond issues between 1883 and 1894; between 1895 and 1913 it took part in 93 such issues.

Very soon after its inception, SKA had become a strong driving force in the economy, a role that was only to intensify in subsequent years.

- SKA promoted the Swiss railways, directly by contributing its own equity capital to rail construction projects, indirectly by helping to raise further capital.
- SKA promoted trade and industry: by helping to finance the large-scale import and export flows that were so vital to the country's development; by extending loans for other productive purposes; by taking equity stakes in new companies; and by helping to turn companies into productive, modern enterprises. The engineering, food and drink, and luxury goods industries were particularly reliant on issuing equities and bonds (the textile industry less so, since this sector was dominated by family companies that could boast considerable capital reserves of their own).
- SKA acted as a model and a source of ideas and, by setting up and taking stakes in companies, stood at the center of the new Swiss banking and insurance sector.
- SKA made a substantial contribution to the electrification of Switzerland by helping to fund numerous energy projects, either directly or through the finance companies it helped set up.

Statue of Alfred Escher in front of Zurich's main station.
The work by Richard Kissling (1848–1919) was officially unveiled in 1889 as a mark of posthumous respect by a private group of admirers. It prompted the artist Karl Stauffer to make the following, rather pointed remark: '... I am of the opinion that the real monument to Escher is the hole through the Gotthard. Period.'

Alfred Escher

SKA's early success was closely tied to the person of Alfred Escher (1819–1882). Escher dominated the political scene in Zurich and Switzerland in a way that would be unimaginable today. The institutions and ideas he initiated in the economic and cultural arenas qualify him as a paragon of 19th century economic liberalism.

Career milestones
1842	Graduated as the University of Zurich's first Doctor of Law
1844–1847	Guest lecturer at the University of Zurich
1844–1882	Member of the Zurich Cantonal Parliament
1848–1855	Governing Council of Canton Zurich (president 1849, 1850, 1851, 1854)
1848–1882	National Council (president 1849/50, 1856/57, 1862/63)
1853–1872	Chairman of the board of the Nordostbahn (NOB)
1854–1882	Vice chairman of the Polytechnikum school council
1856–1877	Chairman of the board of directors of SKA
1858–1874	Supervisory board of the Rentenanstalt
1859–1875	Member of Zurich City Council
1863–1872	Chairman of the standing committee of the Gotthardvereinigung
1872–1878	Chairman of the Gotthardbahngesellschaft
1879–1882	Chairman of the board of directors of NOB
1880–1882	Chairman of the board of directors of SKA

Escher reached the peak of his brilliant political career at an early age, before extending his activities to the burgeoning economy and the nascent railway industry. Towards the end of his life he increasingly ran into difficulties and suffered various setbacks. Having fallen out of favor, Escher, for so long unchallenged as the leading figure in the liberal community, was abandoned by many of his ex-colleagues.[71]

SKA's foundation in 1856: Swiss money for Swiss railways

Various motives and considerations prompted Alfred Escher, along with a number of other important business and political figures, to contemplate the foundation of a new type of large bank for the Zurich region:

- Crédit Mobilier, established in Paris by brothers Emile and Isaak Pereire in 1852, was originally conceived of as a bank with a wide range of business activities, but from the start it concentrated mainly on financing the foundation of new companies in the railway and large-scale industrial sectors. The appearance of this joint-stock bank triggered a wave of new bank openings throughout Europe; in Germany 16 banks of a similar type were founded in 1855/56 alone.
- Switzerland's railway construction projects – those that were planned and those that were already under way – required larger volumes of capital than the existing Swiss banking sector could provide. Escher and some of his colleagues were shareholders in Nordostbahn (NOB) railway company and were thus dependent on the backing of a well-capitalized financial institution.
- Major foreign banks, especially French ones (Crédit Mobilier, Rothschilds, Réunion Financière), had become increasingly active in Switzerland, and controlled large amounts of Swiss investment capital. In addition to the foreign banks, the new financial institutions and traditional private banks of Basel and Geneva were also striving to establish themselves in the railways business.

When the Crimean War ended in the spring of 1856, demand from the USA for manufactured goods shot up. In Switzerland, the ambitious railway construction projects promised a sustained economic boom. Business was blossoming and Swiss companies were full of optimism. Despite this propitious background, the financial negotiations that the chairman of NOB Alfred Escher was conducting with foreign banks were threatening to run into the sand. When it became known that the recently established Allgemeine Deutsche Credit-Anstalt (Leipzig) wanted to open a branch in Zurich, Escher realized that the time had come to put the plans for a well-capitalized, autonomous (or as autonomous as possible) bank into action without delay.

First of all, on the initiative of Christoph H. Hirzel-Lampe – Zurich book publisher, Switzerland's General Consul in Leipzig and founding member of Allgemeine Deutsche Credit-Anstalt – the arguments for and against setting up a Zurich branch of the German institution were examined. Escher and his colleagues, however, insisted on independence. As a compromise, the two parties agreed that Allgemeine Deutsche Credit-Anstalt would take a 50% stake in the new SKA's equity capital. Within a few months the preparatory work was complete. The founders contented themselves with making half of the company's Sfr 30 million capital stock liquid by issuing it in the form of shares. Sfr 7.5 million

The members of the founding committee that on 14 July 1856 constituted itself as the first board of directors of Schweizerische Kreditanstalt:

National Councillor Alfred Escher as chairman

Johann Jakob Rüttimann, Governing Council of Canton Zurich, as vice chairman

Heinrich Abegg of the bank F. Arlès-Dufour, Paris

National Councillor Johann Heinrich Fierz of the cotton-trading firm Heinrich Fierz

Colonel Bernhard Friedrich Fischer of the firm Heinrich Meyer of Brugg, as representative of the Allgemeine Deutsche Credit-Anstalt, Leipzig

Johannes Hagenbuch, owner of Orell Füssli & Co., booksellers of Zurich

Christoph H. Hirzel-Lampe, Swiss Consul General in Leipzig

National Councillor Heinrich Hüni-Stettler, Governing Council of Canton Zurich, chairman of the Zurich Chamber of Commerce

Casimir Friedrich Knörr, private banker of Lucerne

Benedikt La Roche-Stehelin, City Councillor and private banker of Basel

Colonel Johann Rudolf Raschle, owner of the textile mill Raschle & Co. of Wattwil

Adolf Rieter-Rothpletz, of the trading house Rieter, Ziegler & Co. of Winterthur

Jacques Ris, of the bank A. Ris & Co. of Zurich

National Councillor Friedrich Peyer Im Hof, chairman of the Rheinfallbahn, Schaffhausen

National Councillor Rudolf Friedrich Wäffler-Egli of the trading house Wäffler-Egli of Winterthur

of these went to Allgemeine Deutsche Credit-Anstalt, and the other Sfr 7.5 million remained in Swiss hands. Sfr 3 million of shares was allocated to Escher and his group, and the remaining Sfr 4.5 million was earmarked for other shareholders, most of whom came from Zurich. Within three days, interested investors had subscribed Sfr 218 million, clearly reflecting the mood of optimism and renewal that characterized the Swiss economy of the time. On 16 July 1856, SKA opened its doors for business with half a dozen employees at the 'Kleiner Tiefenhof' in Zurich.

What was new for Switzerland about this setting-up process was the fact that businesspeople, primarily from the textile industry, put large sums of money into an investment that was not directly connected to their own business activities.[72] It is also noteworthy that Zurich's private banks, far from opposing the establishment of the new company, actually participated in the initial offering. Ultimately, by buying shares in SKA, all the investors were helping to finance the construction of the Swiss railway system.

The new firm's articles of association defined its business goals more broadly than that of the handful of older commercial banks. Its aim was 'to found and operate industrial and other companies on its own account, to participate in existing or newly created companies, to help with their management or to take them over wholesale, to advise on the formation of companies, and to under-

Zurich's Governing Council approved Schweizerische Kreditanstalt's first articles of association on 5 July 1856. The picture shows the front cover as well as the page of articles covering the bank's purpose and lines of business.

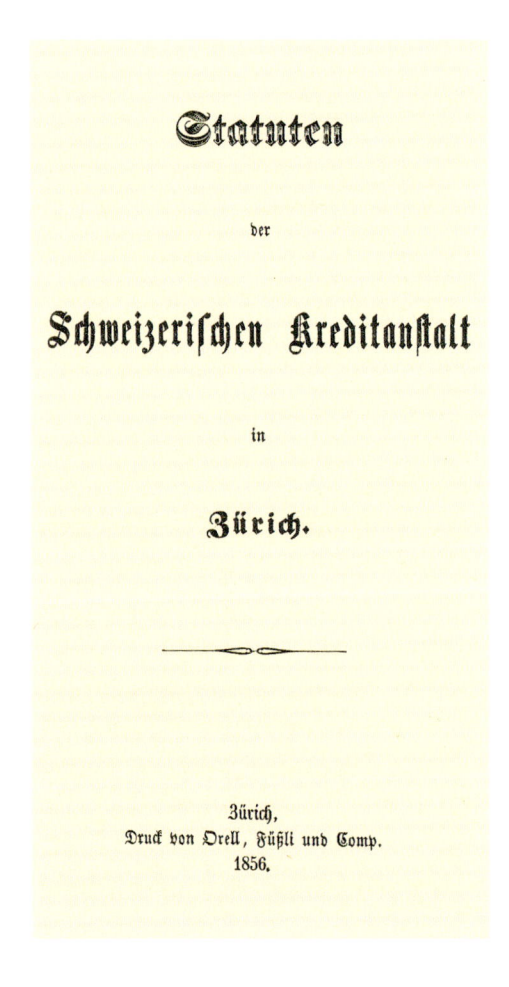

write the equities and bonds of these companies in accordance with the relevant legal provisions' (12c of the 'Statuten' pictured opposite).[73] SKA's business operations also included trading in precious metals, securities and goods, as well as hypothecation, bill and other discounting business, clearing, deposit-taking, lending and collection business, and issuing bonds up to the amount of its equity capital.

Although the general design of the bank came from France, and the impetus to actually found it came from Germany, the critical influence remained Swiss. For one thing, Alfred Escher and the other founders developed an institution which – apart from the company start-ups and railway financing – was very different from Crédit Mobilier in terms of its everyday business practices.[74] Secondly, despite its 50% stake, Allgemeine Deutsche Credit-Anstalt only exerted a minimal influence on the new bank. As early as 1859 it began to dispose of its SKA shares, and after SKA's articles of association were revised in 1885 it withdrew from the board of directors.

SKA's first premises were in the 'Kleiner Tiefenhof' in Zurich. The illustration shows a view of the 'Tiefenhof' and environs around 1840.

1856–1914: growing pains

Trial and error instead of strategy

To start with, the newly established SKA could only boast a moderate degree of expertise in managing a commercial bank or in dealing with long-term industrial loans. The history of the bank up to the 1860s was somewhat fraught, with all manner of business activities conducted on a trial and error basis. As soon as the bank was founded, there were discussions about issuing banknotes and possibly adding a mortgage institution. However it was eventually decided that the bank should not engage in mortgage business, because it would contravene the principles of a commercial bank by tying up funds over the long term without generating sufficient turnover.

For a long time, SKA was regarded with some justification as an elitist bank, which makes it all the more surprising that it cultivated a customer segment, albeit tentatively, that had little in common with the normal target clientele of a joint-stock commercial bank. Possibly in order to fulfill one of the corporate objectives laid down in its articles of association – to promote farming and small businesses – SKA tried in vain to launch a 'project with significance for the agricultural sector' by setting up a sugar beet factory. Furthermore, until 1862 the bank's portfolio contained up to Sfr 25,000 worth of 'Racen-thierzucht-Actien' (shares in animal breeding ventures). Clearly the bank was trying to include agricultural enterprises in its efforts to drive the Swiss economy forward. Even at the birth of the new bank, the *Neue Zürcher Zeitung* newspaper had described this particular business objective as 'fishing for compliments'.[75]

Agriculture and small businesses, which really had little significance to SKA's early operations, were removed from the corporate objectives listed in the

SKA's image → 239

The principle of 'encouraging farming, trade and commerce' contained in SKA's articles of association is 'an innocent captatio benevolentiae, an attempt to curry favor' (*NZZ*, quoted by Jöhr, SKA, p. 43).

articles of association when these were revised in 1897. The articles subsequently only included the promotion 'of trading and industrial companies'.

Start-ups business and real estate purchases

As it became clear just how easy it was to make a loss in the start-ups business (founding and participating in new companies) and in the acquisitions business, especially in the industrial sector, the bank increasingly concentrated on operations that 'could be run directly by our management'.[76] By 1862, the heading 'industrial participations' had disappeared from the balance sheet and in 1873, the last industrial establishment owned by SKA was sold. However, by the 1880s, stakes in industrial companies became worthwhile again as many firms converted into joint-stock companies (Aktiengesellschaften, or AGs).

Real estate acquisitions proved as unsuccessful for SKA as the start-ups business had. A factory that made chalets in Paris, a castle with its own brewery in Bavaria, spinning mills in Switzerland and various other properties were purchased, and then kept on for several years, despite yielding minimal returns or even making losses, before finally being sold.

Commodities trading

Trading in commodities also proved to be a loss making business for the young SKA. Price volatility on the commodities market (particularly for cotton and dyer's madder), and the losses this caused in the years between 1859 and 1861, prompted the bank to extricate itself from the commodities business and from holdings in companies that engaged in commodities trading. Schweizerische Exportgesellschaft, formed by SKA together with a number of merchants and industrialists, was made independent in 1861, though SKA continued to hold shares and sit on the board. Creating an export company did not prove to be a very successful move given the repeated trade crises, and Schweizerische Exportgesellschaft had to be wound up in the 1870s. Nevertheless the idea of running an export company kept cropping up in discussions until well into the 20th century. Even after pulling out of Exportgesellschaft, SKA remained heavily involved in the import-export business through its letters of credit, bills of lading and other bills.

The consequences of all this trial and error are made only too clear by the considerable fluctuations in the dividends paid out during these years: 1858 brought a dividend of 3.8%, the lowest in the whole history of SKA, while 1862's dividend, at 12.5%, was the highest. In 1867 the dividend was 4.5%, a figure that was to be bettered every year until 1939. 1867 was, in fact, SKA's worst ever reporting period. Having endured a year of 'abnormally unfavorable economic conditions' it was the only time until 1996 that the bank as a whole had to report a loss.[78] This potentially fatal crisis made the bank, which by now had been in operation for more than a decade, refocus its business activities. Over the course of the following year, SKA was to move away from start-ups business and long-term financing in order to dedicate itself to commercial banking. Short and medium-term loans, which were easier to secure, and deposit-taking thus

---

SKA's estate in Slavonia

In 1873, SKA joined a consortium to buy an estate of 18,000 joch (about 10,300 hectares) in Slavonia. The idea was to turn the forests on the estate to industrial use and then to sell the land at a profit at a later date. As it happened, the timber stocks proved less productive than anticipated and large investments in infrastructure were required. After its partners either withdrew or went bankrupt, SKA had no choice but to take on the estate on its own. The bank continued to manage the project after a fashion. Board members were repeatedly sent out to look for solutions and opportunities to sell until SKA finally got rid of the estate in 1887.[77]

moved to center stage. 1885's articles of association took account of the change of direction initiated in the late 1860s to the extent that they redefined SKA's range of business activities: credit business and loan negotiation were now listed above proprietary securities transactions and long-term participations.[79] Asset management, safekeeping of valuables, and management services for other banks and finance companies were also included in the articles for the first time.

Railways, shares and factories

Financing the railway network

One of the main pillars of SKA's business in the early decades of its existence was its involvement in the construction of Switzerland's railway network. The financing of Nordostbahn (NOB) was unquestionably the central element of this enterprise. At the end of the bank's first business year, 25% (or almost Sfr 1 million) of its securities portfolio was made up of NOB stock. Accounting for a twentieth of the new bank's total assets, the NOB participation represented a considerable risk. As with the establishment of the Rentenanstalt insurance company in the same year, this showed that in its early years the bank was prepared to take on large accumulations of risk that today would be regarded as extremely hazardous. As mentioned earlier, the motive to take on such risky commitments was not primarily economic, like the speculative business entered into by Crédit Mobilier of France, but political. It should also be mentioned that from the point of view of NOB itself, SKA's stake was relatively small, accounting for only 2.3% of its total capital stock.[80] Once its co-operation with NOB was up and running, the bank reduced its shareholding to less than 20% of its securities portfolio, a percentage that it was not to exceed again right up to the nationalization of the Swiss railways on 1 January 1902.[81] In autumn 1857, SKA began its close cooperation with NOB on bond issues.

Once the initial period of expansion amongst the private railways had come to an end towards the middle of the 1860s, railway construction in Switzerland slowed more or less to a halt. The second great phase of railway construction was then ushered in by the ratification of the first Gotthard agreement in 1869, the creation of the international Gotthard consortium in 1871, and the start of construction work on the Gotthard line during the following year. Although the financial participation of the Swiss banks led by SKA was relatively small, SKA played an important role in the Gotthard project. Quite apart from Escher's personal contribution as chairman of the board of Gotthardbahngesellschaft, the bank provided a variety of services 'in the interest of the country and shareholders'.[82] Not only did SKA help to draft the Gotthard agreement, it also liaised between the international consortium – which consisted of one leading group each from Germany, Italy and Switzerland – and Gotthardbahngesellschaft, the company charged with constructing the railway. When in 1875 the railway crisis and excessive construction costs threatened to derail the project, SKA intervened once again to underwrite a series of bond issues.[83]

Rudolf Koller (1828–1905). The 'Gotthardpost'. 1874. Oil on canvas. Credit Suisse Group Collection.

The 'Gotthardpost' – the name popularly given to the painting – is Koller's best-loved work. The painting shown here, acquired by SKA in 1965, is the second version, which the painter produced a year after the first version of 1873.
The first 'Gotthardpost', which can be seen today at Zurich's Museum of Art (Kunsthaus), was commissioned by the board of the Nordostbahn as a present for Alfred Escher on his resignation as chairman and director of the Nordostbahn.

NOB too suffered from the consequences of a collapsing economy and the intensifying struggle between rival railway companies. In 1872 leading figures from the democratic movement in Winterthur[84] founded Nationalbahn as a direct challenge to Escher's NOB. The two rival companies purchased additional railway lines which, however, soon proved unprofitable and which dragged the railway companies en masse into a deep crisis. NOB shareholders were faced with an unexpected collapse in dividends. After enjoying a healthy payout of 8% in 1875, in 1877 they received nothing at all. All the expansion plans had to be downscaled. Even in this period of crisis, the national interests that were so heavily emphasized at the time were still prioritized: a rescue plan involving a bond issue by a French consortium was rejected after heavy criticism.

Things started to look up in 1878. Elections to the council of Canton Zurich gave a majority back to the Liberals at the expense of the Democrats, thus creating a more favorable climate for investment. Resignations, a moratorium on construction, the forced liquidation of Nationalbahn in 1878, and the establishment of Schweizerische Eisenbahnbank ('Swiss Railway Bank') by SKA in the same year also helped to alleviate the crisis. In 1880, NOB took over Nationalbahn, which had thus far been its main rival. Eisenbahnbank played a decisive role during this time: the new company, the first of its kind in Switzerland, was charged with restructuring NOB in accordance with the principle of 'securities substitution'. Three representatives of SKA sat on Eisenbahnbank's 18-man board of directors, and SKA held around 20% of the firm's equity capital of Sfr 20 million. Despite French collaboration, the autonomy and the Swiss character of Eisenbahnbank, which was wound up in the mid-1880s once the restructuring of NOB was complete, was heavily emphasized. The economically liberal elite that controlled the banks and railways had restored its reputation.[85] Though the two institutions became less close, SKA retained its ties to NOB until 1902.

From 1890 onwards, SKA increasingly used the funds it had invested in railways to buy stakes in newly established finance companies, such as Bank für Orientalische Eisenbahnen in Zurich (1890), the Société Financière Franco-Suisse in Geneva (1892), and Banque Belge des Chemins de fer in Brussels (end of 1894). The focus of its railway investments shifted gradually to Southeastern Europe and Asia Minor – regions that were yet to develop their own railway systems properly.

Securities business

In its first years of business, an average of around 30% of SKA's assets was invested in securities and participations. Documents from 1860 show that securities business was not targeted as a main focus of the bank's operations. Depending on changes in business policy and the general economic conditions, in subsequent years this principle was sometimes observed, sometimes not. Between 1863 and 1868, for example, SKA carried a substantial portfolio of equities. At the end of 1865 this portfolio was worth Sfr 15.4 million, account-

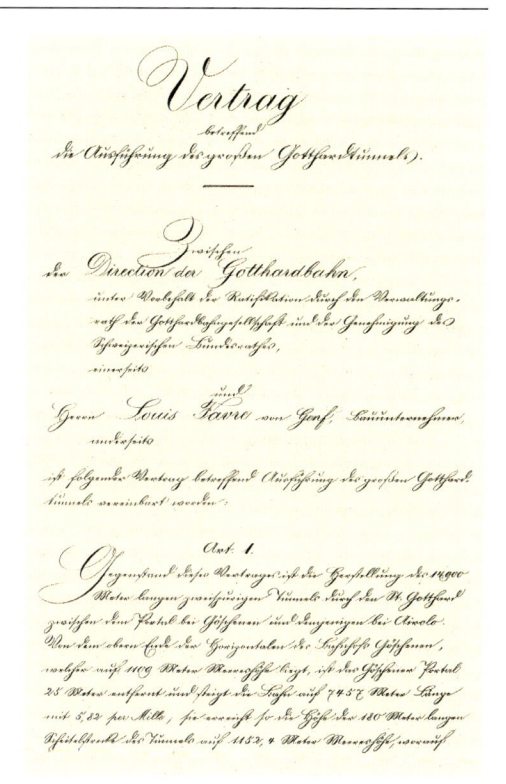

Alfred Escher was chairman of the Gotthardbahngesellschaft from 1872 to 1878. Collaboration between the directors of the Gotthardbahn and the building contractor Louis Favre was governed by an eleven-page contract signed on 7 August 1872. Article 1 of this contract states:
'The object of this contract is the construction of the 14,900-meter long, two-lane tunnel through the St. Gotthard between the portals at Göschenen and Airolo. The Göschenen portal is 25 meters from the upper end of the horizontals at Göschenen station, which lies 1,109 meters above sea-level, and the railway rises for a length of 7,457 meters at 5.82 millimeters per meter; in this way it reaches the height of the 180-meter long stretch that marks the apex of the tunnel at 1,152 meters above sea level...'
On 29 February 1880, the Gotthard tunnel penetrated the entire massif, and only two years later the first trains were running between Göschenen and Airolo.

Die Kreditanstalt in Zürich gegen den Paradeplatz zu.
Nach dem Originalplane des Hrn. Oberarchitekten Wanner ausgeführt von Hrn. Xylograph Bachmann

In the *Bürkli-Kalender* of 1874, 'Kreditanstalt's palace', which was still under construction, was introduced under the title 'A contribution to the beautification of the city of Zurich'. The new building was ready for occupation on 25 September 1876. Since the bank only employed fifty staff at this time, it had to rent out part of the premises. Thus the *Kalender* also noted: 'But while the other financial institutions build their palaces for themselves, the Kreditanstalt has seized the opportunity to use the construction of theirs to do some good business. It is an old rule that a good house-owner should receive as much rent from his tenants as he needs to pay for his own quarters; the Kreditanstalt would appear to have something similar in mind. We don't know if it will have its quarters paid for, but we can be sure that by renting out space it is in a position to construct a great and beautiful building on Zurich's most attractive and best-located square.'

ing for 27% of all assets. In the years that followed, the larger part of this stock was sold, and by the mid 1890s the bank's portfolio, though still worth Sfr 15 million, was by now equivalent to only 11% of total assets.

In 1862, SKA's securities transactions contributed about Sfr 1.5 million to earnings – i.e. about 48% of the total. In the following year, the bank made a loss on securities transactions of some Sfr 770,000. Excessive unauthorized securities buying by senior management prompted the board of directors to dispose of domestic paper and temporarily to keep away from virtually all foreign securities. The new bank's securities portfolio underwent many major changes. In the first few years, the portion of the portfolio devoted to equities was much larger than the bond portion and in 1859, for example, bonds accounted for only about 10% of the bank's securities. Then between 1866 and 1882, a more cautious business policy meant that more bonds were held than equities. Generally the ratio was about 2:1 in favor of bonds at this time, though in 1880 the dominance of bonds peaked when they accounted for 85% of the total securities portfolio. At the end of the 1880s the ratio between shares and bonds gradually began to even out.

Until 1862, the balance between Swiss and foreign securities fluctuated in a range between 3:1 and 2:1. SKA's holdings of Swiss securities consisted mainly of railway shares and bonds, as well as paper issued by individual banks and companies. In 1863 the gathering wave of company start-ups caused the price of Swiss banking and insurance shares to rise. Up till 1861, SKA's foreign securities were mainly those issued by North American and later by German rail companies. There was a marked reduction in holdings of non-Swiss paper between 1864 and 1869, but then 'in response to public interest', SKA turned its attention back to North American railway stocks – especially bonds, and then also started buying securities from Germany, Italy, France and Austria. Its portfolio of Swiss stocks was broadened and sometimes even included the shares of direct competitors such as Bank in Winterthur, as well as of various insurance companies that SKA had founded or co-founded. From 1877 onwards, Swiss and foreign securities took turns to make up the majority of the portfolio. American railway stocks were joined by European bank and railway paper and by government bonds. From the mid 1880s to the start of the First World War, there was a gradual increase in the proportion of foreign securities.

Start-ups and participations in the financial industry

Alongside its commitments in the rail industry, another of the young SKA's major lines of business, and another good example of the bank's significance to the Swiss economy as a whole, was its work on the establishment of new insurance companies and banks. The event that stands out above all others here is undoubtedly SKA's involvement in the creation of Rentenanstalt. On the initiative of Conrad Widmer, Director of the Zurich Penal Institution, and following a resolution of the SKA board of directors, Schweizerische Rentenanstalt (literally translated as 'Swiss Pensions Institution', but known internationally as Swiss Life) was established as an independent life insurance company.[86] In practical terms, the new institution was still a division of SKA. Not only did the bank take the considerable risk of putting up the whole of its equity capital, Sfr 15 million at the time, to guarantee all of Rentenanstalt's liabilities, but it also selected the new company's management and three members of its supervisory board. What is more, to start with it claimed 40% of Rentenanstalt's annual net earnings for itself.

'A healthy company put up by the Creditanstalt is bound to meet with general approval' (Moritz Grossmann, 1863).

Once Rentenanstalt had established itself in the up-and-coming insurance market, it began after 1867 to loosen its ties to SKA. However, the long drawn-out discussion about the introduction of a government insurance regulator and various political disputes with Zurich's democratic government, which ultimately had to be taken to the Federal Council, meant that the two companies did not actually completely split from one another until almost 20 years later, in 1885. The 'Kreditanstalt/Rentenanstalt' model was the closest relationship between a bank and an insurance company in Switzerland in the 19th century. In the light of today's Allfinanz/bancassurance strategies, it is worth taking a closer look at this model.

Relationship between Kreditanstalt and Rentenanstalt → 211

A whole series of new companies emerged in the financial sector in the early 1860s. SKA took equity stakes in the Helvetia Feuerversicherung fire insurance company in 1861 (Sfr 100,000) and in Schweizerische Rückversicherungs-Gesellschaft in 1863 (an initial investment of around Sfr 1.6 million). In the case of the Rückversicherung (popularly known as 'Schweizer Rück', this was the reinsurance company later to become known internationally as Swiss Re), SKA's involvement also included work on the company's foundation charter and arti-

Involvement in setting up insurance companies → 216

The chairmen of the board of directors of Schweizerische Kreditanstalt and Credit Suisse Group. Portraits from the Credit Suisse Group Collection.

Katrin Pillon-Brauer (*1946). Alfred Escher. 1999.

Léon J. R. Bonnat (1833–1922). Carl Abegg-Arter. 1906.

Paul Janowitch (–?). Julius Frey. 1917.

John Quincy Adams (1874–1933). Wilhelm Caspar Escher. 1927.

Schweizerische Kreditanstalt

Marcel-André Baschet (1862–1941). Hermann Stoll. 1937.

Alexandre Blanchet (1882–1961). Adolf Jöhr. 1944.

Alexandre Blanchet (1882–1961). Ernst Gamper. 1957.

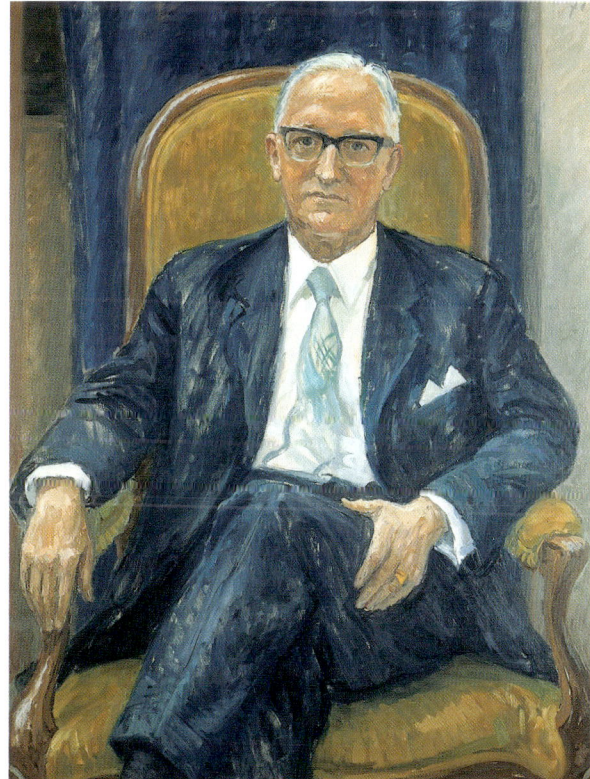

Walter Sautter (1911–1991). Felix W. Schulthess. 1971.

Hermann Alfred Sigg (*1924). Oswald Aeppli. 1985.

George J. D. Bruce (*1930). Rainer E. Gut. 1991.

The chairmen of the board of directors of Schweizerische Kreditanstalt/ Credit Suisse Group (1856–2000)

Alfred Escher	1856–1877, 1880–1882
Heinrich Fierz-Etzweiler	1877–1880
Carl Abegg-Arter	1883–1911
Julius Frey	1911–1925
Wilhelm Caspar Escher	1925–1929
Hermann Stoll	1929–1940
Adolf Jöhr	1940–1953
Ernst Gamper	1953–1963
Felix W. Schulthess	1963–1977
Oswald Aeppli	1977–1983
Rainer E. Gut	1983–2000

Heinrich Fierz-Etzweiler, chairman of the board of directors of SKA from 1877 to 1880, was not painted for the Collection. Photo taken around 1880.

An SKA share from 1890. Some of the images on the certificate illustrate the bank's connections with transportation and trade. Others reflect SKA's close ties to the city of Zurich and to Switzerland.

cles of association, the nomination of several directors and a right of approval over changes to the company's articles. The parties behind the creation of Helvetia and Schweizer Rück were only too happy to have the support of what was then the biggest bank in German-speaking Switzerland.[87]

In 1869, SKA was active on its own account once again when it set up the 'Schweiz' transportation insurance company. Three years later the 'Schweiz' developed into Versicherungs-Verein, which then in 1875 became known as Transport- und Unfall-Versicherungs-Actiengesellschaft 'Zürich'.

SKA had been involved in setting up new banks ever since 1856 when it helped found Bank in Luzern. In 1863 it provided capital and expertise for the establishment of Basler Handelsbank. In the new wave of start-ups that gripped the financial sector, it once again helped to set up more banks by taking up stock, either to issue or to hold temporarily in its own portfolio of participations. These investments included Basler Bankverein, Banca della Svizzera Italiana in Lugano and various banks in neighboring countries. In Italy, for example, SKA held stakes in Banca Napolitana di Credito e di Deposito in Naples, and Banca Italo-Svizzera in Genoa; in Austria, it was Bank für Tirol und Vorarlberg in Innsbruck; in Germany, Berliner Produkten- und Handelsbank; and finally in the Alsace, Bank in Mülhausen. In 1874, at the suggestion of its Viennese representative, SKA set up the Österreichisch-Schweizerischer Credit-Verein. This was conceived as a co-operative and functioned as a discounting bank, issuing discount credits exclusively to members of the co-operative. Three years later SKA called in the loan of over Sfr 2 million that it had granted as a capital investment.[88] An adventurously speculative stake of Sfr 250,000 in Swiss American Bank in San Francisco had to be written off in 1877 when the Californian bank was liquidated.

The number of new bank start-ups gradually decreased from the 1880s onwards. One of SKA's most significant pieces of business at the tail-end of the 19th century was its participation in the foundation of Banca Commerciale Italiana in Milan in 1894, which was to become one of Italy's leading financial institutions. SKA's limited liability participation in the German bank J. Dreyfus & Co. of Frankfurt am Main between 1881 and 1897 constituted a special case: SKA's intention was to secure its own link to the key Frankfurt stock exchange. The relationship came to an end when J. Dreyfus & Co. merged with Commerz- und Diskonto-Bank in Hamburg.[89]

Participations in industrial companies

Apart from its activities in the electricity sector, SKA's involvement in industry was less focused on creating new companies, and more on taking equity stakes in institutions set up by others. In the 1860s and the early 1870s, these holdings often took the form of limited partnership stakes ('Kommanditeinlagen'). As mentioned earlier, many of these investments led to losses for SKA. Then, from the 1880s onwards, most of the bank's industrial interests were associated with the conversion of privately owned industrial companies into joint-stock companies. The intention, or the hope at least, was to benefit from a rising share price when the companies earnings subsequently improved. As Switzerland's industrial base broadened out, SKA realigned its business policy, particularly with regard to domestic operations. Financing industry became increasingly important, and financing the railways less so. The rise of the engineering industry led to an intensification of business relations with this branch of the economy and in the early 1870s, SKA started supporting the development of the machine tool manufacturer Daverio Siewerdt Giesker. In 1876 it took part in its conversion into AG Werkzeug- und Maschinenfabrik Oerlikon (MFO) before gradually growing to be the company's house bank. As the century moved to its close, SKA entered into further significant relationships with engineering companies, including the Georg Fischer iron and steel works, Escher Wyss & Cie., and Brown, Boveri & Cie. From the 1870s, SKA's client list included more and more foreign companies, such as Krupp in Essen and, later on, Germany's AEG (Allgemeine Elektricitäts-Gesellschaft).

Close contacts were also forged with the emerging food and drink industry. Having maintained a business relationship with the Anglo-Swiss Condensed Milk Company of Cham, SKA eventually took part – mainly thanks to the personal commitment of its director Wilhelm Caspar Escher – in the company's merger with Nestlé. The bank also granted loans to Maggi and Sprüngli. Apart from these exceptions, however, until about 1914 contacts between banks and industrial concerns were limited to the bare minimum; industrial companies tended to be family-run, and the owners were often only prepared to take on short-term debt. One of the exceptions was, as mentioned above, the Maggi company founded in Kemptthal in 1869. SKA director Georg Stoll, later to become managing director of Maggi, not only secured capital from the estate of Alfred Escher, but in 1886 also backed the creation of the new limited partnership Julius Maggi & Co. and its conversion into a joint-stock company four years later.[90] Unlike the Swiss federal government, SKA recognized Maggi's market potential and, implicitly, the significance of new forms of food production to the modern world. Furthermore, its support for the company once again demonstrated SKA's commitment to Switzerland as a business location.

Thanks to the bank's relationships with major companies at home and abroad – and thanks also to the increasing breadth of the Swiss money and capital markets – the last two decades of the 19th century saw SKA develop into a significant and respected issuing house. Unlike the dominant banks in larger countries, SKA never acted as principal in the major financing operations, preferring instead to take on subholdings.[91] Between 1895 and 1906, the bank's syndicate business included numerous equity issues as well as 121 Swiss and about 250 foreign bond issues. This average of about 23 foreign bond issues per year was not matched again until the 1950s.[92] As with all the large banking institutions, brokerage business on the capital markets played a more important role for SKA at the turn of the century than commercial lending. From the 1890s, various investment companies were set up with the intention of offering investment opportunities to a broader section of the population. SKA was once again in the thick of things: Zürcherisch-Amerikanische Trustgesellschaft (1895–1902) was formed, like Bank in Zürich and Eidgenössische Bank, in response to the boom in American securities business. It was set up with equity capital of Sfr 8 million, and was the first Swiss investment trust to concentrate on North American securities. When the economic boom in the USA showed signs of slowing down in 1901, gains were realized and the company was closed down. The experience led to the creation of various other companies, such as Zurich American Trust (1904–1917), which was fully owned by SKA and its customers.[93]

If railways dominated SKA's industrial business in the first decades of its existence, giving it the personality of a 'railway bank', towards the end of the 19th century this area of activities was gradually superceded by another important part of the economy: the electricity industry. In 1891, SKA and two other Swiss companies, MFO and Escher Wyss & Cie., set up a research company to look into the development of hydroelectric power in Switzerland. From then on the bank was to play a pioneering role in the electrification of the country. In 1894, SKA helped to finance the construction of the first large-scale power station on the River Rhine, the Kraftübertragungswerke Rheinfelden. In 1895, it cooperated with Deutsche Bank, the AEG Group and various Swiss companies to create Bank für elektrische Unternehmungen, or Elektrobank, which from 1946 was known as Elektro-Watt Elektrische und Industrielle Unternehmungen AG. Bank für elektrische Unternehmungen (also known as the 'Elektrobank'), initially controlled by German capital, proved to be a driving force behind

The age of the finance companies

The age of the finance companies began in 1890. These new financial institutions were important for SKA for various reasons, as the 1897 annual report attests: 'Over the course of the last seven years we have gradually established several financial institutions in Zurich for a series of special tasks which we would not be able to carry out properly within the scope of our normal business operations; some of these have been set up on our own initiative, some at the instigation of and in cooperation with other correspondent banks. [...] All of these institutions, some of them significantly capitalized, have given our bank, which is charged with their special administration, the opportunity to intensify its relations with a number of other outstanding banking institutions and industrial companies, and thus also given us the opportunity for more involvement in large international financing operations.'[94]

Adolf Jöhr, chairman of the board of directors of SKA, also took on the chairmanship of Elektrowatt in 1947. This portrait of Adolf Jöhr – oil on canvas – was painted in 1926 by the German Expressionist Max Liebermann (1847–1935) and is today held in the Credit Suisse Group Collection.

A contract signed on 31 July 1895 marked the start of many years of cooperation between Bank für elektrische Unternehmungen (Elektrowatt) and SKA. In the first article of the contract, the Bank für elektrische Unternehmungen assigns cash services, bookkeeping, securities safekeeping and the associated secretarial and correspondence work to SKA. The remaining articles deal with the diligence and punctuality with which these tasks must be carried out and with various questions of compensation.

Immediately after the Second World War, Elektrowatt still occupied a relatively modest position in the Swiss electricity industry. This changed in 1947 when it founded the Bau- und Betriebsgesellschaft Kraftwerke Mauvoisin AG based in Sion. The photograph shows the Mauvoisin power station in Val de Bagnes during construction in 1955. The 237m high dam was declared operational on 17 September 1958. Between 1989 and 1991 the dam wall was raised to 250m. Mauvoisin is one of the world's highest dams.

In 1910 SKA founded the Schweizerisch-Argentinische Hypothekenbank, domiciled in Zurich. The bank, which was involved primarily in the electricity industry, set up the branch in Buenos Aires pictured here. Photo taken around 1920.

As early as March 1864 the board of directors identified credit and current account operations as the businesses most likely to bring 'the prospect of a handsome and steady return on equity capital'.

the utilization of domestic hydroelectric power, and was gradually transferred entirely into Swiss hands. SKA traditionally had two representatives on Elektrobank's board of directors, and assumed the management of the firm's business operations right from the start.

The new finance and investment companies became increasingly active in markets outside Europe and North America. Encouraged by the head of Elektrobank, in 1910 SKA founded Schweizerisch-Argentinische Hypothekenbank with its head office in Zurich and a branch in Buenos Aires. Again SKA assumed the management of the new company.[95] The creation of this institution, which was primarily involved in the electricity industry, reflected the growing importance of the two most prosperous states in Latin America, Argentina and Chile.

Commercial business and the first branches

Unlike the Crédit Mobilier banks in Paris and Geneva, from its very inception SKA laid greater emphasis on diversifying risk. After the first few years, core banking business increasingly took center stage, ahead of start-ups business and equity participations.

In addition to the bill discounting and mortgage lending that had become standard fare by this time, SKA became the first Swiss bank to begin offering current accounts on a large scale. This new business gradually developed into a lively lending operation, centering particularly on unsecured credits.[96] Since current account transactions, unlike bills and drafts, have remained a mainstay of banking right up to the present day, the following section concentrates mainly on this type of business.

Between 1857 and 1860, an average of 43% (about Sfr 3.5 million per year), and between 1875 and 1880 about 56% (Sfr 16 million) of the current account loans granted by SKA were unsecured. As a result of repeated losses, SKA's practice of granting unsecured loans without carrying out thorough credit checks attracted an increasing amount of criticism. By 1913 the proportion of unsecured loans had decreased to a quarter of total outstanding claims. By analyzing the borrowers who came to SKA for current account loans between 1863 and 1873, we can obtain a clear view of how the bank's client structure changed over this period.[97]

In its early years, SKA tended to concentrate primarily on the Zurich region and on Swiss business people based in other countries. The expansion in the volume of international lending was fuelled on the one hand by business with various trading companies in Europe and abroad, and on the other by the bank's relationships with spinning and weaving mills in Southern Germany, the Vorarlberg (Western Austria), and Northern Italy, many of which were Swiss-owned. From the start, SKA had forged relations with North American companies via the textile trade, and in the 1860s it collaborated with Swiss trading houses like Gebrüder Volkart in Winterthur to establish regular business contacts with companies in other overseas territories. By contrast with its long list of foreign borrowers, the bank had relatively few Swiss borrowers from outside Canton Zurich on its books. This situation began to change in the final decades of the 19th century as the bank's business relationships spread increasingly around the whole of Switzerland.

A look at SKA's commercial clientele during the period shows that the greater part of the bank's customers up to the 1880s were from the domestic cotton and silk industries. This reflected the economic structure of Canton Zurich at the time. Between 1864 and 1870, about half of all the spinning mills in Switzerland, especially medium-sized ones, were located in Canton Zurich.[98] By 1888, the proportion had fallen to about 40% as the total number of mills trended downwards. Because SKA did not tend to lend to companies that would today be categorized as SMEs, the general public regarded the bank, more than any of the other commercial banks, as an institution that served mainly large-scale customers. This image was reinforced further by the perception that in the first decades of its existence, SKA was very much 'Alfred Escher's bank'.[99]

Towards the end of the 19th century, as the first steps were taken in the development of modern retail banking, SKA gradually increased its appeal to a wider customer base. Greater savings activity on the part of the emerging middle classes prompted the major banks to turn their attention increasingly to the funds so generated. The opening of SKA's bureau de change in 1890, and its city deposit counters from 1900, furthered this trend with the declared aim of 'helping the urban population, and especially small businesspeople, to make use of our facilities as much as possible'.[100] Following the example of banks in Berlin and Paris, SKA's bureau de change, and the head office deposit counter that was run as a department from 1900, were followed from 1906 onwards by further deposit counters around Zurich. In about 1900, SKA also started renting out safe deposit boxes in a newly constructed strong room.[101] It also issued bearer medium-term notes and deposit books that once again were aimed mainly at middle-class customers who now had the opportunity 'to invest even small sums of money in a convenient, secure, interest-bearing form'.[102] Money invested by customers in deposit books was used mainly to purchase securities. From 1900, the bank's international depositors, primarily from France and Spain, also increased in number, prompting SKA to open a representative office in Paris in 1910. In 1911, a Spanish private bank was mandated to look after SKA customers in Spain.[103]

Retail strategy → 347

The bank ran a 'strongly centralized operation'[104] up until the turn of the century and stuck to its principle of not opening any branches outside the city of Zurich, even though its articles of association permitted the establishment of branches and so-called 'comptoirs' both at home and abroad.[105] The SKA board of directors repeatedly discussed the issue: in both 1857 and 1882, for example, the possibility of opening an office in Basel came under consideration. But because the bank's business activities were aimed mainly at large customers and companies that could be contacted either from Zurich itself or via SKA's various networks – correspondent banks, affiliated trading firms, representatives – the board saw no reason to set up additional offices. The board further justified this policy by referring to the difficulties that would have been involved in controlling the individual branches to a sufficient degree. It was seen as more

In 1976, SKA took over the Schweizerische Bodenkredit-Anstalt, with which it had been closely associated for many years. This picture of the offices on Zurich's Werdmühleplatz was commissioned as part of the Bodenkredit-Anstalt's 50th anniversary celebrations in 1947.

prudent to do as Bank in Winterthur did, or indeed SBV (Schweizerischer Bankverein – or Swiss Bank Corporation) until 1896, and concentrate operations in a single center. Different views were enshrined in the expansive policies pursued by Eidgenössische Bank and SVB. The former, unlike SKA, had always seen itself as a bank for the whole nation with a branch network to match. Its note-issuing operations also required a broad presence, and by 1890 it had opened seven branches and two agencies.[106] SVB, again unlike SKA, refrained from participating in other banks, but between 1875 and 1900, helped by its co-operative structure, opened 14 branches.[107] SKA's almost painful reticence was also evident outside Switzerland: representative offices were set up in Vienna (1871-1900) and New York (1870–1878), but the bank was not able to maintain them for long.[108]

In 1903, the wave of mergers that had already started in other countries, engulfed Switzerland. Hypothekarbank Zürich, founded in 1896, joined up with SKA in 1903, and after a swift rise from local to national prominence was renamed in 1906 as Schweizerische Bodenkredit-Anstalt (SBKA). 1904 saw the merger of Oberrheinische Bank, in which SKA had recently taken a stake[109], and the Rheinische Creditbank. One year later, SKA decided – 'after overcoming

Schweizerische Kreditanstalt 67

View of the counter hall at SKA's Basel branch. Photo taken around 1920.

The 'Seidenhof' in St. Gallen. After integrating the Bank in St. Gallen and the St. Galler Handelsbank, SKA opened for business in the 'Seidenhof' in 1906. Photo taken around 1910.

strong internal inhibitions'[110] – to take over the Basel branch of Oberrheinische Bank. Thus the SKA branch in Basel was created. In 1906 various deposit counters followed, as well as the branches in Geneva and St. Gallen; in 1912 further branches were opened in Glarus and Lucerne, plus an agency in Horgen. More branches obviously required more staff: in 1904, SKA employed only 277 people, but by the end of 1913, after the end of this first phase of expansion, the bank's headcount had risen to 1,024.

Competition or co-operation?

Like the creators of SKA, the founders of the later major banks, Bank in Winterthur (1862), Basler Handelsbank (1862), and Eidgenössische Bank (1863) were heavily influenced by Crédit Mobilier. Inevitably these three banks also borrowed elements from the SKA model, which had by then proved workable for six years or so. Political, regional and economic differences meant that Bank in Winterthur and Eidgenössische Bank pursued an independent course, but Basler Handelsbank (BHB) – founded in 1862 with SKA participating in one-fifth of its equity capital – regarded itself in its early years as a sister company of Escher's bank. In 1863, SKA and BHB signed an agreement to cooperate on large financing operations. A little later on, Banque Commerciale of Geneva was included in this agreement, meaning that the Zurich-based SKA now had links with Basel and Geneva, Switzerland's other two key banking centers. Various bond issues for the railways resulted from this co-operation, including work on a bond issued by Canton Freiburg that indirectly helped to finance the 'Westbahn' railway. The collaboration, which can be seen as an early prototype of the later bank cartel, came to an end in 1866 as the banks scaled down their long-term holdings and began to build up commercial lending operations.

The various newly established cantonal banks provided the commercial banks with serious competition in domestic business. In 1882, another attempt by SKA to deepen its co-operation with Bank Leu, Bank in Winterthur, Bank in Zürich and Zürcher Kantonalbank by means of an agreement on the exchange of 'acceptances due' failed.[111] Finally, in 1897, the first genuine banking cartel was formed between SKA, Geneva's Union Financière and SBV.[112] By 1905, Eidgenössische Bank, Kantonalbank von Bern, BHB and the Basel private bank Speyer & Co. had signed up to the agreement; Bank in Winterthur, Bank in Luzern and Bank Leu followed in 1908, and finally SVB joined in 1911.[113] Adoption of these banks into the cartel was clearly motivated not merely by a desire for co-operation but also by a desire to control the competition. In fact, partly because of the rise in the number of banking institutions operating on a supraregional level, concerns about competition became increasingly central, providing an ever more pressing rationale for the establishment of branches. In 1911, the Cartel of Swiss Commercial Banks and the Association of Cantonal Banks came together in a syndicate in order to jointly take over and run larger Swiss bond transactions.[114]

Comparison between the major commercial banks (1880/1913)

1880	Share capital (Sfr m)	Shareholders' equity (Sfr m)	Total assets (Sfr m)
Schweizerische Kreditanstalt	20.0	22.1	92.3
Bank in Winterthur	15.0	17.6	59.5
Basler Bankverein	8.0	8.7	41.1
Bank Leu	14.0	14.7	40.6
Eidgenössische Bank	12.0	12.0	40.1
Basler Handelsbank	8.0	8.7	18.1
Volksbank in Bern	1.7	1.8	13.3
1913			
Schweizerischer Bankverein	82.0	110.2	580.4
Schweizerische Kreditanstalt	75.0	100.4	538.8
Schweizerische Volksbank	66.2	80.3	501.0
Bank Leu	36.0	45.3	245.5
Eidgenössische Bank	36.0	44.5	244.2
Schweizerische Bankgesellschaft	36.0	46.1	206.1
Basler Handelsbank	30.0	47.0	162.8
Comptoir d'Escompte	15.0	24.2	98.1

The table clearly shows some of the significant changes that occurred in the Swiss banking sector between 1880 and 1913.[115] In 1880, SKA was the undisputed leader, but by 1913 it had fallen to second place. On the eve of the First World War, the trio made up of SBV, SKA and SVB were clearly set apart from the other banks. SVB in particular had made enormous progress within just a few decades, not least thanks to its extensive network of branches. SBG (Schweizerische Bankgesellschaft, or Union Bank of Switzerland – UBS – as it was known internationally), formed in 1912 from a merger between the Toggenburger Bank and Bank in Winterthur, could only claim the sixth largest total assets of the major Swiss commercial banks in 1913. SBV usurped SKA's position as biggest bank (measured by total assets) for the first time in 1897 following the merger between Basler Bankverein and Zürcher Bankverein.

1914–1945: conflicts, crises and credit

In an era blighted by two world wars and a major economic crisis, SKA more often than not found itself reacting to emergencies and thus increasingly having to combine business interests with public concerns.

Following the end of the First World War, the internationalization of financial business accelerated constantly. Banking activity thus centered more and more on foreign business, which expanded significantly in the second half of the 1920s. In the next two decades, however, the banks had to put most of their energies into coping with various economic and political difficulties and into refocusing their international operations. Engagements in states, such as Germany, that had imposed strict foreign exchange controls were scaled down as much as possible, while business in other countries and regions, such as North America, grew more and more important.

First World War provides a harsh test

The First World War 'knocked everything sideways'[116], creating an exceptional situation for the Swiss banks – a situation that asked questions of both their domestic and international business operations. Neutral Switzerland's sympathies for the warring parties between 1914 and 1918 tended to run along linguistic lines. Exacerbated by the difficult social conditions faced by many sections of society, this division put the country through a harsh test, which manifested itself in numerous political incidents and finally came to a head in the general strike of November 1918.

Soon after the outbreak of war, SKA found itself doing more of its international business with the Central Powers, namely Germany and Austria-Hungary, mainly because of the deprecatory and critical attitude of the English and French towards the Swiss practice of neutrality. Whereas payments business with Germany continued relatively normally after the war started, for example, Swiss assets held by banks in France and Britain were blocked. And if the situation for the bank was 'very bad' in France, 'the situation in London beggars belief'.[117] SKA was seen as being friendly to the Germans and ran the risk of inclusion on the Franco-British blacklist. Tensions were gradually eased, however, as the banks and the Swiss government started to advance money to both sides in the war in return for deliveries of goods required in Switzerland, particularly coal. Nevertheless, the banks had become a pawn in the neutrality game: no sooner had the Swiss extended an advance to France than Germany would demand the same, which would then prompt another call from France. Although SKA, for example, had the better business relations with Germany, while SBV was more in tune with France and Britain, and although attempts were made by both banks to use their respective advantages to gain the upper hand in international business, ultimately both banks ended up pulling in the same direction for the good of the country's economic and political health. In the interests of Switzerland's policy of neutrality and of even-handed relations with all the parties involved, SKA and SBV shared equally the role of go-between, passing on news to major banks in Berlin, London and Paris of what was happening in the other countries.

Back at home, SKA was confronted by a 'panic-stricken' run on deposits by Swiss customers at the start of the war. Ultimately payments had to be restricted following a decree to this effect by the Swiss National Bank. Nevertheless, SKA was able to provide key support for the Swiss economy. It granted payment extensions to producers of foodstuffs and consumer goods, for example, and approved bridging loans to cover the payment of wages and to finance production.[118] Furthermore SKA took on a portion of the federal government's mobilization bonds, which were used to finance costs associated with the war. Together with the other Swiss banks, SKA was also caught up in the social problems of the day. A strike by bank staff on 1 and 2 October 1918 brought operations to a halt and prompted the banks to increase wages. This calmed the situation to the extent that bank employees did not take part in the general strike in November.

Uncertain inter-war years

From 1914 to 1917, SKA once again managed to maintain higher total assets than SBV and thus to confirm its position as the biggest Swiss bank; by 1921, however, SKA had fallen back to third place behind SBV and SVB. After a short, sharp period of growth, driven by its international business, SVB took over the top spot in 1928, though by 1930 SBV had already taken over again as number one. The 1930s bore witness to further major shifts in the relative strength of the major banks. In this time of crisis, all of the banking institutions had to struggle against considerable difficulties, and only SKA and SBV were able to avoid serious restructuring measures. SVB fell behind the other two banks during this period, and was never again able to regain its former eminence.

Main focuses of business within Switzerland

SKA built up its domestic organization in step with the other major banks by making acquisitions and setting up new companies. By the end of the 1930s it had one or more offices in just about every part of the country. For the first time the bank had branches in Eastern Switzerland – having taken over the offices of Schweizerische Bodenkredit-Anstalt (SBKA) in 1916 – in Western Switzerland (branches opened in Neuchâtel in 1919 and Lausanne in 1921), in Bern (branch opened in 1919), in Southeastern Switzerland (acquisition of Rhätische Bank in 1930), in Central Switzerland (acquisition of Bank in Zug in 1936), and in the Bernese Oberland (an agency was opened in Interlaken in 1940 for reasons relating to the war). There was a doubling of the number of offices in Switzerland from 14 in 1913, to 28 in 1940.

Between the wars, the major banks had to narrow the scope of their business as demand for capital throughout the economy settled below the levels seen in the decades prior to 1914. Switzerland's railway network was largely complete, industrialization had already reached a relatively high level and the public sector was increasingly competing with the banks on large projects such as the development of hydroelectric power. Following the easing of political tensions after 1918, SKA ventured into new areas of business. As a reaction to the serious difficulties faced by the hotel industry after the war, in September 1921 SKA participated in the foundation of Schweizerische Hotel-Treuhand-Gesellschaft, which provided consultancy and auditing services and extended loans to struggling hotels.[119] In 1926 the SKA-chaired company wound up its operations after helping to rehabilitate 224 hotel businesses.

Shortly after this experience of fiduciary work in the hotel sector, SKA acquired a majority equity stake in Fides Treuhand, the largest remaining independent auditing and trustee company in Switzerland. Two representatives of SKA joined the board of Fides, which made itself available to the bank's subsidiaries and customers for auditing work, execution of legal business and consultancy in fiduciary matters. In order to be able to engage in bank auditing, SKA and SBV joined together to form Schweizerische Gesellschaft für Bankrevision (Swiss Bank Auditing Association).[120] Few other new companies were established by SKA in the period up to 1945, though the creation in 1942 of the Holzverzuckerungs-AG in Ems, predecessor of Ems-Chemie, is worth mentioning. As a producer of ethanol, fuels and similar products, the company was a central pillar of the Swiss wartime economy. Finally, in 1943 the bank founded Schweizerische Schiffshypothekenbank in Basel. This 'ship mortgage bank' helped to finance the construction and repair of ships, and thus bolstered the development of the Swiss deep-sea fleet.

International underwriting and syndicate activity by the Swiss banks largely fell by the wayside from about 1930, but domestic syndication business remained intact. The threat of war made Swiss customers more interested in overseas assets and in 1939, again in league with SBV, SKA took a stake in Société Internationale de Placements (SIP) in Basel, which had been founded in 1930 and was the first European institution to introduce a system of collective capital investment. Once SIP had become solely Swiss-owned, the Intercontinental Trust was created. The Trust's mostly overseas assets were kept in fiduciary safekeeping by SKA and SBV. After the Second World War, SIP established the 'Schweizeraktien' investment trust, which as one of Credit Suisse's most important equity funds celebrated its 50th anniversary in 1998 – its name by then changed to CS Equity Fund Swiss Blue Chips.

Lending to industry and business continued in the inter-war years. However, not least because of the lack of new large company start-ups, most of this business was done with major customers that had been with SKA since the 19th century. Business with middle-class customers, meanwhile, was heavily affected by the uncertainties of the time. Funds held in deposit-book accounts, for instance, fell from Sfr 156 million in 1931 to Sfr 79 million in 1935. Medium-term notes business suffered a similar fate. By contrast with term money, however, short-term sight deposits experienced strong growth, especially after the devaluation of the Swiss franc in 1936.[121]

The development of the bank's own portfolio of securities between 1914 and 1945 very much reflects the political and economic ebb and flow of the period. During the First World War the portfolio became a less significant asset as it was heavily trimmed in response to falling securities prices and bleak international prospects. Having started the war at Sfr 40 million, the 'Securities and participations' entry in SKA's balance sheet had been reduced by rigorous cutting to only Sfr 17 million by the end of 1920. The book value of foreign securities was now less than Sfr 1 million. Over the course of the following year, the nominal value of securities holdings went up again, though in relative terms it continued to lose ground: accounting for 7.4% of total assets in 1913, by 1929 it made up only 1.9%.[122] In the 1930s, problems in international business triggered marked changes to the portfolio. Foreign paper was sold, disappearing completely from the bank's holdings by the end of 1937. Only after commencing business in the USA at the start of the 1940s did SKA begin to buy foreign – mainly American – securities again. No other balance sheet item reflects the influence of the war more clearly than the valuation of securities and participations. Up to 1944, the value of Swiss and foreign bonds in particular rose continually. The securities portfolio once again became the biggest single balance sheet item. At 26% of total assets it had achieved a relative significance not seen since 1867. This did not mean that the bank had returned to the business policies of its early years, however; it simply reflected the dynamism of the capital markets.

Main focuses of business outside Switzerland

Encouraged by a burgeoning international economy, SKA increasingly looked for investment opportunities outside Switzerland. It was particularly active in the development of the international, especially German, electricity industry. In spring 1920, SKA and Bank für elektrische Unternehmungen participated in the transfer of Deutsch-Überseeische Elektrizitätsgesellschaft (DUEG) in Berlin – originally founded by AEG – to the world famous Société Financière des Transports (Sofina) in Brussels. With the help of a Spanish group, DUEG was then made over to the newly established Compañía Hispano-Americana de Electricidad (CHADE), based in Madrid but with business operations primarily in Argentina. Swiss companies held a third of CHADE's capital, and the firm's main share listing was on the Zurich stock exchange.[123] Thanks to the influence exerted by SKA on CHADE's management, Swiss industrial companies secured many contracts, particularly in Buenos Aires. Meanwhile, by the mid-1930s Chile had also developed into an important Latin American investment partner.

Participation in bond issues for the railway industry led to valuable business relationships, particularly with major Dutch banks and with institutions in France. In order to create its own link between the two up-and-coming financial centers of Amsterdam and Zurich, in 1922 SKA set up a Dutch subsidiary called Effekten-Maatschappij Amsterdam (EMA), which eventually had to be wound up after the Germans invaded Holland in 1940. SBV also moved into Amsterdam when it co-founded Internationale Credit Companie in 1924.[124] Apart from its involvement in the bonds issued by Swiss Federal Railways, the high point of SKA's railway financing activities was its participation in the French railway bond issues of the mid-1920s. These transactions were also very useful as a platform for subsequent success in French banking business. In 1927, SKA took on a French state railways bond by itself, passing on a tranche to Swiss insurance companies.[125] Ten years later, in a greatly changed political environment, cooperation with France was re-intensified. Long-term bonds issued by the French railway companies were converted into 'Emprunt Extérieur Unifié de l'Etat Français'. These financing operations, executed in conjunction with SBV and two Dutch banks, were aimed mainly at strengthening the French government's credit standing in other countries. In Switzerland alone, Sfr 175 million was invested in these conversions, Sfr 60 million by SKA.[126]

The increasing international demand for credit after the First World War opened up many opportunities for collaboration on government bond issues in other countries, and especially on stabilization and reconstruction bonds for Germany and France:

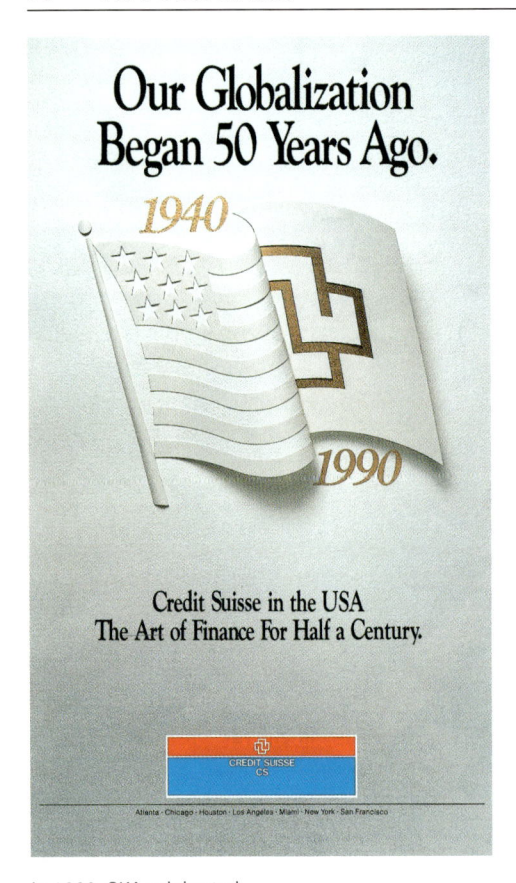

In 1990, SKA celebrated the 50th anniversary of its first foreign branch, the New York Agency.

The New York Agency at Pine Street 24–26 was SKA's first office in the USA. Photo taken in 1940.

- In 1924, the lead management of the Swiss syndicate for the 'Internationale Anleihe des Deutschen Reiches' ('Dawes Bonds') was transferred from J.P. Morgan to SKA.
- In 1926, SKA headed a consortium of Swiss banks that underwrote a Swiss franc bond which, like the bonds to fund the railways, re-established confidence in France's financial strength. This issue for the French government greatly enhanced SKA's international reputation.
- Finally the cartel of major banks led by SKA underwrote Sfr 92 million of the 'Young Bonds' issued in 1930.[127]

At about this time, the bank began building up its international operations on the other side of the Atlantic via the Amsterdam-based EMA. In 1921 SKA purchased a $110,000 holding in International Acceptance Bank (IAB), set up in New York by SBV and a group of German banks. This gave SKA a stake in a US banking institution for the first time in almost fifty years.[128] When Bank of the Manhattan Company took over IAB in 1929, SKA and SBV retained interests in this company of 10% and 25% respectively.[129] In 1939, SKA acquired some of the assets of the Jewish-owned Bank Speyer & Co., New York, and transferred them to a newly established subsidiary called Swiss American Corporation (Swissam). Swissam concentrated mainly on securities and custodian business. Just under a year later, the New York Agency, SKA's first foreign branch, opened its doors for business.

The creation of Custodian Trust Company (CTC), Charlottetown, was a typical response to the threat of war. SKA and Fides set up this organization together with Royal Trust Co., Montreal, Canada's leading trustee company, in order to secure the safety of assets in the event of war in Europe. CTC subsequently maintained custody accounts in its own name at various different banks in the USA. Half of its costs were paid by SKA, which also made use of CTC for its own customers.

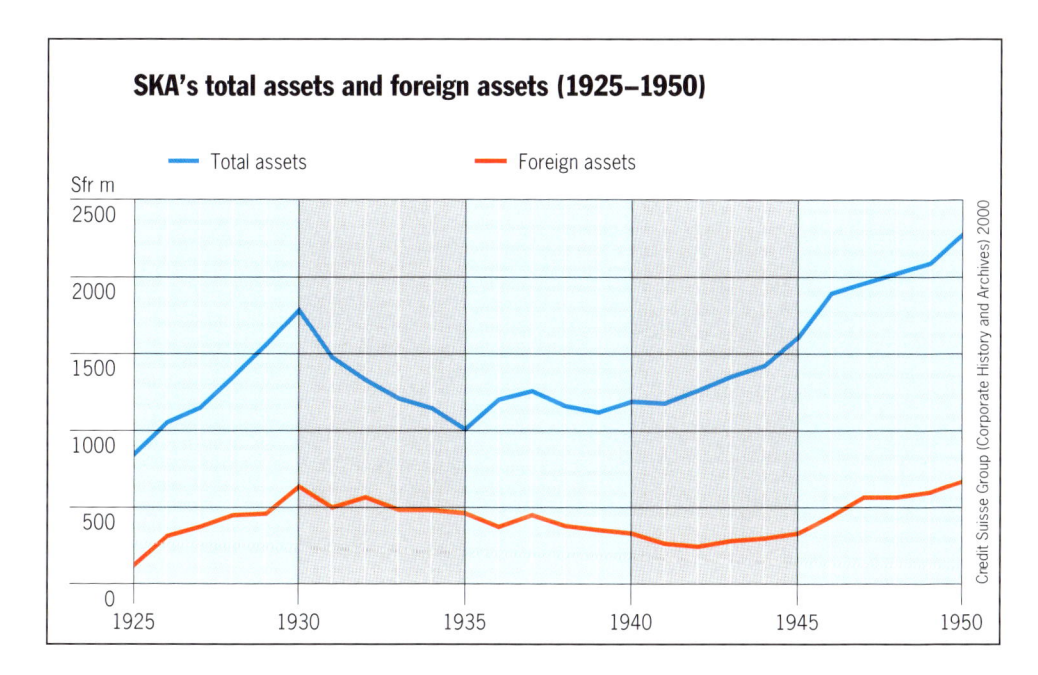

SKA's total assets and foreign assets (1925–1950)

Credit Suisse Group (Corporate History and Archives) 2000

Swissam/New York Agency → 158, 172

The number of custody account holders banking with SKA doubled between 1914 and 1929 to over 38,000. In particular, foreign depositors grew in significance after the end of the First World War. Up until 1930, large sums of domestic and foreign money, often invested only for short periods, flowed into the Swiss banks. Since there was not enough demand for the investment of this capital in the Swiss domestic market, more and more of the money had to be invested abroad. In the period between 1925 and 1930, foreign assets held by SKA rose by approximately Sfr 500 million, or 400%. Over the same period, the bank's total assets more than doubled, increasing by around Sfr 950 million. The years of crisis that followed had a negative effect not only on SKA's foreign business, but also on its total assets, which fell by a third between 1930 and 1935 to Sfr 1.01 billion.

Business activity in Germany experienced a general revival in 1924 following the implementation of the Dawes Plan, and within a few years SKA's investments had grown considerably in value. Sometimes in association with other institutions, sometimes on its own, SKA extended loans to German banks, trading companies and industrial firms; it also increased its credit exposure through export financing and commitments in the energy industry. As part of their business with long-term loans to Germany, SKA, SBV and other domestic and foreign banks set up Internationale Bodenkreditbank in Basel in March 1931, a few months before the outbreak of the banking crisis. Bodenkreditbank, which was soon to be swept aside by ensuing events, had investments in Germany (62%), Hungary (15%) and Switzerland (12%). Acting as a kind of international mort-

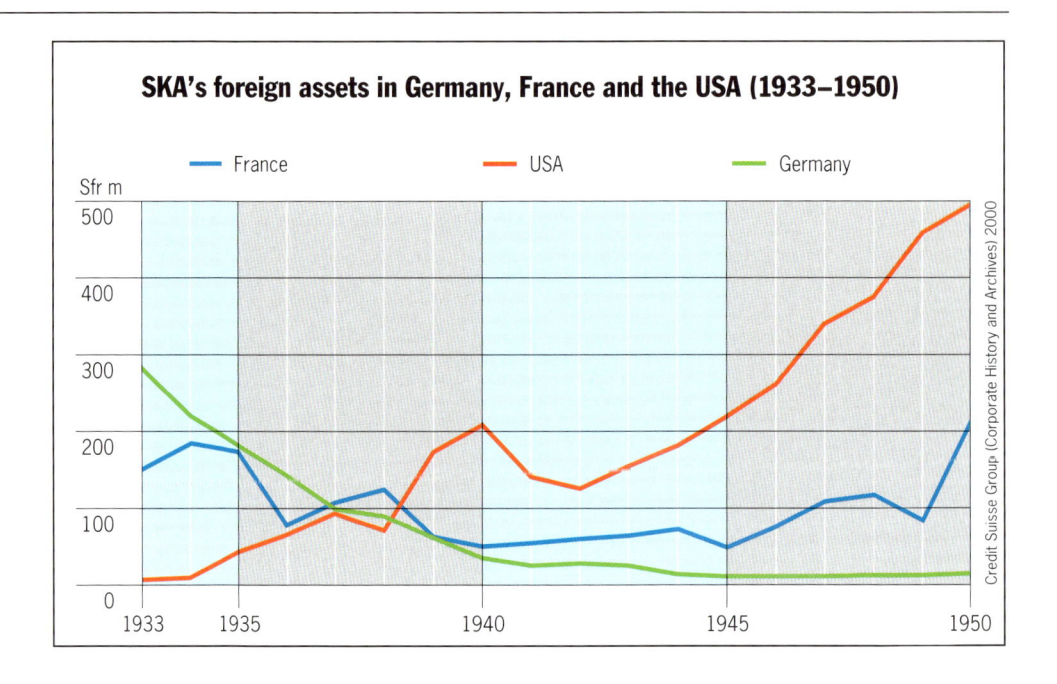

SKA's foreign assets in Germany, France and the USA (1933–1950)

[Line chart showing SKA's foreign assets in Sfr millions from 1933 to 1950 for France (blue), USA (orange), and Germany (green). Germany starts near 300 in 1933 and declines steadily to near 0 by 1950. France fluctuates between roughly 60 and 220. USA starts low, rises sharply after 1940 to about 500 by 1950.]

Credit Suisse Group (Corporate History and Archives) 2000

> 'The executive board, by agreement with the board of directors, is working to reduce German commitments still further by calling in loans, converting the sums into Registermarks and cashing these in' (Minutes of the board of directors, 30 August 1934).

> 'No further loans will be made abroad, except in Egypt where there is a possibility of winning a significant number of attractive business relationships with large Swiss and English firms by extending loans to cover the price of their cotton sales to Switzerland' (Minutes of the board of directors, 17 April 1935).

gage bond bank, it raised money against bonds and channeled these funds into German mortgage loans.

The banking crisis that swept through Germany and Austria, and the imposition of currency restrictions by the Germans in 1931 – i.e. even before the rise to power of the National Socialist Party (the NSDAP) – marked the onset of a destabilization, which a few years later was rapidly made even worse by political events in Germany and the collapse of the gold standard in Britain and the USA. Most of SKA's assets in Germany were frozen, and there was a danger that even the interest payments due on these assets would not find their way back to Switzerland. SKA thus embarked on a painful withdrawal from business with Germany. This entailed a massive and loss-making reduction of assets held in the country.

In 1933, the bank had German-based assets worth Sfr 292 million, but by 1939 this figure had fallen to Sfr 60 million and by the end of the war to a mere Sfr 10 million. Only thanks to its substantial reserves was SKA able to cope with the loss of around Sfr 90 million that it incurred as a result of the pull-out.

Exposure to France was also reduced, though to a lesser extent than was the case with Germany. In fact in 1937 and 1938, French assets constituted the greater part of SKA's foreign holdings. One of the reasons for this was the currency devaluations in the 'gold bloc' countries in 1936, as a consequence of which there was a revival in lending to customers in France, as well as to those in Italy, Belgium and in the countries covered by CHADE. Another reason for the bank's large holdings of French assets can be found in the transactions made in connection with the issue of French railway bonds mentioned above. From 1939, SKA concentrated on the USA. Whereas its foreign holdings fell by about Sfr 370 million or just under 60% between 1930 and 1941, between 1941 and 1945 they increased again by about Sfr 78 million to some Sfr 219 million, thanks to the expansion of business in the United States.

Business interests during the Second World War: caught between adapting to political circumstances and protecting customers' interests

The years between 1933 and 1945 were overshadowed by the National Socialist regime in Germany, which threatened the survival of Europe's democratic states and committed systematic genocide of horrific consequence. The Swiss banks were affected by the National Socialist system in various different ways. During the reign of the 'Third Reich' they were caught between adapting to political circumstances and protecting the interests of their customers. Amidst the turbulent progression of events, and under pressure from the constraints of government and business policy, bank staff were in many cases unable to discern quickly and clearly enough how to proceed in a fashion which was both morally defensible and correct from the business point of view.

The depression of the 1930s and the Second World War affected SKA much more seriously than the First World War had. Managing foreign assets in Switzerland, as well as the whole of the bank's business activities in other countries had become much more important in the intervening years. During this dramatic period, SKA's main concern was to ensure its own survival and at the same time to safeguard the interests of its shareholders, customers, staff and, not least, of the Swiss economy as a whole. Indeed, domestic underwriting business was one of the few lines of business that generated better earnings during the war than in the preceding decades. This was in large part due to the Swiss government's great demand for capital to fund the defense of the country and the development of its electricity industry. As a consequence, by the end of the war, claims on the public sector accounted for 32% of total assets – making them SKA's most important asset item by far.

Foreign business was hit especially hard by the economic and political upheavals of the 1930s and 1940s. For one thing, SKA's assets in the two countries with which it maintained its most intense business relations were made extremely difficult to transfer or were even frozen – by Germany from 1931 and by the USA from 1941. For another, Switzerland's encirclement by the Axis powers and the restrictions imposed by the Allies severely hampered the bank's business dealings. Because the bank's foreign assets were largely frozen, its opportunities to engage in lending business, international underwriting and stock market business, foreign exchange trading and asset management were severely restricted. SKA's securities business also went into decline during the war years. As a further example of the negative trend, the number of safe deposit boxes rented out by SKA fell by almost 30% between the beginning and the end of the war.

As mentioned in the previous chapter, restrictive foreign exchange controls imposed by the Germans in 1931 and the Nazi's rise to power prompted SKA to reduce its assets in Germany, which had increased sharply during the 1920s. This business policy was continued until 1945. For the entire period, SKA had to maintain its business relations with customers in the 'Third Reich' in order

---

Credit Suisse Group is currently working on a detailed research project into the business policies and practices of its banks during the Second World War. Amongst other topics, this project is looking in detail into the issues that are touched on briefly in this section.

SKA customer assets frozen in the USA

The freezing of all Swiss assets in the USA in June 1941 placed a great burden on SKA until well after the war. The main reason for the freeze was the US Treasury Department's supposition that substantial enemy assets could be hidden in accounts at the major Swiss banks and that the Swiss banks located in the USA could possibly be involved in the Germans' 'cloaking' transactions. Several years of audits and various attempts to sequester assets held at the SKA branch in New York weakened the clients' right to banking secrecy and threatened the assets of many customers, which only in exceptional cases could be described as 'enemy property'.

The Swiss Compensation Office, which after the war was charged with examining the Swiss banks, their activities and their customers to the satisfaction of the US authorities, gave the financial institutions a clean bill of health.

to carry out the reduction in assets in an orderly fashion and to keep losses to a minimum.

When looking from today's perspective at SKA's business activities between 1933 and 1945, it is clear that the bank's managers, as well as some individual employees, resorted to behavior that in various respects has to be judged critically. In several instances, SKA cooperated in the process of 'aryanization', for example. It followed instructions from customers to transfer assets even though it must have known that these customers had been forced to issue the instructions by the German authorities. It accepted looted assets and looted gold even though it knew that these assets had been acquired in contravention of international law – or at least should have known this if it had exercised sufficient care and attention.

During the 'Third Reich', National Socialist legislation and policies forced SKA, in common with other banks doing business in Germany, to search for ways and means of continuing their business activities. However, the circumstances under which they were operating deteriorated badly. The main priority was no longer to sustain or expand their day-to-day business, but simply to avoid losses from their existing customer relationships. As well as stealing assets from its own citizens, the Nazi regime introduced various measures, such as forced currency exchange, transfer restrictions and new taxes, which made it difficult for Swiss banks with customers in the 'Third Reich' to conduct their business. Discrimination against Jewish bank customers presented the banks with particular problems, since previously healthy loans suddenly went sour. This exceptional situation often overwhelmed the responsible bank management bodies and staff. Finding the right path between safeguarding business interests and protecting customers' interests became a tightrope walk, and business ethics were not always afforded due respect. In the light of new research, certain behavior, justified at the time by narrowly legalistic arguments, appears particularly reprehensible precisely because details of the shocking circumstances involved were known even back then.

Our judgment today cannot restrict itself to the bank's conduct during the years of the 'Third Reich' and the Second World War, but must extend to the post-war period. Here it becomes clear that SKA showed too little sensitivity and too little resolve with regard to an important issue – namely the treatment of the accounts that have lain dormant since the end of the war. The banks' inadequate and insufficiently responsible approach to this issue after the collapse of the 'Third Reich' constituted a grave omission. Despite constant reminders by Jewish organizations, senior figures at the Swiss Bankers' Association and at the individual institutions failed for years to rise to this complex challenge. In addition to the lack of will to solve the associated problems correctly and quickly, the responsible parties made serious organizational errors. It was wrong not to treat the issue as a board-level matter. Policy formulation was left to the Bankers' Association, but it too assigned the matter to its legal committee rather than to its board of directors, on which the heads of the member banks sat. The individual banks also tended to pass the whole issue on to their legal departments, which might have been appropriate in strictly technical terms, but clearly did not give sufficient weight to the exceptional political and moral implications concerned. Over the years, this catalog of neglect lent the dormant accounts a significance out of all proportion to the assets that were actually involved in 1945. Only with the settlement between the Swiss banks and the Jewish class action plaintiffs – and the associated work of the independent Volcker Committee – could the issue of dormant accounts from the time of the Second World War finally be resolved.

The conduct of the banks with respect to the Nazi's expropriation policy

As a consequence of their lending commitments in Germany, the banks were confronted directly with the National Socialist's policy of expropriating Jewish assets – the so-called 'aryanization' policy. Loans to Jewish companies went sour as these companies were driven to ruin by the targeted action of the Nazi regime. In their attempts to avoid, or at least to minimize, losses on these credit positions, the banks were faced with a choice: either terminate the loans and write them off in whole or in part, or transfer them. For the bank that had granted the loan, the decisive point was not whether a company's predicament was the result of economic recession, management problems or, as in the case of the anti-Jewish boycott, political and economic discrimination. The crux of the matter was whether and how the borrower could remain solvent. In the case of Jewish companies thrown into financial difficulty, banks which did not want to or could not immediately write off their claims had to choose one or more of the following options: participate in the 'Aryan' receiver firm, acquire the property on which the loan was collateralized as part of a compulsory realization, or extend new loans to 'Aryan' companies and receiver companies. Given the unfavorable circumstances, in most cases the aim was not to make a profit, however, but at best to limit the size of the inevitable losses. In some circumstances, banks could derive an advantage – higher dividend payments for instance – by providing representatives to sit on the supervisory boards of companies that carried out 'aryanization' policies. One single example of such conduct by SKA is documented.

However, the banks themselves could also take the initiative on 'aryanization', as demonstrated by a case in Berlin involving SVB (which was integrated into CS Holding in 1993). SVB extended two major loans to a Jewish printer; when the printer had to file for bankruptcy, the bank pressed for the 'aryanization' of the company in order to keep the losses down. There are no records of similar cases involving SKA.

Three concrete examples will help to show exactly what kind of issues were involved:

- SKA – and Bank Leu – made substantial working loans to a Viennese textile company. After this company fell into crisis, Bank Leu and SKA, in 1932 and

From 1931 onwards, Germany's foreign exchange legislation dictated that interest payments due on assets held in Germany, as well as the amortization or repayment of such assets, could only be carried out with permission from the authorities. Such permission was dependent on compulsory exchange of foreign currency payments into 'Registermarks' at a very disadvantageous rate. This special currency then had to be resold (against e.g. Swiss francs) to realize any value from the payments or assets held in Germany, but this could only be done at a substantial loss – sometimes of as much as 90%. The only way that the banks could keep these unavoidable losses within bounds was to leave the assets in Germany, in some cases transferring the loans originally made to Jewish companies to the 'Aryan' receiver firms that took over from them.

> *SKA's first branch in the USA takes offices in the premises of the Jewish-owned bank Speyer & Co. in New York*
>
> In 1938 the Jewish bank Speyer & Co. of New York was up for sale. The firm's elderly founder offered to sell to SKA, but his offer was turned down. One of the topics debated by SKA's management when considering the possible acquisition was the anti-Jewish mood that prevailed in Europe at the time: 'Certain difficulties arise because of the fact that it is a Jewish firm; this could have an influence on our relations with Germany and Italy.' A further objection was that excluding the Jewish partners could be problematic: 'If we take over a Jewish firm, our institution will be identified with it, and if we then remove the non-Aryan partners, this too will be held against us.'
>
> SKA directors Adolf Jöhr and Joseph Straessle spoke in favor of the purchase. Their main line of argument was that political uncertainty in Europe made the opening of a branch in the USA an urgent priority. In order to minimize the economic disadvantages which might be associated with the acquisition of a Jewish bank, they proposed that, 'the Jewish partners be removed from the company as soon as possible by mutual agreement'. Their support for the acquisition was also based on the fact that it represented a 'unique opportunity', i.e. 'the chance to move into an existing institution', thus reducing the high costs required for a launch onto the market. Even the supporters of the acquisition considered the fact that it was a Jewish bank to be problematic in terms of business policy; nevertheless they believed that it would be possible, 'to aryanize the bank by amicable means and perhaps even by changing the company's name'.[130] Despite these arguments, the finance committee decided by majority vote not to take the bank over.
>
> Half a year later, in 1939, SKA rented Speyer & Co.'s offices for its newly founded subsidiary Swiss American Corporation, also taking on some of Speyer's portfolio and staff, including Jewish employees. In May 1940, SKA established its first overseas branch, the New York Agency, in the same premises.

1934 respectively, signed a moratorium on the loans. As part of the 'aryanization' of the German subsidiary in 1937, the two banks became involved with the parent company of the Swiss receiver company, granting it further loans. Subsequently the subsidiaries in Austria, Hungary and Yugoslavia were also assimilated for a time by the receiver company.

- The 1939 'aryanization' of a Moravian sugar works that had maintained an operating loan with SKA since 1928 prompted a claim for restitution after the war. The plaintiff requested documents from SKA that would prove the 'aryanization' took place, but SKA stated that it could not supply the documents because of banking secrecy.
- A representative of SKA sat on the supervisory board of a Berlin joint-stock company that made acquisitions by means of 'aryanization'.

The latest results of internal research by Credit Suisse Group show that SKA was faced with the 'aryanization issue' to a much lesser extent than the other banks that were to become part of Credit Suisse Group: SVB, Bank Leu and Schweizerische Bodenkredit-Anstalt. Owing to their smaller reserves, these banks depended much more on being able to continue their business in Germany than SKA did. Nevertheless, SVB and Bank Leu in particular suffered considerable losses and had to be completely restructured in the mid-1930s.

Dealing with forced transfers of customers' money

SKA also experienced difficulties with the asset transfers forced on customers by the authorities of the 'Third Reich'. Using rigorous currency laws, the Nazis frequently forced the inhabitants of German-controlled and occupied territories – Jews and non-Jews alike – to withdraw their assets from Switzerland and put them at the disposal of the Nazi state. When it received withdrawal instructions signed by such customers, SKA paid out the assets as requested. The means used by the German currency and customs investigators to force the hand of people with foreign assets included threats, 'preventative detention' and the appointment of a Nazi functionary as an 'asset manager'. Bank customers were held in 'preventative detention' until they signed a document releasing the foreign bank – SKA for example – from banking secrecy and authorizing it to pass on banking information to the German authorities. If the information was positive, the prisoner would hopefully be released, but their foreign assets would be brought under government control. Under German currency laws, this meant that the assets would be repatriated to the 'Third Reich'. Some documents from 1938, contained in Credit Suisse Group's central corporate archive and relating to two Jewish customers, show how these forced transfers were carried out. In both cases the customer was required to transfer the securities deposited with SKA to a German foreign exchange bank. Each of these customers was imprisoned until the securities had been sold in Switzerland and the proceeds transferred to a blocked account. On their release, it was made clear to the customers that they ought to leave Germany. Technically, their money was transferred into an 'Auswanderer-Sperrkonto' ('emigrant's blocked account'), but in reality it simply accrued to the 'Third Reich'.

SKA started to receive such instructions in mid-1935. In accordance with the orders received, the bank credited the assets in the account, or the proceeds from the requested sale of securities, in favor of the customer to the account of the Reichsbank or of a foreign exchange bank. These accounts were held at SKA's head office. Many instructions issued under duress were also received from Austria after the 'Anschluss' of March 1938. These were often signed by functionaries in the Nazi hierarchy and most of the assets were to be transferred from SKA to Creditanstalt – Wiener Bankverein or to the Reichsbank in Berlin. However, SKA did not carry out this type of instruction unless the actual owner of the account had personally signed the order alongside the Nazi 'Zwangsverwalter' ('sequestrator'). SKA always refused to comply with instructions or provide information if the customer had previously issued an unambiguous instruction that assets should not be paid out either on the basis of a subsequent written instruction or upon presentation of a document such as an heir's certificate.

After the end of the war, SKA received several hundred requests to investigate assets that may have been subject to forced transfers. Former clients or their heirs wanted to know what was left of their accounts and securities portfolios. Often the customers or legal heirs would require documents from the bank in order to make a claim to the relevant German authority for the restitu-

Asset transfers despite awareness of the customers' predicament

In the mid-1930s, just as the currency crisis in Nazi Germany was intensifying, the Swiss banks began to notice an increasing flow of capital back into Germany. A survey of the members of the Swiss Bankers' Association (SBA) in 1936 revealed that this withdrawal of credit balances by German citizens was in many cases not voluntary, but was being forced on the account holders as a result of German foreign exchange controls. As soon as its law on foreign exchange control came into force on 4 February 1935, the German government could force people who owned assets abroad to offer these assets to the German Reichsbank and, if required, to sell them to the Reichsbank or to a German exchange bank. Once the Reich's law against economic sabotage, which threatened the death penalty as a sanction against capital flight, became effective on 1 December 1936, the Swiss banks expected a further run on German assets deposited in Switzerland. Political considerations kept the SBA from intervening directly with the German authorities since 'Swiss countermeasures ... would be viewed as an economic declaration of war and would be answered as such'.[131] In January 1937, the SBA's 'Schutzkomitee Deutschland' (Protection Committee, Germany), which was chaired by SKA director Adolf Jöhr, informed the Swiss authorities about the way that German assets held in Swiss banks were first being transferred to Germany and subsequently sold to the Nazi regime.

Despite their awareness of the predicament faced by their customers, the Swiss banks, including SKA, continued to carry out these transfers. There is some evidence to suggest, however, that a refusal by the banks to comply could under some circumstances have placed their customers in grave danger.

It is thus impossible to make a general pronouncement about whether SKA acted appropriately overall or not. Each case was different. However, the bank can be criticized for the fact that it did not always look hard enough at the question of what was best for its customers in each particular situation.

---

tion of expropriated assets. In some cases the applicant would request compensation from SKA itself – something that the bank always refused.

When investigating assets, SKA always requested proof of identity before it gave out any information or handed over bank documents. However, internal research was carried out in response to every single request. If the result was negative, the bank would tell the applicant, even if he or she could not provide any proof of identity. In such cases the legal department at head office would inform the applicant of the negative results in what was known as an 'Obschon-Brief' ('although' letter), which would tend to run more or less as follows: '... although the documents which would prove the inheritance rights of M. F. are missing, as an exception, and to avoid unnecessary inconvenience, we write to inform you that in 1944 our bank ... did not transfer any sums on the instructions of and/or in favor of ...'

If in the course of its investigations SKA discovered any closed accounts, the legal department's letter to the applicant would usually state either that the bank was only obliged to keep records for ten years, or that no account existed after a particular date – without explaining, however, that an account had been held at the bank prior to this. The latest research by Credit Suisse Group has revealed that in a few cases, replies to applicants stated that documents from previous years were no longer available, even though the bank actually was in possession of certain records from the years concerned.

Gaps in the source material mean that the scale of forced transfers can only be partially reconstructed today. Documents from the central corporate archive do reveal that transfers of securities into the custody account held by Deutsche Bank at SKA totaled about Sfr 8 million between 1933 and 1939. How-

Bank espionage and denunciation

The German authorities used bank espionage to obtain information required for their cause. As early as 1932/33, it was alleged that the Swiss banking industry was colluding with this espionage, specifically with regard to the German currency control laws that had been in force since 1931. Further accusations about bank espionage at SKA were made in the *Pariser Tageblatt*. The SKA immediately denied the allegations.

In June 1936, Swiss federal prosecutors, acting on information from the Federal Department of Political Affairs, warned the member banks of the Swiss Bankers' Association, that German agents were attempting to procure foreign currency by deceit. The banks were requested to inform the federal prosecutors if their suspicions were aroused.

The only known case of espionage at any of the banks that now belong to Credit Suisse Group was a single one at SKA. Working on his own initiative and without the knowledge of his superiors, an employee of SKA Basel co-operated with the German intelligence service and informed on 74 customer accounts containing deposits worth a total of Sfr 890,000. The case was uncovered when in 1942 and 1943 German currency and customs investigators forced 27 clients of SKA Basel living in Germany to sign instructions to transfer their assets to the Reichsbank and the German Golddiskontbank. According to a report by Basel criminal investigators, the Germans had found out about these assets through bank espionage. The informer was arrested in 1942 and charged with military and economic espionage for the 'Third Reich'. In December 1942, he confessed to having reported the 74 SKA accounts to the Germans, and in March 1943 he was sentenced to life imprisonment for military and economic treason and other crimes, including infringement of banking secrecy.

ever, it is not possible to quantify the more significant – in terms of both number of transactions and sums involved – transfers to Deutsche Bank's current account at SKA, or to SKA custody accounts maintained by Deutsche Golddiskontbank in Berlin, the Reichsbank in Berlin and other German foreign exchange banks.

Treatment of looted assets

SKA also came into contact with assets that the Nazis had expropriated from the territories they occupied. On 10 December 1945, the Swiss government created a special Swiss forum at the federal court to hear claims for these so-called 'looted assets' (Raubgut), especially claims relating to securities and paintings. Applications were to be submitted by the end of 1947; subsequent claims could only be made through the ordinary – and more expensive – civil courts. SKA's legal department, along with the Swiss Bankers' Association, criticized the Federal Council's decision as a 'serious interference in the applicable Swiss law, in that it orders the return of all looted assets in Switzerland, regardless of whether the acquiring party is acting in good faith or not'.[132] According to a list drawn up by the Swiss Compensation Office, the value of the looted assets at stake came to around Sfr 3.5 million. This included the class actions brought by applicants in Luxembourg and the Netherlands, with whom the Swiss government was negotiating a settlement. Following the settlement with the Luxembourg plaintiffs in 1949, at the beginning of 1950 around 700 lawsuits involving Dutch plaintiffs were still pending. These were settled in January 1951, with SKA contributing Sfr 25,000 of the Sfr 635,000 settlement sum. The bulk of the settlement was paid by the federal government – acting

'Name identification' and 'person identification'

In the Nuremberg Trial of the main war criminals in 1945/46, charges were brought against 24 people. In the subsequent trials between 1946 and 1949, a further 177 people were arraigned before the court. For the first time, groups, organizations and representatives of some of the professions were charged (including SS heads, the supreme command of the Wehrmacht, doctors, lawyers and industrialists). A total of 201 persons were thus called to face prosecution in the war crimes trials.

In 1997, the Simon Wiesenthal Center in Los Angeles published the 'Wiesenthal List' in connection with the various US Holocaust class actions. The criteria used to draw up the list of 334 personal and company names were not, however, clear in every case.

Seventy five people on the 'Wiesenthal List' were also included in the list of 201 people who faced criminal proceedings in the war crimes trials; consequently Credit Suisse Group's internal investigations centered on a group of 460 people.

'Name identification' is regarded as having been established if a name on the 'Wiesenthal List' or on the list of the accused at the Nuremberg Trials matches the name of a customer at a Credit Suisse Group bank.

'Person identification', however, not only requires that the relevant name be identified, but also requires concrete proof that the person on the 'Wiesenthal List', or on the list of the accused at the Nuremberg Trials, is one and the same person as the customer with the identical name recorded in Credit Suisse Group's records.

as final indemnitor if previous defendants (i.e. the banks) were found to have acted in good faith – with Sfr 435,000, and by Eidgenössische Bank with Sfr 103,000. SKA was called before the Federal Supreme Court as defendant or indemnitor in a total of 85 'looted assets' actions. Seventy-six of these were settled as part of the Luxemburg and Dutch class actions. One suit was withdrawn, two were successful. The results of six of the suits are not documented in the central corporate archive.

Treatment of 'problematic' customers

With so many customers in Germany, it was inevitable that SKA would also maintain accounts for people and businesses who, because of their position within the Nazi system, were in some way involved in the crimes of the 'Third Reich'. However, current research shows that SKA did not play a significant role, either qualitatively or quantitatively, with regard to 'problematic' customers.

The criterion by which a customer is now identified as having been 'problematic' is based on the various 'blacklists' produced during and after the war. These lists include people who in one form or another were, or might have been, involved in the crimes committed by the 'Third Reich'. Credit Suisse Group's latest internal research is based on the 'Wiesenthal List' and on the list of people who were arraigned before the Nuremberg Trials.

A comparison of the 460 names that appear on these lists with those that appear in SKA and SVB customer records reveals the following:

One hundred and forty eight names on the blacklists also appear at least once in the banks' records ('name identification'). Of these, 13 have been unequivocally identified as the same person ('person identification'). Twelve of these were SKA customers, and one an SVB customer:

- Four of the customer relationships were with people who were condemned at Nuremberg and who maintained business contacts with SKA in the peri-

Illegal transactions by Schweizerische Bodenkredit-Anstalt (SBKA)

In 1945/46 the Swiss Compensation Office (SCO) conducted a thorough investigation of SBKA on the suspicion that it had contravened clearing regulations. This suspicion arose after an informer at SBKA told the Swiss army's secret service that the institution's manager in charge of converting 'Sperrmarks' (a currency introduced by the Nazis as part of their stringent foreign exchange controls) into cash was moving 'substantial amounts of capital from Germany to Switzerland'.[133] Various other of SBKA's activities during the Second World War were also investigated. Ultimately all of these activities were designed to convert Sperrmarks into Swiss francs at much more favorable conditions than were available on the market. Alongside its legal, and from today's perspective unproblematic, transactions, SBKA sometimes used means that according to the SCO did not conform to 'clean business practices'.[134]

One method that SBKA used to convert Sperrmarks into cash between 1942 and 1944 was to arrange delivery to German companies of Spanish tungsten and tin – metals vital to the war effort – and also to facilitate the purchase by IG Farben of tungsten mines in Spain. In return, the German Ministry of Economics authorized SBKA to exchange some of its holdings of Sperrmarks into Swiss francs at a favorable rate. Another transaction was only indirectly associated with the liquidation of Sperrmarks. This was the sale of 518 shares in the Spanish electricity company CHADE, which according to the SCO 'had been stolen in the occupied territories by the German occupying powers'.[135] The proceeds of Sfr 114,933 were transferred to a Genevan company 'whose purpose [was] to camouflage foreign assets'.[136] Although SBKA returned some of the CHADE stock, the SCO condemned the business as being 'morally extremely dubious'.[137] The circumvention of clearing regulations presented another problem. In order to be able to carry out the transactions detailed above, SBKA relied on its agent in Germany, who was one of Hermann Göring's entourage. Commissions were not paid directly to the agent, however, but to his representatives in Switzerland, including a lawyer who placed the money with a Swiss real estate firm. In 1945, details of these investments and of the accounts and assets subject to reporting obligations were withheld from the SCO department dealing with frozen German assets. The SBKA thus contravened the Swiss government's resolution of 29 May 1945, which included the obligation to report German assets held at Swiss banks and fiduciary agents.

Most of the transactions concerned were initiated and carried out by the above-mentioned SBKA manager, but the finance committee of SBKA's board was usually kept informed of the dealings. Apart from one brief interruption, SKA had appointed the chairman or the vice chairman of the SBKA board ever since 1906.

When the SCO auditor's report on these matters was submitted at the start of 1946, SBKA pensioned off the manager concerned prematurely. The finance committee adopted a much more critical stance towards his behavior than it had during the war. In 1946 the SCO charged SBKA with offences against the clearing regulations in the case of its agent in Germany, and considered a charge of failing to report German assets. In the end, in July 1946 the SCO ordered SBKA to pay the sum of Sfr 602,000 into the German-Swiss clearing system. On appeal, SBKA managed to have this amount reduced by half.

od between 1933 and 1945. From what we know today, it appears that two of these customers held assets of about Sfr 10,000 at the bank. The other two only remained with the bank for a short period – in one case only thirty days – closing their accounts in 1935 and 1936 respectively. It is now impossible to determine the size of the assets involved in these two cases.

- Three people who were acquitted at the Nuremberg Trials maintained longer banking relationships with SKA between 1933 and 1945. In two of these cases the assets involved came to about Sfr 1 million.
- Three people who were not arraigned before the Nuremberg Trials, but who do appear on the Wiesenthal List, were also SKA customers between 1933 and 1945; one was a customer of SVB. Again, the amount of the assets involved can no longer be determined.
- None of the other three customer relationships was active between 1933 and 1945.

Bank Leu sells escudos for German customers

During the Second World War, SKA and Bank Leu carried out various foreign exchange transactions on behalf of German customers. Firstly, escudos, dollars or pounds sterling were sold to the German Reichsbank and 'other German banks put forward by the Reichsbank'. The German institutions then usually used the currency to procure Swiss francs that could in turn be used to buy goods and raw materials. Secondly, the major Swiss banks themselves sold Swiss francs to German banks in return for foreign exchange or gold for the purpose of arbitrage. Bank Leu in particular maintained 'good relations with the Reichsbank, to the extent that we [Bank Leu] have become its confidante', because '… our assets in Germany mean that we rely on the goodwill of the Reichsbank'.[138] Most significant of all for Bank Leu were the escudo sales – most of them to the German Reichsbank – which overall were worth a total of around Esc 1 billion (or about Sfr 150 million). Bank Leu stopped this business in autumn 1942, mainly owing to pressure from the Allies.

Gold transactions with German banks

In terms of volume, SKA's and Bank Leu's involvement in the gold business that went through Switzerland remained small throughout the war years. However, the fact is that in 1940/41 gold from the German Reichsbank, including gold it had looted, also found its way to these two banks. Sources in Credit Suisse Group's central corporate archive provide no indication that gold deliveries made to SKA and Bank Leu included gold belonging to Holocaust victims. According to the report of the Independent Commission of Experts Switzerland – Second World War (ICE), the Reichsbank made deliveries of gold worth about Sfr 7.4 million to SKA and worth Sfr 43.8 million to Bank Leu.[139] The sources relating to Bank Leu, however, are contradictory and suggest that the Reichsbank's gold deliveries were actually about Sfr 10 million lower than stated by the ICE.

Independent Commission of Experts Switzerland – Second World War: Gold deliveries by the Reichsbank to the Swiss commercial banks (1939–1945)

	Value (Sfr million)
Schweizerischer Bankverein	151.0
Bank Leu	43.8
Schweizerische Bankgesellschaft	31.8
Basler Handelsbank	9.6
Schweizerische Kreditanstalt	7.4
Eidgenössische Bank	0.1
Total	243.7

In 1943/44, private customers exported gold coins and ingots worth between Sfr 1.6 and 2.6 million from Germany to Switzerland in the name of SKA and with the approval of the Swiss National Bank. This gold, most of which was re-exported out of the country shortly after it came in, was also very probably looted. Given the pressure exerted by the Allies and the allegations about looted gold, of which the banks were undoubtedly aware by 1943 at the latest, it is impossible to understand from today's perspective why SKA carried out these gold imports and why the National Bank granted permission for them to do so. It was not until September 1944 that the SKA management banned all gold transactions with enemies of the Allies.

Before war broke out, SKA's international gold business had been concentrated primarily on British and French customers. Because private ownership of gold was permitted in France for the whole period of the war, which was not the case in Switzerland's other neighboring states, French demand for gold coins from Switzerland continued until 1945. Otherwise, once the war had started, the international gold business shifted to foreign central banks that maintained accounts with the Swiss National Bank in Bern, to Germany, and until the middle of 1940, to the USA. Between March and June 1940, for example, SKA sold just about as much gold to US clients as it acquired from the German Reichsbank during the entire war (about Sfr 7.4 million).

The Swiss National Bank's gold transactions

The Swiss National Bank (SNB) was by far the most significant buyer and seller of gold in Switzerland. It had dealings with both of the warring sides and did not favor one side significantly over the other. In this respect it did not contravene international law. However the SNB also acquired large volumes of gold that the 'Third Reich' had looted from the central banks of the countries it had conquered (especially Belgium, the Netherlands and Luxembourg). Though the responsible parties at the SNB were later to deny the fact, they were aware of the gold's dubious provenance. Only as a result of stern warnings from abroad did the SNB supervisory board decide to urge caution upon its directors in July 1943. Despite this, the directors continued with their practice until the temporary suspension of gold sales in the summer of 1944. By this time the SNB had long 'stopped believing "that this gold was clean"'.[140]

The SNB was working on two levels. On the one hand it continued to deal in gold, make profits and issue declarations of non-objection. On the other, it deliberately suppressed the knowledge that the German's had acquired the gold by questionable means. Although it was within the Bank's power after 7 December 1942 to prevent the private sector from carrying out gold transactions with German customers, in practice it was very generous with its authorizations. Even more serious is the fact that from 1943 onwards, the SNB's sales of gold to Swiss banks put the looted gold into general circulation. Even in 1947, when the SNB in all probability must have been aware of the dubious origins of ingots sold to SKA, it issued a declaration of non-objection in response to the bank's request.

The customs authorities and the SNB were constantly at loggerheads about how to respond to the gold smuggling that took place between 1943 and 1947. The SNB took a relaxed stance on diplomats taking gold over the border and were munificent in their granting of export licenses; meanwhile the customs authorities tried to stem the smuggling by imposing severe penalties. However, their fines often had to be reduced because of the SNB's attitude. Contrary to its official stance, the SNB was keen to see as much gold as possible going back out of Switzerland. By the end of the war, illegal exports of gold from Switzerland were probably between ten and fifteen times as large as the approximately Sfr 20 million worth of official gold exports carried out by the commercial banks (since 1943).

There was a break in private gold trading in Switzerland during the Second World War as a result of a decree issued by the Federal Council on 7 December 1942. Gold trading, which had never been one of SKA's core businesses in previous years, subsequently became even less significant for the bank. The new laws imposed drastic restrictions on what had been a relatively free market in gold, and gave the National Bank dirigiste powers. This led to significantly smaller turnover and margins for SKA and for all the other commercial banks. From 1943, SKA only made a few hundred thousand francs a year in profit from gold business, though earnings were higher in 1941 and 1942. The bank's highest wartime earnings from gold trading were in 1942 when it earned about Sfr 2 million. Its own gold holdings – Sfr 28 million at their peak in 1944 – were insignificant compared with the reserves held by the central banks. During the war, SKA's most important source of gold was the Swiss National Bank, which between 1942 and 1945 supplied SKA with about Sfr 110 million worth of gold. At the end of 1942, security considerations and business policy prompted SKA to build up its gold portfolio in Argentina, buying gold from various American sources. The gold holdings in Argentina had nothing to do with the movement of Nazi flight capital.

The Swiss Federal Council's decree of 7 December 1942 dictated that authorization must be sought from the National Bank for all private gold transactions with foreign countries. A side effect of this law, however, was to boost black-market gold trading by diplomats and private smugglers. One SKA employee, unbeknown to his superiors, was involved in illegal transactions of this sort to the tune of more than half a million Swiss francs.

The 'dormant accounts' issue

After the war, the Swiss Federation of Jewish Communities repeatedly brought up the issue of dormant accounts – i.e. bank accounts, securities portfolios and safe deposit boxes belonging to people who had not contacted the bank since the end of the war. Dormant accounts were also the subject of several surveys by the Swiss Bankers' Association between 1947 and 1956. In addition, they formed part of a settlement between Switzerland and Poland in 1949.

Under political pressure from inside and outside the country, the Swiss government passed a decree on dormant accounts on 20 December 1962. This obliged the banks to report dormant assets to the newly created government Claims Registration Office. Between its head office and branches, SKA reported 503 possible cases in Switzerland. After extensive internal investigations, 141 of these were forwarded to the Registration Office in 1964. From today's vantage point, the main fault with this procedure was that some accounts held by people whose names were determined by Jewish expert advisors to be probably or definitely Jewish, but whose domicile was unknown, were not reported. This is despite the fact that Article 4, Paragraph 1 of the Federal Decree of 1962 stated that cases had to be reported in the event of uncertainty.

The Swiss banks failed to show the required sensitivity in a number of areas: in the survey of dormant assets, in the implementation of the Federal Decree of 1962 and, to some extent, in their responses to the individual applications received. This attitude stemmed from a narrowly legalistic interpretation of banking secrecy. In the case of applications from Eastern Europe, however, the Swiss banks showed particular caution because they, and the Bankers' Association feared that the authorities in Eastern Bloc countries were pressurizing customers and their heirs, as was proved to be the case with certain applications that were made to SKA from Romania.

Since 1989 and with increasing force since 1995 – when various memorial events were held to mark the fiftieth anniversary of the end of the Second World War – politicians have been calling for a legal solution to the dormant accounts issue. The World Jewish Congress, later supported by the US authorities, pushed for a detailed investigation to settle the matter once and for all. As part of their efforts, massive pressure was put on the Swiss banks and on Switzerland's political leaders.

Between 1945 and 1995 SKA reacted to practically all requests about dormant accounts by carrying out research, usually free of charge, into accounts by name, number and pseudonym in all the relevant head office departments and in the general ledger. If the results were negative, the bank would inform the applicants that this was the case, even if a lack of proof of identity meant that it was not obliged to do so. These investigations covered between 95% and 99% of all accounts in Switzerland. For an appropriate fee, the research could be extended to include all of Switzerland or the whole of a specific region. If the result was positive, SKA would not give out any information until the required proof of identity was produced. Where original documentary proof had been lost, the bank often accepted a statutory declaration in its place. SKA always informed the applicants correctly and properly if no existing accounts had been found, but it did not mention any accounts that had already been closed at the time of the request. This was the case with about a quarter of all requests.

In cases where the applicants were able to produce sufficient proof of identity, SKA, SVB and Bank Leu always conducted a comprehensive survey of all Swiss accounts. If the results of this research were negative, the bank would report this and return the documents. If assets were found, Holocaust victims with insufficient documentary proof of identity, especially those from Communist Eastern Europe, would often have to wait a long time before anything was paid out to them.

In individual cases, SKA, SVB and Bank Leu undertook investigations on their own initiative and contacted, for example, the International Committee of the Red Cross, Jewish organizations or the Swiss authorities. As a rule, however, the banks refrained from active research, primarily for reasons of client protection.

Investigations by the Swiss Bankers' Association since 1995 and by the ICEP ('Volcker Committee')

In June 1995 the Swiss Bankers' Association (SBA) conducted an initial investigation into accounts that had been dormant at the key Swiss banks since the end of the war. Three months later, the SBA expanded the investigation to cover all of its member banks and in February 1996 it announced the total amount of money held in the dormant accounts of foreign customers. There were 775 accounts containing a total of Sfr 38.7 million. The announcement attracted heated criticism from Jewish organizations in Switzerland and abroad, which had expected much higher figures. Demands were made for an independent review of the results. These demands ultimately led to the formation of the 'Independent Committee of Eminent Persons' (ICEP), later to be known commonly as the 'Volcker Committee' after its chairman Paul A. Volcker. On the suggestion of the ICEP, in 1997 the Swiss Federal Banking Commission (FBC) requested that the banks publish a list of the accounts of foreign and Swiss account holders and of account holders whose domicile was unknown or impossible to establish with certainty. In July and October 1997, the Swiss banks published the names of 5,570 foreign account holders in the world's press and on the Internet. For its part, the ICEP concluded its wide-ranging research in December 1999 with a detailed report. A total of 53,886 accounts were identified 'as having a probable or possible relationship to victims of Nazi persecution. [...] On the basis of information now available, no valid estimate can be made of the aggregate value of the accounts due to victims of Nazi persecution.'[141] On the conduct of the banks, the ICEP stated: '(a) The auditors have reported no evidence of systematic destruction of records of victim accounts, organized discrimination against the accounts of victims of Nazi persecution, or concerted efforts to divert the funds of victims of Nazi persecution to improper purposes. (b) There is, however, confirmed evidence of questionable and deceitful actions by some individual banks in the handling of accounts of victims,

Dealing with the past and the responsibility of the bank's managers

Over the course of 1997, during a time of great challenges for the bank's staff – a time of restructuring and groundbreaking strategic realignments – an issue arose that could only be tackled successfully at the cost of great effort from the whole of Credit Suisse Group: the issue of the Swiss banks' dormant accounts and the role of the Swiss financial industry during the Second World War. Credit Suisse Group started to take a critical look at its own corporate history during the period in question and embarked on an exhaustive process of research and reassessment. At times, several hundred staff could be found working on the centralization, cataloguing and scrutiny of the central corporate archive, or reading through the stacks of files. Credit Suisse Group wanted to provide the best possible working conditions for the 'Volcker Committee', which had been formed to clarify the issue of dormant accounts, as well as for the auditing firm charged with checking the documents, and for the Swiss government's Independent Commission of Experts (ICE). Together with the other Swiss banks, Credit Suisse Group compiled a list of the beneficial owners of the dormant accounts, and published this list all over the world. On the initiative of Rainer E. Gut, chairman of Credit Suisse Group's board of directors, the Swiss business community created a humanitarian fund that went beyond the immediate issues surrounding Switzerland's conduct during the Second World War. The fund was a 'gesture of gratitude for the fact that Switzerland was spared the ravages of the war and was able to draw maximum benefit from post-war economic developments. The fund should thus be seen as a recognition of the immeasurable suffering of those concerned.'[143] Rainer E. Gut spoke even more clearly at the Credit Suisse Group AGM of 30 May 1997: 'We have long failed to recognize the scale of the problems that have remained unresolved. This is why we feel, why I personally feel, all the more obliged to sort the issues out as much as we can with the documents available to us today. We are not responsible for the things that our predecessors did or left undone in individual cases. Nor should we make judgments from our safe vantage point on the basis of what we know today. But we are responsible for the way we deal with our history here and now. We are prepared, and I give my personal guarantee for this, to investigate our past thoroughly and to publish the results. If we discover that anyone has suffered as a result of unjustifiable conduct, we will of course do what we can to make up for it.'

In a speech made to the critical US media at the invitation of the National Press Club in Washington on 26 June 1997, Rainer E. Gut supported calls for a proper understanding of the difficult role that Switzerland had to play during the war: 'We are not intent on glossing over any unpleasant aspects of our past. Nor do we wish to engage in generalized judgments of the wartime generation. All we are trying to do is to reconstruct the events of the past in as complete a manner as possible in order to achieve a just and balanced perspective.' The chairman of Credit Suisse Group's board of directors was unequivocal: 'Where assets belonging to the victims are discovered, those assets must find their way to the victims' rightful heirs or, where no such heirs exist, to charitable causes providing help to the victims.'

This personal commitment and this general attitude set the tone for the settlement made with the Jewish plaintiffs' lawyers in New York in 1998. The settlement also took account of the banks' corporate responsibility, thus allowing Swiss financial institutions to carry on their business in the USA without the constant threat of boycotts and sanctions. The forging of this solution did a great service not only to the two major banks, but also to Switzerland and its economy as a whole. According to the settlement, the payments made by the banks into the settlement fund satisfied all claims on Switzerland and on Swiss companies and organizations (except for the three life insurance companies Basel, Winterthur and Zürich). In particular they settled the claims associated with Switzerland's refugee policy during the Second World War and with the Swiss National Bank's gold trading operations, but also the claims relating to enforced and slave labor at subsidiaries of Swiss companies.

including withholding of information from Holocaust victims or their heirs about their accounts, failure to keep adequate records, many cases of insensitivity to the efforts of victims or heirs of victims to claim dormant or closed accounts, and a general lack of diligence – even active resistance – in response to earlier private and official inquiries about dormant accounts.'[142]

1945–1976: reticence and stagnation

Losing ground: SKA in competition with the other major banks

In 1945, Basler Handelsbank and Eidgenössische Bank had to relinquish their independence as a consequence of losses suffered over the previous fifteen years. Basler Handelsbank was taken over by SBV (known internationally as Swiss Bank Corporation, or SBC) and Eidgenössische Bank by SBG (Union Bank of Switzerland, or UBS). SKA (Credit Suisse) made no such acquisitions, but still found itself in a healthy position when the war came to an end. In terms of total assets it was only a little smaller than SBV and it boasted substantial equity capital. The bank thus showed itself to be, along with SBV, the most resistant in its peer group to economic problems. In 1946, SKA also led the field in lending business. As far as numbers of Swiss branches was concerned, the three biggest banks were running practically neck and neck. SBG was much smaller than SKA and SBV, but its branch network was second only to SBV's in size. When the various mergers were complete, the apportionment of quotas in the underwriting cartel gave SKA and SBV the highest quotas of 24.5% each, although 'the prevailing feeling in the cartel [was] that we [SKA] could actually have claimed a higher quota'.[144] As the clear number three bank, SBG was given a revised quota of 21% (up from 12%).

A look at the key figures for 1946 and 1956 shows that the competitive relationship between the four major banks shown in the table[145] hardly changed at

Comparison of SKA, SBV, SBG and SVB (1946/1956/1966/1976)

	1946				1956			
	SKA	SBV	SBG	SVB	SKA	SBV	SBG	SVB
Total assets (Sfr m)	1894	2139	1319	892	3169	3392	2651	1708
Shareholders' equity (Sfr m)	196	196	103	93	252	275	182	120
Lendings (Sfr m)	725	638	527	662	1518	1359	1126	1276
Customer deposits (Sfr m)	1338	1603	1041	749	2320	2484	2038	1476
Cost/income ratio (%)	65	70	78	66	56	65	66	67
Return on equity (%)	4.95	4.67	3.67	4.79	9.65	9.81	9.90	6.14
Swiss branches	28	31	32	62	32	35	39	65
Headcount	2282	3153	n.a.	n.a.	2708	n.a.	2746	n.a.

	1966				1976			
	SKA	SBV	SBG	SVB	SKA	SBV	SBG	SVB
Total assets (Sfr m)	10 223	11 294	10 122	4 179	41 664	52 757	52 651	11 343
Shareholders' equity (Sfr m)	576	623	965	244	2 697	3 146	3 229	644
Lendings (Sfr m)	4 499	5 108	4 772	3 373	17 683	17 887	20 920	8 254
Customer deposits (Sfr m)	8 266	8 127	7 214	3 695	24 990	26 366	29 617	9 635
Cost/income ratio (%)	56	66	59	65	62	58	61	71
Return on equity (%)	9.82	9.64	7.90	9.64	7.95	8.05	8.09	8.61
Swiss branches	54	79	100	80	124	158	199	134
Headcount	4 239	6 018	5 729	2 435	9 549	11 226	13 549	4 329

all during the years immediately after the war. The positions remained more or less fixed: only under the item 'shareholders' equity' was there a change, with SBV overtaking SKA. The rise in customer deposits that put SKA in first place for this item in 1966 was based primarily on the bank's Swiss commercial, industrial and wealthy private clientele (cash accounts, deposit books), but not yet on business with small savers.

In each of the years between 1961 and 1966 the total assets of the three leading major banks were almost the same. In 1963, SKA once again had marginally the greater total assets with Sfr 7.9 billion. By 1966 the figures for the three big banks lay between Sfr 10.1 billion (SBG) and Sfr 11.3 billion (SBV) – SBG had thus more or less caught up with SKA (Sfr 10.2 billion). With reference to shareholders' equity, SBG's figure went up enormously with the purchase of Interhandel (1966/67). Its 1966 shareholders' equity of Sfr 965 million was about nine times as high as in 1946. Meanwhile, SBV's Sfr 623 million and SKA's Sfr 576 million for 1966 represented little more than threefold increases on the 1946 equity figures. There were also large differences in the respective size of the branch networks. In 1966 SBG had 100 branches, almost twice as many as SKA's 54, while SBV had 79.

SKA suffered its greatest setback against its rivals in the years between 1966 and 1976, a period during which all the major banks' growth performances were based on international business and on the new discipline of retail banking. By 1976, SBV and SBG had 20% greater total assets than SKA. The deficit in terms of number of branches had increased proportionally since 1966, but SKA was also now clearly the number three bank in terms of shareholders' equity, lending volume and customer deposits.

Two further benchmarks demonstrate how much SKA's position had deteriorated. To start with, the bank not only kept pace with its major rivals in terms of return on equity (RoE)[146], it actually outperformed them on occasion. However, between 1966 and 1976 its less aggressive business policy began to have an effect here too, and its RoE fell back behind that of the competition. SKA's cost/income ratio[147] also looks positive to start with: SKA's ratio was lower until 1966, reflecting a more efficient performance than either SBG or SBV. In addition, SKA had the greatest total assets per head of staff until 1966. However, the lower efficiency rating of the other leading banks was also a sign of their greater spending – on things like acquiring other institutions and tapping into new markets. Thanks to the more or less stable economic boom that lasted till the start of the 1970s, SBG and SBV were thus laying the foundations for their long-term growth.

Fewer risks in domestic business

Despite the principle that 'domestic business comes before international business', SKA remained cautious about building up its Swiss branch network until the end of the 1960s. The first new SKA branch to be opened after the Second World War was in Biel in 1950. By contrast with the developments in the first half of the century, new branches had to be established from scratch in Biel and

'More intensive efforts in our Swiss operations are the main priority if our business is to continue developing healthily. International business, important and valuable though it may be, is only a complementary source of earnings to our Swiss business' (Minutes of the board of directors, 13 January 1955).

in other new locations, since there were no suitable candidates for takeover. Although SKA steadily expanded its branch network in Switzerland, it was still falling further and further behind the other majors, especially SBG. SKA also continued to pursue a more cautious acquisitions policy than SBG and SBV.

In 1968, executive board member Heinz R. Wuffli's comment on SKA's branch policy was that the bank was not going to open as many branches as possible just for the sake of prestige; it was striving for the optimum, not the most extensive branch network.[148] Nevertheless, SKA could not completely avoid the pressure to found new branches or indeed to take over banks, as it did with Bank Gebrüder Oechslin & Co. in Schaffhausen (1962), Bank Wädenswil (1968), Bank Hofmann AG (1972; still exists as an institution) and Schweizerische Bodenkredit-Anstalt (1976).

Unlike the growth period at the end of the 1920s, SKA's expansion after 1945 was based on domestic foundations. Every sector of the Swiss economy used SKA's services.[149] Current account loans played a 'dominant role', with the emphasis on operational and investment loans, which were extended to a broad corporate clientele.[150] Short-term unsecured loans became even more important after 1945 as the buoyant post-war economy helped an increasing number of companies become sufficiently creditworthy. Unsecured loans to Switzerland's leading firms predominated in terms of volume, but this type of credit was now also extended to small and medium-sized companies.[151] SKA's mortgage business, too, had been strengthened by acquisitions such as Bank in Zug in 1936. Later on, full consolidation of SBKA (1976) and Bank in Wädenswil (1978) further consolidated the bank's position in this area.

In asset management business with private customers, SKA benefited from the qualities offered by Switzerland as a financial center. A new client base was opened up, for example, when customers from the Middle East began to invest their oil earnings in Switzerland after the Suez Crisis ended in 1956. One indicator of the increased importance of asset management was the marked rise in the number and value of securities safekeeping accounts:

'After dealing with ongoing business, Dr. Schmidheiny commented on the purchase of smaller banking institutions by the major banks. He found the policy adopted by the Bankgesellschaft in the case of the Bündner Privatbank, which is now being echoed in the cases of the Sparkasse Au and other institutions, as unworthy. This approach is psychologically and economically damaging for all the banks' (Minutes of the board of directors, 15 February 1962).

SKA securities safekeeping accounts (1945–1970)

	Value (Sfr million)	Number
1945	3 877	46 044
1960	13 058	80 437
1970	47 303	188 998

Meanwhile, SKA was making only hesitant steps into the retail market. However, following the example of its rivals, it launched a range of savings products designed to appeal to a wider cross-section of the population. 1953 saw the introduction of the bank's so-called 'bearer deposit books', which had a minimum investment limit of Sfr 3,000, and paid interest on sums up to Sfr 20,000. SBG, SVB and Bank Leu, all of which had already issued similar products, enjoyed a clear headstart in this business.[152] SKA entered more new territory in 1969 with its salary account, and in 1970 with the launch of its savings books and young people's saving books, which replaced the old deposit books and accounts. The bank also introduced a personal checking account in 1970.[153] These efforts to 'attract stable Swiss deposits, even in small and very small amounts, in order to fund domestic lending business'[154] were prompted primarily by the shortage of money from the general public, which was tending to flow instead into Swiss and foreign securities and into other international markets.

As the 1960s got under way, the gold and foreign exchange trading departments gained in significance. Gold trading had been one of SKA's traditional lines of business since the 1930s but, in common with developments at the other major Swiss banks, it only became a mainstay after about 1960. It really came into its own when the free market in gold was created in 1968. Encouraged by this liberalization, as well as by the increased significance of trading in other precious metals, in 1967 SKA purchased the Ticino-based precious metals refiner Valcambi SA, which has since become an important producer of ingots and coins as well as of watch cases and straps.[155]

Foreign exchange trading was primarily run as a service for customers until well into the 1950s. Now, however, it did not just grow in volume terms, but also began to play a central role in the bank's own liquidity policy. This was due to the lack of a Swiss money market and to the increasing internationalization of business. When the Swiss franc was abandoned to the free play of market forces in 1973, it gained in strength against other international currencies. Inflows of money from abroad increased, and areas such as foreign exchange and precious metals became even more important as a result.

Underwriting business was also expanding steadily. Owing to the volumes handled in this area and the increasing importance of capital exports, in 1966 SKA divided its Swiss underwriting business into one department for Swiss issuers and another for foreign issuers. The bank's ability to place issues was a real trump card: until the mid-1970s it managed a greater volume of customer securities portfolios than, for instance, SBG. Although the majority of large infrastructure construction projects in Switzerland had been completed, right up until the 1980s most of the new issues came from the electricity sector. After the Second World War, SKA gradually built up its shareholding in Elektrowatt until for a short time at the beginning of the 1970s it actually held a stake in excess of 50%. In 1971, interest differential business (i.e. borrowing and lending), the single most important source of earnings, was separated from commissions business. This development was prompted not only by the general economic trend but also in no small part by Switzerland's particularly strict rules on the banks' equity capital coverage. Because equity capital is a comparatively expensive source of funds, the banks were compelled to exercise self-restraint in balance-sheet business and to emphasize balance-sheet-neutral activities.

Finally, leasing and factoring business also deserve a mention. During the 1960s, these lines of business grew enough to earn their own separate departments; as the trend continued SKA subsequently set up Finanz AG Zürich (1967), CS Leasing AG (1969), and CS Factoring AG (1971).

Hesitant moves into international markets

After the war, SKA and the other major banks understandably took a rather cautious and reticent approach to international business. The prevailing feeling was that investment in other countries was not compatible with sound business principles. Unlike the foreign banks, the Swiss major banks did not see themselves as the kind of financial institutions that would engage in long-term financing business: they had long ceased to be 'banques d'affaires'. They certainly would lend to foreign borrowers again, but concerns about creditworthiness kept this activity within limits.[156] Consequently, until the 1950s the volume of foreign loans made by SKA remained below the level seen in 1931 – though the loans were spread across a larger number of countries in an attempt to diversify the risk.

Various foreign projects were extensively evaluated but ultimately discarded. Uncertainty about the international business climate often comes up in the board minutes of this time. At the beginning of the 1950s, for instance, the concern was expressed that 'western Europe could turn into a battlefield'.[157] Potential new participations on other continents failed to come to fruition because representatives of Swiss industry sitting on the SKA board showed insufficient interest in such projects. Nevertheless, having founded Swissam in 1939 and EMA in 1922, SKA set up a third foreign subsidiary in 1951: Credit Suisse (Canada) Ltd. in Montreal. Here too, security issues were as significant as the desire to exploit Canada's economic potential: 'Being part of our security measures in the event of a war, the main reasons [for setting up the subsidiary] lie in our efforts to provide an organization that can best meet the desires and demands of many of our investment clients.'[158] In 1955 – in cooperation with First Boston Corporation, SG Warburg Ltd., London, and other companies – the international finance company Transoceanic Development Corporation Ltd. was founded with its head office in Canada. SKA figured as the only Swiss bank amongst the European partners. It took a Can$ 200,000 stake in the company's capital of Can$ 5 million.[159]

At the end of 1958, the key currencies were once again made freely convertible on the basis of fixed but adjustable exchange rates. This facilitated the development of large international money and capital markets – the so-called Euromarkets.[160] Convertibility opened the doors to a revolutionary internationalization of the money economy, and accelerated economic growth around the world. New forms of foreign trade financing emerged in the wake of this trend, including medium-term finance without regress to the exporter ('forfaiting'), which quickly gained in significance, particularly for transactions with developing countries and state-trading countries. Against this background, SKA was gradually becoming a globally active bank. Along with the other Swiss majors, it came under pressure as stamp duties and the restrictive capital export poli-

International expansion → 156

SoGen-Swiss → 180

CREDIT SUISSE NOW HAS A LONDON BRANCH

SKA maintained a representative office in London from 1954. In 1972 it was expanded to become a branch.

cy imposed by the government threatened to compromise the appeal of the Swiss financial center relative to the Euromarkets, which developed particularly quickly after 1967. With Switzerland in danger of losing ground, SKA worked to strengthen its presence abroad. In 1967 it began to build up its international network of offices, which had grown little in the post-war period (there had been a representative office in London since 1954 and one in Buenos Aires since 1959), and to establish further foreign subsidiaries. By converting its representative offices in Los Angeles and London into full branches in 1972, SKA deviated for the first time from its previously unshakeable principle of having no international branches apart from the New York Agency. Even this change was not enough, however, to make up lost ground. SBV in particular was clearly ahead of SKA, having already opened nine representative offices and one branch outside Switzerland between 1951 and 1966. SBG, meanwhile, started to expand its international presence at the same time as SKA, but did so at a faster tempo.

In 1962 SKA, via Bank in Zürich, took over White, Weld & Co. AG, Zurich, from the US investment bank White Weld, New York, and changed its name to Clariden Finanz AG. In 1970, White Weld, New York, and SKA together founded a new joint-stock company in Zug called WW Trust which, amongst other holdings, now owned Clariden Finanz AG.[161] This collaboration formed the basis for SKA's later dominant position in Eurobond underwriting. In 1974, SKA increased its holding to over 40%, at which point the name of the company was changed from WW Trust to S.A. financière du Crédit Suisse et de White Weld.

Meanwhile, in New York itself, an important restructuring took place in 1973. In co-operation with other European banks, SKA created a new investment bank, SoGen-Swiss International Corporation, by merging Swissam, founded in 1939, with SoGen International Corporation, a subsidiary of France's Société Générale. The purpose of the new company was to establish a presence in domestic US underwriting business (corporate finance) and in US investment banking.[162] Customer portfolios originally managed by Swissam were transferred to the newly formed, 100% SKA-controlled subsidiary Swiss American Securities Inc. (SASI).[163] SASI took over SoGen-Swiss International Corporation in 1979.

1977–1996: restructuring and growth

A new dynamic

As late as 1975, Felix W. Schulthess, then chairman of the SKA board of directors, expressed the opinion that in view of the economic recession, 'the time is currently not right for expansion either at home or abroad'.[164] Nevertheless, various developments during the 1970s indicated some fundamental changes in SKA's policy. These developments were: the closer cooperation with the US financial institution White Weld, an imminent generational change in the executive board, and the planned expansion of the bank's retail business. In the end, however, the real break with the past came with the Chiasso Affair of 1977, which shook SKA to its very foundations. For several years, managers at the bank's Chiasso branch had criminally misappropriated certain customer deposits, originally destined for the Euromarkets, to acquire shareholdings and make highly irregular loans via a Liechtenstein company. Neither this money, nor the associated bank guarantees, appeared in SKA's books. The corresponding items on the balance sheet were a group of overvalued assets, most of them located in Italy, against which substantial write-downs had to be made over the years.

In domestic banking, all the Swiss banks found money in extremely short supply. This meant that personal savings business, launched by SKA with a new range of products in 1970, became 'vitally important' for the procurement of stable deposits. The importance to the bank of borrowed funds was reflected not only in the development of new products, but also in the further expansion of its domestic branch network and the creation, under the slogan 'regionalization' of a chain of deposit-taking agencies. The job of these very small units was to establish a firm hold for the bank in all parts of Switzerland. Despite all this effort, however, SKA did not make much progress on increasing the volume of funds deposited by its customers. As part of the push to attract savings, in 1975 the bank set up a marketing committee and introduced modern public relations techniques. The idea was to move away from the image of a 'Zurich bank' and to popularize SKA amongst a much broader public. The Chiasso affair made the need for such a change of image only too clear. The use of market research (from 1975) and the inception of sponsorship activities (1978), further encouraged SKA's transformation into a modern major bank. Finally, in 1977 SKA took over the consumer credit business of its subsidiary Allianz Kredit AG. The idea here was to 'make a long-term contribution to the promotion of sales of consumer goods' for the benefit of all sections of society.[165] In 1983 Allianz Kredit AG and SKA merged. SKA organized an advisory service for small and medium-sized companies, and loans were increasingly made available to up-and-coming firms not yet capable of issuing securities.

International business continued to be characterized by expansion and the development of further cooperative partnerships. Investment banking was a lucrative business as yet only pursued on a very small-scale by the Swiss banks;

Mentalities and images → 235

Generational change → 302
White Weld → 174

Chiasso Affair → 245

Tour de Suisse → 385

but around this time, SKA gradually began to build up a new 'home market' for investment banking in the USA. The relationship with White Weld was followed in 1978 by collaboration with the renowned Wall Street house of First Boston. This partnership, and the majority stake taken by SKA in First Boston's US parent company, put the bank a long way ahead of its European competitors. In addition, SKA had been intensively building up its network of US branches since 1976 (Chicago, Atlanta, San Francisco, Miami, etc.). Later on, the international organization was also strengthened in other key financial centers, such as London and Tokyo. In 1985, SKA acquired Effectenbank-Warburg AG of Frankfurt am Main (as well as Grundig Bank GmbH in Fürth/Nürnberg). It had already taken over Bank für Handel und Effekten (Zurich) in 1981 in order to secure a better position in international trading business (and especially in commodities financing) – a line of business that SBG, by contrast, had been pursuing intensively since the 1950s.[166]

First Boston → 186

Within the ranks of SKA itself, there was a conflict between the generations about the future strategic direction that the bank should take. Managers of the younger generation were all set to conquer new markets. They wanted to make SKA into a leading institution on the international stage in key areas such as raising capital, and trading in securities and foreign exchange. If the bank was to go on to greater success in the future, it was no longer sufficient to concentrate on reducing costs. The bank had to become active in the areas where the business opportunities lay and where money could be earned, i.e. in commissions business rather than just in business that depended on interest rate differentials.

Restructurings

1982 witnessed another milestone in the history of SKA: the creation of a sister company called CS Holding. In a difficult period, the bank used CS Holding to bring together its participation in Financière Credit Suisse – First Boston in Zug, and a small portion of its equity stake in Elektrowatt AG. CS Holding offered four main advantages:

- Optimized capital adequacy requirements
- A platform for future business developments
- Tax advantages
- A ground-breaking investment opportunity for shareholders

In the wake of the establishment of CS Holding, the old SKA was restructured in a series of moves that followed in rapid succession; the new management's signature was becoming clearer and clearer. Various measures to improve efficiency were introduced – some of them in collaboration with the consultancy firm McKinsey. 1982's 'Overhead Value Analysis' (OVA) aimed to break down the different cost factors in order to achieve efficiency gains, first at head office, and then in the branches. A year later SKA introduced the CRAPA (Customer Rela-

Optimization → 339

tionship and Profitability Analysis) management system, which for the first time in a Swiss business revealed the profitability of individual customers.

A new divisional organizational structure was introduced in 1987; the new divisions were Commercial Banking (domestic and foreign), Finance and Investment Banking, Fund Management and Deposit Business, and Logistics. This emphasis on strategic business areas helped SKA to become more flexible and dynamic and to better exploit the potential of the changing markets. 'SKA plus', the project started in 1986, aimed to make retail business more profitable through a more precise segmentation of the bank's customer base. The other major banks had denser branch networks, and were thus in a position to attract more money than SKA. With its smaller available funds, SKA was forced to work more efficiently, more professionally and more systematically at retail banking. In parallel with 'SKA plus', the bank launched the 'Führung ZN Schweiz' (Swiss Branch Management) project, which by the mid-1990s had introduced a new management structure for the regions and rationalized the whole production process by separating front office work from processing tasks.

Divisional organization → 335

In the 1980s, each individual branch of the major banks still operated as a 'full-service bank' in its own right, offering all the different types of products and handling all the necessary processing on site. The 'Führung ZN Schweiz' project ultimately led to a concentration of all production processes in four centers. The branches could thus return to their function as sales offices.

'Führung ZN Schweiz' was an intensification of the earlier OVA project which, having rationalized the cost side, was now looking at how to increase earnings generated from the existing customer base. By making growth and earnings into the bank's central strategic principles and by subsequently launching the measures to put these principles into practice, SKA gained a lead in the market that its rivals were not able to close until years later.

In 1988, the investment banking activities of CS Holding affiliate Financière Crédit Suisse – First Boston, and thus its 40% stake in First Boston Corporation, were integrated into the new CS First Boston, a globally active group headquartered in New York. Rainer E. Gut, chairman of the board of directors of SKA since 1983 and chairman of CS Holding since 1986, set a clear goal for SKA: 'In the 1990s it aims to be one of the few large, highly capitalized, first-class financial institutions that operate a truly international business.'[167]

In 1989, CS Holding was made the umbrella holding company and parent of SKA Group. SKA and CS First Boston were now at the same level in the corporate structure, as were the former SKA subsidiaries Fides Holding and Elektrowatt AG. Elektrowatt proved to be of strategic value to the new grouping thanks mainly to its position in the Swiss electricity industry and the potential underwriting business it could channel through to SKA.

CS First Boston → 191

With the creation of a holding company, SKA was breaking new ground for the major Swiss banks. It was faced with a legislative regime that had until that point been tailored to traditional bank holding companies, but not to 'mixed financial services conglomerates' like CS Holding. When the holding company was first created in 1982, the Federal Banking Commission (FBC) expressed

From SKA to CS Holding (1989)

Before exchange

Shareholders (registered and bearer) and **part. cert. holders** (registered and bearer PCs)

| SKA | CS Holding |

- Bank participations — 94%
- Fides — 43.9%
- Elektrowatt — 1.4%
- CS First Boston — 44.5%

After exchange

Shareholders (registered and bearer)

CS Holding

- SKA — 99%
- CS First Boston — 44.5%
- Fides — 94%
- Elektrowatt — 45.3%

SKA → Bank participations

Exchange offer of 17 April 1989
CS Holding presents SKA shareholders with following exchange offer (17–27 April 1989) …

| 1 SKA registered share nom. Sfr 100 plus 1 CS Holding registered PC nom. Sfr 10 | → | 1.1 CS Holding registered share nom. Sfr 100 |
| 1 SKA bearer share nom. Sfr 500 plus 1 CS Holding bearer PC nom. Sfr 50 | → | 1.1 CS Holding bearer share nom. Sfr 500 |

… plus a capital increase by CS Holding with 15:1 subscription rights at par (29 May – 9 June 1989)

- Simpler structure
- Greater transparency
- Platform for future growth
- Flexibility
- Autonomous development and own identity for subsidiary companies

Credit Suisse Group (Corporate History and Archives) 2000

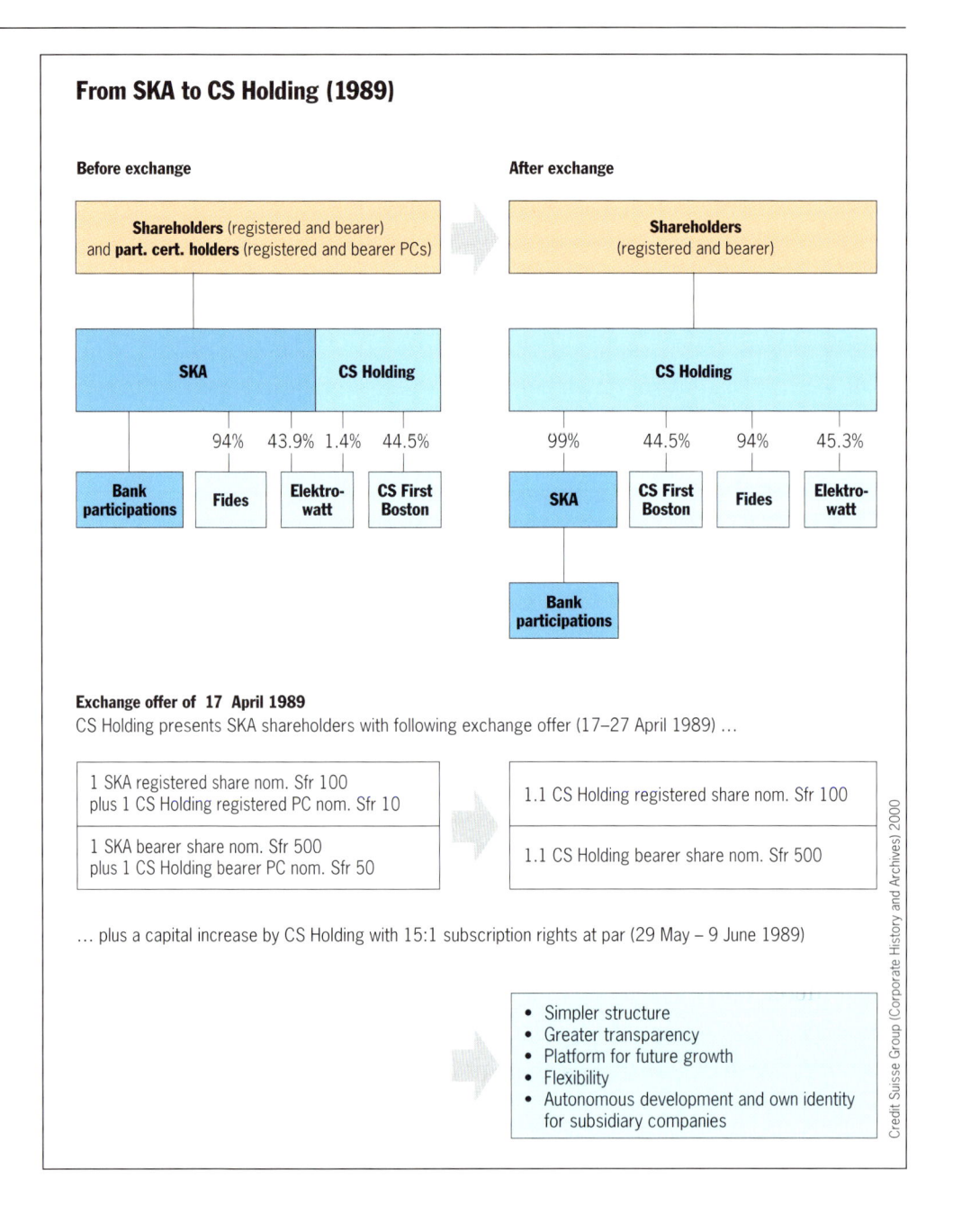

concern that CS Holding would be able to carry out unverifiable transactions under the new structure. Following its transformation into the group's parent company in 1989, the question arose as to how far Switzerland's Federal Banking Law could be applied to CS Holding. Interestingly, some representatives of the regulatory authorities had initially judged CS Holding to be a pioneering organizational structure. Not least because of intervention by rival institutions, the FBC made its views 'more precise'. SKA was thus confronted by an FBC decree that did not make CS Holding subject to Banking Law, but which did demand that its SKA subsidiary maintain sufficient shareholders' equity, as defined in the provisions of the Banking Law, for its sister companies as well as for itself ('effective duty to provide support'). The view of SKA, meanwhile, was that the Banking Law did not require it to provide equity coverage for sister companies that were not included in its own consolidated accounts. However, the FBC assumed that the restructuring of CS Holding was actually an attempt to avoid capital adequacy regulations and to slip through the net of Swiss legislation. The Federal Court backed the FBC's view that SKA, as the most important company in CS Holding, and the one subject to banking law, was obliged in effect to provide support for its sister companies wherever necessary. The only way to ensure that SKA's business activities would not be compromised by this need to provide capital coverage for its sister companies, was for CS Holding, even though it was not subject to FBC supervision, to have available the same amount of shareholders' equity as it would have needed had it been a bank operating on a consolidated basis. As a result of these circumstances, in spring 1991 CS Holding announced a partial 're-going public' for SKA, though in the end an improved earnings situation meant that this step could be avoided: CS Holding itself was now in a position to meet the high capital adequacy requirements and to cover all of its investment banking activities (CS First Boston and Credit Suisse Financial Products) with the equity capital required by the FBC. As far as CS Holding and SKA were concerned, the intervention by the FBC and the Federal Court unfairly favored the traditional monolithic parent company structure used by their competitors. The decision by the Federal Court did limit the benefits of the innovative holding concept, which would have allowed the optimum deployment of the available equity capital, i.e. a deployment that would not have compromised CS Holding's competitiveness at international level. Nevertheless, it remained a more flexible system than the parent bank system, and this flexibility was to be strategically very important for the group's further development.

In 1989, CS Holding took the idea of a full-service bank (or 'universal bank') to a different level, creating a whole range of significant advantages.[168] It allowed the company to satisfy a wide variety of customer needs – whether in volume business or market niches – from under the same roof. It also improved the internal spread of risk and encouraged initiative in business policymaking. Because they enjoyed a great degree of autonomy, it was easier for the individual companies within the holding structure to target their various customer segments with specific brands and products while at the same time benefiting from the strengths of the group as a whole. On top of this, the results of the subsidiary companies were more transparent than those of CS Holding's competitor banks.[169] A variety of different corporate cultures were allowed to develop independently and in the most productive way within the holding framework – without conflicting with one another. Further factors that spoke in favor of the holding structure were the wave of liberalization and deregulation that swept through America and the UK at the end of the 1980s, as well as efforts in various countries to relax previous 'separate banking' systems to accommodate full-service, or 'universal', banks. In addition, with a groundswell of cross-border corporate mergers expected in Europe, CS Holding group companies could exploit synergies and take on leading roles in areas such as mergers and acquisitions. Finally, the creation of CS Holding could also be seen as a product of the economic situation of the time and as a response to expected developments. The economic dynamism of the 1980s demanded more flexible banking institutions and a wider variety of financing and capital-raising opportunities. The aim of the companies brought together within CS Holding was to be able to handle any large financial transaction in any of the major currencies.

Expansion in Switzerland and abroad

CS Holding laid down various markers that were to be decisive for its future development. As part of the restructuring, CS Holding's top managers committed themselves to the 'aggressive' use of electronic data and information processing, which was no longer just an internal tool for the bank but which was becoming a central element of an earnings-oriented business policy. The creation of CS Life in November 1989 marked the first step in the direction of Allfinanz, while the acquisition of Bank Leu in spring 1990 triggered a wave of financial sector mergers throughout Switzerland. Acquiring Bank Leu gave CS Holding an improved position in asset management. It integrated the new company with two of the institutions it already owned, Bank Hofmann and Clariden Bank, to form a new holding company called Leu Holding. Affida Bank and Bank Heusser were soon added to the ensemble, which was restructured into a genuine private banking group. In 1991, as market conditions changed, the Fides Group's auditors, legal department and tax department were spun off and integrated into the internationally active Klynveld Peat Marwick Goerdeler group, which is completely independent of CS Holding, as KPMG Fides.

Refocusing, and the reorganizations that this entailed, became inevitable in international business too. SKA's creation of Credit Suisse Financial Products in London in July 1990 was another milestone in the bank's journey towards becoming a truly worldwide operator. This new company, a joint venture with CS First Boston, became a leading international player in swaps and derivatives business within the first year of its existence – a perfect example of how the synergies between the expertise of an investment bank and the capital and placing strength of a full-service bank could be exploited to the full. In 1990, a new 'home market' emerged in the USA: CS Holding purchased the US asset management company BEA Associates Inc., New York, and secured the approval of the US Federal Reserve Board (the Fed) to acquire a majority stake in CS First Boston. CS Holding thus became the first non-US 'full-service group' to hold a clear majority stake in a major investment bank within the US banking sector, which was divided by the Glass-Steagall Act into commercial and investment banks. This masterstroke gave SKA a considerable advantage over its Swiss and European competitors for many years to come.

In 1992, SKA approved a new strategy for its retail business in an attempt to overcome its persistent earnings weakness in this sector. More precise customer segmentation, new distribution and communications channels, and a streamlined product range provided the foundations for further growth. The integration of SVB into CS Holding at the start of 1993 provided an ideal oppor-

CS Life → 224
Bank Leu takeover → 131

CS First Boston → 199

Glass-Steagall → 165

CS Holding Group (as at April 1994)

SCHWEIZERISCHE KREDITANSTALT SKA

Capital 99.9%
Voting rights 99.9%

As a globally active full-service bank, Credit Suisse (SKA) provides corporate banking, investment banking within Switzerland, asset management and investment advice, and retail banking.
Credit Suisse, together with its subsidiaries, is present in all the world's major financial centers, including Germany and Luxembourg.

Further major subsidiaries:

BEA Associates Inc.,
New York

Credit Suisse
Asset Management,
London and New York

Swiss American Securities Inc.,
New York

CREDIS International Fund Holding AG,
Zurich

Credit Suisse Fides Trust Holding,
Zurich

Credit Suisse Financial Products,
London (50%)

Schweizerische Volksbank

Capital 99.8%
Voting rights 99.8%

As a full-service bank active in Switzerland, Swiss Volksbank concentrates on commercial business, as well as on investment advice and asset management for medium-sized and smaller companies and personal customers.

LEU HOLDING

Capital 99.8%
Voting rights 99.8%

Leu Holding Ltd. serves private and institutional investors in Switzerland and abroad. Its subsidiary Bank Leu Ltd. also provides commercial banking services in the Zurich area.

Major subsidiaries:

Bank Leu AG,
Zurich

Bank Hofmann AG,
Zurich

Clariden Bank,
Zurich

Bank Heusser & Cie. AG,
Basel

Banque Leu (Luxembourg) S.A.,
Luxembourg

CS First Boston

Capital 63.2%
Voting rights 75.7%

CS First Boston Inc. is an international investment bank providing a comprehensive range of services to both suppliers and users of capital throughout the world. It offers financial advisory and capital raising services, is active in securities underwriting and trading, and provides economic and market research reports.

Major subsidiaries:

CS First Boston Corporation,
New York

CS First Boston (Europe) AG,
Zug

CS First Boston Pacific, Inc.,
Tokyo

Credit Suisse Financial Products,
London (50%)

CS Life

Capital 100%
Voting rights 100%

CS Life is a Zurich based life insurance company. Its products, which are targeted at high-net-worth individuals, are sold by investment advisors and asset managers in banks belonging to the CS Holding Group.

FIDES INFORMATIK

Capital 100%
Voting rights 100%

Fides Informatik is a major European supplier of IT systems, software and services. It offers both individual and standard software solutions to banks, insurance companies, public sector institutions and financial information services.

Major subsidiaries

Fides Informatik,
Dusseldorf

Fides Informatik,
Frankfurt am Main

Fides Informatik,
Munich

Elektrowatt

Capital 46.3%
Voting rights 46.3%

Electrowatt Ltd. is the holding company for a group of companies active both nationally and internationally in the fields of energy, industry, engineering and real estate.

Major subsidiaries

Centralschweizerische Kraftwerke,
Lucerne

Elektrizitäts-Gesellschaft Laufenburg AG,
Laufenburg

Kraftwerk Laufenburg,
Laufenburg

Kraftübertragungswerke Rheinfelden AG,
Rheinfelden

Cerberus AG,
Männedorf

Staefa Control System AG,
Stäfa

Elektrowatt Ingenieurunternehmung AG,
Zurich

Sandwell Inc.,
Vancouver, Canada

Göhner Merkur AG,
Zurich

Credit Suisse Group (Corporate History and Archives) 2000

Core Swiss market → 129
SVB takeover → 137

NAB takeover → 142

Creditanstalt-Bankverein → 169

Merger with Winterthur → 227

Union between CS Holding/SBG? → 147

tunity to use SKA's proven retail strategy to increase the profitability of SVB's personal client business. The acquisition of SVB, at that time the fifth biggest bank in Switzerland, changed the face of the Swiss banking scene once again. Far from being a deviation from the strategy of building a global financial services company, this huge domestic transaction simply gave out a clear signal that CS Holding also wanted to maintain its roots in its core Swiss market. The integration of SVB, and one year later of Switzerland's largest regional bank, Neue Aargauer Bank (NAB), gave CS Holding an even larger share of the Swiss retail market, allowing it to overtake its competitors, SBG and SBV. Despite the streamlining prompted by market conditions, and despite organizational considerations, CS Holding now had not only the largest domestic branch network of any Swiss bank, but was also the number one bank by market share. This situation continued until the other two major banks finally merged.

As part of its efforts to build up its strategic position in Central Europe, CS Holding held talks with the Austrian authorities in 1994 about the possibility of buying the government's stake in Creditanstalt-Bankverein. However, party political disagreements in Austria made it apparent that such an investment would be unwise.

SKA also began to forge new strategic alliances with the insurance industry. The first of these came in 1994 with the bank's collaboration with Swiss Re. This partnership was based on a 20% stake taken by Schweizerische Rückversicherungs-Gesellschaft (known in English as Swiss Re) in Credit Suisse Financial Products. The aim was to develop new products and innovative solutions, especially in the area of derivatives, that required both reinsurance and banking expertise. This move was followed in spring 1996 by a cooperation agreement with Winterthur Schweizerische Versicherungs-Gesellschaft (Winterthur Insurance). By selling tailor-made products, the new partners could make better use of their distribution channels and achieve greater efficiency in logistics areas. Then in 1997, the bank and the insurance company merged to become an Allfinanz conglomerate: CS Holding and Winterthur were integrated into the new structure of Credit Suisse Group, which thus became one of the biggest providers of comprehensive banking and insurance services in the world.

In spring 1996, Rainer E. Gut asked the chairman of SBG, Nikolaus Senn, whether a merger between CS Holding and SBG should be considered. SBG – under pressure from a major shareholder, Martin Ebner – suspected a plot, rejected the approach, and by means of a well-targeted indiscretion set off a media furor. CS Holding and its chairman were heavily criticized by some commentators, though this criticism rang rather hollow when SBG merged with SBV only one-and-a-half years later. The reasons given for the merger between CS Holding's two rivals to form the new UBS were actually very similar to the arguments put forward by Rainer E. Gut when he telephoned Nikolaus Senn with his offer, and which were restated in writing to the SBG board of directors ten days later: the reduction in the number of major banks within the Swiss financial center may well have been regrettable, but it was also simply a sign of the times and as such was inevitable. By merging with each other, long-established firms with different cultures could increase their size and strength and use their combined power to thrive in the markets of the future.[170]

From CS Holding to Credit Suisse Group

Following SBG's rejection, CS Holding – from its position of strength as the Swiss market leader – opted for a different solution: restructuring itself to form Credit Suisse Group. In doing this it distanced itself clearly from its old image as a Swiss full-service bank that also ran international operations, establishing itself instead as an international banking group with its head office in Switzerland. The starting point for this far-reaching restructuring was the need to modernize CS Holding so that it could achieve an even better competitive position in the international arena and also root out any duplication of effort within its existing structure.

In its attempt to focus on the business of providing financial services, Credit Suisse Group disposed of all its previous activities outside this core area. The main task here was to sell Elektrowatt AG. Through a spin-off within the Elektrowatt Group in 1977, Elektrowatt's two divisions, industry and energy, were made more attractive for sale. The decision to sell was made because the investment phase in the Swiss electricity industry was coming to an end, which would inevitably have implications for underwriting business. For the purpose of the sale, Elektrowatt AG's energy holdings (electricity companies involved in power sales and power stations) were brought together in a subholding called Watt AG, while the other Elektrowatt companies continued as an industrial conglomerate. Once the technical and legal requirements – including a public purchasing offer addressed to all of Elektrowatt AG's shareholders and a subsequent declaration of invalidity – had been dealt with, CS Holding sold both parts of the company. In autumn 1998, Siemens AG of Berlin and Munich completed its purchase of the industry group, which boasted greater turnover than the energy division. The group was fully integrated into Siemens, but its head office remained in Switzerland (Zurich). Watt AG, the ex-energy division, was sold to a Swiss-German consortium involving Nordostschweizerische Kraftwerke (NOK), Bayernwerk AG (BAG), and Energie Baden-Württemberg AG (EnBW). Credit Suisse Group retained an interest in Watt AG, initially of 20%, to ensure a majority Swiss stake in its capital.[171]

By retaining the tried and tested holding structure, but concentrating on four business areas – Credit Suisse (for Swiss corporates and personal customers), Credit Suisse Private Banking (wealthy private clients), Credit Suisse Asset Management (institutional asset management) and Credit Suisse First Boston (trading business and investment banking) – the restructuring of CS Holding created the basis for further development of the bank's market position. Great benefits were derived from focusing the range of services offered on the relevant markets and on customers' requirements. The four 'business units' were

Break-up of Elektrowatt

Position at 30 September 1997

- Credit Suisse Group — 44.9% → Elektrowatt
  - 56.3% CKW
  - 73% EGL — 8.3% — KWL (76.6%)
  - 69% KWR
  - Industrial holdings

Position at 23 September 1998

- Watt AG: CSG 20%, NOK 31%, BAG 24.5%, EnBW 24.5%
  - CKW, EGL, KWL, KWR
- Siemens 100% → Elektrowatt (now Siemens Building Technologies)
  - Industrial holdings

Credit Suisse Group (Corporate History and Archives) 2000

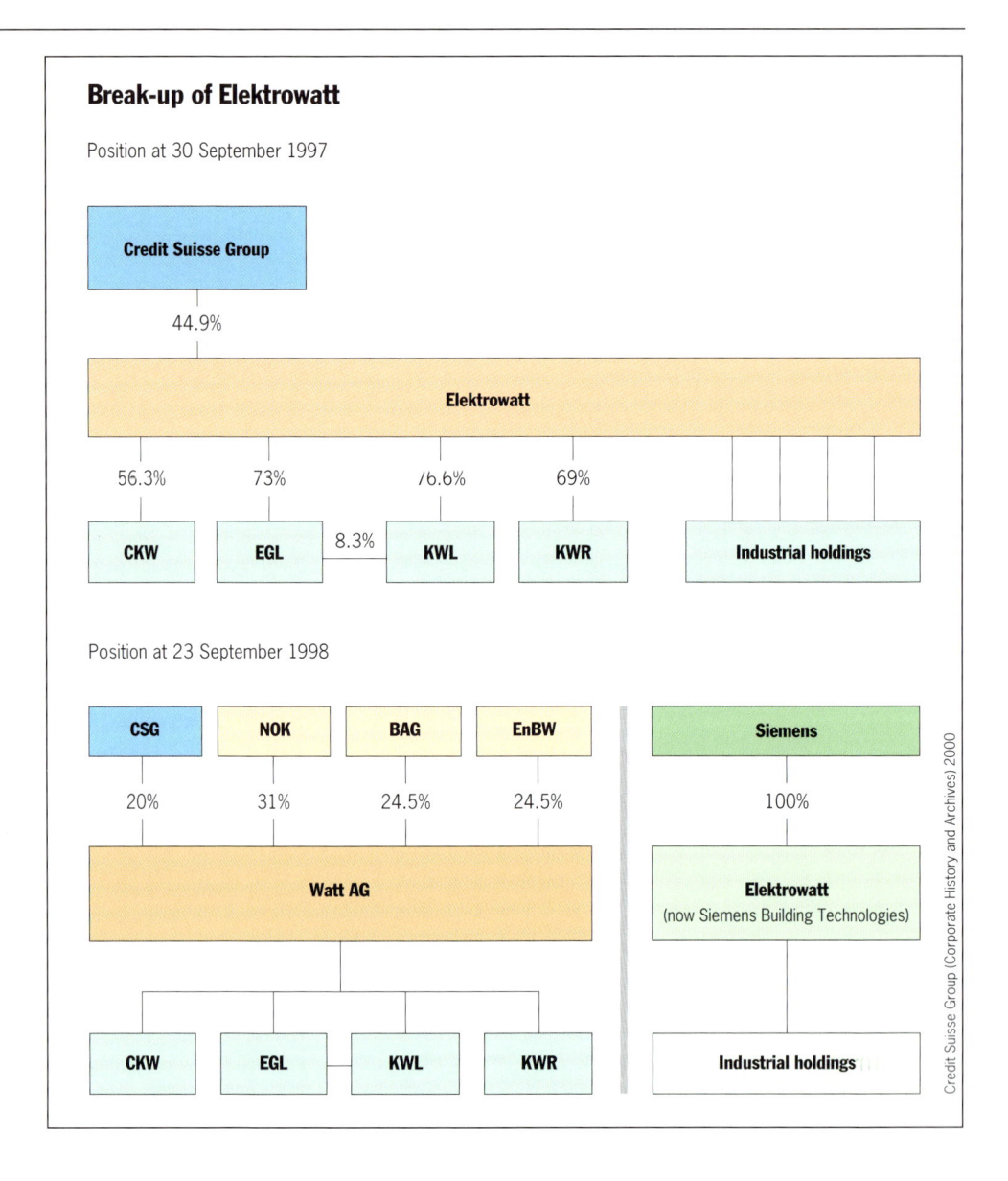

grouped together in pairs under the two legally autonomous Swiss banks: Credit Suisse and Credit Suisse First Boston. From 1 January 1997, CS Holding became Credit Suisse Group. Only half a year elapsed between the announcement of the reorganization (known internally as Project 'Focus') on 2 July 1996 and the actual assumption of business operations by the four independent business units. This represented an impressive feat of planning and implementation by the management, led by Rainer E. Gut, chairman of the board of directors and president of the executive board of CS Holding. Rainer E. Gut also stood at the head of the new Credit Suisse Group as chairman of its board of directors. The new president of the executive board and CEO was Lukas Mühlemann, who joined Credit Suisse Group from Swiss Re on 1 January 1997.

In various areas, restructuring inevitably led to job reductions, though these could be achieved largely through natural attrition, wide-ranging retraining measures, and a generous early retirement scheme. In the end, the downsizing

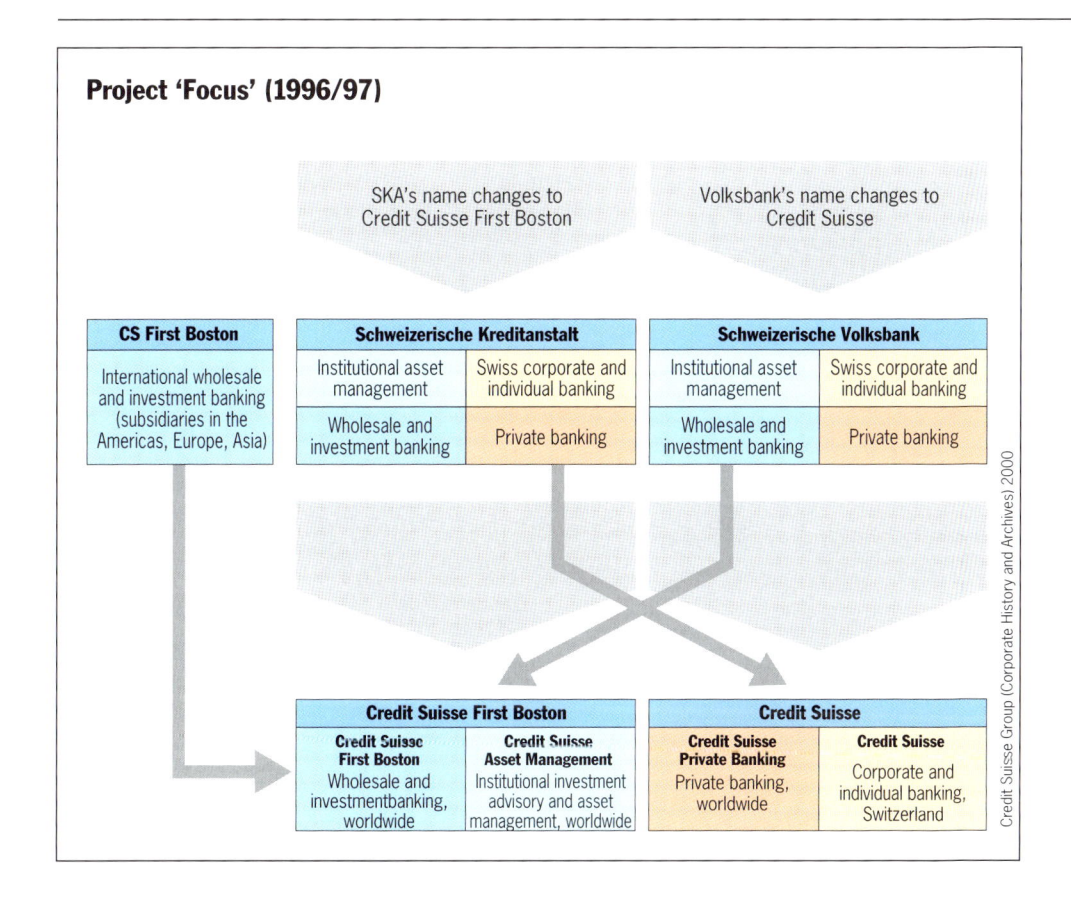

Project 'Focus' (1996/97)

	SKA's name changes to Credit Suisse First Boston		Volksbank's name changes to Credit Suisse	
CS First Boston	**Schweizerische Kreditanstalt**		**Schweizerische Volksbank**	
International wholesale and investment banking (subsidiaries in the Americas, Europe, Asia)	Institutional asset management	Swiss corporate and individual banking	Institutional asset management	Swiss corporate and individual banking
	Wholesale and investment banking	Private banking	Wholesale and investment banking	Private banking

Credit Suisse First Boston		**Credit Suisse**	
Credit Suisse First Boston — Wholesale and investment banking, worldwide	Credit Suisse Asset Management — Institutional investment advisory and asset management, worldwide	Credit Suisse Private Banking — Private banking, worldwide	Credit Suisse — Corporate and individual banking, Switzerland

Credit Suisse Group (Corporate History and Archives) 2000

required virtually no redundancies. Swiss employee associations praised the management of the restructuring as a 'progressive solution by Swiss standards, and one that bears witness to a great sense of social responsibility'.[172] After the restructuring was completed, Credit Suisse Group was also able to create a number of new and attractive jobs. At the end of 1998, the planned reduction of around 3,500 jobs in the Swiss market and about 1,800 jobs abroad could be set against the creation of almost as many new positions. The restructuring also brought with it a new risk management concept. This was soon to be tested by the Asian crisis that began at the end of 1997 and the resulting turbulence on world markets. Further steps to expand Credit Suisse Group in 1997/98 included the creation of a new 'home market' in the United Kingdom – made possible by the acquisition of parts of the British investment bank BZW (Barclays De Zoete Wedd) – and the purchase of Banco Garantia, Brazil's leading investment bank. As early as 1993, SKA had founded Switzerland's first telephone bank, 'CS Firstphone'; four years later, Credit Suisse Group made another technological quantum leap in banking when it launched its Internet banking service. Again, Credit Suisse was the first Swiss bank to apply the new technology with any lasting success.

'First mover' → 370

Reviewing the intensity and quality of the measures implemented during the 1990s to restructure, improve efficiency and adjust the bank's strategic positioning, it is clear that the management and employees of the present-day Credit Suisse Group have succeeded in achieving an enormous amount within a

Organizational structure of Credit Suisse Group (1 January 1997 to 31 March 2000)

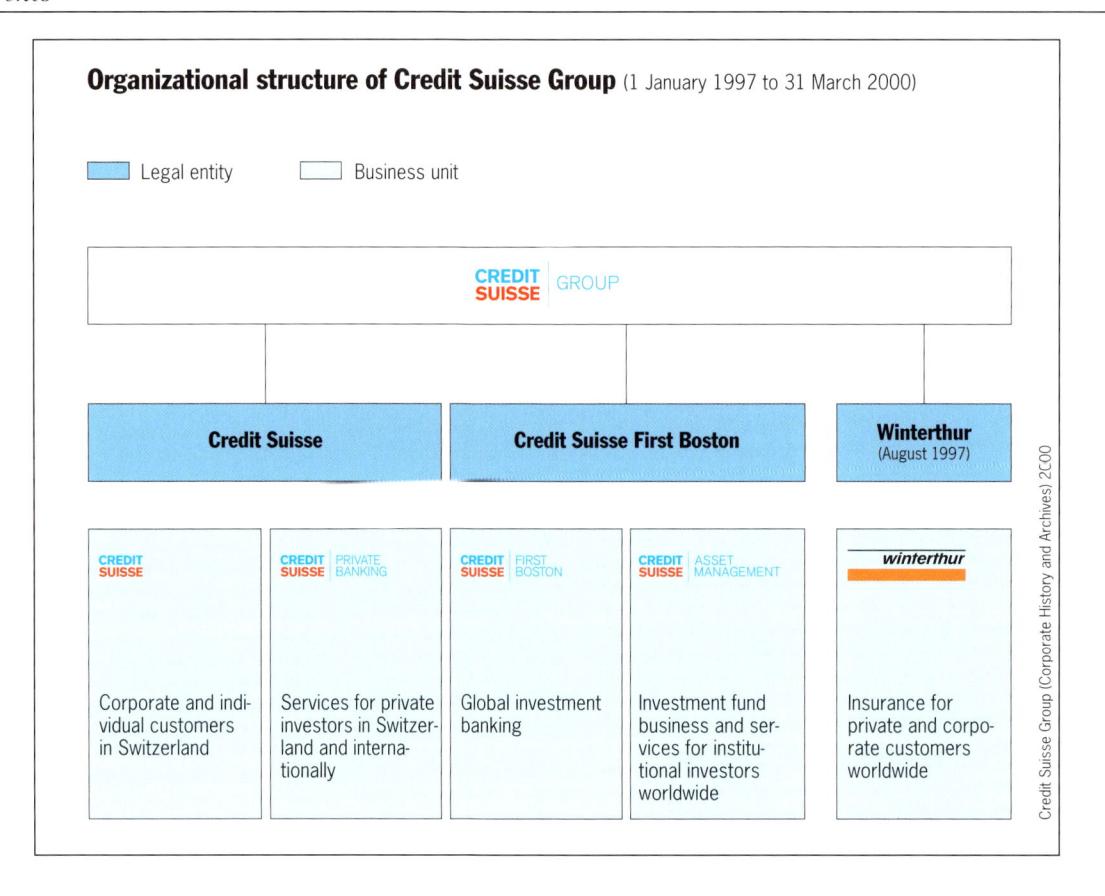

- Legal entity
- Business unit

CREDIT SUISSE GROUP

- **Credit Suisse**
  - CREDIT SUISSE — Corporate and individual customers in Switzerland
  - CREDIT SUISSE PRIVATE BANKING — Services for private investors in Switzerland and internationally
- **Credit Suisse First Boston**
  - CREDIT SUISSE FIRST BOSTON — Global investment banking
  - CREDIT SUISSE ASSET MANAGEMENT — Investment fund business and services for institutional investors worldwide
- **Winterthur** (August 1997)
  - winterthur — Insurance for private and corporate customers worldwide

Credit Suisse Group (Corporate History and Archives) 2C00

Organizational structure of Credit Suisse Group (from 1 April 2000)

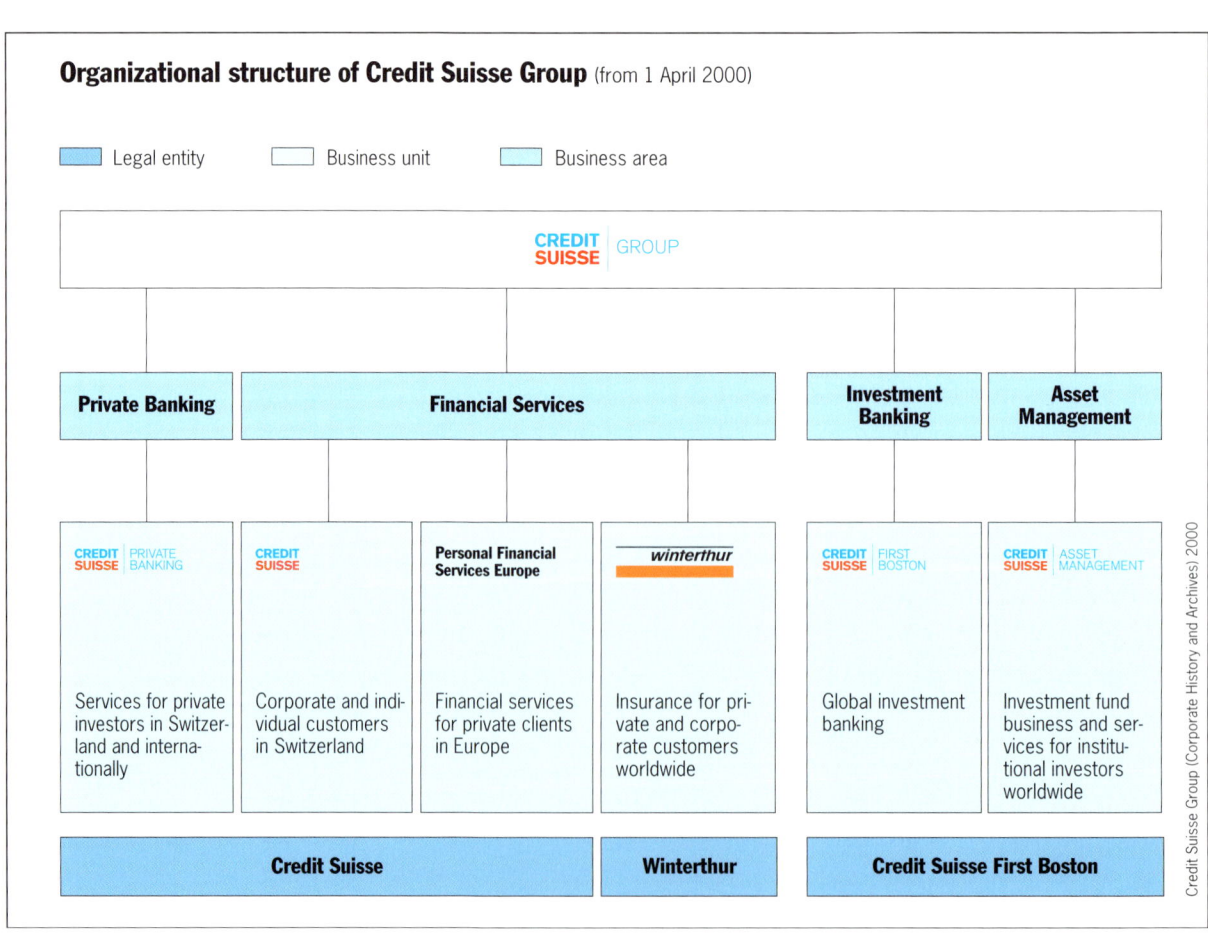

- Legal entity
- Business unit
- Business area

CREDIT SUISSE GROUP

- **Private Banking**
  - CREDIT SUISSE PRIVATE BANKING — Services for private investors in Switzerland and internationally
- **Financial Services**
  - CREDIT SUISSE — Corporate and individual customers in Switzerland
  - Personal Financial Services Europe — Financial services for private clients in Europe
  - winterthur — Insurance for private and corporate customers worldwide
- **Investment Banking**
  - CREDIT SUISSE FIRST BOSTON — Global investment banking
- **Asset Management**
  - CREDIT SUISSE ASSET MANAGEMENT — Investment fund business and services for institutional investors worldwide

Legal entities: Credit Suisse | Winterthur | Credit Suisse First Boston

Credit Suisse Group (Corporate History and Archives) 2000

very short time. Two huge mergers – with CS First Boston and with SVB – were begun almost simultaneously; efficiency and restructuring programs were implemented; and groundbreaking strategic shifts, such as the move towards Allfinanz, were introduced. Economic conditions were difficult at times, and there were various changes in top management, but none of this ever stopped the bank from attracting new customers, and thus continuing on a growth trajectory, or from ensuring that social concerns were taken into account when implementing structural change. The lead that Credit Suisse Group, and with it the whole of the Swiss financial industry, has established over financial services providers in the rest of continental Europe and Japan represents a good platform for further growth and development. Having transformed itself into a comprehensive financial services provider, and with a foothold in the USA – thanks to Credit Suisse First Boston – that is unique amongst European banks, Credit Suisse Group is well equipped to meet the challenges of the future.

Part Two: Strategic Pillars

A poster to publicize the opening of SKA's branch in Bern in 1919.

The core Swiss market

By the 1970s, SKA found that it really needed to act if it wanted to retain its traditional status as one of Switzerland's largest banks. With its much smaller branch network and its image as a bank for large-scale customers, it lagged behind its competitors, particularly in deposit business. Even strengths, such as its excellent position in underwriting business, would not be enough for it to achieve the size it needed to maintain its standing over the longer term.

The integration of Schweizerische Bodenkredit-Anstalt in 1976 kicked off a series of measures aimed at improving SKA's position in Swiss retail business. Despite making some progress, the bank soon exhausted the potential of primarily organic growth – and still there was no sign of a decisive change in its fortunes. As a consequence, CS Holding and SKA took advantage of the removal of banking conventions and the difficulties caused by the collapse of the Swiss real estate market, and between 1990 and 1994 built up a sizeable core market in Switzerland. The acquisition of Bank Leu, SVB and NAB represented a turning point in Swiss banking history, as well as strengthening CS Holding's retail banking business and private banking operations. With a strong Swiss core market behind it, the bank was now able to embark on further expansion in areas such as investment banking and Allfinanz.

SKA's business policy up to the middle of the twentieth century

As a start-ups bank, the young SKA played a leading role in the pioneering days of the Swiss state and Swiss industry, helping to build up a stable and highly developed nation. During the 'Belle Epoque' between the 1870s and the outbreak of the First World War, the bank altered its business focus. Railway financing remained a major strand, but in transforming itself into a commercial and industrial bank, SKA also built up its lending and deposit-taking operations as well as its involvement in the electricity industry. Securities underwriting and stock exchange business also grew in significance, giving SKA an early opportunity to make a name for itself as an underwriter outside Switzerland too. By the end of the 19th century, SKA was the leading 'major bank' in Switzerland. The series of crises that began with the First World War hit the bank hard. Its foreign operations suffered particularly badly, though unlike many other Swiss banks, SKA was able to sort out its problems without recourse to outside help. As Switzerland won international significance as a financial center after the Second World War, commercial lending remained the dominant line of business for SKA.

The 1970s: SKA at a crossroads

The need for a new beginning

SKA stood at a crossroads in the 1970s. Over the previous 30 years it had managed to fritter away its comfortable post-war standing and was now clearly only the number three among the major Swiss banks. Between 1946 and 1976, SKA's total assets had risen from Sfr 1,894 million to Sfr 41,664 million (a factor of 22). Meanwhile, SBG's total assets had gone up from Sfr 1,319 million to Sfr 52,651 million (a factor of 40), and SBV's from Sfr 2,139 million to Sfr 52,757 million (a factor of 25).

The figures clearly show that SKA was posting significant growth rates but still losing ground. The gap between it and the other two major banks, SBG and SBV (or UBS and SBC, to give them their English acronyms), had been widening since the mid-1960s. Even if it now managed to grow in step with the other two, SKA's position as number three bank would simply be cemented even more firmly. If there were to be any hope of closing the gap over the long term, the bank would not only have to work extremely hard, it would also have to implement a rigorous growth strategy. There was no alternative. Size was becoming more and more important in an increasingly tough competitive environment, and if SKA continued to pursue its business activities in the same manner as before, it even risked losing its reputation as the most profitable of the major banks. The first signs of a new era were appearing in American banking. This era would be characterized by liberalized financial markets and an emphasis on shareholder value, and it would bring an abrupt end to the comfortable Swiss way of doing things, in banking as well as in other areas.

During the 1960s and early 1970s, SKA had developed into a broader-based financial institution. In some disciplines – especially underwriting business, foreign exchange and precious metals trading, and business with large customers – it had improved its position relative to its competitors and was able to make the best of its strengths.

However, in balance-sheet business (i.e. lending and borrowing) SKA suffered from weaknesses that manifested themselves most obviously in its lack of customer deposits. The bank simply could not compete properly with its rivals, both of which had many more branches, and thus much greater access to people's savings and investments. It took a long time for the realization to dawn that SKA needed to strike out in a new direction. Even after the bank entered the retail savings market in 1970, chairman of the board of directors Felix W. Schulthess still took the view that, because of the margins involved, it would still be better only to pursue business with large-scale customers. When talking about the rationale for retail business (i.e. savings products, small loans and mortgages) Schulthess mentioned the bank's 'economic obligations', but not the pressure from competitors or the need for a 'universal' bank to serve a truly universal clientele.[173] As a result of this unforthcoming business policy there was a real danger that in commercial banking, at least, SKA might fail to meet the standards required, and thus fall by the wayside in a time of rapid economic growth.

Only one strategy could possibly help the bank to narrow, or even close, the gap between it and its main rivals: growth. If SKA wanted to play a significant role as a full-service (or 'universal') bank in the future, it needed to go on the offensive, especially in retail business. Within the bank, the signs of a general change in attitude had begun to build up from the mid-1970s onwards. It was then that SKA laid the foundations for a professional PR operation, reflecting the strategic importance of future public relations activities. Meanwhile, branch managers were making it increasingly clear that in order to stimulate savings business, SKA would have to shed its image as a bank that was really only interested in large-scale customers.[174]

The merger with Schweizerische Bodenkredit-Anstalt (SBKA) in 1976 marked the first major step towards the required expansion in retail business. After over seventy years of co-operation, SKA fully assimilated SBKA, which was primarily involved in mortgages and savings business, thus achieving a significant increase in both its distribution network and its customer base. At the same time, SKA felt compelled by circumstances to once again completely rethink its policy towards retail business.

This process of realignment was greatly accelerated by the Chiasso Affair, which had shaken SKA to its very core. New ideas of how to take the bank forward, some of which had actually been in the air for a long time, could now be implemented. For the first time ever, the bank included the goal of sharply increasing its market share of 'customer deposits of all types' in its guiding principles.[175] One of the central realizations at this time was that if the bank was to achieve sustained success in its core Swiss market, it would have to become more populist in terms of both image and business orientation. SKA was forced, in effect, to live up to the slogan it introduced in 1979: 'SKA – für alle da' ('SKA, there for everyone'). As a consequence there followed a phase of internal growth that fundamentally changed the bank's operational structure as well as its external image. While the marketing, advertising and sponsorship departments projected SKA's new 'populist' image to the outside world, the process of modernization also progressed on various levels within the bank itself. Under slogans like 'cost consciousness', 'cost reduction', 'efficiency gains', 'customer focus', 'customer segmentation' and 'systematic benchmarking', SKA built up a modern image for itself in domestic business and started to use new distribution channels. Efforts were also made to expand the branch network.

In order to show what effects this paradigm change had on SKA, the next section takes a closer look at some of the individual business areas that played significant roles in SKA's core Swiss market between 1970 and 1990. The main elements as far as retail banking was concerned were deposit business (i.e. savings), as well as loans and mortgages. The expansion of the branch network was also a significant feature during this period. In wholesale banking, securities underwriting was the principal line of business.

What is a core market, what is a home market?

The terminological distinction commonly made within Credit Suisse Group between 'core market' and 'home market' goes back to the mid 1990s when plans were made to expand SKA's business operations geographically to encompass a new 'home market' in Austria. A 'home market' is characterized by a broad-based business presence in the foreign market concerned. 'Core market', by contrast, refers to the bank's business activities within Switzerland.

Marketing and communication → 373

Deposit business

In commercial banking business, healthy, sustained growth is only possible if the liabilities side of the balance sheet is well structured. In other words there has to be the right amount of customer deposits. Money deposited by customers tends to represent a more stable and cost-effective basis for the refinancing of commercial lending than money procured from the more volatile interbank market.

In fact a lack of savings deposits was one of the reasons why SKA fell behind its rivals in the mid-1960s. All three of the leading major banks had entered the savings market late compared with the cantonal banks and SVB (SBG started in 1962, SKA and SBV in 1970) but from the off, SKA found the fight to establish itself in this area particularly difficult – not least because of its image as a bank that was primarily interested in large customers.

At the end of the 1960s, SKA was still only offering its retail customers deposit books; the word 'savings' was not to be found in the bank's range of products (in general terms 'deposit books' had more restrictive withdrawal conditions, but also higher interest rates, than 'savings accounts' and 'savings books'). As broad sections of the Swiss population attained greater material prosperity during the 1970s, there was a change in their savings and payment habits. Retail business swiftly gained in importance.

In 1970, SKA still had the greatest volume of customer deposits on its books, though its rivals were following close behind. Within a few years SBV and SBG had overtaken SKA and they continued to increase their lead steadily until 1990.

A comparison of the relative development of the three banks' customer deposits as a proportion of total assets reveals an even more marked difference in fortunes. SKA was clearly struggling with great problems, especially between 1970 and 1980, during which period the contribution of customer deposits to

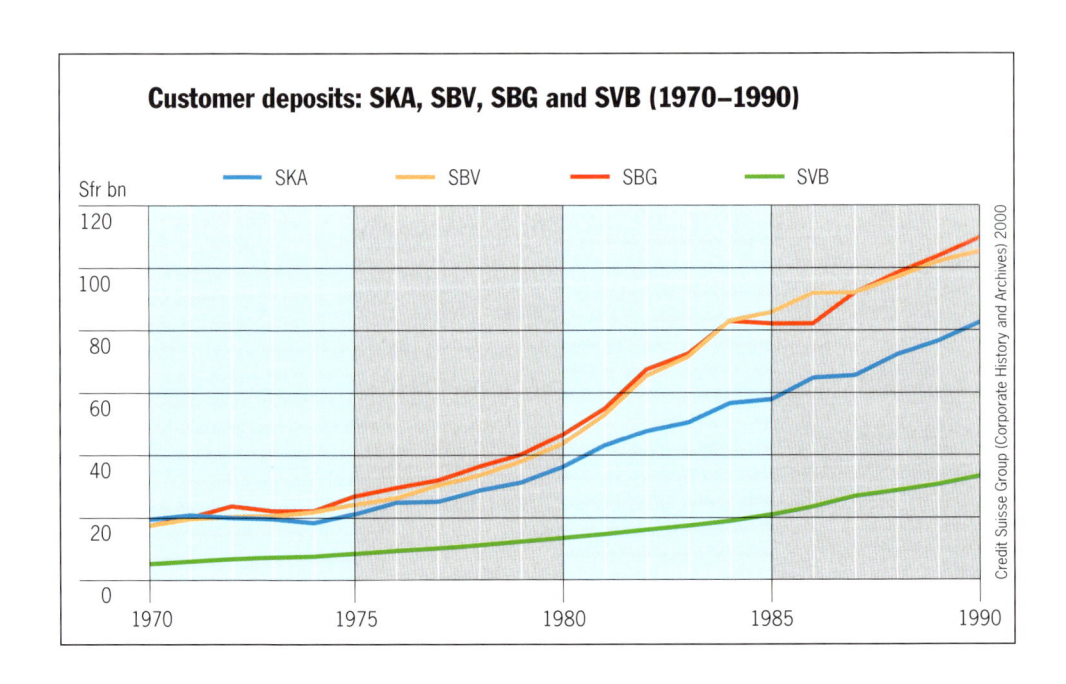

Having remained true for rather too long to its self-image as an elite Zurich bank, in the 1970s SKA began to build up its retail banking operation, developing a whole range of new products within a short space of time.

total assets fell from 70% to 57%. Over the same period SBV witnessed a decline from 63% to 59%, while SBG managed to increase the proportion from 58% to 60%.

SKA was well aware that its lack of deposited funds was a problem, and in 1978, for example, it set itself a new goal: the procurement of customer deposits – especially savings – was to be the bank's highest priority.

In order to achieve this goal, SKA continuously adjusted its range of savings and investment products to suit the prevailing market conditions; it also formulated concrete objectives, trained its staff in technical matters and sales psychology and closely examined any innovation that came onto the market. However, the ideas proposed for generating more retail business went much further. These included a greater amount of direct advertising, special offers for newborn babies and pensioners, more customer-friendly counter opening times, rewards for staff who attracted customer deposits, and promotional gifts for the retail customers themselves.[176] Even if some of the ideas were never implemented, they bore witness to the fresh wind that was now blowing through the bank.

These efforts began to bear fruit during the period between 1980 and 1989, though not, perhaps, to the extent that had been hoped. As the chart detailing savings deposits at the major banks (page 118) shows, the gap between SKA and its two main rivals continued to widen in absolute terms. Consequently, by 1990, SKA had more or less given up the whole idea of improving its market position through internal growth alone.

By 1969, SBG already held savings deposits of Sfr 1,645 million; in 1990 it was still the number one bank for savings. By contrast, SKA and SBV did not even start accepting savings until 1970. SKA introduced its new range of investment products in July 1970 by converting its old deposit books and deposit accounts into personal bank accounts, and its old investment books into savings books. At the same time it also launched a young persons' saving account.

Despite these efforts, SBV was more successful than SKA right from the start, not least because of its more extensive branch network, and was able to maintain its number two position amongst the majors. For a long time – and even after its takeover of SBKA in 1976 – SKA had to make do with the same market share as Swiss Volksbank, which was a smaller company but which could boast a long tradition in the savings business. New products, like the young people's salary accounts introduced in 1975 or the pensioners' saving accounts, took some time to establish themselves at SKA. The bank was also confronted by a testing and increasingly competitive environment, made even more difficult by the Chiasso Affair and the damage this did to the bank's image. Between 1978 and 1981, savings deposits at the major banks actually declined as a result of the very low interest rates that prevailed at the time; during the period in question, long-term interest rates were lower than short-term ones. This inversion of the yield curve prompted customers to move their savings into term deposits and other higher-yielding investments. SKA thus felt compelled to launch a renewed offensive in savings business: savings products should be 'actively sold

Deposits – the raw material of banking.

in all customer areas; but in other areas, too, each individual employee should use whatever opportunities are available to attract new savings customers. Sales opportunities can [also] be found in each employee's private sphere.'[177] At the end of the 1980s, when SKA was using a whole array of other measures to liven up its savings business, it temporarily overtook SVB in terms of savings volumes, but it was still suffering as a result of another inversion of the interest rate structure. The gap between SKA and its two main rivals thus remained more or less the same right up to 1990.

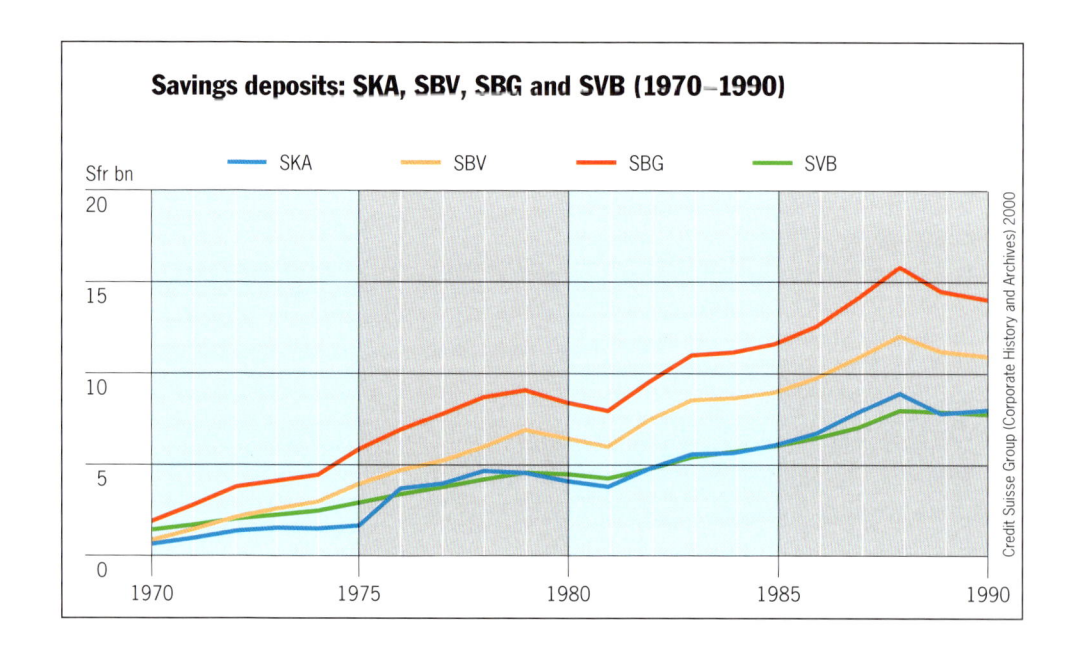

Savings deposits: SKA, SBV, SBG and SVB (1970–1990)

Credit Suisse Group (Corporate History and Archives) 2000

A look at the total numbers of the different savings instruments at SKA and SBG shows just how much effort SKA was making from the second half of the 1970s onwards. At the end of 1970 it had about 165,000 savings books, but by the end of 1980 this number had increased by a factor of 3.4 to about 565,000 and by the end of 1990 by a factor of 5.8 to 965,000. By contrast the equivalent increases at SBG were from 457,000 at the end of 1970 to 1.155 million at the end of 1980 (2.5 times the 1970 figure) and 1.713 million by 1990 (3.7 times more than in 1970).

SKA savings products (1970–1990)

	Saving books	Young people's and pensioners' savings books	Investment savings books	Total
1970	165 127			165 127
1975	234 222	61 843	66 441	362 506
1980	252 876	186 811	125 717	565 404
1985	259 324	282 874	202 380	744 578
1990	332 197	347 516	285 416	965 129

A look at the table shows just how difficult it was for SKA to make significant inroads into the savings market, especially in the 1980s. The annual average growth rate in the number of savings books during these years, approximately 25%, was about the same as at the other major banks and thus far too small to make up the existing deficit. It is also notable that most of the growth was achieved as a result of the higher-interest young people's salary accounts and the pensioners' and investment savings accounts, all of which were introduced in 1975, whereas the normal savings accounts barely showed any growth at all in the first half of the 1980s.

Mortgage business

During the 1960s, the major banks expanded their mortgage businesses mainly by buying up existing specialist institutions. Thus SKA, for example, acquired Banque Populaire de Martigny in 1961 and Bank Wädenswil in 1968 (fully integrated in 1978). SBG bought Crédit Hypothécaire de la Suisse Romande in 1965, as well as Hypothekar- and Sparkasse AG, Aarau, and Ersparnisanstalt Toggenburg AG in 1968; meanwhile SBV took over Bank für Hypothekarkredite Basel in 1960 and Schweizerische Spar- and Kreditbank St. Gallen in 1965. The significance of mortgage lending increased in parallel with that of retail business, and during the 1970s the banks intensified their own efforts in this area, as well as continuing their strategy of taking over other mortgage institutions. The mortgage loan grew to be one of SKA's 'most important products'.[178]

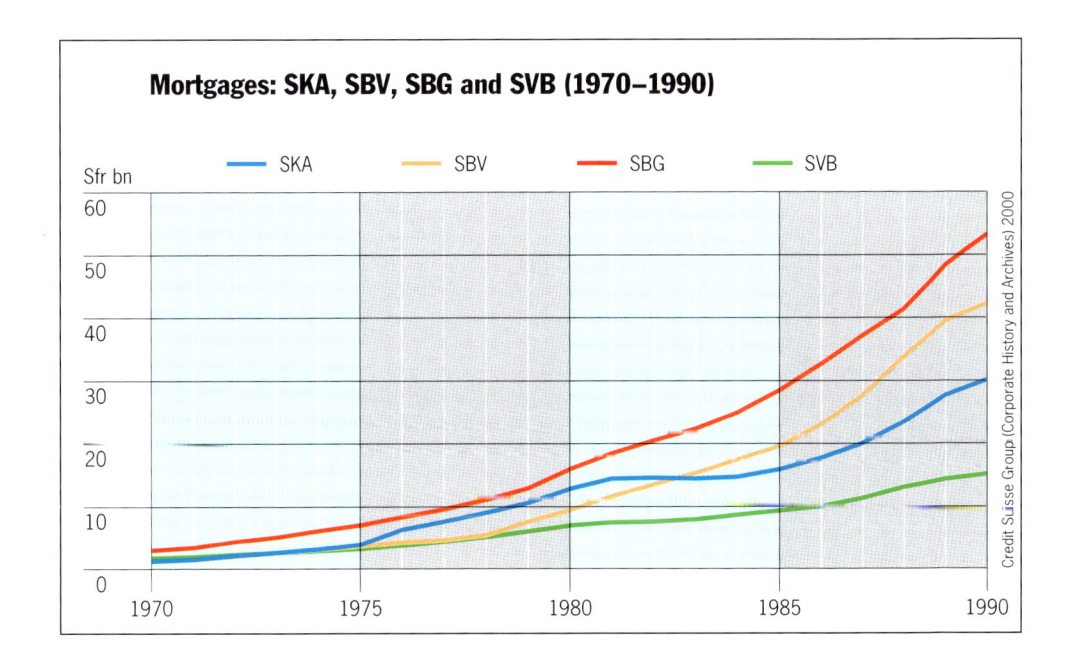

Mortgages: SKA, SBV, SBG and SVB (1970–1990)

Credit Suisse Group (Corporate History and Archives) 2000

A look at the volume of mortgages granted (direct and indirect mortgages) shows SKA lagging behind SBG but keeping just ahead of SBV during the 1970s. In 1972/73 SKA's market share (not including SBKA) of mortgage loans and mortgage-backed lendings rose slightly. By acquiring SBKA in 1976, SKA improved its position still further. In 1983, SBV overtook SKA, also by making

«Wer unser Einfamilienhaus finanziert hat?»

«Die SKA, unsere Bank, mit einer Hypothek.»

Verlangen Sie unsere Broschüre «Die eigenen vier Wände».

SCHWEIZERISCHE
KREDITANSTALT
SKA

During the 1970s, SKA's advertising addressed its new target groups ever more specifically. The above advertisement exemplifies the classic 'testimonial' style: satisfied customers are the best sales pitch.

acquisitions – such as Bodenkreditbank in Basel. While SBG and SBV continued to grow as the 1980s began, SKA suffered a temporary decline. Its mortgage lending volume may have more than doubled between 1980 and 1990, from Sfr 13 billion to Sfr 30 billion, but over the same period SBG increased its mortgage business by a factor of 3.3 to more than Sfr 53 billion, and SBV by a factor of 4.4 to more than Sfr 42 billion. SKA suffered particularly from the fall in mortgage loans as a proportion of its total domestic lendings: having reached a peak of 64% in 1983, this proportion had gone down to 58% by the middle of 1991. This was one of the consequences of SKA's efforts to maintain the 'golden rule' of banking, i.e. trying to refinance mortgage loans using savings deposits of similar maturities. Its competitors, by contrast, raised their market shares by running a more generous lending policy.

At the end of 1990, the Swiss banking industry as a whole showed the following profile. Mortgage lending accounted for 68% of the total volume of domestic lending. Mortgage volumes had increased almost sevenfold over the previous 20 years, while other forms of domestic lending had gone up only fivefold. Between 1980 and 1990, mortgage business accounted on average for about 48% of earnings at the cantonal banks, about 10% at the major banks and about 58% at the regional and local banks. Nevertheless, from 1987 onwards the major banks were market leaders in mortgage business, holding 37% of outstanding mortgage loans in Switzerland.[179]

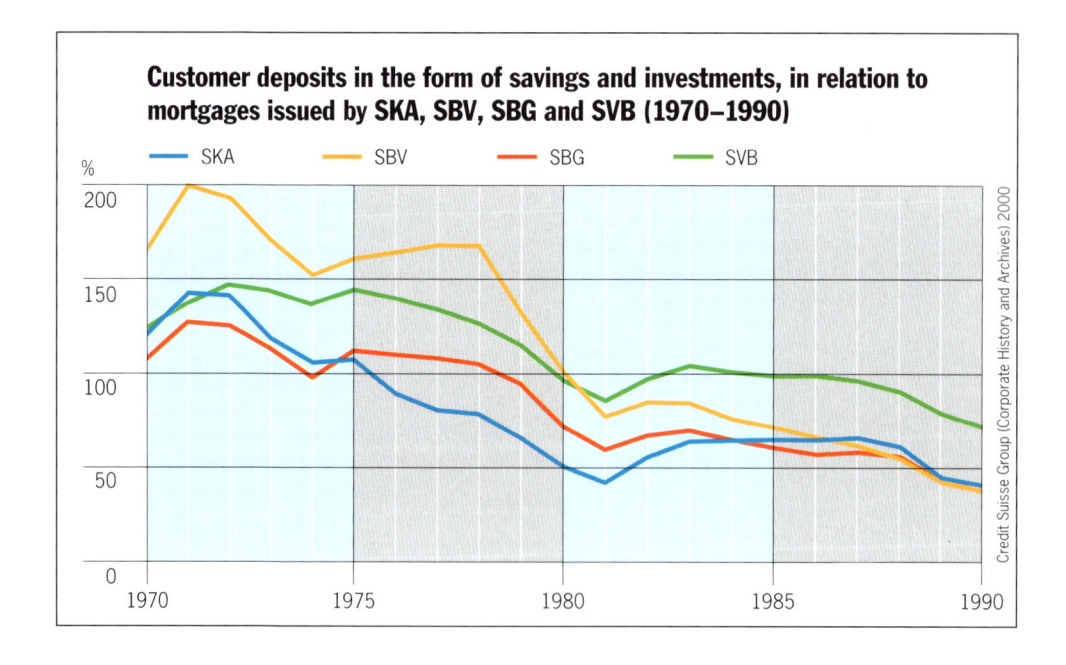

Customer deposits in the form of savings and investments, in relation to mortgages issued by SKA, SBV, SBG and SVB (1970–1990)

Credit Suisse Group (Corporate History and Archives) 2000

Along with mortgage note loans, medium-term notes and bonds, savings and investment products are the central instruments used by the banks to refinance mortgages. If we compare savings and investment deposits with mortgage lendings, we can see how the refinancing structure in Switzerland has changed. Over the period reviewed (1970 to 1990) all of the major banks experienced a marked reduction in the proportion of mortgages refinanced through savings and investment deposits, clearly indicating how difficult it was for the Swiss majors to attract customer funds. Between 1975 and 1985, SKA had the lowest coverage ratio of all the major banks.

After the difficulties caused by the inversion of the yield curve in 1979, the normalization of the rate structure in 1981 had a welcome effect on the quality of mortgage refinancing, which improved at all four of the banks shown in the chart. In the mid-1980s, SKA also began to reap some reward from its efforts to improve its retail business: between 1983 and 1987 it was the only one of the major banks that managed to avoid a drop in its mortgage coverage ratio. In 1988, the negative trend started to intensify at all the banks. Customer deposits fell while mortgage lending increased and the coverage ratio fell to about 42% – once again as a consequence of an inverted yield curve, as well as of customers' increasing yield awareness. Savers were becoming more flexible and were using the whole range of investment vehicles offered by the banks. This produced a rather unbalanced situation, in which customers were being presented with a competitive range of savings products, while the mortgage rate was still influenced by political considerations, rather than also being left to market forces. Owing to its relevance to everyone renting an apartment or house (which meant the majority of the population, since Switzerland has a culture of tenancy rather than home-ownership) the mortgage rate could only be adjusted to market conditions after some delay.

Branches

As a result of general growth and regional diversification within the Swiss economy, the need for commercial finance in Switzerland's outlying regions began to increase after 1945. These regions were soon demanding the services that only internationally active banks could provide. Since the cantonal and local banks could not meet this demand satisfactorily, the major banks had every incentive to expand their branch networks. However, regional offices set up by the majors only began to come decisively into their own when these institutions intensified their involvement in mortgage and savings business from the 1960s onwards. Head offices could deal with activities like underwriting and commercial lending, but customer deposits had to be collected via the branches. Suddenly, the bank with the most extensive network of offices enjoyed a significant advantage over its rivals.

SKA had been building up its branch network steadily, but cautiously, since 1945. During the 1960s and 1970s, when the spiral of new branch openings began to spin faster and faster, SKA, far from being a driving force amongst the major banks, merely 'played along' with the general trend without any real enthusiasm.[180] A comparative analysis of the development of the major banks' branch networks provides another clear example of the fact that SKA, despite its increasingly expansive policy, was not going to be able to make up the distance it had fallen behind its rivals.

Number of branches: SKA, SBV, SBG and SVB (1960–1990)

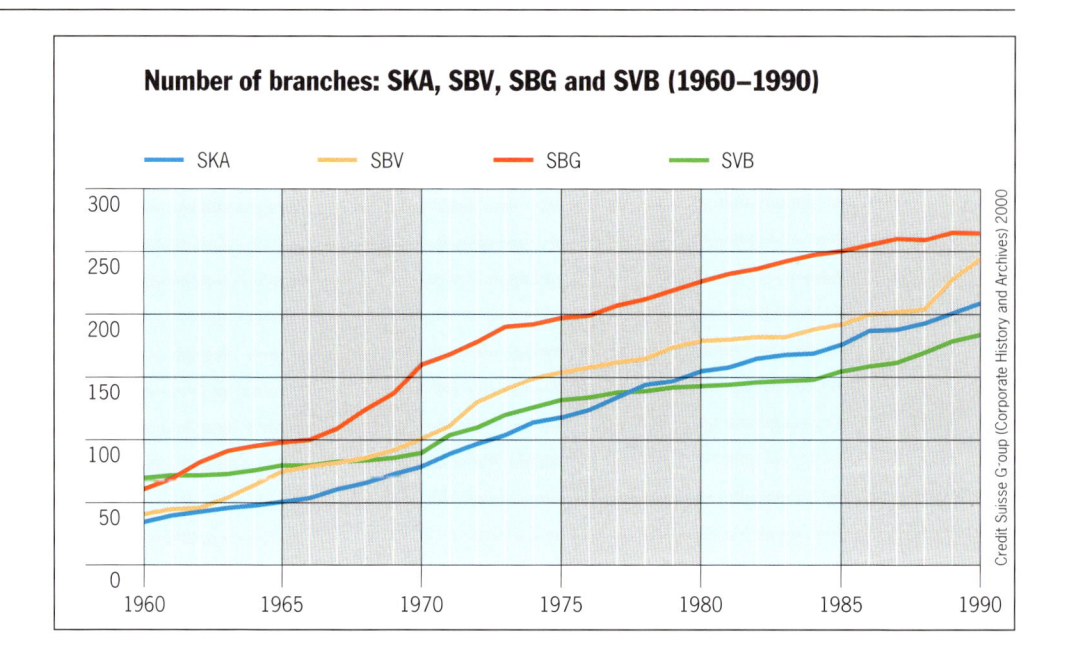

Credit Suisse Group (Corporate History and Archives) 2000

Like the other major banks, SKA had sometimes attracted public criticism for taking over other institutions. Because of this criticism, and because of the fact that it was hard to find suitable acquisition candidates when the economy was doing well, the bank extended its branch network primarily by setting up

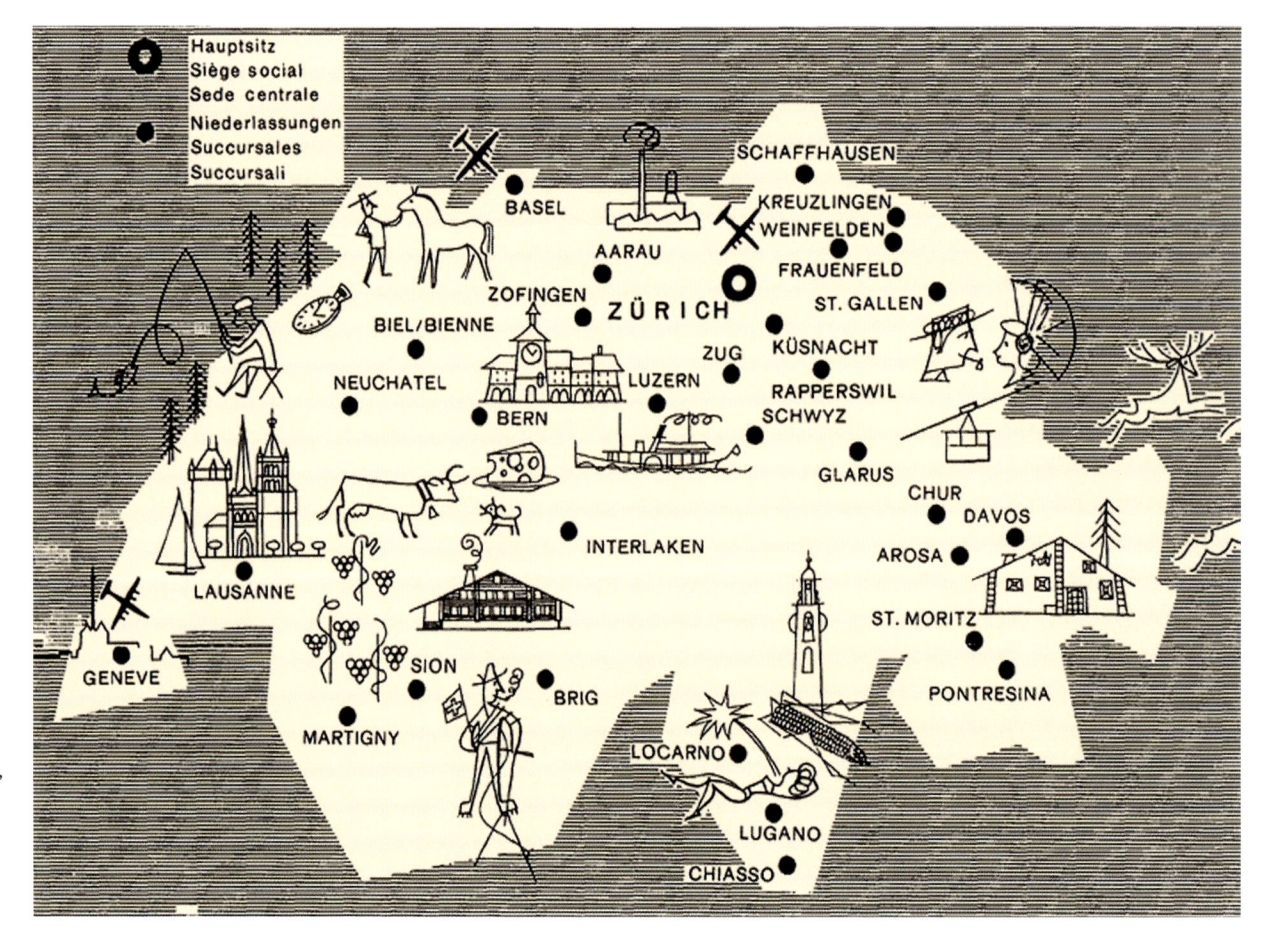

In 1962 SKA used an advertisement to show off its branch network in Switzerland. It had just opened branches in Rapperswil and Zofingen as well as another office in Basel. However, compared with those of the other major banks – SBG, SBV and SVB – SKA's network was not dense enough to allow a really strong presence in retail banking.

new branches from scratch. Nevertheless, the increased presence of the major banks in rural areas and smaller towns made life difficult for some of the local banks, exposing them to the possibility of takeover – a vicious circle which gripped the banking sector until the far-reaching structural adjustment that took place in the 1990s.

Faced by recruitment difficulties and uncomfortable about the threat that their branch networks posed to the local banks, in 1971 the major banks came to a gentlemen's agreement to restrict the number of new branch openings and to operate a cautious policy with regard to the acquisition of local banks. Lulled by this agreement into a false sense of security, SKA's board of directors assumed that they no longer had to worry about falling further behind their competitors.

As a result of this agreement, fewer local banks were taken over by large institutions, but there was no stopping the flood of new branch openings. Between 1966 and 1975, SBG opened ten new offices a year on average, SBV eight, and SKA seven.[181] In mid-1977, the agreement was allowed to lapse by mutual consent, which led to various critical comments in the press. Unlike the other two banks, from the start SKA was against prolonging the agreement. It was aware that Switzerland was becoming saturated with bank branches, but it was also aware that it needed to catch up with the other majors. Even SVB had a denser branch network than SKA at that point.

SKA thus felt it had to 'open new offices in good locations' as a 'defensive measure'.[182] Market research suggested that if SKA wanted to consolidate its domestic strength, it needed 160, rather than the existing 134 branches.[183] At the same time, however, it wanted to continue with its policy of 'not establishing prestige branches and then running the risk of having to close down offices after a few years because they are not earning enough'.[184] Unlike its rivals, SKA tended to invest modest amounts in setting up agencies, which rarely employed more than five or six staff.

Between 1980 and 1983, the four biggest banks in Switzerland agreed to be bound by another pact. Once again they were to ration the number of new branch openings and refrain from taking over local or regional banks. In order to improve its position in its core market, SKA fundamentally realigned its branch structure in the mid-1980s by, amongst other measures, reorganizing its regional management structure (the 'Führung ZN Schweiz' project) and integrating its smallest units, the Einnehmereien (collection offices), more effectively into its overall retail strategies.

The chart below shows the relationship between customer deposit business and the number of branches at each bank. Until about 1975, the four major banks generated about the same volume of savings and investment deposits per branch as each other. The greater the number of branches a bank had, the greater the sum of this type of money it attracted. Towards the end of the 1970s it became clear that the other banks were able to gather more deposits than SKA not just because of their larger branch networks, but also because of the more effective work they were doing at each individual branch. Then, in the years between 1979 and 1981, the various campaigns launched by SKA to promote

'Even if it slows our plans down a little – it does not, after all, allow for the fact that we, as the major bank with the smallest branch network, have some catching up to do – we believe that the agreement is very valuable, particularly from the psychological point of view' (Minutes of the board of directors, 22 April 1971).

In 1905, SKA took over Oberrheinische Bank's office and turned it into its first Basel branch. The photograph (from the 1920s) shows the entrance to the SKA branch on Freie Strasse.

Customer deposits in the form of savings and investments, per branch: SKA, SBV, SBG and SVB (1970–1990)

'Einnehmereien' (collection offices)

The development of 'Einnehmereien', or collection offices, provides a particularly good example of how SKA's attitude towards its branch network changed towards the end of the 1970s and then again at the end of the 1980s. The bank had run a small number of Einnehmereien since the early 1940s. These were located in rural areas and tended to be run by local villagers as a sideline rather than by the bank's own staff. As retail business with small customers began to gain momentum, these Einnehmereien, which concentrated primarily on simple counter transactions[185], proved to be excellent collection points for savings.

By the end of 1978, SKA was operating 47 Einnehmereien, though at this stage there were still no accurate statistical analyses of the costs and benefits of these operations.[186] In an attempt to attract greater volumes of funds from small customers and to boost personal banking business, SKA produced its first ever strategy for Einnehmereien in 1978. It hoped that these flexible, cost-effective units would be able to compete more with the rural credit banks and cantonal banks in areas outside the range of its branches. This led to a phase of expansion that lasted up to the end of 1987, at which point the bank had 92 Einnehmereien. Thereafter, the number and significance of these units, which had now been renamed as 'agencies', fell sharply.[187] This decline was caused mainly by the abolition of banking conventions and the subsequent dismantling of overcapacities in the Swiss banking sector.

The pharmacist as banker: SKA's Einnehmerei in Winterthur-Töss was opened in 1982. The SKA logo can be seen above a stand full of cosmetics. Photo taken in 1982.

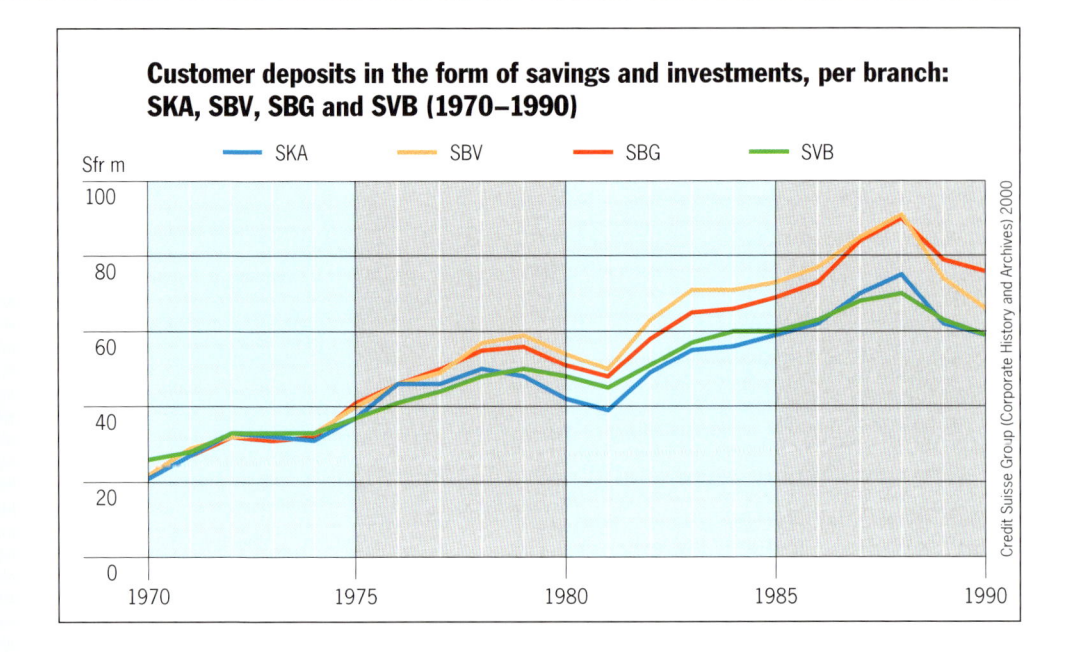

deposit business began to bear fruit in so far as SKA's branches were better able to maintain their position under pressure from the inverted yield curve than the other banks. Otherwise, however, the competitors' branches remained more successful.

After 1982, SKA branches managed to match the growth rates achieved by the rival branch networks in deposit business, but because the rivals' networks were so much bigger, the overall gap between SKA and the others inevitably continued to widen.

Underwriting business

Underwriting is one of the most important lines of banking business, especially for the major banks. The principal aim of underwriting, also known as 'new issues business', is to procure capital for private companies and the public sector by issuing securities. By issuing a bond, the company or public entity can obtain long-term debt capital on the capital market; by issuing new shares it gets long-term, risk-bearing equity capital. By contrast with commercial lending business, the banks' role in this process is usually restricted to that of an intermediary.

SKA started to occupy a leading position in Swiss underwriting and syndication business at around the end of the 19th century. It was able more often than its rivals to take on the prestigious role of lead manager in the underwriting syndicates that were formed at the time. As lead manager, SKA could exert more influence on the actual placement of securities and enjoyed a higher quota of the syndication. More than any other business, underwriting was a board-level matter. Contacts between the bank and the issuer usually took place at the highest level, an approach that further confirmed SKA's image as a bank for big business and large-scale customers.

In 1906, SKA opened its first branch in Western Switzerland at the Place Bel-Air in Geneva. The original building was torn down in 1928 and replaced by a new one. Photo taken in 1930.

In the wake of the very lively issuing activity, a number of consortia were founded. These groups were responsible for maintaining order when bonds were allocated, ensuring that risks were diversified properly, and correcting any excessive imbalances in the relations between competing institutions. The first ever Swiss banking cartel was created in 1897 as a consortium of this type[188], followed shortly afterwards by the creation of the Association of Swiss Cantonal Banks. In 1911, these two consortia agreed to work together on the underwriting and placement of bonds issued by the public sector. Various other consortia were formed to handle bond placements for power stations, big industrial companies and foreign borrowers.[189] In order to qualify for membership of a syndicate, a bank required established business relations with the lead manager, cross-shareholdings with the other banks involved, placing power, and, possibly, reciprocation agreements with the lead institution.

Elektrowatt AG played an important role in SKA's underwriting business. The energy industry was very capital intensive (owing to the large investments required in power stations, but also in transportation and distribution equipment) and the power companies had to raise considerable volumes of money. Thanks to the close capital and personal links between SKA and Elektrowatt, the two companies enjoyed fruitful cooperation on a whole variety of issuing projects. Elektrowatt engaged in a wide variety of activities, diversifying in the decades after 1945 before transforming itself in the 1980s from a 'sometimes rather random collection of parts into a strategically focused conglomerate with

Bank in Luzern was founded in 1856 – the same year as SKA – and was taken over by SKA in 1912. Ten years later, SKA constructed this new building on Lucerne's Schwanenplatz in a Neo-Renaissance style. Photo taken in 1950.

This 'traditional Schwyz-style building is an embellishment to the vicinity and a monument to its builder, master architect Heinrich Peikert of Zug' (1926 annual report of Bank in Zug). SKA opened its first branch in Canton Schwyz in this building, located on Postplatz in the town of Schwyz. Photo taken in 1955.

1913 saw the opening of SKA's first Ticino branch at the Riva Vincenzo Vela in Lugano. In 1917 the bank moved into the building shown here at Piazza Riforma 6. At the end of 1985, larger premises were required – SKA Lugano by now employed about 400 staff – and a new office was built in the Maghetti district. However, SKA continued to maintain its office at the very central Piazza Riforma. Photo taken in 1960.

In 1921, SKA took over Société Suisse de Banque et de Dépôts, based at the 'Lion d'Or' in Lausanne. This subsidiary of the Paris bank Société Générale was thus transformed into SKA's third branch in French-speaking Switzerland after Geneva and Neuchâtel. Photo taken in 1950.

clearly defined business divisions'.[190] Alongside its energy operations, Elektrowatt Group was strengthened by its companies' activities in the industrial and services sectors and, above all, in the real estate business.

As the chart below[191] shows, the volume of underwriting in Switzerland fluctuated considerably between 1970 and 1975. The reasons for this lie in the volatility of interest and exchange rates and in the unstable economic cycles of the period. More than by anything else, the 1970s were characterized by the Swiss government's efforts to dampen economic activity. These efforts included lending restrictions and controls on the underwriting of domestic bonds and equities. In 1973 the first major oil crisis sent prices and interest rates rocketing all over the world. In response, the central banks of the key industrial nations pursued an expansive monetary policy in an attempt to counter the economic consequences of the shock. Demand for capital went up again in 1975, partly because of transactions on behalf of the three major banks themselves, which began to issue registered shares for the first time. Nevertheless, a sharp economic collapse in the mid-1970s hit the stock market hard and made it more difficult to find domestic equity capital.

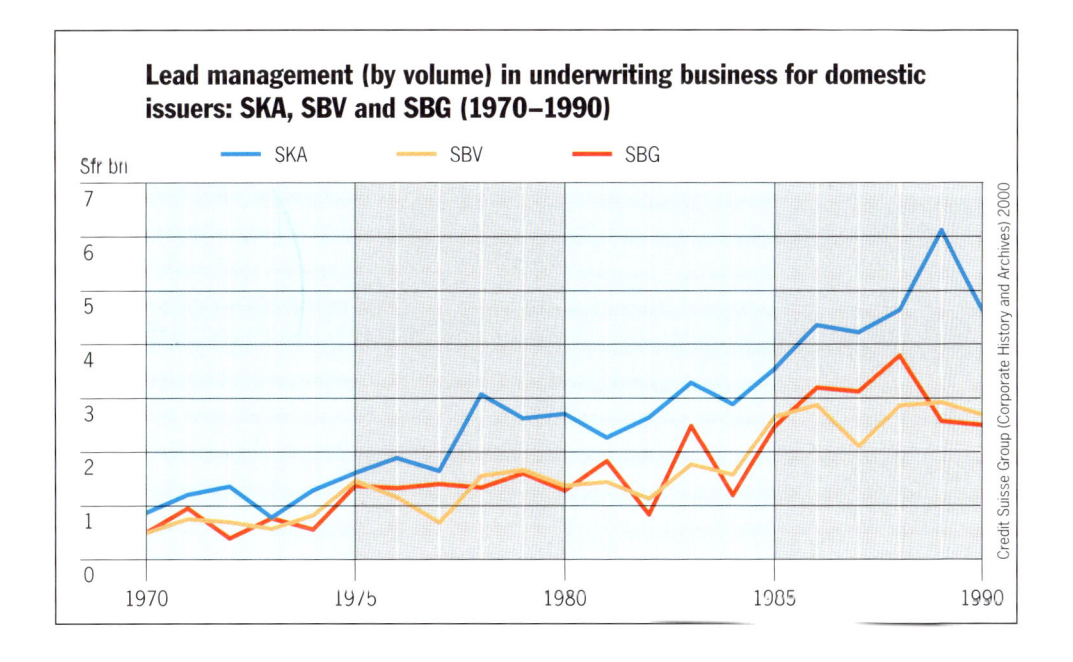

Lead management (by volume) in underwriting business for domestic issuers: SKA, SBV and SBG (1970–1990)

At the beginning of the 1980s, the world economy was confronted by another oil shock and then by the international debt crisis. In the second half of the decade, international bond issues were promoted in a successful attempt to counter the sharp decline in lending business. The Swiss authorities lifted underwriting controls at the end of 1982[192], paving the way for a significant increase in the volume and number of domestic issues. Underwriting business received another boost in the mid-1980s as world economic activity rapidly recovered, interest rates remained low and a highly optimistic mood settled over the stock market. Then, as a result of the stock market crash of 1987 and

In 1930, SKA established itself in Canton Grisons by taking over Rhätische Bank's branches in Arosa, Chur, Davos and St. Moritz. The picture shows the branch in St. Moritz Dorf at Via Maistra 5. Photo taken in the late 1960s.

the high interest rates that resulted from the restrictive monetary policy pursued between 1989 and 1991, underwriting business declined again at the end of the 1980s.

Various developments in the second half of the 1980s subsequently led to far-reaching changes in the Swiss banks' underwriting business:

- The internationalization of the capital markets
- A wave of newly developed products
- New opportunities to circumvent the clear regulations on fees laid down in the Swiss Bankers' Association's Convention VIII (restrictions on the reimbursement of commissions paid to second-line brokers on public issues)
- Increased competition for the established banks from insurance and pension companies

In 1989 and 1990, the restrictions on competition in underwriting business were removed: the conventions between the banks were scrapped and the large syndicate which controlled the issue of domestic public-sector bonds and Swiss franc bonds put out by foreign borrowers was broken up.

Despite economic ebbs and flows and despite various government interventions on the financial markets, SKA has been able to defend its strong position in business involving large-scale customers right up to the present day. In many years, SKA lead managed half the transactions involving the major banks in volume terms, leaving SBV and SBG to share the remaining half of the domestic underwriting market. SKA has also played a leading role in the issue of equities and Swiss-franc denominated foreign paper (public bonds and notes) – a business that expanded sharply from the mid 1970s onwards.

The SKA branch in Gstaad was opened in 1967. Photo taken in 1999.

The 1990s: breakthrough

Increasing pressure to restructure

At the end of the 1980s, the business environment in Switzerland was shaken by profound change, and the banks were forced to realign their business policies. The international securities and foreign exchange markets had not only grown exponentially since the 1970s, they had also been forced to cope with increasingly complex risks in the wake of deregulation. Added to this, the unstoppable march of technology was radically changing the face of the market. The introduction of new financial instruments and processes – such as options, futures and swaps – was giving a greater and greater degree of independence to the financial markets, which had previously been inextricably tied to industrial production on account of the primacy of lending business.

A groundswell of mergers and acquisitions, unprecedented in scale, swept over the Atlantic from the USA to engulf Europe. Various moves towards liberalization in Swiss economic policy combined with the opening up of international markets to expose Switzerland's banks to the raw wind of competition. New and more aggressive strategies were required.

SKA has maintained a branch in Davos Platz since 1930. Photo taken in 2000.

The banks were forced to try and keep up with the gathering pace of the trend towards larger economic zones and globalization, and the unstoppable process of concentration in the industrial sector. All of these new developments meant that internationally active major banks needed to achieve a critical mass significantly in excess of anything the leading Swiss institutions could offer.[193] Large modern businesses not only had to be in a position to develop their own strengths in the most effective way, they also had to ensure the most effective use of their financial resources.[194] The need for comprehensive risk management to protect against the consequences of interest rate fluctuations and escalating country risks, and the rise in fixed costs – unavoidable owing to the growing cost of IT solutions – also meant that banks had to be of a certain minimum size.

By converting CS Holding into an umbrella holding company in 1989, SKA had chosen an appropriate structure for its further growth in the international arena. It was already in a good position in international business, but expansion outside Switzerland also depended on achieving a critical mass in the Swiss domestic market; given the developments of the preceding decades, however, this critical mass was looking more and more difficult to achieve. Despite the introduction at various levels of measures aimed at reducing costs and improving efficiency, and despite the change in mentality amongst the bank's most senior managers, in Switzerland SKA was still very much number three among the major banks. As long as its earnings were greater than those of its rivals, the bank had been able to live perfectly well with this situation, but unless it managed to achieve the required critical mass, there was now no guarantee that it would be able to maintain its position in the future.

SKA continued to struggle in vain with the objective it had set out at the end of the 1970s: namely, to become a leading full-service bank in Swiss retail business.[195] The creation of CS Life marked CS Holding's entry into the Allfinanz business (i.e. the production and sale of both banking and insurance products), an area so far neglected by its rivals; but the success or otherwise of this venture would only become apparent over the long term. By the end of the 1980s, the banks were finding it virtually impossible to achieve organic growth in the Swiss domestic market under their own steam. Owing to the expansion of the major banks' branch networks and the increase in the number of foreign banks over the previous ten years, the Swiss banking sector had reached a growth plateau, leaving the country quite clearly 'overbanked'. Further organic growth through geographical expansion was severely limited in a small country like Switzerland; given the overcapacities that already existed, such a strategy would anyway have been unsuccessful. Consequently, SKA/CS Holding had to choose from three strategic options if it wanted to push for market leadership:

- Establish itself as a niche player in areas such as private client business and investment banking
- Acquire a series of smaller banks in order to make up the deficit bit by bit
- Take over a large bank with a strong position in the domestic market

In view of the commitments already made to expand abroad, the first option was not a serious consideration. Despite successful precedents in the American banking world (e.g. BancOne)[196], the second option would have taken up a great deal of time, entailed major risks and placed enormous demands on the bank's management. Thanks not least to the holding structure and the financial resources generated in the high-earning 1980s, it thus appeared that an ambitious takeover policy, i.e. option three, was the only feasible alternative, assuming, of course, that a suitable candidate could be found. In fact, the bank could be quite confident that opportunities would arise: competition had been intensifying since 1989 and one or other of its rivals could reasonably be expected to fall by the wayside – but SKA would have to act with speed and precision.

Thus it was that the third option was implemented between 1990 and 1994. From about 1990, analysts and observers correctly assumed that there would be an accelerated process of concentration within the banking sector, though they did not expect there to be any major changes in the relative positions of the major banks. Professor Ernst Kilgus, head of the Institute of Swiss Banking in Zurich, for example, was of the opinion that the three largest banks in Switzerland were indeed still some way below the optimum size, but that political factors would prevent what he described as an 'Elefantenhochzeit' (an elephants' wedding – i.e. a union between any of the majors).[197]

1990 was an 'extremely difficult year' for the banks. In quick succession many smaller financial institutions had to surrender their independence. A collapsing real-estate market and the abolition of the conventions between the banks unleashed a 'general insecurity' in the industry and intensified what was already a much tougher competitive environment. The banks faced particular difficulties in mortgage business[198]: owing to the high level of debt carried by their customers, a critical lack of funds suitable for refinancing mortgage loans, the long-term commitment entailed by mortgage lending, and an inverted yield curve, the banks were faced with a serious shortage of liquidity. There were no longer enough customer deposits (especially savings) to fund the mortgage business, so the banks had no choice but to resort to shorter-term, riskier time deposits or expensive inter-bank money. Only a third of the total mortgage portfolio was subject to compulsory amortization; worse still, the free play of the market on the liabilities side was set against a mortgage market that was much less flexible and less quick to react to changing circumstances. In the banks' view, the 'urgent government decree on the subjection of mortgage interest rates to price monitoring' that emerged from Switzerland's price control debate, was a classic example of Swiss interventionism – especially since the mortgage market was so politicized anyway – as well as being a crassly discordant note in the general move towards deregulation.

'Such an entity would be so powerful that it would be practically impossible to avoid a political debate about nationalization. This would, however, be highly problematic' (Ernst Kilgus, 1990).

With the economy in a critical state, the major banks once again turned the screw on costs: stock market departments at subsidiary companies were closed down, for example, and to all intents and purposes there was a freeze on recruitment. The pressure to restructure was most obvious in retail banking, where the Swiss market suffered from the lowest margins in the world. As we have seen, CS Holding and SKA were active in this area too and had tried, though with little success, to improve their position in the domestic market under their own steam by means of innovative retail banking strategies.

The first coup: the takeover of Bank Leu

CS Holding's long-planned first 'coup', the integration of Bank Leu, came during this time of upheaval and crisis. Bank Leu, Switzerland's sixth largest bank by total assets, had been a prospective takeover target for some years. Having survived various crises since the 1920s, and having at times been forced to lean heavily on SBV for support, the bank had generated impressive growth in the years of economic and stock market euphoria. However, Leu had failed to keep up with developments in logistics and infrastructure. During the 1980s it suffered various setbacks, and in 1988 there was a change in management, which simultaneously acted as the trigger for share buying by CS Holding. The managers at Paradeplatz had long taken an interest in what was going on at Zurich's oldest bank, whose offices were located just across the Bahnhofstrasse. Bank Leu was too big to be an agile niche player and too small to act as a globally

Leu 'tired of the freedom of the wild, has taken refuge in the CS zoo!' (*Handelszeitung*, 19 April 1990).

> *'Plans to Take Over Bank Leu:*
> *A Coup by CS Holding'*
> 'Neue Zürcher Zeitung', 11 April 1990
>
> 'Almost exactly 40 days ago at Bank Leu's annual press conference, the bank summed up its optimistic mood with the slogan "resolutely onwards"', noted the *NZZ* on 11 April 1990. 'Chairman of the board of directors Kurt Schiltknecht and representatives of the executive board talked in detail about the measures they had implemented in all areas in order to put the bank at the top of the pile in terms of service quality'. CS Holding's takeover offer thus came as a complete surprise to everyone. It had voted with a 16% shareholding at Bank Leu's annual shareholders' meeting, though in fact it already possessed a larger stake. Following the takeover press conference of 10 April 1990, the comments and headlines in the Swiss press reflected the general surprise (and also made great use of the literal meaning of the word 'Leu' in Swiss-German: lion): 'Leu in the CS Zoo' (*Finanz und Wirtschaft*), 'CS Holding Gets Leu into Its Cage' (*Tages-Anzeiger*), 'CS Holding Has Captured the "Lions"' (*Amriswiler Anzeiger*), 'Leu Moves to a New Zoo' (*Berner Rundschau*).
>
> As well as all the wordplay, the journalists also came up with some salient points. 'Despite its attempts some years ago to break out of its given role and strike out for the new shores of international investment banking, Bank Leu has long since reverted to being a decent provincial bank', wrote the *Aargauer Tagblatt*, also going on to state that SKA's strategy for advancement had intensified since the CS Holding roof was erected: 'With his eyes unwaveringly fixed on the unsleeping global financial market, where bankers tirelessly ply their trade, CS boss Rainer E. Gut is constantly pulling new strings to create a dense network of relationships around the financial world. This time, however, CS Holding wants to broaden its operational base in the domestic financial market.' The *Tages-Anzeiger* wrote: 'Major bank swallows major bank, Bank Leu loses its autonomy. The managers at Bank Leu did not want what the bosses at CS Holding have been planning'; the newspaper described the process as 'unfriendly… even if it is officially being made to sound friendly at the moment'. However, the *Tages-Anzeiger* had not missed the fact that there were serious problems at Bank Leu: 'Bank Leu is simply too big to be an agile niche specialist and too small to be a globally active full-service bank. … [The] noises heard from the increasingly tough competitive environment in the Swiss banking industry are likely to become harsher and louder. If the takeover of a major bank can be so quickly digested, it makes you realize just how easy it would be for a feeding frenzy to erupt in the banking industry.' For all its reserve, the *NZZ* could not help but let slip a certain note of admiration: 'The proposed structure is not without a certain elegance: in Bank Hofmann and Clariden Bank, Bank Leu, founded in 1755, is set to gain two partners that – although smaller – together generate slightly higher commission earnings than Bank Leu alone. Its new subholding also provides CS Holding with a well-funded credit portfolio.'
>
> In its November 1990 issue, *Schweizer Bank* asked Robert A. Jeker, the new chairman of Leu Holding's board of directors, to comment on his strategic considerations. Jeker left readers in no doubt 'that the three banks brought together in Leu Holding have great potential for further development in private banking. All three could certainly have remained successful on their own, but we are convinced that we can greatly improve the performance of all three by exploiting synergies.' Jeker's words prompted *Schweizer Bank* to make the following analogy: 'The "lions" have been adopted, and now must show that they can develop independently and prove themselves within this new family.'

active full-service bank. A proposed capital increase, which was recommended to the shareholders at par and with no indication of the intended purpose, attracted CS Holding's attention. The increase improved the voting strength of existing shareholders and inevitably led to rumors. One of the concerns expressed was that given the large volume of funds already available to the bank, the additional capital could only be intended for 'new adventures in the direction of Martin Ebner's BZ Bank'.[199] Following the annual shareholders meeting of 29 March 1990, CS Holding let it be known that it held a large stake in Bank Leu and laid a share exchange offer before the shareholders. As a consequence of this move, CS Holding came to control about 56% of Bank Leu's equity voting rights and was satisfied that it had managed to acquire a well-refinanced loan portfolio.

Like Bank Hofmann and Clariden Bank, Bank Leu retained its own character within CS Holding, rather than being recast as just another subsidiary of a major bank. When commenting on this, Rainer E. Gut referred to the advantages of the holding structure and quoted the (slightly altered) words of Chairman Mao: 'let one hundred flowers bloom'.[200] Because Bank Leu had been a candidate for takeover for many years, its share price was high. Measured by the ratio between earnings and share price, Bank Leu was in fact the most expensive Swiss bank.[201] Different commentators responded in different ways to the question of whether too much had been paid for a bank that was overcapitalized and not an ideal strategic fit. Some called it a 'clever move' by CS Holding, since it had in effect wrested control of Bank Leu by means of a relatively small capital outlay. Indeed, CS Holding had distinguished itself by introducing a new merger model. By bringing in the two subsidiaries Bank Hofmann and Clariden Bank it created a majority stake for itself in the new public company Leu Holding. The offer to shareholders was made on condition that if 100% of Bank Leu's shares were exchanged, Bank Leu would make up 75% of the new Leu Holding, and Bank Hofmann and Clariden Bank the remaining 25%.[202]

It took longer than expected to integrate Bank Leu and increase its profitability. Inevitably, the media was quick to take advantage of the opportunity to make puns at the bank's expense ('Leu' being the Swiss-German word for 'lion'): 'If his rivals were initially left seething by Rainer Gut's cheek, they are now just happy that they do not have this tired old lion in their own cage.'[203] On top of this, at the end of the 1990s came difficulties with CS First Boston, and a decree by the Swiss government that forced SKA to provide equity capital coverage for CS Holding's subsidiaries. Bank Leu was thus put through another metamorphosis in order to position itself more effectively in the market. 'Normal' bank business was concentrated at the core company (now Bank Leu AG), while its participations (such as Merkur Immobilien AG) and its foreign subsidiaries in Luxembourg, London and the Bahamas were hived off and attached to Leu Holding, which thus found itself with a number of subsidiaries.

In the following year, 1991, Bank Leu embarked on further restructuring. Its domestic branch network was reduced to the role of distribution channel and within two years was cut back from 21 to 12 units. This repositioning meant that Bank Leu finally had to give up its status as one of Switzerland's 'major' banks, a fate that had already become apparent at the end of 1990 when the SNB downgraded Leu from 'major bank' to 'commercial bank' in its banking statistics. Bank Leu now focused its attention primarily on retail and corporate business in the Zurich region and on asset management in the national and international arena.[204] The three banks that now belonged to Leu Holding all had considerable potential in private banking, which consequently became a priority at the expense of retail banking.

As it turned out, Rainer E. Gut and CS Holding were only in 'the lion's den' for a short period.[205] Within a year there was already talk of CS Holding having used its 'drive [to get] out of the trough'[206]. Nonetheless, the company had a bitter pill to swallow when at the start of 1992, as continental Europe languished in recession, the rating agency Moody's downgraded SKA's rating for long-term liabilities from AAA to AA1. The downgrading was prompted by the deteriora-

134 *Part Two: Strategic Pillars*

The so-called 'Leuenhof' at Bahnhofstrasse 32 in Zurich has housed the head office of Bank Leu since 1915. The Neo-Gothic building was constructed by Zurich architects Gebrüder Pfister. Photo taken in 1990.

Bank Hofmann's head office at Talstrasse 27 in Zurich. The bank was taken over by SKA in 1972. Photo taken in 1996.

Price performance of Leu Holding AG bearer shares (Sfr 100 nom.)

(Sfr)	1990*	1991*	1992*	1993
High	675	376	366	695
Low	208	210	245	290
Closing price on 18.11.1993				688

* Adjusted prices, from foundation in May 1990

Price performance of CS Holding bearer shares (Sfr 500 nom.)

(Sfr)	1989	1990	1991	1992	1993
High	2935	2740	2230	2140	3460
Low	2300	1475	1360	1570	1860
Closing price on 18.11.1993					3415

tion of the general economic climate in Switzerland, and especially the real estate crisis, which had a sharply deleterious effect on the bank's Swiss assets. According to the *Wall Street Journal* this came as a 'severe blow both to Credit Suisse and to the image of Swiss banking as a whole'.[207]

In April 1992 Leu Holding's complicated capital structure was simplified by the introduction of bearer shares. At the end of 1993, CS Holding made an exchange offer to the remaining minority shareholders. Both sets of shares, CS Holding's and Leu's, had performed strongly that year.[208]

On 30 April 1995, Leu Holding AG merged with CS Holding; Leu Holding had fulfilled its purpose. It was also assumed, correctly, that the individual banking institutions could reach their goals more effectively through a direct affiliation to CS Holding. In accordance with this line of thinking, Bank Leu AG, Bank Hofmann AG, Clariden Bank, Affida Bank and Bank Heusser & Cie. AG were put together in a private banking group. This group's core activities were asset management and investment advice for discerning private customers and institutional investors in Switzerland and abroad, as well as securities trading, collateralized lending, investment funds business, and foreign exchange, money market and precious metals trading. Bank Leu also kept up its corporate and retail banking operations in the Zurich region. The private banking group was finally integrated into the Credit Suisse Private Banking business unit on 1 January 1997, while its remaining corporate and retail banking operations were transferred to the Credit Suisse business unit.

In April 1992, the press reported, with more than a hint of criticism in some cases, that the majority of CS Holding's business was now outside Switzerland: 63% of its assets where held abroad, and 44% of group earnings were generated in other countries.[209] CS Holding was aware of the imbalance and continued to pursue the policy of growth in its core Swiss market too. However, the conditions were still very difficult for such growth: SKA had decided to be more cautious in its mortgage business in future, granting mortgage loans mainly to customers who were likely to bring in significant additional business as well. A further difficulty came when the local interest rate pacts were abolished and the banks had to pursue a policy of interest rate differentiation. In autumn 1992 a renewed increase in counterparty risk became apparent, especially in Western Switzerland and in the real estate and construction industries. By the end of 1993, the expectation was that another 20 or 30 regional banks were likely to lose their independence.[210]

Bank Heusser's offices in Basel are housed in an imposing corner property in the St.-Alban-Vorstadt. The building, constructed in 1855 by the renowned architect Melchior Berri, is now protected as a historical monument. Photo taken in 1997.

In 1990 Clariden Bank moved into its new head office at Claridenstrasse 22 in Zurich. The building, commissioned by the silk company Stehli Seiden AG, is protected on account of its Art Deco façade. Photo taken in 1995.

Riding to the rescue: the acquisition of EKO Bank Olten

On 22 October 1992 the Federal Banking Commission (FBC) ruled that EKO Hypothekar- und Handelsbank Olten (EKO Bank) would have to close its doors on account of the mountain of debt it had accrued.[211] Motivated by a desire to rescue the venerable regional bank, founded in 1829, and thereby to confirm its commitment to the healthy diversity of the Swiss banking sector, SKA declared itself willing to take on EKO Bank's assets and liabilities and to cover the ailing institution's considerable need for funds. On 26 October the municipality of Olten, which as the owner under public law had also been the guarantor of all EKO Bank deposits, voted to accept the offer.

EKO Bank – one of Switzerland's 15 largest regional banks and the oldest bank in Canton Solothurn – had experienced a huge growth spurt between 1987 and 1991. Lendings to customers had almost doubled over this period, reaching a sum of almost Sfr 1.2 billion. Its closure came for similar reasons to those that had led to the collapse of Spar- und Leihkasse Thun one year earlier: the creditor organization had simply failed to keep pace with this growth. The bank's management had also overstepped its credit authority by carrying out transactions outside its region (especially in Canton Ticino) and risky real estate deals in a deteriorating market. Accumulations of risk and failure to comply with reporting obligations finally broke the bank's back.

In addition, EKO Bank played 'at the very least a compliant role'[212] in the financial maneuverings of an industrialist whose empire collapsed at the start of the 1990s. According to a statement by FBC director Kurt Hauri in the *Oltner Tagblatt* of 27 October 1992, this type of business – where, for instance, a credit officer accepted very dubious 'collateral' for loans, e.g. a mortgage note for Sfr 8.7 million on a completely unproductive gravel pit – 'had become very extensive in recent years' at EKO Bank.

At the end of October 1992, the audit report on EKO Bank by KPMG Fides put the need for write-downs and provisions at Sfr 193.3 million, with more than 100 individual risk items subject to pending legal action. The FBC then determined that the bank's equity capital had been used up, that it was over-indebted and that it could no longer cover its third-party liabilities. Statutory banking regulations left the FBC with no choice but to withdraw EKO Bank's license. This meant that the creditors would lose money, but not even the municipality of Olten could save the bank now.[213]

SKA expressed its willingness to take up the FBC's call for a Swiss solution to this difficult situation. It offered to take over EKO Bank's assets and liabilities, even though the auditors at KPMG Fides had shown that the large volume of provisioning required had wiped out the bank's reserves, endowment capital and participation certificate capital.

Essentially, SKA intervened because it was its turn amongst the major banks to step in as rescuer, and thus safeguard the 'higher interest' of a sound financial industry in Switzerland.[214] Josef Ackermann, CEO of SKA at the time, commented that 'the takeover of distressed regional institutions by the major banks

---

Sfr 190 million of provisions required at EKO Bank: the regulators' early warning systems prove inadequate.

'The bank's managers took on a lot of imprudent and incautious real estate risks' (Silvio de Capitani, chairman of the FBC).

'We do not actually have any interest in taking over EKO Bank; it is not an attractive deal and it brings large risks as a result of over-indebtedness and substantial takeover costs' (Member of the SKA executive board Josef Ackermann at the Olten municipal council meeting of 26 October 1992).

is not an ideal response to structural change within the banking sector'.[215] On 27 October 1992, only four days after its closure, EKO Bank was able to open its doors again for business – this time as an SKA branch office. SKA also took on all of EKO Bank's 107 employees, with the exception of the management. Even when confronted with serious internal problems, the Swiss banking industry had shown that it could sort things out for itself.

But why had another regional bank been forced to close only one year after the disturbing events at Spar- und Leihkasse Thun, before whose doors incensed customers had queued to rescue their assets? Television pictures from Thun had been broadcast all over the world. The Swiss Bankers' Association had been prompted by the collapse in Thun to establish a safety net for regional banks, but clearly even this was not enough to stabilize the situation. In the case of EKO Bank, it was primarily the FBC and the municipal authorities in Olten that had to accept 'certain criticisms'.[216] The FBC should have 'investigated the "state guarantees" situation long before', since the actual worth of these guarantees had been out of all proportion to EKO Bank's total assets for decades.[217] Finally, the municipality of Olten, as the owner, should have intervened to sort out its house bank much earlier, rather than waiting until the 'hole in the bank' had grown too large.[218]

'The opportunity of the century': union with SVB

In 1992, SKA, as part of the retail banking strategy mentioned above, launched a new campaign to increase customer deposits while at the same time reducing costs. While this campaign was being successfully implemented, the retail banking scene was turned on its head. At the start of 1993, Switzerland was confronted with the 'biggest bank takeover in its history', which saw 'Volksbank falling into the lap of SKA'.[219] SVB, fourth largest of the major banks, requested that trading in its securities on the Swiss Stock Exchange be suspended on 4 and 5 January 1993 (Monday and Tuesday). The rumors started to fly. Various foreign institutions, such as Deutsche Bank and Citibank appeared to be in the game. Insurance companies like Allianz also came under the spotlight, and ultimately SBG and CS Holding were also mentioned as possible buyers. While SBG did not want to make any statement with regard to SVB, SKA/CS Holding announced that they were following the situation very closely. One day later the boards of directors of CS Holding, SKA and SVB decided to merge the two major banks on the basis of a stock swap.

SVB had publicly given up its ambitions as a true major player after the silver debacle at its Geneva branch in 1981. Nevertheless, it continued to be tempted by what looked like very profitable foreign business and by other activities over and beyond its core customer base. Between 1982 and 1991, SVB's branch network increased from 148 offices in Switzerland and 5 abroad, to 191 and 12 respectively. In the years between 1986 and 1990, an expansive lending policy brought annual net profits in excess of Sfr 100 million; but it also made the bank more susceptible to crisis. In 1991, after the end of the economic boom and

The SVB building at the Christoffelgasse in Bern, pictured around 1910. Water color and pencil by an unknown artist. Credit Suisse Group Collection.

> *'SVB Is a Dream Candidate for the Kreditanstalt'*
> 'Der Bund', 7 January 1993
>
> 'A short while ago we took over EKO Bank Olten. That move was really in the interests of the Swiss financial center. We acquired a bank that was no longer capable of functioning. SVB, by contrast, was very much a dream candidate for us', said member of the SKA executive board Josef Ackermann in an interview with the *Bund* (7 January 1993). 'We announced our strategy for winning market share in Switzerland some time ago. I believe such a strategy gives us a platform for a successful operation abroad.'
>
> However, some commentators spoke, for example, of 'a risky shopping spree' (*Cash*, 8 January 1993). For Volksbank, which had suffered particularly badly as a result of the real estate slump and which did a lot of its business with the recession-hit small and medium sized business sector, refuge under the wing of CS Holding was simply the best solution. By contrast, CS Holding was taking something of a risk. 'About Sfr 1.5 billion will have to be raised through a capital increase […], which will cause a significant dilution. It will be expensive, too.' Nevertheless, Rainer E. Gut was able to tell *Cash* that he rated the takeover of SVB 'as SKA's chance of the century. Such a leap in size, such an increase in customers and capital (1.1 million new accounts and Sfr 46 billion in assets) would be impossible through organic growth alone. But acquisitions of this size could not be financed during the boom times. Assuming a similar premium to the one CS Holding is paying now, in 1986 Volksbank would have cost five billion.'
>
> The media were torn. On the one hand there was admiration for 'SKA's Great Coup' (*Tages-Anzeiger*, 6 January 1993); *Blick* even showed a picture of 'the man who won the Volksbank bidding war' with the caption 'Rainer E. Gut: from apprentice to the king of Swiss banking'. Meanwhile, other journalists expressed their concern about the purchase. 'Problems Like the Other Banks Have – But a Little More Serious' ran the headline in the *Sonntags-Zeitung* (10 January 1993), following up with: 'CS Holding will be hoping that Volksbank has no more skeletons in its closet.'
>
> To start with, the stock market reacted to the takeover 'unkindly', as the *Handelszeitung* (14 January 1993) put it. In its article 'Hercules Meets Sisyphus' it went on to state that retail banking might offer great potential, but that the practical implementation of the merger represented a problem that was virtually impossible to solve. 'Thus far it would appear that synergies, i.e. a division of activities between SKA and the Leu Group, have by no means been fully exploited, and now the banks face a new task – the redistribution of the branch network between SKA and SVB – that really will need the strength of Hercules. Of SVB's 190 branches, 130 duplicate a part of the SKA network.'
>
> Regardless of these negative comments, SBG was seen as the loser by many newspapers. 'Unlike the Bankverein, which had shied away from restructuring, the Bankgesellschaft is left looking downcast. It had fought hard but once again failed to get what it wanted. For a second time, Rainer Gut has beaten Robert Studer to the prize' (*Cash*, 8 January 1993). 'There were long faces at Schweizerische Bankgesellschaft (SBG). From what one hears, the SVB board committee had originally favored the SBG offer, only for the full board to turn it down – the first time such a reversal has occurred', reported the *NZZ* (9 January 1990).

the start of the real estate crisis in Switzerland, the bank was forced to make disproportionately large write-offs of Sfr 394 million on total assets of Sfr 46.5 billion, with even greater charges expected for the following year. At the end of 1991, SVB lagged a long way behind the 'Top Three' (SKA, SBV and SBG) in terms of its cost-income ratio. Given the prevailing unfavorable environment, it also lacked the necessary financial strength to keep going for much longer. In autumn 1992, SVB announced that it intended to give up its legal status as a co-operative in favor of becoming a joint-stock company. This sent out the signal that it was ready to remove all the formal hurdles that might stand in the way of co-operation agreements or participations. Then the FBC gave the SVB management an ultimatum to find a satisfactory solution; in fact the bank had already been in contact with CS Holding and SBG, as well as with other interested parties. Between Christmas and New Year 1992/93, various secret meetings took place between the different executive boards to discuss strategies for a possible merger.

Price was not the only point of contention in the subsequent fight to take over SVB; the structure of the institutions concerned and the proposed methods of integration also played a role. SBG, for instance, insisted that it would have to integrate SVB immediately and fully into its parent company structure. CS Holding, by contrast, assured SVB that it could retain its separate market identity, brand name and management for as long as market conditions allowed this.

As the new year began, it seemed that the dice were falling in favor of SBG. On 2 January 1993, after the two Swiss suitors had presented their offers in Berne, SVB's board committee made a preliminary decision to accept SBG's offer. However, by adjusting their offer and backing this up with a complementary communications strategy, CS Holding's top executives managed over the next couple of days to turn things around. Media relations work was intensified in the lead up to the merger announcement: the advantages of an SKA/SVB union were emphasized, and serious concern was expressed about the colossal size of an SBG/SVB merger. CS Holding executives continued to talk selectively and directly to key figures at SVB and within two days the SVB board was presented with a reworked offer. On 5 January 1993, Rainer E. Gut and Josef Ackermann paid another visit to Bern. Under almost bizarre conditions of secrecy, the two men were smuggled into the Volksbank head office, where they were allowed to present their offer and their ideas to the assembled board of directors. In the secret ballot that followed, the SVB board voted by a clear majority of 17 to 4 in favor of the CS Holding offer. CS Holding's bosses had achieved the impossible at the very last minute, seizing their 'opportunity of the century' and at the same time preventing the creation of a market-dominating SBG/SVB combine.

As the victor in the takeover battle, Schweizerische Kreditanstalt – now dubbed a 'Volks-Anstalt' by one commentator[220] – had saved SVB from a third massive collapse (following its restructuring by the government in the 1930s and the silver debacle of 1981). In terms of its management, SVB was integrated into CS Holding like any other subsidiary company, in terms of its capital it was tied very closely to SKA. In addition, SKA executive board member Kurt Widmer took over as president of the SVB executive board. Within a short period it was possible to harmonize SVB and SKA operations while maintaining SVB's customer base and keeping a clear separation between the two institutions' business activities. SVB continued to concentrate on business with medium-sized and smaller personal and corporate customers in Switzerland. Together with SKA, which was to concentrate primarily on foreign operations, underwriting, and business with large customers, SVB was able to secure a leading position for CS Holding in Swiss retail business. Although its total assets were only about a third of the size of SKA's, SVB had 1.1 million savings books, compared with SKA's 0.992 million (1991). There were also many opportunities to exploit synergies and cost savings in the banks' distribution networks, logistics operations, international organizations and in various individual business areas. Furthermore, SVB still enjoyed a good reputation in Switzerland, and its local roots were a real plus. The new SKA/SVB pairing now topped SBV in terms of total assets; it also became Switzerland's biggest mortgage lender, with a market share of 14.3% (1991), and could boast the largest number of ec-cards.

Effect of SKA/SVB merger on Swiss market share[221] (1991; as percent of total market)

	SKA	SKA/SVB	SBG	SBV
Total assets	15	21	23	20
Mortgages	10	14	14	14
Swiss lendings	11	17	17	14
Swiss customer deposits	11	18	14	14
ec-cards	12	20	16	13
Branches	7	14	9	10
Headcount	11	16	16	13

Most commentators welcomed the merger.[222] Markus Lusser, chairman of the Swiss National Bank, highlighted the point that, unlike in other countries, market forces in Switzerland were strong enough to push forward the process of structural adjustment without the need for special state regulation. The fact that there were now three internationally competitive, strong and roughly equal institutions with solid home bases was also welcomed, as was the fact that Swiss businesses could continue to benefit from a good supply of money and credit from a well-diversified banking system. As far as the foreseeable job reductions were concerned, the general feeling was that it could have been worse, especially if SVB had been taken over by a foreign company! While acknowledging that there was obviously an urgent need for action at SVB, the FBC emphasized the point that it was not in a position to step in and do anything itself.

What criticism there was came primarily from those who were concerned about the temporary fall in the price of CS Holding stock. Despite the obvious synergies and the complementary profiles of the two new partners, it was apparent that the two banks faced a testing time over the medium term. On the one hand, CS Holding's overall performance would suffer, which would pose a further threat to its credit rating; on the other, it was inevitable that the number of branches – and thus headcount – would have to be reduced. A month after the merger deal was concluded, SVB's annual report made it obvious just how urgent it had been that the bank forge a union with another institution. Owing mainly to the large write-downs on non-performing loans and to massive provisioning, SVB's accounts for the 1992 business year showed a loss of Sfr 68 million, its worst performance for 50 years. Because it had to take on these liabilities, SKA was downgraded a second time by Moody's in April 1993 to leave it with a rating of Aa2 for its long-term liabilities.

In the meantime, retail banking business was proving unprofitable owing to the excessive costs involved. A further clean-out was inevitable. After the newly created SVB registered shares had been exchanged for CS Holding stock, the go-ahead was given for an ambitious fitness program. This continued a streamlining campaign already underway at SVB, but also included elements from SKA's retail banking strategy. As well as sealing the conversion of SVB into a joint-stock company, within two years this program led to a reduction of the branch network from the original joint figure of 400 offices down to 330. This still left CS Holding with the densest branch network in Switzerland. At the same time about 600 jobs were cut, though virtually all of this downsizing was achieved without the need for compulsory redundancies. The changes were more significant in the higher echelons of SVB, and between April 1993 and June 1995, almost half of the bank's management was replaced.[223]

Despite all these changes, and despite the ongoing restructuring of retail business, care was taken to ensure that the affected business areas still had a certain amount of autonomous room for maneuver. With further rationalization in mind, SKA and SVB agreed to share the same logistics and IT platform in Switzerland. Integrating the two existing platforms was not only a highly complicated project, it also had to be completed under great time pressure. For SVB,

SBG's minutes stated that 'the chalice had passed them by' (*NZZ*, 7 January 1993). We can probably assume that this was not a completely accurate reflection of SBG's true feelings at having been thrown out of the race at the very last minute.

By taking over SVB, SKA had 'in a way saved the honor of the Swiss financial services industry' (Urs Tschumi of the Swiss Association of Bank Employees in the *NZZ*, 9 December 1997).

this operational reorientation represented 'the biggest challenge in its history'.²²⁴ 'Match', as the project was called, was launched in the shape of a four-year implementation plan due for completion at the end of 1997. By mid 1995, the operational savings achieved through the merger had already come to Sfr 437 million.²²⁵

An ideal complement: the acquisition of Neue Aargauer Bank

Against a background of privatizations and partial privatizations amongst the cantonal banks, and as a result of a tough line from the FBC, which compelled institutions outside the regional bank holding network to look around for strong

Head office of Neue Aargauer Bank (NAB) in Aarau. NAB was formed in 1989 from the merger of Allgemeine Aargauische Ersparniskasse, Aarau, and Aargauische Hypotheken- und Handelsbank, Brugg. It was brought under the CS Holding umbrella in 1994. Photo taken in 2000.

In 1992 SKA took over the Gewerbebank Baden, founded in 1864. It was integrated into the NAB in 1995. Photo taken in 1990.

*'SKA Wants NAB to Retain Its Identity
as a Regional Bank'*
'Aargauer Tagblatt', 21 September 1994

The headline above the *Aargauer Tagblatt*'s report on the press conference of 20 September 1994, where Neue Aargauer Bank and CS Holding announced a close co-operation with each other backed by a takeover offer to shareholders, read: 'SKA Wants NAB to Retain Its Identity as a Regional Bank'. 'SKA Wants to Buy the Biggest of the Small Banks', said the *Luzerner Neuste Nachrichten*, while the *Solothurner Zeitung* went with the headline: 'SKA Chosen as Bride'. It was generally assumed that NAB would have to turn for help to a larger bank, but its actual choice of partner came as a surprise to most of the media. Towards the end of 1993, according to *Finanz und Wirtschaft*, there had been an increase in 'rumors about the integration of by far the biggest regional bank into the SBG group', further fuelled by the fact that SBG was NAB's largest shareholder with a stake of 12.5%. Under the headline 'The Great Guzzling' the *Tages-Anzeiger* pointed out that SBG had already 'swallowed up' five regional institutions in 1994 and that SBV had not been standing idle either. 'The Kreditanstalt has been more restrained since swallowing the mighty Volksbank and Bank Leu. But with its offer to NAB, SKA is now signaling that the "digestion period" does not last forever – especially when a tasty little morsel sits up and offers itself.' The *Tages-Anzeiger* continued by saying that the motive 'for the "thieving spree" by the big three' was clear: synergies. 'It is still true that a bank has to be at least a certain size if it is to survive in the tough competitive environment. Because of technical advances, especially in information technology, the "optimum" size for a bank has increased continuously over recent years. [...] The Kreditanstalt has shown itself to be particularly adept at this policy of expansion. Led by its chief strategist Rainer E. Gut, it introduced the holding concept, which facilitated the development of a flexible and global group structure beneath the broad umbrella of CS Holding. The successful fishing trips to catch Bank Leu, Volksbank and now NAB show that the concept is attractive for the target banks too: the acquired institutions get to keep their names and their autonomy – at least as far as external image is concerned.'

SBG's unconcealed desire to integrate the regional bank straight away seems to have been the main reason why NAB turned instead to SKA. Various newspapers addressed this issue; the *Blick*, for example, talked of a 'severe setback for SBG boss Robert Studer. [...] "The answer to our absolutely central question of whether we would keep our independence after the takeover was so vague that we went to SKA instead", admitted NAB chairman Bruno Hunziker. Studer had allowed himself to be lulled into a false sense of security.' At CS Holding 'the NAB board of directors believes that the bank really can maintain its own identity and that the potential for synergies in the logistics area can be exploited', wrote the *NZZ*. In its editorial it reminded readers that in 1989 the 'dream couple' that formed NAB –Allgemeine Aargauische Ersparniskasse, Aarau, and Aargauische Hypotheken- und Handelsbank, Brugg – had been presented as sound to the core. Now, however, the confirmation had come, 'that merger euphoria has to be followed by hard graft – in the operational and logistics areas, but also within the board of directors'. 'The merger simply did not happen as far as information technology was concerned', commented a rueful Bruno Hunziker to the *St. Galler Tagblatt*. NAB had fallen upon hard times mainly as a result of its insufficiently professional lending operations; the new auditors Atag Ernst & Young had discovered an enormous need for new provisions on doubtful loans in 1993. CS Holding responded by granting a subordinate convertible loan of Sfr 200 million, which, together with the NAB shares it had bought on the stock market, gave it a stake of 34%.

partners, it was in CS Holding's interests to keep planning further expansion – expansion that it could accomplish at a lower cost than its rivals thanks to its structure. The chance to acquire Neue Aargauer Bank (NAB), Switzerland's biggest regional bank, in autumn 1994 thus came as a welcome opportunity. Once again, CS Holding's holding structure and management culture allowed it to steal a march on SBG, despite the fact that SBG had traditionally maintained close relations with NAB and was the regional bank's most powerful shareholder with a stake of 12.5%. Once again, CS Holding's approach allowed the target bank to continue operations under its own name and thus continue to exploit its strengths in retail business. NAB was an ideal complement to Gewerbebank Baden, which CS Holding had acquired in 1992, and allowed SKA to bolster its position in one of Switzerland's most important economic regions. Over the period between 1995 and 1997, NAB, Gewerbebank Baden and SVB's branches in Canton Aargau were merged together under the Credit Suisse Group umbrella.

A restructured Swiss core market

Market leader in savings and investments

In 1995, Paul Meier replaced Kurt Widmer as the president of SVB's executive board. In order to rid SVB of its backlog of non-performing loans and to give the bank its operational freedom back, a 'lifeboat' company called Vertika AG was set up. Vertika took on all of SVB's high-maintenance, risk-laden assets, both within and outside the real estate sector. These problem assets amounted to Sfr 6 billion. Three years after the SKA/SVB merger, Josef Ackermann, president of SKA's executive board, was able to announce that the integration of SVB had been completed successfully and on schedule.

CS Holding had substantially increased its business base in the core Swiss market; it had more than caught up with its two competitors, SBG and SBV (UBS and SBC) and could now build on a strong domestic base to grow into a global financial conglomerate. It should also be remembered that the task of expanding the core market had to be accomplished in a difficult economic environment. Switzerland had failed to achieve any economic growth since 1991, the number of bankruptcies in the corporate sector was constantly high and real estate prices had slumped. According to estimates by the regulatory authorities, Switzerland's banks had to set aside about Sfr 19 billion of value adjustments and provisions for mortgage-backed loans between 1991 and 1995.[226] Retail business, especially for small and medium-sized companies, was still insufficiently profitable. In the face of these difficulties, the fact that SKA, and subsequently also SVB, were the first significant Swiss banks to define their retail business strategically proved to have a positive effect in the medium term. The new CEO Lukas Mühlemann, who took over at Credit Suisse Group on 1 January 1997, following on from his successful restructuring of Swiss Re, described the takeover of SVB four years before as an outstanding strategic move.

The bank's strong position in domestic retail business not only gave it a more stable platform for refinancing its business and thus a greater degree of scope in its international operations, it also gave credibility to SKA's image abroad as the leading Swiss bank.

The integration of SVB was also extremely important to CS Holding's later metamorphosis into Credit Suisse Group. Only once SVB had been slimmed down

---

The takeover of SVB represented a milestone for CS Holding on its journey towards critical mass in its core market. It created the key conditions that allowed the bank to assume its place amongst the world market leaders.

'There are no successful, globally active players who do not also have firm roots in their core domestic market. Retail banking is a key pillar for the Group and in forthcoming years it will contribute to the Group's prosperity' (Lukas Mühlemann, 1997).

and made more efficient could it be fitted into the new business unit concept adopted by Credit Suisse Group. The many and varied experiences of the 'Match' process, not just at the structural and organizational level but also in the emotional and social sphere, had a considerable influence on the new operational structure announced by the bank on 2 July 1996 and on the 'Focus' project. The aim of 'Focus' was to transform CS Holding and its subsidiaries into Credit Suisse Group and its four business units. In the wake of the project, Josef Ackermann resigned after serving as president of SKA's executive board since 1993. In order to achieve a consistent market and brand image, the names SVB and SKA were replaced: SVB now conducted Swiss retail business under the name Credit Suisse. Within Credit Suisse Group, the emphasis on the identity of individual banking institutions was replaced by a concentration of business activities on specific customer segments and markets. The Credit Suisse Private Banking business unit, which incorporated key parts of SKA, looked beyond the Swiss market to establish itself as one of the largest private banks in the world.

A look back at the years from 1990 to 1996 shows that CS Holding's acquisitions strategy had allowed it at last to achieve its central aim of expanding in the core Swiss market and thus making up the ground it had lost to its rivals.

In 1996, the CS Holding banks could boast the densest branch network in Switzerland. Although the process of restructuring branch operations was yet to be completed, the problem with which the bank had wrestled for so long – namely, its inadequate foothold in the core Swiss market – had been solved once and for all. By building up their strength in retail business, the CS Holding banks were now the clear leaders in Switzerland's savings and investments market. While comfortably maintaining their eminence in underwriting business[227], CS Holding's mortgage lending operations, an area in which SKA had lagged

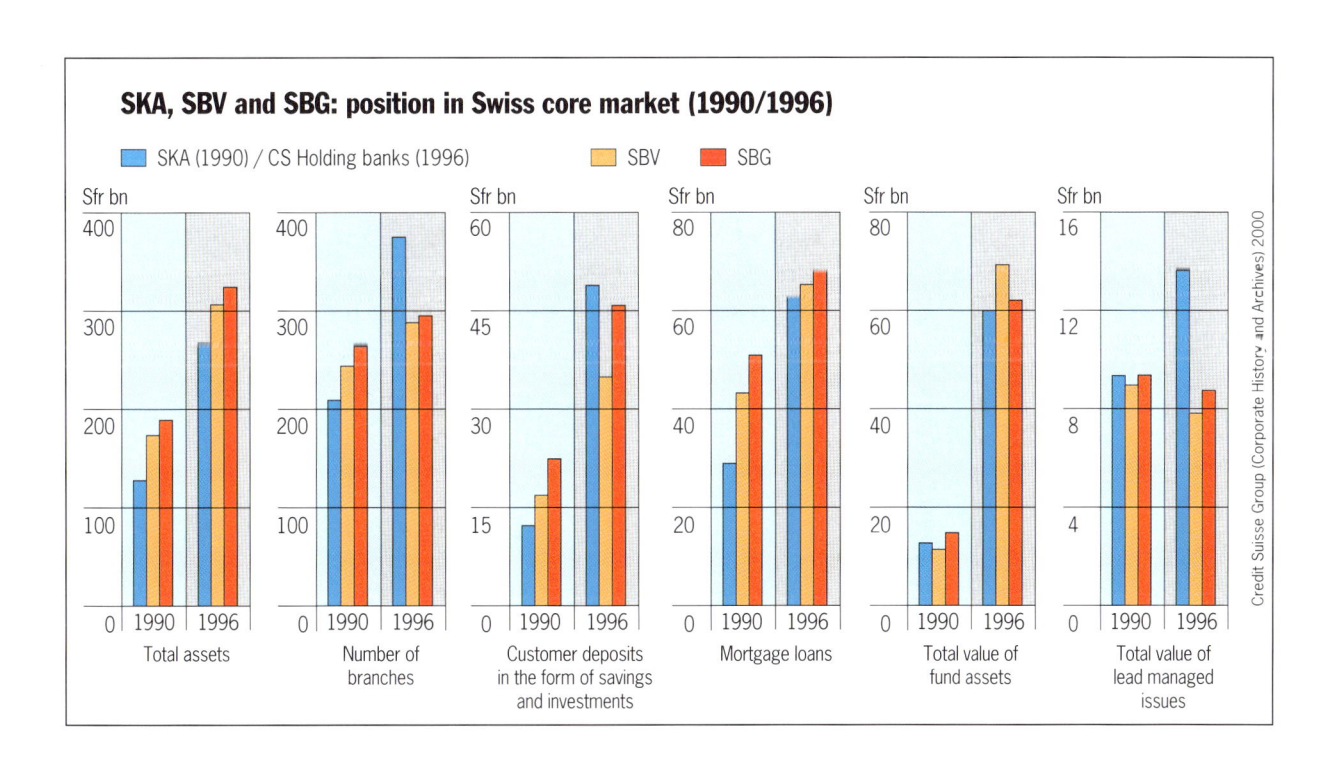

SKA, SBV and SBG: position in Swiss core market (1990/1996)

Finanz und Wirtschaft gave its readers a taste of the ambience of Credit Suisse Private Banking in November 1999. From top to bottom: Bank Leu, Bank Hofmann, Clariden Bank.

particularly far behind in 1990, had caught up with those of SBG and SBV in one fell swoop.

Investment funds had become increasingly important since the end of the 1980s (see chart on p. 145: Total value of fund assets). Having grown only slowly during the 1980s against a background of rising stock market and real estate prices, investment funds business enjoyed a boom in the 1990s. The main reasons for this were the continuing health of the stock market and low interest rates, which made traditional savings products much less attractive. Assets held in investment funds grew at about the same pace at all of the major banks until 1993, at which point SBV began to move ahead of the competition.

Another line of business also gained added significance during the 1990s: banking for wealthy, often foreign, private customers, i.e. private banking. From the banks' point of view, the chief characteristic of this business, which had expanded steadily since the Second World War, was that it involved a relatively low level of risk but would generate a continuous earnings stream as long as customers were offered good products and services. As we have already seen, Switzerland was, and still is, a very appealing place for foreign private customers, hence the quip: 'Money alone won't make you happy; not unless you keep the money in Switzerland!'[228] In 1989, SKA began to consolidate its administration of large private portfolios into central portfolio management units. It also started to push ahead more rapidly with the development of existing, and the creation of new, private banking units abroad. While the private banking clientele in Switzerland was concerned primarily with security, discretion, loyalty to their bank and with banking secrecy, international customers focused more on issues such as capital growth, performance and comprehensive service. As part of a dedicated private banking strategy that aimed to make Credit Suisse Private Banking one of the 'best established, most reliable and most profitable banks in the private banking business', the first half of the 1990s saw a raft of further innovations. Most significant of these was the expansion of financial advisory services (tax and inheritance advice, real estate advice and trust business).[229] The takeover of Bank Leu greatly strengthened CS Holding's private banking business, and in the second half of the 1990s business with wealthy private customers increasingly challenged classic lending business as the bank's flagship activity. Since 1990 alone, the Swiss banks have seen annual growth rates averaging almost 10% in private banking.[230] Success has also had its darker side, however, the main problem issues being money laundering and 'potentate money'.

Attempted alliance between CS Holding and SBG

Before the task of transforming CS Holding into Credit Suisse Group was taken up, the chairman of the CS Holding board of directors Rainer E. Gut had put forward a spectacularly daring alternative: a merger with SKA's competitor of many years, SBG (UBS to its international customers). Despite the extensive structural adjustment that had taken place within the Swiss banking industry,

The Credit Suisse Private Banking customer zone at Paradeplatz, designed in 1997 with works by Silvie Defraoui (this page) and by Niele Toroni, Balthasar Burkhard and Roland Gfeller-Corthésy (facing page).

a merger between any of the country's three largest banking institutions had thus far been seen as a pretty unrealistic scenario. We have already mentioned Ernst Kilgus' 1990 analysis, and similar sentiments had been expressed by, for example, Robert Studer, then president of the SBG executive board. In March 1992 Studer made it very clear that he could hardly conceive of a merger between any of the majors, backing up this position with a number of arguments: duplications in domestic business, political problems, the closure of hundreds of branches, and the sacking of thousands of employees. 'Unless there were a completely unforeseen and dramatic emergency', Studer ruled out the possibility of a fusion between two of the major banks in the foreseeable future.[231]

As it happened, SBG did run into trouble over the course of the following year as more and more of its stock was bought up by Martin Ebner of BZ Bank. The pressure increased still further when the bank's former partner Winterthur Insurance announced that it was to cooperate closely with CS Holding and sever its traditional ties with SBG.[232]

The power struggle between SBG and Martin Ebner, as well as the trench warfare raging within SBG itself, came to a head in the run-up to SBG's general meeting of shareholders on 16 April 1996. On 1 April, Rainer E. Gut picked up the telephone and called the out-going SBG chairman Nikolaus Senn in Florida. Gut began the conversation by denying the rumors that CS Holding intended to support Martin Ebner's BK Vision against SBG at the forthcoming shareholders' meeting. The chairman of CS Holding then went on to sound out the question of whether it would be appropriate to consider the possibility of a merger between Switzerland's two biggest banks. Given the dispute between

'CS Wants Control over SBG'
'Tages-Anzeiger', 9 April 1996

On 9 April 1996 the *Tages-Anzeiger* ran the headline 'CS Wants Control over SBG'. The article that followed hit Switzerland like a bomb. It said that Rainer E. Gut had phoned the out-going SBG chairman Nikolaus Senn to deliver an ultimatum and force a merger. This was 'blackmail of the worst sort' according to the splash quote. Furthermore, CS Holding had not even digested the takeovers of SVB and NAB. The SBG bosses were not perfect, 'but what Ebner, Blocher and Frey are doing from one side, Spälti, Bremi, Gerber and Gut are doing from the other – irresponsibly attempting to destabilize Switzerland's biggest bank'. All the top managers 'who vote with Martin Ebner on 16 April out of a thirst for power or even revenge, should be reminded: they are gambling with money that we have entrusted to them in our capacity as customers, insurance policy holders or employees. Neither a weakened SBG nor a forced merger would be in the interests of Switzerland as a financial center.'

On the 10 April, there was barely a Swiss newspaper that did not have something to say about the by now legendary telephone conversation. 'The purpose of the leak may well have been to torpedo the merger negotiations', speculated the *Basler Zeitung*; the *Zürichsee-Zeitung* went as far as to report that the *Tages-Anzeiger* journalist who had used phrases such as 'Gut approached SBG and put a knife to its throat', had years ago been a war reporter in Central America. Without having heard the conversation, how could the author talk about blackmail and at the same time pillory the chairman of CS Holding in such an accusatory and condemnatory fashion? 'He should not have done this; not even if Gut, who has given much thought to the future of Swiss banking, did indeed sketch out some daring proposals to Senn', the *Zürichsee-Zeitung* continued. Under the headline 'Banking Revolution', *24 Heures* expressed its concern about possible job reductions: 'The rash of mega-mergers continues – at the cost, if it comes to pass, of thousands of jobs.'

By contrast, the *NZZ* endorsed CS Holding's indignation: 'CS Holding is very put out – and here it's worth reading the text [the CS Holding press release] several times – by the nature of the answer to this confidential testing of the waters between two bank chairmen: it received SBG's response, combined with what CS Holding says is a distorted portrayal of the question asked, through the *Tages-Anzeiger* article of 9 April. This is certainly not the style that has previously characterized conversations between the highest representatives of Switzerland's major banks.' The *Frankfurter Allgemeine Zeitung* took the merger plans seriously: 'A united "Swiss major bank" would carry much greater weight, especially in the international arena, than is the case with either of these two majors on their own. Frankfurt, too, would have to sit up and take notice.'

One and a half years later, on 8 December 1997, SBV and SBG announced that they were merging to form UBS. On the next day the *NZZ* reported that: 'Chairman of the SBV board Georges Blum made it clear at the press conference that he and his predecessor had been convinced of the great potential for synergies between the two banks, and the ideal complementarity of their strengths since 1995. In April 1995, he had taken the initiative.' One year, as it happened, before the controversial telephone conversation between Rainer E. Gut and Nikolaus Senn. Robert Studer – who was portrayed by the media as the big loser in the bank deal – now explained to the *Tages-Anzeiger* why SBG had refused CS Holding's advances in 1996: 'Even back then our discussions with the Bankverein were so intense that it would not have been correct to negotiate with another major bank.'

On 22 December 1997, *Bilanz* revealed that the Bankverein had first knocked on SBG's door after acquiring the investment bank Warburg: 'But [Senn] sent Blum away. Colonel Senn wanted nothing to do with the measly Bankverein and its uncultured, non-Swiss-army-trained managers.' 'Financially Strong, But Weak Management', was the headline on 10 December 1997 above another *Tages-Anzeiger* article on the merger: 'According to observers, the Bankgesellschaft's inward-looking management culture encourages promotion motivated by tactical considerations and personal friendships. This takes its toll in emergencies such as the ones that resulted from the Meili affair or from the pressure exerted by the major shareholder Martin Ebner. With a chairman, Robert Studer, who is incapable of action, and a fragmented management team, Cabiallavetta took the bull by the horns. But SBG was in no position to make great demands.' On the same day *Finanz and Wirtschaft*'s editorial stated: 'Within Schweizerischer Bankverein the idea of remaining a small major bank, by Swiss standards, with correspondingly limited resources in the global arena, released new energies', though the newspaper also made it clear that ultimately SBV too had been forced to act. *Facts* conducted an interview with Lukas Mühlemann (11 December 1997) to discuss Credit Suisse Group's position following the merger between SBG and SBV. This included the following exchange:

Facts: Do you now expect to see an influx of ex-UBS and SBC customers who are against the merger and the associated job reductions?

Mühlemann: The merger certainly will bring us more customers and further strengthen our position. The United Bank of Switzerland now finds itself in the kind of restructuring process that we have been through in recent years. From our own experience we know that in these circumstances, a lot of energies can be tied up by internal matters.

Facts: Where do you see your opportunities?

Mühlemann: Our specific opportunities are in investment banking, where we enjoy a unique position, in Allfinanz and in Europe. We will be bringing new ideas to the table here. Our other divisions also have the required size to be successful.

Facts: Maybe so, but Credit Suisse Group is now the big loser.

Mühlemann: Certainly not. In merging with Winterthur Insurance, we opted to take a different course and to expand our range of services in Allfinanz business. In addition we have established a second main point of focus abroad – because ultimately international business, not business in Switzerland, will be decisive. In investment banking we enjoy a very good position both in Europe, especially since the acquisition of BZW, and in the USA.

SBG and its major shareholder Martin Ebner, and in view of the changes to SBG's shareholder structure, Rainer E. Gut thought that it would be very useful to have an initial view on the matter before the shareholders' meeting. Nikolaus Senn said that he was willing to think about it and that he would get back to Gut.

On 11 April, SBG delivered its answer through the media, sharply rejecting Rainer E. Gut's suggestion and declaring itself 'put out' by CS Holding's behavior. Two days earlier, SBG had leaked the news of the conversation between the two chairmen, triggering an enormous furor in a press already sent into a state of excitement by the Ebner controversy. The international media's measured response to the idea of a merger contrasted with the sometimes overheated reporting in Switzerland. In the Swiss press, the talk was of CS Holding taking over SBG and of an ultimatum delivered by Rainer E. Gut to his colleague Nikolaus Senn almost in the 'form of blackmail'. A more objective appraisal of a possible merger between SBG and CS Holding, however, would probably produce the following picture: the considerable implications for domestic business – branches would have to close and jobs would be lost – would be countered by an enormous increase in the scale of international business. A merged CS Holding/SBG would have been the biggest non-Japanese bank in the world and would have played a decisive role on the international financial markets.

In a letter to shareholders, Rainer E. Gut set straight the facts that had been reported so sketchily, subjectively and distortedly in the media. Nobody could dispute that the Swiss financial industry faced further restructuring or that long-term success in the global competitive environment could only come from a position of size and strength; nor could there be any argument that a voluntary merger between two major banks would be much better than one forced on them by a crisis. Numerous mergers in the financial sector in other countries (the takeover of Barnett Bank by the Bank of New York in 1994, the merger between Chase Manhattan and Chemical Bank in 1996, etc.) and within Swiss industry (Novartis) clearly showed the way forward. Rainer E. Gut closed his letter with a look into the future that was later to be borne out in reality – without the help of Credit Suisse Group.

'SBG has chosen to follow the conservative path today. But like the Swiss financial services industry as a whole, it will not be able to avoid the issues concerned over the long term' (Rainer E. Gut, April 1996).

Nikolaus Senn spoke once again about his conversation with Rainer E. Gut when he addressed SBG's general meeting of shareholders on 16 April 1996. Senn said that personally he had been 'very put out, not to say shocked' by Gut's behavior, but that the pros and cons of a merger had nevertheless been discussed intensively within SBG. The board of directors had come to the conclusion, he said, that a merger with CS Holding would entail such large financial costs and place such a huge burden on the management that the further successful performance of SBG group would be compromised and its whole strategy would be called into question. Taken as a whole, a merger would have no advantages for the company or its shareholders. However, 18 months later, the new chairman of the UBS board made it clear that the then-SBG had actually been talking intensively about a merger with SBV since as long ago as 1995, and that this was the real reason why it could not start negotiating with another major bank.[233]

The pressure for restructuring within the Swiss financial sector continued without bringing any respite to SBG, which was being pulled in different directions by its various alliances. Finally, in April 1997, the ongoing talks with SBV resulted in concrete negotiations about a possible merger. On 5 December 1997 the boards of directors of the two institutions gave the go-ahead and three days later the merger was announced. As expected this 'elephants' wedding' led to huge restructuring costs and presented the two partners with the difficult task of melding together their very different corporate cultures. In the view of many who commented on the giant merger, SBG had in fact been rescued by the much smaller SBV.

CS Holding

Strictly Confidential

To the
Board of directors of Schweizerische Bankgesellschaft
Bahnhofstrasse 45
8021 Zurich

Zurich, 11 April 1996

Chairman of the board
Ladies and Gentlemen

I think it is appropriate for me to summarize and make more precise the idea of a merger between our two companies, which I outlined in my telephone call with Mr Senn on 1 April.

There is no doubt that both SBG and CS Holding are in a position over the medium term to play in the premiere league of the global financial services industry. However, we believe that if we joined forces, we would be far more effective still, and thus that we could generate substantial added value for our shareholders and ultimately for all 'stakeholders'.

There is no stopping the trend towards consolidation in the global financial industry; the reasons for this are well known to us all. With many mergers in the past, the strong have had to take over the weak, and no doubt we will be confronted with this phenomenon in the future too. However, what are far more interesting are the mergers that take place between two strong partners, especially if each is capable of helping the other to a quantum leap forward. A whole series of US and Japanese banks have shown us the way over the last few months, most recently Chemical Bank and Chase Manhattan, and Mitsubishi and Bank of Tokyo. It is safe to assume that the institutions produced by these fusions will contribute greatly to an intensification of the competitive environment around the world. In strategic terms, well-timed partnerships or fusions between strong companies are undoubtedly preferable to defensive mergers 'late in the day'.

In our country, as elsewhere, the process of restructuring within the banking sector is a long way from complete. Everyone agrees that job losses will be inevitable. We believe that ultimately, it would also be in the best interests of our employees if we can control this process from a position of strength early on in the game. Such a strategy would give our joint management the greatest possible scope to manage the consolidation process and would give our employees the best chance of profiting from the benefits and the expanded job opportunities that are undoubtedly available now, and which will be created in future, for well qualified people.

We would like to propose that a small team be appointed from our two boards of directors and executive boards to evaluate the potential of a merger. Ideally we would have done this 'in camera' but over the last few days we have been confronted with a situation in which the media and the market have been evaluating this potential, instead of us. It is time that we retook control.

Our own analysis suggests that the net earnings of a combined entity would be increased from the current Sfr 3 billion or so to between Sfr 4.5 and Sfr 5 billion, perhaps more. Earnings would undoubtedly fall in some divisions, but it is just as certain that they would rise in others. Over the short and medium term, potential cost savings would contribute greatly to the increase in net profits. We estimate this potential to be about Sfr 2 billion per year. Many other good analysts share this view – indeed they regard the figure as rather conservative. Like us, they also believe that the task represents a tough challenge.

This reduction in costs would have a considerable influence on earnings per share for our group's shareholders. We are assuming 30–50%, depending on the scenario. The added value for our shareholders would come to Sfr 20 billion or more. The new entity's ROE would increase to about 13–14%. None of these figures take account of the strategic opportunities that would arise.

Obviously our preliminary analysis would have to be verified by a joint group of experts. We have only mentioned these numbers here because they cannot be ignored. We believe that we are obliged to our shareholders to pursue this project further. Now that the idea is out in the open, we have to proceed all the more carefully.

In our view the business case for a merger between our two companies is so promising on initial examination that we need to act quickly. The potential is enormous. The advantages of the global strategic position that we would attain through a merger, and which we could then jointly build upon, go far beyond the cost reductions mentioned above. Today's *Financial Times* says that the project would 'represent a new wind blowing through the ... banking scene'. This new wind – some are even calling it a storm – is unavoidable. Rather than being swept along by the wind, we should be the ones that start it blowing.

Yours sincerely
[signed by Rainer E. Gut]

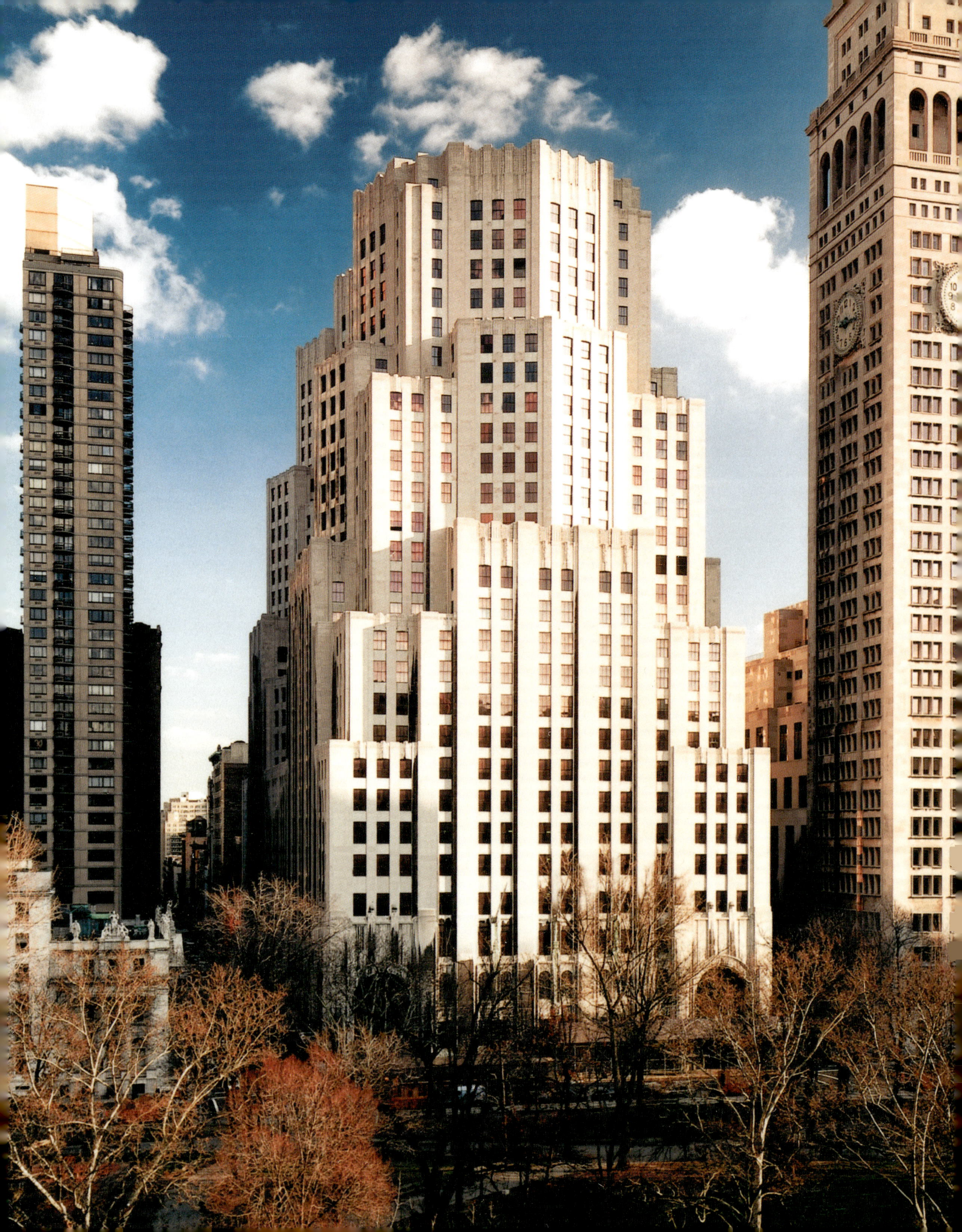

Global investment banking

Ever since it was established, SKA has regarded itself as a globally active bank. For a long time the bank conducted its international business through a series of jointly owned companies and a network of correspondent banks. It was not until just before the outbreak of the Second World War that it set up its first permanent international office – in New York. In global investment banking, the bank soon lived up to its reputation as an institution for large customers. Together with its US ally White Weld, SKA played a decisive role in the creation and development of the Euromarkets – the first international capital markets – in the mid-1970s. 1978 saw the beginning of the partnership between SKA and the renowned investment bank First Boston, an association that soon led to top rankings in the key league tables. In 1990 CS Holding upped its stake in CS First Boston to become the first non-US company to gain a majority holding in a US investment bank. Thanks to Credit Suisse First Boston, Credit Suisse Group now has two home markets in addition to its core market of Switzerland – one in the USA and the other in the United Kingdom.

Credit Suisse First Boston moved into its headquarters at Eleven Madison Avenue in New York in 1996. Photo taken in 1998.

Expansion in the global arena

Between its inception and the present day, SKA has gone through four phases of growth, each of them distinct from the others in terms of the lines of business, geographical regions, organizational forms and partnership structures involved.

The first phase: 1856 to the end of the 1950s

From the very start, SKA worked on building up a worldwide network of correspondent banks. The founders of Switzerland's first major bank recognized that their institution would need the help of such a network if it was to provide the services that were increasingly being demanded by the Swiss export industry. Since the risks involved were difficult to calculate, the young SKA favored the correspondent banking approach over the more expensive tactic of building up its own branch network. In fact it was 80 years before the bank would start to create its own permanent organization of international offices, setting up a subsidiary (1939) and a branch (1940) in New York. The dates speak for themselves: any lingering doubts were over-ridden by SKA's primary objective during the Second World War of establishing a base outside Europe in case Switzerland was occupied.

The second phase: from the end of the 1950s to the end of the 1970s

The financial markets had been growing ever more rapidly beyond national borders since the late 1950s, and competition between the internationally active major banks was becoming increasingly fierce. SKA began, rather cautiously, to build up its own international organization, starting by setting up representative offices and then moving on to full-scale branches. In the mid-1970s the decision was taken to develop into a globally active bank, concentrating outside Switzerland on wholesale banking and private banking. SKA quickly made a name for itself in commercial banking business in North America, the Middle East and Europe, though in investment banking it did not at first have the expertise to keep up with its rivals in the United States.

The decision was taken that it would be too risky to build up the bank's own capabilities in this area, so SKA started to look out for a US investment bank that would make a suitable partner. The bank's existing financial stake in White, Weld & Co. Inc., New York, was upgraded in 1974 to a strategic participation; and then finally, in 1978, the bank chose to begin its partnership with The First Boston Corp., New York.

The third phase: from the end of the 1970s to the end of the 1980s

Right up to the end of the 1970s, SKA's expansion plans in commercial banking business lacked a clear strategic direction. Only in 1983/84 did the bank begin to focus its efforts on the basis of its 'Strategy 1990'. By contrast with its second phase of development, the bank now concentrated even more strongly on North America and Europe, but also built up its presence in Asia.

White Weld → 174

Collaboration with First Boston on investment banking became more intense. From 1988 onwards the investment bank operated as CS First Boston – a subsidiary of CS Holding, which was founded in 1982 and which had a minority stake in the US company. In 1990 CS Holding acquired a majority equity holding, marking a decisive milestone on the road to establishing a home market in the USA.

For a long time, SKA's international business had been divided across various departments at its head office in Zurich; but then in 1987 the introduction of a new division-based structure helped to streamline all of the bank's international operations.

First Boston → 182

From White Weld to CS First Boston: organization charts → 185

The fourth phase: the 1990s

Following the end of the Cold War, CS Holding and SKA tapped into new growth markets in Eastern Europe and built up their position in Southern Europe and the Far East. It proved difficult, however, to establish additional home markets, as the example of Germany showed very clearly. Private banking operations were successfully developed, helping the bank to get even closer to its wealthy personal clients. In 1993, the revision of the divisional structure brought all of the bank's international commercial banking operations together into one central unit at head office – the International Division, making it easier to implement a coherent international strategy. The decisive event in this fourth phase of development was the transformation of CS Holding into Credit Suisse Group on 1 January 1997. SKA's International Division, investment banking operations, large parts of its securities business and trading activities (including the corresponding parts of SVB) were merged together with CS First Boston to form the new business unit Credit Suisse First Boston.

Disappointment in Germany → 164

Strategy for Eastern Europe → 167

No home market in Austria → 169, 170

Hesitant steps up to the end of the 1950s

At the beginning of the 1880s, SKA was conducting regular business with nearly 250 Swiss and foreign correspondent banks. The network soon embraced the whole world, meaning that the many services supplied to Swiss exporters could also be offered across the globe. Representative offices had already been opened a decade earlier in New York (1870) and in Vienna (1871). The Viennese office had been set up 'because of the particular business environment in Austria', and was primarily concerned with promoting SKA's current account transactions with Austria.[234] The New York office, meanwhile, was established to improve the processing of trading business. Neither representative office was able to gain a long-term foothold, however. The agency in New York was closed in 1878 and was not opened again, 'due to difficulties finding a suitable person to run it'.[235] The office in Vienna closed down in 1900.

On the prompting of its Viennese representative, SKA established the Österreichisch-Schweizerischer Credit-Verein in Vienna in 1874. Formed as a cooperative organization, it aimed to be a discount bank that would offer discount credits exclusively to members. Three years later, tax problems and an economic downturn caused SKA to withdraw from the project and call in the Sfr 2 million loan it had originally made as a capital contribution.[236] In 1910 the bank set up another representative office in Paris, though again this was unable to survive for long.[237]

The series of economic and political crises that hit Europe during the 1930s forced SKA to realign its business operations. In the summer of 1936 the bank's board of directors held its first proper in-depth discussions about the question of foreign branches and subsidiaries. As was the case thirty years before when the first Swiss branch was discussed, the board did not find the matter easy. It hoped that it would be able to stick to its established principle of not opening branches abroad. Once again the main fear was that a branch in another country could escape from head office control.

The possibility of setting up a branch in the UK was rejected, 'owing to the current circumstances' (1939), but the growing threat of war increased the bank's interest in a presence overseas: 'Given the situation in Europe it is apparent that we need to take steps in this direction'.[238] Because the United States of America's 1933 Glass-Steagall Act prevented the bank from participating in a New York securities house as a 'special partner', the possibility of founding a subsidiary was discussed. On 11 July 1939 the Swiss American Corporation (Swissam) opened its doors for business at the premises of the bank Speyer & Co. Swissam was intended as a possible precursor of a full SKA branch – as a 'business corporation' that would pursue underwriting business and securities trading and that could broker stock exchange orders.[239]

Swissam's activities soon proved to be severely limited. After war broke out in Europe and after influential figures in Washington promised that 'America would never carry out orders emanating from a possibly occupied Switzerland', SKA's board of directors decided – only seven months after Swissam started business – to open its own branch in the USA.[241] The New York Agency opened on 9 May 1940.

Even after the end of the Second World War, there was still a great reluctance to forge ahead with expansion abroad. SKA continued to maintain domestic business as its unchallenged first priorty.[242] Nevertheless, the bank took some initial steps to expand its international organization, with a number of participations and the establishment of a Canadian subsidiary in 1951. London, the center of the British Commonwealth and the most important banking center in Europe, became an obvious target and on 15 July 1954, SKA opened up a representative office there. However the office's business was restricted to sourcing transactions that still had to be processed in Zurich.[243] By the second half of the 1950s, SKA thus had only two offices abroad, excluding subsidiaries, namely the branch in New York and the representative office in London. In 1951 it became the first Swiss major bank to operate a direct teleprinter link to New York.

'The most important decision that SKA's board of directors has taken for decades'

The bank had previously rejected the idea of international branches because, given the large amount of write-offs required in domestic business, it did not want to incur yet more costs unless there was a very good chance of making large profits. Now, in 1939, however, there was an irresistible reason to gain a foothold in a territory that was far away from European affairs – and thus safe – and that was not subject to currency controls. The fact that SKA's competitors wanted to set up in New York, too, also played a significant role.[240]

Acceleration in the 1960s and 1970s

SKA had traditionally maintained good business relations with Argentina and in 1959 it opened a representative office in Buenos Aires. From the mid-1950s onwards, the bank also increasingly turned its attention to the Middle East, especially Beirut.[244] The board of directors had debated the merits of expanding into this region for years and in 1967 SKA finally opened a representative office in Beirut; this was later replaced by a subsidiary on account of local laws. Numerous voices had spoken in favor of an even greater commitment to the Middle East ever since the early 1960s. SBV and SBG had already established footholds in Kuwait for business with private clients, and SKA wanted to follow suit. There was some delay, but finally the bank was able to tap into this lucrative region, with representative offices in Tehran (1974) and Bahrain (1975).[245]

At the end of the 1960s, the economic boom in East Asia gave rise to the idea of setting up there too. The bank's choice fell upon Hong Kong (1969), Singapore (1971) and Tokyo (1972); it was felt that this was where the best conditions and the greatest prospects for success in business within South East and East Asia lay.[246]

In the USA, the bank's attention turned primarily to California. The state's GDP was exceeded by only seven countries in the world, making it an exceptionally attractive market. The job of a branch here would be to promote commercial banking ties on America's west coast and to nurture contacts with local banks. In the end, the bank chose to set up in Los Angeles, since no Swiss bank had yet established a presence there. In 1972 the representative office that had been established in Los Angeles four years earlier was converted into a branch. It was hoped that this branch – unlike the branch set up by SBV in San Francisco in 1965 – would start to turn a profit after only three years.[247]

Meanwhile, the representative office set up by SKA in England in 1954 was finding it more and more difficult to compete with SBV and SBG, which had maintained full branches in London since 1898 and 1967 respectively. This problem was recognized by SKA's board of directors: 'If we wish to avoid a disproportionately large negative impact on our balance sheet, we have no choice but to adapt to circumstances and establish a branch in London.'[248] The existing London representative office was thus converted into a branch in 1972.

In 1976 SKA set up a representative office in Moscow in partnership with Svenska Handelsbanken. The main purpose of this new office was to provide advice and support particularly to corporate clients interested in doing business in the Soviet Union.[249] However, cost/benefit considerations led to the closure of this office in 1982.

To pick a sample period from this second phase of international expansion, SKA opened a total of 16 representative offices between 1968 and 1976, the main emphasis being on North America, London and East Asia. Over these same eight years, the bank also set up four international branches – in London, Los Angeles, Singapore and in Nassau (Bahamas). In addition, it was also active in the

South America became an increasingly attractive market towards the end of the 1960s. Thanks to the representative office it had already set up in Buenos Aires in 1959, SKA found itself in a better position to exploit this trend than its competitors. Advertisement from 1960.

In 1971, SKA was the first Swiss bank to establish a representative office in Singapore. The brochure issued to mark its opening was decorated with this drawing of the 'Tiger Balm Garden'.

Arab region and in South America, markets that had become lucrative thanks to a wealthy private clientele.

Conditions change and expansion explodes at the end of the 1970s

During the 1970s the trend towards the internationalization of the financial services industry accelerated continuously. Driven by the twin motivating forces of 'globalization and securitization', international business grew to become a central activity at all three of the big Swiss full-service banks, SBG, SVB and SKA.[250]

As Robert Lang, member of SKA's executive board, noted in a presentation in 1974, the Swiss banks' international assets had already increased by a factor of eight between 1963 and 1973, with foreign liabilities expanding to almost six times the level recorded at the start of this ten-year period. Meanwhile, Swiss domestic assets and liabilities had merely doubled over the decade in question. SBV traditionally had the largest volume of foreign assets amongst the Swiss banks. The worldwide recession that was triggered by the oil shock of 1973 and the collapse of the Bretton-Woods system led to sharp market fluctuations.[251] Nevertheless, SKA's careful management of its balance sheet and its adherence to the so-called '50:50 rule'[252] worked well, enabling it to maintain its image as a 'Swiss bank' despite its expansion abroad.[253]

As early as 1970, chairman of the board Felix W. Schulthess had observed that: 'We have to measure ourselves against powerful international institutions, which are building up multinational branch networks, often with scant regard for traditional structures.'[254] The overriding principle for the future was that SKA had to maintain and continue to strengthen its position as an international commercial bank. At SKA's 1971 management conference, Robert Lang explained that there was already a network of ten representative offices in key markets that were able to supply services to international customers and keep an eye on local markets.[255] He was particularly committed to the development of the bank's representative offices in Hong Kong and Tokyo.

That same year, a study was produced entitled 'SKA's international business activity'. The study stated that such activity must include credit business, deposit taking, fiduciary investments, portfolio business, underwriting, foreign exchange and stock market trading, and investment funds business. The accompanying analysis revealed that, depending on the precise business area, between 27% and 75% of all SKA's transactions (including off-balance-sheet business) involved customers based outside Switzerland. The study described the state of international business as successful, but also called for a decisive push for expansion in order to take advantage of the good earnings opportunities. Three options were discussed:

- Continue the close cooperation with correspondent banks
- Build up SKA's own organization
- Work within a 'club of internationally active major banks'

Regardless of which option was ultimately chosen, there could be no argument about the fact that SKA had to act: 'Today we are one of the three major Swiss banks. We must not allow the gap to widen against the other two institutions [SBG and SBV]. If we do, we may remain attractive to foreign banks, but we will no longer be the most attractive partner.'[256] The direct comparison between the three alternative models for future development helped to crystallize their respective advantages and disadvantages. If the bank continued as before, co-operating with correspondent banks, perhaps augmented by the establishment of a few individual offices, there was a danger that SKA would 'dwindle to the status of a regional bank'.[257] Building up its own organization might give SKA a greater degree of independence, but the question was raised as to 'whether such a move would be appropriate considering our size'.[258] The 'club banking' option was judged to be promising, but because there was a possibility that the club would 'look to one of our competitors to be its Swiss member, we might perhaps prefer to operate on the basis of the Swiss banks in general keeping their distance from such a club'.[259] Even though the study did not unequivocally call for the development of a proprietary organization, it came to the conclusion that this would be the most flexible option and the one that would most closely meet the needs of the bank's commercial clients.

Against this background, at the beginning of 1972 Eberhard Reinhardt, president of the executive board, instructed Rainer E. Gut – who was shortly to be called to the executive board himself and who, as a former partner in the investment bank Lazard Frères, knew all about international and especially US business – to improve SKA's position in the international arena. In doing so, all efforts were to be directed at the development of wholesale banking to the exclusion of deposit-taking business.[260] The start of the migration of the Euromarkets to London in the mid-1970s confirmed the wisdom of SKA's newly established strategy of processing more and more of its business through its own foreign offices.[261]

In the bank's first 'Guiding Principles' printed in 1976, the 'International' section stated that promising new markets should be explored, though the emphasis should be on supporting the Swiss exporting sector. A presence in all the international financial markets was laid down as an express objective. In addition, a worldwide network of correspondent banks should be maintained and nurtured. Particular importance was attached to the central international secretariat at head office, which was responsible for coordinating country limits and international customer relations. The general feeling was that strong growth was only possible outside Switzerland, because Switzerland itself was too heavily regulated by conventions laid down by the Swiss Bankers' Association and other bodies.[262]

The risks and limitations of expansion

In 1977 the board of directors discussed the suitability of a new country limits system, which would take due account of the 50:50 rule mentioned above, as a means of restricting the amount of risk taken on by the bank as it expanded

'Put Credit Suisse on the map in international business' (Eberhard Reinhardt's instruction to Rainer E. Gut, 1972).

its foreign operations. Board member Max Schmidheiny was skeptical about forcing the pace of expansion abroad because SKA's engagements were concentrated on a small number of countries, and levels of debt were increasing continuously around the world. It was quite possible that certain states might declare debt moratoria. Neither should currency risk be underestimated. Chairman of the board Oswald Aeppli explained that SKA was well aware of the risks inherent in international business, and that the bank was actually pursuing a rather conservative policy on business outside Switzerland by comparison with SBG and SBV. Ultimately SKA had no choice but to participate properly in this type of business. Executive board member Rainer E. Gut added that the current situation could not be compared with the situation in the 1930s. International money and capital markets were now so closely intertwined with one another that it was almost impossible to imagine that individual markets could collapse on their own.[263]

In SKA's Guiding Principles of 1976, it was stated that the bank maintained a network of branches, subsidiaries, representative offices and majority participations in the key international centers. The bank was not generally interested in minority participations.[264] At the 1979 management conference it was emphasized once again that additional PR work was required to increase awareness of SKA's worldwide presence. Senior managers were encouraged to spend more time at conferences put on by organizations like the International Monetary Fund and the Asian Development Bank, or at the management symposium in Davos.[265] In November of that year, the board of directors had occasion to discuss the bank's business in North America; commercial banking operations in the region had grown strongly since the mid-1970s on the back of new representative offices and increased staff numbers. Great significance was placed on a marketing mentality and on sales training. The representative offices were issued with 'hunting licenses'. These were stocks of approved credit limits that the bank's staff could go and offer directly to customers. Using such tactics, the bank managed to increase both its total assets and its profits in the USA.[266]

In parallel with the growth of the international organization, 1980 saw the creation of the 'multinational services' subdivision at head office, which catered for the particular financial needs of globally active foreign firms. This was followed in 1987 by the 'multinational services Switzerland' subdivision. The progressive internationalization of the bank left its traces in the names of other units at head office too; departments, which had previously been known by their German names, were given English titles instead, such as 'corporate finance' and 'asset management'. Similarly in 1990 the whole foreign exchange/precious metals/bank notes/money market/liquidity area was renamed 'global treasury'.

The need for a focused strategy for international expansion

Regular meetings of department heads were arranged to improve the co-ordination of international activities. Different markets were discussed and SKA-specific solutions developed.[267]

In the mid-1980s, SKA's board of directors held intensive discussions about Mexico, Brazil and other highly leveraged countries. Certain lending commitments had gone sour, which led to urgent questions about credit and limit policy. As solutions to the debt problem were sought, the discussion focused on the issue of granting additional bank loans – except in Argentina, it seemed that the situation in Latin America had actually been improving since 1984. Nevertheless, SKA cut its exposure sharply. Loans to Sub-Saharan Africa were also chopped back rigorously. In 1984, 69% of the bank's commercial loans outside Switzerland were to the countries with the best credit ratings in the world, while only 12% were to regions where the borrower risk was high.[268]

Nevertheless, until now there had been no clear strategy behind the bank's expansion abroad. On the one hand, SKA wanted to be present in all the key financial centers; on the other, there was intensive debate about building up business activities in the OPEC countries, in Southern Africa, in the emerging markets of Asia, and in Australia. The rather tangled organizational structure at the bank provided a further complication. The foreign offices were allocated to individual members of the executive board – to four of them in 1976, for example[269] – who were also responsible for Swiss branches and other functional areas of the bank. International business was, therefore, not centralized, making it difficult to implement a coherent worldwide strategy.

Main focuses of 'Strategy 1990': North America, Western Europe and East Asia

Finally, at an executive board meeting held in January 1984, the focus of the bank's international business activities was defined in 'Strategy 1990'. SKA wanted to remain one of the three leading Swiss banks, but at the same time it also wanted to play in the top league internationally. In fact no less than 24% of the bank's earnings were already being generated outside Switzerland by 1983. The most profitable branch was the one in New York, which accounted for 40% of foreign earnings, followed by the ones in London and Nassau.[270] International business would make a substantial contribution to the bank achieving its ambitious targets for return on equity (ROE) and return on assets (ROA).

According to 'Strategy 1990' it was particularly important to take into account that many of the products involved were already being offered by Financière Crédit Suisse – First Boston (FCSFB) and First Boston. Customer relations had to be managed locally, except in cases handled by the multinational services subdivision. Trade finance and export finance – business areas used mainly by the bank's international clientele – also counted as international business.[272] Customer relations and capital market advisory for central banks and insurance companies also had to be intensified and extended in collaboration with FCSFB and First Boston. The general expansion of international business should concentrate mainly on the USA, Canada, the United Kingdom, West Germany and Japan, though off-balance-sheet business could also be pushed forward in other economic regions.[273]

Business activities in the USA

The difficult political and economic situation, and the threat of war in Europe prompted SKA to set up the Swiss American Corporation (Swissam) in 1939 to conduct securities trading and handle the processing of securities transactions. It soon became clear, however, that Swissam's business goals were too restrictive, which is why the bank founded a branch in New York on 9 May 1940.

In 1964, SKA was granted a license as a full-service bank, allowing it to take deposits and carry out all other types of banking in the USA. Nevertheless, until the 1970s, SKA operated almost exclusively as a classic foreign bank, concentrating mainly on commercial banking services for large non-US customers. Once the presence in New York was established, the bank built up its branch network continuously, not least because it was now serving more and more of the 'Fortune 500 companies', i.e. the biggest listed companies in the USA. When deregulation came in the 1980s, SKA was able to develop into one of the most respected foreign banks in the US in specialist areas such as project finance, and to become a market maker in foreign exchange and precious metals business. Staff at the bank's branches in the USA were sourced locally, with the exception of a few Swiss employees, helping to establish strong roots throughout the region. The bank's performance can be judged from the development of its headcount, which more than doubled from 41 to 102 between 1940 and 1950, and which had reached 1,074 by 1985.[271]

New home market in the USA – disappointment in Germany

SKA wanted to retain its status as a significant international bank, though it was careful to sort its markets and customers into different segments. Alongside greater cooperation with FCSFB and First Boston, this led the bank to target countries with key investment currencies for development into home markets. Creating these 'home markets' was a priority in four main countries: the USA, the United Kingdom, the Federal Republic of Germany and Japan[274] and it was not long before the bank started setting up or acquiring the companies it needed to accomplish this aim. In 1991 SKA purchased the New York asset management company BEA Associates Inc. It also built up its presence massively in the UK and in the Channel Islands. After 1986, the liberalization that swept through London's financial services industry allowed brokers, too, to be members of the stock exchange. In response, SKA strengthened its position by buying the long-established brokerage house of Buckmaster & Moore, which perfectly complemented the activities already being pursued by Credit Suisse First Boston Ltd., London.[275] 1990 saw another important step in SKA's cooperation with CS First Boston when the two companies set up the derivatives and swaps specialist Credit Suisse Financial Products, also based in London.

In 1985 SKA bought two banks in Germany. This move was prompted by the conviction that it was essential to have a base in the country that is Switzerland's most important trading partner, firstly to encourage local client acquisitions, and secondly to monitor commercial customers more effectively. However, the board of directors believed that setting up a branch would prove too time-consuming and expensive.[276] First of all, therefore, SKA took over Grundig Bank GmbH, a local bank based in Fürth with total assets of DM 1.3 billion and a staff of 140. Shortly afterwards it was able to acquire Effectenbank-Warburg AG of Frankfurt, which had total assets of DM 1.6 billion and 300 staff. SKA's mission in Germany was clearly set out in the so-called 'Adler-Papier' of November 1985: the aim was to combine commercial banking and investment banking services to set the bank apart from its competitors.[278]

Glass-Steagall Act

The stock market crash of 1929 drove many US savings and loans institutions to ruin, prompting the introduction in 1933 of the 'Glass-Steagall Act'. The purpose of this law was to separate commercial banking from investment banking. This led, for example, to the division of Morgan Bank into the commercial bank J.P. Morgan and the investment house Morgan Stanley. Nevertheless, the authorities repeatedly allowed exceptions to this rule. Attempts were made to revise or abolish the law on many occasions, but for many years differences of opinion between interest groups and the authorities, particularly with regard to the conflicting responsibilities of different regulators, prevented any compromise. It was not until October 1999 that the US Congress decided to repeal Glass-Steagal and to issue a new banking act that would facilitate an agreement on regulatory authority. It was also decided that the 'Community Reinvestment Act' should remain in force. This compelled the banks to offer a retail banking service to poorer sections of society. It was now possible to create American full-service banks and financial services conglomerates like Citigroup. At the same time, however – and this is viewed by experts as a step backwards given the current state of technological progress – industrial and trading companies, including firms like the supermarket chain Walmart, are excluded from the financial services industry.[277]

'Grandfathering'

In 1978 the 'International Banking Act' subjected foreign banks to the same conditions that the 'Bank Holding Company Act' had imposed on US banks since 1956. However, some of the activities already pursued by foreign banks went beyond the lines of business permitted by the 'Bank Holding Company Act'; so the 'International Banking Act, Section 8 (c)' was introduced to allow foreign banks to continue such activities, i.e. the rights originally given to them were maintained, or 'grandfathered'. To prevent 'protected' foreign banks from exploiting this competitive advantage to the detriment of US banks, 'grandfathering' was tied to various conditions, which placed certain restrictions on their activities.

Both of the newly acquired German banks were run as subsidiaries, renamed as Credit Suisse Grundig Bank GmbH – later to become SKA (Deutschland) GmbH – and CSFB-Effectenbank AG. On 1 July 1986 the two merged to form SKA (Deutschland) AG, though the CSFB-Effectenbank brand was retained for German and international underwriting business, an area in which SKA soon attained first place amongst the foreign banks operating in Germany. A new branch in Nuremberg, as well as representative offices in Munich and Stuttgart, further enhanced the bank's presence. By 1986 SKA (Deutschland) AG could boast total assets of DM 4.2 billion and a staff of 550. Within a year, SKA (Deutschland) AG had thus become the largest entity in the whole of the bank's international organization. However, in 1989 the president of the executive board Robert A. Jeker used his speech at the management conference that year to remind managers that not everything was rosy for the bank in Germany.[279] He was referring, amongst other things, to the high turnover of management-grade staff, the many reorganizations that had been carried out, problematic credit positions and a generally unsatisfactory market penetration.

In 1995, the international division finally came to the conclusion that the split market presence used until that point did not match up with the demand for a wholesale service from a single source. It was decided, therefore, that all the bank's various activities in Germany should be brought together under the 'new' Credit Suisse Deutschland AG. With this new structure, and thanks to the cost reductions facilitated by the consolidation, it was assumed that the potential of the market could be exploited more effectively.[280]

In 1985, SKA strengthened its presence in Germany by taking over Grundig Bank GmbH, Fürth, and then Effectenbank-Warburg Aktiengesellschaft, Frankfurt am Main, whose head office is pictured here. Photo taken in 1985.

Credit Suisse representative office in Chicago
Représentation du Crédit Suisse à Chicago
Rappresentanza del Credito Svizzero a Chicago
SKA-Vertretung in Chicago

The Standard Oil Building in Chicago was the fourth tallest building in the world when SKA opened its representative office on the 65th floor in 1976.

Despite all these efforts, however, the attempt to build up an additional home market in Germany proved unsuccessful. This was quite different from the bank's experience in the USA, where within a short period in the mid-1970s SKA opened a whole series of commercial banking branches on both coasts as well as in key business hubs such as Chicago and Houston. By the middle of the 1980s, the bank had created a comprehensive network of branches and representative offices for commercial banking, which in combination with FCSFB's investment banking operations covered the entire wholesale banking spectrum. When deregulation came in the 1980s, SKA was able to develop into one of the most respected foreign banks in the United States in specialist areas such as project finance, and to become a market maker in foreign exchange and precious metals business. However, the really decisive factor in the bank's success in the USA was its partnership with First Boston. Without this globally active investment bank it would not have been able to leap into the uppermost reaches of the league tables as it did.[281] In Germany, meanwhile, SKA simply did not have the same kind of opportunity.

At SKA's 1988 shareholders' meeting, the chairman of the board of directors, Rainer E. Gut, declared that the bank was pursuing a very clear goal: in the 1990s it was going to be one of the very few well-capitalized, blue-chip financial institutions that could run a truly worldwide wholesale banking operation, using partners where necessary. The Guiding Principles of 1990 emphasized once again that in international business, the North American, European and Far Eastern economic regions were the strategic keys to success, but that outside Switzerland the only customer segments which should be cultivated were multinational firms, wealthy private individuals and institutional investors.[282]

Robert A. Jeker was aiming in the same direction when in 1990 he delivered his 'Visions for SKA' speech: the bank should use subsidiaries and branches to become one of the leading providers of financial services in wholesale banking and private banking in all of the industrialized nations, but particularly in markets which kept the different types of banking separate, such as the USA and Japan. Robert A. Jeker went on to state that business in the Far East had to be expanded and that the bank should also extend its influence southwards by intensifying business in the southern EC countries, too. He expressed concern about the situation in the developing world, and especially the debt situation in developing countries, which was placing massive restrictions on opportunities for direct investment.[283] At a press conference in 1991, Jeker predicted that SKA would achieve enormous growth primarily outside Switzerland. It was clear that growth abroad would be greater than domestic growth, not least because of the insufficiently attractive tax regime in Switzerland. The prediction was backed up by the figures: in 1989 only 18% of SKA's gross earnings had come from abroad; by 1991 this figure had risen to about 34%. Another third of its earnings came from international business conducted from within Switzerland.[284]

The growth of SKA's, SBG's and SBV's international organizations

In the 1950s, SBV had significantly more foreign offices (branches and representative offices) than SKA and SBG.[285] Then in the 1960s all three major banks embarked on a general expansion abroad, though SKA continued to lose ground to its two rivals. It was not until the 1970s that the bank was able to make up this deficit. In the 1980s and up to the middle of the 1990s, SKA's foreign operations grew at a much faster rate; in terms of the numbers of offices it ran, it was able to catch up with and overtake SBV, which was traditionally very well represented outside Switzerland.[286]

SKA, SBV and SBG: number of branches and representative offices outside Switzerland (1959–1996)

	SKA		SBV		SBG	
	Branches	Rep. offices	Branches	Rep. offices	Branches	Rep. offices
1959	1	2	2	6	n. a.	1
1969	1	8	3	15	1	11
1979	8	21	10	24	7	20
1989	12	27	12	28	8	19
1996	17	37	11	29	15	26

The 1990s: tapping into new markets

Having established itself well in its traditional Swiss and US markets, after the end of the Cold War SKA wanted increasingly to make the most of the new business opportunities that were arising in Eastern Europe and the Soviet Union. The collapse of the communist eastern bloc in 1989/90 and the fall of the Soviet Union in 1991 led to a fundamental change in the prevailing political and economic systems; but this did not necessarily mean that conditions were right everywhere for the immediate introduction of a market economy. The demand for the know-how and capital needed for the transformation opened up international business opportunities for European and American banks. SKA and other CS Holding companies perceived that there were indeed chances to tap into new markets, but that a differentiated approach was needed. Distinctions had to be made according to the specific developments in the different countries, not to mention the variations in creditworthiness throughout the region.

Based on a 'Strategy paper for Eastern Europe', which had been approved by the executive board at the beginning of 1990, SKA decided to get in early by establishing a strategic foothold in Moscow. In autumn 1991, SKA thus became the first Swiss bank to set up a representative office in Moscow. Thanks to this local presence and the much more effective access to information that it provided, the bank was able to push ahead vigorously with establishing and developing business relations. In 1994, SKA founded its subsidiary Credit Suisse (Moscow) Ltd. with starting capital of $20 million – again the first Swiss bank and one of the first international banks of all to make such a move. The new

Number of employees in non-Swiss branches and representative offices relative to number of employees at SKA head office (1959–1996)

	Employees in non-Swiss branches	Employees in non-Swiss rep. offices	Employees at head office
1959	114	n. a.	1271
1969	130	n. a.	2244
1979	482	102	4615
1989	1271	136	7067
1996	1992	241	7585

1959, 1969, 1979, 1989: actual number of people
1996: number of full-time posts

'Credit Suisse Group's Expensive Russian Adventure'
'Basler Zeitung', 17 March 1999

Credit Suisse First Boston, which had become involved earlier and more systematically in Eastern Europe than other banks, was hit particularly hard by the severe financial, economic and governmental crisis that ravaged Russia in 1998.

As the collapse of the ruble accelerated, Credit Suisse Group's share price fell rapidly. 'Its registered shares have fallen by 4.59% in a single day', reported the *NZZ* on 21 August. 'According to its own figures, over 40% of total foreign investments … were in Russian fixed interest paper. Hardly surprising, then, that investors have turned their backs on the Swiss bank's shares since the Russian central bank declared a moratorium on foreign debt repayments on Monday.' The *Tages-Anzeiger* also noted that, 'Russia has put CS under pressure'. At the same time the *Basler Zeitung* wrote that the US securities house Goldman Sachs had taken Credit Suisse Group's shares off its 'recommended' list. One day later, *Finanz und Wirtschaft* reported that around 8% of Credit Suisse Group's shares had suddenly changed hands. However, it also talked about an 'excessive reaction to the Russian situation', and even came to the conclusion that, 'the current price level can thus be seen as a good opportunity to buy CS Group registered shares.'

On 26 August, Credit Suisse Group officially revealed the effects of the Russian crisis in a press release. Net profit for the first half of the year had fallen by no less than Sfr 365 million to Sfr 735 million. This prompted *Cash* to state in a headline two days later that the bank had 'Lost at Russian Roulette'. Working from Credit Suisse First Boston's overall results for July and August, on 29 August *Finanz und Wirtschaft* ('Russia Overshadows CS Group') estimated that the bank's losses in Russia had to be between Sfr 660 and 680 million. 'Despite Mühlemann, who had previously always maintained that CSG would go it alone, takeover speculation had begun again', commented *Cash* after the bank's autumn press conference on 9 September, pointing out that the share price had risen disproportionately following the rumors of a merger with Deutsche Bank, J. P. Morgan or Chase Manhattan in the first half of the year. 'No Mercy for Credit Suisse Group' from the stock market, wrote *Finanz und Wirtschaft*, referring to the open secret of Credit Suisse First Boston's difficulties. On 13 September 1998, Lukas Mühlemann was forced to deny the rumors that he would resign: 'I will face the new challenges with relish', he stated in the *Sonntags-Zeitung*. At the same time the bank announced that about half of its 350 staff in Moscow would have to go. Some time later, *Weltwoche* passed harsh judgment on Credit Suisse Group, saying that the investment bankers in Moscow believed that there could only be two possibilities: 'Either Credit Suisse First Boston's strategists were brilliant, or they were hiding their losses.' (29 October 1998).

The annual results press conference on 16 March 1999 brought more information. 'Dark Russian Shadows On a Stronger CSG', was the *NZZ* headline; 'CS Loses 1.9 Billion in Russia' screamed the *Blick*. By contrast the *Tages-Anzeiger* looked to the future: 'CS Wants to Minimize Risks.' According to the press release, the changes to risk management policy at Credit Suisse First Boston centered on the creation of a strategic risk management unit, an increased focus on risk management issues by senior managers, and the avoidance of risk clusters in all areas.

'Project Europe' – activities in Eastern Europe and the CIS

In 1993 SKA's 'Project Europe' defined the countries of Eastern Europe and the CIS as one of the bank's four business regions in Europe. The target markets remained the same – Central European countries, plus Russia, the Ukraine, Uzbekistan, Turkmenistan and Kazakhstan – and the client focus continued to center on banks and sovereign risks (republic and state authorities). As far as products were concerned, the bank concentrated on short-term trade financing, treasury business and participations in co-financing and project finance with the European Bank for Reconstruction and Development (EBRD) and the International Finance Corporation (IFC). Encouraged by the improved credit rating of certain countries in the region, the bank also began cautiously to extend loans to large blue-chip companies, mostly in the form of credits or participations in syndicate deals.

Thanks to previous marketing work and intensive traveling around the region by key staff, SKA was soon widely known throughout Eastern Europe and the CIS states. The bank generated a lot of goodwill, especially through its generous support for the education and further training of bank staff at a large number of on-the-spot seminars on trade finance and treasury business (including in Almaty, Ashkhabad, Yekaterinburg and Riga as well as at SKA's head office in Zurich). The bank also scored a great success with the Russian edition of its documentary credits manual, which many CIS banks subsequently used for their own training programs.

SKA in Central Asia

In March 1995, SKA opened a representative office in Tashkent (Uzbekistan), which acted as a marketing hub for all five of the Central Asian states. Once again SKA was the first Swiss bank in the area. It had previously been able to develop a 'special relationship' and close business ties with Uzbekistan, for example signing a co-operation agreement on the occasion of the 1993 World Economic Forum in Davos. The representative office in Tashkent contributed greatly to the successful establishment of fruitful relationships and increasing volumes of business in the region.

company concentrated on marketing basic bank products 'at high margins' to the Russian subsidiaries of foreign companies (joint ventures and representative offices), to Russian companies, as well as to Western and Russian banks.[287] By 1996, Credit Suisse (Moscow) Ltd.'s staff had increased fourfold to 200, the volume of business it was conducting had risen sharply, and it was successfully expanding its local and international customer base. Significant income was coming from securities and foreign exchange trading as well as from trade finance. Credit Suisse (Moscow) Ltd. had established itself as one of the leading foreign banks in the Russian market.[288]

In 1994, CS First Boston, too, set up a subsidiary company in Moscow, which was merged with Credit Suisse (Moscow) Ltd. on 1 January 1997. From then on, the Moscow arm of what was now Credit Suisse First Boston was able to cover the entire spectrum of wholesale banking services.[289]

Finding itself confronted with massive economic problems, in August 1998 the Russian government set the ruble free to float and declared a moratorium on all public-sector debt denominated in the local currency. As a result of this step, Credit Suisse First Boston, which was the market leader for Russian government issues and debt instruments, had to make write downs and provisions of Sfr 1.86 billion for the 1998 business year. Business in Russia suffered a general and dramatic collapse and the bank had to significantly reduce both its business presence and its staff numbers.[290]

1993 brought new opportunities for business in the Central and Eastern European markets when the Austrian government announced that it was looking for a strategic partner to take on its stake in the country's second biggest bank, the Creditanstalt-Bankverein (CA) in Vienna. The government approached CS Holding, having been impressed with the example of its participation in CS First Boston. However, during negotiations CS Holding made it clear that if it was to take an initial minority position in the bank, this would have to be expanded into a majority stake later on. Only then would it be able to make effective use of the CA in Austria and its business activities in Eastern Europe. Unlike the Austrian government, the CA board was skeptical about CS Holding's offer, preferring a broader distribution of its equity capital. Negotiations became more and more entangled in the contortions of Austrian domestic politics, which were becoming increasingly fraught in the run-up to 1994's parliamentary elections. As a consequence, and to the regret of many Austrian commentators, CS Holding withdrew its offer on 12 September 1994. When the Austrian government made a fresh approach in 1995, CS Holding turned it down again because there had been no substantial change to the basic offer.

The idea of creating another home market in Austria thus came to nothing. However, this disappointment could be set against the bank's success in Southern Europe: SKA, and after 1997 Credit Suisse Group, successfully established themselves in France, Italy and Spain.

*'CS Holding, Zurich /Creditanstalt-Bankverein,
Vienna: a victory despite empty hands.
Swiss decide to withdraw in the face
of party political wrangling'*
'Handelszeitung', 15 September 1994

'After months of searching, it seems that Creditanstalt (CA) has come to a preliminary decision about a new partner', reported Vienna's *Standard* on 27 April 1994. 'Schweizerische Kreditanstalt (SKA), part of Credit Suisse Group, has emerged as the clear first choice for finance minister Ferdinand Lacina, who as a representative of the main shareholder – the federal government – wants to sell a 20% stake in the bank's share capital (4.1 billion Austrian schillings) before the summer as part of the bank's ongoing privatization.'

This was followed by a huge backlash in the Austrian media against the possibility of any type of foreign solution, particularly since the management of CA wanted to maintain the power to take its own decisions. 'Rainer E. Gut turns on the charm in Vienna – but fails to win everybody over', was the comment from the *Sonntags-Zeitung* on 8 May 1994. As well as the patriotic objections, internal Austrian politics also played a role: CA was dominated by the conservative Austrian People's Party (the ÖVP), while the country's largest bank, Bank Austria, was controlled by the Austrian Social Democratic Party (the SPÖ). Accusations were made that Lacina, a Social Democrat, was being driven by party-political motives: he wanted to remove control of CA from his political opponents. At the same time, an Austrian-international consortium came up with a counter-offer to 'keep CS Holding out' (*Sonntags-Zeitung*, 15 May 1994). As the pressure on Lacina increased, he decided to postpone his decision until October – i.e. until after the parliamentary elections – and, according to the *NZZ* of 29 June 1994, stated, 'that contrary to the widely expressed assumption, he did not intend to make over a majority holding in the country's second biggest bank to foreign investors'.

In this fraught atmosphere, little attention was paid in Austria to Rainer E. Gut's comment to the *Weltwoche* that: 'Over time we will hopefully be able to prove that we can be good citizens in Austria and that Creditanstalt can retain its Austrian personality even with the participation of a Swiss bank. [...] CS Holding is a group of various significant companies, all of which have their own identity. [...] This would apply to CA too. We are not going to shoehorn the Swiss cross into the CA logo. We believe in the concept of home markets and with the help of CA, Austria will become a new home market for us – a market which will be taken care of for us by CA' (26 May 1994).

The *Handelszeitung* thought that the 'tide was turning' (14 July 1994), whereas the *Sonntags-Zeitung* (17 July 1994) still believed that: 'CS Holding holds the ace.' Hopes were raised again in August when Lacina decided that a foreign investment bank should evaluate the two offers – the *Tages-Anzeiger* heard that this would be Goldman Sachs (17 August 1994). But then on 12 September, CS Holding unexpectedly withdrew its offer. 'Dream Wedding Falls Through', announced the *Tages-Anzeiger* next day; 'Nothing Going On But The Fees', sniped the *Basler Zeitung*.

'CS Shares in Demand After Project Collapses', was the *NZZ*'s contrasting and more sober assessment; as far as investors were concerned, what was important was that the feared dilution of earnings had been avoided. Furthermore, the 'capitulation before the forces of economics and politics', did not represent a change of strategy at Paradeplatz. On 14 September *Finanz und Wirtschaft* stated that, 'CS Holding Will Not Hang Around Moping About CA', and ventured – despite the denials from CS Holdings press office – that what had tipped the scales was the fact that the only bank left to evaluate the two offers was J. P. Morgan, a direct competitor of Credit Suisse First Boston. In an article headlined, 'A Victory Despite the Empty Hands' (15 September 1994), the *Handelszeitung* delivered further background. According to a rumor that kept cropping up, 'the SPÖ and ÖVP had long before agreed in secret that the finance minister would sell the government's stake in CA to the Austrian-Italian-German consortium, creating a rightist banking giant to act as a counterbalance to the leftist Bank Austria. In return, the SPÖ would earn the right to appoint the President of the National Bank, until then a post in the gift of the People's Party.'

---

*CS Holding's strategic considerations
with regard to a union with Creditanstalt-
Bankverein (Vienna), 18 March 1994*

'Given the competitive position of the Austrian banks in general and of Creditanstalt in particular, we are of the opinion that CS Holding could bring its great expertise to bear and help to improve the financial situation. [...] The Austrian banks' results leave something to be desired in terms of both earnings and costs. [...]

*The potential strategic role
of Creditanstalt for CS Holding*

We see an alliance between CS Holding and Creditanstalt not just as an extension of our existing activities, but believe that the company could play a precisely defined, key strategic role within CS Holding Group. As part of CS Holding and within the parameters of our organization's overall strategy, Creditanstalt would:

1. Maintain its own identity
2. Be CS Holding Group's anchor in an Austrian home market
3. Together with CS First Boston and Credit Suisse make a significant contribution to CS Holding Group's business in Central and Eastern Europe.

Creditanstalt has a leading market position in the Republic of Austria, but one of the biggest advantages it enjoys over its European peers lies in its historical links with Central and Eastern Europe. Our analysis suggests that this unique market position brings with it significant potential for the future, especially if the company can build up its product expertise, improve its efficiency and effectively nurture its business operations in Central and Eastern Europe. We believe that CA would find it much easier to achieve these aims in an alliance with CS Holding.

Operational implications for Creditanstalt

A strategic alliance with CS Holding would naturally have operational consequences for Creditanstalt. If it were to become a strategic partner, we would try to strengthen its competitiveness and bring its finances and operations more into line with those of banks in other European countries, as well as of Credit Suisse and CS Holding. [...] In the operational area, we see some major challenges and opportunities for Creditanstalt over the medium term:

1. The first major requirement is that Creditanstalt increases its earnings power in Austrian domestic business. [...]
2. The second major challenge is to nurture and intensify the bank's traditional strengths in Central and Eastern Europe. [...]
3. As a part of CS Holding [...] the company would be an integral part of a strong, globally active financial services organization. [...]
4. Creditanstalt also has to improve its financial results substantially. [...]'[291]

Global investment banking **171**

In February 1970, SKA's New York branch and its subsidiary Swiss American Corporation – joined later by SASI – moved into the newly built skyscraper at 100 Wall Street, where they were to remain for more than 20 years. Photo taken in 1973.

Staff at the offices of Swiss American Securities Inc. (SASI) in New York. Photo taken around 1975.

From White Weld to Credit Suisse First Boston

The beginnings

Ever since it was first established, SKA saw the whole world, rather than just Switzerland, as the stage on which it wanted to operate. In commercial business it was for a long time much more strongly bound to the domestic market than the other Swiss major banks, but this was not the case with investment banking. As a traditional commercial bank and a major underwriter, it was already involved in all areas of securities business with Swiss and foreign customers in the 19th century: from underwriting and stock market business, to investment advice and placements, to securities trading.

Nevertheless, SKA did not feel obliged to build up an international organization to back up this business until well into the 20th century. As we have seen, it took the deterioration of the political climate in Europe in the mid-1930s to persuade the bank to examine the possibility of setting up a foreign branch or subsidiary. New York was chosen for business as well as security reasons: during the inter-war years, the city's financial center had become the most important market for foreign bonds. In July 1939 SKA founded a subsidiary called Swiss American Corporation (Swissam), which concentrated on underwriting and placement business as well as investment advice. One year later the 'Credit Suisse New York Agency', SKA's first international branch, was opened in the same building as Swissam to facilitate commercial banking operations. This twin-track approach was necessitated by US legislation (the Glass-Steagall Act of 1933), which demanded that securities houses and commercial banks be kept separate.

Setting up a securities bank in New York put SKA way ahead of its Swiss competitors. SBV opened a branch in New York in 1939, and the smaller SBG set up a representative office there in 1946, but it would be about 30 years before these two banks established subsidiaries in the Big Apple: SBV in 1969 with the Basle Securities Corporation, and SBG in 1970 with the American UBS Corporation, which was integrated into the UBS-DB Corporation at the end of 1971.

The Eurobond market

The 1960s brought many new opportunities and developments in business and finance. The decade was characterized by high economic growth rates – especially in Europe – numerous mergers and acquisitions, the creation of a European Economic Community (EEC) and the emergence of the Euromarkets. Unsurprisingly, international banking also underwent rapid change as a result.

The Euromarkets developed thanks to the introduction of free convertibility in 1958. Foreign exchange restrictions were removed, meaning that the world's key currencies could once again be freely traded against one another. As national financial markets diverged – each imposing its own different regulations on lending and deposit-taking business, its own interest rates and its own tax

SCHWEIZERISCHE KREDITANSTALT
CRÉDIT SUISSE / CREDITO SVIZZERO

GEGRÜNDET IM JAHRE 1856
AKTIENKAPITAL UND RESERVEN: Fr. 190 000 000

Nachdem sich der Geschäftsverkehr mit Übersee nun wieder zu normalisieren beginnt, kann unsere New Yorker Niederlassung

CREDIT SUISSE NEW YORK AGENCY
30, Pine Street • Telegramme: Credsuis
NEW YORK CITY

den schweizerischen Importeuren und Exporteuren in mancher Hinsicht gute Dienste leisten. Dank ihrer vorzüglichen Beziehungen in den Vereinigten Staaten ist sie in der Lage, bei der Anbahnung neuer Verbindungen behilflich zu sein durch Einführungen und Besorgung von Auskünften. Ganz besonders gut eingerichtet ist sie für die Eröffnung von Akkreditiven. Die reiche Erfahrung unserer in allen Zweigen der schweizerisch-amerikanischen Wirtschaftsbeziehungen spezialisierten Filiale und ihre moderne Organisation bieten Gewähr für eine zuverlässige und rasche Abwicklung sämtlicher Bankgeschäfte mit den U.S.A. und den andern Dollarländern. Unser Hauptsitz sowie unsere Niederlassungen in der Schweiz stehen jederzeit gerne zur Verfügung für nähere Angaben, Empfehlungsschreiben und Weiterleitung allfälliger Wünsche.

INHALT DIESES HEFTES:
Die internationale Währungslage am Kriegsende S. 75.
Finanzielle und wirtschaftliche Rundschau S. 89. — Börsenbericht S. 96.
Effektenkurse S. 98. — Unkotierte Werte und Devisenkurse S. 103.

Advertisement for the SKA branch in New York; *Monats-Bulletin*, October 1945.

Convertibility

Convertibility is defined as the free exchangeability of different countries' currencies at the prevailing exchange rate. During the Second World War and immediately thereafter, international payment transactions were subject to rigorous state controls for economic and political reasons. Only at the end of 1958/start of 1959 did the countries of Europe return – in some cases in stages – to free convertibility. Without currency convertibility, multilateral trade and capital transfers would never have become as significant as they are today.

regime for borrowed funds – the Euromarkets, which were initially established only for short-term money market transactions, began to grow faster and faster. In 1963 the USA introduced an interest equalization tax in an attempt to sort out its balance of payments deficit. This worked as an indirect foreign exchange control and made it much more expensive to issue bonds in New York. However, the real trigger for the Euromarket's decisive breakthrough came in 1965 when the USA imposed restrictions on the export of capital, again in an attempt to improve the country's balance of payments situation. The restrictions forced a large proportion of US companies to finance their foreign subsidiaries with funds sourced from outside the USA. Europe was awash with investable funds, so these large corporations had no choice but to come to the Euromarkets for financing. With blue-chip American firms on board, the Eurobond market quickly gained in significance and grew to become the biggest international capital market of them all.

Partnership with White Weld

On 12 June 1962, SKA acquired the shares of White, Weld & Co. AG, Zurich, from the US investment bank White, Weld & Co. Inc. of New York, one of the USA's leading brokers and underwriters. White, Weld & Co. AG, Zurich had been founded in 1955 and specialized in portfolio management and stock market business. Owing to tax considerations and the fact that it now wanted to operate abroad only as a stock market company and not as an asset manager, White Weld (New York) had decided, 'to sell its Zurich company in good faith, but only to a first-class institution'.[292] The official stated purpose of the acquired firm was, 'the processing of financial transactions of all types for its own account and for the account of others; financing for its own account and for the account of others; the purchase, sale and brokering of securities for its own account and for the account of others; the management of assets of all types; the representation of similar Swiss and foreign companies; and participation in similar Swiss and foreign companies'.[293]

SKA replaced the name White, Weld & Co. AG with Clariden Finanz AG, and cooperation between SKA and White Weld (New York) became even closer. In 1970, the two institutions founded WW Trust, Zug, in order to co-ordinate White Weld's non-American business (the company had been involved in international business for over 40 years). SKA brought Clariden Finanz AG into this holding company.

White Weld (New York) had been set up in 1895 and was one of the largest underwriting houses in America. In 1974 it had 14 offices in the USA and Canada, four in Europe (London, Paris, Zurich and Geneva), one office in South America (Caracas) and one in South East Asia (Hong Kong), and employed 1,400 staff. It occupied an impressive position in the key ranking lists throughout the 1970s: measured by the volume of lead-managed international equity and debt capital transactions[294] it was an almost permanent member of the top fifteen.

White, Weld & Co. AG, Zurich, and Clariden Bank

1955: White, Weld & Co. AG, Zurich, is founded as a 100%-owned subsidiary of the US investment bank White, Weld & Co. Inc., New York. Its main activities are portfolio management and stock market transactions.

1962: Via its subsidiary Bank in Zürich, SKA acquires White, Weld & Co. AG, Zurich, which now employs 28 staff. From this point on, White, Weld & Co. AG's operations focus on managing client assets and the transactions related to this type of business. The company is renamed Clariden Finanz AG after the name of the Zurich street on which its head office is located: Claridenstrasse.

1970: SKA and White, Weld & Co. Inc., New York, found WW Trust, Zug; SKA integrates Clariden Finanz AG into this holding company.

1973: Clariden Finanz AG is given bank status and becomes Clariden Bank.

1974: SKA is the biggest shareholder in WW Trust. This is now renamed as Société anonyme financière du Crédit Suisse et de White Weld (CS&WW).

1978: Merrill Lynch & Co., the parent company of Merrill Lynch Pierce Fenner & Smith Co., takes over White Weld Holdings Inc. in New York, which has 100% control over White, Weld & Co. Inc., New York. From this point on, SKA's strategic partner in America is the investment bank First Boston Inc., New York, parent company of The First Boston Corporation, New York. CS&WW becomes Financière Crédit Suisse – First Boston (FCSFB).

From 1979: Clariden Bank has established subsidiaries and runs representative offices in Geneva (since 1970), Basel, Olten, Lugano, the Cayman Islands, Singapore, Hong Kong, New York, Guernsey, São Paulo, Buenos Aires, Oslo, London, Bogotá, Mexico City and Santiago de Chile.

1990: Clariden Bank becomes a subsidiary of Leu Holding, an associated company of CS Holding.

1996: Clariden Bank and all of its subsidiaries are consolidated under the umbrella of a new holding company, Clariden Bank Group.

1998: Clariden Bank Group mergers with another of Credit Suisse Group's bank's, Bank Heusser & Cie. AG of Basel, which is henceforth run as a branch and renamed as Clariden Heusser, Basel. Clariden Bank Group employs around 400 staff and generates a profit of Sfr 117 million.

White Weld's rank, volume and market share of global equity and debt capital transactions (1970–1977)

	Equity capital transactions			Dept capital transactions		
	Rank	Volume ($ m)	Market share (%)	Rank	Volume ($ m)	Market share (%)
1970	5	388	5.8	13	768	3.2
1971	8	508	3.5	13	643	2.5
1972	5	874	6.2	13	416	2.0
1973	10	184	2.8	9	772	4.4
1974	18	18	0.6	16	355	1.2
1975	9	166	2.1	12	908	2.4
1976	10	216	2.4	9	1201	3.6
1977	14	126	1.8	10	762	2.6

White Weld (New York)'s image centered on its international focus, and in the early 1970s it considered three strategic options for extending its geographical reach still further[295]:

- Expand business activities, especially towards the Netherlands, Belgium and Germany, in an attempt to become a pan-European group. For this option, White Weld (New York) was prepared to offer SKA an equal 40:40 stake in the founding capital of the new company. The remaining 20% would be reserved for the management.
- Alliance with a large commercial bank, such as First National City Bank (which changed its name in 1976 to Citibank), mainly in order to develop

Part Two: Strategic Pillars

On the pulse of the global financial markets: Wall Street, New York. Photos taken in 1997.

The subsidiaries of Société anonyme financière du Crédit Suisse et de White Weld (1974–1978)

- CSWW, London (Euroissues business)
- Banque Française de Dépôts et de Titres, Paris (commercial bank)
- Clariden Bank, Zurich/Geneva (investment advice and asset management)
- Forinvest, Paris (financial analysis)
- Sodefi Holding AG, Zug (acquisition, management and sale of participations)
- Valeurs White Weld SA, Geneva (issue of options on and trading in precious metals and commodities, etc.)
- White Weld Asia Ltd., Hong Kong/Tokyo (merchant bank)
- White Weld Securities Ltd., London (Eurobond trading)
- WW Finance SA, Geneva (short and medium-term Eurofinancing)
- WW Services AG, Zurich (accountancy and administration)

Minority interests
- Banco de Investimento do Brasil, Rio de Janeiro (investment bank)
- Sumitomo & East Asia Ltd., Hong Kong (merchant bank)
- Sumitomo White Weld Ltd., Zug/London (merchant bank)
- White Weld Holdings Inc., New York, with White, Weld & Co., Inc., New York (investment bank)

medium-term business and to offer customers a broader range of services (i.e. the entire range of maturities as well as business with public and private-sector, national and international partners).
- Tie-up with a London merchant bank.

Meanwhile, SKA's main expectation of more intense cooperation with White Weld (New York) was that this would facilitate a rapid strengthening and consolidation of its position in international underwriting business. Since SKA also wanted to act as lead manager in domestic US business, rather than just content itself with the role of second-line underwriter, the model established by the UBS-DB Corporation would not suffice. This meant that the prerequisite for closer cooperation with White Weld (New York) was that WW Trust would first have to become an operational arm of SKA.

SKA's influence increases

At the start of 1974, SKA strengthened its participation in WW Trust by carrying out a capital increase of about Sfr 39 million, raising WW Trust's equity capital to Sfr 117 million. Following this capital increase, the ownership structure looked like this: SKA 40.9% (previously 19.9%), White Weld (New York) 29.2% (previously 43.9%), the Swiss private Ludwig-Institut for cancer research 12.6% (previously 18.9%), members of the executive board and other shareholders 17.3% (unchanged).[296] The conditions attached to SKA's commitment were as follows:

- SKA is the largest shareholder in CS&WW, with a minimum stake of 25%.
- 'Credit Suisse' appears first in the names of the group companies.
- SKA and White Weld (New York) exploit their respective potential customer bases to the full.

Where SKA had previously taken a rather passive role in WW Trust, regarding its commitment primarily as a financial one, it was now able to exercise a

From left to right: John C. G. Stancliffe, president of the executive board of White, Weld & Co. Ltd.; Robert L. Genillard, chairman of the board of directors and president of the executive board of WW Trust; John F. Cattier, vice chairman of the board of directors of WW Trust. Photo taken around 1970.

greater influence over business policy. This change was also made apparent in WW Trust's new name: Société anonyme financière du Crédit Suisse et de White Weld (CS&WW). The group's most important unit, White, Weld & Co. Ltd. in London, was also given a new name: Credit Suisse White Weld Ltd. (CSWW). CSWW was active as a manager and underwriter of public Euroissues and private placements, an arranger of Eurosyndicate loans, international corporate mergers and corporate acquisitions, and as a trader of dollar-denominated deposit certificates.

CS&WW's purpose was defined as: 'Acquiring, holding, managing, selling or otherwise disposing over financial participations in other companies (especially banking, financial, insurance, securities and real estate companies, or companies involved in the extraction and trading of raw materials); financing and financial transactions of all types; underwriting, placement and distribution of, and participation in, securities issues of all types; acquiring, holding, managing, selling or otherwise disposing over such securities or any other assets of a material or immaterial nature. Providing services for individuals, companies and public-sector bodies, particularly services in the area of corporate or public-sector finance and asset management.'[297]

SKA further benefited from the fact that, except in underwriting business, the collaboration with White Weld also extended to the United Kingdom, France, Brazil and the Far East, where CS&WW had already established itself via its subsidiary companies.

Along with White Weld (New York) and CSWW, other institutions, including SG Warburg, Deutsche Bank, Kuhn Loeb, NM Rothschild, Banca Commerciale Italiana, Paribas, Hambros Bank, Morgan Stanley, and later SBV and SBG, also recognized the potential of the Euromarket. Initially, however, there was a great deal of uncertainty about the future of the first ever truly international capital market, so it was important that internationally renowned bankers like Siegmund Warburg (SG Warburg), Hermann J. Abs (Deutsche Bank), Jocelyn Hambro (Hambros Bank) and Jacob Rothschild (NM Rothschild) gave their backing to the idea of the Euromarket. The principal key to the market's success, however, was the fact that the new ideas could be translated into innovative products. The creative – and for this era still very young – partners and staff of White Weld (New York) and CSWW played a leading role here. No other financial services group initiated or co-developed as many products as White Weld (New York) and CSWW. White Weld (New York) and CSWW were the first to issue a Eurodollar bond, which was soon followed by a convertible Eurobond. They also underwrote a straight bond for a European company and issued London Certificates of Deposit before anyone else.[298]

Following the injection of capital by SKA, CSWW quickly rose to become the leading institution in Eurobond business. It introduced innovations such as bonds denominated in special drawing rights, floating rate notes and Euro-convertible notes, lending the Euro-underwriting business significant momentum in the process. While Deutsche Bank could take advantage of its size and assume a particularly strong position in D-mark issuing business (which in 1977 accounted for 26% of the total volume of all internationally syndicated Eurobonds), CSWW was market leader for Eurodollar bonds. Although there was no Euromarket in Swiss francs, between 1973 and 1977 CSWW was number two in the ranking list of lead managers for all Eurobonds, behind Deutsche Bank but ahead of SG Warburg and Morgan Stanley.

Rank, volume and market share of the main banks in Eurobond business (1963–1977)

	1963–1967			1968–1972			1973–1977		
	Rank	Volume ($ m)	Market share (%)	Rank	Volume ($ m)	Market share (%)	Rank	Volume ($ m)	Market share (%)
White Weld	8	215	4.5	3	941	5.4			
CSWW							2	3379	7.2
Deutsche Bank	1	665	14.0	1	2163	12.3	1	6505	13.8
SG Warburg	3	394	8.3	4	925	5.3	3	3104	6.6
Morgan Stanley	5	350	7.4	2	1771	10.1	4	2876	6.1
Kuhn Loeb	2	420	8.8	6	800	4.6			
Dresdner Bank				5	912	5.2	7	2008	4.3
SBG							6	2113	4.5

In 1974 the new CS&WW used most of the proceeds of the equity issue by WW Trust to purchase a 29.6% stake in White Weld (New York)'s newly created parent company White Weld Holdings Inc. of New York.[299] Robert L. Genillard, Partner at White Weld (New York) and chairman of the board of directors of CS&WW, explained the alliance with SKA as follows: 'We'd had a long historical relationship with Credit Suisse and felt that, of the three big Swiss banks, they were the most investment-banking minded.'[300] However, the union with SKA was also forced upon White Weld (New York) to a certain extent by the difficult situation it found itself in at that time. In 1973 White Weld had sustained heavy losses from two large underwriting projects; the firm's relocation to larger premises in 1972 had also led to a massive deterioration in its cost structure. Finally the investment bank fell victim to the poor performance of the stock market in 1973. White Weld (New York)'s activities in block trading and in the over-the-counter market for insurance shares, which it had conducted as a market maker, proved to be a particularly burdensome load on the bank's finances.

As CS&WW's largest shareholder, SKA insisted that White Weld (New York) work more closely with it in the international arena. Its main concern was that the two institutions should coordinate and expand their respective customer bases. SKA preserved its full freedom to do what it wanted in commercial and general banking business, while White Weld (New York) was obliged to hold such business back for SKA. Although the USA and Switzerland were expressly excluded from the arrangement with White Weld (New York), SKA still profited from activities in the US market thanks to the fact that its stake in CS&WW also made it indirectly the biggest shareholder in the parent company, White Weld (New York). SKA worked at expanding its position in the US market primarily because it expected capital markets business to shift more towards the USA once

The goal that SKA aimed to achieve with CS&WW was to strengthen its position in international underwriting business and in investment banking. If it had decided to pursue this aim on its own, the road would have been much longer and harder.

Major international partnerships at the start of the 1970s

- EBIC Group (European Banks International Corporation), formed in 1970 by Amsterdam-Rotterdam Bank, Deutsche Bank, Midland Bank and Société Générale de Banque (Belgium); augmented in 1971 by Creditanstalt-Bankverein and Société Générale (France) and in 1973 by Banca Commerciale Italiana.
- Orion Group, formed in 1970 by Chase Manhattan Bank, National Westminster, Royal Bank of Canada and Westdeutsche Landesbank Girozentrale; augmented in 1971 by Credito Italiano and Mitsubishi Bank.
- Europartners Group, formed in 1970 by Commerzbank and Crédit Lyonnais; augmented in 1971 by Banco di Roma and in 1973 by Banco Hispano Americano.
- ABECOR Group (Associated Banks of Europe Corporation), formed in 1971 by Algemene Bank Nederland, Banque de Bruxelles, Bayerische Hypotheken- und Wechsel-Bank and Dresdner Bank; augmented in 1974 by Barclays Bank, Banca Nazionale del Lavoro and Banque Nationale de Paris; and in 1978 by Banque Internationale à Luxembourg and Österreichische Länderbank.

In the early 1970s, international business was regarded as extremely vulnerable, especially because of the liquidity risks on the Euromarkets.

the country's authorities removed their capital controls. On top of this, if it wanted to do business with the petrodollar billions, SKA needed a global network of relations, a powerful international organization and a substantial capacity to place securities. Its stake in CS&WW, allied with White Weld (New York)'s contacts in industry, allowed SKA to fulfill these conditions.[301]

Aiming to make its corporate finance business even more efficient, in 1974 SKA created a competence center at its head office in Zurich, which offered 'finance concepts', 'going-publics', 'venture capital', 'participation financing', and 'company acquisitions and mergers'. By bringing all these services, previously spread across several departments, together the bank was able to deploy its capabilities more effectively.

Joint ventures with international major banks

If SKA wanted to offer its international clientele a comprehensive service, it had to go down one of two paths: it could either enter into partnerships or set up joint ventures with other institutions. Both forms of cooperation would help the bank gain entry to important financial centers, and in both cases, the costs and risks involved could be shared.

In the early 1970s, the Swiss major banks SKA, SBV and SBG (or Credit Suisse, Swiss Bank Corporation and Union Bank of Switzerland, as they were known internationally) were confronted with the fact that foreign major banks were increasingly working together in international groupings. However, owing to concerns about the structural weaknesses and cumbersome decision-making mechanisms that characterized these large conglomerates, the Swiss banks decided to forego such arrangements, instead agreeing to follow a uniform, coordinated policy.

The three banks put together a declaration of intent in which they agreed that they should not join the above-mentioned 'banking groups…, which aim to focus their international business activities on the joint organization or on their partner banks according to general preferences, and to afford these banks a certain exclusivity. […] However cross-border agreements or "joint ventures" that relate to more narrowly defined areas of business or specific territories are not affected by this declaration of intent.'[302]

Instead of joining in with so-called 'club banking', therefore, SKA took part in a series of joint ventures. At the beginning of 1970 it worked with the major UK and US banks Baring Brothers, Chemical Bank and Northern Trust Company of Chicago to found London Multinational Bank Ltd. ('Multibank').[303] Then at the end of 1972 it set up SoGen-Swiss International Corporation ('SoGen-Swiss') in New York together with the other European major banks Société Générale, Société Alsacienne de Banque, Société Générale de Banque, Sofina (Belgium) and Amsterdam-Rotterdam Bank.

Multibank's main activities were medium-term Eurocredit business and international placements, though it also took part in the underwriting of international public issues. However, as SKA set up more and more of its own offices to handle Eurocredit business – as when it converted its London representative office into a branch in 1972, for instance – this participation became less and less significant. In March 1974 SKA increased its stake in the White Weld Group, which, as mentioned earlier, now ranked among the leading institutions in international underwriting. The other founding members of Multibank took similar courses and by the end of 1976 the decision was made that the best solution for all concerned would be for a joint-stock bank to take over Multibank. In August 1977 the US Federal Reserve Board (Fed) approved Chemical Bank's plan to acquire Multibank, allowing the other partners to sell their stakes to Chemical Bank.

At the beginning of 1972, Société Générale asked SKA whether it would be willing to merge together SoGen International Corporation, founded in New York in 1968, with Swissam, established in 1939, to form a new company in which other top European institutions could also participate. Subsequently it became apparent that two other international underwriting heavyweights, Amsterdam-Rotterdam Bank (Amro-Bank) and Société Générale de Banque (in cooperation with Sofina) would welcome a partnership of this type. The purpose of the new company was to engage in domestic US underwriting business and associated activities (securities trading, placement business and the full range of corporate finance activities). However, negotiations proved difficult and rather unpleasant for SKA inasmuch as the other banks were determined that SKA 'would have to pay to enter the inner sanctum of the 'bachelors' club' [i.e. the EBIC group]'.[304] The partners agreed that in future they would direct all relevant securities business to the newly created company, though SKA made it clear that it would continue to manage its US securities portfolios – as it had so far – through Swissam, as well as taking care of the related payments business. Against this background, the subsidiary company Swiss American Securities Inc. (SASI) was established. Additional agreements had to be concluded between the banks involved in order to prevent the three members of the EBIC group (Amro-Bank, Société Générale de Banque and Société Générale) acquiring a majority stake in the new company. Such a majority arrangement – which could have been created because of the EBIC's existing stake in the European-American Banking Corporation and the European-American Bank & Trust Corporation, its two most significant joint ventures in the USA – would have been prohibited under US legislation. Once SKA had taken over the role of main shareholder, the new company could begin operations under its name of SoGen-Swiss International Corporation on 1 July 1973.[305]

From this point on, the business that SKA did in cooperation with White Weld (New York) had to be agreed with its SoGen-Swiss partners. This did not cause any difficulties, however, because SKA was not obliged to route its US business to White Weld (New York). The agreement with White Weld (New York) related exclusively to Euro-issues business, international investment banking, and merchant banking, provided this was not of a commercial nature.

In underwriting business, the partners involved can only bring their full combined weight to bear on the market if all activities are rigorously coordinated and openly discussed. This was the case when SoGen-Swiss first started

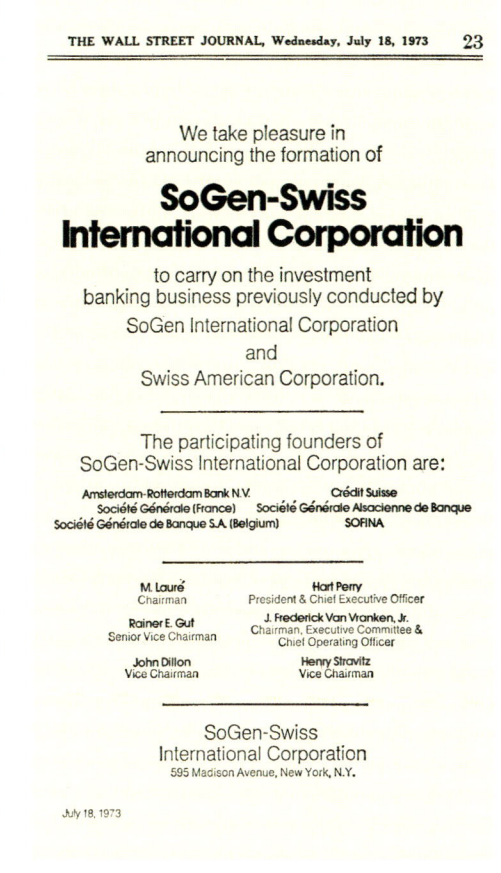

SoGen-Swiss International Corporation advertises its opening in the *Wall Street Journal* of 18 July 1973.

In November 1982 SKA, via its SASI subsidiary, becomes the first Swiss bank to gain a seat on the New York Stock Exchange. The imposing stock exchange building designed by George Post was opened in 1903. Photo taken in 1999.

'It all began in Zurich at 11 a.m. on April 4, 1978, when the telephone rang for Rainer Gut, chairman of Credit Suisse...' (*International Herald Tribune*, 29 November 1978).

up, but things changed relatively soon. Up until 1977 SoGen-Swiss had managed to post a profit every year, but in 1978, the negative price trend on the US stock market led to a loss of Sfr 10.5 million. Given that the company only had total assets of Sfr 74.9 million and equity capital of Sfr 11.4 million, this came as a heavy blow, and the SoGen-Swiss partner banks searched for ways of at least using the loss for tax purposes. Eventually the banks decided in 1978 to merge SoGen-Swiss with the profitable SASI. SKA held a 75% stake in the new SASI (90% of voting rights), Amro-Bank held 12.5% (5% of voting rights), Société Générale de Banque 7.5% (3% of voting rights) and Sofina 5% (2% of voting rights). In November 1982, SASI was admitted as a member of the New York Stock Exchange, making SKA the first Swiss bank to own a subsidiary with a seat on the NYSE.

Other major European banks also began to find that joint ventures and partnerships were becoming less useful. These banks had become better acquainted with international business and realized that it was increasingly important for them to maintain their own presence in the world's key financial centers.

Alliance with First Boston

The late 1970s brought difficulties for the entire investment banking industry. The landscape was being changed by corporate takeovers such as the purchase of Kuhn Loeb by Lehman Brothers, Shield Model Roland by Bache Halsey Stuart (both in 1977) and Reynolds by Dean Witter (1978). Inflation, growing government deficits and uncertainty about the strength of the dollar contributed to the trend.

Against this background, talks about a merger were held between White Weld and Merrill Lynch. SKA was willing to discuss a possible cooperation between CS&WW and Merrill Lynch as long as two important conditions were met: SKA had to remain the principal shareholder in CS&WW's successor company, and, furthermore, it had to be given the option after the merger of buying White Weld's 31% stake in CS&WW from Merrill Lynch. This second condition was designed as insurance in case the cooperation between Merrill Lynch and CS&WW failed to materialize.

SKA and Merrill Lynch agreed to devote a maximum of three weeks to an intensive and constructive examination of cooperation opportunities. In the end SKA decided that Merrill Lynch's complex international organization would make cooperation too difficult, and the talks were broken off by mutual agreement. On 12 May 1978, SKA exercised its option and purchased the remaining 31% of CS&WW's equity capital from Merrill Lynch for Sfr 47.5 million. Together with its existing stake, which had grown in the meantime to 44.8%, the bank now held a majority participation in CS&WW of 76%.

Once Merrill Lynch had taken over White Weld for approximately $50 million in one of the biggest mergers seen thus far on Wall Street, SKA had to review its strategy for US business. Should it go for internal, organic growth, or external growth? In response to this core question, SKA decided that it would be best to work with an established investment bank; it had seen that the only way to carve out a leading position within a split banking system without outside help was to invest a disproportionately large amount of money and effort. The decision to go for external growth was also encouraged by the success of CSWW, which had developed into a significant London investment bank with an outstanding track record. Having established this platform, it was time to attempt the great leap into the ranks of the top international investment banks.

This is the first ever work of research into banking history to make an analysis of the long-term performance of individual investment banks. It documents global equity and debt underwriting (1970–1999), as well as global high-yield securities business and M&A business (1980–1999). The data includes business volumes, league table positions, market share and the number of transactions executed by the top 20 firms each year.[306]

The choice is made

The beauty contest could begin. John A. Craven, chairman of the board of directors and chief executive officer of CSWW in London, and John F. Cattier, chairman of the board of directors of CS&WW, proposed a merger with Dillon Read. Michael von Clemm, vice chairman of the CS&WW executive board, was of the opinion that the bank should only consider one of the five leading 'bulge-bracket' firms on Wall Street. Dillon Read was an excellent firm with a first-rate customer base, but its position in the international league tables was little better than White Weld's. Brief negotiations were held with Dillon Read later on, but SKA's top management ultimately concurred with the view that it should concentrate primarily on the 'bulge-bracket' banks.

Rank, volume and market share of Dillon Read and First Boston in global equity and debt capital transactions (1970–1977)

	Dillon Read						First Boston					
	Equity capital transactions			Dept capital transactions			Equity capital transactions			Dept capital transactions		
	Rank	Volume ($ m)	Market share (%)	Rank	Volume ($ m)	Market share (%)	Rank	Volume ($ m)	Market share (%)	Rank	Volume ($ m)	Market share (%)
1970	14	180	2.7	10	922	3.9	2	462	6.9	1	4070	17.0
1971	23	194	1.3	12	685	2.7	6	566	3.9	1	4268	16.7
1972	15	246	1.7	15	376	1.8	4	894	6.3	1	3808	18.1
1973	13	121	1.8	14	324	1.8	6	567	8.6	2	2138	12.1
1974	n.a.	n.a.	n.a.	10	715	2.5	2	473	16.6	2	4294	14.8
1975	8	260	3.3	11	1342	3.5	3	1281	16.1	3	4309	11.2
1976	15	90	1.0	8	1237	3.7	3	925	10.4	3	4438	13.4
1977	15	123	1.8	9	769	2.6	4	517	7.5	3	3336	11.3

the global force in investment banking

At this time there were five bulge-bracket investment banks: Merrill Lynch, Morgan Stanley, Salomon Brothers, Goldman Sachs and First Boston. All of these renowned firms, apart from Goldman Sachs, got in touch with SKA's head office in Zurich. The decisive issue for SKA was the extent to which the potential partner would participate in the new company that would have to be set up. Once again, SKA's basic conditions were that it had to have control over the new company and that 'Credit Suisse' would again appear at the start of the new company's name. It soon became clear that First Boston would be the ideal partner for SKA in every respect.

In the meantime it had become known that the International Banking Act would be coming into force in the USA in 1978. The Glass-Steagall Act already

Since 1993, the London branch of Credit Suisse First Boston has been located at One Cabot Square in Canary Wharf, the new business district in the city's Docklands. Photo taken in 1993.

stipulated that commercial banks and investment banks had to operate separately, but the International Banking Act would for the first time extend the Glass-Steagall restrictions (no securities business, full banking activities in only one US state) to foreign banks. However the 'grandfathering' clause would ensure that rights already granted could be maintained. Time was of the essence, because the new legislation was due to be approved on 26 July 1978. Thereafter, other European banks would not be in a position to follow SKA's example.

In the second half of the 1970s, First Boston had had to fight not only against the ups and downs of the market, but also with internal tensions, which soon began to have a deleterious effect on the company's profitability. First Boston's business operations were focused mainly on the US market, but now it saw an opportunity to build up its standing in Europe. SKA could contribute its position as one of the seven triple-A banks in the world, its capital strength and its extensive international business operations. CSWW saw that a partnership would deliver a larger sales market thanks to First Boston's excellent client list. A combination of SKA, First Boston and CSWW would have topped the league tables in 1977: first place in bond underwriting on the international market, first place on the Eurobond market, first place on the Eurodollar bond market, first place for foreign public bond issues in the USA (the 'Yankee Bond' market).[307]

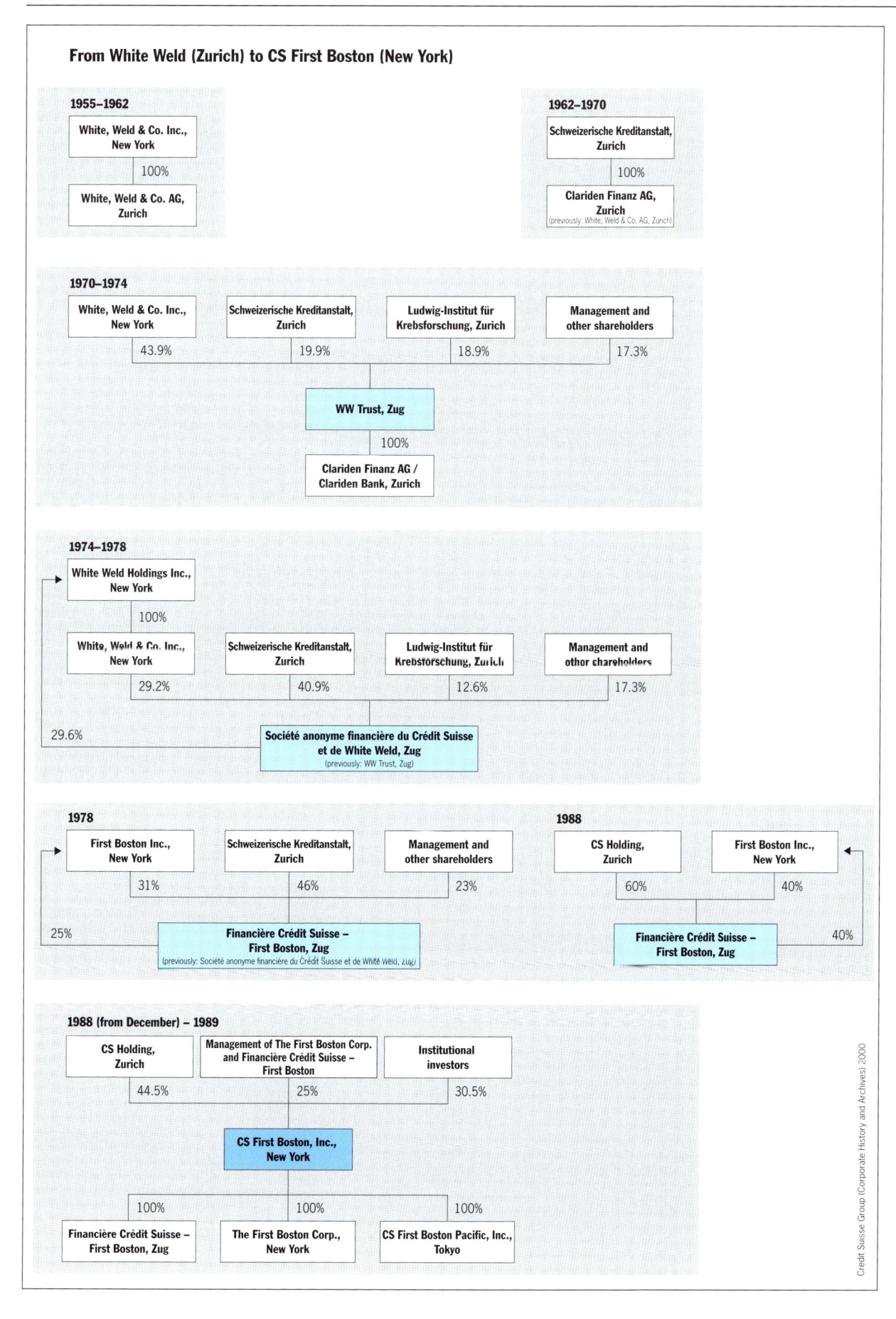

From White Weld (Zurich) to CS First Boston (New York)

1955–1962
- White, Weld & Co. Inc., New York — 100% → White, Weld & Co. AG, Zurich

1962–1970
- Schweizerische Kreditanstalt, Zurich — 100% → Clariden Finanz AG, Zurich (previously: White, Weld & Co. AG, Zurich)

1970–1974
- White, Weld & Co. Inc., New York — 43.9%
- Schweizerische Kreditanstalt, Zurich — 19.9%
- Ludwig-Institut für Krebsforschung, Zurich — 18.9%
- Management and other shareholders — 17.3%
- → WW Trust, Zug — 100% → Clariden Finanz AG / Clariden Bank, Zurich

1974–1978
- White Weld Holdings Inc., New York — 100% → White, Weld & Co. Inc., New York
- White, Weld & Co. Inc., New York — 29.2%
- Schweizerische Kreditanstalt, Zurich — 40.9%
- Ludwig-Institut für Krebsforschung, Zurich — 12.6%
- Management and other shareholders — 17.3%
- White Weld Holdings Inc. — 29.6%
- → Société anonyme financière du Crédit Suisse et de White Weld, Zug (previously: WW Trust, Zug)

1978
- First Boston Inc., New York — 31%
- Schweizerische Kreditanstalt, Zurich — 46%
- Management and other shareholders — 23%
- First Boston Inc. — 25%
- → Financière Crédit Suisse – First Boston, Zug (previously: Société anonyme financière du Crédit Suisse et de White Weld, Zug)

1988
- CS Holding, Zurich — 60%
- First Boston Inc., New York — 40%
- First Boston Inc. — 40%
- → Financière Crédit Suisse – First Boston, Zug

1988 (from December) – 1989
- CS Holding, Zurich — 44.5%
- Management of The First Boston Corp. and Financière Crédit Suisse – First Boston — 25%
- Institutional investors — 30.5%
- → CS First Boston, Inc., New York
  - 100% → Financière Crédit Suisse – First Boston, Zug
  - 100% → The First Boston Corp., New York
  - 100% → CS First Boston Pacific, Inc., Tokyo

Credit Suisse Group (Corporate History and Archives) 2000

Credit Suisse First Boston's London trading floor. Photo taken around 1993.

The contract with First Boston Inc., New York, was signed on 26 July 1978 and came into effect on 25 August 1978. According to the agreement, First Boston Inc. would take on the 31% stake in CS&WW that SKA had acquired, and CS&WW would take over about 25% of the capital of First Boston Inc., New York, the parent company of The First Boston Corp., New York. The agreement also allowed both firms to increase their respective minority stakes at a later date in order to ensure parity of interests.

Organizational arrangements

CS&WW and its London subsidiary CSWW were renamed as Financière Crédit Suisse – First Boston (FCSFB) and Credit Suisse First Boston Ltd. (CSFB) respectively. FCSFB was entered in the commercial register of the Canton Zug on 14 September 1978. The official purpose of the new company can be summarized as follows:

- Acquisition, management, sale, etc., of financial participations in other companies
- Execution of financings and financial transactions of all types
- Underwriting, placement, acquisition, management and sale of securities of all types
- Provision of services for individuals, companies and public institutions

At this time, regional financial markets were still to a large extent separate from one another, which is why the partners decided to divide up all of their activities according to geographical criteria: SKA was responsible for the Swiss

---

Federal Banking Law

'Under the International Banking Act of 1978, as amended (the "IBA"), a foreign bank having a branch located in the United States such as Credit Suisse is not generally permitted to engage in non-banking operations in the United States or to own or control, directly or indirectly, 5% or more of the outstanding voting shares of a company engaged in non-banking operations in the United States (such as First Boston) without first receiving the approval of the Federal Reserve Board. Such approval could not be obtained for a company engaged in First Boston's activities. However, the interest of a foreign bank in a non-banking company at the time the IBA was enacted in 1978 was grandfathered on the conditions that such foreign bank engage in the future essentially in only those activities in which such foreign bank was engaged, directly or indirectly through an affiliate, on July 26, 1978, the effective date of the IBA, and not make acquisitions of non-banking businesses after that date.'[308]

'In this regard, the Federal Reserve Board has indicated that the activity grandfathered under the First Sentence is investment banking, which includes underwriting and dealing and trading in all types of securities, including asset-backed securities, asset management, brokerage, interest rate and currency swaps, and other derivative products and foreign exchange. The Federal Reserve Board has also stated that the Company may continue to make investments in the equity of other companies in connection with the conduct of its investment banking business provided that such investments, when aggregated with the investments of its affiliates, including CS Holding, do not exceed 25% of the voting shares of the stock of a company and are not made for the purpose of exercising, nor result in the exercise of, operational control of any company.

Following consummation of the Issuance, in order to preserve CS Holding's grandfather rights under the First Sentence, the Company will be permitted in the United States to engage only in investment banking activities and expand its United States businesses only through internal growth. The Company will be prohibited in the future from making any acquisitions in the United States of going concerns, regardless of the business in which such concerns may be engaged. Foreign acquisitions, however, will be permissible and the Company's foreign investment banking activities will not be affected.'[309]

*Extracts from the report on the
IFR AWARDS 1974–1999,
IFR 25th ANNIVERSARY, 1974–1999*

CREDIT SUISSE FIRST BOSTON
Best Bank of the past 25 years

CREDIT SUISSE FIRST BOSTON
Best Bond House of the past 25 years

'In many ways a full-service US investment bank, a London-based capital markets franchise and a Swiss universal bank would appear to make poor bed fellows. But although the relationship was at times tortuous, it did give the firms a global reach. Today, CSFB has the most balanced business mix (between the US and Europe) of the bulge-bracket firms, employs roughly the same number of people on both sides of the Atlantic, and derives roughly the same amount of profit from each location. [...]'

'A great factor in CSFB's success has been the nature of Credit Suisse's involvement. Rainer Gut, chairman of Credit Suisse Group, is the man credited with the early vision. Crucially, the bank has always operated at arm's length. [...] Gut was and is cognizant of the destructive force of culture clashes, and was careful not to stifle the creative forces needed to make his project work. [...]'

'CSFB [...] was an avowedly capital markets operation. It eschewed the advisory game and focused purely on originating, selling and trading new-issue bonds. To win mandates, it developed a raw, aggressive and gregarious culture that is now the stuff of legend. [...] CSFB almost single-handedly created the Euromarkets model. It was a genuine pioneer, regularly introducing firsts, whether in the form of new structures or new borrowers, pushing the envelope on size, and opening up the market to new pockets of demand. [...] The firm has brought more debut borrowers to the market than anyone else – not just sovereigns and supranationals, but in the financial, high-yield and emerging market sectors, too. [...]'

'First Boston did the first unbundling of residential mortgages to create the first-ever mortgage-backed security. It also led the first-ever 144a deal, the first public asset-backed security, the first oil-indexed note, and the first taxable municipal note. [...] As influential as CSFB was in the evolution of the Eurobond market in the 1980s, First Boston was equally influential in the creation of the modern M&A market, with Bruce Wasserstein and Joe Perella at the helm of the group. Its M&A deal roster since the late 1970s is awesome.'

capital market, and First Boston for looking after customers in North and South America and Australia; finally, FCSFB was responsible for Europe and the rest of the world.

One of FCSFB's strategic aims was not to be dependent on any single currency or on issuers from any single country, but instead to broaden its customer base still further through collaboration with the two parent companies, First Boston and SKA. This approach allowed the optimum play of synergies. First Boston, for example, could carry out an M&A deal[310] and finance it through syndicated bonds in which SKA took part. This meant that CSFB was in a position to carry out a number of debt and equity transactions that would ultimately bring additional earnings for other parts of the group, too. Transferring most international investment banking business to CSFB or First Boston meant that the commercial banking and investment banking cultures remained separate from one another, though both banks could continue to profit from each other's activities. As a consequence SKA in combination with First Boston and CSFB commanded a very high position in the key league tables – e.g. for Euromarkets business, global equity and debt financing and M&A business – throughout the 1980s. M&A business in particular became increasingly important and in 1988 the volume of announced M&A transactions came to $480 billion: five times the figure recorded in 1983. Together with Goldman Sachs and Morgan Stanley, First Boston controlled the lion's share of this market. Throughout the eighties (except in 1980, 1982, 1984 and 1989) these firms consistently occupied the top three spots in the M&A league tables, though in various different orders.

'The combined potential of First Boston und Credit Suisse First Boston will offer large-scale customers – investors and borrowers – a previously unheard-of breadth of services. A leading firm on the United States capital market, the biggest capital market in the world, has now teamed up with a leading group on the international capital market, the fastest growing capital market in the world' (George L. Shinn, chairman and chief executive officer of First Boston, *Finanz-Revue*, 1 September 1978).

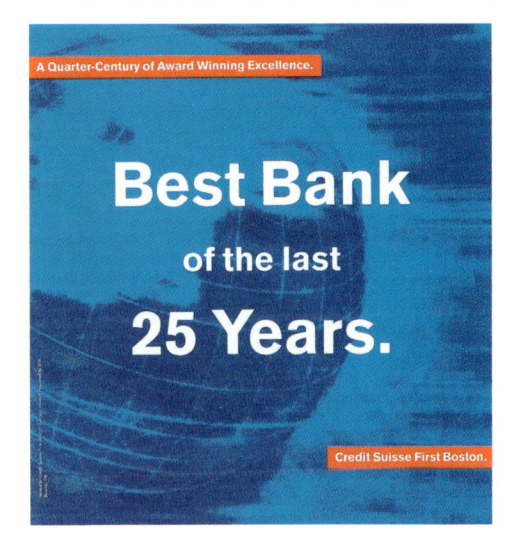

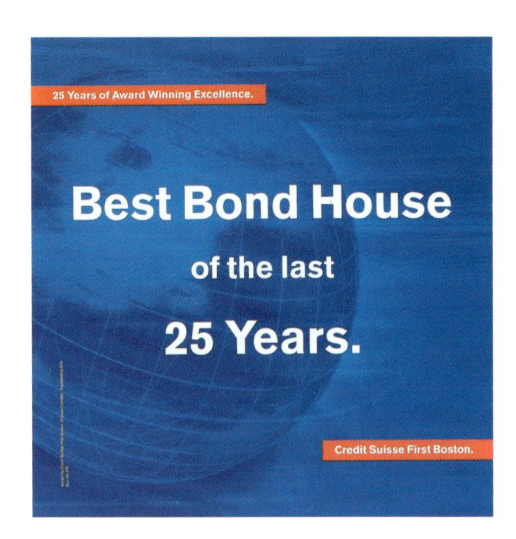

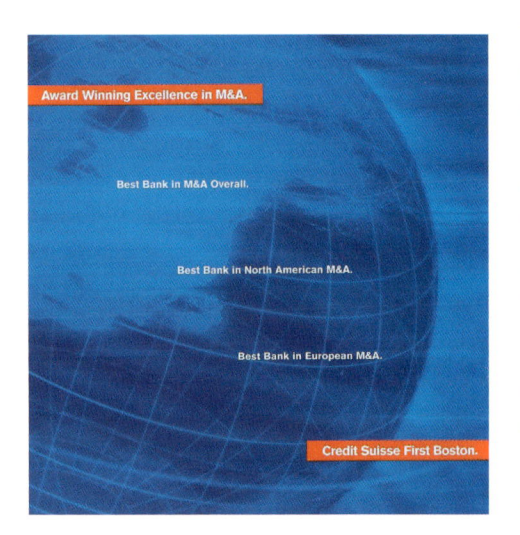

By the middle of the 1980s, SKA's operations in the USA were based on four main pillars:

- Its own branches and representative offices in Atlanta, Chicago, Houston, Los Angeles, New York, Miami and San Francisco
- Swiss American Securities Inc. (SASI), New York
- The First Boston Corp., New York
- Various external brokers and banks

SASI acted as a 'service station', managing US securities for SKA and its customers. It also took care of just about all of SKA group's stock market orders for the United States and continued to work for a whole range of US brokers, offering stock market clearing and custodian services. First Boston gave SKA constant and direct access to the latest market information as well as to new ideas, which in an ever-more volatile and increasingly Americanized financial world provided an indispensable basis for decision-making. SKA and SASI used other firms for specialist research and underwriting services. Because their lines of business and their business philosophies were sufficiently distinct from one another, there was essentially no conflict of interest between SASI, SKA and First Boston.

Geographical and cultural differences

Following the exchange of shareholdings between SKA, FCSFB and First Boston in 1978, and after a few teething problems, the arrangement worked well for all the partners. Two factors were responsible for the initial losses made by FCSFB. Firstly, internal tensions caused by the cultural differences between Swiss and US/British banking, but also problems between London and New York, temporarily impacted on business operations. Secondly, business suffered from the volatile exchange rates that characterized the period. Subsequently, however, profitability improved enormously and FCSFB was able to build up its market position continuously. Despite the unstable conditions on the international capital markets, in 1979 CSFB reached the number one spot in the Eurobond league table for the first time, coming ahead of Deutsche Bank, Merrill Lynch and SG Warburg.[311] This performance was further reflected in the company's total assets, which had fallen more than 30% to Sfr 766 million in 1978, but which had reached Sfr 1.362 billion by the end of 1980.

Thanks to FCSFB, its subsidiaries and First Boston, SKA enjoyed a leading position in international underwriting business throughout the 1980s. Its main competitors were a number of US banks, followed by Deutsche Bank, Japan's Nomura Securities and SG Warburg of the UK. From 1984 to 1990 (with the exception of 1988), for example, SKA together with First Boston and CSFB was the number one for global equity financing every year. The CSFB group carved out a market share of around 11–15% in this area.

It was a similar story in global debt financing. In this much larger market by volume (difference between size of markets 1984–1990: factor 10) the bank's share was around 9–15% and the CSFB group was amongst the top three institutions in every year between 1984 and 1990.

In 1987, CSFB lost its mantle as the king of the Eurobond market. It still held a leading position, with market shares of between 7% and 8% in 1987 and 1988, but this was only enough to put it in second place behind Nomura Securities, which enjoyed a share of between 10% and 13%.[312] This development was hardly surprising when one remembers that at that time the Japanese bank was one of the most important players on the international capital market and that the yen was the preferred currency for debt issues. It was cheaper to raise money in yen and then to exchange it into other currencies by arbitrage. This meant that Japanese banks, especially the 'big four' Nomura Securities, Daiwa Securities, Yamaichi Securities and Nikko Securities, were able to increase their underwriting volumes massively. However, these investment banks did most of their business in yen and remained relatively weak in other currencies. For example, 95% of the transactions carried out by Nomura, the biggest Japanese investment bank, were either denominated in yen or carried out on behalf of Japanese customers.[313] At the end of the 1990s, however, it became clear that this failure to diversify on the part of the Japanese investment banks brought risks with it: Sanyo Securities and Yamaichi filed for bankruptcy in 1997; Nikko had to enter into a joint venture with Salomon Smith Barney that was virtually tantamount to a takeover; finally, Nomura and Daiwa had to form alliances with the Industrial Bank of Japan and Sumitomo Bank and continually lost market share.

Consolidation of global activities

The situation became more difficult for the CSFB group in 1988, prompting the decision by SKA, First Boston and FCSFB to merge First Boston and FCSFB's worldwide activities. Shareholdings in the two companies were also restructured. The whole industry was beset with problems in the second half of the 1980s, but the difficulties at First Boston were more pronounced than elsewhere. Management problems and bloodletting amongst the key staff made the situation even worse. The highest-profile disturbance of all was the departure of 'Wall Street's merger kings', Bruce Wasserstein and Joseph Perella in 1988.[314] They left partly because of disagreements about the strategic direction taken by First Boston. Wasserstein and Perella wanted to expand merchant banking operations and thus strengthen their position within the firm. However, still haunted by the stock market crash of 1987, First Boston's top management was determined to reduce their exposure to this risky area of business.

Ultimately, the changes made in 1988 resulted in equal measure from organizational and structural factors. In 1978 the geographical split between the three partners' activities had been thoroughly appropriate, since financial markets in different regions of the world still maintained quite separate existences back then. But now the increasing globalization, interlinkage and liberalization of the capital, equity and foreign exchange markets was leading to structural problems. The three partners were increasingly divided by rivalries, operational overlaps, differences of opinion over how to divide up earnings, and conflicts of

'In the 1980s we were told we would take over the world. Now we wonder whether any Japanese company can really stay a serious global player' (Senior employee of a Japanese investment bank, *Financial Times*, 29 January 1999).

The leading figures at CS First Boston (from left to right): Allen D. Wheat, John M. Hennessy, Archibald Cox jr., Hans-Jörg Rudloff, Rainer E. Gut. Photo taken around 1993.

Business Day

The New York Times

Swiss Bank Turns Aggressive

Crédit Suisse Builds Its Investment Bank

By STEVEN GREENHOUSE

Special to The New York Times

ZURICH — Rainer E. Gut, the chairman of Crédit Suisse, Switzerland's third-largest bank, squirmed the other day when a visitor described his bank as aggressive.

Like any Swiss banker, Mr. Gut prefers to think of himself as conservative and risk-averse, yet in pursuing his vision he has clearly come down on the side of aggressiveness.

As the world's financial markets have become more interconnected, Mr. Gut, a 56-year-old Swiss native, has moved far more quickly than other European bankers to build a global investment banking firm. Indeed, the new firm he helped create, CS First Boston Inc., with operations in North America, Asia and Europe, is called by some analysts the first truly global investment bank.

Tapping Asia's Growth

CS First Boston's two prominent subsidiaries are the First Boston Corporation, based in New York, and Financière Crédit Suisse-First Boston, the hugely successful investment banking joint venture based in London. The new firm's third, and newest, pillar is CS First Boston Pacific, which aims to tap into Asia's explosive growth as a financial market.

"You have to move with the times," said Mr. Gut, a relaxed, charcoal-haired man, from his austere third-floor office overlooking Zurich's bustling Paradeplatz.

For Mr. Gut, moving with the times meant last October's decision to set up CS First Boston, 44.5 percent owned by Crédit Suisse and 25 percent by its employees. Mr. Gut is chairman of the new firm, which is negotiating with several large institutions, including Japanese ones, to buy the other 30.5 percent from an interim investor, the Olayan Group of Saudi Arabia.

"We want to create an organization in partnership with others that allows us to be a major player in every area of financing activity around the globe," said Mr. Gut, who leads a company that has $79 billion in assets and that offers commercial, retail and investment banking services in Switzerland.

John M. Hennessy, deputy chairman of CS First Boston, said the new firm, with three independently run subsidiaries, will make it easier to place issues like the $1.5 billion that CS First Boston is raising for Rupert Murdoch's new company, Media Partners Inc.

"We now have three legs in the

Continued on Page D2

Rainer E. Gut, chairman of Crédit Suisse, in Zurich, the third largest bank in Switzerland, which is building an investment banking firm with divisions in Europe, the United States and Asia.

Crédit Suisse's Recent Performance

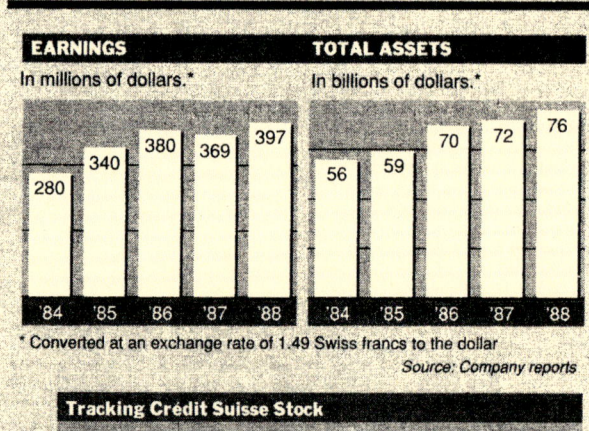

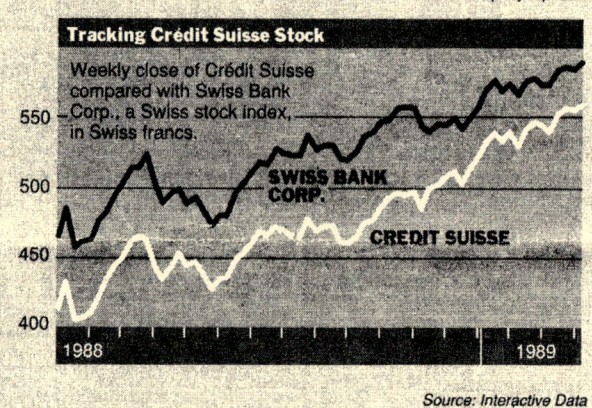

EARNINGS — In millions of dollars.*

'84	'85	'86	'87	'88
280	340	380	369	397

TOTAL ASSETS — In billions of dollars.*

'84	'85	'86	'87	'88
56	59	70	72	76

*Converted at an exchange rate of 1.49 Swiss francs to the dollar

Source: Company reports

Tracking Crédit Suisse Stock

Weekly close of Crédit Suisse compared with Swiss Bank Corp., a Swiss stock index, in Swiss francs.

Source: Interactive Data

The New York Times/April 10, 1989

The New York Times, 10 April 1989.

authority. Worst of all, these divisions were beginning to irritate clients more and more.

Finally, at the end of 1988, the partners agreed that the three group companies should be merged and run under the name of CS First Boston, Inc., with a head office in New York. Within this new structure, Financière Crédit Suisse – First Boston was responsible for Europe, the Middle East, and Africa; The First Boston Corp. looked after North and Latin America; and the new unit CS First Boston Pacific, Inc., Tokyo, would be responsible for the Far East and Australia. It was also decided that CS Holding would own 44.5% of this new group's equity capital, 25% would go to senior employees of the new CS First Boston[315] and institutional investors would hold 30.5%. Legislation prevented SKA from holding a stake of more than 45%. The bank had all the more reason to be grateful that in 1982 a proposal for amendment to the International Banking Act of 1978 had paved the way for SKA to take a direct stake in First Boston. Previously SKA had only held 24% of First Boston through its 60% participation in FCSFB. The 30.5% stake originally held by Suleyman S. Olayan was later placed with various institutional investors including Metropolitan Life Insurance Company, Crescent Diversified Ltd., The Mitsui Trust & Banking Co. and other investors from the Far East, the USA and Europe.

For tax reasons, and because the 'management partnership' form of participation was only permissible in the USA, SKA chose New York as the new holding company's domicile. This also meant that the company could go to the US capital market for finance – an enormously important advantage since this new, globally active operation could not have been sustained on an exclusively Swiss funding basis. In any case, the existing laws on equity capital coverage made it virtually impossible for a Swiss bank to take over a larger foreign institution. Furthermore, the International Banking Act dictated that CS Holding could not account for more than 20% of the board of directors or 20% of the executive board.[316]

One of the challenges faced by the new holding company was that the traditions and mentality of a Swiss full-service bank were not easy to transfer to a different country. CS Holding decided to tackle this problem by establishing subsidiaries and giving them both room for maneuver and autonomy. However, this strategy did not always have the desired effect, since many difficulties resulted not from the regulatory format but from the diversity of corporate cultures.

The importance of a US base

Because SKA had been so early to establish itself in financial centers outside Switzerland, it now found itself in a unique position in the international arena. The following charts[317] show how important it is for a bank to be firmly anchored in the USA if it wants to survive as an international financial services provider. SKA took steps to establish such a firm base earlier than the other internationally active major banks, and since other non-US banks were not able to enjoy the advantages of the 'grandfathering' clause, SKA's rivals were not able to catch up with it for a long time. Although SKA was repeatedly faced by problems, its strategy proved to be the right one: no other major European bank was able to keep pace with the development of US investment banking.

By contrast with SKA, both of the other Swiss major banks, SBV and SBG, did not enter into comparable co-operative partnerships for a long time, committing themselves instead to building up international investment banking operations under their own steam. Only in 1985 did this strategy change, when SBG purchased the London broker Phillips & Drew. SBV waited even longer, but then scored a series of impressive successes by taking over O'Connor of Chicago (1989), SG Warburg of London (1995) and the US firm Dillon Read (1997). Despite strengthening their hands in the Anglo-American banking industry in this way, both SBG and SBV had let a gap open up that they had still not been able to close by the end of the 1990s. The other internationally active major banks also missed the boat by waiting too long to acquire a suitable investment bank; and because M&A business was for a long time only conducted in the USA, the negative consequences of this delay were unavoidable. Against this background it was inevitable that CS Holding, thanks to CS First Boston, would occupy a prominent place in the ranking lists for this key area of business.

Measured by volume of M&A transactions, Credit Suisse First Boston's lead over its main non-US competitors narrowed in the final quarter of 1999. The bank still managed to complete no less than 335 M&A transactions – around 100 more than Deutsche Bank and 50 more than UBS (Warburg Dillon Read) – confirming its strong market presence; but it did not take part in any of the four largest M&A transactions in the fourth quarter of 1999. These accounted for a transaction volume totaling $440 billion, equivalent to an eighth of all transactions in the previous year. Nevertheless, Credit Suisse First Boston retained its outstanding position in M&A business.

New opportunities and risks

At the end of the 1980s Hans-Jörg Rudloff, then the chairman of the board of directors and president of the executive board of FCSFB, advocated investment in Eastern Europe on account of the political changes that were taking place in the region. Once the Iron Curtain had been swept aside, demand for privatizations, joint ventures and strategic partnerships grew rapidly. Within a very short period of time, CS First Boston had set up offices in Budapest (end of 1990), Prague (spring 1991), Warsaw (also spring 1991) and Moscow (end of 1991). Countries, industries and companies were analyzed minutely and their market potential assessed. Eastern European bankers were brought to London for further training so that they would have the know-how required for the transition to a free market economy. By the summer of 1998 this strategy was bearing fruit to the extent that Credit Suisse First Boston had become one of the most important foreign banks in Eastern Europe. But then Russia was hit by economic chaos; Credit Suisse First Boston suffered massive losses as a result, and sharply reduced its commitments in the country.

Transaction volumes in global underwriting business: Credit Suisse First Boston compared with non-US banks (1987–1999)

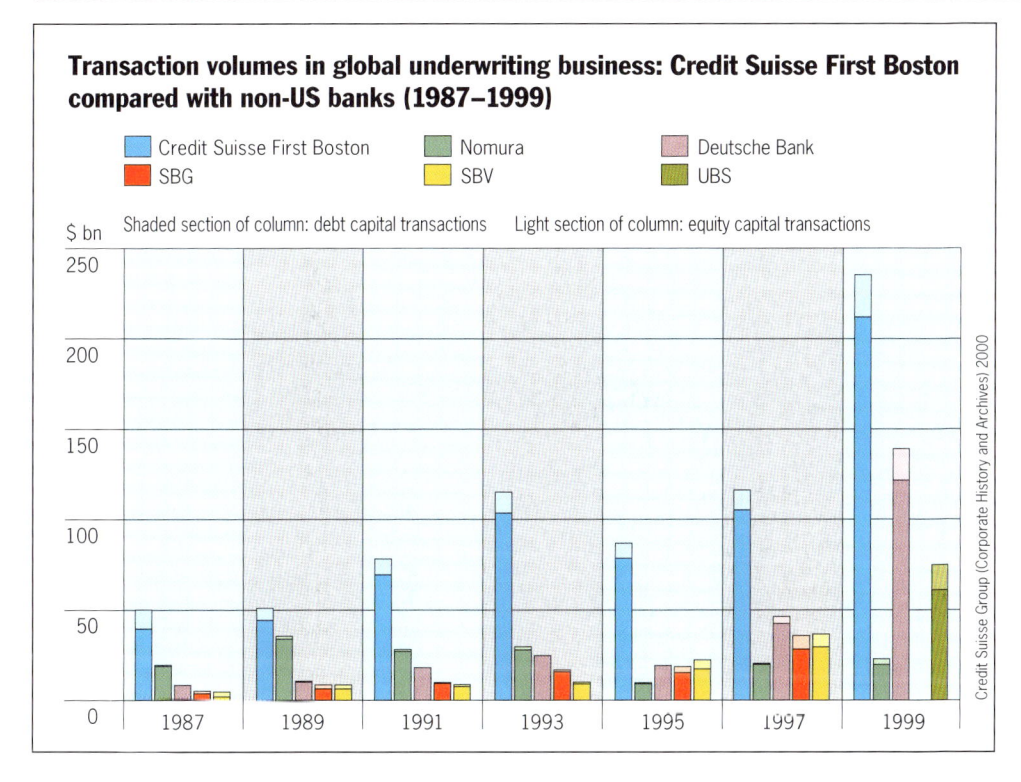

Legend: Credit Suisse First Boston, Nomura, Deutsche Bank, SBG, SBV, UBS

Shaded section of column: debt capital transactions   Light section of column: equity capital transactions

Transaction volumes in global underwriting business: Credit Suisse First Boston compared with the world's other major investment banks (1984–1999)

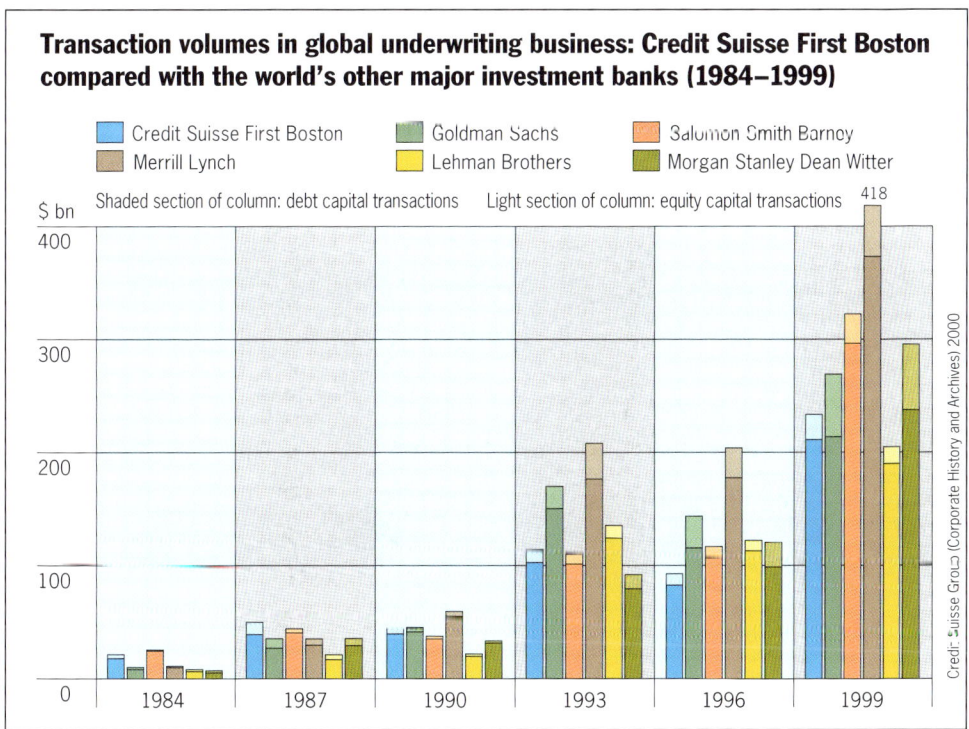

Legend: Credit Suisse First Boston, Goldman Sachs, Salomon Smith Barney, Merrill Lynch, Lehman Brothers, Morgan Stanley Dean Witter

Shaded section of column: debt capital transactions   Light section of column: equity capital transactions

Alongside the work it was doing to fill the geographical holes in its business, in 1990 CS First Boston closed a gap in its product portfolio with the creation of Credit Suisse Financial Products (CSFP), London. Allen D. Wheat, who had recently left his position as chairman of Bankers Trust Int. Ltd. in London to join CS First Boston, headed the new company's executive board, managing a team of specialists brought over from Bankers Trust. CSFP developed derivative prod-

Transaction volumes in global M&A business: Credit Suisse First Boston compared with non-US banks (1987–1999)

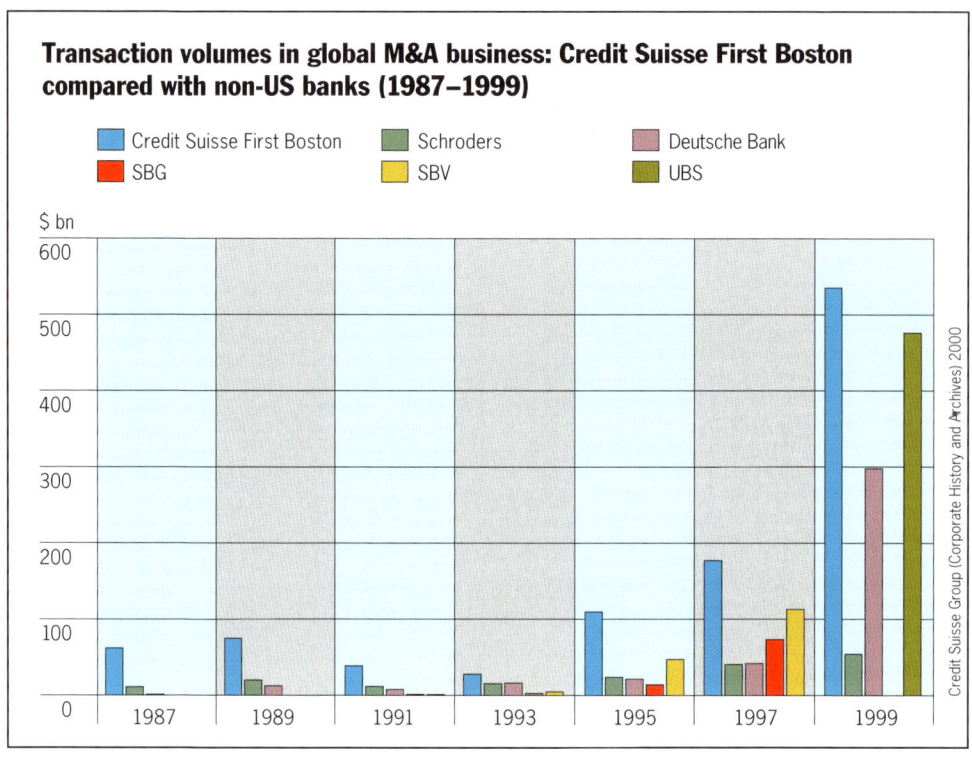

- Credit Suisse First Boston
- SBG
- Schroders
- SBV
- Deutsche Bank
- UBS

Credit Suisse Group (Corporate History and Archives) 2000

Transaction volumes in global M&A business: Credit Suisse First Boston compared with the world's other major investment banks (1984–1999)

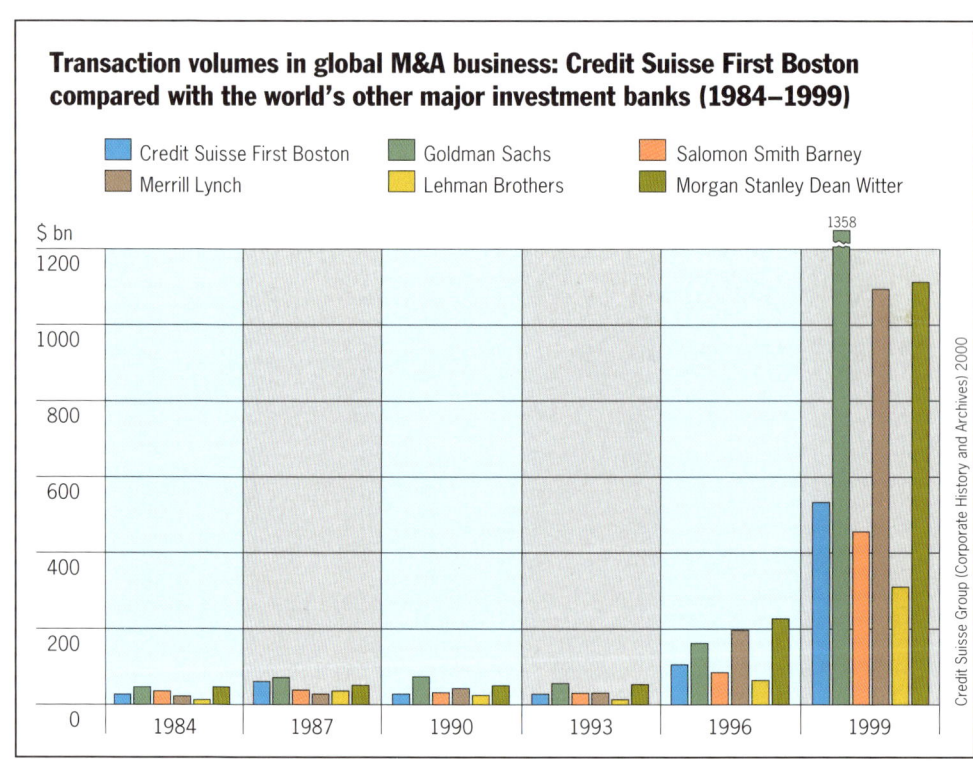

- Credit Suisse First Boston
- Merrill Lynch
- Goldman Sachs
- Lehman Brothers
- Salomon Smith Barney
- Morgan Stanley Dean Witter

Credit Suisse Group (Corporate History and Archives) 2000

Global investment banking **195**

Credit Suisse Financial Products specialise exclusively in risk management products and services.
Like all true specialists, because that's all we do, we do it best.

No.12: Simon Moore, Glass Designer

CREDIT SUISSE | Financial Products

True Specialists

London +44 171 888 2000 / New York +1 212 325 5900 / Zurich +41 1 332 6400 /
Tokyo +813 5403 4000 / Hong Kong +852 2101 6357
Or please contact us at Credit Suisse First Boston in Sydney +61 2 394 4400

A subsidiary of CREDIT SUISSE FIRST BOSTON

In 1998, Credit Suisse Financial Products used photographs of original works of art to advertise its highly specialized products. Pictured here: works by Simon Moore.

CS First Boston established itself in Eastern Europe in the early 1990s, setting up branches in (clockwise from top left) Prague, Moscow, Budapest and Warsaw.

ucts and made them available to group companies and their customers. Thanks to the support of SKA, with its strong balance sheet, its worldwide network of customers and its commercial banking contacts, the new company managed to break even extraordinarily quickly. By the end of 1990, only about six months

Global business with high-yield US securities:
CS First Boston and the other major investment banks (1983–1990)

	CS First Boston			Drexel Burnham Lambert			Merrill Lynch		
	Rank	Volume ($ m)	Market share (%)	Rank	Volume ($ m)	Market share (%)	Rank	Volume ($ m)	Market share (%)
1983	13	75	1.2	1	3 228	53.4	2	559	9.2
1984	8	269	2.6	1	6 411	62.6	6	312	3.0
1985	6	455	3.6	1	7 670	60.3	8	277	2.2
1986	6	1372	4.9	1	12 856	46.4	2	2622	9.5
1987	2	3645	13.7	1	11 197	42.2	4	3129	11.8
1988	2	3673	14.6	1	11 034	43.7	4	1997	7.9
1989	5	1815	7.7	1	9 009	38.8	3	2253	9.6
1990	–	–	–	–	–	–	3	100	14.5

	Goldman Sachs			Morgan Stanley			Shearson Lehman Hutton		
	Rank	Volume ($ m)	Market share (%)	Rank	Volume ($ m)	Market share (%)	Rank	Volume ($ m)	Market share (%)
1983	10	113	1.9	–	–	–	6	202	3.4
1984	10	99	1.0	7	306	3.0	5	335	3.3
1985	5	497	3.9	3	846	6.6	4	759	6.0
1986	7	1072	3.9	4	1707	6.2	5	1689	6.1
1987	5	1925	7.3	3	3560	13.4	10	257	1.0
1988	7	805	3.2	3	2358	9.3	12	350	1.4
1989	4	2195	9.3	2	2350	10.0	6	1714	7.3
1990	1	250	36.4	–	–	–	–	–	–

People

Rainer Gut's Wall Street headache

BY KEVIN MUEHRING AND BETH SELBY

There was only one item of any importance on the agenda as the nine members of CS First Boston's executive committee gathered in New York last March: How was the group's First Boston Corp. unit going to deal with its $257 million bridge loan to Robert Campeau's bankrupt Federated Department Stores? It was senior management's first meeting since the collapse of Drexel Burnham Lambert the month before, and CS First Boston was struggling to quash market rumors of trouble with the bridge and with First Boston's junk bond exposure in the wake of Drexel's demise.

All eyes fixed on William Mayer, who in January had been unceremoniously relieved of his duties as CEO of First Boston and put in charge of a new merchant bank created mainly to look after the firm's shaky bridge loans. Despite the gloom that pervaded the boardroom on the 44th floor of Park Avenue Plaza, Mayer was remarkably upbeat. "We are expecting a good Christmas season [at Federated]," he told the group. His words hung in stony silence as the others stared at him in stunned disbelief. The fate of First Boston, the prestigious bulge-bracket American investment bank whose brains, breeding and bravura style had seemed to define the heady 1980s, now depended on the whims of holiday shoppers — nine months into the future? On the health of the already shell-shocked U.S. retailing sector? "I couldn't *believe* this guy," recalls one of those who had flown in for the meeting. "I thought to myself: 'A good Christmas season? Are you out of your frigging tree?'"

The March meeting was one of dozens held during the next nine months — in New York, London, Zurich, Tokyo and, amid broken August holidays, Spain — that led CS First Boston and its partners at Credit Suisse to conclude that counting on Father Christmas was not the wisest strategy for saving the floundering firm. On Monday, December 10, shareholders approved a two-stage, $1 billion "restructuring" of CS First Boston — parent of First Boston, London-based Euromarket powerhouse Credit Suisse First Boston and CS First Boston Pacific (see page 69). The deal, the product of a volatile mix of First Boston mismanagement, Federal Reserve Board jitters over the prospect of yet another financial crisis and a long-held desire by Swiss shareholders to consolidate control over their Wall Street arm, amounted to the first-ever takeover of a full-line U.S. investment bank by a foreign or domestic bank — in this case, Credit Suisse.

Central to this saga from the beginning has been **Rainer Gut**, chairman of both Credit Suisse and CS Holding. The Swiss banker is not only the architect of last month's bailout of First Boston and of the 1988 modus vivendi — through the agency of CS First Boston — between First Boston and CSFB, but he has also been the guiding force behind what had until recently been an immensely profitable, albeit stormy, twelve-year collaboration among First Boston, CSFB and Credit Suisse.

Gut's efforts to turn the U.S. investment bank around and simultaneously strengthen the global capabilities of CS First Boston will in effect be a referendum on his leadership — and on his firm belief in decentralized management. Above all it will be a trial by ordeal of his vision of CS Holding — under whose universal banking umbrella are Credit Suisse and CS First Boston — as one of a handful of dominant players in the international financial markets of the 1990s. Says Gunter Kaser, who heads the Zurich-based research boutique KKR Swiss International: "We like Mr. Gut's strategy, and I'm sure they will clean up First Boston. But they still have to prove that it will be a successful and profitable company, and you have to ask how they see getting their money back."

Separate cultures

The 58-year-old Gut, described by one American observer as "Europe's most powerful bank chairman," joined the No. 3 Swiss bank in 1973, after having dispensed with a university degree and having left

Credit Suisse's Gut: "We had to have our conditions met. We would not put money in without getting control"

after receiving its license, CSFB had produced an after-tax profit of $14 million. It has been one of the most successful and comprehensive providers of derivative financial products ever since.

At the end of the 1980s, business with high-yield bonds – 'junk bonds' – collapsed.[318] The volume of the market for these high-risk securities had grown at a phenomenal rate to start with, but it did not take long for the first signs of tension to appear. One of the reasons for this was that the US authorities not only stopped financially vulnerable savings banks from investing any more in junk bonds, but also demanded that they reduce their existing holdings. At this point, about an eighth of all outstanding junk bonds were held in the savings banks' portfolios. Illegal activities such as the insider dealing by Ivan Boesky and 'junk bond king' Michael Milken finally caused the market leader in junk bond business Drexel Burnham Lambert, to collapse and disappear from the scene in 1990. Other investment banks, such as Shearson Lehman Hutton, Kidder Peabody and Prudential-Bache Securities also fell into difficulties, forcing their parent companies (respectively American Express, General Electric and Prudential Insurance) to step in and shore them up with additional capital. Similarly, CS Holding had to help out CS First Boston in order to support First Boston.

To the rescue

In the mid-1980s, investment banks had begun to grant bridge loans to allow their customers to carry out leveraged buyouts (LBOs) – typically under the supervision of the lending bank. These bridge loans were refinanced by selling high-yield securities (junk bonds). CS First Boston was very active in LBO financing and the bridge loans business. It increased its exposure to US high-risk paper after 1985 to such an extent that by 1988 it controlled about 15% of the market, helping it to achieve second place in the relevant league table. Following the surprise fall of pack leader Drexel Burnham Lambert and difficulties at other investment houses, the market for US junk bonds collapsed from $25.24 billion (1988) to $0.69 billion (1990). Suddenly the investment banks could not find anyone to buy their long-term junk paper any more, leaving them stuck with their short-term bridge loans. In 1989, for example, CS First Boston was involved in a bridge loan of $257 million to Federated Department Stores, a subsidiary of the Robert Campeau retailing empire. Burdened by excessive debt, the company found itself chronically short of liquidity and at the beginning of 1990 had to seek protection from its creditors (i.e. it had to file for 'Chapter 11').[319] CS First Boston was carrying another $935 million worth of junk bonds on its books issued variously by the mattress manufacturer Ohio Mattress Comp., the holding company of the Jerrico Inc. Fast-Fish restaurant chain, and the well-known US hospital group American Medical International. After creating provisions for these problem loans, the bank's net profit for 1989 was reduced to a mere $11 million.

CS First Boston completed further structural changes in 1990. Massive provisions had to be set aside for investments in illiquid companies, low-value bridge loans and vacant premises. With the rating agencies threatening to downgrade its credit rating, CS First Boston reduced its exposure to bridge loans, but the outbreak of the Gulf Crisis made the situation even more fraught. CS First Boston was now put on the rating agencies' watch lists, and because everyone in the market knew what a predicament the company was in, it was very difficult to sell any bridge loan backed by CS First Boston.

CS Holding had no choice but to step in and rescue its subsidiary. With CS First Boston's reserves under threat, CS Holding took over the whole portfolio of bridge loans, the shares of the distressed companies, and the junk bonds. The total value of these positions was $ 1.139 billion and CS Holding set up a lifeboat company especially for them. By spinning off the bridge loans in this way, an inflow of funds was created and liabilities could be reduced. CS First Boston also received an injection of $ 300 million from CS Holding and $ 15 million from Metropolitan Life. In the wake of these urgent restructuring measures, the company's top management in the USA was replaced and CS First Boston's headcount was reduced by 14% from 6,252 to 5,494. At the end of 1990 CS First Boston showed a loss of $ 587 million and total assets of only $ 38.195 billion, a 17.8% reduction on the previous year.

Thanks to the creation of the lifeboat company and the capital injections, the agencies were able to maintain CS First Boston's rating at its previous level and the situation became calmer. However, in the light of the 'grandfathering' clause, this procedure was not without its complications, since CS Holding certainly did not want to loose its rights completely (as a result of taking too high a stake in the US company). Nevertheless, CS Holding was the only shareholder that could supply First Boston with the capital it needed to survive. In return, and with the permission of the Federal Reserve Board, it gained majority control of the company and now held 64.2% of the capital. This made CS Holding, together with SKA, the first internationally active commercial bank to own a majority stake in a US investment bank. The Fed's approval, granted on 7 November 1990 was not conditional on any significant restrictions with regard to CS First Boston's activities or to the presence of CS Holding appointees on the board of directors. As well as having to give up some investments in the data processing and asset management sectors, CS First Boston now also had to refrain from granting bridge loans; but given the bad experiences the bank had been through, this was in CS Holding's interests anyway. Otherwise, there was a continuation of the restriction limiting the bank's stake in any non-banking US company to a maximum of 25%.[320]

Big Three or Big Four?

Within a very short period at the start of 1993, the heads – and with them many of the staff – of the energy, high-yield securities, fixed interest and M&A departments all left CS First Boston. The underlying reason for the defections was the low level of bonuses compared with those paid by its competitors, but the process was accelerated by the fact that the bank's rivals, especially Merrill Lynch and Morgan Stanley needed experienced investment bankers and were prepared to offer attractive terms to lure them.

Part Two: Strategic Pillars

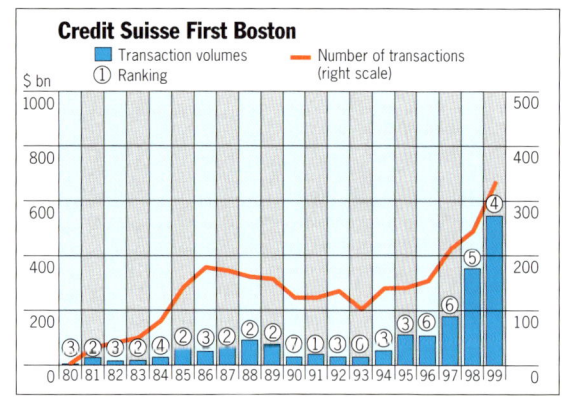

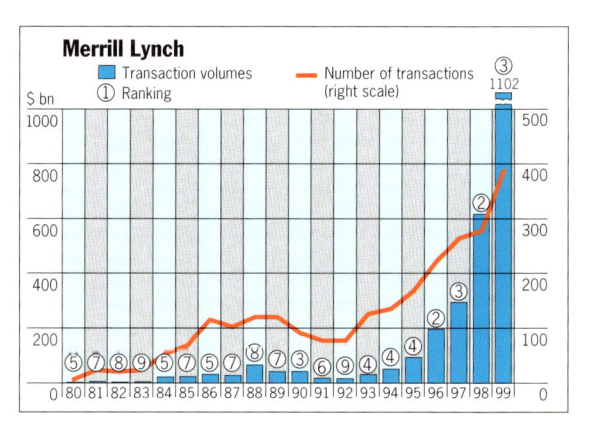

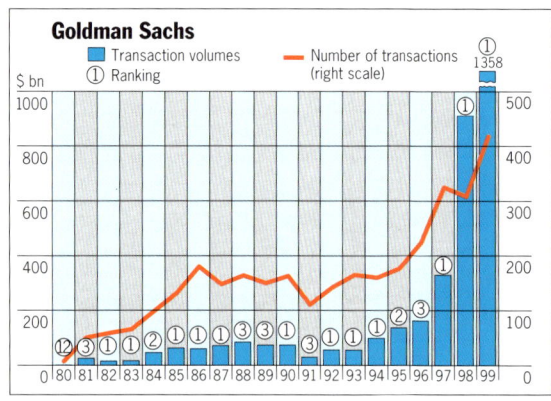

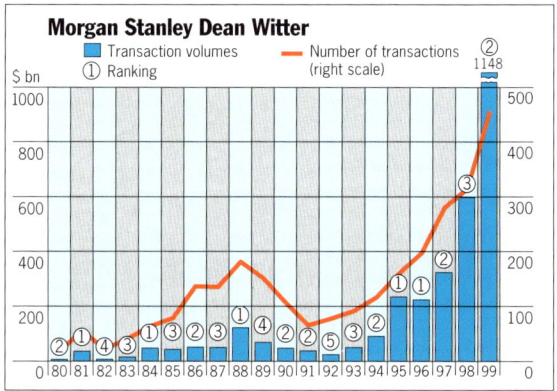

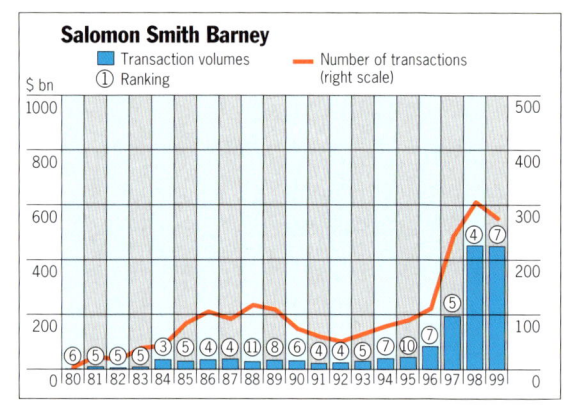

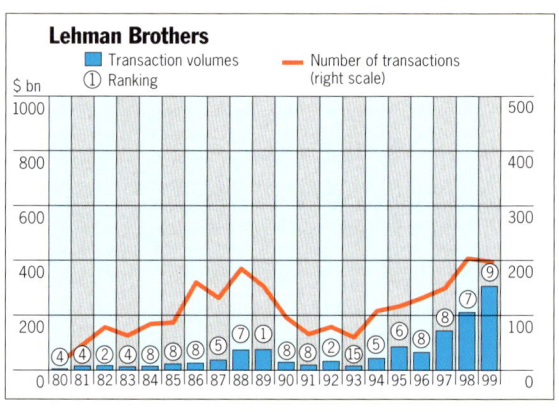

Global M&A business: comparison between the major investment banks (1980–1999)

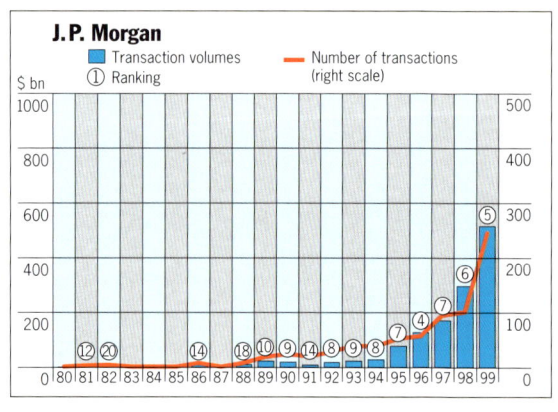

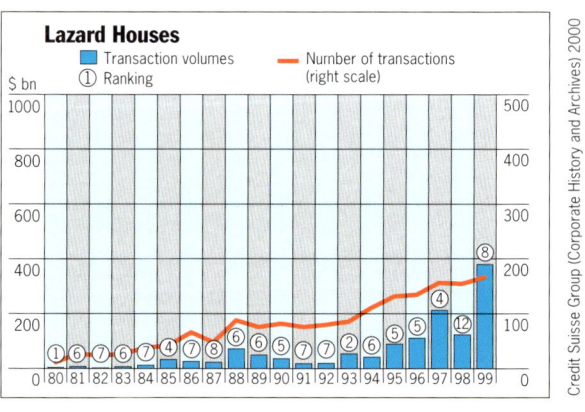

Global investment banking 201

Global underwriting business: comparison between the major investment banks (1980–1999)

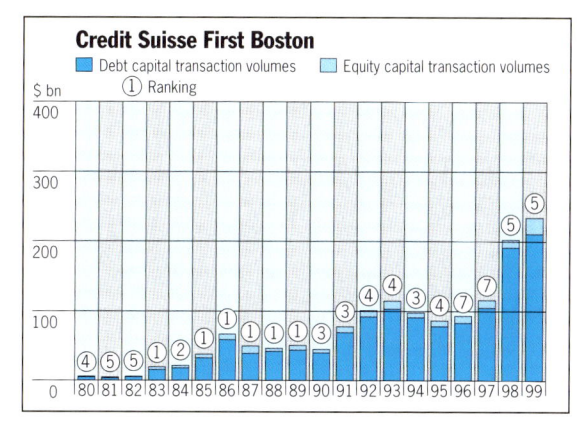

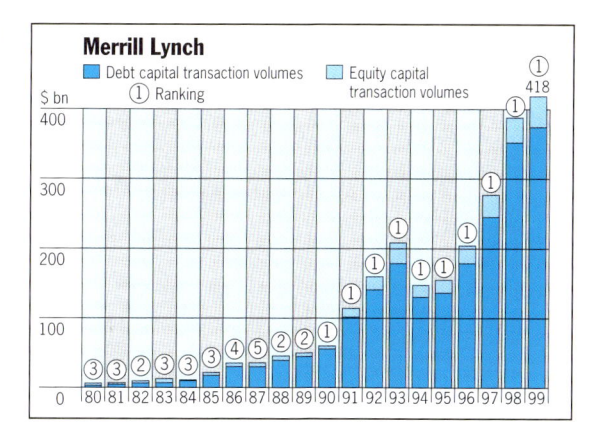

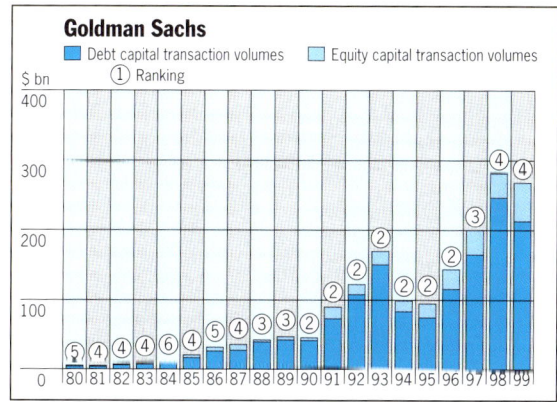

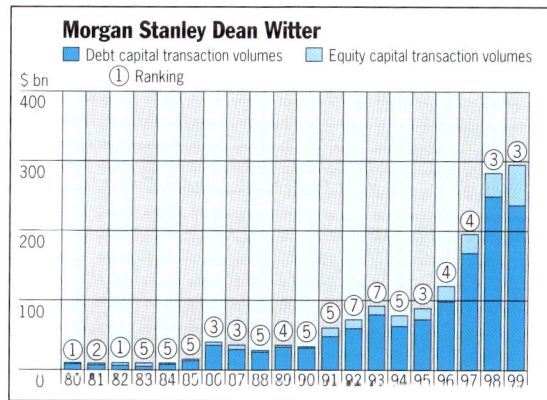

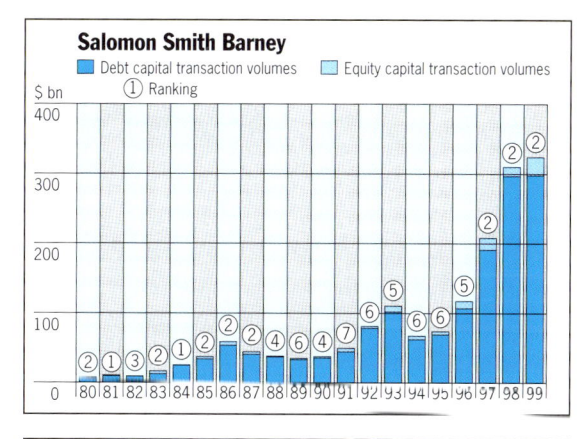

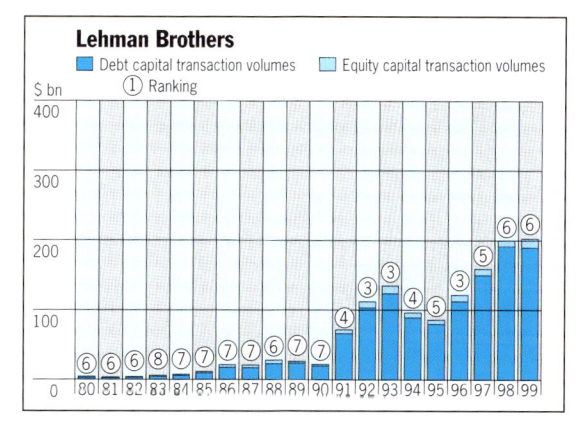

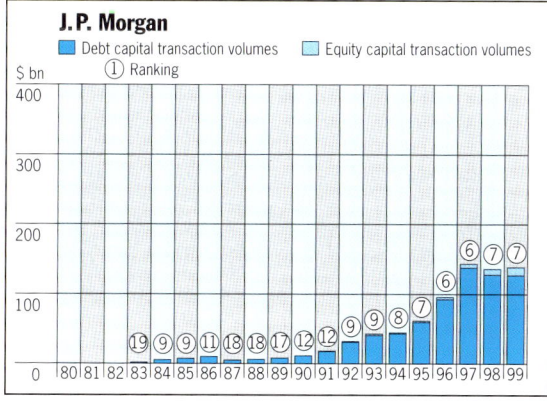

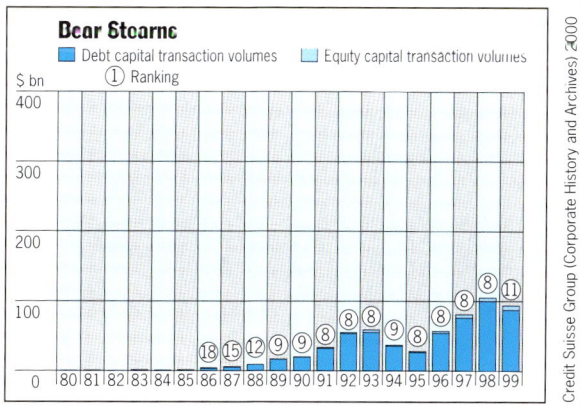

Credit Suisse First Boston's trading floor at Eleven Madison Avenue in New York. Photo taken in 1998.

Consolidation

In September 1993, Allen D. Wheat was appointed chairman and chief operating officer of CS First Boston. He carried out a comprehensive reorganization of the bank, breaking up the group's three geographical units and dividing its operations by product instead. The general view in the industry was that, '… issues like compensation, formal review processes, career planning and management information systems all play to Wheat's strengths. His ability to build team spirit, motivate people and inspire loyalty is well documented.'[321] Over and beyond the restructuring measures, Allen D. Wheat was also determined to strengthen the firm's corporate culture. This required a lot of work since it had been shown in the past that people often only identify with a company if doing so also serves their personal interests.

Despite all the internal difficulties, 1993 saw CS First Boston recording the highest ever earnings in its history. Favorable market conditions helped the bank to post record results and achieve a return on equity higher than direct competitors like J. P. Morgan, Morgan Stanley, Salomon Brothers and Lehman Brothers.[322] By 1994, the situation had deteriorated once more. Turbulence on the international bond markets impacted on profits at all the US securities houses, confirming once again that earnings from investment banking can be very volatile. At this time CS First Boston had less equity capital than its main rivals, meaning that it was not able to engage in proprietary trading to the same extent as the other big-name investment houses – such as Salomon Brothers – which suffered much greater losses as a result.

Even though CS First Boston's equity capital had increased by an annual average of more than 50% over the previous three years, the bank's equity base was still not as solid as it would have liked; this situation was becoming increasingly problematic.[323] If CS First Boston wanted to improve its position in the league tables, it needed more than just a good return on equity. It was clear to the management that action was required.

On top of everything else, Allen D. Wheat had more internal problems to cope with when another batch of employees, mainly bond dealers, jumped ship at the beginning of 1996. Although Wheat had helped to make the compensation system more transparent, it seemed that bonuses were still reason enough to abandon any loyalty to the company.

The creation of Credit Suisse First Boston

In order to achieve lasting success, an investment bank must have three things: highly skilled staff, sufficient capital, and customer relations that promise to bring a lot of profitable business. The creation of the Credit Suisse Group ensured that these three conditions were met: the associated restructuring gave the new Credit Suisse First Boston a greater number of skilled specialist staff as well as a significant boost to its overall capital. Compared with 1991, for example, by 1 January 1997, its headcount had risen by about 8,500 to more than 12,000, while its total assets had increased tenfold to $ 304.4 billion and its equity capital had gone up eightfold to $ 6.55 billion. The figures increased again in 1998 with the acquisition of the leading Brazilian investment bank Banco de Investimentos Garantia, São Paulo, and the takeover of the M&A department as well as the equity underwriting, equity trading and equity research departments of the famous British investment house Barclays De Zoete Wedd (BZW). These acquisitions helped the bank to establish a third home market – after Switzerland and the USA – in the United Kingdom.

Along with the provision of advice on equity and debt finance, M&A is the flagship business within investment banking. The charts on pages 200 and 201 show the most important banks in global M&A business and in global underwriting business over a period of 20 years. The data make it clear just how rapidly these business lines have developed at all the firms concerned. Size seems to have become the only applicable criteria both with regard to the number and the volume of transactions.

The 1980s saw the start of a golden age for M&A business. A favorable tax regime in the USA, the competition authorities' relaxed interpretation of the anti-trust law, the increase in privatization and restructuring activity, as well as the accelerating globalization and deregulation of the financial markets all

'The backbone of the business is a small number of people who you must pay as much as possible, because you need them to protect the franchise. [...] Maybe some people thought they were part of that group, when they were not' (Editorial in *Euromoney*, no. 5, 1996).

helped to usher in the boom years.[324] In 1988 the volume of announced transactions reached what for then was the almost inconceivably large figure of $ 480 billion. Nevertheless, the achievements of the 1980s pale in comparison to the business volumes generated in the late 1990s. In 1998 the total size of announced M&A transactions was 56% higher than in the previous record year of 1997 at more than $ 2.3 trillion. In 1999 worldwide M&A volume, measured by the number of announced transactions, reached about $ 3.5 trillion: 'One day a company is a very big player in its market place, the next day it's on everyone's shopping list. [...] These days you're either the toaster or you're toast.'[325]

In this environment, larger and more diversified financial institutions kept being created.[326] Corporations merged with the aim of expanding their product ranges, broadening their earnings bases, saving costs and improving their distribution channels. The need to achieve critical mass within the global environment will probably ensure that this trend towards consolidation and merging will continue.

The increasing importance of cross-border deals meant that investment banks with a presence in the USA, where M&A business had always been significant, enjoyed an advantage. With deals becoming progressively larger and more complicated, potential customers tended more and more to seek the help of the big 'bulge-bracket' firms. Only the biggest banks were able to offer the required infrastructure and the necessary human capital – bankers, lawyers, industry specialists, analysts and finance specialists who were familiar with local, country-specific and continent-specific practices. And as if this were not already enough, the cost of bonuses, information technology and compliance/risk controls was rocketing, while global competition was leading to narrower margins. The charts on page 200 show that the average volume of M&A transactions at the most important banks has risen continuously in recent years. The consequences of this are not hard to discern: the market share of the giant 'bulge bracket' investment banks became larger and larger at the expense of the somewhat smaller 'major bracket' investment banks.

The trend towards greater and greater size was also apparent in international corporate finance, which proved beneficial above all for companies with strong balance sheets. There were several reasons behind the growing use of the capital markets. M&A business had become so important because it often brought additional business – financial advisory, underwriting, derivatives – in its wake. In addition, mergers, takeovers and privatizations were increasingly being financed through the issue of bonds and equities rather than through more expensive commercial loans. Finally, the trend was also fuelled by low interest rates, strong equity markets and positive prospects for growth. As the charts on page 201 show, underwriting business nevertheless remained a cyclical business, whereas M&A proved to be relatively resistant to cyclical influences.

All of these developments and trends confirm that a top ranking in the league tables is a 'must' for any investment bank that wants to achieve real success. The alternative is to pursue a niche policy and thus becoming a specialized 'investment boutique' – an approach which simply would not fit with Credit

---

The most significant reasons for the sharp rise in mergers at the end of the 1990s

- Deregulation in the financial services and telecommunications sectors
- Consolidation in the pharmaceuticals, engineering and technology sectors (the combination of the tendency towards mega-companies and the trend towards specialization means that mergers are often followed by spin-offs)
- Diversification and broad geographical coverage of products
- Strategic privatizations and restructurings (especially in Europe)
- Demand for improved efficiency (primarily through managing costs)
- Increasing significance of the shareholder value approach

AUGUST 16, 1999

FORTUNE

Is CSFB Now Ready to Play In The Big Leagues?

BY ANDREW SERWER ■ ONE OF THE PERENNIAL TOPICS of discussion on Wall Street is, Will any other firm rise up to challenge the three-headed supremacy of Goldman Sachs, Merrill Lynch, and Morgan Stanley? (Okay, Morgan Stanley Dean Witter.) Increasingly during the past decade, the Big Three have come to dominate the Street simply because they do an awful lot of things awfully well. That's not to say the other guys—DLJ, Lehman, Bear Stearns, Paine Webber, etc.—don't have some great businesses. They do. It's just that they aren't in the same league.

Yes, there are firms with mega-aspirations. Citigroup with Salomon and Smith Barney is formidable, but it's lacking top-tier clout in key areas such as equity underwriting and M&A. Walter Shipley has forged a powerhouse over at Chase, but it's still far from a full-service investment bank. And as for Deutsche Bank, well, let's just say it breaks into the big leagues in the U.S. the day monkeys fly out of my you-know-what. So for my money (and it is my money!), I'm picking another candidate as the most likely to turn the Big Three into the Big Four. I'm talking about CSFB. Yup, Credit Suisse First Boston.

Of course, First Boston once *was* at the top of investment banking. Back in the roaring 1980s, the firm's M&A department, run by ("bid 'em up") Bruce Wasserstein and Joe Perella, was a Wall Street juggernaut. Then in 1989 the firm just about OD'd on some toxic bridge loans and was subsequently 100% absorbed by Credit Suisse in a couple of transactions.

Autonomy for the New York headquarters: *CEO Allen Wheat has hired a slew of topnotch bankers and "redeployed" the firm's loan book.*

But wait a minute. What's so great about CSFB? Isn't it getting spanked by the Japanese government for impeding an investigation? Wasn't there speculation about problems in its real estate lending business? And didn't it get creamed in Russia last year? Yes, yes, and yes. But the Japanese imbroglio turns out to be basically a molehill. Besides, name me a Wall Street firm that *hasn't* been hit by some sort of scandal over the past few years. (What is it with this business, anyway?) Meanwhile, CSFB's real estate exposure has been scaled back. And as for Russia, well, yes, CSFB frittered away huge money there—like $1.2 billion—which wiped out profits last year. But CSFB wasn't alone in losing its shirt on the march to Moscow.

What CSFB does have is a parent with a huge market cap ($52 billion), a significant and growing presence in the U.S. securities markets (far and away the crown jewel of global investment banking), and a topflight international business, particularly in Europe. Perhaps most important, CSFB—which in good times generates about 50% of Credit Suisse's profits—is run with considerable autonomy by Allen Wheat, a veteran U.S. investment banker. That's not to say there aren't turf wars at Credit Suisse. (Please!) It's just that they haven't been crippling, like those at, for instance, Deutsche Bank.

I recently spoke with the press-shy Wheat from CSFB's offices in London, and he talked about his game plan. "Basically, what we have done since 1996 is to take a huge loan book, which had a very low return on assets, and redeploy it into client-oriented businesses." Wheat (a former Bankers Trust derivatives guy, regarded by some as having a pretty sharp pencil) has been doing things like hiring away Frank Quattrone, George Boutros, and the entire technology banking group from Deutsche Bank. (CSFB just brought in DB's health-care bankers too.) Wheat bought Garantia, a giant Brazilian bank, in a transaction that some scoffed at initially but that now looks as if it's panning out. And he picked up the whole of BZW (except for its fixed-income business).

Now I'm not one for paying much mind to league tables—the bankers always massage the figures until they come out No. 1 in *something*—but I can tell you that CSFB has been gaining market share across the board. And this year the firm will even make money! Analysts expect CSFB to earn about $840 million on $7.45 billion in revenue.

So will CSFB ascend to the top ranks of investment banking? It could. Increased globalization helps this bank. Conversely, that means debacles like last year's international meltdown hurt. Wheat has done a credible job of maximizing CSFB's growth (i.e., the hiring of Quattrone et al.). Now he must minimize the firm's black eyes. If he can do that, it's move over, Merrill and Morgan, and get back, Goldman!

Fortune, 16 August 1999.

> The willingness to take risks is not only reflected in the ranking lists and growth rates, but also in setbacks like the enormous losses in Russia (1998) and the withdrawal of CSFP's license in Japan (1999).

Suisse Group's global orientation. 'Is CSFB now ready to play in the big leagues?'[327] is the question that various financial analysts have been asking recently. The consensus view seems to be that Credit Suisse First Boston is the one firm that could be in a position to catch up with the three biggest US investment banks, Morgan Stanley Dean Witter, Goldman Sachs and Merrill Lynch. A look at the league tables over the last few years confirms that Credit Suisse First Boston is undoubtedly the 'pretender to the crown'.[328] As part of Credit Suisse Group, it boasts a solid equity capital base, it is profitable and it is well represented in all the rankings. Finally, Credit Suisse First Boston is one of the few genuinely global investment banks that can claim a strong presence in both the USA and Europe.

The entrance hall of Credit Suisse First Boston's head office at Eleven Madison Avenue in New York. Photo taken in 1998.

Wo immer Sie sind. Was immer Sie tun. Wann immer das ist. Wir sind für Sie da.

Leben Sie Ihr Leben. Und lassen Sie uns an Ihre Sicherheit denken. An Ihre Zukunft. Dafür sind wir da. Vierundzwanzig Stunden am Tag. Telefon 0800 809 809. Heute. Morgen. Übermorgen.

CREDIT SUISSE WINTERTHUR mit CREDIT SUISSE, ein starkes Versicherungs- und Bankteam.

winterthur

Allfinanz

Deregulation, liberalization and globalization brought far-reaching change to the financial markets at the end of the 20th century, rendering traditional categories increasingly irrelevant. The breathtaking advances made in information technology, the creation of the EU internal market and the European Monetary Union paved the way for this change. One of the main features that characterizes today's financial services market is the blurring of the boundaries between different sectors. SKA, and later CS Holding, reacted quickly to the changing situation: the bank developed an Allfinanz strategy as early as 1988, and in 1990 CS Life was created as an insurance company within the CS Holding fold. Then in 1997, a much stronger competitive position was achieved through the merger between Credit Suisse Group and Winterthur. Today, Credit Suisse Group is one of the world's leading Allfinanz conglomerates.

One of the advertisements from Winterthur's 1999 campaign. 'Wherever you are. Whatever you do. Whenever you do it. We are there for you.'

The term 'Allfinanz'

The modern concept of Allfinanz has its origins in the USA of the late 1970s, where terms such as 'integrated financial services', 'one-stop financial shopping' and 'financial supermarket' were used to describe the same concept. The central point was that all the different types of financial services were being offered from under one roof.

In practice the term 'Allfinanz' is used for just about every form of cooperation between banks and insurance companies, from sporadic exchanges of business right up to full blown merging of the two disciplines. Various degrees of integration are thus often subsumed under the catch-all description of Allfinanz, which can be confusing.

In France, Belgium and Southern Europe, the combination of banking and insurance services is also known as 'bancassurance' and 'assurfinance', expressions which emphasize the fact that the main focus is on cross-selling: either selling insurance products over bank counters ('bancassurance') or bank products via an insurance company's distribution network ('assurfinance').

By contrast, the term 'Allfinanz' implies proper integration, comprehensive financial advice, cross-disciplinary products and innovative solutions to customers' problems.

'In the not-too-distant future there will cease to be two separate markets for banking products and insurance products. Instead there will be a single, integrated market for financial services' (Thomas Wellauer, CEO Winterthur, June 1998).

Nowadays it seems that you can read about some new development in the financial world just about every day, whether it is a change in the operating environment, a new partnership agreement or a full blown merger. It is also notable that this process of change involves institutions beyond the traditional banking and insurance sectors. As long as they have the right IT capabilities and customer bases, companies of all types can tap new sources of growth and income by moving into finance of one kind or the other. Thus it is quite common nowadays for car manufacturers or retailers, not to mention the post office, to provide customers with financial services.

Nonetheless, the banks and insurance companies continue to be the major players in the financial services market. Because the barriers to entry into financial business have become much lower, and because the boundaries between the traditional sectors are increasingly permeable, it is not surprising that banks and insurance companies are moving closer together. This convergence marks the path to Allfinanz.[329]

Banks and insurers also face mounting pressure 'from below': they are being forced to adjust their services and structures to the new realities of the market. Independent brokers and sales organizations are positioning themselves as financial advisors, selecting and bundling together products that they think will appeal to their customers, and thus covering the whole range of financial requirements from a single source. This leaves the banking institutions and insurance companies to function merely as product suppliers.

Up to the mid-1980s, banks and insurance companies divided the financial services sector between them. There was hardly any competition between the two different types of company. Quite the opposite in fact: the services of one complemented those of the other.

The rapid transformation of the capital markets has set off a wave of product innovations by the banks and insurers. For both sectors, the decisive change is that they no longer have to sit back and accept the risks associated with their business operations, but can manage this risk actively. Globalized capital markets, new information technology and innovative financial instruments allow the companies to evaluate risk and then to pass this on to the desired extent to the financial markets, i.e. to trade in risk. This opens up interesting new prospects for both banks and insurance companies, rendering their traditional products increasingly substitutable.

Cooperation between a bank and an insurer in the 19th century: Schweizerische Kreditanstalt/Rentenanstalt

Despite the dynamic rise of industry in the first decades of the 19th century, manufacturers usually managed without recourse to debt capital. Firstly, there was still relatively little need for investment, and secondly, yields were very high, meaning that companies tended to be able to finance themselves. Thirdly, the financial institutions of the time were not capable of financing large investments. Financial services did not really get going as an industry in Switzerland until the dawning of the age of railways. Railway construction demanded investment on a hitherto unknown scale. This created new risks, which had to be covered in some way.

At the same time, the industrial sector was consolidating: new technology had made investment in replacement equipment more expensive and had squeezed profit margins. The self-financing model was being stretched to its limits and in order to keep up with the dynamic development of the economy, industrial concerns had to find new sources of capital.

The wave of new financial company start-ups which began at this time was prompted more than anything else by the desire to prevent well-established foreign competitors from snapping up all the lucrative new financing and insurance business.

SKA was a catalyst for Swiss economic development in the second half of the 19th century.

As a provider of capital, SKA helped with the foundation of five insurance companies. From left to right: Schweizerische Lebensversicherungs- und Rentenanstalt (Zurich, 1857), 'Helvetia' Schweizerische Feuerversicherungsgesellschaft (St. Gallen, 1861), Schweizerische Rückversicherungs-Gesellschaft (Zurich, 1863), 'Schweiz' Allgemeine Versicherungs-Aktien-Gesellschaft (Zurich, 1869), 'Zürich' Allgemeine Unfall- und Haftpflicht-Versicherungs-AG (Zurich, 1872).

Johann Conrad Widmer (1818–1903), from Canton Thurgau, came to Zurich in 1851 as the director of the Cantonal Penal Institution. In 1857 he proposed the establishment of Rentenanstalt, which he headed until 1892. Widmer was one of the pioneers of the Swiss insurance industry.

The liberal lawyer and politician Johann Jakob Rüttimann (1813–1876) – member of the Governing Council of Canton Zurich from 1844 to 1857, and member of parliament from 1848 to 1854 as well as from 1862 to 1868 – was also a co-founder of SKA and a member of its first board of directors. It was thanks to his good offices that the close ties between Kreditanstalt and Rentenanstalt first came about in 1857.

'In 1857 SKA decided to provide a guarantee to allow the creation of an institution which would be recognized as a necessity for Switzerland and which would bring economic benefits for our country' (SKA annual report, 1867).

The creation of Rentenanstalt

In 1857, a total of about 20 French, German and British life insurance companies were operating in Switzerland. From an early stage, the Swiss people showed a great predilection for life insurance and pensions (pensions = 'Renten' in German, hence 'Rentenanstalt', which literally means 'pensions institution'). Unfortunately, this meant, 'that every year money flows out to other countries, which could just as easily be kept in Switzerland, if Switzerland had a well funded insurance company of its own'.[330]

The far-reaching change wrought upon Switzerland by the new federal constitution of 1848 created favorable conditions for the development of a Swiss life insurance company. Conrad Widmer, who came from Canton Thurgau, saw the way things were going and together with Zurich's commissioner of finance Johann Jakob Sulzer-Ott planned the foundation of a company that was later to become Schweizerische Lebensversicherungs- und Rentenanstalt (or Swiss Life, as it has come to be known internationally).

Widmer and Sulzer-Ott envisaged a life insurance company built on the principles of mutuality – a plan that relied on the confidence of a large section of the population. Both men agreed on the central requirements for a successful insurance business: firstly, premiums could not be set too high; secondly, policyholders had to be confident that the insurer was financially sound enough to meet its obligations. At that point in time, life insurance providers were faced with the danger that they would lose their financial equilibrium if there were suddenly a disproportionately large number of deaths. Since the creators of the new insurance company insisted on fixed premiums and did not want to have to ask policyholders for extra payments, the company had to offer insurees a reliable additional guarantee over and above the money they had paid in themselves.

The founders first went to Bank Leu to ask whether it would be willing to stand guarantee with its entire equity capital, at that time Sfr 10 million, for the new company's liabilities. In return, Bank Leu would be assigned all of the insurance company's funds to manage, provided it could guarantee a minimum yield of 4% on these funds. Bank Leu refused the offer because it was worried about the possible effects on its liquidity, so the founders considered setting up a joint-stock company in order to obtain the necessary capital for the guarantee. However, a general financial and trade crisis at the time meant that this project, too, came to nothing.

Thanks to the good offices of the then vice chairman of the newly founded Schweizerische Kreditanstalt, Johann Jakob Rüttimann, the guarantee problem was solved. What was even more significant was the concept that SKA came up with for a collaborative partnership between the bank and the insurance company, a solution that, especially in view of current developments in Allfinanz, deserves to be recognized.

The Governing Council of Canton Zurich approved Rentenanstalt's application for a license in November 1857, and the company was able to open for business at the beginning of 1858.

Guarantee and profit participation

Because the new insurance institution was a mutual organization, SKA did not have to provide any equity capital beyond the guarantee amount. Nevertheless, SKA retained most of the control over Rentenanstalt for almost 30 years. Without the determination and audacity of the Kreditanstalt, which itself had only recently been created, Rentenanstalt in its early years would not have been able to take on its extensive liabilities. To start with, it was by no means certain that Rentenanstalt would be able to establish itself successfully in the market, or whether it would need to fall back on the Kreditanstalt's guarantee. The fact that the bank put up the guarantee in the first place can thus be seen as unusually bold.

SKA also provided Rentenanstalt with the funds it needed to operate for the first few months of its existence. As business began to go well, however, the insurance company soon expressed a desire for greater independence. In 1862, SKA agreed to reduce its share of profits by half to 20% in order to help Rentenanstalt compete more effectively against rival companies and support its further development. Furthermore, SKA offered to waive its right to any further claim on profits as long as it could withdraw its guarantee. This offer came in part as a result of the pressure the bank felt from repeated 'criticism in the press about profit rates that were perceived as excessive'.[331]

In 1867 certain policyholders demanded that SKA withdraw completely from Rentenanstalt.[332] However, the bank's executive board and supervisory board did not think that the time was right to sever all ties.

In 1873 SKA raised its fully paid-up equity capital from Sfr 15 million to Sfr 20 million, leaving Schweizerische Rentenanstalt with the following financial cover[333]:

'Considering the great entrepreneurial spirit that ruled at that time – the spirit that contributed to the establishment of Schweizerische Kreditanstalt itself – it comes as no surprise that the new financial institution also turned its attention to the insurance sector and set up an organization devoted to this type of business' (Roesle, SKA, p. 149f.).

'Schweizerische Rentenanstalt submitted its revised articles of association and sought the Kreditanstalt's approval for these new articles' (Minutes of the SKA board of directors, 21 November 1859).

- Own assets   Sfr 8 million
- Annual premium and interest income   Sfr 2 million
- SKA's fully paid-up guarantee capital   Sfr 20 million

Schweizerische Rentenanstalt thus rested on a massive financial foundation, which provided a very solid guarantee for its members.

Further disputes about SKA's share of profits came in 1874, and in 1875 a report to Rentenanstalt's supervisory board recommended that SKA's guarantee be maintained, but that its share of profits be reduced. That same year, Zurich's Democrat government rejected a proposed revision of Rentenanstalt's articles of association. The canton's Governing Council decided that the draft articles should first be presented to SKA for approval, since Rentenanstalt, 'in essence is no more than an organization set up and managed by Kreditanstalt, with the necessary external autonomy, to manage the members' premiums and deposits – i.e. a division of Kreditanstalt which happens to present itself as an independent entity to the outside world'.[334]

In order to overcome the Zurich government's resistance to the new articles of association, Rentenanstalt even considered changing its domicile. In 1877, SKA agreed in principle to give Rentenanstalt its independence on condition that it was released from its guarantee obligations.

At a conference chaired by Swiss Federal Councillor Numa Droz and attended by representatives of the Zurich government and Rentenanstalt, three experts selected by the Federal Council came up with a report which was to form the basis of the solution to the conflict and facilitate the drafting of new articles of association.[335] Amongst other things, the report contained an agreement that SKA would gradually reduce its share of profits. It also called for a complete abolition of SKA's guarantee as soon as Rentenanstalt's assets reached Sfr 20 million, i.e. as soon as it was in a position to 'offer the same guarantee as the surety put up by the Kreditanstalt'.[336]

At the beginning of 1885, Rentenanstalt's assets reached this Sfr 20 million threshold. SKA continued, at the request of various policyholders, to guarantee certain policies and received a commission of 1‰ for doing so. However the total sum of these guarantees reduced over time: in 1886 it was still as high as Sfr 1.3 million, but by 1900 it was down to Sfr 0.5 million, and by 1910 to Sfr 0.3 million.[337]

Control over the management

SKA had insisted on maintaining the right to appoint Rentenanstalt's president, vice president, accountant and three members of its supervisory board.[338] The following examples show the way in which the bank exercised this right.

On 10 May 1872, Conrad Widmer wrote in a letter to SKA: 'I would like to raise with you the issue of selecting a vice president for our institution.'[339] SKA responded not only by choosing the person to be made vice president, but also determining his salary.[340] When on another occasion the company accountant's post became vacant, Rentenanstalt had to keep SKA informed in detail about the

> Rentenanstalt expressed the hope and pleasure it felt as a result of the fact, 'that after a prosperous 27-year alliance, the final act can now be completed in the same harmonious spirit that has ruled thus far' (Letter from Conrad Widmer to SKA, 25 March 1885).

new appointment and the terms and conditions being offered. In concrete terms this meant having to submit proposals for possible appointees. 'Please approve the choice of Mr. Jacob Wegmann as accountant (initially for one year), to be responsible for a part of the bookkeeping and cash desk as directed by the executive board; also the choice of Mr. J. Keller from Aussersihl to help with bookkeeping and the cash desk, and Mr. Jacob Ruckstuhl from Aadorf as a second assistant.'[341]

When these employees' salaries and terms of employment came up for review in 1880, SKA's board of directors once again laid down the conditions: 'The executive board is directed to inform Rentenanstalt's supervisory board in suitable form and in the name of the board of directors that the board of directors intends to revise the conditions of employment of the Anstalt's president, vice president and accountant as follows.'[342] The choice of a person to fill a post was only legally binding once SKA's board of directors had approved the appointment. Furthermore, employees who wanted to resign had to go to SKA to explicitly gain release.[343]

Interlinked management bodies

Rentenanstalt's six-man foundation committee included three members of SKA's board of directors. These were chairman of the board Alfred Escher, who remained on Rentenanstalt's supervisory board for 17 years until 1874; vice chairman of SKA's board of directors Johann Jakob Rüttimann (a member until 1876); and Johann Friedrich Peyer-Im Hof, who was a member of the boards of directors of both SKA and Rentenanstalt until 1868. Another member of Rentenanstalt's 1857 foundation committee was Heinrich Stapfer, who in 1867 was also elected to SKA's board of directors, where he remained for ten years.

The board-level links between SKA and Rentenanstalt developed in phases. The period between 1857 and 1885 was marked by close ties between the two organizations. Throughout this period, either three or four members sat simultaneously on the boards of directors of Rentenanstalt and SKA. Ten people in total shared these roles, of which four started off on SKA's board, and two began as members of the Rentenanstalt board. A major break came in 1885, after which there was no board-level tie between the two companies until 1905, at which point the tradition was restarted. Between then and 1976, the two boards always shared either one or two members.

Between 1976 and 1983, nobody held a director's mandate at both companies. Then former Federal Councillor Fritz Honegger (1983–1987) became the last person to be a member of both boards. Since then, Rentenanstalt has no longer had anyone on the board of SKA or CS Holding / Credit Suisse Group, and the bank has similarly maintained its distance from Rentenanstalt's board.

The regulatory environment

Switzerland's federal constitution of 1874 declared private insurance a matter for the government. Federal legislation would create the regulatory environment for the operation of private insurance companies. Once the time limit

Kreditanstalt and Rentenanstalt: The bank dominates the relationship

- SKA stands guarantee with its entire equity capital of Sfr 15 million.
- For as long as is required, it advances the funds needed to run Rentenanstalt at an interest rate of 5%.
- In return it is entitled to 40% of the profits.
- It selects Rentenanstalt's management (executives, accountants).
- It has the right to appoint three delegates to Rentenanstalt's supervisory board.
- It is allowed to intervene in all strategic and operational processes.
- It is Rentenanstalt's preferred institution for all banking business.

In fact, there were parties critical of Rentenanstalt who thought that the company was 'nothing more than a simple office of Schweizerische Kreditanstalt, and that Rentenanstalt's articles of association were no more than internal regulations issued by Schweizerische Kreditanstalt, and that the only name that should appear on documents was "Schweizerische Kreditanstalt, Rentenanstalt department"'(*Der Landbote*, 8 April 1876).

SKA's involvement in the establishment of insurance companies

SKA took a prominent role in the birth of many of the major insurance companies that were established during the second half of the 19th century. Its part in the creation of banks and insurance institutions continually enhanced its position on the capital markets. The precise nature of its involvement would vary depending on the legal form adopted by the insurance company. If it was a joint-stock company, SKA would help to raise the necessary operational capital. If it was a cooperative, like Schweizerische Lebensversicherungs- und Rentenanstalt, SKA would put up the required guarantee capital.

The bank's first participation in a joint-stock insurer came in 1861 when the Helvetia Feuerversicherungsgesellschaft was founded as a sister organization of the existing Helvetia Allgemeine Versicherungsgesellschaft in St. Gallen.

In 1863 SKA – again in collaboration with the Helvetia Allgemeine Versicherungsgesellschaft and the Basler Handelsbank – established Schweizerische Rückversicherungs-Gesellschaft (Swiss Re) in Zurich. SKA drafted the foundation agreement and the articles of association and took a Sfr 1²/₃ million stake in the company's equity capital of Sfr 6 million. It also had two representatives on the foundation committee: member of the executive board Caspar Huber and member of the board of directors Heinrich Hüni-Stettler. Conrad Widmer of Schweizerische Rentenanstalt was also on the committee. The new company quickly achieved success as a reinsurer of transportation, fire and life insurance.

In June 1869 the transportation insurance company 'Schweiz' Allgemeine Versicherungs-Aktiengesellschaft was established in Zurich on the initiative of SKA and interested parties from the silk and cotton trading and textile industries. SKA controlled a quarter of the initial Sfr 5 million set aside as the new company's equity capital, though it was to reduce its stake later on.

In 1872 Versicherungs-Verein (renamed 'Zürich' in 1875) was founded as a sister company to the 'Schweiz'. The founding committee that met on 22 October 1872 had exactly the same members as the board of directors of the 'Schweiz'. Again the new firm was created to a large extent on the initiative of SKA. Although the original plan was to set the company up with capital of Sfr 5 million, only 1,000 shares with a nominal value of Sfr 1,000 each were issued in the first instance. The amount paid up was initially fixed at 10%. Private individuals were not allowed to own more than 20 of the company's shares. SKA took on a large tranche of stock. In 1881 the company stopped underwriting transport insurance and in 1894 it changed its name to 'Zürich' Allgemeine Unfall- and Haftpflicht-Versicherungs-AG.

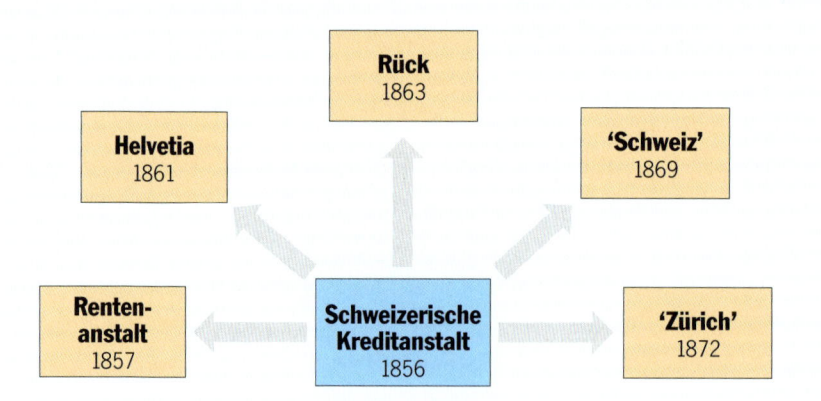

```
         Rück
         1863
Helvetia        'Schweiz'
  1861            1869
Renten-  Schweizerische  'Zürich'
anstalt  Kreditanstalt    1872
 1857        1856
```

for a counter-referendum in response to this proposal had expired, the 'Federal Law on Supervision of Private Companies in the Insurance Sector' came into effect on 1 November 1885. This prohibited private companies from carrying out insurance business in Switzerland, 'without the approval of the Federal Council'.[344] Particularly important was the ban on insurance companies pursuing 'non-insurance business' – which in the first instance meant banking. Insurers were soon also banned from offering life and non-life products at the same time.

> **J. J. Bäschlin zum Jordan in Schaffhausen** verzinst Kapitaleinlagen, Ct.-Ct.-Gelder zu 5%; besorgt den gütlichen und gerichtlichen Einzug von Forderungen jeder Art; vermittelt; Kapitalaufnahmen, Verkäufe von Liegenschaften, Werthschriften; Lebens- und Feuerversicherungen; Inserate in alle bestehenden Zeitschriften: ertheilt: Auskunft über Credit- und Vermögens-Verhältnisse von Firmen des In- und Auslandes.

In the 19th century it was not unusual for business people like Johann Jakob Bäschlin of Schaffhausen to run a private bank and also offer insurance products. Advertisement from the Schaffhauser Intelligenzblatt *of 24 June 1875.*

This split between the two types of insurance was to be enshrined in the Insurance Supervision Act.[345] As a result, various insurers that offered accident, personal liability and property insurance set up or purchased life insurance subsidiaries.[346]

Until prohibited by the law on supervision, there was no statutory ban at federal level on Allfinanz activities. Meanwhile, in Canton Zurich, for example, when a revision of the Cantonal Banking Act was discussed in 1878, a council proposal that would have obliged the Zurich Kantonalbank to start offering life insurance, was rejected. The idea behind the proposal was that less well-off sections of the population would thus be given access to life insurance products.[347] It is worth noting that according to the rejected draft law, the Kantonalbank's reserves could no longer have been used to cover damage by acts of God, thus challenging an old-established link between banking and insurance business.

Federal supervision of the banks was first introduced in Switzerland in 1935, though the banks were indirectly affected by insurance supervision prior to this date, specifically by the provisions which for a long time prevented them from entering into the insurance business.[348] The aim of the state regulation of Swiss private insurance companies at the end of the 19th century was to avoid risk clusters and to protect policyholders from loss. As a consequence, a 'division of labor' between the banks and the insurance companies was established that went unchallenged until well into the second half of the 20th century. Non-life and life insurance companies alike were, however, able to conduct the other form of insurance through subsidiary companies. One example of this is provided by the 'Schweizerische Unfallversicherungs-Actiengesellschaft in Winterthur' (Winterthur-Unfall, or 'Winterthur Accident'), which in 1923 set up a subsidiary for life insurance business (Winterthur-Leben). Nowadays an insurance company can obtain a license from the regulatory authorities to practice 'non-insurance business' – to run a bank, for instance, and a bank can operate an insurance arm, as long it has a license from the Federal Office of Private Insurance. According to the Swiss Federal Banking Law, there is no objection at all in principle to banks participating in insurance companies.[349]

Similar laws on the separation of the different disciplines and on 'non-insurance business' were also in force elsewhere in Europe. In Germany, for example, certain institutions, such as the Bayerische Hypotheken- und Wechsel-Bank, did for a time run banking and insurance operations under the same roof, but the central insurance company regulator introduced by the German authorities in 1901 put a stop to such 'cohabitation'. Even in the United Kingdom and the

Financial and capital markets in flux

In the last quarter of the 20th century, the development of the financial and capital markets was marked by exponential growth in the volume of international financial flows, and by numerous innovations:

- Globalization and deregulation of the financial markets facilitated round-the-clock international trade.
- Technological developments made worldwide 'real-time' transactions possible.
- The securitization of credit liabilities created ways of assigning risk to the financial markets and increased the banks' financial power.
- New financial market instruments, such as futures and options, created new and far-reaching ways of hedging individual transactions and entire portfolios.

Netherlands, which had the most liberal supervisory regimes, there were no significant Allfinanz companies until the second half of the 20th century.

In Switzerland, as in other countries, the laws still prohibit or require a license for non-insurance business by insurance companies; the same applies to the operation of life and non-life insurance under the same roof. However, innovations by the companies themselves, and a generous approach to granting licenses on the part of the Federal Office of Private Insurance, have smoothed the way for the creation of Allfinanz groups.

Financial services in the 20th century

The USA leads the way

The development of Allfinanz in its modern incarnation was influenced by the dynamic growth of the financial markets, and can be traced back to the USA of the 1970s. Despite the rigid regulation of banking in the United States of America, new forms of financial services provision emerged as a result of certain exceptions made by the US authorities.

Efforts were made by both banks and insurers to move into the other type of business. These attempts to break down the divide between the two financial services disciplines were encouraged by innovative new products that were not covered by the existing regulations. Such products were first introduced by companies that were not subject to banking supervision. Though the regulatory regime might have appeared at first sight to be bent on stifling innovation, in fact it only encouraged the spirit of discovery. In 1981, the giant US retailer Sears Roebuck & Co. entered the securities and real estate business when it purchased Dean Witter Reynolds and Coldwell Banker & Comp. The American Express Company, traditionally a credit card provider, also expanded its business activities by acquiring various financial institutions and thus becoming involved in insurance, mutual funds business and investment banking. Numerous other providers steadily broadened their range of products and so helped to make the traditional boundaries between various financial services disciplines increasingly permeable. More and more partnerships were forged under the influence of deregulation, globalization and advances in information technology. Banks, retailers, credit card organizations and insurance companies jointly developed a growing range of financial services. Eventually this trend led to the creation of new types of Allfinanz conglomerates that were able to sidestep the supervisory regulations.

Variable life insurance ('variable life', 'universal life', etc.), which varied interest rates and benefits according to developments on the capital markets, also had a groundbreaking effect in Europe. During the period of high interest rates, previously very conservative US life insurance companies were forced to develop such products because they feared their assets would be whittled away by policy loans (where customers used their policies to secure loans at low, contractually stipulated interest rates and then invested the loaned funds at a higher rate on the money market).[350]

The EU internal market and pension investments act as catalysts

To start with, Europe's financial services providers were content merely to closely monitor developments on the other side of the Atlantic. Then when high interest rates hit in the 1980s, the new trends were transplanted to Europe, making the competition between insurance companies and banks much tougher. A variety of factors now conspired to force Europe down the path of Allfinanz:

- The freedom to set up branches, and later to offer services, granted by the new EU internal market
- The forthcoming introduction of the euro
- The liberalization of the insurance industry through the relaxation of material supervision and the introduction of 'home country control'
- The liberalization of investment regulations
- The removal of localization restrictions

The main reason for the intensification of competition, however, was the battle for pension investments. If they wanted to be able to extend their operations in the direction of Allfinanz, the banks and insurance companies had to choose from the following options:

- Systematic cooperation with a bank or an insurer as appropriate
- Take over an existing bank/insurance company and run it as a group company
- Establish a new bank/insurance company

All of these strategies for entry into Allfinanz were feasible both in Switzerland and abroad. Initially they proved most successful in Latin countries, where today up to 50% of life insurance business, and an increasing proportion of non-life

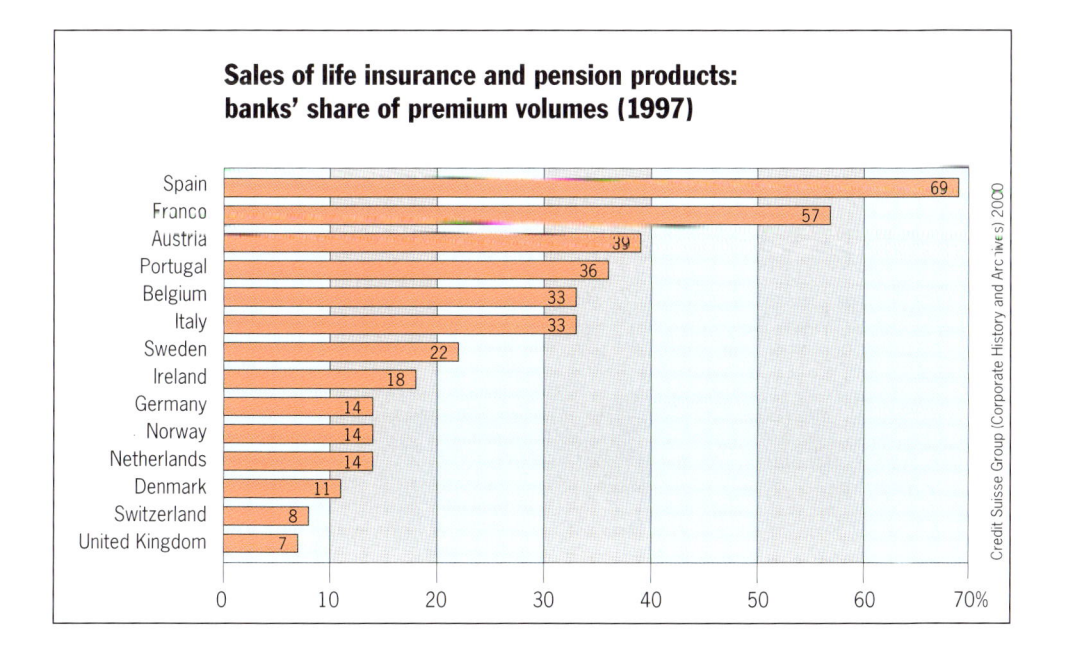

New banking legislation in the USA

The purpose of the United States' new banking law, the Gramm-Leach-Bliley Act of 1999, is to eliminate the restrictions previously imposed on Allfinanz companies that operate simultaneously as banks, securities traders and insurance firms – particularly significant for Credit Suisse Group as the parent company of Winterthur. In addition, the new law envisages a simpler regulatory regime for such companies and affords better protection of customers' privacy. Aside from a few exceptions, banks are now prohibited from passing on non-public, personal customer information to external third parties (though this information can be given to companies within the same group). However, the more extensive protection afforded by Swiss banking secrecy is not affected by this new law.

Sales of life insurance and pension products: banks' share of premium volumes (1997)

Country	%
Spain	69
France	57
Austria	39
Portugal	36
Belgium	33
Italy	33
Sweden	22
Ireland	18
Germany	14
Norway	14
Netherlands	14
Denmark	11
Switzerland	8
United Kingdom	7

Credit Suisse Group (Corporate History and Archives) 2000

SKA-Vorsorge 3. Säule.

Die 3. Säule bei der SKA. Vorsorge im rechten Alter.

aktueller Zinssatz 5%

SCHWEIZERISCHE KREDITANSTALT SKA

Switzerland's federal law on occupational old age, survivors' and invalids' insurance came into force at the beginning of 1985. The tax breaks made 'pillar three' (personal) pensions particularly attractive.

business, is conducted over bank counters under the name of 'bancassurance'. In these cases, the banks dominate most of the partnerships concerned.[351]

Customers' attitude to investment

Until the 1960s, most Swiss households regarded savings books and savings deposits as the most important instruments for capital formation. Savings were generally understood to be an accumulation of short and medium term reserves of liquidity, or a nest egg set aside for large purchases. In addition, better-off investors might put money into medium-term notes and bonds issued by public bodies and other borrowers. Longer-term provision was arranged through life insurance policies, which had maturities of 20 or more years and which were usually financed by regular payments. Equity investments were the preserve of the wealthy. At the end of the 1960s and the start of the 1970s, investment funds became increasingly common in Switzerland as elsewhere, though they then suffered a massive loss of popularity on account of the long bear run on the equity markets.

As economic growth continued, more and more households were able to save and invest money, prompting them to take a greater interest in levels of return. They noted that the prevailing very high rates of inflation were cancelling out most of the earnings generated by their savings, so they started to look for new places to put their spare money, turning increasingly to bonds and tax-privileged life insurance policies.

The introduction of compulsory 'pillar two' (occupational) pensions and optional, tax-privileged 'pillar three' (private personal) pensions in 1985, changed the situation in Switzerland. Pillar two opened up huge growth potential for pension institutions, and the banks wanted to make sure they would benefit too. The main thing that alarmed the banks and made them worry about

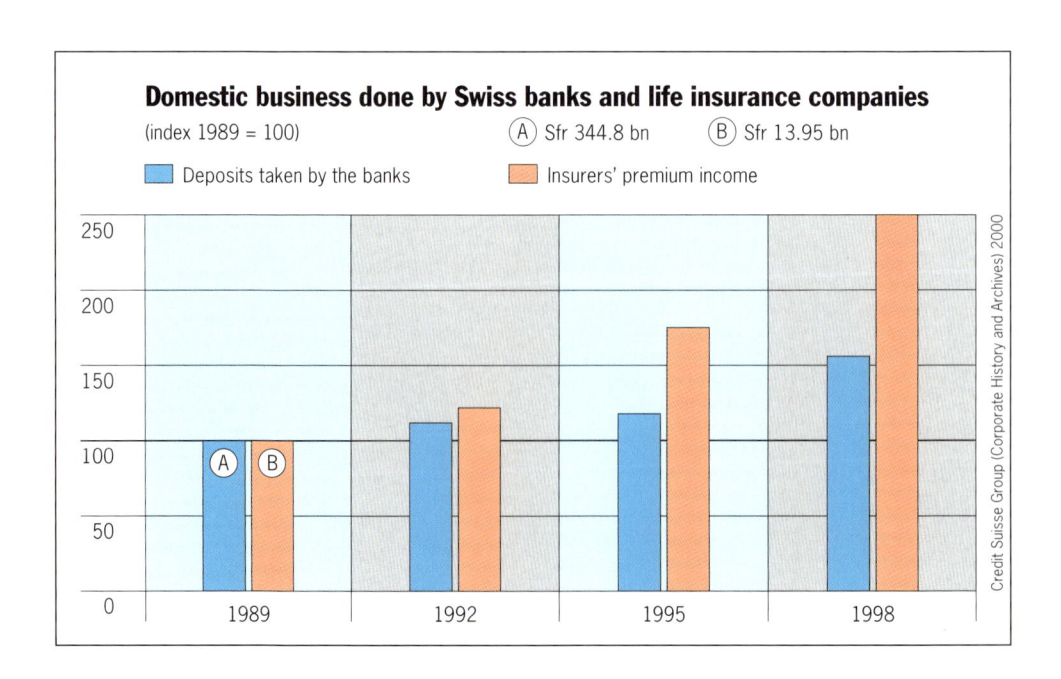

Domestic business done by Swiss banks and life insurance companies
(index 1989 = 100)   (A) Sfr 344.8 bn   (B) Sfr 13.95 bn
■ Deposits taken by the banks   ■ Insurers' premium income

Credit Suisse Group (Corporate History and Archives) 2000

their market position was the danger that savers would defect to the life insurance companies. Consequently they set up their own pension funds and subsequently their own insurance companies to fight for the money going to the autonomous and semi-autonomous funds, thus becoming direct competitors of the life insurance companies. In parallel, the banks also developed new products in response to the new 'pillar three' personal pensions option. Investors thus had a free choice between banking or insurance solutions.[352]

Thanks to the booming equity markets of the 1990s, investment funds, which allowed small and medium-sized investors to participate in a diversified equity investment without incurring too much risk, enjoyed enormous success. Investment funds were broadened out to become vehicles for systematic investment, thus creating serious competition for the life insurers.[353] Similar developments occurred in other Western European countries.

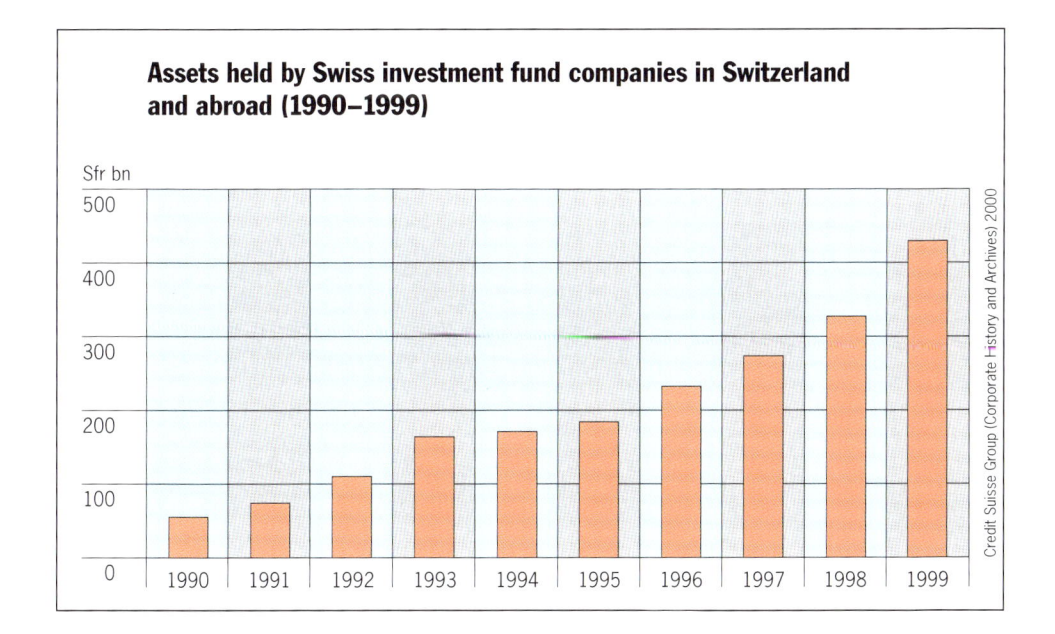

Assets held by Swiss investment fund companies in Switzerland and abroad (1990–1999)

Credit Suisse Group (Corporate History and Archives) 2000

Allfinanz activities in Switzerland

Even before the spectacular developments in the USA, the Swiss retailers Coop and Migros had set up their own banks and insurance companies. Indeed Coop had been in the business for a very long time, setting up the Coop Leben life insurer in 1918 and Genossenschaftliche Zentralbank (later Coop Bank) in 1927. It added legal insurance in 1974, and in 1994 established a direct insurance sales company. All of these companies are still operating today. Meanwhile Migros founded its own bank in 1957, the Secura insurance company in 1959 and Secura Leben (for life insurance) in 1977. In the final months of 1999, the Manor retailing group announced that it, too, was entering the financial services market.

Both Coop and Migros run their banks and insurance companies separately from each other, and so cannot be described as pursuing any clear Allfinanz strategy. Both only use the powerful sales capabilities of their many stores to a

'Winterthur Connects'
'Finanz und Wirtschaft', 9 December 1995

There was nothing to suggest that 1995 would witness the decisive turning point in the major Swiss banks' Allfinanz strategies. When Rentenanstalt (Swiss Life) invited the media to a press conference in mid-September, is was generally expected that 'Switzerland's biggest life insurer would announce its long-expected conversion from a cooperative to a joint-stock company' (*NZZ*, 16 September 1995). Indeed it did do this, but it also announced an alliance with SBG – though this was subsequently revoked.

The *NZZ* could see the logic of a joint venture, but was 'surprised by the choice of partner'. In a detailed report on 22 September *Cash* talked about 'this awkward situation with Winterthur'. And it was not just a matter of finer feelings: 'UBS chairman Senn does not sit on the Winterthur board of directors just to make up numbers; he belongs to the board's central strategy and control committee, which oversees the fate of the company. The law obliges Senn to "shoulder full responsibility for the management of the company". […] Senn left Winterthur in the lurch because a greater self-interest prevented him from ever telling it the truth: namely that his bank was cuddling up to its competitor, Rentenanstalt. On the other side too, in SBG's board committee, Senn had to deceive his friend Spälti.'

'Winterthur certainly does not have to cancel its Allfinanz plans yet. Within Switzerland, the SKA group, with its extensive branch network, could be interested in working with Winterthur. In Germany, a partnership with Commerzbank could work', stated *Finanz und Wirtschaft* on 20 September, though it contradicted itself shortly afterwards (*Finanz und Wirtschaft*, 7 October 1995), saying that CS Holding was more or less tied up already and asking, 'will Winterthur look to the ranks of other banking groups (for instance private banks, cantonal banks)?'. Peter Spälti himself saw 'no strategic need' for cooperation with a Swiss bank. He would remain on the SBG board of directors according to a quote cited in the *Tages-Anzeiger* on 3 October.

'At the end of September, the chairman of Winterthur Insurance, former National Councillor Peter Spälti called the chairman of CS Group Rainer Gut, and proposed an intensive cooperation. The goal: an Allfinanz conglomerate', is how *Cash* later described events in its 15 December 1995 issue. 'One week later, a Saturday, a delegation of four or five experts and top managers from each side met at the new SKA training center at Bocken close to Lake Zurich for a brainstorming session. This was followed by a series of secret talks.'

The media did not have any concrete details, but on 2 December *Finanz und Wirtschaft* reported some of the rumors that were flying around. ('The race for Winterthur is in full swing'). On 8 December the newspapers could finally tell their readers: 'Winterthur and CS Holding Shake Hands' (*Tages-Anzeiger*), 'CS Holding and Winterthur Create a New Bancassurance Hub' (*Le Nouveau Quotidien*), 'CS Holding, Winterthur set Swiss Tie-Up' (*Wall Street Journal*). The *NZZ* talked about 'the at times breathtaking speed of restructuring within the group', which aimed at, 'consolidating its reputation as an attractive investment for internationally oriented investors'. Meanwhile, the boards of directors of the Allfinanz companies had to disentangle themselves: Peter Spälti announced that he would be departing the SBG board of directors at the end of 1995, thus forcing Nikolaus Senn to leave the Winterthur board. On 15 December 1995 *Cash* asked Peter Spälti about what exactly happened in September: 'We never felt that we were under pressure, but we did discuss the Allfinanz issue in the executive board at the start of the year and talked to SBG in the middle of the year about working together. […] After thinking about it for a while they came back with a negative answer. When we approached them, the SBG/Rentenanstalt deal was almost tied up. […] I was not upset, just disappointed. I was always 100% loyal to SBG myself, including during the BZ saga. SBG's treatment of Winterthur was not acceptable to me. But that is all history now.'

Four-and-a-half months later, on 22 April 1996, Winterthur and CS Holding announced their firmed-up ideas to the media. The *Börsen-Zeitung* in Frankfurt went with the headline 'CS Group and Winterthur United in Allfinanz'. Allfinanz has a new leader, said the *Tages-Anzeiger*: 'The partnership between banking and insurance launched by CS Holding and Winterthur Group is broader and deeper than anything seen before.' The *NZZ* also reported in full on the 'multi-track cooperation,' and quoted Peter Spälti, for whom the new partnership was, 'broader and deeper and has greater creative power than anything that has previously come to the market under the name of "Allfinanz"'.

very limited extent to distribute financial services. Since insurance business no longer plays a part in Migros' plans for the future, it sold Secura to Generali in 1999. Likewise, in an attempt to focus more on its core competencies, Coop reduced its stake in the Coop Bank and gave up its majority voting rights to Basler Kantonalbank at the end of 1999.

Winterthur Insurance took a modest step towards Allfinanz in 1989 when it built up the stake it had held in Hypobank Winterthur since 1965 to a majority holding of 65%, thus becoming the first Swiss insurance company to control a bank. However, because of Hypobank's limited regional catchment area and its specialist focus on mortgage business, it was not able to fulfill Winterthur's expectations with regard to Allfinanz and was finally sold to SBV in 1993 (also in part owing to the deepening crisis in the real estate sector).

In 1992, Zurich Insurance and SBV set up a cooperation arrangement primarily for the purpose of systematically cross-selling each other's products. In order to further this aim, they created a joint sales company. In 1996 and 1997 Zurich took over two US mutual fund and asset management companies and in 1999 it founded the Zurich Invest Bank in Switzerland. The Zurich Financial Services Group thus ploughed its own furrow in the direction of Allfinanz.

In 1993, SBG founded a life insurance company. This company is still operating today under the name UBS Life – contrary to the original intention – in the single-life insurance market. In 1995 the bank took a 25% stake in Rentenanstalt, thus ending decades of cooperation with Winterthur. It seems that this minority holding did not fit into the strategy of the new UBS – the company formed from the merger of SBG and SBV – as it was sold on in 1999. For its part, Rentenanstalt acquired the Gotthard Bank and the asset management operations of ATAG, thus also taking some initial steps towards Allfinanz.

In addition to this activity, a number of cooperative partnerships were forged between cantonal, regional and private banks on the one hand, and insurance companies on the other, though these were not really strategically significant for the parties involved. Experience so far suggests that it is difficult to develop Allfinanz solutions solely on the basis of co-operation agreements, and that minority stakes in other companies are jeopardized by subsequent acquisitions and mergers.

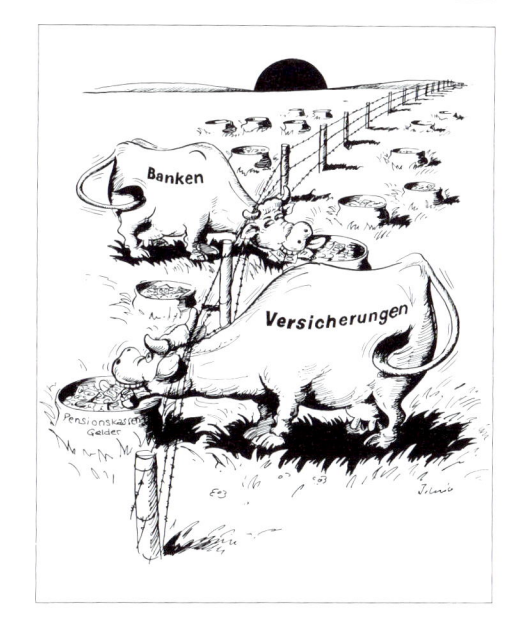

Cartoon by Johann Sonderegger, in *Finanz und Wirtschaft*, 19 October 1985.

Allfinanz at SKA

On the way to CS Life

In the mid-1980s, SKA had to face the fact that competition from the insurance companies was eating into its deposit-taking business. As the insurers were mopping up more and more customer money, the flow of funds into SKA was being seriously undermined. The bank felt compelled to conduct a far-reaching analysis into the various points of contact between banking and insurance business and thus come up with a basis for the formulation of a strategic reorienta-

Increasing competition between the banks and the insurance companies brought many different and far-reaching changes to the Swiss financial services industry.

Made in Switzerland

Wenden Sie sich an Ihren Anlageberater.

Sicherheit mit mehr Rendite.

CS Life.

CS Life opened its doors for business in 1990. On 1 April 1998 it was integrated into the Winterthur Group.

Different forms of Allfinanz

- There have always been loose partnerships between banks and insurance companies at the local level. Insurance agencies and bank branches have often passed business on to one another, though this has usually been based on personal relationships.
- The next level up is a partnership between a bank and an insurance company based on a formal co-operation agreement. The bank sells insurance over its counters and the insurance company sells bank products, especially mutual funds, through its distribution channels.
- Closer integration still comes when the two companies hold an equity stake in each other, possibly augmented by the foundation of a joint venture subsidiary for Allfinanz services. However, the two companies continue to maintain their own separate profiles.
- The highest level of Allfinanz is represented by the Allfinanz group that uses a holding structure. The different types of business are run by subsidiary companies, but structure, product design and sales can be controlled centrally. One of the advantages of this model is that an overall strategy can be applied. It is very important that there are opportunities for each business to make use of the other's potential customer base.

tion. To this end SKA set up an internal project group at the beginning of November 1987, which reported to a steering committee of three executive board members.

Supported by the McKinsey consultancy firm and working on the basis of numerous market analyses, external interviews and intensive discussions, the project group produced a report at the end of March 1988 that summarized and compared the strengths and weaknesses of the banks and insurance companies.

The main competitive advantages enjoyed by the insurance companies were identified as:

- Great potential for the future thanks to their strong position in pillar two and three pensions business
- 'Constitutional' advantages (tax advantages, minimal capital adequacy and liquidity requirements, low transaction costs and preferential bankruptcy treatment)
- A stronger and more customer-focused sales operation
- Widespread customer demand for additional protection against risk

Competition from insurers in mortgages and lending business did not appear to be particularly threatening, but the business that the bank did with insurance companies as customers (payment transactions, securities trading and management, foreign exchange business, capital raising, etc.) was shown to be a real weak point. This deficit was particularly critical because, given SKA's placing power, this type of business had real strategic significance. The extent of the unfulfilled potential can be seen from the fact that in business with insurance companies, SKA only had a market share of 5%. Only Zurich Insurance and Rentenanstalt (Swiss Life) used SKA as a preferred banking partner. The analysis also showed that SKA came out negatively overall with regard to insurance business done with banks (i.e. covering bank risks, and brokering risk cover for banking customers).

Based on their situation analysis, the project group formulated various options, ranging from expanding SKA's business with insurance companies and improving competitiveness by creating attractive products, to partnerships and joint ventures with insurance companies, to establishing a majority stake in an insurance company.

The founding of CS Life

At the beginning of 1989, SKA's executive board held further intensive discussions about the different options during a special seminar. In the end they decided that the best option was to found the bank's own life insurance company. In the meantime, additional analysis had shown that the time and effort that would be required to make such a solution work were not as extensive as originally thought. In particular it had become apparent that the development of such a company could be speeded up by rigorously pursuing a niche policy. Encouraged by these new findings, the executive board issued the instruction to carry out a feasibility study as quickly as possible. This study was ready by July 1989.

The project group was then mandated to formulate a formal proposal for the creation of SKA's own life insurance company, to be called CS Life. On 30 October 1989, this proposal was submitted to the bank's board of directors. It was thought that 12 to 15 months of preparatory and development work would be required before the first policies could be sold. CS Life was to be set up as an independent company under the CS Holding umbrella.

Another careful evaluation of the arguments in favor of and against had been conducted prior to the proposal's submission. The advantages that a new company would enjoy included the bank's existing extensive distribution network. Special mention was also made of the fact that SKA had more customers than any Swiss insurance company. The bank's own surveys had shown that insurance products with an investment element would be very popular with customers. Furthermore, thanks to their investment expertise, the bank's relationship managers should be quite capable of selling life insurance products, too. Ultimately, the clinching argument for the launch of the bank's own company was that the investment required for this option was considerably smaller than the investment that would have been needed to buy an existing insurer.

However, setting up a new company also had disadvantages compared with the other options. Three points in particular were mentioned. Firstly the bank would have to employ specialists to bolster its insurance know-how. Given the state of the labor market at the time, this was not regarded as too problematic. The risks associated with building up a new infrastructure were also regarded as relatively insignificant, because no great investment was needed for the development of new infrastructure. Finally, it was accepted that a new company would take a relatively long time to start turning a profit.

The SKA board of directors approved the proposal, as did the CS Holding board, and CS Life was established as a 100% subsidiary of CS Holding.

In line with the underlying aim of offering attractive life insurance products with a more substantial investment component, the new company cultivated an image as a niche player right from the start.

Setting up a new life insurance company gave the CS banks the chance to benefit from the 'constitutional advantages' of the insurance sector, and thus to improve their own competitive position quite considerably without having to expand their own infrastructure.

'Chairman R. E. Gut believes that rival companies have no choice but to move in the same direction. The signs of the time are clear' (Minutes of the CS Holding board of directors, 9 November 1989).

Dynamic development

CS Holding was the first Swiss banking group to expand so decisively into the insurance business. In 1990, CS Life began operations with about 20 staff, equity capital of Sfr 25 million and an organization fund of Sfr 15 million. The timing of the implementation of this visionary idea proved fortunate, coming as it did at the start of the 1990s, when a favorable interest rate trend made operating conditions much more comfortable than they might otherwise have been. The ambitious plan was realized so quickly thanks in no small part to consistent pressure from the top: pressure exerted by chairman of the board of directors Rainer E. Gut on SKA's executive board, and pressure from president of the executive board Robert A. Jeker on the individual divisions and subdivisions. Only ten months after CS Life was founded, it had developed two new life insurance

Factors in CS Life's success
- Sales efforts concentrate on wealthy private customers, and especially existing customers of the Group.
- CS Life does not build up its own sales organization but sells its products exclusively via CS Holding's banks.
- CS Life only offers a limited range of products focusing on capital investments.
- Only single deposit policies with a minimum investment of Sfr 100,000 are sold.

> For CS Holding the creation of CS Life was an important step on the road to becoming an Allfinanz group. It set off a long-term learning process that brought many valuable experiences.

products, its IT infrastructure was up and running, and it had trained 1,500 bank staff how to sell life insurance products.[354]

Ambitious goals had been set for the new company. In the original proposal, it had been assumed that within five years CS Life would have a premium volume of between Sfr 400 million and Sfr 500 million and a guarantee fund of Sfr 1 billion. It was scheduled to reach break-even point two years after foundation.

Thanks to an aggressive business strategy, which aimed to set the company apart from its competitors by virtue of higher interest guarantees, a clearer premium structure and lower costs, CS Life managed to generate premium income of Sfr 290 million in only its first year of operations. The ambitious goals were exceeded by a substantial margin: at the end of 1995, premium volume was twice as high as planned at Sfr 819 million, and the guarantee fund topped the Sfr 2 billion mark. In a mere five years, CS Life had conquered a share of around 5% of the Swiss single-life insurance market. Apart from the attractiveness of the products themselves, this great success can also be attributed to the fact that the company was able to sell its products through banking distribution channels to the existing customers of the CS Holding banks. It is worth noting that 14% of the new insurance customers had never previously been customers of SKA.

CS Life met, and indeed exceeded, the expectations placed on it sooner than expected. It was generating a considerable amount of new customer money and it was also preventing the outflow of existing money by offering products that investors could use to restructure their portfolios without going to another company. Finally, CS Life also expanded the Swiss life insurance market in general by opening up new customer segments that had previously been more or less out of the reach of traditional life insurance companies.

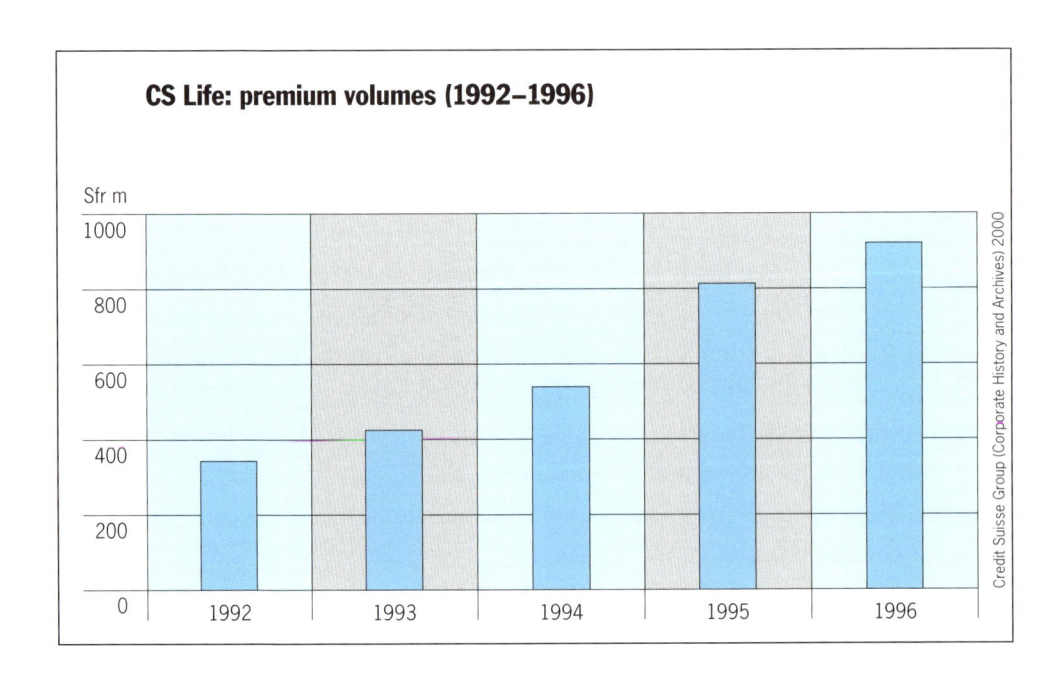

CS Life: premium volumes (1992–1996)

Credit Suisse Group (Corporate History and Archives) 2000

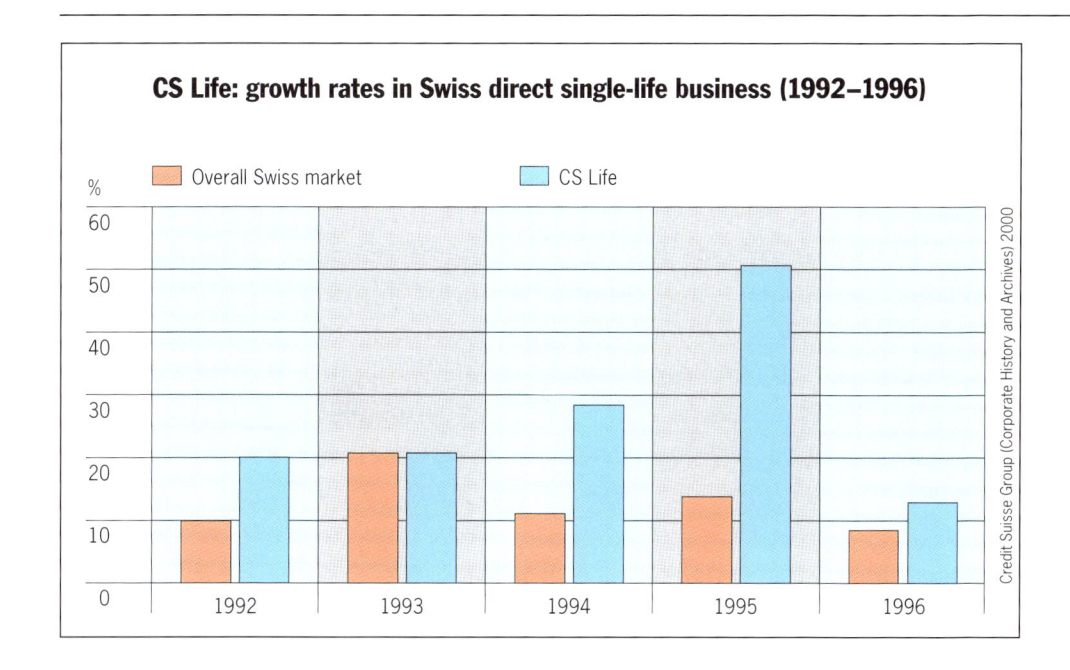

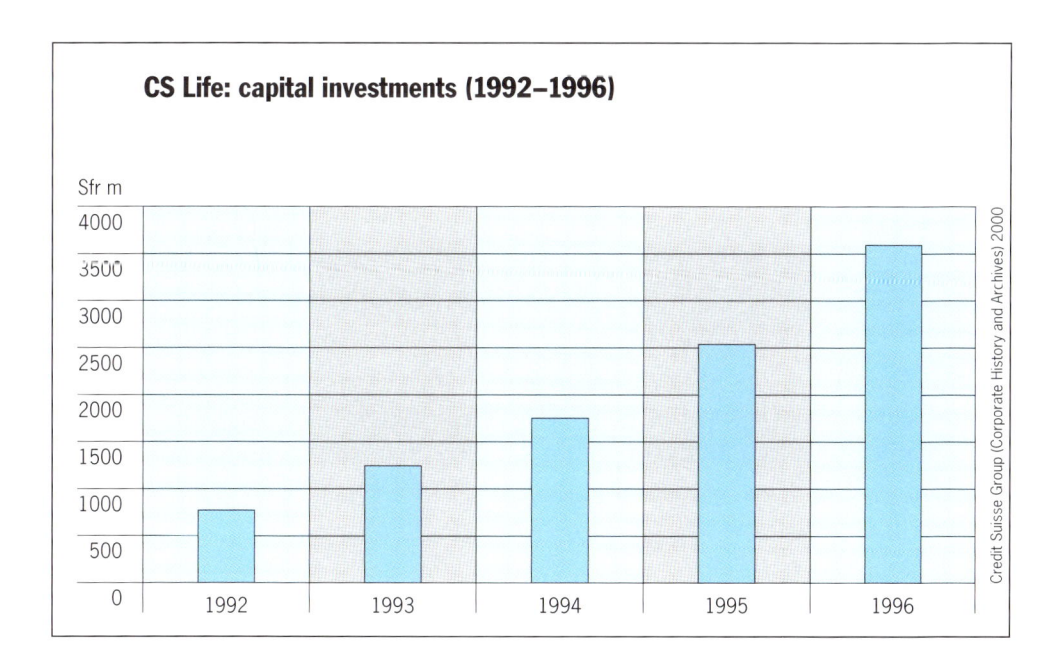

CS Life: growth rates in Swiss direct single-life business (1992–1996)

CS Life: capital investments (1992–1996)

Merger between Winterthur and Credit Suisse Group

Once SBG had severed its ties with the Winterthur insurance company in 1995 – ties which were forged as a result of the two firms' shared origins in the town of Winterthur and which had lasted for many decades – the way was clear for Winterthur and CS Holding to examine the possibility of working together. In 1996, CS Holding and Winterthur decided to enter into an alliance in order to open up new joint sales opportunities for their products. The most important result of this alliance was the Winterthur-Columna joint venture, which brought together all of Credit Suisse's and Winterthur's 'pillar two' pension activities.

Thanks to the combined know-how of the bank and the insurance company, Winterthur-Columna enjoyed a unique competitive position.

> Experience of cooperation between CS Holding and Winterthur soon made it clear that an even greater degree of partnership would unleash considerable additional potential.

> The merger between Credit Suisse Group and Winterthur in August 1997 created an Allfinanz group that could offer its customers more than most other institutions in terms of know-how, technology and range of products.

Both partners brought their core competencies to the new company: Winterthur contributed its extensive specialist expertise and many years of experience in the insurance business, while the CS banks brought their skills in portfolio management and investment consultancy to the table. Where previously the customer had been obliged to choose between banking or insurance products, the new company's Allfinanz approach offered comprehensive advice and a new range of products which combined the advantages of insurance-based and conventional bank savings.

1996 also saw the Winterthur Group take a stake in Reinsurance Finance Consultants, which had been set up earlier by CS Holding and Schweizerische Rückversicherungs-Gesellschaft (Swiss Re). This groundbreaking joint venture facilitated the development and sale of tailor made risk-management solutions for multinational companies.

At about this time, Martin Ebner's BZ Group had systematically been buying Winterthur shares, building up a stake of more than 30%. Winterthur was thus forced to undertake a fundamental strategic realignment. Consequently it approached Credit Suisse Group to explore the mutual benefits of an even closer partnership.

It had also become clear that the loose ties between Winterthur and Credit Suisse Group had reached the point where urgent restructuring was required – the situation had arisen where Winterthur and CS Life were starting to compete with each other, and clearly this internal conflict had to be sorted out as soon as possible. Another factor was that considerable investment would be required if the Allfinanz business was to be extended to foreign markets. Talks between Credit Suisse Group and Winterthur went well and in August 1997, the two companies merged. With assets under management of about Sfr 700 billion, the new group was at the time one of the biggest asset managers in the world.

The integration of Winterthur into Credit Suisse Group went according to plan, and by the start of 1998, the company had already come up with a new product line – the 'Wohneigentümerpaket' ('home-owners package') that brought together the specific skills of the banking and insurance sectors. Credit Suisse Group contributed savings and pension products, land and construction loans, as well as various types of mortgage to the package, while Winterthur added building and owners liability insurance, contents insurance, whole life cover and mixed life insurance.

Integration and new prospects

As far as risk management was concerned, the first job was to harmonize Credit Suisse Group's and Winterthur's strategies and structures. The basis for this harmonization was the shared goal of managing the use of risk capital so as to maximize corporate value. The risk exposures created by the companies' insurance business and capital investments were systematically recorded so that cross-industry assessment criteria could be established on the basis of comparable data.

More than 80 Credit Suisse branches were merged with Winterthur agencies, on the one hand to create synergies, and on the other to start the move towards offering 'comprehensive financial services from a single source'.

Aiming to become one of Europe's leading providers of pension solutions as soon as possible, CS Life and Winterthur-Columna were merged with Winterthur-Leben (Winterthur Life) to form a product center, and then integrated into the Winterthur Group as its new 'private and occupational pensions' division.

Various approaches and products were brought together in this division, which made it easier to exploit the Allfinanz potential. One of the most important developments was the institutionalization of collaboration between Winterthur and Credit Suisse Asset Management (CSAM) on the distribution of mutual funds. CSAM made its range of products available and Winterthur marketed funds selected from this range via its dense sales network.

Thanks to a retail organization that extended to many countries within the European single market, Winterthur was able right from the start to expand the group's capacity for selling fund products. CSAM benefited further from the opportunity to combine its investment products into fund-linked life insurance products. These hybrids – true Allfinanz products – were sold via both Winterthur's organization and the Credit Suisse Group banks.

Particularly in its life insurance business, Winterthur held significant volumes of investment capital, which it used to cover guaranteed insurance benefits. The performance of these investments was becoming increasingly important from both the income as well as the marketing point of view. Cooperation between the asset managers and insurers within Credit Suisse Group thus helped to generate considerable added value for customers, staff and shareholders.

Before the merger with Winterthur, Credit Suisse Group's only offices in Spain, for instance, were the SKA (as it was then) branches in Madrid and Barcelona. Winterthur, by contrast, had a much more impressive Spanish presence, consisting of more than 4,000 agencies and two million customers in the country. Many synergies were created by the merger, in logistics and communications as well as in the shared use of products and distribution channels. The introduction of the 'Eurotop 100' investment fund in spring 1998 paved the way for the launch of jointly developed Allfinanz products. From the very start, the coordinated sale of mutual funds simultaneously through the Winterthur's dense sales network and through Credit Suisse Private Banking's channels was crowned with success. A great deal of this success could be attributed to the quality of the products and the performance of the agents, who were specially trained to sell these types of fund.

Focusing on strengths in European Allfinanz

Winterthur's goal is to become a leading provider in key European markets. In the light of this goal, the company reviewed and modified its strategy within the context of its new position in Credit Suisse Group.

Winterthur-Columna was formed on 1 January 1997 from the merger of CS Columna and Winterthur Life's collective insurance business. The new company offered both banking-based and insurance-based pension products.

Zusammenschluss

Ausserordentliche Generalversammlung vom 5. September 1997

Sehr deutliches Ja zum Zusammenschluss

Nachdem die Aktionärinnen und Aktionäre der Credit Suisse Group dem Zusammenschluss mit der Winterthur bereits am Morgen klar zugestimmt hatten, war es am Nachmittag an den 1541 anwesenden Aktionären der Winterthur, den Zusammenschluss gutzuheissen. Mit einem Ja-Stimmen-Anteil von 98,4 Prozent fiel der Entscheid für den Zusammenschluss nach fast dreistündiger Versammlung überwältigend aus. Insgesamt waren an der ausserordentlichen Generalversammlung 4 521 384 Stimmen vertreten.

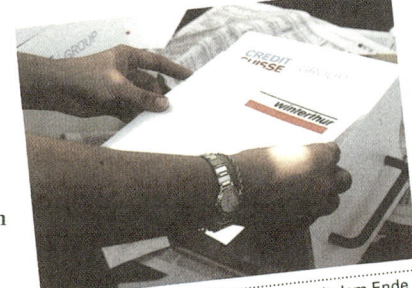

13.00 Uhr: Die Wahlurnen erhalten nach dem Ende der Generalversammlung der Credit Suisse Group das Logo der Winterthur.

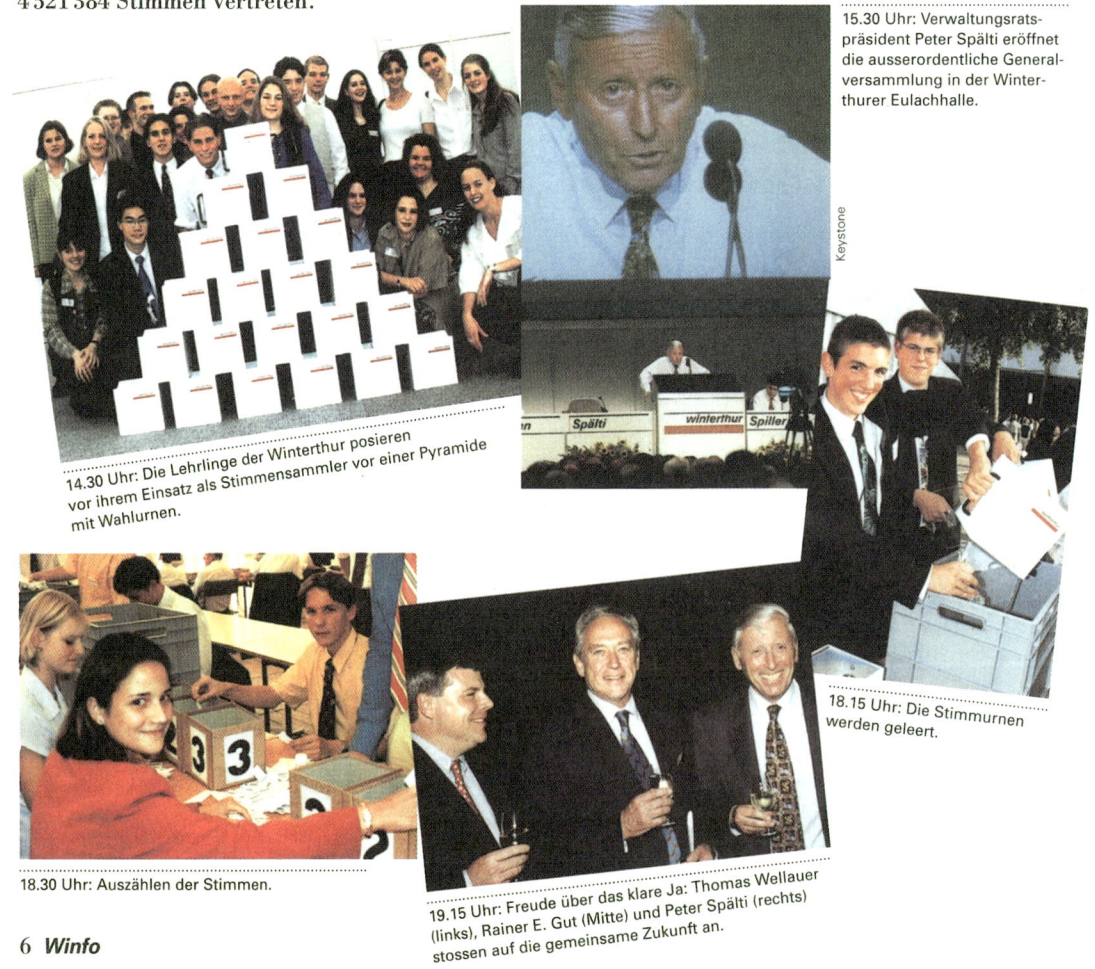

15.30 Uhr: Verwaltungsratspräsident Peter Spälti eröffnet die ausserordentliche Generalversammlung in der Winterthurer Eulachhalle.

14.30 Uhr: Die Lehrlinge der Winterthur posieren vor ihrem Einsatz als Stimmensammler vor einer Pyramide mit Wahlurnen.

18.15 Uhr: Die Stimmurnen werden geleert.

18.30 Uhr: Auszählen der Stimmen.

19.15 Uhr: Freude über das klare Ja: Thomas Wellauer (links), Rainer E. Gut (Mitte) und Peter Spälti (rechts) stossen auf die gemeinsame Zukunft an.

6 **Winfo**

Winfo, Winterthur's staff magazine, 9/1997: 'A resounding Yes to the merger'.

The key markets for Winterthur are Switzerland, Germany, Italy, Spain and the United Kingdom. In other European markets, Winterthur wants to consolidate its market position and then build on it through the use of international (rather than country-specific) products. In addition, it aims to develop its position in selected Eastern European and Asian markets, and to bolster its status as one of the leading providers in global insurance and pensions business with large companies.

In order to be able to concentrate on its core business, in 1998 Winterthur sold its majority stake in HIH Winterthur of Australia as well as its active reinsurance business. The funds realized by these sales were used to strengthen the company's position in Europe and to build up its business activities in Eastern Europe and Asia.

In Germany, the operating conditions changed for DBV-Winterthur in 1998, when equity capital links were established between Commerzbank and the Generali Group. Winterthur and Commerzbank had both enjoyed success as a result of their previous cooperation, but now this alliance had to be given up and new alternatives found for distribution in Germany.

Personal Financial Services (PFS)

In 1998 the Allfinanz strategy was taken a step further as preparatory work was begun on the Personal Financial Services (PFS) concept. The basic idea of PFS was to use a variety of distribution channels – e-business, personal bankers, investment centers and call centers – to offer a comprehensive range of high-quality financial products and services covering pensions, investment and insurance. Customers benefit from a personal advisory service tailored to their individual needs and suited to the stage of life they find themselves in.

Previously, little attention had been paid to the customer segment targeted by the PFS strategy – so-called 'affluent clients' with assets of somewhere between Sfr 80,000 and Sfr 1 million. However, market research has shown that it is one of the groups with the highest potential. With PFS, Credit Suisse Group can cover a segment of 20 million customers out of a population of 300 million living in the EU.

On 5 May 1999, Credit Suisse (Italy) was established, marking the launch of the PFS project in the Italian market. By the end of 1999, thanks to cooperation between Credit Suisse Private Banking, Credit Suisse Asset Management and Winterthur, 230 personal bankers were already working in Italy, and several branches and a call center were up and running. The strategy is due to be extended soon from Italy to other high-potential European markets – initially Germany, the United Kingdom and Spain.

The timing of the launch of the PFS strategy has been determined, amongst other things, by the profound changes currently sweeping through Europe. Various developments suggest that customer relations will be realigned over the next three to five years. These developments include: ever-greater general prosperity and the simultaneous corrosion of state social security systems, both of

Banking and insurance services from under one roof. The Horw branch near Lucerne. Photo taken in 2000.

which are increasing the emphasis on self-provision for the years after retirement; the marked rise in the significance of brands and brand names, including in the financial services sector; new distribution channels such as the Internet; and finally the convergence of the European market as a whole with the introduction of the single currency. By implementing the PFS strategy, Credit Suisse Group has put itself in a position to exploit the new opportunities as they arise.[355]

Part Three: A New Paradigm

Ein Portal öffnet sich...

Hinter diesem Portal erwartet Sie wohl das
emsige Geschäftsleben einer Grossbank,
aber auch die stets zuvorkommende Bedienung
und der freundschaftliche Empfang
Ihres persönlichen Beraters.

SCHWEIZERISCHE
KREDITANSTALT
Paradeplatz

Advertisement from 1965.

Mentalities and images

Until the end of the 1970s SKA lagged a long way behind its two great rivals, SBV and SBG. Having been the clear number two amongst the Swiss major banks in 1946, as measured by total assets, 30 years later it had just as clearly been relegated to third place; what is more, the distance between it and the two market leaders was growing all the time. Thanks to a sustained economic boom, SKA was still able to record steady growth, but it was quickly overtaken by SBG, which had started from a much worse position than SKA after the war. The different rates of equity capital growth at the three major banks were particularly telling. Until 1966, SKA just about kept pace with SBV in this regard, but SBG had locked on to a much steeper growth trajectory. While SKA's equity capital increased from Sfr 252 million to Sfr 576 million between 1956 and 1966 (a growth factor of 2.3), SBG's went up from Sfr 182 million to no less than Sfr 965 million (a factor of 5.3). And though SBG did take over a number of large financial institutions, such as Interhandel in 1966, during this period, this is still not sufficient to explain the discrepancy in growth rates. So what happened?

The starting point

After the end of the Second World War, and following a bout of structural adjustment by the major banks, SKA's management was not prepared to fundamentally change its approach in response to the dawning of the new era. The great boom of the late 1920s and the subsequent collapse of international business was still fresh in the minds of the men running the bank. Throughout the years of crisis and war they had maintained a policy of caution, and in 1945 it was still very uncertain which way the world economy and world politics would develop. Conditions were still difficult for international business, and business operations were hampered by numerous obstacles as a result of the nationalization of banks and continuing problems with transfers. Various experts predicted that conflict with the USSR would break out in the near future and that this would lead to another economic crash. Fear of a post-war depression was widespread in Switzerland as elsewhere. Caution thus appeared to be an appropriate attitude. A leading proponent of the pessimistic view, Walter Adolf Jöhr, professor at the St. Gallen Handelshochschule, exerted a great influence over his father Adolf Jöhr, who served as chairman of SKA's board of directors from 1940 to 1953.[356]

Soon, however, the omens for economic development changed. In 1949 the Marshall Plan for the reconstruction of the European economy was launched, and Europe entered into a phase of economic upswing on the coat-tails of the USA. Unfortunately, SKA's managers failed to respond to this new dynamism. Even more unfortunately they felt that the wisdom of their cautious stance was actually confirmed by the Korean War (1950–1953), the Hungarian uprising (1956), the Cuban missile crisis (1962), and generally by the threat that the Cold War would escalate.

The flagship of Swiss banking is overtaken

> The attempt to maintain the luster of the old days made it much more difficult for the bank to conquer new markets.

After 1945, SKA operated primarily as a commercial and business bank, as it had done in the 19th century. It paid little attention to customers with smaller portfolios, but had an extensive constituency of large customers built up over the course of several decades. The bank thus retained the image that had set it apart throughout the years: that of a prestige, superior bank serving the wealthiest clientele in Switzerland.

In these terms, SKA was still regarded as the flagship of the Swiss major banks – even after it had been thoroughly overtaken by its two competitors in terms of size. Its core client base of industrial companies and the haute bourgeois elite remained loyal to the bank, confirming its prestigious image. In their high-handed complacency, SKA's top executives failed to notice that new customer segments were quickly gaining in significance, and that SBV and SBG had already secured large slices of this fresh market for themselves. SKA had not prepared itself for – and for too long was simply not interested in – courting new customers from amongst the companies operating in high-potential segments of the market.

With its classical banking culture, better suited to maintaining the status quo than to innovation, SKA maneuvered itself further and further away from the accelerating trend towards modernization in business and society in general. The more the competing banks – especially SBG – opened themselves up to modern trends and prospects, the more anachronistic SKA's position began to appear.

Even though its rivals were enjoying considerably more success, SKA still could not bring itself to change. SBV, which took the same conservative view as SKA in some areas, was respected to a certain extent by the men at Paradeplatz – unlike SBG. When in 1945/46, for example, the rumor started going round that SBG would have to close down, SKA barely took note. SKA, as the bank for Zurich's old money, saw itself as a Swiss version of the prestigious US bank J. P. Morgan, while SBG was cast in the role of the populist Citibank. Meanwhile, SBG, which was still standing on shaky ground even after taking over the bigger (by total assets) Eidgenössische Bank in 1945, had little to lose. Consequently it adopted a forward-looking strategy that made full use of the dynamism of the time, and that by the 1960s had transformed the former 'peasants' bank' into the number one Swiss major bank. Even the meteoric rise of its rival failed to elicit much of a response from SKA, however. Symptomatic of its head-in-the-sand attitude was the astonishment and outrage shown when SBG took over Bündner Privatbank in 1962. Having maintained good relations with this venerable private bank for many years, the SKA's executive board simply had not expected that the 'shirt-sleeved upstart' could possibly swallow it up. Finally, SKA was left trailing when SBG entered wholeheartedly into savings and mortgage business and, as part of this strategy, carefully built up its network of branches in Switzerland. Within ten years it increased its number of domestic branches from 39 (1956) to 100 (1966). During the 1960s, while SBG was racing ahead with the development of its branch operations, SKA failed to take the necessary steps to finally transform itself from a hidebound Zurich institution into a truly Swiss bank. Between 1956 and 1966 it expanded its domestic branch network by only 22 new offices, to 54.

Ruled by status

Unshakeable in their convictions, the managers of SKA continued to cultivate their 'sensible and moderate approach'.[357] This attitude becomes more comprehensible when seen in the light of the bank's central concern with saving money. The whole bank was obsessed by economy. Everything had to cost as little as possible. Even short-term costs that promised to yield long-term returns were viewed with skepticism. The doors at Paradeplatz were closed for a long time to innovative ideas and to attempts to make the most of the new market potential. SKA did not seem to need to open up and change. And the figures only confirmed this view. It might no longer have been the biggest bank, but it was still the most profitable.

'You often get the feeling with us that customers are expected to feel fortunate merely to be able to talk to SKA' ('White Book', p. 7).

This reluctance to look at what was happening in the outside world was also due to a large extent to the social make-up of the executive board. Even in the 1960s, the bank was still recruiting executive board members from remarkably similar backgrounds. Entry to this closed circle was granted on the basis of origins (Zurich), religion (protestant), academic training (law) and banking background (career at head office).

Perhaps the most fundamental characteristic of SKA's corporate culture was that the bank was not really 'managed', since each member of the executive board – and each senior manager – essentially did what he thought best.[358] Allocation of responsibilities was based not on an executive board member's skills and strengths, but on the number of years he had served at the bank. Until 1977, no agenda was drawn up for executive board meetings, and no order of priority was established for the business at hand. Members of the board spoke by order of seniority, reporting on whatever they thought important. Minutes were not kept. The individual operational units did not report measurable, transparent results, and senior managers enjoyed such confidence that controls were neglected – a situation that was to blow up in the bank's face with the Chiasso Affair.

Central planning and support units and management bodies were barely visible and there was no sign at all of the kind of benchmarking against competitors that has become so vital to modern businesses. At SKA, thought and action were governed by a strict, internal, and closed system of values. This sometimes took an absurd form, as at the bank's management conferences, which well into the 1970s used a seating plan that ensured that everyone was placed relative to everyone else in a way that exactly reflected his or her position in the SKA hierarchy.

Forced to become a 'super-universal bank'?

'As far as competition with the other banks is concerned, Felix W. Schulthess, chairman of the board of directors, is of the view that SKA cannot let too big a gap grow, because then there would be a danger that SKA would be forever fixed in the public mind as the number three bank. The battle is being waged partly via the opening of branches, though experience shows that new branches contribute relatively little – and only slowly – to the procurement of deposits and to the growth of total assets. [...] Our overall policy must accord with our own views and not be influenced too much by what the others are doing. The question of whether to introduce savings books is germane here. The continual growth of the major banks has its darker side, and in the long run is not a good thing. The Swiss people do not regard such large-scale consolidation very favorably. Concern may also be expressed at the political level. Nonetheless, the question must be asked as to whether Bankgesellschaft's actions force us to move towards becoming a "super-universal bank".'[359]

One thing was becoming ever clearer: SKA had failed to keep up with its more dynamic competitors. The fact that some lessons had been learned even

Credit Suisse was run like a country club.

SKA is only for big customers

The difficulties which started to pile up in 1973 – the oil crisis, the increasing exodus of customer deposits from the banking sector, and the incipient recession – affected the economy as a whole and thus hurt all of the Swiss banks. Owing to the difficult position it was already in, SKA was, however, hit hardest of all. The following extract from a letter written on 18 November 1975 by Karl Reichmuth, branch manager at SKA Schwyz, to executive board member Heinz R. Wuffli illustrates the problem.

In response to the question of why SKA only managed to increase its savings deposits by 2% in the first half of 1975, the worst figure of all the major banks, Karl Reichmuth referred to the comparatively small size of the bank's branch network and SKA's overriding image as a bank for large customers – a point that had been brought home to him by a conversation in a Schwyz inn: 'A senior civil servant said he would have to cash in his savings book with us because the savings bank was paying $1/2$% more interest than us. When told that SKA's investment book would in fact pay $5 1/2$%, he said that that was not the same as a savings book. A small businessman added that we were there for the big customers, not the small ones, and that when loans had been restricted, we made sure we looked after the large clients first. As a major bank we had not even granted a small mortgage loan to a former employee who had worked for us for eleven years. By contrast, the small savings bank that we were talking about had been able to make the loan even in the bad year of 1973.'

Karl Reichmuth's letter went on to comment on this conversation: 'You can see that amongst the middle classes, a slogan like "Your Partner" just doesn't work, because the word-of-mouth is that quite the opposite is true. [...] Since our image in this area of business has become even worse in the meantime, I see it as my duty, ... to raise the question of whether the team responsible for our range of products is paying sufficient attention to the situation in the middle class market.'

before the great crisis hit the bank in 1977 did not help much. The bank had acknowledged that business with private customers was another key strand alongside commercial banking and that efforts had to be made in savings business, but this was still not enough. Unless SKA was prepared to tailor its services to new client needs and to build a core market for itself in Switzerland, its descent into mid-table obscurity was inevitable.

Given this background at home it may seem surprising that in the mid-1970s SKA upgraded its financial stake in a US investment bank to a strategic participation. This far-sighted move laid the foundations for one of the three strategic pillars of the 'new' SKA, leading to its later significant position in investment banking and to the creation of its new home markets in the USA and the United Kingdom.

1965–1975: SKA's image – from within and without

Increasing prosperity created new demands and new forms of consumer behavior. Demand for banking services grew, helping the banks to attract more and more customers; but while its competitors tackled the new challenges head on, SKA persisted in prioritizing its traditional self-image. It was not until the 1960s that the bank's managers began to acknowledge that something needed to be done, and from 1965 the bank commissioned a variety of external studies aimed at identifying and analyzing its image amongst the general public. At the same time these image studies identified specific underlying values on which the bank could base its new marketing activities. From the 1960s onwards, the banks became generally more interested in image analysis and in targeted advertising and marketing campaigns, having seen how useful such tools had been for other industries, particular the consumer goods industry and the marketing pioneers of the food and detergents sectors.

Essentially, all of the external studies commissioned by SKA between 1965 and 1975 confirmed that the bank's image had not changed very much at all. SKA was regarded as a Zurich bank and as an institution for large customers. It was generally believed that SKA had little interest in small savers, women or young people. The bank was regarded as a serious organization, but also as conservative and not particularly open to innovation. It became clear that the bank's PR work left a lot to be desired: though SKA customers were more than averagely satisfied with their bank, non-customers rated SKA as much worse than the other majors.

Farbstein, Farner and Explora

In 1965, the so-called 'Farbstein Study' came to the conclusion that SKA's image was being impaired in part by its very name[360]: 'The term "Anstalt" [institution] … has very impersonal and functional connotations, thus reinforcing the bank's image of "anonymity".' It went on to say: 'The associations conjured up by SKA tend to be things like "safe", "rather cautious", "not happy about taking risks", etc.' Large sections of the general public regarded SKA as a 'typical' major bank. 'Its very "impersonal" image creates preconceptions like "minimal contact", "insufficient advice", etc. The current situation is not very good in that "passive" savers already have the even safer alternative of the Kantonalbank, while "active" savers tend to prefer other banks.'

The Farbstein Report formed the basis for a 'Study of the use of public relations and advertising to increase Schweizerische Kreditanstalt's customer funds in all areas'. This study, which was conducted by the advertising agency Rudolf Farner, proposed that SKA introduce some new elements to its advertising and PR activities:

- Publishing articles in selected newspapers
- Press conferences
- Creation of an 'SKA prize' for outstanding performances within the bank
- Competitions and direct marketing via mailings

In addition, the bank should offer new services to meet the growing demand for savings and investment vehicles.[361] The Farner Report's central recommendation was for a 'critical review and, where necessary, a change, in all the elements of SKA's operations that impact directly on customers (conduct and appearance of contact persons; premises…; printed materials)'. Farner wanted to give SKA a personal face. To do this, SKA's advertising needed to address customers primarily on an emotional level, conveying the message that: '… Schweizerische Kreditanstalt is your friend and expert adviser on all money matters. Whether you have small sums of money or large, you can turn to the bank at any time and you will always be given open and valuable information.'

The Explora Study of 1975 showed once again what the general public thought of the major banks[362]: SBG was clearly the most popular major, and the one that was most attractive to small savers; SBV was the 'most neutral'; and SKA was perceived as the major bank 'from which the small saver was psychologically most distant'. The study went on to say that: 'The selective effect of SKA's image means that savers who do not see themselves as being financially strong do not feel comfortable about investing their money with SKA. The feeling that a bank might not accept them represents an insurmountable barrier to small savers.' Survey results also showed a negative response to the bank's logo: 'SKA trails the other two major banks in terms of spontaneous recognition of its logo and house colors. The calm, undynamic blue of SKA matches its current image. It would be worth examining whether an optimal realignment of SKA's image could be supported by the introduction of more dynamic house colors.' The study concluded that: 'In general, the public's image of SKA, which currently tends to be characterized by a rather colorless, undynamic seriousness and a distance from average savers, should be given more emotional content. The bank's current style of advertising is too one-sided and too intellectual for many savers. As far as memorability of advertising is concerned, SKA lags a long way behind its two main rivals.'

The 'White Book'

SKA was not content, however, merely to commission external reports, and in 1975 it surveyed the views of its entire senior management. The results, which were collated in the so-called 'White Book'[363], revealed a clear picture: while some senior managers spoke out in favor of the status quo and wanted to stick to SKA's traditional image, the clear majority expressed a desire to pay more attention to retail business and to subject the whole bank to a process of thorough modernization.

At first glance, two things are surprising: the sheer fact that SKA's public image had hardly changed over ten years (although several studies had come to a similar conclusion); and the fact that the view from within was so similar to the view from without. In the context of the bank as a whole, however, none of this is perhaps as surprising as it first seems. It was never going to be enough for SKA just to introduce new services – in retail banking for instance – or to try and appeal to previously neglected customer segments like women or young people. The gradual changes that the bank made in these directions in the late 1960s and early 1970s did not amount to a reorientation. And if the bank was not willing to accept the new social and economic reality as a challenge and to address this challenge head-on, then there was no reason for its image in the public's eye to change very much. Public image was ultimately not a matter of advertising: it was a reflection of SKA's business policy and business practice – a reflection of the bank's innermost being.

'Advertising and the press department have to be rethought. Alongside our classic general advertising in SKA blue, we need to sell ourselves with brighter colors' ('White Book', p. 38).

'In French-speaking Switzerland we have to get rid of our image as a "Zurich" bank. We ought to make an overture to the French-speakers' ('White Book', p. 40).

Reawakening

This, then, was the situation that prevailed when in 1977 the Chiasso Affair broke, calling into question all the measures used thus far in the attempt to improve the bank's image. 'Chiasso' forced SKA to take extreme action. There was no alternative but to embark on an uncompromising, forward-looking strategy. The only thing that could rescue SKA's position as an independent major bank was a fundamental reorientation.

First of all, SKA's image, which had been severely damaged by the events of 1977, had to be reconstructed by means of a campaign stretching over several years. The measures launched in 1978 to enhance the bank's public image focused on the core messages of 'popularization' and 'regionalization'. On the one hand, SKA aimed to position itself as a 'populist' bank that would gladly look after anybody's financial needs. On the other, it also wanted to revise its branch policy and markedly increase the number of branches it maintained in Switzerland. It thus hoped to be able to position itself as a locally based provider in every region of the country.

SKA was now also trying new methods to unlock the creative potential of each of its employees, a fact that is demonstrated very clearly by the slogan competition held in spring 1977. This competition was advertised in the bank's *bulletin* magazine and carried a prize of SKA shares for the winners.[364] The jury had to choose from a great number of entries in German, French, Italian and English.[365] Winning entries included the following suggestions: 'In Bankfragen – SKA fragen!' ('For banking – ask SKA!'), 'Wer Bank sagt, meint Kreditanstalt' ('If you say bank, you mean SKA'), 'Qui dit banque suisse dit Crédit Suisse' ('If you say Swiss bank, you mean Credit Suisse'), 'The bank you cannot miss – Credit Suisse' and 'Banca sicura – CS su misura' ('Secure bank – CS is tailor-made').

The worth of this effort can be measured by its success. Both the German slogan that was later used for the bank's advertising 'SKA – für alle da' ('SKA – there for everyone') and the French slogan 'De père en fils au Crédit Suisse' ('From father to son: Credit Suisse') were actually based on suggestions submitted to the competition. The German was a shortened version of the entry 'Von Hänschen klein bis Grosspapa – die Kreditanstalt ist für alle da' ('From the little boy to grandpa – SKA is there for everyone'), and the French slogan was based on the suggestion, 'Pour Papa, Maman, fille et fils – la meilleure banque: le Crédit Suisse' ('For father, mother, daughter and son – the best bank is Credit Suisse').

The decisive expansion of advertising activities and the increasingly professional use of marketing had an effect. By taking the bull by the horns, within a short space of time the bank was able not only to make up the damage done to its image by the Chiasso Affair, but also to launch a process of genuine transformation: the upper-class Old Maid of Paradeplatz was turned into the new and dynamic SKA. An independent study carried out in 1979 characterized SKA's image as follows: 'Switzerland's third-biggest bank ... has recently been negatively impacted by the Chiasso Affair, but it has been able to overcome most

---

SKA's entry into sports sponsorship marked the bank's breakthrough to modern communication techniques.

of the negative influences thanks to active PR work. [...] The bank's sponsorship of the "Tour de Suisse" cycle race, the dissemination of information in its vibrant house colors and a large number of campaigns besides are clearly helping to make the bank more popular on a national level.'[366] By 1980, SKA was already being regarded by companies as the most dynamic of the major banks and at the board of directors meeting of 10 September 1981, the spokesman for the executive board, Rainer E. Gut, was able to state that: 'As far as public awareness levels are concerned, we and SBG are far ahead of the rest. [...] Our logo [is] almost as well known as that of SBG, which until recently had a clear lead over everyone else. Even more significant is our position amongst young people: no less than 62% of under-21-year-olds ... name us as their preferred bank.'[367]

Der SKA-Gigant

Sie sind in hellen Scharen erschienen. Doch die 3099 Teilhaber der Kreditanstalt hatten an der Generalversammlung zum «Fall Chiasso» nichts zu bestimmen. Die grosse Schau für die kleinen Aktionäre war gelungene Kosmetik. Die Chiasso-Pleite kann den Geschäften der drittgrössten Schweizer Bank nichts anhaben. Das SKA-Imperium am Zürcher Paradeplatz steht so fest wie eh und je

Der Gigant kam nicht ins Zittern

'The Giant is Not Quaking' The article went on to say: 'General meeting at Zurich's Züspa-Halle: spotlights lit up the members of the executive board on the podium. In the middle stood chairman of the board of directors Oswald Aeppli, his face visible to all shareholders on a giant television screen. The SKA chief's central statement was that "the bank's earnings power has not been compromised".'
Schweizer Illustrierte, 27 June 1977.

The Chiasso Affair

In April 1977 it became apparent that the managers of the SKA branch in Chiasso had massively exceeded their powers of authority and had broken the law: instead of putting customer deposits totaling Sfr 2.2 billion into blue-chip investments, they had taken this money off the branch's balance sheet and invested it in Texon Finanzanstalt of Liechtenstein and its associated companies. The affair resulted in the biggest loss SKA had suffered in its entire history and shook confidence in the Swiss banking industry as a whole. 'Chiasso' filled the pages of the Swiss and international media for many months. On the political level, the subject of actively assisting capital flight became a hot topic and there were calls for greater control, or even nationalization, of the banks.

Realignment and fundamental reform were needed if the banks were to avoid over-hasty and excessive state regulation. The Chiasso Affair triggered a change in the mentality at work in the Swiss banking sector, quickly leading to the development of new forms of self-regulation. At SKA itself, the crisis of 1977 prompted the bank to strike out for new shores and transform itself from a traditional Zurich institution into an international financial services provider. The Chiasso Affair thus triggered a sea-change in the self-image and the strategic orientation of SKA.

Ernst Kuhrmeier on the relationship with Texon Finanzanstalt

'At the start of the 1960s, business at Chiasso began to expand. Alongside our large lira transfers, we were also approached for loans. Since these would not always have been sufficiently collateralized by current assets, the limits requested were rarely approved. Owing to the fact that nearly all the credit applications came from very respectable parties, however, I was sorry not to be able to do the business. My desire to secure good business for the bank led me to seek alternative solutions, and I soon began to process lending business through Texon. I was helped by the fact that a very good customer ... was willing to make several million francs available to Texon. Over the course of the years, more and more customers invested their cash with Texon.'[369]

From secret investments in an network of companies to the discovery of irregularities

The creation of Texon Finanzanstalt, Vaduz

Chiasso is a town in Canton Ticino, located right on Switzerland's border with Italy. On 17 April 1961, Ernst Kuhrmeier, at that time the deputy manager of SKA's Chiasso branch, set up Texon Finanzanstalt, Vaduz, which was entered into the Commercial Register of the Principality of Liechtenstein on 25 April 1961. The first, and for the time being only, member of the board of directors was Alessandro Villa, a tax advisor at the Studio legale Maspoli & Noseda legal practice. The new company's foundation capital amounted to Sfr 50,000, which was certified as having been deposited at SKA's Chiasso branch.[368]

Over subsequent years Ernst Kuhrmeier steadily expanded Texon's business activities. He was helped by several of the staff at the Chiasso branch, but most particularly by Studio legale Maspoli & Noseda. Deposit-taking was the main priority. Ernst Kuhrmeier set the ball rolling – and once it was rolling it could not be stopped. When a bank makes a fiduciary investment on the Euromarket on behalf of a customer, the customer bears the risk, of course; but it is up to the bank to ensure that the customer's money only goes into first-class investments. Texon did not fulfill the latter criterion, so customers were only prepared to put their money into Texon if the investment was also guaranteed by SKA Chiasso branch. 'Many of the customers, all of whom were also customers of the bank, were also given guarantees.'[370] A further attraction for customers was that Texon offered higher interest rates than other institutions. SKA's branch in Chiasso thus became the preferred bank for Italian clients. Rivals began to get jealous.

From loans to participations

To start with, the short-term loans made to Texon were usually paid back in the proper manner, but in the mid-1960s, the first major problem became apparent. 'A loan ..., secured only by ... shares, could not be paid back owing to the collapse in the share price. [...] Almost at the same time, two loans, one to the Ampaglas plastics factory and ... [one to a] wine company, started to deteriorate. I had to do something. After much intense consideration I came to the conclusion that I should convert these loans into equity participations by Texon.'[371]

Ernst Kuhrmeier had built up a large network of contacts in Italy and Switzerland. He was a 'doer' who always seemed to have a solution, whatever the problem was. His reputation was such that other SKA branches would even refer their customers to him when restrictions on their powers of authority meant that they could not handle the business themselves.

In Texon, Ernst Kuhrmeier had a vehicle that permitted him, for example, to issue an additional loan alongside one approved by SKA head office. The following example, from 1963, shows how the mechanism worked. A customer needing a bank loan went to SKA's Lugano branch, which referred him to SKA Chiasso. Ernst Kuhrmeier approved the loan and issued part of it through the branch and the rest through Texon. When the customer inquired, Kuhrmeier informed him that Texon was a financial company run by Studio legale Maspoli & Noseda. The customer had no reason to doubt that this was so, and assumed that head office in Zurich knew all about this financial company. The manager of SKA Lugano, Ugo Primavesi, was left wondering how the Chiasso branch could grant a loan to a customer when head office had not given his own branch approval for the same loan.[372]

The withholding tax problem 1968/69

By a rather circuitous route, in autumn 1968 head office in Zurich got to hear of some irregularities involving withholding tax at the Chiasso branch. During a tax audit at head office, an employee of the Federal Tax Administration dropped several hints to Hans-Ulrich Frey, head of the SKA tax department, that a 'major withholding tax affair' had been discovered at one of the branches. 'I finally got it out of him that the branch in question was Chiasso. We never heard anything at all from the branch itself, although … all the other banks in Chiasso were talking about it. We deliberately did nothing ourselves because we wanted to see whether and when the branch itself would report in'.[373]

Finally the matter was discussed with Ernst Kuhrmeier at the management conference of 14 February 1969. However, the initiative did not come from Kuhrmeier himself – instead the matter was raised as a result of complaints made by Alfred Hartmann, a member of SBG's executive board, to his SKA colleague Hans Escher about the Chiasso branch, which 'was using guarantee agreements with customers to circumvent interest rate conventions for third party borrowers'.[374] Hans Escher brought the head of the tax department along to his interview with Ernst Kuhrmeier.

Hans Escher and Hans-Ulrich Frey were given the standard explanation about the relationship between the branch and Studio legale Maspoli & Noseda, and no action was taken as a result of the interview of 14 February 1969. Hans Escher did not inform his colleagues in the executive board, or anyone else within the bank, about the matter.

Competitors intervene

Julius Weibel, who was responsible at head office for interbank relationships, was surprised to find during a routine visit in autumn 1969 that various Ticino-based banks were complaining about unfair competition from SKA's branch in Chiasso. Banca Cantonale Ticinese in Bellinzona, Banco di Roma in Lugano, and Banca della Svizzera Italiana in Lugano referred specifically to the fact that the Chiasso branch was accepting funds on a fiduciary basis from Swiss and foreign customers to invest on the Euromarket, and guaranteeing full coverage of the risk involved. These rival banks were considering making an official complaint to SKA's executive board. They were also determined to lay the matter before the Federal Tax Administration.[376]

Julius Weibel informed the executive board member responsible for the Chiasso branch, Hans Escher, of his findings. In a letter dated 19 September 1969,

---

The Chiasso branch's earnings performance was excellent. When asked, Ernst Kuhrmeier always described Texon as a financial institution owned by Studio legale Maspoli & Noseda, and mentioned the good business that this legal practice forwarded to the branch. Ernst Kuhrmeier enjoyed the confidence of his superiors in Zurich, who saw no reason not to believe what he told them.

Hans-Ulrich Frey's notes on the interview with Hans Escher und Ernst Kuhrmeier included these observations: 'As far as tax is concerned, the following has been established: Italian money was credited to the account of one Texan [sic!] Finanz-Anstalt, Vaduz. This institution is managed by the Maspoli law practice in Chiasso, with which our branch maintains close relations. The Chiasso branch stood guarantee for the investors' money. Some of the investors were customers of the branch, some were customers of the Maspoli practice. In return for its guarantee, the bank received a commission of 1/8% from Texan. The investors were paid their interest of 5–6% in the form of a normal credit payment debited to Texan. It is not completely clear whether the investors were familiar with the name of Texan. Presumably in most cases they were not.'[375]

Hans Escher and Julius Weibel reminded Ernst Kuhrmeier – 'personally and in confidence' – of the complaints made some time before by Ticino banks about certain practices involving fiduciary investments. 'These complaints have now been repeated more forcefully during a brief visit by J. Weibel ..., as you can see from the enclosed photocopy of a memorandum. [...] Since these rumors refuse to die down, please give us a detailed report on the situation in writing, as the whole problem is of great concern to us.'[377]

On 25 September 1969, Ernst Kuhrmeier gave his response in a long letter. He started off by conceding that various Ticino banks had indeed complained about the SKA branch about a year before on account of its acceptance of deposits at unusually high interest rates. Neither had withholding tax been deducted from the interest payments. 'I explained at the time that it could only be pure fiduciary business, though I did not mention our relationship with TEXON-FINANZANSTALT, Vaduz, which is owned by Studio Avv. Maspoli-Noseda-Pedrazzini.'[378]

Kuhrmeier explained that this financial company had been set up in 1961 by the law practice in response to the capital flight that was beginning at the time, and to the transfer of Italian assets to Swiss holding companies. 'These lawyers now serve more than a thousand holding companies, some of which are very significant. A large proportion of the customers involved also made investments in Texon. [...] Over the last few years we have often had to put up guarantees in connection with investments in Texon made by these customers.'[379]

Ernst Kuhrmeier kept his explanations very vague. He did not talk directly about the branch's customers, though at the end of his letter he did mention the dispute with the Federal Tax Administration. 'However, since our bank only guaranteed repayment of the capital, and because we made no interest payments, we never thought that these transactions would be subject to withholding tax. [...] Contrary to the view of highly qualified experts at Studio Maspoli, namely Dr. E. Gada and Dr. A. Villa, both former senior officials of the Cantonal Tax Administration in Bellinzona, Bern decided that withholding tax should be charged on money which came from Texon under our guarantee. Texon subsequently had to pay arrears of [around] Sfr 450,000.'[380]

Texon as a bank within the bank

Ernst Kuhrmeier also expressly confirmed that his investments in the Euromarket were always made in accordance with the existing directives, so that there could be no question that he was indulging in unfair competition. The rival banks simply did not like the fact that his branch was doing so well with Italian clients. 'I very much hope that my explanations will help finally to clear up the whole matter. We have been exposed to sometimes veiled attacks from within the ranks of the Ticino Bankers' Association as a result of our excellent relations with the very active gentlemen of the Studio Maspoli-Noseda-Pedrazzini, so I am happy if our close relationship with TEXON, which is now practically a bank within the bank, is clearly explained. Please contact me at any time if you require further information.'[381]

Hans Escher took note of these explanations and passed them on to SKA's tax department. Meanwhile the Banca della Svizzera Italiana had been to see Julius Weibel again and given him a copy of one of the Chiasso branches 'guarantee letters'.[382] On 8 October 1969, Hans-Ulrich Frey and Albert Nägeli, head auditor, paid a personal visit to the branch. By taking samples at random, they established that fiduciary loans and fiduciary investments in the Euromarket had indeed been carried out in accordance with the directives issued by head office. They then investigated the transactions conducted with Texon Finanzanstalt, Vaduz.

Hans-Ulrich Frey and Albert Nägeli learned nothing new about the Texon investments to which formal guarantees had been attached: the investigation carried out by the Federal Tax Administration and the subsequent payment of Sfr 457,356.45 of withholding tax had since become common knowledge. However, further questioning revealed that the Studio legale Maspoli & Noseda had adjusted its business practices as a result of the intervention by the Federal Tax Administration. 'Our branch was no longer asked for formal joint and several guarantees for Texon investments. Instead Chiasso expressly confirmed to customers who asked Texon that the investment would be repaid on the due date.'[283] This 'new trick', which 'evidently' upset the competition, was categorized by the head of the tax department as a tax evasion maneuver that could not be tolerated.

Hans-Ulrich Frey passed on his conclusions to Hans Escher. Department N – the body responsible for approving all lending business that did not fall within the authority of a branch – was told to instruct Ernst Kuhrmeier in writing on behalf of the executive board that he was not allowed to carry out transactions of this type any longer, and furthermore that he should make sure that by the end of 1969 all existing Texon investments were sorted out so as to accord in every way with SKA's directives. 'If the law practice of Maspoli-Noseda-Pedrazzini should come to you again with proposals of this kind, please submit them to us for review before you act on them or carry out any new types of transaction.'[384] On 23 October 1969, the branch wrote to thank head office for the letter. 'We assure you that we will adhere strictly to your instructions when carrying out our business.'[385] This assurance from the branch, addressed to the tax department, was brought to the attention of Hans Escher and department N. It was not thought that any further investigations – for example into Texon Finanzanstalt, Vaduz, which had been mentioned throughout the correspondence – would be necessary. Not even Ernst Kuhrmeier's remark that Texon was 'now a bank within the bank', prompted any kind of reaction. Ernst Kuhrmeier's word was good enough for the Zurich head office.

Hans Escher received fresh complaints from rival banks in February 1970. On his instruction, Gerhard Stuker of the tax department phoned Ernst Kuhrmeier about these on 20 February 1970. 'Mr. Kuhrmeier explained to me in the clearest possible terms that his fiduciary investments were made precisely in accordance with our instructions. [...] Mr. Kuhrmeier is sure that the transactions he has carried out since our intervention could not have given any cause

'Texon belongs to Studio Avv. Maspoli-Noseda-Pedrazzini, with which Chiasso enjoys a close working relationship. All of the Studio's Italian customers are referred to our branch for their banking needs. Roughly speaking, one can say that the Studio's Italian customers are also our banking customers' (Memorandum from Hans-Ulrich Frey, 16 October 1969).

for complaint and that the objections which had reached the ears of Dr. Escher either had no basis in truth or could only be referring to previous business.'[386] Hans Escher thanked Gerhard Stuker for his clarifications, which were also passed on to department N. Once again, no further investigations were made.

These events have been described in such detail to show that by the end of the 1960s, SKA's head office had already received enough information to warrant a thorough investigation of the relationship between the Chiasso branch and Texon. Such an investigation did not take place.

In 1970 head office believed that the matter was once and for all under control; but in Chiasso, the business with Texon was going on as before.

During this period, there was a significant increase in the number of staff at Chiasso, from 106 at the start of 1969 to 153 by the start of 1971. Business was booming at the branch, and the management team was strengthened. On 1 January 1975 Ernst Kuhrmeier was promoted to executive vice president, the highest grade below executive board level. He was already being touted as a future member of the executive board.

> Zurich found the constant complaints from its competitors extremely irritating, especially since Ernst Kuhrmeier kept assuring head office that he was adhering strictly to the existing directives.

Chiasso was repeatedly praised at the quarterly management conferences in Zurich, and the branch's results were held up as a model to others. Meanwhile Ernst Kuhrmeier had long become a prisoner of his own success, and business with Texon was expanding inexorably. Liquidity problems at the companies in which Texon had invested constantly had to be bridged with new funds; if any of the companies had been allowed to go bankrupt, the whole house of cards would have come tumbling down. Problem loans were converted into equity participations. It went so far that even loss-making transactions at the branch were transferred to Texon. By doing this Ernst Kuhrmeier was able to 'cure' risk positions that were of concern to head office without any negative consequences for the branch – which earned him yet more points in the eyes of his superiors. The rival banks kept quiet during this period. They too were doing good business with Italian clients in their own way.

> 'In fact, over time Texon had become the branch's "dustbin" for ill-advised loans' (District attorney Paolo Bernasconi during the trial, 19 June 1979).

Starting from very rudimentary beginnings, over the course of the years Ernst Kuhrmeier had built Texon up into a veritable empire of equity participations. Up to 1970, his secretary kept the accounts, but to the outside world Texon was represented by employees of Studio legale Maspoli & Noseda. In 1965 Alfredo Noseda and Elbio Gada joined Alessandro Villa on the Texon board of directors; they also sat on the boards of many of Texon's associated companies. They knew the financial circumstances of the individual companies – including their financial problems – and only they, alongside Ernst Kuhrmeier, had a complete overview of the business. In 1970, Texon moved into its own premises very close to the Studio legale and the SKA branch. Two branch employees now handled the accounts. Apart from Claudio Laffranchi, no SKA employee, not even branch managers, were allowed to enter the new premises or look at Texon's accounts.

Texon was well known throughout the Chiasso branch. Many staff were seconded to carry out special duties for Texon. Ernst Kuhrmeier and Claudio Laffranchi, his deputy, continued to maintain, even to these people, that Texon was simply a very good customer of the branch and that it was owned by the Studio legale. There seemed to be no reason not to trust the generous boss Ernst Kuhrmeier, especially since he paid separately for work done on behalf of Texon.

Management discontent

Ever since Meinrad Perler had been appointed vice president in 1970, a certain amount of discontent had been evident in the ranks of the branch's top employees. Perler noticed from the branch's balance sheet that most of the guarantees that SKA had issued for Texon liabilities had not actually been booked to the accounts. The first major argument between Meinrad Perler and Ernst Kuhrmeier came at a meeting of the branch's managers on 13 July 1972. Contrary to his better knowledge, Kuhrmeier claimed that the branch had a guarantee limit of Sfr 20 million approved by head office for Texon. Meinrad Perler remained skeptical, though he – like his colleagues – continued to profit from the advantages bestowed by Texon.

On 26 February 1975 there was a meeting of the whole management team. Texon was one of the subjects on the agenda. Meinrad Perler acted as spokesperson and expressed the suspicion that the branch had issued unbooked guarantees, and that the money invested with Texon was in jeopardy. Once again Ernst Kuhrmeier claimed that there were no losses at Texon. For the first time he actually named some figures. Texon held customer deposits of Sfr 1.3 billion, while the branch had guaranteed only Sfr 200 million.[307]

As well as Meinrad Perler, his management colleagues Claudio Künzli and Giorgio Belloni also found themselves in a dilemma. They were convinced that Ernst Kuhrmeier was not telling them the whole truth, but they did not know the full extent of the Texon web. They persuaded themselves that Zurich must also know all about Texon. Meinrad Perler and his colleagues did not want under any circumstances to endanger their own positions by denouncing their boss. If they had done this, they would undoubtedly have missed out on the generous unrecorded bonuses that Ernst Kuhrmeier paid out at the end of every year for work done for Texon. In addition, Texon often proved very convenient for them personally: when Ernst Kuhrmeier booked ill-advised loans or currency transactions to Texon, his staff did not have to account for them to head office. Reports to head office, which had long been urgently required, were thus simply not made. With a certain fatalism, the staff just sat back and waited to see what would happen next.

Warnings at the highest level

Zurich thus received no concrete information from the Chiasso branch about possible irregularities. However, rival banks had become active once again. Two interventions came at the highest level in 1976. On 14 January 1976, member of the executive board Heinz R. Wuffli was visited by his SBG counterpart Philippe de Weck, who warned Wuffli about business practices at SKA's Chiasso branch, and handed him a copy of a guarantee issued by the branch to cover liabilities held by Texon to the tune of more than Sfr 900,000. Wuffli did not rule out the possibility that he had already come across the name 'Texon'. He subsequently talked to department N and found out that Texon had a guarantee limit of Sfr 12 million secured against current assets with the Chiasso branch. He then telephoned Ernst Kuhrmeier, who explained to him that the business brought up by de Weck was a special case that he had been obliged to carry out for a friend. Kuhrmeier promised not to issue any more guarantees like this and confirmed once again that all due withholding tax would of course be paid. Heinz R. Wuffli was reassured. He produced no memorandum of his conversation with Philippe de Weck, and he kept the copy of the guarantee that de Weck had left with him in his files. At the executive board meeting of 27 January 1976 he reported the meeting with Philippe de Weck to the best of his recollection. None of his executive board colleagues reacted particularly to his report; the tax problems of 1968/69 were no longer of any interest. As was usual for this time, no minutes were kept of the executive board meeting.[388]

In April 1976, SBG made another attempt to raise the matter, though this time they went directly to the chairman of SKA's board of directors. On 14 April 1976, the chairmen of the boards of SBG and SKA, Alfred Schaefer and Felix W. Schulthess, drove together to Winterthur for a board meeting of Sulzer. Alfred Schaefer used the opportunity to give his colleague Felix W. Schulthess the hint that he should keep a close eye on Ernst Kuhrmeier's business practices in Chiasso. Felix W. Schulthess was at last confronted directly with the complaints about Ernst Kuhrmeier, which had now been raised on several occasions. He thanked Alfred Schaefer for the tip and mentioned Philippe de Weck's visit to Heinz R. Wuffli in connection with the matter. Felix W. Schulthess was sure that the executive board had since reacted. As far as the chairman of SKA's board of directors was concerned, the matter was thus dealt with. Nevertheless, as far as he could remember, he did inform one or more members of the executive board about his conversation with Alfred Schaefer, though nobody on the executive board could later confirm that he had.[389] In any case, the conversation between Alfred Schaefer and Felix W. Schulthess led to no further investigation of activities at the SKA branch in Chiasso.

The first direct warning signal from Chiasso

In fact, business in Chiasso went on as usual. At the end of 1976, it was time for the annual round of promotions. Following Claudio Laffranchi's elevation in 1975, it was now Meinrad Perler's turn for preferment. He was appointed as a manager of the Chiasso branch as from 1 January 1977. At the management conference in Zurich on 17 December 1976, chief auditor Bernhard Henggeler congratulated Perler, but to Henggeler's astonishment, Perler responded by saying that he did not know whether to accept the promotion or not. Amongst the reasons he gave was the fact that he suspected that Ernst Kuhrmeier might still be maintaining unrecorded guarantees. This was the first direct insinuation by a Chiasso employee about serious irregularities at the branch. Bernhard Henggeler was disturbed. As head of the audit department he could not just ignore Meinrad Perler's remarks. He told him that he would be informing the executive board about their conversation.

At the budget meeting of 5 January 1977, member of the executive board Heinz R. Wuffli (soon to become president of the executive board) was told about the conversation with Meinrad Perler. The chief auditor suggested that the matter be discussed directly with Ernst Kuhrmeier during the audit of the Chiasso branch's balance sheet, which was scheduled for March 1977. There did not appear to be any need for greater urgency.

The collapse of Weisscredit Bank

The event that finally shook the executive board in Zurich out of its complacency was the collapse of Weisscredit Bank, Chiasso. There had been several shakeouts in Ticino's banking community over past years, but none of these had given much cause for concern in Zurich.[390] This situation changed dramatically when Weisscredit Bank, Chiasso, fell into dire trouble at the end of 1976. Deputy executive board member Sergio Demiéville – who before joining SKA had been head of the Weisscredit branch in Lugano, which he had also helped to found – received a cry for help from the troubled bank. In January and February 1977, SKA's accounting and legal departments conducted intensive investigations into Weisscredit's position. It soon became clear that Weisscredit was running a 'bank within a bank' in the form of a Liechtenstein institution called Finanz- und Vertrauenshandelsanstalt, Vaduz, which was over-indebted. SKA thus viewed a possible takeover of Weisscredit as too risky. It informed Weisscredit's managers of this decision on 23 February 1977.[391]

At the end of January 1977, during discussions about the possible acquisition of Weisscredit, the executive board talked for the first time about the rumors that Texon played a similar role for SKA as the Finanz- und Vertrauenshandelsanstalt played for Weisscredit. Oswald Aeppli, who was coming to the end of his term as president of the executive board, was disturbed, and instructed Sergio Demiéville to look into the matter. Again, there seemed to be no need for particular urgency. Finally on 2 March 1977, Demiéville instructed the head of the bank's central accounting department Josef Müller to investigate Texon. Before he could begin, however, Heinz R. Wuffli told Müller on 7 March 1977 that he had already asked the audit department to look into the affair and that these investigations would begin in mid-March. On the weekend of 12/13 March 1977, Robert A. Jeker also became involved. Hoping to learn some details about Texon, he invited Claudio Künzli, who he had known from his time at the Chiasso branch, to dinner. Künzli admitted to Robert A. Jeker that the Chiasso branch's relationship with Texon was indeed 'a copy of the relationship between Weisscredit and the Finanz- und Vertrauenshandelsanstalt'. Jeker was filled with consternation and told Claudio Künzli that he would ring the alarm in Zurich.[392]

On Monday 14 March 1977, Robert A. Jeker told his executive board colleagues what he knew. In a meeting on 15 March 1977 it was decided to call Ernst Kuhrmeier to Zurich on 18 March for questioning by a delegation of the

On 25 March 1977 deputy member of the executive board, Sergio Demiéville was given the 'SITUAZIONE PATRIMONIALE MARZO 1976' (balance sheet as per March 1976) in Chiasso, signed by the Texon directors Alfredo Noseda, Alessandro Villa and Elbio Gada. This showed assets of Sfr 1.4705 billion and liabilities of Sfr 1.45 billion. Sfr 950 million of the liabilities were listed as 'Clienti Studio' and Sfr 460 million as 'Altri clienti'. The assets included five conglomerates, including 'PIROGA (Albarella)', 'AMPA' and 'WINE AND FOOD', with a total value of Sfr 1.26 billion. In an accompanying letter, the three members of the board of directors confirmed 'in good faith' that a customer of their Studio legale had deposited the certificate for Texon's founders' rights with them.[393]

executive board (Heinz R. Wuffli, C. Walter Fessler and Sergio Demiéville). Ernst Kuhrmeier arrived in Zurich on 18 March for his interrogation. He had no documentation with him. Responding to the questions posed he confirmed that Texon existed, but that the situation was under control. Fiduciary investments of a few hundred million Swiss francs had been forwarded to Texon. The executive board delegation demanded that they be shown the balance sheet.

Meanwhile, the auditors had been at work in Chiasso since 14 March. Contrary to all expectations, their investigations yielded no concrete results, and Zurich waited with growing impatience for Ernst Kuhrmeier to submit the promised balance sheet.

Early in the morning of 28 March, an emergency meeting was held in Zurich, attended by Oswald Aeppli, Heinz R. Wuffli, Sergio Demiéville, Hugo von der Crone and Bernhard Henggeler. These men discussed the Texon 'balance sheet', of which they now had a copy, as well as the investigations carried out so far in Chiasso. At last the situation was judged to be very serious; Ernst Kuhrmeier was called to appear in Zurich once again on 30 March 1977.

The shareholders' meeting of 29 March 1977

SKA's 1977 general meeting of shareholders took place on 29 March. That same morning, the Chiasso problem was discussed once again at an executive board meeting. However, it was decided that the facts were as yet so unclear that the matter should not be mentioned at the shareholders' meeting. It would not be responsible for the executive board to tell the shareholders about a problem before they were absolutely sure about all the details. The shareholders meeting thus passed harmoniously and according to the scheduled agenda. Oswald Aeppli had informed the out-going chairman of the board of directors Felix W. Schulthess about the problems at the Chiasso branch on 28 March. By contrast, Hans Schwarzenbach, vice-chairman of the board of directors, was not informed at all – which explains why he was able to say at the shareholders' meeting that Schulthess was leaving his successor a bank 'avec un bilan impeccable' ('with an impeccable record').[394]

On 30 March 1977, Ernst Kuhrmeier came to Zurich and admitted for the first time that Texon had liabilities of Sfr 2 billion, though he continued to maintain that the assets of the participations were available to the bank as long as there was sufficient time to liquidate the exposure.[395]

On the evening of 30 March, Josef Müller and Ernst Kuhrmeier drove to Chiasso. By this time, the executive board had relieved Josef Müller of his other duties and appointed him as full-time commissioner for Texon. His first urgent priority was now to obtain a clear and comprehensive overview of Texon's liabilities. To help him do this, Josef Müller seconded Franz-Josef Groth, a specialist from the auditors' department. By 12 April, the figures had been prepared.

The Texon balance sheet prepared by Franz-Josef Groth as per 31 March 1977 showed a loss of more than Sfr 400 million. Customer deposits came to Sfr 2.2 billion. The assets side included, amongst other items, Texon participations with a book value of Sfr 1.4 billion, though large provisions had to be set aside for these items. There were no individual valuations, however, and the figures were based exclusively on balance sheets and information from staff at the Studio legale Maspoli & Noseda.[396] Heinz R. Wuffli came to Chiasso at lunchtime on 12 April. Josef Müller and Franz-Josef Groth explained the figures to him. Müller said he suspected that a loss estimate of Sfr 300 to 500 million was probably on the low side.[397]

Heinz R. Wuffli returned to Zurich with this unpalatable news. On 13 April a meeting of the executive board, in agreement with the chairman of the board of directors, decided to suspend Ernst Kuhrmeier, Claudio Laffranchi and Meinrad Perler on a provisional basis. The director of the Federal Banking Commission (FBC) and the chairman of the Swiss National Bank (SNB) were informed without delay. The members of the SKA board of directors' finance and credit committee were immediately informed verbally, and the other members of the board of directors were given the news in writing.

On Thursday 14 April 1977, Josef Müller was instructed by the executive board to inform Ernst Kuhrmeier, Claudio Laffranchi and Meinrad Perler of their provisional suspension. He then informed the staff at the branch, immediately triggering a wave of shock and consternation.

On the evening of 14 April 1977, the executive board published a press release.[398] Prior to this, staff reporting directly to Heinz R. Wuffli at head office were told about the irregularities at the Chiasso branch and about the consequences for the employees involved. Head office too was thrown into a state of confusion. Many staff knew Ernst Kuhrmeier as a brilliant banker and a valued colleague. By that evening, 'Chiasso' was already making headlines on radio and television.

Managing the debacle

Initial reactions

The SKA executive board's press release of 14 April 1977 hit Switzerland like a bombshell. Reporting in the media, which had started off rather cautiously, became much more aggressive[399] – the *Tat* talked about a 'Multi-million-franc scandal at the Kreditanstalt'.[400]

This overwhelming response from the media took the executive board completely unawares. Strategic PR platforms were unknown at the time. The executive board's first priority at this point was to secure Texon's assets. In addition, the regulatory authority (the FBC) and the SNB wanted information quickly. There was a great deal of concern that currency controls and the withholding tax laws might have been violated.

Meanwhile, the Chiasso branch was besieged by mainly Italian customers looking for their relationship managers; but with the entire branch management suspended, there was initially nobody left for them to talk to. Many of these customers wanted to withdraw their assets or at least obtain a guarantee that their money was still safe at SKA. Head office arranged to have money taken down to

'Radio Silence From SKA' (*NZZ*, 20 April 1977).

Telex message from SKA to the Swiss media, 14 April 1977.

Translation:
'Statement by the general management of SKA:
Investigations by the bank's internal auditors have revealed that a major foreign client of the Chiasso branch – a financial holding company with various participations in Europe and abroad – is encountering profitability and liquidity problems. In flagrant disregard of its due diligence obligations and powers of authority, the management of the Chiasso branch has concealed the existence of these difficulties for some considerable time. As a result, the bank is likely to incur a substantial loss, though this will be covered by general del credere provisions. The persons responsible have been suspended from their posts until the comprehensive and time-consuming investigations into the matter have been completed. Customers of the Chiasso branch of SKA will not suffer any losses.
The negotiations that the bank is about to complete with regard to taking over the assets and securities portfolio of Weisscredit-Bank are not affected by this matter. Further information will be given to the general public at the appropriate time.'

```
       ☩
33307 ddp ch    momm☩
52521a rco ch   momm☩
22300 upige ch  momm☩
33393a spk ch   momm☩
75304 wicks ch
1818/ca
58412x skal ch       credit suisse zuerich    14apr77


pressecommunique

die generaldirektion der schweizerischen kreditanstalt teilt
mit:

untersuchungen der internen revisionsorgane haben ergeben,
dass bei einem auslaendischen grosskunden der filiale chiasso
– einer finanzholding mit verschiedenen beteiligungen in
europa und uebersee – rentabilitaets – und liquiditaetsprobleme
bestehen, deren vorhandensein durch die dortige filialdirek-
tion unter massiver verletzung ihrer sorgfaltspflichten und
kompetenzen seit laengerer zeit verheimlicht wurden. der bank
duerfte daraus voraussichtlich ein erheblicher verlust erwach-
sen, der jedoch durch die allgemeinen delkredere-rueckstellun-
gen gedeckt ist. die verantwortlichen funktionaere wurden in
ihren aemtern einstweilen eingestellt, bis die im gange be-
findlichen umfangreichen und zeitraubenden abklaerungen abge-
schlossen sind. kunden der filiale chiasso der ska kom-
men nicht zu schaden.

die vor dem abschluss stehenden verhandlungen der bank in
bezug auf die uebernahme von aktiven sowie der werschriften-
depots der weisscredit-bank werden durch diese angelegenheit
nicht beruehrt.

die oeffentlichkeit wird zu gegebener zeit weiter informiert
werden
       credit
```

the Ticino so that the branch could remain liquid even in the event of large-scale withdrawals.

It was more than a week before SKA went public with further information in a second press release of 25 April 1977. In the meantime, speculation had become rife. 'Chiasso' was the main talking point for the media over the weekend of 16/17 April 1977. It was clear to everyone that the Swiss banking industry had suffered more than a mere flesh wound from this affair and that the consequences would inevitably be serious. The size of the expected loss became an increasingly hot topic for debate over the next few days. Information was urgently required, but SKA was maintaining radio silence. Media people started to do their own research and the rumor mill began to turn furiously.[401]

Stock-taking and initial responses

The executive board still only had sketchy information about what had gone on. It had become apparent from the initial statements made by the responsible parties that a vast network of participations, mainly in Italian companies, had been built up via Texon. It had since also become clear that Texon had been financed by 'misappropriated fiduciary funds' from the Chiasso branch.[402]

SKA demanded that Texon pledge all of its assets immediately. On 18 April the pledge agreement was signed in Chiasso. This charge served 'to secure all claims that Schweizerische Kreditanstalt already has on Texon Finanzanstalt or which it may acquire in future, no matter on what legal basis these claims may be based'.[403]

As the pledge-holder and executive agent, SKA was authorized to look into all of Texon's files without restriction and to take whatever action was necessary to maintain the value of the assets involved. Ernst Kuhrmeier was no longer denying that it was he, and not the Studio legale Maspoli & Noseda, that had founded Texon; but Elbio Gada, Alessandro Villa and Alfredo Noseda were only reluctantly helping to clear up exactly what had happened.

Investigations in Chiasso were conducted at a furious pace and the picture of Texon's activities was becoming ever more complex. Texon's principal holdings included the conglomerates Winefood, Albarella-Mare[404] and Ampaglas. It soon became clear that the empire extended through these holding companies to more than a hundred firms, but that nobody knew their value because the balance sheets that were available were incomplete. On 25 April 1977, the bank mandated Fides Revision to audit and value all of the companies in which Texon had an interest. More than 50 auditors were put to the task.

At SKA, the realization was dawning that the bank would have to accept responsibility for the Sfr 2.2 billion of customer money invested in Texon, regardless of whether the branch had issued sureties or guarantees. To start with, the investors were advised to leave their money where it was, even though Texon was no longer liquid. It was vital to reassure the investors and win some time.

> In the worst case, SKA would have to answer to its customers for about Sfr 2.2 billion of Texon liabilities.

From suspension to arrest

It was not just the press that sat up and took notice when the Chiasso branch's managers were suspended; the public prosecution office for the Sottoceneri region also took a keen interest. District attorney Paolo Bernasconi, an expert in business crime, approached SKA with an offer to investigate the case in cooperation with each other. He was very concerned not to take measures that could compromise that bank's efforts to secure the assets involved and minimize the potential losses. Arresting the guilty parties was not, therefore, a priority for him as long as SKA needed the people involved to help clear up the exact facts of the case. Nevertheless, Paolo Bernasconi demanded full cooperation from SKA and a binding assurance that no documents would 'disappear'. Furthermore, he wanted to be kept up to date at all times with the results of SKA's internal investigations.[405] SKA itself did not press charges, since the offences under investigation were a matter for public prosecution.

At this time, questions of responsibility and possible criminal guilt were not the executive board's top priority,[406] an attitude that met with a degree of incomprehension amongst the general public and, especially, the media. Very little attention was paid, therefore, to SKA's press release of 25 April 1977. What reaction there was concentrated mainly on objections to what had been left out of the release. The official text mentioned 'criminal machinations by the management of the Chiasso branch and the risk of losses ... from the issue of unregistered guarantees for misappropriated fiduciary funds', that had been used 'by Texon to buy participations in companies'.[407] But SKA could not yet make any statement about the size of the losses. This gave further fuel to speculation of all types. It did not help either that the press release expressly confirmed that, 'the bank's hidden reserves and provisions exceed the maximum conceivable risk of loss by a considerable margin'.[408]

> SKA's executive board was accused of having deliberately misled shareholders at the annual general meeting.

There was another reason why little notice was taken of the press release of 25 April 1977. The day had begun with another bombshell: on the evening of Sunday 24 April 1977, district attorney Paolo Bernasconi had ordered the arrest of Ernst Kuhrmeier, Claudio Laffranchi and Meinrad Perler.[409] The news spread like wildfire on 25 April 1977. The affair had gained a new, criminal dimension and the media surpassed itself in the propagation of suspicions, rumors and half-truths. The *Tat* took a particularly aggressive line. For its editor in chief, Roger Schawinski, the Chiasso Affair was the only story worth pursuing. Taking a muck-racking approach previously unknown in Swiss journalism, he and his team pounced on every possible informant, even if they had nothing to contribute to the investigation of the actual facts beyond vague suspicions. For the *Tat*, events at SKA were the real page-fillers and, as it turned out, the very lifeblood of the newspaper. In its sensationalist reporting, the *Tat* stopped referring to SKA by its real name and instead coined the phrase 'SKAndalbank'.[410]

Customer assets are frozen

On the same day, 25 April 1977, the executive board was confronted by further, quite different problems. In its talks with the SNB and the Federal Tax Administration, it had been made clear that these two bodies would look to SKA to make good unpaid withholding tax and negative interest (at that time, foreign investors had to *pay* interest on their Swiss franc deposits; the Swiss government had introduced this measure to deter the huge influx of foreign funds seeking to take advantage of the strength and stability of the Swiss franc). Faced by this situation, SKA decided to redeem the customer money held at Texon, but only to release 75% of these investments to the customers concerned. The remaining 25% would be frozen in a non-interest-bearing Swiss franc account. These funds would only be released after the money due to the public authorities – a sum that had not yet been determined – had been paid. This procedure was communicated to all Texon customers in a circular[411], and a storm of indignation ensued. Customers were outraged. They had believed the assurance from Ernst Kuhrmeier and his people that their investments would not be subject to either withholding tax or negative interest. The Chiasso branch bore witness to incredible scenes. One customer suffered a nervous breakdown, others threw around threats and insults. All of them were convinced that they were the victims of severe injustice; their previous blind faith in the solidity and serious nature of Swiss banks, especially SKA, had been shaken to the core.

Many customers refused to wait around in Chiasso, instead traveling to Zurich to speak to the executive board. But even these people failed to gain access to the frozen 25% of their Texon assets. The customers were in uproar; claims for compensation were threatened, and the first demands for payment were received.

'Ho creduto in Credito Svizzero come in Gesù Cristo!' ('I believed in SKA like I believe in Jesus Christ!' – Texon customer, end-April 1977).

The Sfr 3 billion standby credit

During these days of unrest and spiraling rumors, the executive board's primary concern was liquidity. When district attorney Paolo Bernasconi announced in connection with the arrest of Ernst Kuhrmeier and his accomplices that around Sfr 2.2 billion of customer money had flowed into Texon [412], it was feared that this figure might be misinterpreted by the general public as well as by SKA's correspondent banks. At SKA's request, the SNB invited the heads of the three major banks to a meeting on 25 April 1977. SKA had suggested that the meeting should look at the possibility of creating a pooled fund in order to support the banks' share prices, all three of which had been falling. To SKA's surprise, the chairman of the SNB, Fritz Leutwiler, instead proposed a standby credit of Sfr 3 billion. SBG and SBV representatives agreed with this suggestion, the idea being to demonstrate to the whole world that there was absolutely no question about SKA's ability to meet its obligations. SKA's original plan was not even discussed. Unfortunately, when news of the loan was released by the Schweizerische Depeschenagentur (SDA) press agency, it had exactly the opposite of the intended effect. There was widespread concern about the ability of SKA to fulfill its obligations. It did not help that SKA's press department explained when asked that SKA would not be making use of the stand-by credit because it did not need to.[413] This only made the situation more uncertain[414] and SKA shares came under even more pressure.

Meanwhile, the Chiasso Affair had acquired a political dimension. In a meeting of 27 April 1977, Switzerland's Federal Council, in the presence of Fritz Leutwiler, discussed the problems that the events at the SKA branch in Chiasso created at the national level. The Federal Council took note of the measures, 'which the National Bank has taken to keep developments on the financial markets on an even keel'.[415]

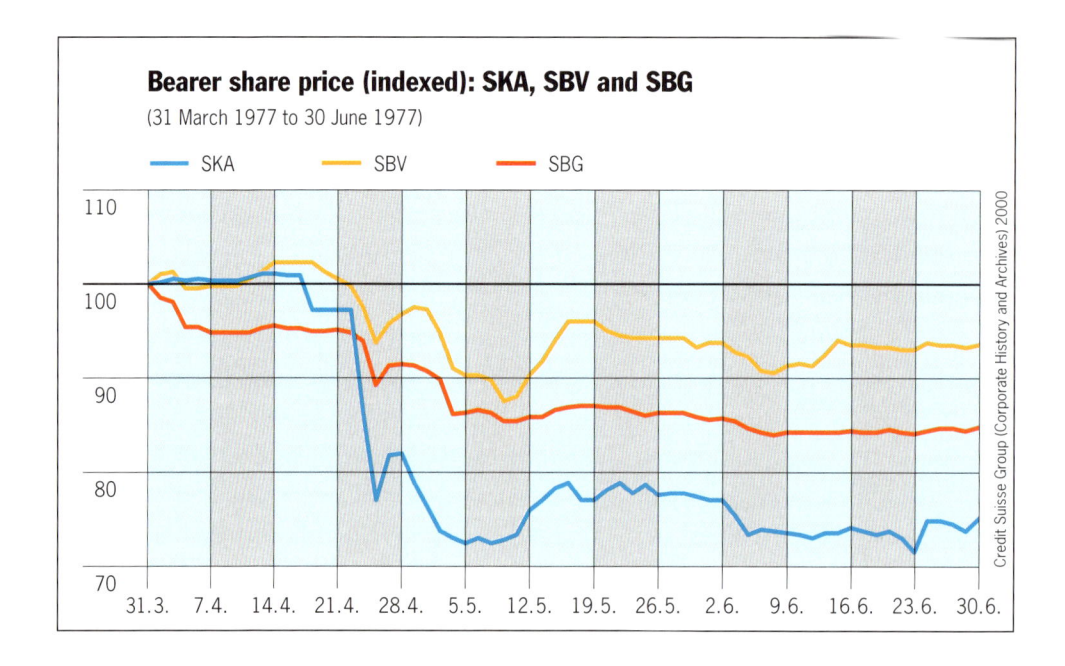

Bearer share price (indexed): SKA, SBV and SBG
(31 March 1977 to 30 June 1977)

Credit Suisse Group (Corporate History and Archives) 2000

Consequences for SKA employees

At its extraordinary meeting of 2 May 1977, the entire board of directors of SKA was told in detail by the executive board about what had happened at Chiasso, about the measures that had been taken in the interim, and about the problems that were to be faced. As far as provisioning was concerned, the board of directors was informed that the freely available and formally allocated provisions were in any event more than sufficient to cover the maximum possible loss.[416]

The board of directors was well aware that in this highly unusual situation it was now obliged to take action itself. The chairman ordered the formation of a special commission of selected board members whose job it would be to discover the people responsible for the affair at all levels at head office and in the branch itself. The members of this commission, which was given a list of key tasks approved by the board of directors, were: E. Luk Keller, Peter Schmidheiny, Rudolph R. Sprüngli and Eberhard Reinhardt. On Oswald Aeppli's request, Max E. Eisenring also joined the commission.

The appointment of this special commission was made public in a press release from the board of directors. The board was unable to say exactly how much damage had been done but it thanked the bank's customers and supporters for the loyalty they were showing at this difficult time and declared how impressed it was by the willingness of staff at every level 'who had nothing to do with this matter, which represents a great burden to them all' to carry on working so hard.[417]

Even the creation of the special commission failed to bring the calm for which the board of directors had hoped. For a start, there was much criticism of the fact that the commission was an internal one; the *Tat* later disparagingly called it a 'Whitewash Commission'.[418] *Schweizer Illustrierte*'s edition of 2 May 1977 included a smug title story about 'The SKA Bomb'.[419] On 4 May 1977, the Swiss parliament held a debate on the 'Chiasso scandal'. On behalf of the national government, Federal Councillors Georges-André Chevallaz and Hans Hürlimann explained the affair to the lower and upper houses of parliament respectively. It was acknowledged that the reputation of the whole country was at stake.[420]

Following this 'rather sketchy'[421] explanation from the Federal Council, the lower house (Nationalrat, or National Council) held a debate. The rightist politicians (National Councillors Luigi Generali of the FDP, Remigius Kaufmann of the CVP, and Georg Brosi of the SVP) expressed their dismay, but at the same time tried to take the heat out of the situation. By contrast, the Social Democratic Party Councillors Helmut Hubacher and Andreas Gerwig, and the PSA/PdA Councillor Werner Carobbio called for the banks' power to be curtailed. In their eyes SKA had done great damage not only to Switzerland but also to Italy.

In this emotionally fraught atmosphere, the special commission began its enquiries on 2 May 1977. The first interviewee was Oswald Aeppli. Then between 4 and 6 May, members of the executive board Rainer E. Gut, C. Walter Fessler, Robert A. Jeker, Hans Hartung and Sergio Demiéville were questioned, as were former executive board members Robert Lang and Hans Escher, plus Josef Müller, Bernhard Henggeler, the heads of department N, and the tax, foreign exchange and personnel departments, as well as other employees of these areas. Rumors about the sackings that the special commission's work would inevitably entail swept around the bank. This new bout of unrest was triggered by a statement from the president of the SBG executive board Robert Holzach, who told a Reuters correspondent that SKA had been warned at the highest level by its rival bank. This prompted questions about who in Zurich might have been responsible for the affair. In the press, the credibility of Oswald Aeppli and Heinz R. Wuffli became a topic of hot debate.[422]

Against this background, the board of directors once again went to the press on the evening of 6 May 1977. In a statement that was also sent by telex to branches and agencies in Switzerland and abroad, the board related that the special commission had 'so far carried out numerous thorough enquiries at all levels'. With regard to the latest rumors, the special commission thought that 'it was only fair to inform the board of directors that the investigations into the con-

On 2 May 1977, the board of directors and executive board wrote to SKA staff and pensioners to inform them about events at Chiasso.

Translation:

'Dear colleagues

The criminal activities of the management of our Chiasso branch and the resulting publicity have placed a great strain on our bank. It is hard to understand how a small group of Credit Suisse employees could cause such damage. The board of directors has set up a commission to investigate thoroughly all aspects of the affair and to determine who at head office and at the branch itself can be held accountable. Thanks to its large reserves, the bank can cover the resulting losses, the exact extent of which we will not know till a later date. However, it will be a long time before we can make good the negative impact of the affair on the reputation and standing of the bank. Given the circumstances, we have been impressed by the loyalty and the sense of responsibility shown by the bank's employees. For the time being, we may have to adopt a more cautious business policy in some areas and may have to adjust our objectives, but the damage we have sustained will not in any way affect the bank's salary policy or its pension and insurance provisions; it certainly won't affect job security. We will, of course, be doing everything humanly possible to ensure that our institution never has to face such a setback ever again. However, it will be impossible to manage Credit Suisse unless there is trust at every level.

The immediate task is to restore the excellent reputation that Credit Suisse enjoys around the world. In order to do this, we need all the help you can give us. For this we would like to express our heartfelt gratitude to you all, and especially to those who are having to take on more work – in some cases significantly more – as a result of the serious misdemeanors that have occurred. It goes without saying that we will be keeping you informed.'

SCHWEIZERISCHE KREDITANSTALT

ZÜRICH 2. Mai 1977

Liebe Mitarbeiterinnen und Mitarbeiter,

Die kriminellen Machenschaften der Filialleitung von Chiasso und die dadurch ausgelöste Publizität stellen für uns alle eine grosse Belastung dar. Es ist unfassbar, dass eine kleine Gruppe von Mitarbeitern der SKA derartigen Schaden beifügen konnte. Der Verwaltungsrat hat eine Kommission eingesetzt, die den Auftrag hat, die Verantwortungen in dieser Sache bei Hauptsitz und Filiale vollumfänglich und unter allen Aspekten abzuklären.

Auch wenn die Kreditanstalt den entstehenden Verlust, dessen Ausmass wir erst zu einem späteren Zeitpunkt kennen werden, dank den bedeutenden Reserven verkraften kann, so wird doch eine längere Zeit verstreichen, bis die negativen Auswirkungen dieses Falles auf den Ruf und die Stellung unseres Institutes wieder wettgemacht sein werden. In dieser Situation sind wir beeindruckt von der Loyalität und dem Verantwortungsbewusstsein unseres Mitarbeiterstabes gegenüber unserer Bank. Wenn unsere Geschäftspolitik in einzelnen Bereichen in nächster Zukunft auch etwas zurückhaltender gestaltet und unsere Zielsetzung teilweise korrigiert werden muss, so hat der uns entstehende Verlust keinerlei Auswirkungen auf die Lohnpolitik und die Fürsorgeeinrichtungen unseres Institutes oder gar auf die Sicherheit unserer Arbeitsplätze. Selbstverständlich wird alles Menschenmögliche unternommen, um sicherzustellen, dass unserem Institut in der Zukunft derartige Rückschläge erspart bleiben. Ohne Vertrauen auf allen Stufen wird sich die Schweizerische Kreditanstalt aber auch in Zukunft nicht führen lassen.

In nächster Zeit geht es darum, den ausgezeichneten Ruf, den die Schweizerische Kreditanstalt weltweit genoss, wiederherzustellen. Dazu brauchen wir Ihren vollen Einsatz. Wir danken Ihnen allen und ganz besonders denen, die als Folge dieser schwerwiegenden Verfehlungen eine zum Teil bedeutende Mehrbelastung auf sich nehmen müssen, dafür herzlich.

Es versteht sich von selbst, dass wir Sie weiter informieren werden.

Mit freundlichen Grüssen

Der Präsident des Verwaltungsrates: Für die Generaldirektion:

Dr. O. Aeppli   Dr. H.R. Wuffli   R.A. Jeker

Zur Kenntnis an
alle Pensionierten unseres Institutes

duct of Dr. Aeppli, chairman of the board of directors, were complete and that they showed that Dr Aeppli can in no way be blamed for the transgressions committed by the Chiasso branch management'. The board of directors concluded in its release that its chairman Oswald Aeppli, 'who assumed his position ... in particularly difficult circumstances', enjoyed the full confidence of the board.[423]

Heinz R. Wuffli resigns

It is interesting to note the timing of this public statement. On the morning of Friday 6 May 1977, the board of directors' special commission questioned president of the executive board Heinz R. Wuffli for the first time about Chiasso. From the questions and comments of the commission members, it is clear that they were very concerned about the blind faith shown in Ernst Kuhrmeier by everyone at head office.

The questioning of Heinz R. Wuffli broke off at midday and recommenced at seven o'clock in the evening.[424] At this point, the board of directors' statement about Oswald Aeppli was already featuring in evening news broadcasts. The special commission's discussion with Heinz R. Wuffli now turned specifically to the question of responsibility. The commission could not understand why in 15 years nobody had ever thought to take a closer look at the 'good' customer Texon. 'There were also dubious creditors. And suspicions should also have arisen when bad loans suddenly disappeared en masse.'[425] The main focus of the interrogation was the warning delivered by SBG executive board member Philippe de Weck during his visit to Heinz R. Wuffli. 'We cannot get away from the fact that this should have set the alarm bells ringing.'[426] This discussion with Wuffli thus crystallized the central point. The minutes of the comments made by those present document in striking fashion how the commission wrestled to come up with a result. Heinz R. Wuffli was in a dilemma; he recognized his formal responsibility. 'Subjectively I do not feel guilty; objectively it is perfectly clear to me that I am.'[427]

Heinz R. Wuffli wondered whether he would be doing SKA a service by resigning. He never sought to shirk his responsibility and the commission members were deeply upset. They saw the human tragedy of the situation and recognized Wuffli's outstanding qualities as well as his great commitment to SKA's interests. At the same time they had to take account of the fact that a 'storm was raging'.[428] Philippe de Weck's visit was being played up by, amongst others, SKA's rivals. The special commission did not want to come to a decision that evening. It was not at all easy to answer the question of whether Heinz R. Wuffli's resignation would be in the bank's best interests or not. One thing that the special commission did agree on unanimously was that if Wuffli did resign, the board of directors would have to issue a statement defending his honor. For all concerned it was 'a great human dilemma'.[429]

Over the next weekend and the following two days, Heinz R. Wuffli, the members of the special commission, and the entire board of directors grappled with the problem: which decision would best serve the interests of SKA? There

'If you leave, the bank will be suffering a substantial loss' (Rudolph R. Sprüngli to Heinz R. Wuffli, 6 May 1977).

Die Erklärung des Bundesrates zum Bankskandal

Hb. Der Bundesrat nahm am Mittwoch morgen *im Nationalrat und im Ständerat* Stellung zur Affäre Chiasso der Schweizerischen Kreditanstalt. Die Erklärung hat folgenden Wortlaut:

Der Bundesrat ist über die schwerwiegenden Unregelmässigkeiten in der Geschäftsführung der Filiale in Chiasso einer grossen Schweizer Bank *besorgt;* sie sind geeignet, den guten Ruf eines wichtigen Zweiges unserer Wirtschaft zu beeinträchtigen und diesem Schaden zuzufügen. Der Bundesrat muss jedoch darauf hinweisen, dass es in einem solchen Fall Aufgabe der Strafverfolgungsbehörden der Nationalbank und der Bankenkommission ist, die sich aufdrängenden Sofortmassnahmen zu treffen. Es sind dies Institutionen, die nach dem Willen des Gesetzgebers von der politischen Gewalt unabhängig sind.

Die Eidgenössische Bankenkommission und die Nationalbank halten den Bundesrat über die Entwicklung der Vorfälle auf dem laufenden. Bisher wurden drei Direktoren der Filiale Chiasso der Schweizerischen Kreditanstalt unter Beschuldigung der ungetreuen Geschäftsführung und der Urkundenfälschung verhaftet. Es scheint erwiesen, dass die Angeschuldigten ausländische Treuhandgelder bei einer Finanzanstalt mit fiktivem Sitz in einem Nachbarland angelegt haben, wo solche Gesellschaften in einem beunruhigenden Ausmass aus dem Boden schiessen. Es erscheint ebenfalls als erwiesen, dass die Direktoren der Filiale Chiasso der Schweizerischen Kreditanstalt bestimmten Gläubigern für solche Treuhandgelder unverbuchte Bankgarantien gegeben haben. Genaue Zahlen über die Verluste der geschädigten Bank und der Umfang der Verfehlungen werden in einer bereits laufenden Untersuchung ermittelt. Diese wird noch einige Zeit in Anspruch nehmen, denn die Abklärung der fraglichen Handlungen wird teilweise wegen fehlender Belege verzögert. Der Bundesrat kann jedoch versichern, dass die Oeffentlichkeit keinen Grund zur Beunruhigung hat und dass diese Affäre restlos aufgeklärt wird.

Sache der Nationalbank war es, darüber zu wachen, dass diese Vorkommnisse *nicht zu Störungen des Geld- und Devisenmarktes* führten. Als die sich verdichtenden Gerüchte übertriebene Reaktionen der ausländischen und der schweizerischen Kundschaft befürchten liessen, sicherte die Nationalbank zusammen mit zwei Grossbanken der betroffenen Bank zu, ihr nötigenfalls in sehr grossem Umfange die benötigten Mittel bereitzustellen, um damit ihre Solidität zu demonstrieren. Obwohl dieses Angebot da und dort kritisiert wurde, ist der Bundesrat überzeugt, dass diese *Massnahme zur Entspannung der Lage* beigetragen hat. Es ist ebenfalls Sache der Nationalbank, festzustellen, ob und wie weit Vorschriften des Bundesbeschlusses über den Schutz der Währung verletzt wurden. Wenn dies zutrifft, hätten die zuständigen Behörden die vorgesehenen *Sanktionen* auszusprechen. Die Eidgenössische Bankenkommission führt eine Untersuchung, um die Ursachen und Verantwortlichkeiten für das Versagen der Kontrolle festzustellen. Sie prüft zudem, ob Widerhandlungen gegen das Bankengesetz begangen wurden und ob die mit Verwaltung und Geschäftsführung der Banken betrauten Personen Gewähr für eine einwandfreie Geschäftstätigkeit bieten. Die Eidgenössische Steuerverwaltung wird ihrerseits feststellen müssen, ob die im Zusammenhang mit den fraglichen Geschäften bezahlten Zinsen der Verrechnungssteuer entzogen wurden. Die Schweizerische Kreditanstalt hat Massnahmen zur Sicherstellung einer allfälligen Steuerschuld getroffen.

Der Bundesrat anerkennt, dass das Parlament und die Oeffentlichkeit *Anspruch auf eine rasche und umfassende Orientierung über diese Affäre* haben. Er kann jedoch heute keine zusätzlichen Angaben machen, ohne der Untersuchung vorzugreifen. Diese muss mit Sorgfalt und Strenge, aber auch unbeeinflusst durchgeführt werden. Schon während die Untersuchung ihren Lauf nimmt, gilt es, nach Mitteln und Wegen zu suchen, um neue Fälle dieser Art zu verunmöglichen. Es wird sorgfältig zu prüfen sein, ob die gesetzlichen Bestimmungen ausreichen. Letztes Jahr sind auf Grund eines Beschlusses des Bundesrates vom 14. Januar 1976 eine Reorganisation und ein Ausbau der Organe der Eidgenössischen Bankenkommission in die Wege geleitet worden, der noch im Gange ist. Wir werden uns einer zusätzlichen Verstärkung der Kommission nicht verschliessen, wenn sich dies auf Grund der Erfahrungen als notwendig erweisen sollte.

So bedauerlich die Affäre von Chiasso auch ist, sie wird die Banken auf eine ihrer wesentlichsten Aufgaben aufmerksam machen, nämlich darauf, *ihre Geschäfte mit doppelter Wachsamkeit und Strenge zu führen*. Es geht dabei nicht nur um das eigene Interesse, sondern auch um jenes des ganzen Bankengewerbes, nicht zuletzt auch um das Ansehen unseres Landes.

Neue Zürcher Zeitung, 5 May 1977: 'The Federal Council's Statement on the Bank Scandal'. The article detailed the Swiss government's reassurances about the investigation into the Chiasso Affair and described the measures taken to maintain the stability of the Swiss banking system in general.

was no sign of the storm abating; in fact it was gaining in intensity. Now that Oswald Aeppli had been declared innocent, Heinz R. Wuffli came under particularly heavy fire.[430] Nevertheless, the press release issued by the board of directors on 10 May 1977 announcing the resignation of Heinz R. Wuffli came as a shock to the general public and especially to SKA's staff: 'In the interests of Schweizerische Kreditanstalt, its staff, its customers and its shareholders, I have decided after much deliberation to tender my resignation to the executive board.' The board of directors accepted the offer and, at Wuffli's express request, published his letter of resignation.[431]

'This sacrifice [i.e. the resignation] is hard and perhaps even unfair on those concerned', said the *Tages-Anzeiger*; 'but it helps to clear the air for the bank and the Swiss financial sector as a whole.'[432] Similar sentiments were expressed by the rest of the media, though the tone taken by the tabloid newspapers was somewhat more aggressive.[433]

In losing Heinz R. Wuffli, SKA and the Swiss financial center had lost a high-profile banker who also enjoyed a great deal of respect outside Switzerland.

Owing to the great amount of interest excited by Wuffli's resignation, little attention was paid to the subsequent statements and finer points contained in the release. Felix W. Schulthess had relinquished the title of honorary president given to him on 3 March 1977. 'He wishes in this way to accept his share of the responsibility.'[434] The press release also expressly stated that the personal integrity and honor of Heinz R. Wuffli and Felix W. Schulthess were not in doubt.

Almost in passing, the press release of 10 May also contained news of a further departure from the executive board. Sergio Demiéville, who had been responsible for the Chiasso branch since 1 April 1976, had resigned his post. However, the statement did not expressly defend Demiéville's honor as it had the honor of the other two men concerned. All that was said was: 'In his case too the investigation remains to be completed. The investigating committee has no reason to suppose he acted dishonorably in the Chiasso Affair.'[435]

On the day after these momentous resignations, Oswald Aeppli wrote to the bank's shareholders on behalf of the board of directors. The board was concerned to tell shareholders about the satisfactory progress of business in the first quarter of 1977, and about the fact that gross earnings had increased by over 10% compared with the same period in the previous year. For the first time, actual figures relating to the Chiasso affair were given: the substantial loss had 'grown out of the misappropriation of fiduciary funds and the issue of unregistered guarantees'.[436] Customer deposits totaling Sfr 2.17 billion, which should have been invested in blue-chip companies, had instead been channeled off the balance sheet and into Texon and its associated companies.

Following these developments, the board of directors' special commission continued its work. Its report to the board was expected at the end of May 1977 and an extraordinary general meeting of shareholders had been scheduled for 24 June 1977.

Criticism of the special commission's work

The resignation of the president of SKA's executive board was the outstanding event of the special commission's tenure. Later on, Heinz R. Wuffli himself was not slow to criticize the composition and the methods of the special commission. He expressed his reservations when giving evidence on 18 June 1979 during the trial against Ernst Kuhrmeier and his accomplices.

Wuffli's main bone of contention was the personal make-up of the commission and the consequent fact that it worked virtually under the chairmanship of Eberhard Reinhardt, the former president of the executive board. In Heinz R. Wuffli's view, Reinhardt, who had joined the executive board in 1948 and who had headed it from 1963 to 1973, was determined to concentrate on what had happened since 1976, and to avoid looking into everything that had occurred between 1961 and this date.[437] Wuffli complained about the press release of 6 May 1977, which, as he saw it, had put the chairman of the board of directors under 'a protection order'[438], making his own position untenable – he had not even finished giving evidence when the release was put out. Wuffli conceded that he had to take the formal responsibility. But: 'The formal responsibility lies with a whole herd of scapegoats. It's just that late-comers must expect to be unlucky.'[439]

In making this criticism, Wuffli was overlooking the fact that his formal responsibility was not the only matter under discussion. Certainly the board of directors' press release about Oswald Aeppli put him in a difficult position. The press was full of speculation about the imminent resignations of both Oswald Aeppli and Heinz R. Wuffli. Ultimately, though, Wuffli was undone by the simple fact that he had not reacted to Philippe de Weck's warnings – by the fact that at this decisive moment, as he said in his deposition of 6 May 1977 to the board of directors' special commission, he 'simply lacked the imagination'.[440]

From crisis unit to Texon special unit

Ever since the Texon Affair had broken, a crisis unit had been working on the matter under the leadership of Heinz R. Wuffli. SKA was under remorseless pressure from the Swiss authorities. The SNB and Federal Tax Administration came to Chiasso to find out at first hand how much negative interest and withholding tax was owed. The Federal Banking Commission let it be known in public that SKA's control mechanisms had failed.[441]

Apart from all the trouble in Switzerland, the crisis unit also had to devote its attention to relations with banks in Italy. Heinz R. Wuffli himself, but also Sergio Demiéville and Hans Hartung visited correspondent banks in Rome and Milan. It was made clear to them that it would not be acceptable for SKA simply to abandon the Italian companies in which Texon had invested: the avoidance of job losses was a particularly sensitive topic in Italy. But the bank also received spontaneous offers of help. Roberto Calvi, chairman and CEO of the Banco Ambrosiano, for instance, came to see SKA chairman Oswald Aeppli. As well as putting the services of his bank and of a specialist finance company at SKA's disposal, he also offered to broker contacts with the Italian government

> 'The most upsetting experience of my career was the Chiasso crisis of 1977. There was enormous pressure from the general public and the media. My colleagues and I on the executive board had to deal with an extreme situation. For most of the time we were acting from one moment to the next, often without proper information on which to base our decisions' (Rainer E. Gut in *Group News*, December 1998).

and the Banca d'Italia. Nello Celio, member of the SKA board of directors and former Federal Councillor, was also willing to talk to the Italian government: 'I can intervene from Leone via Andreotti to Berlinguer', he wrote in a letter to Oswald Aeppli dated 3 May 1977.[442]

A virtually complete copy of Texon's accounts had since been found in the Texon files in Vaduz, raising the hope that there would soon be at least a rudimentary foundation on which to base the decisions that had to be taken about the individual Texon companies.

On 6 May 1977, district attorney Paolo Bernasconi announced that he was widening the current criminal investigation to include Alfredo Noseda, Elbio Gada and Alessandro Villa. At the same time, he arranged for Meinrad Perler to be released on bail. Perler's release triggered a tumult of speculation in the media, and Perler was sought after for interview by a horde of journalists.[443]

On 18 May 1977, the board of directors promoted Robert A. Jeker and Hans Hartung, previously deputy executive board members, to full members of the executive board. With effect from 23 May 1977, Hugo von der Crone, Hans R. Frey and William Wirth were promoted to deputy executive board members. Of the two remaining existing executive board members, C. Walter Fessler and Rainer E. Gut, the latter was appointed as spokesman for the executive board.[444] By appointing Rainer E. Gut above C. Walter Fessler, who had worked for the bank for longer than Gut, the board of directors was emphasizing the fact that SKA was making a new start.

Without further ado, the new-look executive board continued working on the Chiasso Affair. A provisional organization chart of Texon and its associated companies had been available since the middle of May 1977. Alongside the companies already mentioned – Winefood, Albarella and Ampaglas – it had since transpired that Texon also owned FICI (a finance and real estate firm), Olbiacard (which operated in the textile machinery sector), and the haulage company Gottardo Ruffoni. Texon's portfolio of accounts receivable ran to more than Sfr 300 million and included a number of rather dubious items.[445]

Finally the executive board came to the conclusion, already expressed by the old crisis unit, that the work and the problems now facing the bank could only be dealt with by a full-time, dedicated special unit. An executive board directive of 20 May 1977 confirmed the creation of the Texon special unit (internal codename 'Texo'), headed by vice president Klaus Jenny and consisting of about 20 staff, including several members of senior management.[446] The new unit's first job was to take stock of the situation in Chiasso and provide the executive board with the material they needed in order to make the crucial decisions. Within the executive board, Robert A. Jeker, Hans Hartung and Hugo von der Crone formed a special Texon committee.

The mood prior to the extraordinary meeting of shareholders

Having created the special Texon unit, from 23 May 1977 onwards SKA was able to tackle the matter systematically; but though the necessary structures had been put in place, there was still no sign that the situation would calm down as hoped. The next milestone on the calendar was the extraordinary meeting of shareholders called for 24 June 1977.

To a certain extent, the tradition-led image that SKA had built up over the course of many decades was turned on its head by the Chiasso Affair. Amongst the general public, the idea had taken root that the respected major bank had actually been mixed up in illicit and dubious business. 'For large sections of the general public, the Chiasso scandal has become the SKA scandal.'[447]

The daily publicity about the affair made it difficult for staff to work properly. It became harder for them to identify with their employer, although, conversely, the media siege did create a growing sense of team spirit amongst the ranks. Every morning, staff would turn to the *Tat* fearing the next devastating revelation. The attacks on SKA intensified in the run-up to its extraordinary meeting of shareholders. On 20 June 1977, the *Tat* summarized its view of the affair in a two-page diagram (reproduced on pages 270 and 271).[448]

In the week of the extraordinary meeting, the various bodies of the Swiss government once again discussed the Chiasso Affair.

As well as the politicians, the FBC had also gone into action. At its meeting of 27 May 1977, it mandated Kontroll & Revisions AG (KOREAG), Basel, to carry out an extraordinary audit in relation to the case of SKA's Chiasso branch and Texon. KOREAG's list of duties included: identifying the facts of the case, identifying the extent of the damage done, assessing the existing control mechanisms and evaluating the action taken by SKA.[449] The FBC thus ensured that it would have complete freedom when deciding how best to sort out the financial, organizational and personal aspects of the affair.

The Swiss National Bank was particularly concerned about the damage that SKA had done to the Swiss financial center as a whole. On the initiative of the SNB, and following initial resistance from the Swiss Bankers' Association, the Agreement on the Swiss Banks' Code of Conduct with Regard to the Exercise of Due Diligence was signed on 1 June 1977; it came into effect on 1 July 1977.

Extraordinary meeting of shareholders on 24 June 1977

'After weeks of frosty silence from the Kreditanstalt the bank's shareholders are to gather for an extraordinary general meeting. [...] The moment of truth comes on Friday', wrote the *Tat* on 20 June 1977.[450] With headlines of this sort, the media psyched the public up for what was in the truest sense of the word an extraordinary meeting. The bank had brought in the Farner PR agency to help ensure that the meeting was prepared professionally.[451]

An impressive number of shareholders and journalists turned up. The meeting was held at Zurich's Züspa-Halle congress center, and 3,122 shareholders looked on as chairman of the board of directors Oswald Aeppli opened proceedings at 3 p.m.[452]

Aeppli started off by delivering a comprehensive report on the facts of the Chiasso affair, the dates on which the misdemeanors had come to light and details of the action taken since.[453] He referred to the conspiratorial collaboration between several senior figures at the branch and the support given to them

Texon's financial structure

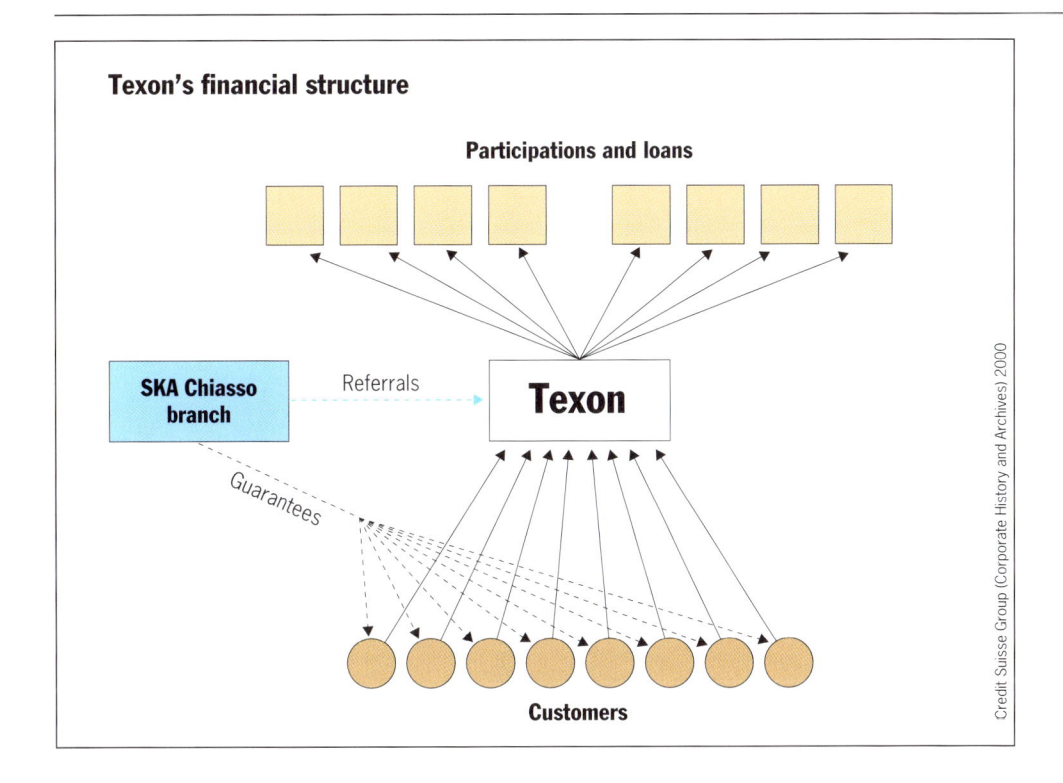

[Diagram: SKA Chiasso branch provides Referrals and Guarantees to Texon; Texon channels funds to Participations and loans (top) and connects to Customers (bottom). Source: Credit Suisse Group (Corporate History and Archives) 2000]

by a well known firm of lawyers. Aeppli said that, 'under these circumstances it becomes difficult to discover transgressions'. He used a chart to illustrate how Texon had been financed using the branch's customer deposits.

In the meantime, SKA had assumed liability for these customer deposits in return for a corresponding claim against Texon. This claim had been secured by means of Texon pledging its assets, including numerous companies in which the financial company had invested, to SKA. However, Oswald Aeppli still could not give any concrete details about the value of these assets. It would not be possible to make a rough estimate of the extent of the bank's potential losses, he explained, until these assets had been valued.

After the chairman had given his overview of the situation, it was time for the eagerly awaited report of the board of directors' special commission. Peter Schmidheiny read out the 60-page report of 31 May 1977 in its entirety.[454] The report centered on the question of who was responsible for what had happened. Discussions with the district attorney had shown, 'that according to the files currently available, the chain of guilt stops at the Chiasso branch and at the offices of Maspoli & Noseda, and that it does not extend to head office'.[455]

The special commission was referring here to the guilt arising from the abuse of decision-making and control functions. As far as the commission was concerned, it was questionable, given the criminal conspiracy and subterfuge employed, and given the fact that Texon's files were kept outside the branch premises, whether the bank's auditors would have come across the background to Texon even if they had carried out a full and thorough audit. Given these circumstances, the signals received by head office in Zurich over the course of the years – including the withholding tax case of 1968/69 and the supposed clear-

Das Bild des SKAndals

Seit Mitte April ist der gute Ruf der Schweizer Banken auch für den kleinen Mann schwer lädiert. Dafür sorgte die Schweizerische Kreditanstalt. Männer dieser drittgrössten Grossbank des Landes machten die Polemiken des Jean Ziegler zur Wahrheit.

Weit weg von den Gesetzen lockten und schmuggelten sie italienisches Geld im Wert von mindestens 2,2 Milliarden Franken in die Schweiz. Sie spekulierten damit und verloren gegen eine Milliarde. Hier zeigen wir, wie der SKAndal ablief, und wer damit zu tun hat.

Ständerat Fritz Honegger (FDP-Parteipräsident) ist Mitglied der SKA-Kontrollstelle.

Die Bankenkommission wurde erst kurz vor der Öffentlichkeit von der SKA-Zentrale über den SKAndal orientiert. Entgegen den Vorschriften hatte die SKA über die interne Untersuchung nicht sofort informiert.

Die Untersuchung im SKAndal liegt bei Staatsanwalt Paolo Bernasconi. Zweiter Staatsanwalt des Sottoceneri: John Noseda, der Sohn von Alfredo Noseda. Bernasconi liess nach dem offiziellen Platzen des SKAndals rund zehn Tage verstreichen, bis er die drei angeschuldigten Direktoren Kuhrmeier, Laffranchi und Perler in Untersuchungshaft nahm. Perler wurde gegen Kaution wieder freigelassen, während Kuhrmeier und Laffranchi noch immer sitzen. Schliesslich leitete Bernasconi auch Ermittlungen gegen die Anwälte Noseda, Villa und Gada ein. Der junge Staatsanwalt gilt im Tessin als integer.

Alfredo Noseda (CVP), Advokat, sass bis zu seinem Umzug im Gebäude der SKA-Filiale in Chiasso, wo er einen direkten Zugang zur Bank gehabt haben soll. Mit ihm waren in der Texon-Sache engagiert Alessandro Villa und Elbio Gada. Ebenso der ehemalige Bundesratskandidat Maspoli, der vor einigen Jahren gestorben war. Zusammen mit Kuhrmeier, Laffranchi und Perler bildete das Anwalts-Trio unzählige Verwaltungsräte von Finanzgesellschaften. Viele dieser Briefkasten sind in SKA-Filialen untergebracht.

Josef Müller (SKA-Jargon: «Pistolen-Müller») war Chef der internen Kontrolle. Nach Ansicht von Insidern hätte er die faulen Geschäfte längst entdecken müssen. Er ermittelte anfänglich noch in Chiasso, bis er an den Hauptsitz zurückbeordert wurde. Offenbar schöpfte man doch Verdacht. Müller war ein guter Bekannter des Hauptverantwortlichen Kuhrmeier.

Die Bankenkommission diagnostizierte «objektives Versagen» der internen Kontrolle.

Sergio Demiéville, Mitglied der Generaldirektion, war zuletzt für die Chiasso-Filiale verantwortlich. Er stolperte aber nicht direkt über den SKAndal, sondern wurde zum Rücktritt gedrängt wegen der Affäre um Moline Certosa. Dort soll die Kreditanstalt 40 Millionen verloren haben. In dieser Sache wurde Anzeige gegen ihn und Wuffli erstattet.

Heinz Wuffli, SKA-Generaldirektor, musste demissionieren. Bis Frühjahr 1976 war er für die Filiale Chiasso verantwortlich. Andere Bankiers haben ihn mehrfach auf die Machenschaften seiner Tessiner Verantwortlichen hingewiesen. Wuffli erkannte aber das Ausmass der Texon-Geschäfte nicht. Er vertraute den falschen Leuten.

SKA-Hauptdirektor Ernesto Kuhrmeier war Initiator der Texon. Als treibende Kraft liess er nicht nur die Texon-Buchhaltung in seiner SKA-Filiale führen, sondern bemühte sich in Mailand aktiv um italienisches Fluchtgeld. Der als erfolgreich geltende Kuhrmeier sah sich bereits in der Generaldirektion am Hauptsitz – sein Haus in Meilen wäre bald bezugsbereit gewesen.

SKA-Direktor Claudio Laffranchi, bis letzte Woche CVP-Kantonsrat, gilt als zweiter Hauptbeschuldigter. Zusammen mit Kuhrmeier soll er den Geldfluss organisiert, Bank-Garantien abgegeben und den Hauptsitz hinters Licht geführt haben.

SKA-Direktor Meinrad Perler wurde vom Hauptsitz vermutlich zu früh schuldig gesprochen. Perler hatte immer seine Unschuld beteuert und wurde bald aus der Untersuchungshaft entlassen.

Fabio Vassalli, Tessiner Regierungspräsident, kann der SKAndal den Kopf kosten. Sein persönlicher Freund Croci Torti soll über die Texon ruiniert worden sein. Zu diesem Zeitpunkt war Vassalli Anwalt im Büro Noseda & Maspoli. Und zwar seit Jahren schon. Er vertrat Croci Torti. Von den ganzen Texon-Geschäften will auch er nichts gewusst haben.

Tat, 20 June 1977.

> 'A visit by a member of the executive board of one bank to his counterpart at a rival bank in order to deliver a warning is extremely unusual in banking, and as such deserves special consideration' (Report by the special commission).

ing up of that situation on the basis of Ernst Kuhrmeier's assurances (assurances which were never subsequently checked out!) – gained even greater significance. In the special commission's view, however, head office's assessment of the situation in Chiasso should certainly have changed at the latest when SBG executive board member Philippe de Weck visited his SKA counterpart Heinz R. Wuffli on 14 January 1976 to give him a copy of a guarantee and bring his attention to the dangerous business practices at the Chiasso branch. Wuffli had neglected to bring in the auditors at that point, instead trusting Ernst Kuhrmeier's explanation of the guarantee in question.

In addition, the special commission found it impossible to understand the reaction of ex-chairman Felix W. Schulthess to the warning delivered to him by the chairman of the SBG board of directors in May 1976. It was also hard to comprehend the conduct of the chief auditor, who had been told by Meinrad Perler about the unbooked guarantees in Ernst Kuhrmeier's desk on 17 December 1976. As the report stated: 'This in itself should have come as a very serious warning for an auditor.'[456]

The special commission's report also examined the relationship between other members of the executive board and other head office senior managers to Texon. The commission dealt in detail with the fact, which had been discovered during the course of their investigations, that Josef Müller had taken a loan of Sfr 120,000 from Alfredo Noseda and Texon in December 1969 – i.e. at a time when he was already chief auditor; the loan had not been paid back in full until the spring of 1977, shortly before the Texon Affair blew up.

In the view of the special commission, this acceptance of a loan could possibly suggest a certain lack of impartiality on the part of Josef Müller. It noted with approval that the executive board had immediately released Müller from his investigative work in Chiasso; consequently the commission did not recommend that charges be brought against him.[457] However the special commission did propose that the chief auditor be replaced, though they harbored no doubts about his integrity, and also said that the audit department should be strenghtened.[458] Referring to the declarations of 10 May 1977, the commission declined to pass further comment on the persons of Heinz R. Wuffli, Felix W. Schulthess and Sergio Demiéville. 'Mr. Demiéville's resignation, however, was connected to another event which had compromised the necessary relationship of trust.'[459]

Immediate consequences

Following the detailed report by the special commission, the extraordinary meeting of shareholders was given an assessment of the implications of the affair for the bank by chairman of the board of directors Oswald Aeppli. If business continued to do as well as it was, he believed that it would be possible to pay out an unchanged dividend despite the Chiasso Affair. 'Our profitability continues to be excellent.'[460] He also told the meeting about the planned complete reorganization of the audit department.

Oswald Aeppli finished his presentation by going into some of the individual questions and criticisms that had been raised in public. He admitted that the bank had made certain mistakes in its information policy. 'I have no hesitation in admitting that we, with the benefit of hindsight, could perhaps have operated more effectively.'[461] He went on to defend the action taken to shore up the share price in the first days after the Chiasso Affair had been discovered. 'What we were trying to do for a few days was avoid a price fall – in the interests of our shareholders and in order to calm the market. But the pressure was too strong. From 25 April, we could not justify further support for the share.'[462]

In his closing remarks Oswald Aeppli stated unequivocally that no investor would suffer any loss. Within the bank, every conceivable precaution had been taken to prevent a repetition of the kind of machinations that had led to the Chiasso Affair. He thanked the bank's employees at every level for their loyalty and perseverance. 'The entire staff has suffered badly from the Chiasso Affair.'[463]

'We can only deeply regret what has happened, but we cannot undo what has been done. Nevertheless, we want to and can overcome this blow. We need your help to do this. And the entire staff of the bank at every level is dedicating its strength, its knowledge and its loyalty to the task. Our highly skilled banking operation and our earning power remain intact: our customers are remaining loyal to us. We have to build on this foundation. There is only one path that we can take: the path that will restore our bank to its full health. We have to take this path in your interests as well as in the interest of our 9,000 loyal employees.'[464] With this appeal to the shareholders, Oswald Aeppli ended his presentation.

In the following open discussion, there was a roughly equal balance between critical and appreciative voices. Particularly strong opposition came from the group of shareholders represented by lawyer Jürg Meister.[465] The work done by the board of directors' special commission was widely praised. Certain doubts were expressed about whether head office could really have been ignorant of what was going on at the Chiasso branch. 'The sparrows were singing from the roofs about it.'[466] Some shareholders still could not believe that Ernst Kuhrmeier could have been responsible for such chaos – after all he had been *the* banker in the Ticino. One Ticinese shareholder earned some laughter when he explained that Kuhrmeier was seen as the 'Eddy Merckx' of banking in the Ticino.[467]

At 8.25 that evening the discussion came to an end, and Oswald Aeppli was able to close this memorable extraordinary meeting of shareholders. It had lasted for more than five hours.

Results for the 1977 business year

The extraordinary general meeting marked a turning point in the handling of the Chiasso Affair. The response to the meeting from the media was cautiously positive[468], and there was a general impression that the board of directors and the newly constituted executive board had the situation under control. Work on minimizing the damage was well under way, but would take time.

Meanwhile the Texon special unit was in Chiasso reviewing the initial results of the investigations. Most of the companies owned by Texon had liquidity prob-

TAT Mittwoch, 7. Dezember 1977   **NACHRICHTEN** ⑦

Die Kreditanstalt steckt nach dem Chiasso-Fiasko in einer tiefen Krise, denn:

Kunden geben Fersengeld!

ZÜRICH – Jetzt laufen die Kunden der Kreditanstalt davon! Im vergangenen halben Jahr büsste die SKA im Sektor Privatkunden (Sparbüchlein, Salär- und Anlagekonti) 70 Millionen Franken ein. Und die wichtigeren Geschäftskunden zogen gar 400 Millionen ab. Fest steht: Die Krise der SKA, die mit dem Verkauf von Jelmoli offenkundig geworden ist, ist viel ernster als bisher angenommen wurde!

Trotz des negativen Geschäftsverlaufes weist die SKA für das letzte halbe Jahr mit 3,1 Prozent den grösseren Geldzuwachs auf als die Bankgesellschaft (+ 2,8%) oder der Bankverein (+ 2,7%).

Dieses erstaunliche Wachstum – der eigentliche Gradmesser des Geschäftsganges einer Bank – ist aber einzig und allein auf die Erhöhung der Einlagen von anderen Banken bei der SKA zurückzuführen!

Zu diesem Sachverhalt, den das linke Politmagazin «Focus» in seiner jüngsten Ausgabe darlegt, wollte die Kreditanstalt ohne Angabe von Gründen «keine Stellung nehmen».

Nicht genannt sein wollende Bankexperten bestätigten allerdings der TAT den massiven Kundenverlust der Kreditanstalt und die vorgenommene Bilanzkosmetik.

Unter anderem wird im «Focus»-Artikel festgehalten, dass die Einbussen in den einzelnen Geschäftssparten durch geänderte Bewertungsgrundsätze und beeinflussbare Geschäftsvorfälle in anderen Sparten so «korrigiert» werden, dass sie in den Globalzahlen der Bilanz nicht auftauchen.

Klar ist: Die SKA hätte das sich ausweitende Chiasso-Desaster nicht überlebt, wenn sie in den letzten Jahren nicht dank grossen Gewinnen riesige stille Reserven angelegt hätte. Überlebenshilfe boten auch die anderen Grossbanken und die Nationalbank sowie andere – auch ausländische – Banken.

In Bankkreisen ist man sich einig: Die SKA darf nicht in die Mittelmässigkeit absacken oder gar Pleite gehen.

So trug die Nationalbank der bedrohlichen Lage der SKA auch bei ihrem Entscheid über die Negativzinsen Rechnung. «Dies war ein wesentlicher Grund», so ein Nationalbank-Sprecher, dass der SKA nur 62 Millionen an Negativzinsen verlangt werden und nicht, wie vom Finanz- und Zolldepartement angeregt, 290 Millionen.

Denn: In Bankkreisen wird damit gerechnet, dass die SKA den 25-Prozent-Rückbehalt der Texon-Kunden diesen vollumfänglich zurückzahlen muss. Das heisst, die SKA müsste dann die ausstehenden Negativzinsen und die 200 Millionen Verrechnungssteuer aus dem eigenen Sack bezahlen!

Dieser wichtige Entscheid dürfte schon bald fallen, denn verschiedene Rechtsanwälte, die italienische Texon-Grosskunden vertreten, haben Gerichtsverfahren gegen die SKA angestrengt.

Die TAT erfuhr weiter, dass die SKA nicht nur Jelmoli verkauft hat, sondern weitere Beteiligungen abgestossen hat. Offiziell ist der Verkauf des 30-Prozent-Anteils an der London Multinational Bank Limited. Bisher nicht bestätigt ist hingegen der Verkauf von zwei weiteren Bankbeteiligungen in Brüssel und New York. Ebenfalls nicht bestätigen wollte die SKA den Verkauf des (Texon-)Chiasso-Hotels «Corso» an den Geschäftsführer der SKA-Tochter Valcambi S. A., Emilio Camponovo, «da dies – wenn es so wäre – eine interne Transaktion ist».

Im Gegensatz zu «Bankkreisen» sieht die Kontrollinstanz der Schweizer Banken, die Bankenkommission, die Lage der SKA offiziell als rosig an. Geschäftsführer Bernhard Müller: «Aufgrund unserer Unterlagen erachten wir die Ertragskraft der SKA als in Ordnung. Ein Liquiditätsproblem besteht nicht. Auch im Ausland ist das Vertrauen in die Kreditanstalt wieder hergestellt.»

Ein Nationalbank-Vertreter indessen: «Das höhere Bedürfnis der SKA nach Liquidität ist unbestritten...»

Hanspeter Bürgin

Tat, 7 December 1977. The headline says: 'Kreditanstalt is plunged into a deep crisis after the Chiasso Affair as: Customers Flee the Bank!' The article goes on to claim that SKA was losing customers in droves and that it was selling off assets and dressing up its accounts to make the situation look better.

TAT Mittwoch, 7. Dezember 1977 — **UNSERE MEINUNG** — ⑬

Wenn's schlecht geht, schadet die Wahrheit

Roger Schawinski

Jeden Tag wird es deutlicher: Die Kreditanstalt ist im Lebensnerv getroffen. Beteiligungen werden abgestossen, eine nach der andern. Und auch die Bilanz-Kosmetiker schaffen es nicht, genügend Rouge auf die eingefallenen Bank-Wangen zu schmieren.

Das Chiasso-Desaster frisst die Bank von innen her auf. Die Auszehrung wird auch durch Geldspritzen der anderen Grossbanken und Vitamin-Schübe der Nationalbank nicht aufgehalten.

Denn die SKA wird zwiefach zur Ader gelassen. Einmal wurden ihr mit der Texon eine Vielzahl fauler Eier ins Nest gelegt, die es jetzt mit Zuschüssen vor dem Konkurs zu retten gilt. Dem schlechten Texon-Geld muss also wider jede Bankregel gutes SKA-Geld nachgeworfen werden. Deshalb wurden stille Reserven aufgelöst, Kredite aufgenommen und jetzt auch die während Jahren gehätschelten Parade-Beteiligungen meistbietend verhökert.

Zum andern war der Vertrauensschwund viel grösser als zuerst angenommen. Zwar tut die Bank-Konkurrenz alles, um der SKA über die Runden zu helfen. Aber für die Privat- und Geschäftskundschaft ist die SKA nicht mehr immer eine «erste Adresse».

Das ist das Dilemma jeder Bank, die ins Gerede gekommen ist: Die Wahrheit über Verluste ist geschäftsschädigend. Das heisst, für Aktionäre, Kunden und Angestellte kann es vorteilhaft sein, wenn das Management sie belügt.

Doch diese Taktik verfängt nur kurzfristig. Denn wenn eine Gerüchtewelle nicht bald durch harte Fakten gestoppt wird, kann sie das Rest-Vertrauen wegschwemmen.

Bericht Seite 7

'S KALLGIRL

Tat, 7 December 1977: 'When Things Are Going Wrong, the Truth Hurts'. The editorial stated that the losses caused by Chiasso would inevitably do great damage to the bank and undermine customer loyalty, but that the only way to stop wild rumors was to be open about the facts.

'It is to the great credit of our chairman that the general meeting passed as we would have wished. Thanks to his mastery of the situation, we were able to restore the confidence of the shareholders, the customers and the staff' (Vote of thanks by vice-chairman Hans Schwarzenbach to chairman of the board of directors Oswald Aeppli; minutes of the board of directors, 30 June 1977).

lems, and there were still no reliable figures or budgets available. Clearly there was much to be done.

The work went well and on 25 August 1977 the unit was able to come to the meeting of the credit committee and the board of directors as planned with an initial record of Texon's exposure.[469] After SKA took on 1,700 Texon creditors, Texon's (non-interest-bearing) current account overdraft came to Sfr 2.079 billion. One hundred and thirty-six more creditors, accounting for about Sfr 112 million, were yet to be processed, leaving the probable overall outstanding balance at around Sfr 2.2 billion. Guarantee exposure to the Texon companies came to Sfr 406.8 million, and overdrafts and time loans came to Sfr 115 million.[470]

'Chiasso' remained a hot topic for the media in Switzerland and abroad.[471] The interest of the general public moved on to the Italian companies taken over by SKA. An exception to this general trend was the reporting by the *Tat*, which continued to publish its tendentious articles. Josef Müller and the head office auditors came under particularly heavy fire: 'The Sweet Life of SKAndal Bankers' ran the lurid headline of 19 July 1977. According to the *Tat* 'exposé' Ernst Kuhrmeier had pampered the auditors in Chiasso with expensive meals, generous gifts and even call girls.

SKA sells its stake in Jelmoli

These discreditable and defamatory articles prompted the bank to lodge a complaint with the Migros co-operative, owners of the *Tat*, though in the end this intervention came to nothing. The idea of pressing charges was considered, but ultimately rejected out of concern for the time and unwanted publicity that a trial would entail. Then, as preparations for the 1977 year-end bookkeeping and the associated sale of the bank's stake in Jelmoli to UTC International AG, Basel, were underway, the last straw came. Hanspeter Bürgin's *Tat* article of 7 December 1977, headlined 'Kunden geben Fersengeld!' ('Customers Flee the Bank!'), and the supplementary editorial by Roger Schawinski went too far for SKA.[472] The newspaper accused the bank of throwing good money after bad by selling its Jelmoli stock to cover Texon losses; it also said that confidence in the bank had slipped to the extent that it was no longer regarded as a 'first-class address'. The bank pressed charges for defamation and secured an injunction preventing Migros from publishing further articles of this type.[473] 'We were ... forced to take these measures in order to maintain the good name of the bank and the confidence of our customers and staff ... We have shown that we will not tolerate any further comments from this paper that could in any way be defamatory to us.'[474]

Selling Jelmoli was painful. The investment in one of Switzerland's premiere department store chains had always been a very good one for SKA in every respect[475], but the sale would produce another Sfr 205 million for the bank's reserves, which in the prevailing circumstances would be very welcome indeed.[476] This was also how the move was interpreted by the business press.[477]

As the publication of the 1977 annual report approached, smoothing the waves in the media was seen as an urgent priority. The philosophy behind the 1977 financial statements was discussed at the board of directors meeting of 15 December 1977. There was unanimous support for the maintenance of the dividend pay-out, even though some board members had wondered about reducing it slightly in order to protect the bank's hidden reserves. However, Oswald Aeppli and Rainer E. Gut opposed this idea because cutting the dividend would greatly harm the bank's prestige and increase the risk that the bank's bearer share price would fall significantly below Sfr 2,000.[478]

By the end of 1977, Fides and KOREAG were coming to the end of their work. KOREAG proposed that write-downs and provisions of Sfr 1.2 billion be made for the Texon investments, a proposal that was approved by the Banking Commission. As part of a private enforcement of its right of lien, at the end of December 1977 SKA took over the assets that Texon had pledged to it on 18 April 1977 as its own property.[479] According to the objective estimate made by KOREAG, these assets (which in future came to be known as the KOREAG assets) were worth Sfr 977 million. The main items were Winefood at Sfr 316 million, Albarella at Sfr 268 million, and Ampaglas at Sfr 110 million. The asset side of SKA's balance sheet contained the claim against Texon, which had been adjusted to Sfr 2.239 billion. In order to cover the required write-downs and provisions of Sfr 1.262 billion, Sfr 29 million had to be taken from the bank's ongoing business, and Sfr 736.2 million from appreciations, liquidation gains, extraordinary dividends from subsidiary companies, and the realization of hidden reserves; another Sfr 400 million had to be charged against existing reserves and provisions, and Sfr 97 million came from the revaluation of bank premises and real estate.[480]

Creation of the Texon press unit

These figures were not published in detail. The 1977 annual report only gave Texon's total exposure, the overall value of the assets taken on by SKA and the resulting requirement for write-downs and provisions. Even from these figures it was clear that cleaning up the Texon mess would result in a loss of about Sfr 1.2 billion for SKA.[481] If the assets taken over from Texon went up in value, the loss could theoretically be smaller, but a realistic appraisal suggested the bank could count itself lucky if these mainly Italian assets retained their current value. If the proposed sale was to have any success, it was important first of all to create a positive atmosphere. Consequently, in January 1978, a full-time press office was set up within the Texon special unit – a development that had first been planned in autumn 1977.[482]

The new press office addressed the public with an article printed over several pages of the February 1978 edition of SKA's *bulletin* magazine. Publication of the article was motivated primarily by the transfer of the Texon investments to SKA's balance sheet at the end of 1977. 'Thanks to the great dedication of everyone involved, all the work being done has now progressed so far that the bank has a clear overview and control over just about all the Texon companies. […] This does not mean that we should expect quick sales. SKA is acting on the

'The financial statements are based on the facts that the hidden reserves are sufficient to cover the entire loss from the Texon Affair, … that our bank's earning power is unbroken, and that we are in a position to pay out an unchanged dividend. These facts have not been contested in any way by the Banking Commission' (Robert A. Jeker, minutes of the board of directors, 17 December 1977).

> 'All the guesswork and speculation about the size of SKA's losses from the Texon Affair have been brought to an end by the presentation of the annual accounts. The figure of Sfr 1.2 billion is towards the upper end of what the public and experts had expected'
> (NZZ, 3 March 1978).

principle that solutions have to be found on a case-by-case basis and that they have to be right not only for the bank, but also for the company concerned, its staff, customers and suppliers.'[483]

By making this statement, SKA was giving a clear indication of the style in which it would be tackling the Texon problem from now on. The time for being defensive was over. The second part of the *bulletin* article outlined the prevailing situation at the key Texon participations such as Winefood, Albarella, FICI, Olbiacard, Ampaglas, Gottardo Ruffoni and others.

Reasonably favorable conditions were thus created for the annual general meeting of shareholders on the 1977 business year. This was scheduled for 4 April 1978. On 1 March 1978 at the press conference on the annual results, traditionally held straight after the board of directors' meeting, Rainer E. Gut, Robert A. Jeker and Hugo von der Crone were already presenting the bank's new self-confident face to a lively crowd of journalists. Thanks to its financial strength, SKA was starting to recover from the blow it had suffered. Its earnings power was undiminished and the bank had reasserted its solid market position.[484]

The annual general meeting of shareholders of 4 April 1978

At the annual general meeting, Oswald Aeppli talked confidently to shareholders about SKA's 1977 business year. In his chairman's address he dispensed with the customary review of a general economic topic. After 'the most upsetting year in the 122-year history of Schweizerische Kreditanstalt' he wanted to concentrate exclusively on the bank's situation.[485]

First of all, Oswald Aeppli explained how the Chiasso Affair was being dealt with in terms of the financial statements. He only had good things to report about the state of the balance sheet. Overall the bank had made a net profit of Sfr 235 million in this memorable year, allowing the board to approve a dividend payment unchanged on the previous year.[486]

In the second part of his speech, Aeppli talked about the measures taken within the bank since Chiasso. The board of directors had restructured its activities, and the flow of information from the executive board to the board of directors had been streamlined.[487] Members of the board of directors who served in special committees had been given new lists of duties, and each member of the board now belonged to at least one committee. A chairman's committee had been set up to advise the chairman of the board on issues pertaining to general business goals and business policy. The responsibilities of the control committee had also been greatly extended, and it would henceforth carry out audits of operations at Swiss branches.

The executive board had also rethought its own working methods. The number of direct reports had been greatly reduced, and now only the biggest branches would report directly to an executive board member. Minutes were now being taken of the weekly executive board meetings, and members of the board would gather at least four times a year for a one or two-day seminar to discuss underlying issues and take major decisions on business policy.

Wide-ranging steps had also been taken in the area of controlling and auditing. The audit department, which now reported directly to the chairman of the board of directors in functional and management terms, was being strengthened by the addition of significant numbers of extra staff. New people were brought in from outside to fill the positions of chief auditor, deputy chief auditor and various other senior managerial posts. Finally SKA had decided to change its external statutory auditor. From 1978, Schweizerische Revisionsgesellschaft, rather than Gesellschaft für Bankrevisionen (GBR), would review the bank's books. This change was intended to avoid any remaining partiality or awkwardness that might have carried over from the earlier financial relationship between SKA and GBR.

On the question of responsibility, Oswald Aeppli told the shareholders that SKA had started to instigate civil proceedings against the main culprits Ernst Kuhrmeier, Claudio Laffranchi and Meinrad Perler, as well as against Alfredo Noseda, Elbio Gada and Alessandro Villa. However, civil action could not be started properly until the results of the ongoing criminal investigation were in. Consequently, the proceedings were unlikely to begin before 1979.

Withholding tax and negative interest

With its decree of 12 September 1977, the Federal Tax Administration put the total amount of withholding tax unpaid by Texon between 1972 and 1977 at Sfr 193 million. These arrears were paid out of the account that had been created for this very purpose from the frozen 25% of assets belonging to former Texon investors.[488]

The situation with regard to negative interest was rather different. In its resolution of 28 February 1978, the SNB had fixed the amount of negative interest due at Sfr 81.7 million. The government suddenly decided that the negative interest would be a welcome source of revenue and wanted to up the amount to Sfr 293 million. It had already announced that it would be lodging an appeal to the administrative court of the Federal Supreme Court to secure this increase.[489] In response to the government's additional claim, SKA would also be seeking redress from the Supreme Court.[490]

This brought Oswald Aeppli's report on the Chiasso Affair to an end. To close he reminded the assembled shareholders of his appeal to the extraordinary general meeting of 24 June 1977. At that time, Oswald Aeppli had left no doubt that SKA was willing and able to overcome the blow dealt by Chiasso. The only path to take was the path forward towards the restoration of the bank's health and strength.

The annual general meeting, attended by 2,168 shareholders, passed off peacefully; all of the resolutions proposed by the board of directors were approved with only a handful of opposing votes. The dividend, the two-step capital increase and the annual report and accounts were all accepted unanimously.

'Despite some shareholders' criticism of the management's conduct in the Chiasso Affair … it seems that the successful financial results have reinforced the shareholders' faith in the bank' (*NZZ*, 5 April 1978).

Rehabilitation

The end of the 1977 business year and the presentation of the results at the annual general meeting of shareholders of 4 April 1978 marked the beginning of the bank's period of consolidation. The size of the loss suffered was now generally known, and Texon's participations had been identified.

Public interest concentrated primarily on the criminal investigation of Ernst Kuhrmeier and his accomplices. Meanwhile the business press was directing its attention towards SKA's ongoing efforts to deal with the Chiasso debacle, and particularly towards gathering information about Texon's companies, most of which were domiciled in Italy. The sale of these participations would ultimately determine whether SKA's losses would remain at Sfr 1.2 billion.

Disputes with former Texon investors

A further risk for SKA was represented by the claims for compensation that had been threatened, and in some cases already made, by the former investors in Texon. These investors refused simply to swallow the retrospective debiting of withholding tax and negative interest. The potential amount at risk here for SKA was the Sfr 250 million owed in total to the public authorities. One thing in SKA's favor was that many investors were keen to avoid attention from the tax authorities, and thus wanted to avoid a legal dispute and the publicity this would bring. SKA was not prepared to discuss compensation until the courts had made a predetermination on the matter. It took more than ten years for this to happen. According to two ground-breaking judgments by the Zurich commercial court, confirmed by the Federal Supreme Court on 2 November 1988 and 10 March 1989 respectively, SKA could only be compelled to make compensation payments if the investors concerned earned less from their Texon investments (after the negative interest and withholding tax had been deducted) than they would have done from an alternative investment available at the time.[491] When the settlements were calculated on this basis, most investors had a rude awakening: their Swiss franc Texon investments had as a rule done very well compared to the alternative investment instruments available at the time. These two judgments at last provided a basis for a whole series of settlement payments to former Texon investors totaling around Sfr 20 million. Admittedly, the investors themselves were left with rather a bitter taste in their mouths. As far as they were concerned, their investments with SKA had lost them money. They felt that the bank had deceived them, having given assurances when the affair was first uncovered that none of the Chiasso branch's customers would suffer any loss.[492] SKA had to live with this image problem for some time to come.

The conclusion of the criminal proceedings

The criminal investigation was finished at the end of November 1978. KORE-AG, already working for the FBC, had also been chosen as an expert witness and had given its view of the losses involved in a comprehensive set of reports.[493] Only at the end of 1978 were all parties, including SKA, given full access to the files.

With his bill of indictment of 8 February 1979, district attorney Paolo Bernasconi brought the case before the 'Corte delle Assise criminali' in Mendrisio.[494] The trial by jury was set for 28 May 1979. Ernst Kuhrmeier and Claudio Laffranchi remained in custody until the trial began.

With the trial now imminent, emotions were once again running high, and memories of the affair, now two years old, were refreshed.[495] Tension reached a peak when the trial was opened on 28 May. The court met at the hall of the Chiasso council buildings, attended by a remarkably large contingent of public and press. Ernst Kuhrmeier, Claudio Laffranchi, Elbio Gada and Alfredo Noseda took their places on the defendants' bench. Alessandro Villa was excused from attending in person for health reasons, but had agreed that the trial could be conducted in his absence.

Senior judge Plinio Rotalinti presided over the trial, supported by two other senior judges and five jurors. District attorney Paolo Bernasconi spoke for the prosecution, and SKA as civil plaintiff was represented by Professor Stefano Ghiringhelli.

Over the course of the six-week-long trial, the Texon story was once again laid out in all its detail. The warnings not heeded by Zurich were described in full. Right from the start Ernst Kuhrmeier accepted full responsibility for what had happened; Claudio Laffranchi also conceded that he was guilty as charged.[496] By contrast, the defendants from the Studio legale tried to put most of the blame on Ernst Kuhrmeier and even on SKA's head office.[497] Kuhrmeier referred to the value of the companies taken over by Texon, saying that in his view, SKA's losses could have been kept much smaller if it had not been for the publicity generated by the criminal proceedings.[498]

Once the evidence had been heard, district attorney Paolo Bernasconi left no doubt in his address to the court that the crimes in question were committed in Chiasso. However, he chastised the Swiss banks in general, saying that in recent years they had put their own profits ahead of their customers' security.[499]

As the civil plaintiff, SKA asserted a claim for compensation of Sfr 20 million jointly and severally against all the accused in the form of a partial claim.[500]

On 3 July 1977, after rigorous discussions behind closed doors, Plinio Rotalinti delivered the eagerly awaited judgment: Ernst Kuhrmeier and Claudio Laffranchi were sentenced to four-and-a-half years imprisonment and a fine of Sfr 10,000 each on counts of continuous disloyal business practices for their own gain, embezzlement, falsification of documents and infringement of various federal decrees (including the Banking Law). The defense strategy adopted by Elbio Gada, Alessandro Villa and Alfredo Noseda did not succeed. As professionals who sat on all the boards of the Texon companies, it was not possible that they could have remained ignorant of the crimes being committed. Quite the contrary in fact: they had actively collaborated and derived personal benefit from doing so. These three accused were thus sentenced, for the same crimes as the other two, to 16 months in jail and to fines of Sfr 200,000 each. The jail sentences were suspended for a probationary period of five years. The civil charge was upheld, leaving all the accused jointly and severally liable for the payment of Sfr 20 million in compensation to Texon and thus to SKA.[501]

The reasons for the judgment, read out by Plinio Rotalinti, attracted even more attention than the sentences themselves. He denounced the boom time of the 1960s that had made such transgressions possible in the first place, and then made it clear that the court was in no doubt that certain control mechanisms had failed. The accused had exploited this situation shamelessly for their own criminal purposes.

The press heaped praise on the judgement.[502] Shortly before the period prescribed for appeal had elapsed, Ernst Kuhrmeier died of a heart attack on 10 July 1979[503], meaning that the judgment against him was never made absolute. The other convicted men lodged appeals with the cantonal and subsequently with the federal courts, but the appellate courts upheld the central judgement.[504] The original pronouncement on the civil charge was also upheld by the Ticino court of appeal.[505]

Liquidation of the Texon companies

Once the criminal proceedings were over, public interest increasingly turned back to the fate of the companies taken over by SKA. Following the annual general meeting of shareholders on 4 April 1978, the Texon press unit had already conveyed a generally positive view of the companies to the media. It organized meetings with journalists in Italy and Zurich, at which the various members of the Texon special unit introduced the particular companies that they were looking after. In October 1978 the press unit arranged for journalists to visit Winefood's key group companies. The trip attracted lively interest.[506] A press trip to Albarella was planned for 1979.[507]

All of these activities had a single goal: to prove to the media that these companies were essentially perfectly sound, though the journalists were not shown any figures. The prevailing impression was that SKA had the Texon Affair under control; in fact there was widespread admiration for what the bank had managed to achieve in such a short space of time. This general impression was strengthened by another article by the Texon press unit published in the *bulletin* of March 1979 under the headline 'Streamlined Italian Investments'.[508] The article reported the first results of attempts to sort out the implications of 'Chiasso'. Group structures had been simplified and various companies had been sold, merged or liquidated. Winefood was to concentrate on the wine business, meaning that the firm could be expected to eliminate its loss by the end of 1979. Albarella stood before a new beginning. The article mentioned that certain problems remained unresolved at Albarella, but that the contract signed with a large German travel agent for the 1979 season showed that there were also positive signs for the future.

This upbeat reporting had the desired effect on public opinion. 'Consolidation in SKA's Italian Investments', was the headline over the editorial in the *Neue Zürcher Zeitung* of 6 March 1979. The basic tone of the report on SKA's 1978 financial year was also positive. 'We have made remarkable progress in the

'The Patients Are Recovering' (*Schweizerische Finanz-Zeitung*, 12 July 1978).

restructuring of the group of companies bequeathed to us in 1977 by the Texon Finanzanstalt, Vaduz, ...; the resulting operational losses have been written down. We will not know the final value of these interests until they have been sold. It will depend greatly on the success of our efforts to improve the earning power of these participations. We have moved much closer to this goal during the year under review.'[509] After the 1979 financial year, the Texon participations were no longer a subject of discussion in the bank's annual reports.

However, the confident view of the Texon companies conveyed to the public was not necessarily reflected by reality. The problems discovered were more numerous and varied than first assumed. The main difficulty was that the companies lacked sufficient earning power. Consequently it was very difficult, if not impossible, to sell the companies without further injections of finance. Additional funds were required to complete the necessary restructurings, especially since the Italian trade unions had such a large influence when it came to redundancies.

1979–1982: the difficult years

A striking picture of the real problems facing the bank can be gleaned from the minutes of the board of directors from this period. Until 1979, the assets of the individual Texon participations were carried in the books at their 1977 values. This was only possible because SKA was funding the companies' operational losses. In 1979 and 1980, investments totaling Sfr 44.13 million had to be made in Albarella just to make sure that the company could keep operating.

In fact SKA seriously considered exiting from Albarella. 'In certain circumstances it may be better to get out'[510], said Ulrich Albers at the board of directors meeting of 16 September 1979.

Although the Texon subsidiaries continued to operate at a loss, SKA's annual results for 1979 and 1980 were satisfactory. Nevertheless, the accounts for the 1980 financial year included provisions for the Texon investments of Sfr 100 million.[511]

The bank's 1981 results were poor. A sharp inversion of the yield curve had made the interest rate environment for Swiss business very difficult. 'The bank's situation has fundamentally changed since Chiasso. The money that we have had to use for write-downs has not been working for us', is how president of the executive board Rainer E. Gut put it to the SKA board of directors. He went on to say: 'We are also missing the revenue from the companies we have sold. Basically our underlying approach is still determined by the effort to put Chiasso behind us.'[512]

By the end of 1981, SKA's interest account showed a negative balance of Sfr 63 million, a deterioration of Sfr 173 million on the previous year. Against this background, the continuing negative performance of the Texon companies weighed particularly heavily. The positive projections for 1981 were not fulfilled, and the companies continued to languish in the red. Another Sfr 98.8 million had to be set aside as provisions, plus another Sfr 48.4 million for write-downs necessitated by the fall in the value of the lira and the French franc.

'There is no good solution for Albarella; we can only choose the one which is least bad for us. We can hardly wind it up altogether, since this would entail a virtually intolerable value adjustment' (Oswald Aeppli, minutes of the board of directors, 16 September 1979).

In this financially unsatisfactory situation, SKA reorganized its group structure. The trigger for this restructuring was the introduction of new capital adequacy and consolidation regulations by the Federal Banking Commission. SKA shifted its entire Sfr 124.2 million stake in Financière Crédit Suisse – First Boston, plus 5,000 Elektrowatt shares worth Sfr 11.5 million, into the newly created CS Holding. Shareholders received an unchanged dividend as far as the overall sum paid was concerned; out of the net profit for 1981 of Sfr 275,778,461.94 they were paid a cash dividend of Sfr 30 per bearer share and Sfr 6 per registered share, plus a dividend in kind of Sfr 50, or Sfr 10 for registered shares, in the form of CS Holding participation certificates, which were inseparable from SKA shares.[513]

The board of directors and the general meeting of shareholders approved this distribution of earnings for the 1981 financial year.

The 1982 financial year was a better one for SKA – a point emphasized with some satisfaction in the control committee's presentation to the board of directors on 24 February 1983: 'In the previous year we were confronted with the dilemma of maintaining the size of the dividend despite the poor results. Thankfully we face no such problem this year.'[514] The comment once again demonstrates how difficult 1981 had been, making clear why the dividend in kind had to be introduced. From the point of view of the Texon problem it was a good job that 1982 was such a good year for business: SKA still had to set aside additional provisions of Sfr 159 million for the troubled companies.

1983: turning the corner

1983 marked the turning point. SKA put in an outstanding performance for the year. 'For the first time', said Rainer E. Gut, 'we have been able to achieve a return on equity higher than the average for the years 1970 to 1976. In other words we have put the events of 1977 behind us and can, if all the signs are correct, look forward to the future with confidence.'[515] A further Sfr 196.2 million worth of write-downs and provisions were, however, still required for the Texon positions in 1983. In 1984 the figure was Sfr 165.8 million, and finally in 1985 Sfr 180 million.

In 1985, the president of the executive board Robert A. Jeker had told the board of directors that SKA was doing everything it could to sell the assets relating to Texon.[516] These efforts bore fruit in summer 1986 when the bank was finally able to dispose of Winefood. However, the sum realized was only a fraction of the value originally set by KOREAG. Following further write-downs and provisions of Sfr 79.6 million in 1986 and Sfr 41.2 million in 1987, the total Texon exposure came to Sfr 115.2 million. 'The Texon investments have thus reached a size that no longer requires special reporting'[517] the SKA board of directors was told by the control commission. Finally, on 9 September 1988, the bank was able to sell Albarella; again the price achieved was well below the value ascertained in 1977.

The facts are sobering. The money raised by selling the three main Texon companies Ampaglas, Winefood and Albarella in 1982, 1986 and 1988 respec-

---

In a wide-ranging report on Texon and its participations entitled 'Is a Golden Goose Hatching From the Rotten Egg?' published on 10 July 1979, *Schweizer Illustrierte* reasoned: 'It is also possible that the huge general store put together by Kuhrmeier and friends as Texon could one day do a roaring trade.'

tively, totaled about Sfr 150 million. In return for the sales, SKA had to waive its claim to Sfr 100 million of loans to group companies owned by these Texon participations.

The bare figures show how painful the Texon exposure was for SKA. They do not, however, reflect very clearly the enormous efforts that were made at all levels to keep the damage down. In 1977/78 most of the Texon companies were in such a critical financial situation that they would have had no choice but to file for bankruptcy. Such a radical solution would, however, have required that SKA immediately write off more than Sfr 2 billion, which at that time would have cast the bank into severe difficulties. Consequently, there was no alternative but to embark on the laborious strategy of keeping the companies afloat and gradually writing off the Texon portfolio over a period of more than ten years.

Amongst the general public, the impression stuck that SKA had ultimately managed to keep the financial damage done by the Chiasso Affair within bounds. Some journalists were even moved to speculate that the Texon companies could one day produce a gain for the bank. 'At least at the international level, the Texon Affair – strange though it may seem – actually strengthened confidence in SKA.'[518]

'Despite all the damage to our image, the whole thing did have a positive side for our bank: the crisis welded me and my colleagues on the executive board together; we developed a real team spirit which helped us to set a successful course for our company in the years that followed' (Rainer E. Gut in *Group News*, December 1998).

Solothurner Zeitung,
11 February 1989.

Testing times for the Swiss banking industry

After the Chiasso Affair, calls intensified for a tightening up of the Swiss banks' internal control mechanisms and of banking regulation in general. A banking initiative proposed by the Swiss Social Democratic Party in 1977 was based on similar concerns. The banks reacted quickly. Within a short space of time, they had taken a decisive step towards self-regulation by producing an ethically motivated code of conduct in partnership with the Swiss National Bank. The code was to set the benchmark for various national and international efforts in the fight against money laundering. Self-regulation was also the main theme of the battle against insider dealing: by closing a regulatory loop-hole and introducing an enforceable legal standard, the Swiss Bankers' Association's Convention XVI helped to prevent a serious legal conflict between the USA and Switzerland.

*The Agreement on the Swiss Banks' Code of Conduct
with Regard to the Exercise of Due Diligence*

'The cry that "something must be done" is booming out. But what exactly can be done? Are new banking laws required? Does our private sector banking system need tougher regulation, perhaps by a much better-staffed Federal Banking Commission? Or do we perhaps even have to consider the nationalization proposed by the Social Democratic Party?' (*Weltwoche*, 25 May 1977).

The Agreement on the Swiss Banks' Code of Conduct with Regard to the Exercise of Due Diligence (Vereinbarung über die Standesregeln zur Sorgfaltspflicht der Banken, or VSB) is a shining example of successful self-regulation and a 'milestone in the ethical development of banking business'.[519] As its president Fritz Leutwiler pointed out several times in the mid-1970s, the Swiss National Bank had 'striven for a long time' for such an agreement. However, 'its actual realization' was 'ultimately triggered by the Kreditanstalt affair'[520] of spring 1977, which had badly shaken the Swiss financial services industry. The affair had also developed into a political matter. In their June sessions, for example, both chambers of the federal parliament dealt with 17 motions relating to the Swiss financial services industry. Banking secrecy was one of the main subjects of criticism in the debates that followed, and parliamentarians tamely accepted various sweeping condemnations of Swiss bank secrecy laws that had come from abroad. At the same time, the Swiss Social Democratic Party (SP) announced its 'banking initiative', the main aim of which was to increase the direct influence of the state on the banking sector. Like most of the motions put before the Swiss parliament, the banking initiative was at heart intended 'ultimately to change the system in a fundamental way'.[521]

The pressure placed on the banks was too intense to be overcome merely by conciliatory words. Even in conservative circles, the prevailing view was that 'a

Neue Zürcher Nachrichten, 13 February 1989. The picture shows one of the half-dozen floats at the Zurich carnival that chose money laundering as their theme that year.

«Suberi Nötli» für Zürich

Mindestens fünf Gruppen kümmerten sich vor Tausenden von Besuchern am Zürcher Fasnachtsumzug um die Geldwäscherei, so auch auf diesem Wagen, ausgerüstet mit Waschmaschine, Waschhafen und Fegbürste. Neben den Themen Geldwäsche und Kopp-Affäre standen die Marronihäuschen und verschiedene Umweltprobleme im Brennpunkt fasnächtlicher Scherze. **Seite Zürich**

*The 17 parliamentary motions dealt with by the Councils
of the Swiss parliament in the June Session of 1977*[522]

National Council (Nationalrat – lower chamber of the Swiss parliament)
Motion by Werner Carobbio of 22 March 1977 (Banking Law; revision)
Motion by the Social Democrats of 4 May 1977 (banking control)
Motion by Jean Ziegler of 4 May 1977 (bank secrecy)
Postulate by Heinrich Müller of 2 May 1977 (banking regulation)
Postulate by Walter König of 20 June 1977 (small savers)
Interpellation by Felix Auer of 9 March 1977 (bank secrecy)
Interpellation by the Social Democrats of 2 May 1977 (Chiasso bank scandal)
Interpellation by the Radical Democrats of 2 May 1977 (Schweizerische Kreditanstalt, Chiasso branch)
Interpellation by Werner Carobbio of 2 May 1977 (Schweizerische Kreditanstalt, Chiasso branch)
Interpellation by the Swiss People's Party of 2 May 1977 (Schweizerische Kreditanstalt)
Interpellation by the Christian Democrats of 2 May 1977 (banking developments)
Interpellation by the Independents of 3 May 1977 (Schweizerische Kreditanstalt, Chiasso branch)
Ordinary question by Werner Carobbio of 7 March 1977 (banking control)
Ordinary question by Jean Ziegler of 22 March 1977 (French flight capital)
Ordinary question by Jean Ziegler of 25 March 1977 (numbered accounts)
Urgent ordinary question by Jean Ziegler of 9 June 1977 (Kreditanstalt affair; role of Councilor Vassalli)

Council of States (Ständerat – upper chamber)
Interpellation by the Radical Democrats of 2 May 1977 (Schweizerische Kreditanstalt, Chiasso branch)

remedy was needed to correct the deficiencies and abuses that have come to light – and not just because of the Chiasso Affair – in the Swiss banking industry', and that this remedy should be 'in the form of a credible, manageable, universally binding and rapidly effective set of tools'.[523]

Taking the bull by the horns, the Swiss National Bank worked together with the Swiss Bankers' Association, which after initial hesitation cooperated very purposefully, to produce a code of conduct within only two months. The key principles formulated in the code paved the way for a whole raft of subsequent measures, including new regulations on due diligence at financial companies (Article 305ter of the Swiss Penal Code; in force since 1 August 1990), the guidelines on money laundering issued by the Federal Banking Commission (FBC) in 1991, and the Federal Law on Combating Money Laundering in the Financial Sector of 1 April 1998 (Geldwäschereigesetz / GwG). In the international arena too, the high professional standards set by the code of conduct were used as a model for various efforts to fight money laundering. The recommendations on identifying customers made by the Financial Action Task Force on Money Laundering (FATF), for example, were heavily based on the Swiss due diligence agreement. These FATF recommendations were in turn incorporated into the EU's money laundering regulations, and from there into the national money laundering legislation of EU member states.

One sign of the code of conduct's quality is its endurance; following its revision in 1998 the code was adopted for another five years. Its core principles, as restated in the preamble to the 1998 version, have remained the same throughout:

- 'With a view to preserving the good name of the Swiss banking community nationally and internationally,

> The VSB was 'even used as a model for the international code of conduct proposed by the countries of the Club of Ten in December 1988' (Paolo Bernasconi, former Ticino district attorney, in: *Der Beobachter*, no. 8, 1989).

- with a view to establishing rules ensuring, in the area of banking secrecy and when entering into business relations, business conduct that is beyond reproach,
- and in an effort to provide effective assistance in the fight against money laundering,

  the banks hereby contract with the Swiss Bankers' Association in its capacity as the professional body charged with safeguarding the interests and reputation of Swiss banking:

  a) to verify the identity of their contracting partners and, in cases of doubt, to obtain from the contracting partner a declaration setting forth the identity of the beneficial owner of assets;
  b) not to provide any active assistance in the flight of capital;
  c) not to provide any active assistance in cases of tax evasion or similar acts, by delivering incomplete or misleading attestations.'[524]

Two aspects of this preamble in particular deserve to be highlighted:

- the duty to identify the customer beyond all doubt (the 'know your customer' rule) and
- the courage to 'put the "beneficial owner" (a concept that is essentially alien to the Swiss legal system) first'.[525]

Alongside the technical details, the provisions of the code contain a number of basic clarifications relating to its intent and purpose. It is stated, for example, that the code does not seek to incorporate foreign legislation on currency, tax and business in general into the Swiss legal system or to make such laws apply to the Swiss banks, nor to undermine current practices in international law. However, by introducing the obligation to carefully ascertain the identity of each individual bank customer and, where appropriate, the beneficial owner, the code enabled the authorities to enforce the duty to testify and provide information as defined by federal and cantonal law. The Bankers' Association emphasized that the code of conduct would not make daily banking business more difficult; it simply laid down the rules 'in binding form for running a bank in accordance with good practice'.[526]

'The Swiss banks want to ensure good order in their own affairs and also, together with the National Bank and the Banking Commission, to take tough action to prevent or punish unacceptable behavior' (Letter from Swiss Bankers' Association, 10 June 1977).

The first version of the code, published in 1977, was conceived of as an agreement between the National Bank on the one hand, and the Bankers' Association and its member banks on the other. Following the revision of 1987, the National Bank stepped back; from then on the agreement was continued as a contract between the Swiss Bankers' Association and its member banks. The fact that the Swiss National Bank, with all its natural authority, took a leading role in the project in its early years contributed greatly to its success. It is also clear that the legal effect of the agreement could not have been achieved fast enough by Switzerland's slow and cumbersome legislative machinery. By autonomously regulating a key part of banking practice, the agreement on the code of conduct made it unnecessary for the government to frame analogous or similar national laws. Consequently it de facto constitutes the law in this area. Furthermore, its main thrust is emphatically ethical in a way that a government law would find very hard to match.[527]

With the VSB code of conduct on due diligence, the banks had well and truly lived up to a claim they had always made for themselves: the Swiss financial community had shown that it was in a position to overcome a crisis by joining forces, and to use the situation as an opportunity.

The banking initiative

The Chiasso Affair, which was made known to the public on 14 April 1977, prompted a debate on the banks at the next session of the Swiss parliament. On 20 June, five interpellations were made regarding the events at SKA's Chiasso branch.[528]

The interpellation by the Social Democrats (SP) was of particular interest. According to its leader Helmut Hubacher, 'the Chiasso banking scandal ... has become a Swiss affair. [...] The excessiveness of the attempts to maximize profits went beyond any measure of responsibility. The worship of private ownership led to a search for profit at any price. [...] What has become public with the Chiasso Affair is not the exception but the rule. [...] The apparently perfect scam supported by conservative politicians, some of whom actually sat in the national government, has been systematically and profitably exploited, giving the scandal even more of a semi-official air.'[529] The interpellations by the Radical Democratic Party (FDP), the Swiss People's Party (SVP) and the Christian Democratic People's Party (CVP) also expressed concern about the good name of the Swiss financial services industry. The Federal Council was called upon to take the necessary legislative measures to prevent a similar scandal from occurring in the future.[530] 'Chiasso' also took up the National Council's time on the following two days. On 21 June 1977, National Councillor Lilian Uchtenhagen explained the SP's motion of 4 May 1977, which demanded from the Federal Council, amongst other things, 'a tightening of the statutory internal and external controls, and a strengthening and expansion of the Banking Commission'.[531]

The Federal Council's answer to this plethora of parliamentary motions was presented in a detailed exposition by the head of the Federal Department of Finance Georges-André Chevallaz. First he emphasized the importance of the financial services industry as a central pillar of the Swiss economy, before moving on to a thorough examination of the problem of flight capital raised by the parliamentarian's submissions. He stated that as far as could be determined at the present time, the fact that serious transgressions had escaped the control mechanisms for so many years was incomprehensible. The matter certainly would have implications, but the Federal Councillor rejected the astonishingly unguarded opinion expressed by National Councillor Hubacher that the Chiasso Affair was the rule rather than the exception in the Swiss banking system.[532]

This statement from the Federal Council prompted a long and sometimes heated debate in the National Council. Conservative criticism focused particularly on the 'rhetorical lunacy'[533] of National Councillor Helmut Hubacher. At the

VSB code of conduct, Art. 11, Para. 1: Violation of the agreement, sanctions

In the event that this agreement is violated, the culpable bank is required to pay the Swiss Bankers' Association a fine of up to Sfr 10 million. In fixing this fine, due account is taken of the seriousness of the violation, the degree of culpability and the bank's financial situation. Measures imposed by other authorities with respect to the same issue may also be taken into account. [...] The Swiss Bankers' Association allocates the amount of the fine to a charitable cause of its choice.

'The shadow of the golden calf has fallen ... across the Swiss cross' (Helmut Hubacher on the Chiasso Affair, 1977).

same time, however, the prevailing view in the council was that 'Chiasso' could not be left without consequences. There was general agreement that a revision of the Banking Law should be considered, and that the staff of the Banking Commission should be strengthened. In the end, the SP's motion, against the party's will, was forwarded by a vote of 56 to 86 to the Federal Council merely as a postulate, which has rather less force than a full motion.[534]

On 23 June 1977, Federal Councillor Chevallaz stated his views about the events at the SKA branch in Chiasso to the Council of States (Ständerat). The upper chamber of Switzerland's parliament also agreed that the affair could not simply be passed over without further action.[535]

The press gave extensive coverage to the parliamentary debate: the Chiasso Affair had become a 'political issue'.[536] 'Chiasso: Exception or Systemic Failure?'[537] The conservative parties' views on this question were diametrically opposed to those held by the leftist faction.[538] For the SP, the rejection of their motion in the National Council ultimately led to their submission of the so-called 'banking initiative'. This initiative – the name given in Swiss politics to a motion put to a general referendum of the electorate – called for a vote against 'the abuse of banking secrecy and the power of the banks'[539], and was launched by the SP at its party conference in Basel on 20 May 1978. It was then submitted to the electorate with 124,291 signatures on 8 October 1979 (at least 100,000 signatures are required before a referendum can be considered).

The banking initiative, divided into four 'packages', aimed at a relaxation of banking secrecy, a strengthening of the rules on disclosure, the disentangling of interests between banks and other companies, and an obligation for banks to guarantee deposits. The first package, which is of particular interest in the current context, demanded that the banks be obliged to provide information to the Swiss tax authorities, and to 'provide help in criminal proceedings in other countries, including in the case of tax and currency offences'.[540] The aim was to help fight tax evasion at the international level.

The Swiss Bankers' Association and the banks opposed the initiative because they thought that the implementation of such demands would be equivalent to an 'amputation' for the financial industry, and that the changes would lead to economic damage as well as destroying jobs and wealth creation opportunities. Rejection of the initiative was also recommended by the Federal Council in its 1982 report, though this did not prevent the government from expressing criticism about illegal capital transfers from abroad. Correctly, however, it also referred to the strict regulations since laid down by the VSB code of conduct.

In the end, the Swiss parliament (in 1983), people and cantons all followed the Federal Council's recommendation with impressive majorities. In the referendum of 20 May 1984, 73% of the electorate and all the cantons rejected the initiative.

Leo Schürmann, former member of the Swiss National Bank's directorate, believed that the unequivocal rejection of the SP initiative was not least due to the indirect effect of the Swiss Banks' Code of Conduct with Regard to the Exercise of Due Diligence.[541]

> 'In politics it is acceptable to choose the right timing for political motions. The SP did not invent the SKA Chiasso/Zurich affair. But as a political party it reacted to the affair and presented what it believed was the necessary answer' (Helmut Hubacher at the SP press conference, 9 November 1978).

> 'There is no desire for banking secrecy to be relaxed' (Minutes of the SKA board of directors, 24 May 1984).

Swiss Penal Code, Art. 161

Exploitation of knowledge of confidential facts.

1. A person who, in his capacity as a member of the board, an officer, an auditor, or a mandated person of a company or of a corporation dominating this company or dominated by it, in his capacity as a member of a public authority or as a public officer, or in his capacity as an assistant to such persons, obtains for himself or a third party a pecuniary advantage through the exploitation of a confidential fact whose disclosure can be anticipated to have a significant influence on the market price of the shares, other securities or equivalent negotiable instruments or interests of the company, or on the market price of options thereof, traded on or ancillary to any Swiss stock exchange, or through the disclosure of such a fact to any third party, shall be punished by imprisonment or by a fine.
2. A person to whom such a fact is communicated directly or indirectly by any person described in subsection 1, and who obtains for himself or a third party a pecuniary advantage through the exploitation of this information, shall be punished by imprisonment for not more than one year or by a fine.
3. A fact within the meaning of subsections 1 and 2 is defined as an imminent issue of new equity rights, a combination of companies, or similar circumstances of comparable importance.
4. When it is envisaged to bring together two corporations, subsections 1 to 3 apply to both corporations.
5. Subsections 1 to 4 apply by analogy when the exploitation of the knowledge of a confidential fact relates to shares, other securities or negotiable instruments or interests, or options thereof, of a cooperative corporation or of a foreign company

Insider trading law: a 'Lex Americana'?

The story of how the law on insider trading (Swiss Penal Code Art. 161) was created stands as an excellent example of just how quickly, flexibly and innovatively the Swiss banking system can react to new challenges.

In 1981, the Securities and Exchange Commission (SEC), which is responsible for stock market regulation in the USA, requested that various Swiss banks, including SKA, provide information about securities purchased on US exchanges: the SEC believed that insider trading had been going on in connection with some forthcoming mergers. US law had long ago prohibited trade in securities on the basis of information that is not available generally and that could have a significant influence on price movements. The SEC's request to the Swiss banks thus focused in particular on details of the identity of the customers behind these transactions.

Because of the strict Swiss laws on banking secrecy and disclosure of business information, the banks, which had acted in their own names, but on the instruction and for the account of their customers, had no choice but to decline to give the customer names. Although insider transactions were taboo within the Swiss banking industry, this taboo was not yet enshrined in any civil or criminal laws. Consequently the US authorities were denied judicial assistance: the prevailing view was that because insider transactions were not punishable by law in Switzerland, the agreement on judicial assistance could not be applied. The issue very quickly developed into a serious legal dispute between Switzerland and the USA, which threatened to prevent Swiss banks and their customers from trading on US securities markets. In one case, a New York district judge brought in by the SEC wanted to exclude a Swiss bank from US stock exchanges under threat of a $50,000 daily fine, seize its assets in the USA and put its managing bodies and employees under coercive detention until they gave the information required! Matters were not allowed to get that far because

'We regard the abuse of insider information ... as reprehensible and will move decisively against such abuse' (SKA's Guiding Principles 1976).

'In addition, SKA will take particularly tough action against insider transactions by its own staff' (Rainer E. Gut in *bulletin* [staff edition] 12/1981).

TRAFIC DE MORT
A Bellinzone, Dick Marty requiert de 6 à 17 ans de réclusion

Le Démocrate, 13 April 1989.

Argent de la drogue • *Les révélations de Dick Marty sur les flux d'argent sale donnent une nouvelle dimension au procès de Bellinzone.*

For various reasons, US public prosecutors would attach great importance to taking the 'Gnomes of Zurich' to task in the event of a 'Swiss Connection' – 'A Swiss case is a good case' (*NZZ*, 12 April 1989).

the customer concerned eventually gave consent for the bank to reveal his identity.

The seriousness and urgency of the problem, which ultimately involved the governments of both countries, brought calls in Switzerland for the immediate creation of a criminal law against insider abuse. Such a law would allow the Swiss authorities to give the USA rapid judicial assistance in similar cases. Although the Federal Council acted quickly, and intended to present draft legislation to the Swiss parliament by 1983, the acuteness of the conflict meant that more immediate action was required.

Once again, the way out of the dilemma only came when the banks decided to impose self-regulation. With its Convention XVI the Swiss Bankers' Association created a provisional arrangement whereby a bank could obtain authorizations from customers in advance that allowed it to give the SEC details of the customers' identity. Another prerequisite for such a revelation was that a Swiss review committee, put together by the Bankers' Association, must first have determined that there was sufficient suspicion of insider dealing.

At the political level, Convention XVI was underpinned on 31 August 1982 by a Memorandum of Understanding between the governments of Switzerland and the USA, though the legal status of this memorandum was never made completely clear.

Finally, on 1 July 1988, after completion of the legislative procedure, the new insider dealing law came into effect as Article 161 of the Swiss penal code. This meant that Convention XVI, which constituted a rather unusual commitment by the Swiss Bankers' Association to a foreign government, could be rescinded.

Money laundering

At the beginning of November 1988, a flood of media reporting about the affair known as the 'Lebanon Connection' aroused a great deal of interest. The reports claimed that the three major Swiss banks had accepted banknotes worth around Sfr 1.5 billion from the well-known 'money changers', the Magharian brothers. A large part of this money was said to have been generated by drug dealing. Jean and Barkev Magharian, who had been held in custody in the Ticino since July 1988, faced a number of charges. These included the accusation that they had used Swiss banks to launder billions of francs worth of funds from drug dealing in Turkey and the USA, and that they had transferred this money on to finance further drug deals. SKA in particular, which the Magharians used for a great deal of their banknote, precious metals and foreign exchange transactions, came in once again for criticism, though it later transpired that the accusations leveled at the bank were largely unjustified.

As the media storm grew, SKA repeatedly tried to refute the charges to the best of its knowledge and ability, especially those accusations relating to the handling of forged banknotes. However, the bank's attempts to tell its side of the story largely fell on deaf ears, and the executive board decided as a last resort to take out full-page advertisements in various daily newspapers (overleaf).

As soon as the Federal Banking Commission heard about the affair, it launched an investigation into the three major banks, SBG, SBV and SKA. In its press conference of 11 April 1989, the FBC said that after researching the facts thoroughly, it had come to the conclusion that there was no need for any action to be taken under banking law against the 'guarantors' of the banks involved. Furthermore, the Banking Commission stated that the banks had correctly examined and documented the identity of the Magharian brothers as contracting partners, as well as ascertaining their beneficial ownership of the deposited assets in accordance with the VSB code of conduct on due diligence. The banks had also thoroughly investigated the Magharians' activities when the business relationships were first opened, and then repeatedly checked up on their plausibility thereafter. None of these enquiries by the banks had suggested that there was any reason to doubt the Magharian brothers' integrity.

On the basis of its investigations, the FBC decided that professional banknote trading, which in Switzerland was only practiced by the major banks, would henceforth be allowed only with its express permission. It subsequently issued strict regulations on the way the banks organized such business internally.

The shock of the whole affair prompted the Federal Council to immediately submit the legislation that would make money laundering a criminal offence – actually drafted by an expert commission in 1986 – to parliament. The legislative process was pushed ahead as swiftly as possible, and on 1 August 1990 the Swiss Penal Code was revised to qualify intentional money laundering (Art.

'In purely economic terms, money from criminal sources represents an insignificant sum for the Swiss banking industry' (Paolo Bernasconi, in: *Der Beobachter*, no. 8, 1989).

'A banker's duty to exercise due diligence includes having to clarify the economic background of transactions where there are indications that these transactions could be illegal or unethical' (Paolo Bernasconi, in: *Der Beobachter*, no. 8, 1989).

Erklärung der Schweizerischen Kreditanstalt

Die Generaldirektion der Schweizerischen Kreditanstalt legt Wert darauf, ihre Kunden, Mitarbeiter und Aktionäre sowie die Öffentlichkeit in Ergänzung zu ihren Interviews und weiteren Verlautbarungen in den Medien aus ihrer Sicht direkt zu orientieren.

Im Anschluss an das Communiqué der Tessiner Staatsanwaltschaft zur sogenannten «Libanon-Connection» und die breite Medienreaktion ist die SKA Zielscheibe von massiven Anschuldigungen geworden. Dazu sind unter anderem eine ganze Reihe von Fragen aufgetaucht, welche die Geschäftspolitik unserer Bank betreffen.

Hiezu halten wir grundsätzlich folgendes fest:

Der Drogenhandel, wozu auch die sogenannte «Geldwäscherei» gehört, wird von einem international organisierten Verbrechertum betrieben, das von einer ganzen Anzahl günstiger Rahmenbedingungen profitiert.

Zu diesen Rahmenbedingungen gehören das internationale Bankensystem, die liberalen Kapitalmärkte und nicht zuletzt das zum Wohle seiner Kunden in der Schweiz hoch entwickelte Bankwesen.

Selbstverständlich verurteilt auch die SKA die missbräuchliche Nutzung dieser Möglichkeiten durch den Drogenhandel. Sie ist bereit, alles in ihrer Macht Stehende zu tun, um dem entgegenzuwirken. Sie wird allenfalls weitere, sich aufdrängende staatliche und private Gegenmassnahmen, die Erfolg versprechen, unterstützen.

Bereits bisher dienten SKA-interne Weisungen und Kontrollen der Verhinderung von solchen Missbräuchen von Dienstleistungen unserer Bank; wir würden bedauern, wenn es trotzdem gelungen wäre, einige unserer Mitarbeiter und Organe zu täuschen. Toleranz solchen Machenschaften gegenüber entspricht jedenfalls nicht unserer Geschäftspolitik.

Die SKA bemüht sich nicht zuletzt um ihrer Kunden und Aktionäre willen um gute Geschäftsergebnisse. Sie belässt ihren Mitarbeitern die notwendige Handlungsfreiheit und Eigenverantwortlichkeit, nimmt aber, wo nötig, mit Weisungen und Vorschriften Einfluss auf die Geschäftstätigkeit. Einzelne Vorfälle, bei denen solche Weisungen zu wenig beachtet wurden, hat sie veranlasst, ihre Führungsrichtlinien einmal mehr zu überprüfen. Ziel ist optimaler Service durch motivierte Mitarbeiter unter Vermeidung von Risiken und Fehlverhalten.

Da wir die Angelegenheit Magharian ernst nehmen, haben wir alle unsere Mitarbeiterinnen und Mitarbeiter über den uns heute bekannten Sachverhalt informiert. Wir legen Wert darauf, die Öffentlichkeit ebenso detailliert zu orientieren.

Zu den aktuellen Einzelfragen:

Die Brüder Magharian, die sich im Zusammenhang mit einem gegen sie gerichteten Ermittlungsverfahren zur Zeit im Tessin in Untersuchungshaft befinden, waren seit mehreren Jahren (1979 bzw. 1984) Kunden der SKA. Nach eigenen Angaben war Barkev Magharian zuvor für M. Shakarchi, Zürich, tätig. Später machte er sich selbständig. Für die SKA war die Konkurrenzsituation zwischen Shakarchi und Magharian kein Grund, diesen Kunden abzulehnen. Bei Eröffnung der Geschäftskonten wurden Informationen eingezogen und die für den Geldhandel übliche Überprüfung durch unseren Sicherheitsdienst veranlasst. Das Resultat war gut; insbesondere lagen keine strafrechtlichen Tatbestände vor.

B. Magharian, ein Notenhändler, unterhielt Konten in verschiedenen Währungen sowie Edelmetallkonti, über die Noten-, Edelmetall- und Devisengeschäfte in bedeutendem Umfang abgewickelt wurden. Ein grosser Teil der Noten stammte nach Angaben des Kunden aus dem Tourismus in Nahen Osten und in der Türkei, ein anderer Teil aus Notenrückflüssen türkischer Gastarbeiter. Diese Angaben waren plausibel; sie wurden durch die tatsächlich abgewickelten Notenumsätze sowie die typisch verlaufenen saisonalen Schwankungen mit ausgeprägten Spitzen jeweils im dritten Quartal (Ferienreisen) bestätigt.

Im Rahmen einer ordentlichen Revision des Sektors Change am Hauptsitz wurde das Inspektorat auf den Kunden Magharian aufmerksam. Seine grossen Umsätze gaben Anlass zu einer vertieften Überprüfung; diese erbrachte keinerlei Hinweise auf eine deliktische Herkunft der Mittel; sie lenkte jedoch die Aufmerksamkeit auf das Geschäftsdomizil in einem Hotel in Zürich.

Uns gegenüber gab Magharian Syrien als seinen Wohnsitz an. Aufgrund seiner häufigen Präsenz in Zürich waren wir jedoch bezüglich der Wohnsitzfrage unsicher. Wir wählten den Weg der Vorsicht und lösten die Konti mit Barkev Magharian auf.

Daraufhin folgte Magharian dem Beispiel anderer professioneller Notenhändler und gründete eine Firma mit Geschäftssitz in Beirut, die Magharian Frères S.à.r.l. Für dieses Vorgehen brauchte er keine Empfehlung. Nachdem weiterhin keine Hinweise auf eine deliktische Herkunft der Mittel auch der neuen Firma vorlagen, erklärte sich die SKA bereit, die Geschäftsbeziehungen mit ihr aufzunehmen. Die erneut eingeforderten Auskünfte waren vorbehaltlos positiv. Sollten sich die Brüder Magharian damals mit Drogengeldern beschäftigt haben, so haben sie uns getäuscht.

Ein Teil der aus den Notenverkäufen stammenden Guthaben wurde für den Ankauf von Edelmetallen verwendet, welche die Brüder Magharian physisch bei uns bezogen. Die Überweisungen im Interbanken-Zahlungsverkehr erfolgten hauptsächlich in D-Mark und in US-Dollar. Die Vergütungen wurden über 300 verschiedenen Banken im In- und Ausland getätigt. Die Empfängerbanken befanden sich grösstenteils wieder in der Türkei.

Zur Behauptung von M. Shakarchi, die SKA vor den Geschäften der Magharians gewarnt zu haben, ist festzuhalten, dass sich unser Kadermitarbeiter nicht erinnern kann, je eine konkrete Warnung erhalten zu haben. Wäre er wirklich gewarnt worden, hätte er eigene Recherchen angestellt und den Vorgesetzten informiert. Wenn derartige Hinweise auf eine Verwicklung von Magharian in Drogengeschäfte oder andere strafrechtlich relevante Aktivitäten für uns erkennbar zutage getreten wären, hätten wir unsere Geschäftsbeziehungen unverzüglich abgebrochen.

Was die Behandlung von als Falschgeld erkannten Banknoten betrifft, so hat sich im professionellen Geldhandel in den letzten Jahren die Praxis herausgebildet, die Falsifikate mittels Stempel zu entwerten und an den Absender zurückzugeben; in aussergewöhnlichen Fällen werden die Behörden informiert.

Wir haben aber eingesehen, dass die Praxis des Abstempelns ungenügend ist. Deshalb haben wir mit sofortiger Wirkung festgelegt, dass bei der SKA Falsifikate weder entwertet noch dem Kunden zurückgegeben werden dürfen, sondern in allen Fällen den Behörden abzuliefern sind.

Immerhin ist festzustellen, dass nach allem, was branchenweit an Informationen verfügbar ist, sich die Falschgeldumsätze, gemessen am gesamten Handelsvolumen, in engen Grenzen bewegen. Bei der SKA wurden von 1985 bis 1988 von den Magharians lediglich 266 falsche Noten im Gegenwert von 21 000 US-Dollar eingeliefert.

Zum da und dort erhobenen Vorwurf, Mitarbeiter unserer Bank seien von den Brüdern Magharian bestochen worden, halten wir folgendes fest: Mitarbeitern der Bank ist es nach der geltenden Weisung untersagt, «für Verrichtungen im Rahmen ihrer Arbeitstätigkeit Geld oder andere Geschenke anzunehmen oder sich einen mittelbaren oder unmittelbaren Vorteil von dritter Seite zuwenden oder zusichern zu lassen. Ausgenommen sind Gelegenheitsgeschenke von geringem kommerziellem Wert. Im Zweifelsfall entscheidet der direkte Vorgesetzte».

Neben geringfügigen Gelegenheitsgeschenken hat ein Mitarbeiter aufgrund der regen Geschäftsbeziehungen zu B. Magharian auch den Rahmen der Geringfügigkeit überschreitende Geschenke erhalten. Pflichtgemäss hat der Mitarbeiter seinen Vorgesetzten informiert und dessen Einverständnis eingeholt. Die Annahme der Geschenke erfolgte nicht im Hinblick auf die Tätigkeit des Beschenkten bei unserer Bank. Es ist zu betonen, dass der Kunde dadurch keine Bevorzugung in irgendwelcher Hinsicht genossen hat. Aufgrund der Sachlage sehen wir keine Veranlassung, unsere bestehende Weisung zu ändern.

Die Schweizerische Kreditanstalt hofft, mit dieser Darstellung des uns bis heute bekannten Sachverhaltes zur öffentlichen Information beizutragen und den zum Teil stark verzerrten Darstellungen oder Unterstellungen entgegenwirken zu können.

SCHWEIZERISCHE KREDITANSTALT SKA

Neue Zürcher Zeitung, 14 February 1989. This is the statement placed by SKA in the Swiss press regarding the Magharian money laundering affair.

305bis) and insufficient care when carrying out financial transactions (Art. 305ter) as criminal offences.

Over and above this, in December 1991, the FBC issued its 'Guidelines on the Prevention and Combating of Money Laundering', which came into legal force on 1 May 1992. According to the FBC itself, these guidelines made the due diligence practices of the 'first-class Swiss banks' into 'generally applicable minimum standards'.[542]

Switzerland's efforts in the fight against money laundering were expressly praised by the FATF in 1992 and 1993 during their so-called 'country examinations'. The Federal Banking Commission's money laundering guidelines (Circular no. 91/3), as well as the mechanisms for identifying contracting parties and determining beneficial ownership laid down by the VSB, were singled out for particular commendation. However, the FATF also criticized Switzerland for not giving financial institutions a legal right to inform the authorities if they came across indications that money laundering might be taking place.

This justly criticized gap in Switzerland's defenses against money laundering was closed initially by the introduction into the Penal Code of a law on the duty to inform the authorities (Art. 305ter, revision of 1 August 1994), and – in a second step – by the adoption of the Money Laundering Law (Geldwäschereigesetz, or GwG). This not only created a right to report, but established a duty to report (Art. 9 GwG). The GwG adhered to the system that had functioned for years in the Swiss banking sector, whereby legal prescription is combined with self-regulation. The GwG extended the defense mechanisms and standards already employed by the banks to the rest of the financial sector, thus closing the regulatory gap that had existed in the non-banking sector. Financial intermediaries, which had not previously been subject to any form of official control, were compelled either to arrange an acceptable form of self-regulation by 1 April 2000, or by this same date to apply for direct control by the Federal Department of Finance.[543]

Finally, at the beginning of July 1998, the FBC brought its revised guidelines on money laundering into effect. The main innovation was that financial intermediaries were no longer allowed to accept money, 'which they knew, or should assume, was a product of corruption or the abuse of public funds'[544]: 'In some ways this anticipates the proposed revision of the criminal law on corruption.'[545]

The banks thus faced a variety of new demands with regard to the fight against money laundering, including the obligations to verify their customers' identity, identify the beneficial owner of assets, clarify the economic background to unusual transactions, and report suspicions to the Office for the Prevention of Money Laundering. In response, SKA – and subsequently the business units of Credit Suisse Group – translated these new requirements into a comprehensive, pragmatic system of internal directives, which functioned as a valuable instrument for relationship managers, helping them to adhere to the correct practices. If attempts to launder money were to be recognized and stopped, 'alertness, proactive thinking and presence of mind' were required. 'This Direc-

> 'As far as money laundering is concerned, Switzerland has become a shining example internationally' (Minutes of the SKA board of directors, 21 June 1990).

> The fact that, 'in Switzerland financial services function efficiently', can 'also be exploited to launder money' (*Handelszeitung*, 15 December 1999).

> 'To combat money laundering, the banks should issue internal directives which take account of these guidelines' (Money Laundering Guidelines in FBC Circulars nos. 91/3 and 98/1).

The article by Hans J. Mast, 'Focus on Banking Secrecy', which appeared in *bulletin* in July 1975, was also made accessible to a wider public when published as no. 2 in the series 'Aus der Sicht des Bankiers' ('Banker's View') in five languages.

Extract from Oswald Aeppli's address to the general meeting of shareholders of 25 March 1983, published as no. 16 in the 'Banker's View' series.

SCHWEIZERISCHE KREDITANSTALT

Aus der Sicht des Bankiers

Das Bankgeheimnis im Blickfeld

von Dr. Hans J. Mast, Hauptdirektor der Schweizerischen Kreditanstalt

Aus der Sicht des Bankiers

Gesetzgeber und Banken

Dr. O. Aeppli
Präsident des Verwaltungsrates der Schweizerischen Kreditanstalt

SCHWEIZERISCHE KREDITANSTALT SKA

tive, therefore, cannot and will not do more than simply require that basic common sense be applied. But basic common sense also tells us that money laundering is the exception to the rule and that the overwhelming proportion of all the business we transact on behalf of our clients is entirely proper.'[546]

As well as formulating clear and binding rules, SKA also devoted a lot of effort to the specific further training of its employees. In cases of doubt, staff could go for help to either the legal department or the compliance department, which were developed into specialist technical and advisory units for all questions regarding money laundering. These departments had to be contacted immediately if there was any suspicion of an offence. The compliance department's job was, and still is, to recognize any threat to the bank's reputation or any illegal activity early on, to take the necessary countermeasures, and thus to ensure that business is always conducted correctly in every respect.

'Integrity, honesty and professionalism at every level are crucially important to the reputation and success of our bank' (Credit Suisse Private Banking directive W-1050, 3 August 1998, section 3).

300 *Part Three: A New Paradigm*

The SKA executive board in 1973 (from left to right): Rainer E. Gut, Heinz R. Wuffli, Robert H. Lutz, Robert Lang, Hans K. Escher, Oswald Aeppli, C. Walter Fessler.

The social profile of executive board members

SKA's realignment in the mid-1970s was also reflected in the social profile of the members of the executive board. Until this time, the typical executive board member could be distinguished by a very narrow set of social characteristics; thereafter, career paths and social backgrounds became increasingly diverse.

The social profile of executive board members underwent a number of changes in the years between 1945 and 1996. The following analysis of this process of change covers such aspects as age, education, place of study, career up to entry into the executive board, activities after leaving the executive board, regional origins and religion, military career and membership of guilds and service clubs.

Using extensive statistical data, these aspects are examined to identify key characteristics, which are illustrated in charts and, finally, interpreted. The main value of this analysis is that the changes in the executive board's profile can be seen to reflect the changing values at work within SKA.[547]

Age structure

Main features:
- From 1945 to 1949, the median age rose from 55 to 58.
- From 1949 to 1953, the median age fell to 45.
- From 1953 to 1972, the median age rose to 60.5 years.
- From 1972 to 1977, the median age fell to 48 years.
- From 1977 to 1996, the median age was 51 on average.

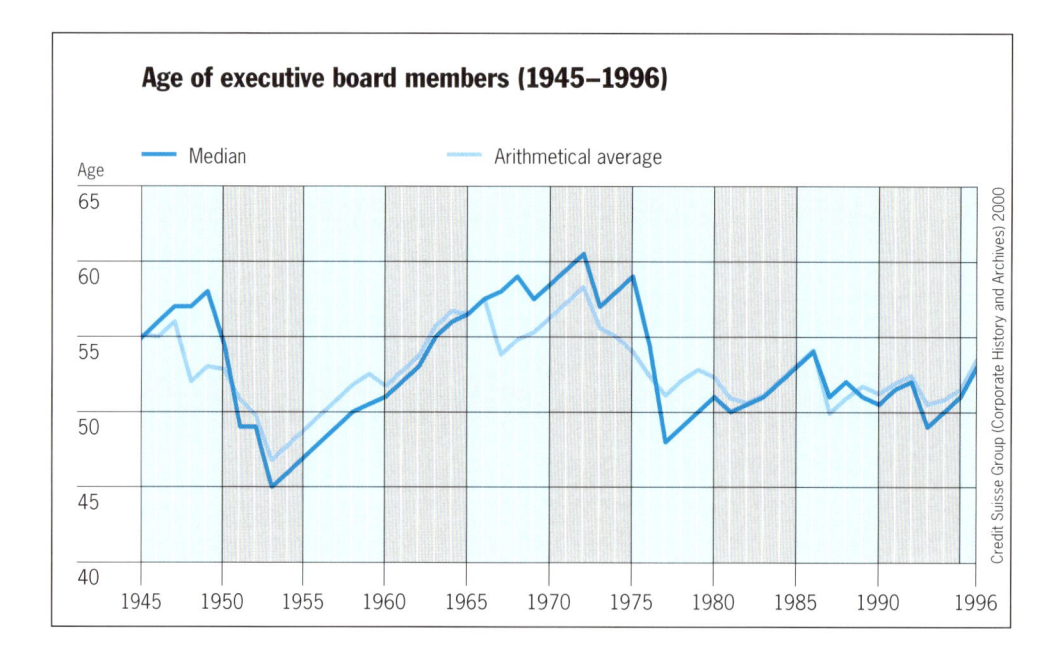

Age of executive board members (1945–1996)

An examination of the development of the age structure[548] clearly shows two sudden dips in the median age of the executive board, the first in the early 1950s, and the second after 1975. The cause of the first rejuvenation was a natural changeover of the generations. For years, executive board members who left on reaching retirement age or who died while in office were replaced by much younger successors. The second sudden rejuvenation – between 1975 and

1977 – was caused by the replacement of almost the entire executive board. Only two members of the board retained their places during this period. SKA was faced by a difficult operating environment at this time – accentuated by the 1977 Chiasso Affair – and was forced into an uncompromising process of modernization. Several younger senior managers were elevated to the executive board with the intention of giving the traditional old bank on Paradeplatz a new lease of life.

Throughout the late 1960s and the first half of the 1970s, the median age of the executive board remained constantly high. The highest median age in any year came in 1972 when it reached 60.5. In the previous 20 years from 1953 to 1972 – with the sole exception of 1969 – SKA's executive board had grown progressively older. This trend passed its peak by 1973 and then came to an abrupt end in 1975.

However, there were some great age differences between individual board members in the late 1960s and the first half of the 1970s. During this period, the executive board was composed of men of around 60 or significantly older, but also of men from a completely different generation. In 1968, for example, of the five executive board members, three were about 60 years old, one was 54 and the other only 41. In 1973, there were seven executive board members; two were about 65, three about 58, one was 46, and the other 41.

Education

Main features:
- From 1945 to 1959 – except between 1948 and 1951 – and from 1977 to 1980, non-university graduates were in the majority.
- From 1981 to 1996, university graduates were in the majority.
- Up to 1989, all the graduates were either lawyers or economists.
- Up to 1958, there was – with a few exceptions – an even balance between economists and lawyers; this was also the case from 1987 to 1989.
- From 1959 to 1966, all the graduates were lawyers; from 1967 to 1986, lawyers accounted for the majority of graduates.
- From 1990 to 1996, economists accounted for the larger proportion of graduates.

Until the end of the 1950s, non-graduates dominated the executive board in all but a few years, but thereafter, their relative numbers declined; between 1967 and 1972, only one executive board member was a non-graduate. In 1973 another two non-graduates were appointed to the executive board. Up to 1979, the number of non-graduates rose to five out of eight board members before declining again. From 1983 to 1996, university graduates accounted for roughly a 70% majority of the executive board, the peak coming in 1987 and 1988 when the figure went up to over 75%.

Graduates/non-graduates on the executive board (1945–1996)

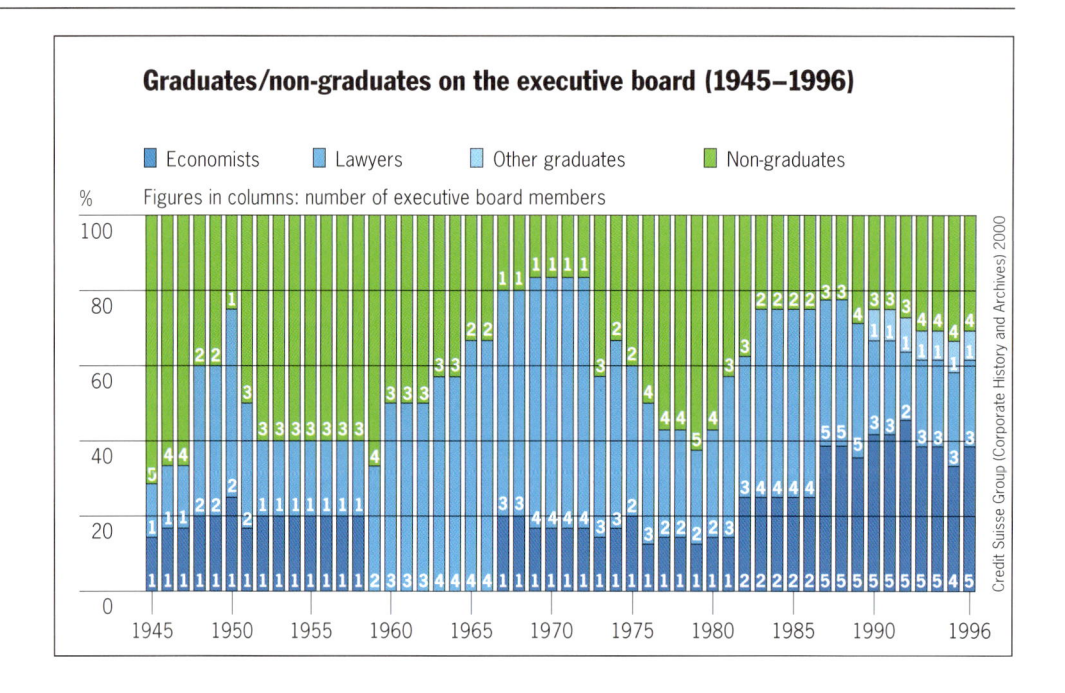

Over the decades, the numerical supremacy clearly swung in favor of graduate members of the executive board, though this certainly did not mean that non-graduates ceased to play key roles within SKA. Between 1983 and 1993, for example, both the president of the executive board and the chairman of the board of directors were non-graduates – the first time in SKA's history that this had been the case.

The increase in the proportion of economists at the expense of the previously dominant lawyers is interesting. From 1990 to 1994, and again in 1996, the economists were actually in the majority, while in 1995 they were still the largest group of university graduates. In 1990 and 1991, for example, five of the total of twelve members of the executive board were economists (out of nine graduates) – the same number as in 1996, when there was a total of 13 executive board members overall. Clearly, the greater weighting towards economists in the 1990s reflected the increasing influence of economics throughout society.

In 1990, for the first and only time, a graduate was appointed to the executive board who had studied neither law nor economics, but the humanities.

Place of study

Main features:
- Of all the university graduates who served on the executive board between 1945 and 1996, the majority graduated from the University of Zurich.
- The proportion of graduates from the University of St. Gallen rose in the late 1980s.

Universities from which graduate executive board members earned their degrees (1945–1996)

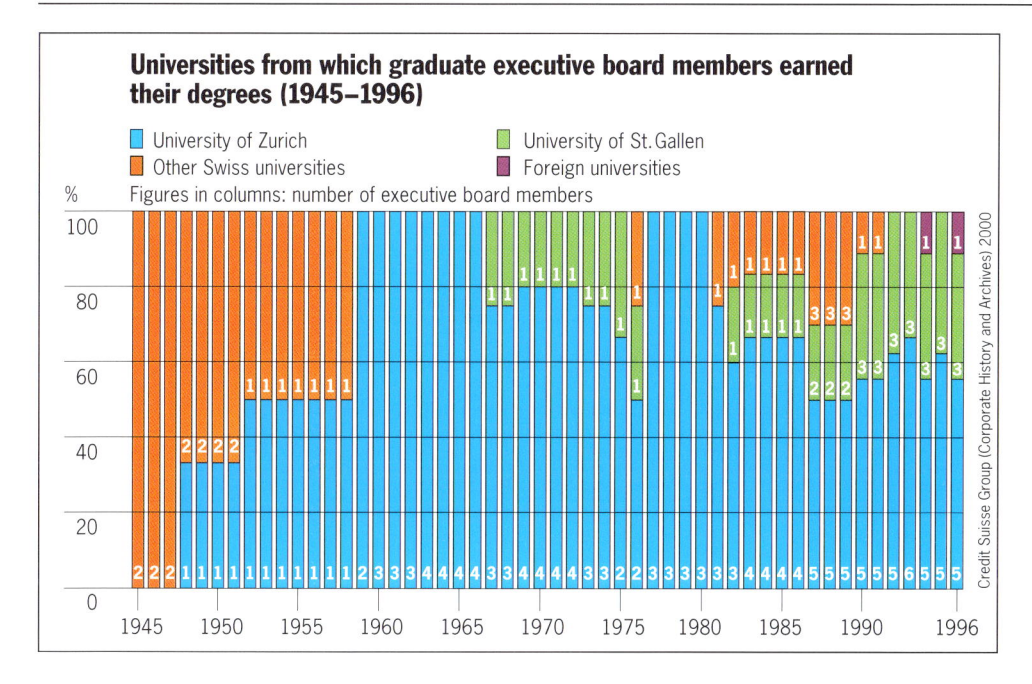

Of the 27 university graduates who served on the executive board between 1945 and 1996, 14 had studied at the University of Zurich. In the years between 1959 and 1966, and then again from 1977 to 1980, all of the graduates on the board were alumni of Zurich. Of the graduates on the executive board between 1967 and 1996, five had earned their degrees at the University of St. Gallen (Hochschule St. Gallen, or HSG), which is hardly surprising given HSG's particular focus on economics and business disciplines. Four executive board members graduated from the University of Bern, two from Basel and two from universities outside Switzerland (Hamburg and Tucson, Arizona).[549] The first SKA executive board member with a degree from a non-Swiss university was appointed in 1994.

Career prior to membership of the executive board

Main features:
- Out of the total of 47 post-war executive board members, 35 had previously had careers at SKA's head office in Zurich.
- The first executive board member to move directly onto the board from a subsidiary was appointed in 1973.
- In 1976, a person was appointed to the executive board directly from a branch for the first time since 1945.

Up to 1980 – apart from in 1950 and 1951 – and then again from 1983 to 1996, the majority of executive board members had worked at SKA head office before their elevation to the executive board.[550] The dominance of head office in the recruitment of people for the highest managerial rank is further reflected by

Appointments to executive board (1945–1996)

- From head office
- From branches
- From outside bank
- From SKA/CSH subsidiaries or companies in which SKA had a stake

Figures in columns: number of executive board members

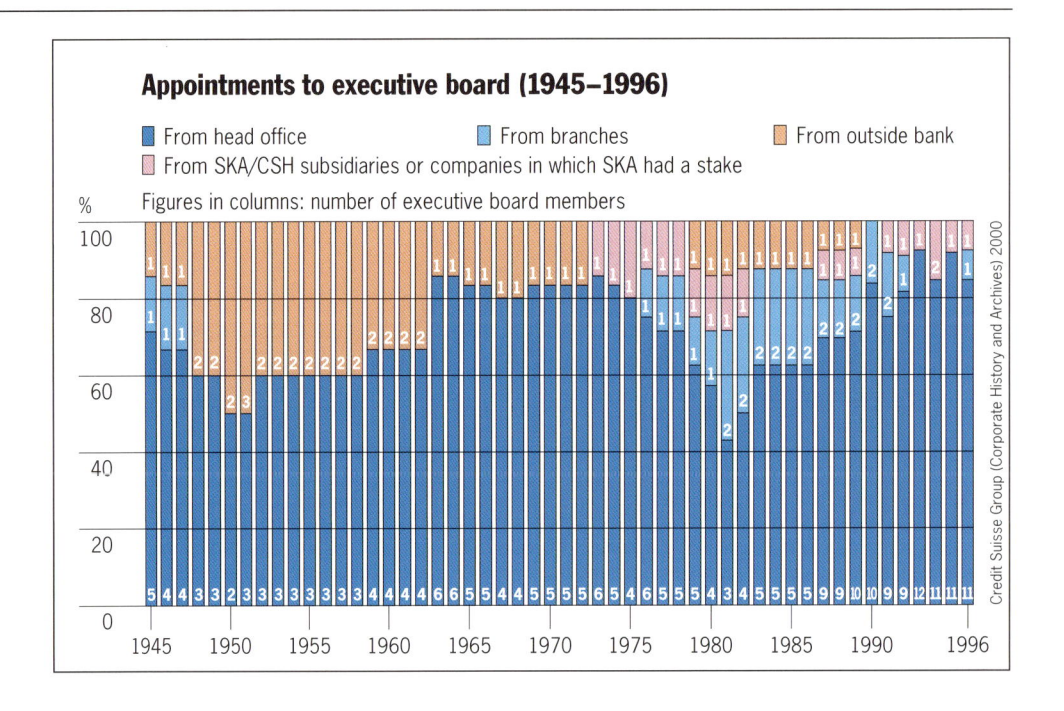

Credit Suisse Group (Corporate History and Archives) 2000

the fact that in the post-war period only three members of the executive board were appointed directly from SKA branches: in 1976, a person was elevated directly from a branch (Basel) for the first time since 1945. Subsequently one person was promoted to the board directly from the Bern branch (1981), and one from the New York branch (1996). However, there were many instances of future executive board members who had spent most of their career at head office going to work at branches for shorter or longer periods in order to expand their skills and experience.

In 1973 someone managed to make the jump directly from a subsidiary – and a foreign subsidiary at that – to the executive board for the first time ever. Such a career path remained an exception, however. One person later moved onto the SKA executive board from Financière Crédit Suisse – First Boston (1987), and two from CS First Boston (1991, 1994).

Three men who had never previously worked at SKA were appointed directly to the executive board: one of these had been in the federal government before his appointment (1948), one had worked at the Swiss National Bank (1951) and one had worked at a US financial institution (1979).

Departures from the executive board

Main features:
- Seventeen members of the executive board sat on the executive board until retirement; four died while still in office.
- Ten men went on from the executive board to assume other management functions within the group.

- In 1977, for the first time, two members of the executive board resigned and took up jobs outside the group, but not with a competing institution. This happened again in 1993.
- In 1992, for the first time, a member of the executive board resigned and went over to a rival company. This happened again in 1996.
- In 1993 and 1994, two more (former) executive board members went over to rival companies having initially taken up other management functions within the group when they left the board (in 1990 and 1989).

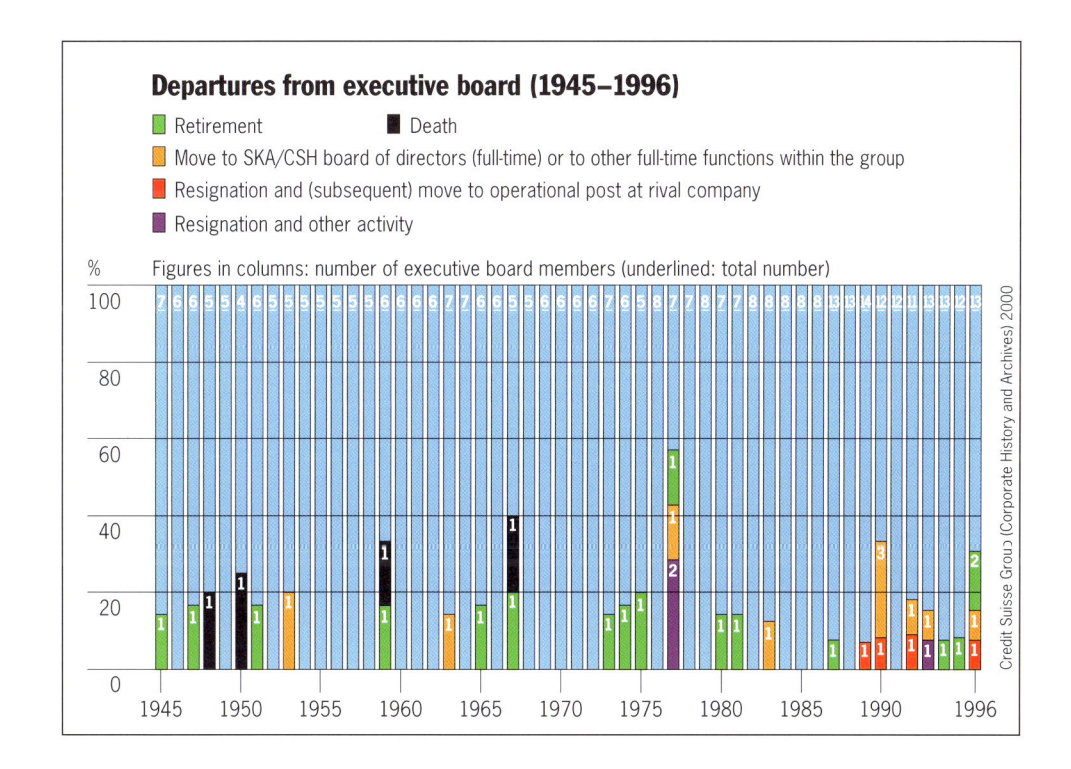

Departures from executive board (1945–1996)

- Retirement
- Death
- Move to SKA/CSH board of directors (full-time) or to other full-time functions within the group
- Resignation and (subsequent) move to operational post at rival company
- Resignation and other activity

Figures in columns: number of executive board members (underlined: total number)

Credit Suisse Group (Corporate History and Archives) 2000

Until the 1990s, it was very much the norm for people only to leave the executive board if they were retiring or if they had been called to the board of directors. Prior to 1970, four men died while still in office. Two members left SKA altogether in 1977 – as a result of the Chiasso Affair and the problems with the Italian company Molini Certosa – and took up positions elsewhere.

In the United States it has long been quite normal for a top manager to leave a bank to continue his career at another company, but the phenomenon only became more common in Switzerland in the 1990s. 1992 saw the first ever direct defection of an executive board member to a rival company. Overall, four of the 24 members who sat on the executive board between 1989 and 1996 left the group and took up operational posts at rival companies: one man went over to the Berner Kantonalbank (1992), one to SBV (1993), one to Investmentbank MC-BBL Group (1994), and one to Deutsche Bank (1996).

One person left the SKA executive board in 1993 in order to pursue a full-time career as a member of various boards of directors.[551]

Regional origins and religious confession[552]

Main features:
- In the second half of the 1940s, there was an even balance between executive board members from the city of Zurich and those from elsewhere.
- In the 1950s, members from the city of Zurich were slightly in the minority.
- In the 1960s, members from the city of Zurich were very much in the majority.
- In the 1970s, a small majority of executive board members were from the city of Zurich.
- In the 1980s and 1990s, members from the city of Zurich were very much in the minority.

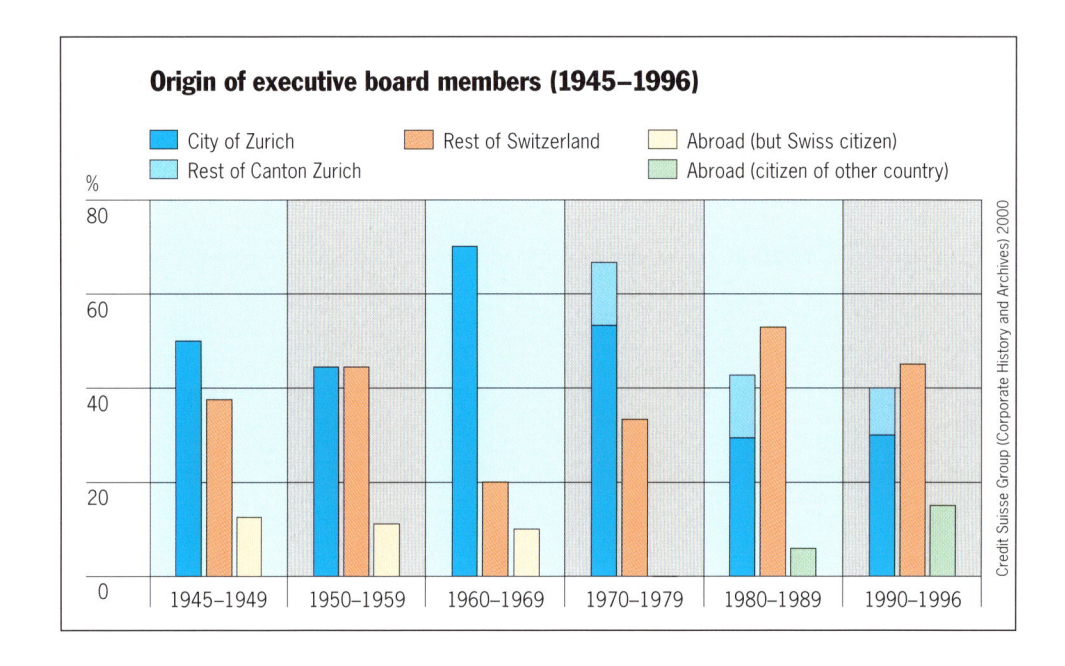

Origin of executive board members (1945–1996)

	City of Zurich	Rest of Switzerland	Abroad (but Swiss citizen)
	Rest of Canton Zurich		Abroad (citizen of other country)

Credit Suisse Group (Corporate History and Archives) 2000

The chart showing the regional origins of the members of SKA's executive board after the war reveals a clear weighting towards men from the city of Zurich up to the end of the 1970s. The place of origin here is defined as the place where the executive board member grew up rather than the place where he lived over the course of his career.[553]

Of the 42 men who joined the executive board after 1945 – the five executive board members who joined before 1 January 1945 but who were still serving after this date are not counted here – 16 came from the city of Zurich and another four from elsewhere in Canton Zurich. Men from the city of Zurich were a very strong influence on the board especially between 1960 and 1969, accounting for seven of the ten executive board members who served during this period. There have always been people from other regions in German-speaking Switzerland on the executive board, but they did not make up the majority of board members until the 1980s.

A total of 16 members of the executive board in the post-war period came from other parts of Switzerland: six from Aargau, two each from Basel-Stadt and Glarus, one each from Appenzell Innerrhoden, Lucerne, St. Gallen, Solothurn and Zug. Whole regions, such as Canton Bern or large parts of Central Switzerland were completely unrepresented on the board between 1945 and 1996. After 1945 there was only one board member who came from non-German-speaking Switzerland: a man from the Ticino who joined in 1976 and left again in 1977.

Until the end of the 1970s, SKA was unequivocally a 'city of Zurich bank' in terms of the make-up of its executive board. This is certainly how the bank, headquartered as it was on Zurich's main square, Paradeplatz, was perceived by the general public.[554] Thereafter, however, the overweighting of executive board members from the city began to disappear. At the same time, SKA changed from being a Zurich institution into a Swiss major bank with increasingly international leanings.

Two members of the executive board in the post-war period held Swiss citizenship but had grown up abroad (Germany, Italy). The first executive board member who was not a Swiss citizen joined the board in 1987. During the 1990s, three further non-Swiss were appointed to the executive board.

The dominance for many years of executive board members from the traditionally Protestant city of Zurich inevitably influenced the composition of the board in terms of religious affiliation. Between 1945 and 1973, everyone who joined the executive board was Protestant.[555] From 1974 to 1996, 23 executive board members were Protestant, ten were Roman-Catholic and one was Old Catholic. From the 1980s onwards, there was an increasingly balanced mix of Protestants and Roman Catholics on the board.

Military careers[556]

Main features:
- From 1945 to 1958, officers were in the minority.
- From 1959 to 1972, officers made up at least half, but no more than two-thirds, of the executive board.
- From 1973 to 1996, more than two-thirds of the board were officers in the Swiss army. Of these, between 1983 and 1995, staff officers (brigadiers, colonels, lieutenant colonels, majors) were in the majority.

All Swiss males have to complete a course of basic military training at around the age of 19. They remain part of the Swiss army, attending refresher courses on a regular basis.

There have been great fluctuations in the number of serving Swiss army officers on the SKA executive board. In the years immediately after the war and in the 1950s, an above average proportion of board members were either not eligible for military service, or served as ordinary soldiers or non-commissioned officers. Prior to 1953, only three members of the executive board were officers

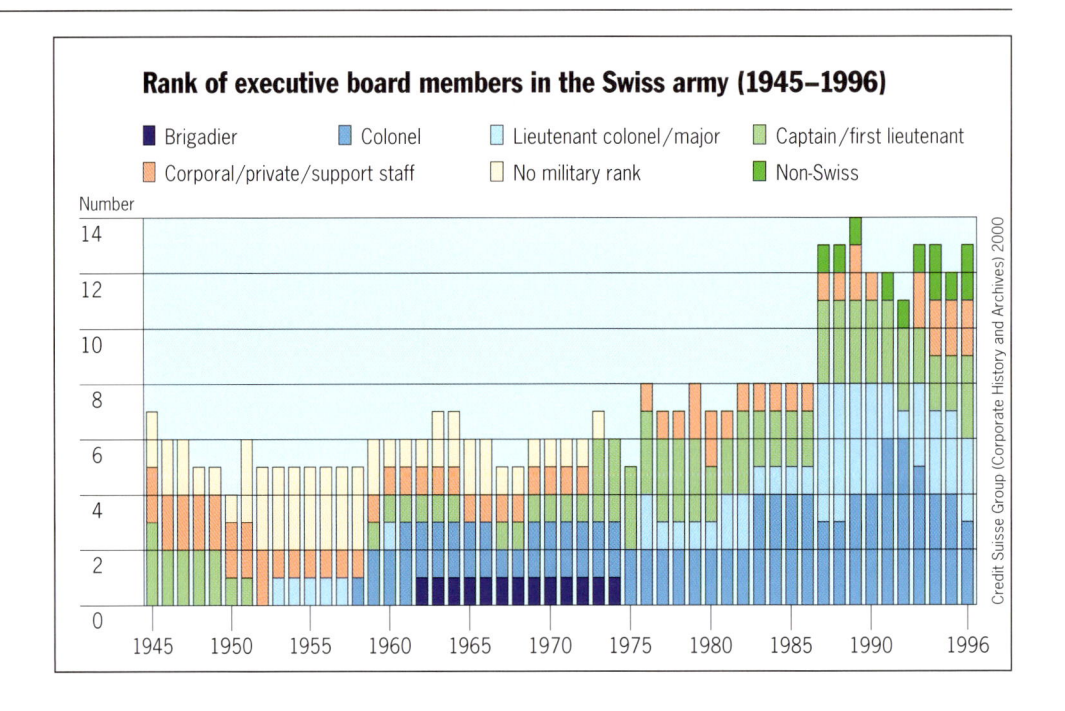

Rank of executive board members in the Swiss army (1945–1996)

- Brigadier
- Colonel
- Lieutenant colonel/major
- Captain/first lieutenant
- Corporal/private/support staff
- No military rank
- Non-Swiss

Credit Suisse Group (Corporate History and Archives) 2000

in the Swiss army – one lieutenant colonel and two captains. In 1958, an executive board member rose to become a colonel in the army for the first time in the post-war period.

From the start of the 1960s onwards, an increasing number of officers, and more senior officers, joined the executive board. This trend reached its first peak in 1962 when an SKA executive board member was promoted to brigadier – the highest rank that a part-time soldier can attain in Switzerland. Out of an executive board of six in 1962, two other members were colonels. The proportion of officers remained high over the following years, peaking again at the end of the 1980s and beginning of the 1990s. In 1991, for example, six of the twelve executive board members were colonels, and the remaining Swiss members of the board were also officers: one was a lieutenant colonel, one a major, one a captain and two were first lieutenants.

Membership of guilds[557] and service clubs

Main features:
- From 1945 to 1958, non-guild members were in the majority – except in 1951 and 1952.
- From 1959 to 1973, guild members were in the majority.
- From 1974 to 1986, non-guild members accounted for at least half of the executive board, and from 1987 to 1996, at least two-thirds.
- Service clubs gained in significance from 1976 onwards.

In Zurich many business leaders are members of the city guilds that developed from the craftsmen's associations of the Middle Ages. Out of the 47 executive

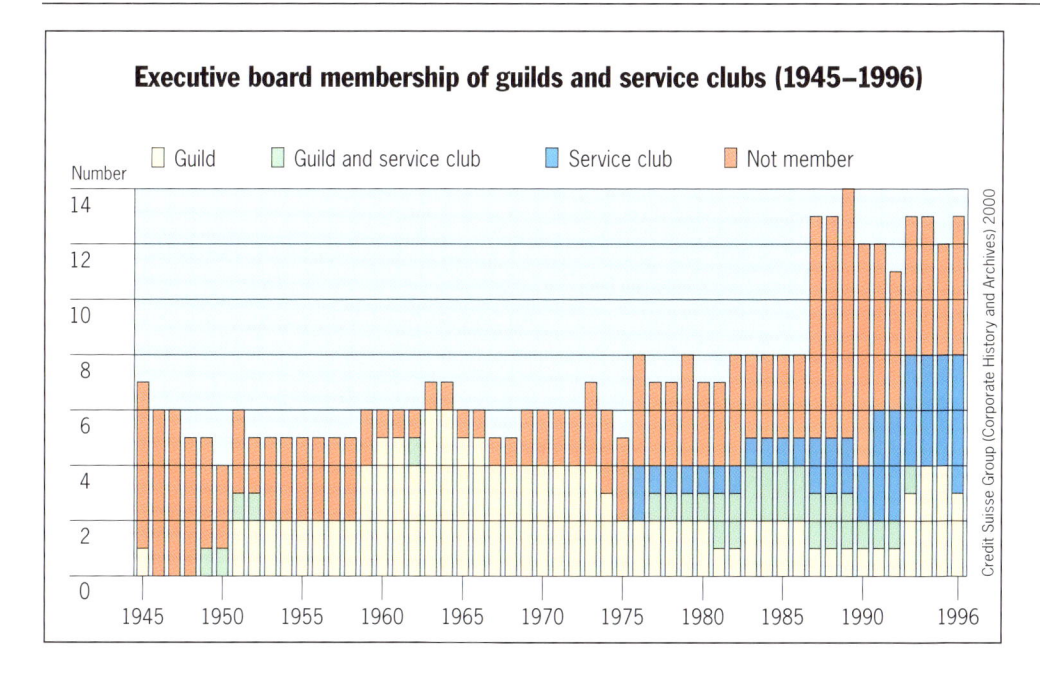

Executive board membership of guilds and service clubs (1945–1996)

board members who served after 1945, 18 were members of guilds and 12 were members of service clubs. Four belonged to both a guild and a service club. If we look only at the 1980s and 1990s, nine executive board members were in service clubs, and eight in guilds. Membership of service clubs, which gradually gained significance in Switzerland only after the Second World War[558], became more common in the late 1970s. At the same time, the falling number of executive board members from the city of Zurich meant that fewer executive board members were members of guilds.

The relative weighting of the different service clubs is also worth noting. A total of ten executive board members were Rotarians, and two were members of the Lions Club.

Conclusion

A look at the development of the social profile of executive board members between 1945 and 1996 shows that there were two typical types of executive board member during this period: one type dominated between 1945 and 1972, the other between 1973 and 1996.

In broad terms, the typical executive board member prior to 1973 grew up in the city of Zurich; he was Protestant and a member of a guild; he was either not a university graduate or he had studied law at Zurich University; he either held an officer's rank in the Swiss army or did not serve in the military; he originally worked at head office in Zurich, went from there into the executive board, and remained in office until retirement.

After 1973, the typical member of the executive board grew up either in the city of Zurich, or elsewhere in German-speaking Switzerland; he was either a non-graduate or he had studied law or economics at Zurich or St. Gallen; he was either Protestant or Roman Catholic and was more likely to be in a service club than in a guild; he held a high rank in the military; he could have come to the executive board either from head office or directly from elsewhere. He left SKA on reaching retirement, or in order to take up a post outside the group, perhaps even to join a rival company.

It is interesting that the typical career model from 1945 to 1973 reached its apogee in the 1960s. For the post-1973 period, the model is most notable for the greater diversity in the social profiles of individual executive board members.

With SKA recruiting most of its executive board from head office in Zurich until the 1970s, it comes as no surprise that Protestants brought up in the city of Zurich dominated the board. The predominance of executive board members from the city of Zurich during these years also explains the high proportion of guild members and the dominance of the University of Zurich as alma mater.

However, between 1945 and 1996 there were always also executive board members that had grown up somewhere other than the city of Zurich, so we can conclude that throughout the period, regional origin was never an absolute criterion of executive board membership.

The question of whether someone was a university graduate or not was never a decisive factor either; nor was guild or service club membership. This observation is further backed up by the fact that several managers did not join a guild or service club until after they joined the executive board.

The fact that the executive board has always included non-officers and officers suggests that officer training was not a crucial requirement for elevation to the executive board either. This is reflected in SKA's image: unlike its rival bank SBG, SKA was never regarded by the general public in Switzerland as a typical 'military bank'[559], despite the fact that SKA's executive board also included numerous, sometimes very senior, officers.

The fluctuating proportion of officers in the ranks of the SKA executive board has to be seen in the socio-cultural context of the time. During the Second World War, senior officers were so involved in active service that it was barely possible for them to work on the executive board as well. This phenomenon carried over to the years immediately after the war and only began to change gradually during the 1950s. Men who had pursued civil and military careers in parallel were now in demand, because it was thought that a senior army officer in particular would possess very sound leadership qualities.

The sea-change that hit SKA in the mid 1970s and that continued even more intensely in the 1980s was based as much on the general social situation in Switzerland as on developments specific to SKA. In order to overcome the Chiasso Affair, SKA was compelled to pursue an uncompromisingly forward-looking strategy. This explains why the CVs of more and more executive board members began to differ from the ones that had predominated in the past. So it was that within a short space of time during these years of change, several non-graduates and non-Protestants who had not grown up in Zurich, and who had not worked at head office, joined SKA's executive board.

Die SKA zum Thema Ausbildung

Unsere besten Lehrlinge fliegen.

SCHWEIZERISCHE KREDITANSTALT SKA

Die SKA honoriert Spitzenleistungen. heute mit dem Swissair-Flug 110 für eine unseren Sitz in New York. Als Belohnung Deshalb fliegen diese sechs jungen Leute Schnupperwoche an die Wall Street 100, dafür, dass Kerstin Abraham aus Basel, Francesco Gasparini aus Baden, Daniel Gerber aus Bern, Urs Kaufmann aus Solothurn, Gabriela Oetiker aus Liestal und Ruth Bretscher aus Zürich dieses Frühjahr die besten Lehrabschlussprüfungen aller SKA-Lehrlinge gemacht haben. Herzliche Gratulation. Wir sind stolz auf Euch!

SKA - die Bank mit Perspektiven.

Human resources management

Optimum staff recruitment, training and development have long been part of SKA's recipe for success. After improvised beginnings, the bank's training program has been developed and improved along very clear strategic lines. The CS Communication Center in Horgen, which was opened in 1994, has given the bank an ideal venue in which to implement Credit Suisse Group's modern training and development strategy in the most effective way.

The bank pursues a long-term management and talent development strategy, involving banking apprenticeships and specific programs for high-school and university graduates. Credit Suisse Group is also a progressive employer in terms of the social provision it makes for its employees.

Further motivation for apprentices to do well in their exams was provided by the prize offered by SKA for outstanding results: Swissair flights to New York. Advertisement from 1990: 'Our best apprentices fly.'

Training

The first training and retraining courses: the bank needs a workforce

The origins of SKA's internal training program go back to the late 1950s. To start with, the program was more or less improvised as a spontaneous response to the economic boom of the time. During this period there was a sharp increase in demand for workers, and the Swiss labor market was quickly exhausted. The expanding bank was as little prepared for this development as many other companies in the country.

There was a lack of skilled employees in all departments of the bank, so SKA began to take on young women who had a basic grounding in commerce, organizing training courses to give the new workers the specific banking knowledge required. These were then supplemented by 'retraining courses' directed at people who had worked in non-commercial professions. For three months, the new recruits were prepared for routine tasks, which were, however, 'often very demanding in terms of the precision and concentration required'.[560]

Applicants from all sorts of backgrounds were employed and then prepared for work by means of these internal courses. The 're-trainees' included some real talent. There was a former pig dealer, for example, who joined SKA's gold trading operation. Within two years he had earned an outstanding reputation as a gold inspector. Sometimes the bank published advertisements aimed specifically at certain professional groups, particularly doctors' and pharmacists' assistants and saleswomen. These adverts tended to highlight the agreeable working hours – no night or Saturday work – and the good salaries. In this way SKA was able to recruit 40 or 50 new staff each month. Its success in finding enough new people was also partly due to its 'white collar' image and to the respect that a job at a major bank brought.

The Credit Suisse training center at Bederstrasse 115 in Zurich, opened on 22 May 1992. Cafeteria in the inner courtyard. Photo taken in 1995.

Intensified training and development

In the late 1960s, SKA's personnel department decided to redesign its range of courses so that instead of being merely reactive to the market situation, as had been the case thus far, the bank's training would be guided by strategic concerns. The rather patchy program of courses was revised and expanded, leading in 1967 to the establishment of a training center in Zurich. Amongst other target groups, the new courses were aimed at, for example, 'between 50 and 60 school-leavers each year', who 'for whatever reason' had not completed an apprenticeship.[561] SKA offered these young people a banking or office-skills course that would give them the theoretical training and practical experience they needed to become clerical workers. A thorough program of further training was also developed for tellers after the bank realized that 'the teller – the person behind the counter – is one of the most important people in terms of interaction with the customer and thus in terms of the bank's image'.[562] From 1969 onwards SKA ran a special course lasting several months for university graduates. Participants worked in various departments to gain experience of all the main areas of banking business. In spring 1970, SKA broke new ground when it opened its specialist school for apprentices. This aimed to transfer the principles of the apprentice workshops common in industrial companies to the white-collar sector. A diploma from the apprentices' school greatly enhanced a young person's chances in the labor market.

The first 'Rigi Seminar', named after the Rigi mountain that overlooked the seminar venue, took place in 1971. This course offered senior mangers a systematic program of management training and helped to institutionalize the concept of continual training and development. It also promoted a team spirit amongst the bank's managers, helped them to identify with their employer and to form 'peer groups'. Indeed, one of the main aims of these training sessions was to enable participants to build up a network of contacts throughout the bank that could be nurtured and utilized once they returned to work. From 1974, the personnel department also carried out management seminars for middle and lower management ranks.

Training for non-managers focused increasingly clearly on improving and expanding specialist skills. However, since the bank was also keen for staff to gain a broad knowledge of its operations, and thus to 'avoid over-specialization'[563], SKA also organized more than 60 generalist courses a year for a total of about 1,000 participants. The bank also kept an eye out for new training methods. It eventually became convinced that for certain courses, 'teaching machines' could be just as effective as human speakers and presenters. Such machines were used in particular for teaching associated with the introduction of new projects and for sales training. In 1977 the bank acquired 100 teaching computers. In subsequent years this system was developed into the bank's PC-aided teaching (PAT) programs. These programs offered staff the opportunity to gain knowledge about a whole variety of subjects through self-study.

Art at the Credit Suisse training center: Bignia Corradini (*1951). Untitled, 1992. Credit Suisse Group Collection.

Systematic development and promotion

The second half of the 1970s brought a phase of accelerated modernization and professionalization to SKA, prompting another fundamental revision of the bank's training program. A stocktaking exercise showed that the relevant issues were being actively addressed, but that there was no overall strategy. Training was being offered to an excessively broad range of employees without first identifying their real needs. The seminar for lower and middle-level managers, for example, had been offered to all middle-ranking staff, regardless of whether they had, or were earmarked for, any kind of management responsibility. Consequently, all staff of this level had been trained, but in a completely unfocused way.[564] The bank's senior managers also found it unsatisfactory that there was no effective system of staff appraisal, meaning that promotions had to be made without reference to any objective data about the candidates' potential.

As a result, in 1979 SKA began a complete overhaul of its human resources activities. The central aim was to use systematic training – in specialist areas, management skills, as well as sales and personal skills – to achieve an above-average level of professional competence at all levels of the bank's hierarchy. One of the key elements was management development. SKA began to carefully select future leaders, training and assessing them so as to ensure that all of its managers would henceforth possess a high degree of professional skill. The structure of the new system was based on three 'dimensions'. The 'planning' dimension involved periodically identifying the short and long-term need for managers at all levels of the hierarchy. The 'training' dimension concentrated on practical training and development on the job. 'Assessment' focused on the evaluation of performance and conduct based on a regular analysis of strengths and weaknesses. Another important instrument introduced at this time was the new appraisal system, which represented a complete change in the way staff were assessed. Previously, managers had merely filled in assessment forms by choosing between different categories and prescribed key words. This characteristics-based approach was now replaced by a system that focused on an employee's specific role using measurable, goal-oriented parameters. Employee and manager would agree on the criteria 'Fulfillment of role as defined in job description', 'Conduct at work', 'Personal contribution to achievement of goals' and – for managers – 'Fulfillment of management responsibilities'. Before someone at SKA could be promoted to become a member of senior management, the bank first had to decide whether the candidate had the necessary management skills. Experiences at a number of major US and German companies indicated that an Assessment Center (AC), a concept first developed in the USA, was a good tool for analyzing management potential. The AC used a combination of several techniques to identify strengths and weaknesses with regard to a series of predefined assessment dimensions. A participant's behavior in realistic simulations of various situations was observed, assessed and recorded by trained line managers. SKA introduced a pilot AC in 1979 and then implemented the idea definitively one year later. At that time no other Swiss company was using a comparable method of assessment. The AC subsequently became a key feature of the way SKA developed its managers.

GESUCHT

für Eintritt im Frühjahr 1956:

Telephonistin

mit mehrjähriger PTT-Praxis und guten Kenntnissen in der französischen und englischen Sprache. Italienische Sprachkenntnisse erwünscht, aber nicht Bedingung. Erforderlich ist auch Gewandtheit im Maschinenschreiben zur Verrichtung leichterer Büroarbeiten.

Jüngling

nicht über 20 Jahre alt, für Botengänge und verschiedene Hilfsarbeiten.

Handgeschriebene Offerten mit Lebenslauf, Photographie und Zeugnisabschriften werden erbeten an die **Personalabteilung** der

SCHWEIZERISCHEN KREDITANSTALT

Paradeplatz 8, Zürich 1

Advertisement in the *Neue Zürcher Zeitung*, 5 December 1955.

Auf das Frühjahr 1961

bietet die **Schweizerische Kreditanstalt Zürich**

jungen Mädchen

mit **abgeschlossener Sekundarschulbildung**, die von einer dreijährigen Lehre absehen möchten, wiederum eine

einjährige Einlernzeit fürs Bürofach

mit unentgeltlicher Tagesschule. Die Mädchen haben gleichzeitig Gelegenheit, die hauswirtschaftliche Fortbildungsschule zu besuchen.

Für diesen Lehrgang stehen 15 Plätze zur Verfügung. Wir bevorzugen ordnungsliebende Anwärterinnen mit guter Kinderstube, rechtem Arbeitswillen und befriedigenden Zeugnissen.

Kurze schriftliche Bewerbungen sind an unsere **Personalabteilung**, Paradeplatz 8, Zürich 1, zu richten.

Advertisement in the *Neue Zürcher Zeitung*, 29 August 1961. Both of these ads were aimed at attracting young women to work at the bank.

Networking and communication

Against a background of general liberalization and continuing internationalization, the bank had laid great emphasis since the 1980s on external training for its most senior managers. Top managers could select from courses at famous US seats of learning such as MIT, Harvard University and Stanford University. These courses enabled SKA managers to network with executives from other companies and thus to measure their capabilities in an international context. One of the useful things about contact and comparison with peers from a wide range of other countries and cultures is that it sharpens self-awareness and leads to a more realistic and constructive assessment of one's own abilities.

From 1987, the Swiss Banking School provided another excellent platform for international networking. SKA played a vital role in the establishment of the school, which offered professional training for managers from banks and other financial institutions in Switzerland and abroad. Attendees were made aware of the developments in the sector that would be important to the strategic management of a bank, thus helping them keep up with the rapid changes that were occurring in banking and finance. Each year SKA sent up to 15 employees to the Swiss Banking School.

Alongside such external courses, SKA continuously expanded the training offered within the bank. As a consequence, the personnel department also grew.[565] The executive board discussed whether it was right to continue delegating responsibility for staff development to the 'training' department. It proposed that personnel policy should in fact come under the authority of the executive board and line management.[566] At the same time it emphasized that the careful selection, training, promotion and nurturing of young talent required the full attention of managers at all levels.

This refocusing of the bank's training and development program also brought a change in the way people were promoted. Until the end of the 1980s, the bank maintained a complicated hierarchy consisting of more than thirty different titles and seven different levels of management. As a result, there were about 1,000 promotions made every year, with all the administrative costs that this entailed. According to the new concept, this complex structure would be reduced to three basic ranks with effect from 1991: associates, members of senior management, and members of the executive board. The new system would mean a radical flattening of the hierarchy, allowing function and performance to come to the fore. This was a pioneering move for Switzerland, and many other companies were to follow SKA's example.

By setting up the CS Communication Center 'Bocken' in Horgen, close to Lake Zurich, in 1994, SKA created a forum that set new standards for strategic training and development. The Communication Center quickly became a catalyst for a new learning culture as well as establishing itself as a place where SKA employees could further their technical, social and conceptual abilities in a stimulating and interactive environment. In 'Bocken' learning is largely freed from hierarchical structures. During a problem solving process, all staff who have the technical and social skills required to make a useful contribution are

---

'The main battle is no longer, or at least not exclusively, being fought on the field of capital or technology, but most especially in the further development of our human resources' (SKA executive board, 1988).

'The new approach to learning ... is more the lighting of a torch than the filling of an empty vessel' (Forum Horgen, text no. 8, undated).

'We have much more to learn from each other than to teach each other' (Peter Ustinov, quoted in: Forum Horgen, text no. 8, undated).

Thousands of apprentices trained

SKA has always been very serious about its social responsibility to give young people a chance at professional training. This attitude has, of course, been in the bank's own interests too, since so many of its trainees have remained loyal to the bank after completing their courses. The first reliable figures are from 1913, when SKA had 63 apprentices – 6.2% of the bank's total headcount. In 1921 there were 102 apprentices, marking a first peak. Between then and 1948 the number fluctuated between 56 (2.6% in 1943) and 86 (3.8% in 1939); the negative effect of the economic crisis of the 1930s and of the Second World War clearly had an influence on the figures for this period. As the economy picked up after the war, the number of apprentices and trainees jumped from 82 in 1948 to 138 in 1949. In 1949, a group of apprentices were trained at head office for the first time. The 200 mark was exceeded in 1959, and in 1964 the number of banking apprentices at SKA reached more than 300. Statistics from 1967 give the first detailed overview of all 'Staff in training in Switzerland'. A total of 362 staff were involved in training programs that year, including 280 bank and office apprentices, 37 high school graduate trainees and 45 university graduate trainees. By 1974 the number of staff in training had reached 1,081, thus rising from 8.3% to 11.4% of total headcount in Switzerland. If we look only at bank and office apprentices, the absolute peak was reached in 1982, with 932. The highest number of high school and university graduate trainees (961) and staff in training (1,959) came in 1990. Thereafter, the number of employees undergoing training fell, partly as a result of the recession and continuing rationalization. In 1996, a total of 8.3% of SKA's staff were in training, including 521 apprentices and 719 high school and university graduate trainees.

involved in producing a solution, no matter what their rank. Consequently, courses are no longer offered for specific management ranks. An open exchange of ideas, and interaction in small groups are always the priorities.

A huge influence was exerted by the philosophy that learning was not a choice but a permanent necessity for companies that wanted to keep pace with rapid changes in their environment. Furthermore, what is learned is not the only important factor. How it is learned and – more than anything else – how fast it is learned are also vital.

Management development

From the end of the 1960s, SKA followed a strategy of long-term management development. The strategy stated that 'staff in training' should always account for a set percentage of total headcount. This percentage was progressively raised throughout the years: at the start of the 1970s it was 10%, by the end of the 1980s 12%. Over the same period, the bank's headcount in Switzerland doubled. As well as fulfilling its training policy, the comparatively high proportion of trainees and apprentices at SKA had a positive effect on its image. The bank always adhered to the principle that apprentices would be offered a job once their training had come to an end.

The economic downturn that began at the beginning of the 1990s forced SKA to adjust its apprentice policy, especially since the restructuring and rationalization measures used to cut costs were leading to a decline in demand for apprentices. The executive board decided to reduce the proportion of staff in training to around 9% – still a very respectable level by comparison with rival banks.

SKA deliberately persisted with offering training opportunities to school-leavers. It developed a program called 'CS-challenge' as a thorough and forward-looking training course for graduates of commercial high schools. The

SKA set up its sports and leisure facility at Fluntern in 1927. Following its renovation and expansion in 1972, it was one of the most up-to-date corporate sports centers in Switzerland. Photo taken in 1997.

courses, three of which were started each year, lasted for 16 months and delivered a comprehensive grounding in banking. Even under the more difficult labor market conditions of the 1990s, SKA had virtually no problem placing graduates of this practice-based program.

SKA also created the management and talent development programs 'CS-academic' and 'CS-performance' for university graduates. The aim was to secure the best-qualified representatives of this target group as employees.

SKA's social, health and accident insurance schemes

As far as social provision for its staff is concerned, SKA has been a modern and progressive employer right from the start.[567] This is shown most clearly of all by the history of the SKA pension fund. As early as 1919, the bank established a pension fund, organized as a cooperative, for 1,206 members. But the roots of this institution reach even further back, the board of directors having set up a pension fund in 1897 that paid out benefits to staff after their retirement.

At the national level, a referendum in 1972 approved the establishment in Switzerland of the 'three-pillar principle' for old age pensions. This system distinguished between state pensions, occupational pension schemes and voluntary contributions by employees. One of the effects of this was to make pension funds compulsory for everyone working in Switzerland.

SKA encouraged individual ('pillar 3') pension provision amongst its staff by means of a share participation scheme. This was introduced on 1 January 1986 with the dual aim of supporting employees' efforts at capital formation, and strengthening their ties to the bank. All staff who had worked at SKA for five or more years were able to buy a set number of SKA shares at a preferential price every year.

In addition to this, SKA paid substantial sums into a non-occupational accident insurance scheme, which according to the law had to be funded by employers. It also set up collective contracts for health insurance, following the principle that 'costs can be reduced and better conditions achieved by bringing a large number of people into a large group'.[568] Staff were allowed to remain in the collective health insurance scheme even after their retirement, thus continuing to benefit from preferential conditions.

Alongside these facilities aimed at helping former staff to enjoy the best possible lifestyle after retirement, SKA also set up a welfare foundation entirely funded from the bank's coffers. Through this foundation, the bank provides support for staff, or their survivors, who have fallen on hard times through no fault of their own. Right up to today, the bank continues to receive between 30 and 100 applications each year, which are treated very discretely and – if the findings are positive – very generously.

However, the bank's concern for the welfare of its retired staff is not just limited to financial matters, but extends to a communications policy designed to meet their needs. In the Zurich region since the 1980s, for example, two events a year have been organized for staff who are about to enter retirement: one at the Forum St. Peter and the other at the Zunfthaus zu Zimmerleuten. At these events, put on together with the Pro Senectute organization and financed by SKA (since 1997 by Credit Suisse Group), experts give presentations on subjects such as early retirement, health provision, and inheritance and tax issues. The pension fund also organizes annual trips for retired SKA staff.

bulletin, February 1972. The article talks about careers for women in the bank.

The executive board has remained purely a 'gentlemen's club'. SKA has never had a female executive board member.

Promoting women at SKA: 'Deeds Not Words'

In 1876, SKA took on its first female employee, a cleaner, and in 1881 recruited a second woman, to the accounting department[569]; it was not until 89 years later that women were first employed as cashiers. Two years after that, two women members of staff were promoted for the first time to the rank of vice president.[570] Personnel statistics show that by 1987, women made up 40% of all staff, but that they were seriously under-represented at management level, making up only 9% of staff in managerial ranks.[571]

The fight for equal opportunities became an ever more important feature of the social change of the 1980s. From this time on, SKA committed itself to systematically promoting the position of women at the bank, though it has to be said that the real trigger for these efforts was the general lack of workers, further exacerbated by the fact that at that time a number of well-qualified women were leaving the bank. In 1987, Rainer E. Gut decided that 'in the most vital interests of our bank's further fruitful development, we have to make better use of the potential of our female employees'.[572]

In 1986, various leading figures from the worlds of politics and business, including Rainer E. Gut, had initiated the Swiss-wide project 'Deeds Not Words' ('Taten statt Worte'), which was committed to improving the position of women at work on a national level.[573] Within SKA, several working groups debated specific aspects of the issue at various levels, looking at questions like, for example, how targeted information could be used to break down prejudices about women. Other groups planned the establishment of a crèche within the bank and discussed the issue of specialist and management training for women.

Thanks to the clearly structured organization of the project and a rigorously applied top-down strategy, it was not long before these efforts bore fruit. The proportion of women in middle and senior management posts increased steadily and wage equality was monitored as part of an annual comparative study; female staff enjoyed six months maternity leave and benefited from the services of SKA's crèche.

In 1991, the project was enhanced by the setting of a new objective: to integrate the equal opportunities process more effectively into the bank's existing staff and management structure. Lukas Mühlemann currently represents Credit Suisse Group on the national initiative committee of 'Deeds Not Words'.

We Mean is published by Credit Suisse Group's special unit for equal opportunities. Pictured: the July 1999 issue.

The crèche at the Üetlihof

After two years of preparation, SKA staff's desire for professional childcare was finally fulfilled on 1 September 1988 with the opening of the Üetlihof crèche, run by two carers in an apartment in the Brunaupark (the residential estate next to the bank's Üetlihof service center). The great success of the original crèche led to expansion at the beginning of the 1990s into a second apartment and then in 1997 to a third. By the start of 2000, the crèche employed seven trained leaders and infant educators – some working part-time – as well as three assistants. They looked after a total of 21 children every day, aged between two months and six years. While the facility was first set up to allow single parents to continue working at SKA, in recent years it has also increasingly been used by children of families in which both parents are working. In a spirit of social fairness, the cost of the crèche is determined by the level of the parents' wages. In order to better meet the goal set when the crèche was first set up – 'to offer a genuine opportunity to combine family and career in the best possible way'[574] – the Üetlihof crèche has been working with the 'Childcare' organization since 1 January 2000. This has made it possible to offer a wider and more varied range of services for parents.

326 · Part Three: A New Paradigm

Organizational and management structure

SKA has always adjusted its organizational structure to suit external operating conditions, its own growth and, especially, its business strategies. In the very first years of the bank's existence, the board of directors had to carry out operational management responsibilities in addition to its supervisory and strategic functions, a situation that lasted until the 1880s. From 1900 onwards SKA's management was continually expanded, and in 1928 the executive directorate was replaced by an executive board. As a result of strong expansion in Switzerland and abroad, it became apparent that the organizational structure based on traditional banking disciplines was reaching the limits of its effectiveness, prompting SKA to introduce a division-based structure in 1987. Amongst other things, the new structure reflected the now less dominant role of commercial banking more accurately. Ten years later, Credit Suisse Group was formed with its four business units. Shortly afterwards, Winterthur joined as a fifth unit.

Board of directors meeting chaired by Felix W. Schulthess in SKA's board room at Paradeplatz. The members of the executive board were also present. Photo taken around 1970.

Organizational structures

The organizational structure of a bank constitutes a central element of its management and strategy. A history of SKA's organizational structure will thus inevitably reflect the key points in the company's development. These developments are influenced by three main factors: the market, the regulatory environment and corporate growth. 'The question of whether a bank can assert itself in the market is actually equivalent to the question of whether the core areas of its organizational structure can endure.'[575]

In the Swiss industrial and banking world of the mid-19th century, it was normal for a board of directors to exert a significant operational as well as strategic influence on the management of a company. At the beginning of the 20th century, the opening of its first wave of branches presented SKA with new issues and problems of decentralized management. In response, it produced several operational directives. Owing to the rapid expansion and changing customer requirements that marked the years after the Second World War, the functional structure organized according to traditional banking disciplines gradually reached the limits of its effectiveness. As a result, the bank found itself encumbered by lengthy and complex decision-making processes. First of all, the executive board tried to solve the problem by means of piecemeal changes to structures and processes, and by setting up a corporate planning and development department at the end of the 1960s. The Chiasso Affair of 1977 then forced SKA to accelerate the reform of its organizational structure. The necessary changes – primarily in the areas of auditing and controlling – were made that same year. Ten years later, in 1987, the bank took a decisive step towards a clear, customer-focused reorientation of its domestic and international business when it introduced a divisional structure and completely reorganized its Swiss operations. These measures paved the way for a new paradigm and increased the importance of investment banking and funds management business relative to the previously dominant commercial banking operation.

Thanks to all these efforts, by the beginning of the 1990s, SKA was well equipped to tackle the difficult integration work associated with the takeover of Bank Leu (1990) and SVB (1993), as well as the challenges presented by the increasingly close cooperation with CS First Boston.

The operational role of the board of directors in the difficult early years

As prescribed in the founding articles of association approved by Zurich's Government Council on 15 July 1856, the governing bodies of the new Schweizerische Kreditanstalt consisted of the general meeting of shareholders, the board of directors and the managing director. Appointing a suitable director proved to be a difficult task, since there were few professionals at that time with the required knowledge of how a commercial bank actually worked. The director or his deputy was to be charged with running the bank on behalf of the board of directors and reporting to the board.[576] On the basis of these reports from the director, the board, at that time composed of 15 members, would take the operational decisions.[577] In order to relieve the full board of some of its work, the individual members divided the bank's business between them and then submitted their proposals to the plenary session.

In the early years, a member of the board of directors took on the role of managing director as an interim measure. The first member chosen to perform the role was Heinrich Abegg, the second was Johannes H. Fierz. In 1859, Caspar Huber, previously a vice president, was promoted to managing director. When some speculative securities purchases led to heavy losses at the bank, the board of directors felt compelled in 1864 to form a committee that could monitor the management of the bank more closely. In 1877, this body was replaced by a number of special committees (the credit, control, finance, legal, and building committees), each with between three and five members.[578]

Article 12 of the founding articles referred to SKA's fields of business, stating that its activities could be pursued not only at head office, but also via subsidiary offices, branches and agencies in Switzerland and abroad. However, concern about the cost of building up its own branch network led SKA to restrict itself initially to cultivating contacts with a growing number of Swiss and foreign correspondent banks.[579]

Operational responsibility handed to senior management and the executive board

Between 1873 and 1885, the reins of operational power were held by executive director Georg Stoll, 'which allowed the board of directors to relax its supervision to a degree'.[580] The board was thus relieved of responsibility for daily busi-

The 'management committee' ('Leitender Ausschuss') was formed by five members of the board of directors. First page of the minutes of the first meeting on 4 April 1864.

Management responsibilities at SKA

Organization chart as at 1 January 1906 (names and titles as per original)

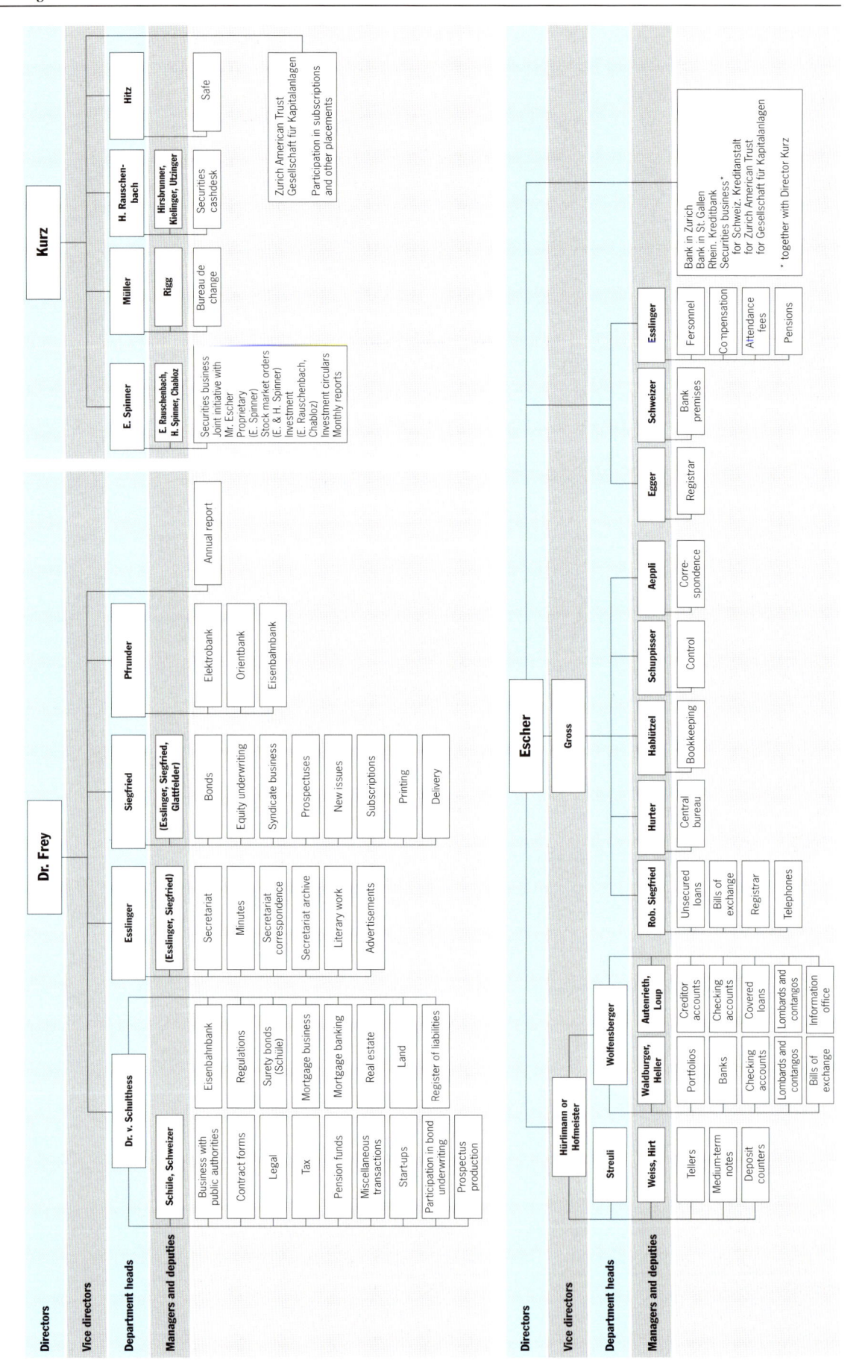

Directors: Dr. Frey

Vice directors: Dr. v. Schulthess | Esslinger | Siegfried | Pfrunder

Department heads / Managers and deputies:

- **Schüle, Schweizer** (under Dr. v. Schulthess):
  - Business with public authorities
  - Contract forms
  - Legal
  - Tax
  - Pension funds
  - Miscellaneous transactions
  - Startups
  - Participation in bond underwriting
  - Prospectus production
  - Eisenbahnbank
  - Regulations
  - Surety bonds (Schüle)
  - Mortgage business
  - Mortgage banking
  - Real estate
  - Land
  - Register of liabilities

- **(Esslinger, Siegfried)** (under Esslinger):
  - Secretariat
  - Minutes
  - Secretariat correspondence
  - Secretariat archive
  - Literary work
  - Advertisements

- **(Esslinger, Siegfried, Glattfelder)** (under Siegfried):
  - Bonds
  - Equity underwriting
  - Syndicate business
  - Prospectuses
  - New issues
  - Subscriptions
  - Printing
  - Delivery

- **Pfrunder:**
  - Elektrobank
  - Orientbank
  - Eisenbahnbank
  - Annual report

Directors: Kurz

Vice directors: E. Spinner | Müller | H. Rauschenbach | Hitz

Managers and deputies:

- **E. Rauschenbach, H. Spinner, Chabloz** (under E. Spinner):
  - Securities business
  - Joint initiative with Mr. Escher
  - Proprietary (E. Spinner)
  - Stock market orders (E. & H. Spinner)
  - Investment (E. Rauschenbach, Chabloz)
  - Investment circulars
  - Monthly reports

- **Rigg** (under Müller):
  - Bureau de change

- **Hirsbrunner, Kielinger, Utzinger** (under H. Rauschenbach):
  - Securities cashdesk

- **Hitz:**
  - Safe
  - Zurich American Trust Gesellschaft für Kapitalanlagen
  - Participation in subscriptions and other placements

Directors: Escher

Vice directors: Gross

Department heads: Hürlimann or Hofmeister | Wolfensberger

Managers and deputies:

- **Streuli**
- **Weiss, Hirt:**
  - Tellers
  - Medium-term notes
  - Deposit counters
- **Waldburger, Heller:**
  - Portfolios
  - Banks
  - Checking accounts
  - Lombards and contangos
  - Bills of exchange
- **Autenrieth, Loup:**
  - Creditor accounts
  - Checking accounts
  - Covered loans
  - Lombards and contangos
  - Information office

- **Rob. Siegfried:**
  - Unsecured loans
  - Bills of exchange
  - Registrar
  - Telephones
- **Hurter:**
  - Central bureau
- **Hablützel:**
  - Bookkeeping
- **Schuppisser:**
  - Control
- **Aeppli:**
  - Correspondence
- **Egger:**
  - Registrar
- **Schweizer:**
  - Bank premises
- **Esslinger:**
  - Personnel
  - Compensation
  - Attendance fees
  - Pensions

Bank in Zurich
Bank in St. Gallen
Rhein. Kreditbank
Securities business* for Schweiz. Kreditanstalt
for Zurich American Trust
for Gesellschaft für Kapitalanlagen

*together with Director Kurz

ness and could concentrate instead on overall direction, control and supervisory functions. In 1900, Theodor Spühler expanded the executive directorate, marking the change from individual responsibility to a collegial system. During this phase, three executive directors held office: Julius Frey, Wilhelm Caspar Escher and Hermann Kurz. These were assisted by three vice presidents, ten heads of department and more than 20 assistant vice presidents. The official organization chart governed all powers of authority and signatory powers.

As business expanded and competition increased after the turn of the century, SKA – in marked contrast to its previous policy – began to build its own Swiss branch network. After the first SKA branch had been opened in Basel in 1905, senior management issued a directive creating a 'central bureau' at head office. This was responsible for maintaining continuous control of business operations at head office, the branches and deposit counters, processing the accounts for business with the external offices and producing balance sheets at all levels.[581] The first written instructions on the management of the external offices date back to the period between 1906 and 1912. These instructions contained decrees that from the modern perspective appear to have the character of guiding principles.[582]

The continuous development of SKA made it necessary to carry out further organizational adjustments in the second half of the 1920s. Senior management had to be strengthened and its standing had to be enhanced in the eyes of customers and the general public. Thus it was that the executive board was created in 1928. To start with, it had four members: Rudolf Bindschedler, Adolf Jöhr, Fritz Autenrieth and Walter Fessler.[583] Because Bindschedler was elected to the board of directors at the same time, he was given the newly created title of 'Delegierter des Verwaltungsrates' (literally 'delegate of the board of directors', but more commonly known these days as 'managing director').[584] Until the mid-1970s, the executive board always consisted of between four and seven members.

On 1 March 1935, Switzerland's new Law on Banks and Savings Institutions came into effect. Amongst other things the new Swiss Banking Law, as it was known, stipulated that major banks had to separate the functions of operational management on the one hand, and overall direction, supervision and control on the other.[585] As far as the regulators were concerned, this meant that members of boards of directors were no longer allowed to assume any operational responsibilities. At SKA, this separation had been made in practical terms since the end of the 19th century.

Functional structure unable to cope with rapid expansion

In 1953, the board of directors appointed Albert Linder as the first president of the executive board (1953–1959). Linder assumed the key strategic task of co-ordinating management decisions to ensure a uniform business policy.[586] Nevertheless, the newly created post was not always filled in subsequent years, remaining vacant between 1959 and 1963, and between 1973 and 1977. When Eberhard Reinhardt ascended to the office in 1963, the president was given

> 'SKA is there for the customers, not the customers for SKA; the interests of the customers must be considered always and in all circumstances, even if there is no direct advantage to SKA; no business must ever be carried out that runs contrary to Switzerland's interests; but despite all the care that must be taken to safeguard the interests of our clients and our country, we must never forget that the purpose of SKA is to earn money' (Instruction from the SKA executive, 1912).

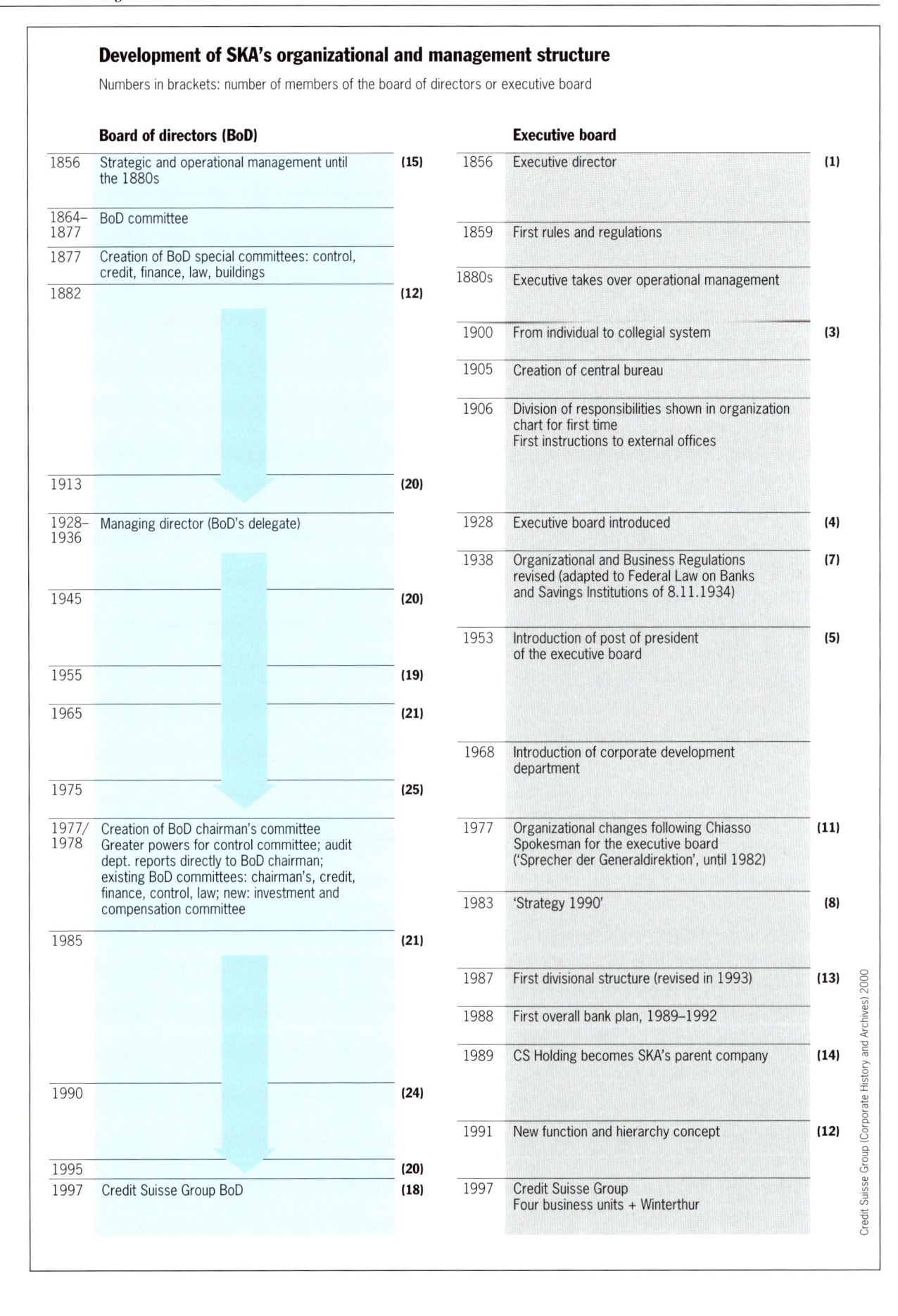

Development of SKA's organizational and management structure

Numbers in brackets: number of members of the board of directors or executive board

	Board of directors (BoD)			Executive board	
1856	Strategic and operational management until the 1880s	(15)	1856	Executive director	(1)
1864–1877	BoD committee		1859	First rules and regulations	
1877	Creation of BoD special committees: control, credit, finance, law, buildings		1880s	Executive takes over operational management	
1882		(12)			
			1900	From individual to collegial system	(3)
			1905	Creation of central bureau	
			1906	Division of responsibilities shown in organization chart for first time; First instructions to external offices	
1913		(20)			
1928–1936	Managing director (BoD's delegate)		1928	Executive board introduced	(4)
			1938	Organizational and Business Regulations revised (adapted to Federal Law on Banks and Savings Institutions of 8.11.1934)	(7)
1945		(20)			
			1953	Introduction of post of president of the executive board	(5)
1955		(19)			
1965		(21)			
			1968	Introduction of corporate development department	
1975		(25)			
1977/1978	Creation of BoD chairman's committee; Greater powers for control committee; audit dept. reports directly to BoD chairman; existing BoD committees: chairman's, credit, finance, control, law; new: investment and compensation committee		1977	Organizational changes following Chiasso Spokesman for the executive board ('Sprecher der Generaldirektion', until 1982)	(11)
			1983	'Strategy 1990'	(8)
1985		(21)			
			1987	First divisional structure (revised in 1993)	(13)
			1988	First overall bank plan, 1989–1992	
			1989	CS Holding becomes SKA's parent company	(14)
1990		(24)			
			1991	New function and hierarchy concept	(12)
1995		(20)			
1997	Credit Suisse Group BoD	(18)	1997	Credit Suisse Group Four business units + Winterthur	

Credit Suisse Group (Corporate History and Archives) 2000

additional responsibilities in the areas of economic research, human resources and work with professional associations. Eberhard Reinhardt also remained active in his original discipline of foreign underwriting business. His successors Heinz R. Wuffli (1977) and Rainer E. Gut (1982/83; 1977–1982 spokesman for the executive board) also retained responsibility for their original areas of business alongside the role of president of the executive board.

Robert A. Jeker (1983–1993) was also in charge of key support areas (economic research, communication), one of his objectives being to focus the bank more rigorously on strategic challenges such as market and customer-orientation. After the introduction of the divisional structure in 1987, Robert A. Jeker was also responsible for the bank's general secretariat and for corporate planning and development. These responsibilities were also taken on by his successors Josef Ackermann (1993–1996) and Hans-Ulrich Doerig (1996).[587]

Until the 1960s, the following ranks were used at the bank: ordinary employee (Mitarbeiter), assistant treasurer (Handlungsbevollmächtigter), treasurer (Prokurist), assistant vice president (Direktionsassistent), vice president (Vizedirektor), first vice president (stellvertretender Direktor), senior vice president (Direktor), deputy member of the executive board (stellvertretender Generaldirektor) and member of the executive board (Generaldirektor). The new ranks of deputy vice president (Chefprokurist) and executive vice president (Hauptdirektor) were added in 1974. This extensive system of ranks, which was created during a phase of rapid expansion in staff numbers, helped to encourage loyalty by offering numerous opportunities for promotion. Such loyalty was at a premium at this time because of the economic boom and the consequent tightness of the labor market.

As early as 1967 the planning department had produced a paper on 'The efficiency of Kreditanstalt' as part of the attempts to counter increasing bureaucracy at the bank.[588] In the mid-1970s the executive board felt compelled by increasing competitive pressure to discuss the bank's organization; there was concern that the rapid growth of the structure was creating complicated reporting lines. Further investigation confirmed the suspicion that the executive board had become too embroiled in day-to-day business at the expense of its core duties. It also became clear that business areas were not divided up equally within the executive board. Other deficiencies finally convinced the bank that it needed to review its organizational structure in order to exploit its strengths more effectively. The new structure would be based on divisions (from 1982: commercial banking in Switzerland and abroad, finance, logistics), regions (Switzerland/international), central functions (economic research, for example), and customer groups (personal customers, for example).[589]

The Chiasso Affair in 1977 accelerated the process of change that had already been instigated. The audit department and the secretariat of the chairman of the board of directors had been producing reports for the chairman since 1974. These two support units were now given more staff and assigned to report directly to the chairman of the board of directors. The audit department also took on extra duties, such as reviewing internal control systems.

'We want to be characterized by a clear, systematic and purposeful organizational structure. [...] Our management must be organized in such a way that decisions can be taken quickly' (SKA Guiding Principles 1981).

The presidents of the SKA executive board from 1953 to 1996

1 Albert Linder (1953–1959)
2 Eberhard Reinhardt (1963–1973)
3 Heinz R. Wuffli (1977)
4 Rainer E. Gut (1982/83; 1977–1982 spokesman)
5 Robert A. Jeker (1983–1993)
6 Josef Ackermann (1993–1996)
7 Hans-Ulrich Doerig (1996)

The duties of the control committee and the statutory external auditors were also expanded. The board of directors formed a seven-man chairman's committee to advise and support the chairman of the board.[590]

The executive board streamlined its internal working procedures in order to improve its controlling cababilities.[591] It also increased its size to eight, a number that was maintained until the introduction of the divisional structure in 1987. By 1979, however, the board of directors and the executive board had noted that despite the measures taken, fundamental organizational problems remained. There were, for example, nine international departments, which reported to four different executive board members, and five areas responsible for managing Swiss branches. Such widely spread management responsibility made it much more difficult to implement a coherent business strategy.[592] In 1982, the executive board held a week long seminar and came up with the idea of a division-based organizational structure.[593] However, the complicated planning and implementation process lasted until 1987.

Similar ideas about how to improve the bank's management and organizational structure had already been proposed at the end of the 1960s, following a general analysis of SKA's operational processes by the Federal Institute of Technology in Zurich.[594] On 23 September 1968, the executive board decided to create a central unit for corporate planning and development, which would produce information on which to base a strategic realignment of the bank. The new department would enable the bank to carry out 'simulations' rather than the more expensive 'trial and error' method for testing new processes.[595] Regular studies were produced by the department in collaboration with external specialists, and it organized seminars for the executive board, like the one in April 1971 on 'Modern Trends in the Theory and Practice of Managing Major Banks'.[596] The bank's first ever Guiding Principles, published in 1976, also concentrated on subjects such as the organizational structure and management culture. Using the business policy laid down in the Guiding Principles as a basis, the executive board started to set annual objectives. These were used in turn as a starting point for the formulation of detailed goals, action plans and budgets.[597]

Over time, all of these individual measures came together in a comprehensive planning cycle, leading in 1988 to the first overall bank plan for the period from 1989 to 1992.[598] Another four overall bank plans followed in the years up to 1996. Based on analyses of the competition and the general environment, these produced further plans for the individual divisions and areas and established the functional strategies to be followed.

A new paradigm in corporate management: the divisional structure

In the 1980s, the deregulation of the Swiss banking sector led to intensified competition. The market was also being transformed rapidly by the influence of internationalization and the introduction of new products, such as derivative

Organizational and management structure

Management responsibilities at SKA
Organization chart as at 1 January 1987

Head office

J — R. A. Jeker, President of the executive board

Annual accounts, management development
- (s) General secretariat, marketing services, public relations — Dr. V. Erne (A) [Gs]
- (s) Corporate development — (A) [Up]

Reporting directly to the chairman of the board of directors:
- Internal auditors — U.P. Hanni [Isp]
- Secretariat to the chairman — H.R. Tischhauser [Svris]

Commercial banking

L — E. Schneider, Member of the executive board
- (k) Commercial banking in West Germany, the United Kingdom and English-speaking Africa — H.-J. Heun (Y) [Br]
- (k) Commercial banking in Latin America — J. Müller (Y) [Fs]
- (k) Export financing, operations services for international subdivisions — Dr. B. Hausermann (Y) [Ha]
- (s) Planning and support: commercial banking — Dr. P. Sailer (Y) [Spk]

Y — Dr. M. Koup, Member of the executive board
- (k) Commercial banking in France, Belgium, Italy, Spain, Portugal and French-speaking Africa — R. Berthoud (Z) [Rk]
- (k) Commercial banking in the Far East, Australia and the Pacific Region — A.E. Lett (L) [Fo]

F — Dr. K. Widmer, Member of the executive board
- (k) Commercial banking in the Zurich region — J. Dreher (Z) [Ze]
- (k) Commercial banking in Switzerland and Liechtenstein, except the Zurich region — M.M. Meier (Z) [H]
- (k) Commercial banking in Austria, Scandinavia, Turkey, Eastern Europe and Israel — G.G. Goetz (L) [Bo]

Z — Dr. K. Jenny, Member of the executive board
- (k) Special financing in Switzerland — F.J. Groth (from 1.1.) (F) [Sf]
- (k) Financial holdings in Switzerland and consumer credit — Dr. M. Wetter (F) [Fb]
- (k) Commercial banking in the Middle East (excl. Israel) — A. Gremli (Y) [Mo]

U — Dr. R. W. Hug, Member of the executive board
- (k) Commercial banking in North America — Dr. R. Andermatt (U) [Fe]

Finance/investment banking

M — Dr. J.-J. Doerig, Member of the executive board
- (k) Multinational services in Switzerland — Dr. J. Ackermann (F) [Mu]
- (k) Multinational services international — R. Stalder (L) [Mai]
- (s) Fanning and support: finance — H. Hiffmann (from 1.1.) (B) [Spf]

S — H.-J. Rudloff, Member of the executive board
- (k) Capital markets and corporate finance in Switzerland — P. Kappeler (M) [S1]
- (k) Str capital market international — Dr. A. Hirs (M) [S2]
- (k) Securities sales — H.R. Zehnder (M) [S3]
- (k) Securities trading — Dr. J. Fischer (M) [Eh]
- (s) Administration of securities portfolio — F. Mani (M) [Ee]

B — Dr. H. Geiger, Member of the executive board
- (k) Foreign exchange, precious metals, bank notes; money market, liquidity — C. Willi (S) [D]
- (k) Banks in Switzerland — E. Locher (S) [Jw]

Funds management and deposits business

V — Dr. W. Wirth, Member of the executive board
- (k) Asset management — Dr. H.C. Maurer (H) [Vm]
- (k) Investment funds — M. Vogel (H) [Aw]
- (k) Economic research — A. Bischofberger (H) [Rw]
- (k) Investment research — Dr. H.C. Maure (H) [Vf]
- (s) Planning and support: funds management — P. Klauser (H) [Spa]

H — H.P. Sorg, Member of the executive board
- (k) Investment management — A. Muggler (V) [k]
- (k) Investment counseling for private clients — E. Scheller (V) [G]
- (k) Investment counseling for institutional investors — Th.J. Zimmermann (V) [k]
- (k) Deposits, savings business — Dr. R. Kormann (V) [Jp]

Logistics

A — Dr. H. von der Crone, Member of the executive board
- Organization and information systems — Dr. W. Guyer (R) [Oi]
- Accounting and controlling — Ch. Ammann (R) [s]
- Buildings and premises — A. Buhler (R) [Ch]
- Legal department — Dr. W. de Capot (R) [Lg]
- Tax and inheritance services — Dr. K. Arnold (R) [As, Ae]

R — Dr. R. Rasi, Member of the executive board
- Personnel — C. Vela (A) [Pers]
- Operations and services head office — K.F. Baumann (A) [X]
- Security — J.P. Huwyler (A) [Si]

Branches

Basel (F) — G. Utzinger
London (U) — Dr. J.F. Burkart

Bern (U) — M.B. Wischi
Geneve (U) — Dr. J.L. Deschaux
Lausanne (U) — G. Studer
Tokyo (U) — P. R. Horer

Zurich-Enge (Z) — H. Emch
Zurich-Rathausplatz (Z) — P. Grunenfelder
Zurich-Werdmuhleplatz (Z) — P. Meier

Branches in West Switzerland, Valais and Bern — J.J. Guinand (U) [New]
Branches in the Zurich region — E. Neuenschwand (Z) [Nz]
Branches in Grisons, Glarus, left shore of Lake Zurich, Ticino — P. Fankhauser (F) [Ng]
Branches in Northwest and Central Switzerland — V. Senn (F) [Nm]
Branches in East Switzerland and Zug — E. Schlauri (F) [No]

Chiasso (F) — M. Koller / S. Zoppi
Lugano (F) — Dr. A. Bernasconi

Aarau (F) — K.W. Staub
Luzerne (F) — R. Jung
St. Gallen (F) — A. Angehrn
Zug (F) — B. Bächer
New York (L) — P. Bosshard

Dr. H.R. Frey, Member of the executive board (until 26 March 1987)

Key
Areas
- k = customer and trading area
- p = production area
- s = support and development area

[ ] Internal department code
( ) Reporting line in absence of division head

Chief executive officer of Credit Suisse Group

1 Lukas Mühlemann (since 1997)

Chief executive officers of the business units

Credit Suisse:
2 Paul Meier (1997–2000)
3 Rolf Dörig (since 2000)

Credit Suisse Private Banking:
4 Klaus Jenny (1997/98)
5 Oswald J. Grübel (since 1998)

The divisional structure from 1987

After four years of planning, SKA introduced a new division-based structure in 1987.[599] The four new divisions – commercial banking, finance and investment banking, funds management and deposit business, and logistics – also determined the make-up of the executive board, which in response to the new organizational structure was expanded from eight to thirteen members.[600] The main focuses of attention had changed decisively compared with the structure of 1982, which had only distinguished between Swiss and international commercial banking, logistics and finance. The commercial banking division now had five executive board members (four after 1991), the finance and investment banking division that had been formed from the old finance area had three, and the funds management and deposits business division had two. The relative significance of logistics remained the same with two executive board members, and the functions exercised by the president of the executive board also remained more or less unchanged. As a result of the restructuring, the number of staff reporting directly to each member of the executive board was reduced, narrowing the breadth of management responsibility and reducing the length of decision-making processes.[601] The newly created executive board committee consisted of one representative from each division, plus the president of the executive board.[602]

financial instruments. A paper called 'Strategy 1990', produced in 1983/1984, clearly showed that if the motto 'organization follows strategy' was true, fundamental structural change was required.

The divisional structure represented the introduction of a new paradigm in the management of SKA, with investment banking and funds management business finally being accorded the significance they warranted. The increasing importance of these areas had been apparent since the 1970s.

This sea-change was also expressed at the same time in the fundamental shift away from generalists and towards specialization.

With effect from 1 January 1993, the bank was restructured into the Switzerland, international, investment and trading business, and logistics divisions. The new names are interesting in that they were no longer strictly tied to functional bank businesses, but also took account of geographical criteria (the Switzerland and international divisions). The number of executive board members responsible for the investment and trading division was increased to three, reflecting its greater contribution to the bank's earnings: commission and trading income had increased greatly by comparison with interest earnings. The main aim was to structure the divisions to better cope with the latest developments in the financial services industry and to better cater for the bank's now clearly defined customer segments. Further aims were to separate domestic and international business and to successfully manage the integration work generated by the acquisition of Bank Leu (1990) and SVB (1993). The newly created group was made up of two parts: on the one hand, SKA, which consisted of the parent company, plus Credit Suisse Financial Products (a derivatives specialist), other subsidiaries and, from 1994 the investment fund company, Credis; on the other, SVB, which also took on NAB in 1995.[603]

From SKA to CS Holding to Credit Suisse Group

In 1989, SKA was integrated into CS Holding as a subsidiary company by means of a two-step capital market transaction. Rainer E. Gut, chairman of the boards of directors of SKA and CS Holding, and simultaneously the chief executive of CS Holding, continued to ensure that ties between the two companies were close. In the end, the members of the boards of directors of SKA and CS Holding were identical but for a few exceptions. Following a thorough restructuring, CS Holding became Credit Suisse Group, which opened for business on 1 January 1997. Since that date, Credit Suisse Group has worked as a global financial services company, operating in the market through its four customer-focused business units Credit Suisse, Credit Suisse Private Banking, Credit Suisse First Boston and Credit Suisse Asset Management. In mid-1997 Winterthur Insurance joined the group as its fifth business unit.[604]

Credit Suisse First Boston:
6 Hans-Ulrich Doerig (1997)
7 Allen D. Wheat (since 1998)

Credit Suisse Asset Management:
8 Philip M. Colebatch (since 1997)

Winterthur:
9 Thomas Wellauer (since 1997; also head of the Financial Services business unit since 2000)

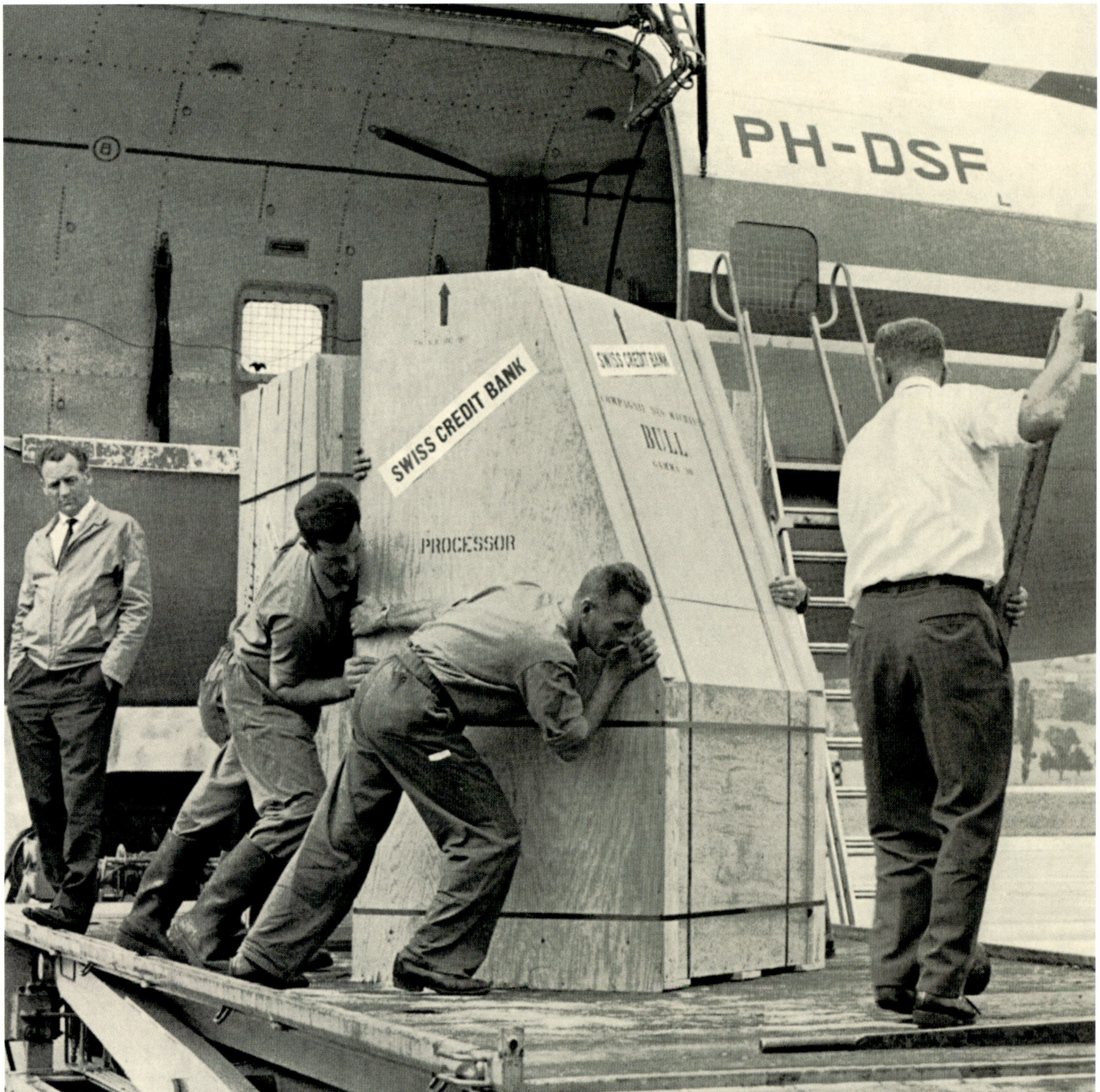
PH-DSF
SWISS CREDIT BANK
SWISS CREDIT BANK
BULL
PROCESSOR

Optimization as a constant of SKA's culture

Various demanding projects launched in the final quarter of the 20th century helped to rationalize, professionalize and modernize SKA. In order to regain its strong position in the core Swiss market, establish itself as a global operator in investment banking and private banking, and implement its Allfinanz strategy, the bank worked hard to ensure that all of its products and services were tailored to the individual customers that used them. In addition, the bank standardized its operations and internal processes. In this way SKA was able to modernize the traditional full-service banking concept, achieve a sustained improvement in earning power and create added value for customers and shareholders. It is significant that the desire to continue optimizing all operations has become a distinctive characteristic of the bank's culture.

Technological innovations have always had a major influence on banking and thus on SKA. In the 1880s, for instance, the telephone was introduced, and in 1948 the first punch card machine opened the doors to electronic data processing. The 1990s saw the start of the irresistible onward march of the Internet. SKA has always played a leading role in the automation and rationalization of business processes and in the introduction of new, computer-supported banking products.

The Bull Gamma 30 data-processing machine, imported from the USA. Photo taken in 1962.

Effectiveness and efficiency-improvement programs at SKA

At the end of the 1960s, the Swiss banks were confronted with a completely new phenomenon: margins were getting smaller and smaller, while costs were rising. Earnings power was under threat, as was the banks' international competitiveness. The Swiss banks lagged a number of years behind several of their

One of the early booking machines used by SKA. Photo taken in the 1920s.

international rivals in these areas, as well as behind other branches of Swiss industry. Great efforts were needed, therefore, if SKA was to find the dynamism and flexibility required to cope with the challenges of the future. The first effective action aimed at meeting these challenges was taken in 1972 with the introduction of a cost center accounting system (KOSKA), and in 1974 with the 'administrative rationalization' project. In 1976 the 'White Book' called for a fundamental reorganization of the bank and for the division of its operations into two sections: one for large-scale customers and one for retail customers. The Guiding Principles of 1976 also expressly confirmed the need for reorganization processes and cost reduction programs.

The real push did not come, however, until the Chiasso Affair of 1977. Finding itself suddenly short of funds, SKA was forced to increase the effectiveness and efficiency of its operations. The main direct effect of the crisis was on the bank's control processes.[605]

In order to avoid internal resistance, but above all in order to benefit from tried and tested expertise, SKA worked closely with external partners on all these changes. At the end of the 1960s, its relationship with the Institute for Swiss Banking (Institut für Schweizerisches Bankwesen) at the University of Zurich, gained in importance. During the crucial changes of the 1980s and 1990s, the bank's dialogue with the consultancy firm McKinsey proved particularly important for the future of the bank.

The 'Overhead Value Analysis' (OVA) project, which started in 1982, was the last attempt made by SKA to achieve bank-wide increases in earnings through organizational improvements and cost cutting (i.e. through a bottom-up approach). Since then, the bank has favored a top-down approach based on fundamental structural adjustments. Initially the primary focus was on general cost reduction, but in 1983 'Strategy 1990' acknowledged the necessity of selective growth and cost control; the implementation of such a strategy was made possible by the great progress that had been made in information technology, operational bookkeeping, and controlling. The first element in this more targeted process was the CRAPA project, which for the first time enabled the bank to measure customer profitability and to implement differentiated customer segmentation. This was followed by a number of key projects – either running in parallel or overlapping – in operational, technical and organizational areas.

From the strategic point of view, 1986's 'SKA plus' program marked a crucial turning point: instead of focusing purely on bank products, SKA started to concentrate on customers. At the same time, the bank systematized customer segmentation and product management. The analysis of segment-specific break-even analysis revealed a large-scale and undesirable cross-subsidization between various products. As a consequence, in the 1990s individual products were redesigned, tailored more specifically to the relevant customer segment, re-priced to ensure that costs were covered, or simply taken out of the range. A new planning and support unit for segment and product management was formed to help implement the associated projects.

Bill Gates' statement that 'Banking is essential for a modern economy, banks are not' has not lost its relevance. In fact it has become a constant challenge.

1974: administrative rationalization

In the first half of the 1970s, various measures introduced by the corporate development department (Ap), the organization department (Oa) and the central bureau (Cb) began to have an effect. In 1970, systematic premises planning led the bank to purchase a large site on the edge of the city of Zurich that was to be developed into the new Üetlihof administration center.

In 1972, cost center accounting (KOSKA) was introduced, providing a basis for a modern budgeting and accounting system. KOSKA was based on an improved accounts structure, and made it possible for the bank to allocate all expenditure to a cost center or to a product; it did not, however, allow unit cost accounting. The system was continuously refined and developed, and eventually replaced by the operational cost accounting system (BEKO). As well as cost center accounting, this also covered cost classification and was adopted as the bank's internal accounting system. Finally, the integrated management information system FISKA became operational in 1987.

Following a positive initial attempt at rationalization at the Basel branch – as a result of which 34 employees were able to deal with a 15% higher volume of work than 42 employees had done previously – a 1973 pilot run using a new methodology suggested that staff costs could be kept under control through systematic and continuous rationalization, but without major capital investment. There was certainly a need for urgent action in this area: at head office alone, the number of staff had increased by 2,287, or almost 120%, between 1968 and 1973. This prompted the launch of the 'Administrative Rationalization' project in spring 1974.[606] For half a year, a rationalization team went through every single cost center at head office to determine how each department could cope with the future volume of work without taking on more staff, but while maintaining the same level of quality.

1982–1986: Overhead Value Analysis (OVA)

In 1980/81 headcount at head office increased by no less than 692 staff, or 15%. Even given the sharp growth in business volumes, analysis showed that this was a disproportionately large rise. Thus it was that after six months of planning, the OVA cost reduction project was introduced at head office and at the Basel and Lucerne branches in the first half of 1983 – marking the bank's first collaboration with the McKinsey consultancy firm. The desire to continuously improve and optimize operations became a characteristic feature of SKA, as well as a key component of its corporate culture and a driving force behind subsequent projects.

OVA's bottom-up approach generated almost 2,500 suggestions for improvements, ranging from standardized records of customer visits to the closure of the now unprofitable 'Autobank' (drive-in bank, see box on page 360). By mid-1985, the implementation of such ideas had brought cost savings of Sfr 60 million, of which Sfr 1.5 million were made in Lucerne and Sfr 4 million in Basel. At head office, the project freed up 700 staff, 15.8% of the total, for new tasks. Owing to its success, OVA was introduced to all Swiss branches in 1984, and to the London and New York branches and other foreign offices in 1986/87.

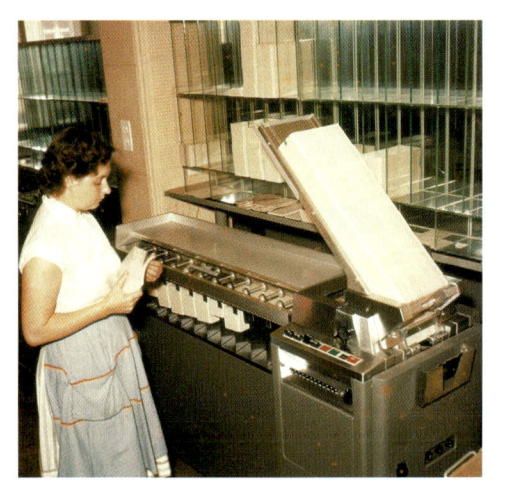

Punch card processing underwent continuous improvement at SKA. Photo taken around 1958.

An open plan office at SKA. In those days, women and men tended to work in separate rooms. Photo taken around 1950.

The effect of the simultaneous development of a more acute cost awareness amongst staff should not be underestimated. OVA encouraged a cost culture and a willingness to be flexible and think beyond the confines of one's own department, thus laying the foundations for the success of future cost management programs.

1983–1987: CRAPA (Customer Relations and Profitability Analysis)

Project CRAPA, planning for which began in 1983, initiated a fundamental change within SKA by creating the structures needed for the planned segment strategy. CRAPA answered the central question of 'who in the bank is earning how much, and with which customers?', i.e. it measured how profitable different customers were. The system thus became a key management information tool, monitoring earnings, turnover and costs. CRAPA allowed the bank to divide its customer base into different segments, thus facilitating the shift from a product-focused to a customer-focused approach.

The implementation of CRAPA involved giving a points rating to the average revenue generated by 150 bank products. Technically, the project proved to be extremely complex, but the system was continually improved and frequently

The Bull Gamma 30 data processing machine could handle 60,000 booking entries per minute. Photo taken in 1962.

linked up to other projects. CRAPA really came into its own from 1986 onwards when 'SKA plus' was introduced.

Project CRAPA measured not only the profitability of different customers, but also the performance of every member of staff with customer responsibility. Consequently it had a direct effect on the attitude of front office employees: while OVA had increased cost awareness, CRAPA was now making staff think more about performance and revenue.

CRAPA also brought some sobering statistics to light, and led to a radical reappraisal of the market: 80% of customers produced no income for the bank and used three bank products at most. Furthermore, retail and commercial banking, the area with the largest turnover, actually operated with a negative revenue contribution – unlike commissions and funds management business. This revelation had a decisive effect on SKA's new corporate strategy.

1986–1990: 'SKA plus'

Now that it was in possession of detailed information about the profitability of each of its customers, SKA launched a wide-ranging, growth-oriented marketing strategy in what was a largely saturated retail banking market. SKA quickly earned itself a reputation as a dynamic bank. A segmentation strategy for personal customers – providing added value for customers by improving the features of certain standard products – had already begun on a selective basis in 1982 with the 'Salary account plus', but thanks to CRAPA, 'SKA plus' could now be planned and implemented between 1986 and 1990 as a comprehensive, bank-wide sales improvement strategy.

The cost-benefit ratio of every product was now continuously assessed using CRAPA. In addition, continual market research provided more and more detailed information about customer needs and about the activities of rival institutions. By analyzing the potential of various types of customer, the bank was able to launch acquisition campaigns aimed at specific segments, with advertising strategies to match.

Staff training was of central importance to the whole effort. As far as SKA was concerned, the days of bank clerks waiting around for customers to come in and see them were over. Staff were now active salespeople and expert customer advisors. Specially trained 'market campaign teams' were formed to put the strategy into action.

As a result of 'SKA plus', customers undoubtedly used and purchased more bank products. However, the additional cost of customer advisors was sub-

An SKA computer center in the second half of the 1970s.

The M81 programmable switchboard at SKA's call center in Horgen. This digital telephone system from Nortel provided the technology needed for the launch of a phone banking service. Photo taken in 1995.

stantial, even leading in some individual cases to negative revenue contributions. The bank's profit and loss account was burdened in particular by the innumerable small customers, who only used low-revenue, cost-intensive retail products.

1987–1995: 'Management of Swiss Branches'

It became ever more clear to SKA that if cost and revenue management was to be implemented rigorously across the board, it would be impossible for every branch to function as a small full-service bank in its own right. The branches did not have the necessary resources to produce and sell the full range of services. The aim of the 'Management of Swiss Branches' project, initiated by the executive board members responsible for the commercial banking division, was to optimize the range of management responsibilities and to relieve front office staff of production tasks. As with other projects, the key to success here was the cooperation between SKA's project staff and the consultants from McKinsey.

SKA decentralized management responsibility by creating management units and regions. Thanks to the FISKA integrated management system, it also made it possible to carry out management tasks more efficiently and flexibly. FISKA delivered analyses of risks, customer segments, financial business volumes, costs and revenues. By getting more information to the right people and by creating far more transparency with regard to costs and income, the bank created a clearer communications structure between head office and the branches.[607]

At the same time, back office and front office were linked together in terms of production by the newly created logistics centers, helping to reduce costs through rationalization. By 1991, regionalization had more or less been completed. The 'Management of Swiss Branches' project had increased revenue contributions in SKA's 17 Swiss regions by between 30% and 100%. Despite this success, there was no doubt that the process had only run half its course when it had to be halted for political reasons. If the bank had wanted to achieve the full effect of rationalization, it would either have had to increase the volumes processed to a substantial degree, or it would have had to reduce the number of logistics centers.

As part of project 'Match', which in 1993/94 merged the logistics operations of SKA and Swiss Volksbank (SVB), the number of regional centers was reduced in an initial phase from 17 to 14 – despite the large increase in business volumes.[608] In project 'Focus' in 1997, the further consolidation required by the drive for rationalization resulted in the survival of only four service centers within the Credit Suisse business unit (located in Zurich, Bern, Geneva and Mendrisio).

1992–1995: retail banking strategy

The abolition of the Swiss Bankers' Association's conventions at the end of the 1980s paved the way for a wave of deregulation that produced, amongst other things, more flexible pricing policies. In the past, SKA had offered all of its one million retail customers the same standard products at the same standard prices through the same distribution channels. At the start of the 1990s, the CRAPA customer profitability records showed a negative revenue contribution of Sfr 100 million. According to the new retail banking strategy, the transparency of the cost/earnings structure had to be increased, customer segmentation had to be further refined, new distribution channels had to be created, and the product range had to be streamlined and run more profitably.

Analysis of the cost/earnings structure revealed the stark truth that only 30% of customers produced a profit for the bank, while the other 70% generated a loss. It was clear that cost/earnings considerations meant that it was no longer appropriate to maintain an undifferentiated approach to customer service.

As a result, in August 1992 SKA's executive board approved a new retail strategy. Its main elements were as follows: introduce a more needs-oriented, differentiated service organization with different products and prices; implement a new distribution and service channel (a telephone bank); and exploit the potential for growth by acquiring existing organizations.

As part of the new project, personal retail customers (defined as customers with invested assets of up to Sfr 300,000) were, from January 1993, divided in two groups for the purposes of customer care. About 300,000 'individual customers' (the 'PKI' group) who needed more advice and had assets of more than Sfr 25,000, were looked after by a personal advisor at their branch and were offered products at preferential prices. Meanwhile, the approximately 700,000 'universal customers' (PKU), who had less need of financial advice, were served by regional telephone service teams, and were offered products at prices which reflected their true cost.

On Sunday 15 May 1993, SKA opened CS Firstphone in Horgen – Switzerland's first telephone bank. The PR success of this innovation was so great that more than a third of the people who used Firstphone had never previously been customers of SKA. After only 18 months, Firstphone's 7×24-hour service had reached break-even.

The third strategic objective (growth through acquisitions) was achieved much sooner than the project team had anticipated thanks to the union with SVB and the integration of the NAB. After three years, the retail banking strategy project could be brought to a close having produced a positive revenue contribution of more than Sfr 100 million.

1993–1998: corporate customer strategy

In the 1980s and at the beginning of the 1990s, Swiss banks suffered massive losses as a result of the collapse of the real estate market, but also because of lending policies that did not always take full account of the risks involved. In 1993, the combined corporate clientele of SKA and SVB generated a negative revenue contribution of Sfr 1 billion. Though making up only 5% of all customers, the corporates accounted for 30–40% of lendings, kept 30–40% of the bank's front office personnel busy, tied up 60% of SKA's equity capital, and generated about 75% of all the provisions that had to be made. Segment analysis revealed the unpalatable fact that 10–20% of customers were generating 80% of the revenue contribution.

In 1994, the commercial banking division created its own corporate customers subdivision to run its new project. The project strategy centered on a new method for dividing up customers. Until this point in time, SKA had used the number of people working for a company as the sole criterion for corporate customer segmentation. This meant that the same segment could contain a very varied mixture of customers from all sorts of different industries, and with all sorts of different needs.

The new strategy involved the creation of five new segments: companies big enough to raise funds on the capital market (F1), large firms with special needs (F2), medium-sized customers (F3), smaller firms with investment needs (F4), and small firms without investments (F5). A customer-oriented service organization allowed the bank to offer a better service, to increase sales, and to achieve the cost reductions required by rationalization. Communication with multinational companies in segment F1 was the exclusive preserve of head office, while F2 companies were looked after either by the regions or by head office, depending on the specific circumstances. Special teams in 50 selected branches were responsible for F3 customers. Segment F4 was looked after by the branches, and F5 by regional service centers.

Project 'Focus' modified the corporate customer strategy's service organization further still. Multinational, capital-market-compatible firms (F1) were allocated to Credit Suisse First Boston, while large Swiss customers (F2) were looked after by the Credit Suisse business unit's Swiss corporates department from its eight offices located around Switzerland.

By 1998, the project had achieved its aims: gross income had been increased, costs had been optimized, the whole credit and risk management system had been overhauled, and the bank had introduced a segment-specific service concept with a pricing structure that took full account of the attendant risks. What is more, the bank had done all this while achieving slightly higher business volumes. Credit Suisse thus became the market leader for large firms with special needs; it also carved out a better-than-average market share in business with medium-sized firms (F3).

1994–1997: Credit and Risk Management (CRM)

'Credit and Risk Management' (CRM) was of central importance to the sustainability of the effectiveness and efficiency improvement programs described above. It ultimately led to a crucial strategic development: the separation of credit approval and monitoring on the one hand, and customer service on the other. The CRM project was launched in 1994 as a sub-section of the 'Match' project, which also included the corporate customer strategy. Though the creation of a central credit unit for the entire bank was the highest priority within CRM, it was not possible to achieve this as quickly as planned. There were also some significant IT problems, which is ultimately why the CRM idea was adapted for the individual business units as part of project 'Focus', and then implemented by each unit on its own. The separation between credit and customer responsibility was achieved through the establishment of 'credit units' within the Credit Suisse and Credit Suisse Private Banking business units.

Information technology as the key to successful banking

Looking back at the history of SKA, one might be tempted to think that technological developments were only modest in the first hundred years of the bank's existence. In fact, however, there were several major leaps in technological progress during this time: the introduction of the telephone (1880), the calculating machine (1904), the telex (1935) and the punch card machine (1948). These new technical facilities made the communication of business information easier and faster, as well as improving bookkeeping and settlement processes. In particular, the telephone, introduced at SKA in 1880, remains vitally important to the bank's existence; telephony has also been developed further to produce such innovations as Firstphone (1993) and today's call center technology.

Technology determines the nature of bank processing until the 1980s

SKA entered the data processing age in 1948 with the introduction of the first punch card machine – the first step taken by the bank on the road to office automation.[609] Over the next two decades, various EDP-based technical aids were introduced to back office operations. These helped to speed up office tasks and order processing to a massive degree, and allowed the bank to cope with

Introduction of technology at SKA

1880	Telephone
1890	Typewriter
1904	Calculating machine
1920	Bookkeeping machine
1935	Telex machine
1948	Punch card machine
1957	Pneumatic post
1962	Bull Gamma 30 (1st generation computer)
1967	IBM/360-40 (2nd generation computer and first query screen)
1974	IBM/370-168 (3rd generation computer)
1985	First PCs
1993	Call center technology
1995	Internet

Credit Suisse Group (Corporate History and Archives) 2000

the high-volume retail payments and deposits business that became more important in the 1960s. The main innovations here were the Bull Gamma 30 data processing equipment introduced in 1962, which could process about 60,000 bookings per second, and the IBM 360 and 370 systems. As international business began to play an ever more significant role for the bank, at the end of the 1960s SKA took the strategic decision to commit itself entirely to a global partnership with IBM. The rapidly increasing importance of electronic data processing led to the creation of a dedicated subdivision for organization and automation (Oa) in 1967.

In 1970, SKA took a trail-blazing decision. Instead of a piecemeal approach, it would from that point on use EDP to rationalize its information storage needs and the technical processing of its banking transactions. The computers available at the time promised to solve two basic technical problems: the storage of data volumes running to billions of characters, and the automation of technical banking processes at hundreds of workstations.

In 1972, the first central computer center for online services – essentially a large EDP factory – was opened at the bank's Giesshübel site in Zurich. Between 1980 and 1983, a second center was developed at the nearby Üetlihof site. Finally in 1994, SKA created a state-of-the-art computer center at Horgen.

In April 1973, the booking system and the CIF (Customer Information File) system for managing customer master data became operational. In securities business, SKA took a decisive leap forward with the 'Securities for the 1980s' (WS 80) project, which was started in 1978 and completed in 1984.

Over the course of the 1970s and 1980s, the bank pursued its aim of linking up back office and front office departments by installing various automation systems for payments and foreign exchange processing, as well as creating system packages for foreign branches. Notable innovations during this period included electronic tools such as Credimat, Contact Bank and Videotex. New opportunities were also opened up by PIAS (Personnel Information and Administration System), the LSV direct debit system and the AIS investment information system. Despite all of this technical integration, the branches – as mentioned earlier – continued to function as small, stand-alone, full-service banks handling their own production needs.

Further IT support was provided at some key locations in the form of computer screens ('dumb terminals') and printers connected to the computer center. By 1978, over 2,000 terminals were already in use. By mid-1983, the number had risen to 3,000, and in 1985 SKA could celebrate the installation of its 5,000th terminal. The first 300 personal computers were installed at the bank, initially as stand-alone machines, in 1985; only one year later SKA could boast 1,000 PCs.

The development of interbank clearing – a key prerequisite for cash-free payment transactions – is another example of the Swiss banks' efforts at automation and rationalization. In 1972 the manual clearing system based on the time-consuming processing of endorsements was replaced by new standardized forms and optical character readers. International collaboration was

Securities trading in the Üetlihof administration center. Photo taken in 1992.

made much easier by the SWIFT (Society for Worldwide Interbank Financial Telecommunication) payments system. June 1987 saw the introduction of the new SIC (Swiss Interbank Clearing) online clearing system.

From the 1980s onwards: business strategy determines IT developments

An IT development plan was produced as long ago as 1969/70, but the first comprehensive IT strategy was formulated in 1983. This strategy covered the period up to 1990; it was implemented in the form of annual IT programs and updated to keep pace with the latest developments. At the beginning of 1988, a five-to-seven year IT strategy was developed containing proposals and objectives with regard to applications development, IT operations, users and PR work. 1988 also witnessed a major shift: until then, the priority had been the automation and implementation of information systems. Now, however, the most important criteria for the development of IT applications became profitability and the maintenance of earnings power. New tools were expected to produce produc-

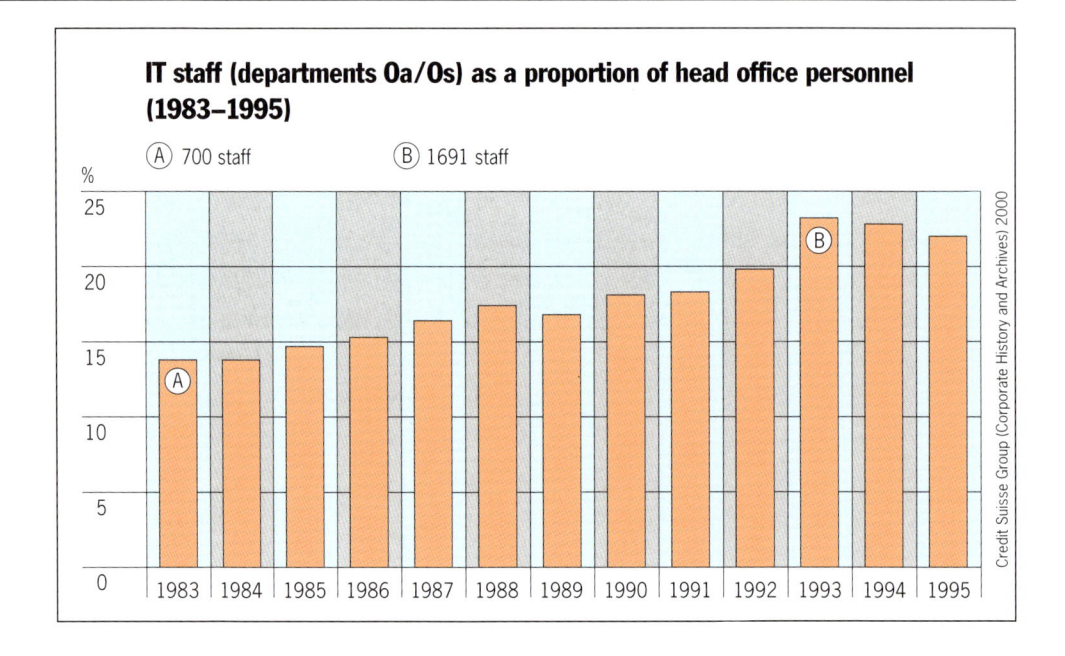

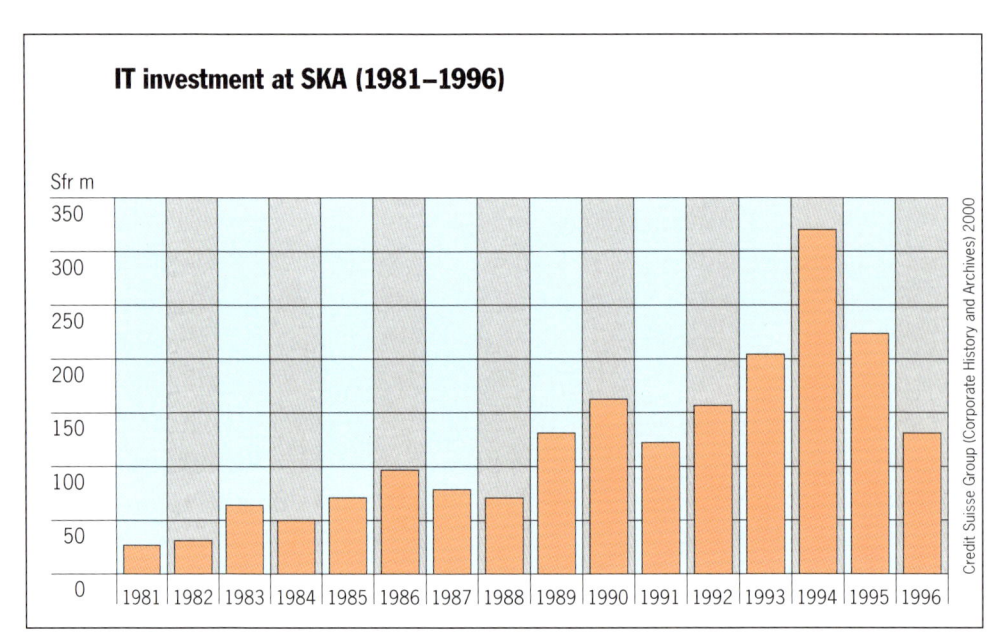

IT staff (departments Oa/Os) as a proportion of head office personnel (1983–1995)

Ⓐ 700 staff   Ⓑ 1691 staff

IT investment at SKA (1981–1996)

'Business strategy determines IT strategy. Information technology is a key element of business strategy' (SKA executive board, 1990).

tivity gains. What is more, the bank had to be able to measure the reduction in the length of projects and the decrease in development costs. As a result, SKA began to buy more services from external firms, restricting its in-house development work to the essentials.

In 1990, the executive board held an IT seminar at the IBM center in La Hulpe, Belgium. The top management's desire to make IT an increasingly important component of corporate strategy was made extremely clear.

In 1991, the 1988 IT strategy was augmented by a further dimension: it was stated that the underlying concept for IT had to be flexible enough to keep up with changes in bank strategy and to keep ahead of technical developments. This new way of looking at the issue can be better understood in the light of the increased personal and financial resources that were being committed to information technology (see the two charts on p. 352).[610] This greater investment reflected the growing importance of IT to the bank's business strategy.

Integrating newly acquired banks and launching new distribution channels: the challenges of the 1990s

The substantial growth achieved by CS Holding in the 1990s by means of external acquisitions presented a great challenge. The takeovers of Bank Leu, SVB and the NAB had to be digested within a very short period of time. From the IT point of view, the necessary acceleration of implementation projects meant that compromises had to be made; inevitably this also led to problems with the system architecture. On 1 January 1997, the 'Focus' restructuring project created four business units under the umbrella of Credit Suisse Group: Credit Suisse, Credit Suisse Private Banking, Credit Suisse First Boston and Credit Suisse Asset Management. Once again the IT departments had to adapt to the new structure under great time pressure.[611]

If SKA's new multi-channel strategy was to be implemented properly, it would not be sufficient simply to renew existing systems: new distribution channels had to be created. In particular, in 1993 retail banking volumes were given a large boost by the opening of SKA's 7×24-hour telephone bank. The call center technology used by Firstphone (1993) and Direct Invest (1995) reduced the amount of cost-intensive personal contact with customers over the counter. Despite the huge progress made in data technology, telephony is still the most important medium for direct communication between the bank and its clients.

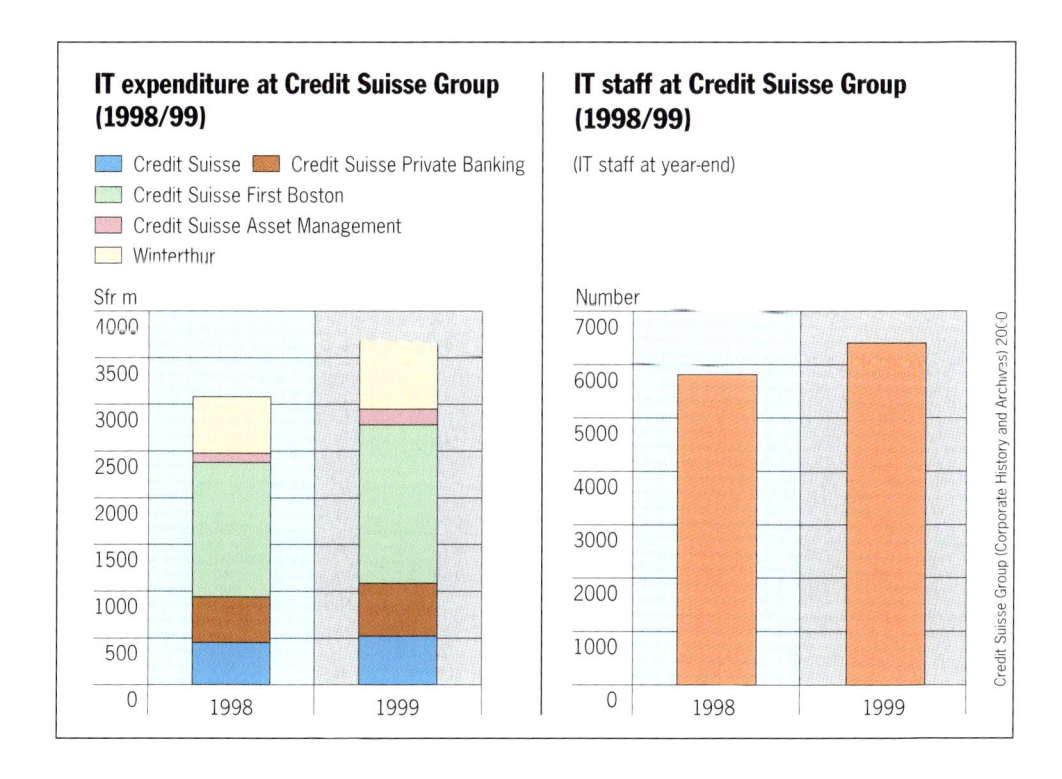

IT expenditure at Credit Suisse Group (1998/99)

- Credit Suisse
- Credit Suisse Private Banking
- Credit Suisse First Boston
- Credit Suisse Asset Management
- Winterthur

Sfr m

IT staff at Credit Suisse Group (1998/99)

(IT staff at year-end)

Number

Credit Suisse Group (Corporate History and Archives) 2000

The introduction of telephones was one of the most important milestones in the bank's technological development. Telephony is central to the exchange of information with customers as well as to communication within the bank itself.

At the end of April 1997, Credit Suisse made a major technological leap in the direction of virtual banking with the introduction of the Direct Net system. Two years later 'youtrade' enabled customers to trade in securities at favorable prices over the Internet and telephone ('discount online brokerage'). There is no doubt that in future, mobile telephony and the further development of e-commerce will change the organizational structure of banks even more quickly and fundamentally than call-center telephone technology did in the 1990s. The IT revolution in the financial services sector will also further strengthen customers' desire for total market transparency and for freedom of choice with regard to the optimum relationship between price and performance.[612]

Development of communications and information technology from c. 1950 (SKA/Credit Suisse Group)

	Key objectives / strategies / measures	Technical equipment
1950s	First moves to rationalize account and portfolio bookkeeping	• Data: Typewriters, bookkeeping machines, punch card machines and electro-magnetic drums; pneumatic post at head office • Telephony: Manual jack switchboard
1960s	**Key objective: cope with burgeoning retail business** Introduction of technical aids in back office. Each branch functions as a 'stand-alone bank'; IT centers in Zurich, Basel and Geneva	• Data: Bull Gamma 30 and IBM/360 systems for bookkeeping and securities business; first circuit-based machines (Nixdorf) • Telephony: Mechanical dial telephones and N52 mechanized switchboard
1970s	**Key objective: automation and link-up between back and front office areas** Major system innovations: CIF, bookkeeping, foreign exchange and online information capability, credit administration, payment transactions, etc.	• Data: Development of first computer center and online screen access ('dumb terminals') • Telephony: Electro-mechanical switchboards
1980s	**Key objective: intensified automation and first information systems, improved retail customer service through introduction of electronic tools** Formulation of first IT strategies (for 5 to 7-year period) and annual IT plans; comprehensive IT strategy paper in 1988 Major system innovations: • Contact Bank, Videotex, direct TEL • CRAPA, PIAS, online securities system • Processing systems for banknotes and precious metals, standing orders, SWIFT, SIC (development of Swiss Interbank Clearing), AIS (investment information system), etc.	• Data: Dumb terminals; from c. 1985 first stand-alone PCs • Telephony: Semi-electronic ESK-8000 switchboard and introduction of digital technologies
1990s	**Key objectives: IDP (individual data processing), office automation, implementation of paperless office, exploit synergies through 'Match' and 'Focus' projects, Internet banking, e-commerce** New distribution channels and updating of existing systems, reorganization of retail business, introduction of Firstphone Major system innovations: • Text processing, electronic mail and archiving, forex trading systems, Direct Net • Outsourcing of IT disciplines outside core competencies (ITS), and specialization of business units with their own systems • Internet technologies increasingly influence construction of proprietary banking systems • IT strategies for individual business units	• Data (first half of 1990s): Linking up PCs within LAN, WAN and server architectures, plus Internet technologies (WAN telecommunications over public telephone lines) Data (second half of 1990s): Migration from IBM (OS/2) to Windows NT; in general: overall packages ('solutions') rather than individual systems • Telephony: Introduction of mobile telephony and call center technologies • Internet, September 1995: First public-access Web server (CS Info Kiosk) • Data warehousing and data mining, WebTV, smart cards, Java, etc.

Credit Suisse Group (Corporate History and Archives) 2000

SKA-Spar-Service plus

Möchten Sie den American dream live erleben?

Macht Fr. 140.– im Monat.

Wenn ein exklusives Ferienziel am Horizont auftaucht, sollten Sie sich rechtzeitig den SKA-Sparplan plus chartern. Mit einem monatlichen Beitrag von Fr. 140.–, 3½% Zins und Bonus erarbeiten Sie sich in 6 Jahren die perfekte Reisebasis von Fr. 11 496.10 für alle Staaten in den USA. Spartips finden Sie in der Sparbroschüre der SKA. Bestellen und Konto buchen.

Coupon
Bitte senden Sie mir gratis die SKA-Sparbroschüre «Richtig sparen – mehr erleben».

Name/Vorname:

Strasse/Nr.:

PLZ/Ort:

Tel. P: G:

Coupon einsenden an die nächstgelegene Niederlassung oder Schweizerische Kreditanstalt, Abteilung Pvz, Postfach, 8021 Zürich.

**SCHWEIZERISCHE KREDITANSTALT
SKA**

From the 1988 advertising campaign for SKA's 'plus' range of services.

From agreements and protectionism to competition

For decades, the conventions of the Swiss Bankers' Association and the so-called 'Platzkonvenien' (local agreements) ensured that banking services and business processes were more or less uniform throughout Switzerland. These agreements ('conventions') prevented free competition and protected structures that were becoming increasingly obsolete. Once they had been abolished, the banks very swiftly developed new products and distribution channels – not least as a result of advances in information technology. In an increasingly tough competitive environment, banks differentiated themselves from each other initially through pricing policy and product ranges. In the age of the Internet and the virtual bank, however, optimum customer advisory services, tailored solutions and branding are becoming the decisive elements in the battle for market share.

From personal dialogue over the counter, to multi-channel management: a revolution in communication with customers.

New products for new customers

For more than a hundred years, SKA communicated with its personal customers exclusively by means of personal dialogue – at the bank counter, in the bank's offices or over the telephone. For many years the bank's products, which covered the classic range from personal accounts to custody accounts, from collateralized loans to safe deposit boxes, were aimed at a clearly defined, relatively narrow customer base.

Then the economic growth of the 1960s forced SKA to adopt a new strategy. Rising incomes meant that ever-wider sections of the population could be considered as potential new customers. Until then, the usual practice had been for the bank to wait for customers to come through its doors, but now investment advisors began to go out and actively look for clients. They visited specific key groups, organizing specially tailored events such as investment seminars for women, doctors and dentists. Such presentations served first and foremost as opportunities to build up and nurture personal contacts.

The bank's range of products was systematically expanded to appeal to new customer segments. SKA, for example, entered the consumer credit market through its subsidiary Allianz Kredit AG.

From 1977 onwards, personal and consumer loans were offered directly by all of SKA's branch offices.[613] This was a strategic move, since the bank hoped that it would be possible to persuade loan applicants to entrust their deposit business to SKA too. A similar motive lay behind the bank's involvement in leasing business, which was initially offered exclusively to corporate customers. CS Leasing AG was founded in 1969 and dealt primarily with finance for movable capital goods.[614]

In 1969, SKA began to court another new target group with the introduction of its salary account. As far as the bank was concerned, this was a tool for the acquisition of customer deposits: the expectation was that once customers had diverted their monthly payments from these accounts, a basic amount of money would remain with the bank at all times – another welcome source of deposit funds. The bank also hoped that these accounts would provide the foundation for a lasting banking relationship. Out of a desire to tap into future potential, the bank also made the account available to 16 to 20-year-olds, even if they were only being paid modest apprentice's wages.[615] In 1970, SKA introduced its savings book and personal account, backing up these product launches with targeted advertising campaigns.

Cash any day, at any time

The possibilities first suggested by the drive-in bank were brought to fruition in 1968 with the introduction of the Bancomat ATMs: the banks were opening up new distribution and communication channels that gave them direct access to customers and allowed them to sell their products more efficiently. SKA was in the vanguard of this process in Switzerland.

1981 brochure advertising the bank's personal loans.

CS Auto Leasing

Es gibt nur wenige Autos, die Sie bei uns nicht leasen können.

Kinderträume und Spielzeugautos kann man natürlich auch bei uns nicht leasen. Wenn Sie aber einen Autowunsch haben, fahren Sie mit der CS Auto Leasing AG, einer Tochter der Schweizerischen Kreditanstalt, besonders gut. Sprechen Sie doch einmal mit dem Berater in der nächsten SKA-Niederlassung oder direkt mit dem Spezialisten bei der CS Auto Leasing AG, Tel. 01/305 42 11. Oder senden Sie ihm den Coupon und Sie bekommen postwendend Unterlagen.

Mein Wunsch: Ich möchte mehr Informationen über das CS Auto Leasing. Einsenden an: CS Auto Leasing AG, Postfach 590, 8021 Zürich oder an Ihre nächste **SKA-Niederlassung.**
Name, Vorname:
Firma:
Strasse, Nr:
PLZ, Ort: Tel:

CS AUTO LEASING AG

So gut wie gekauft.

From CS Auto Leasing AG's 1988 advertising campaign.

Banking from your car

SKA opened Switzerland's first 'Autobank' (drive-in bank) – at the time the biggest and most modern facility of its kind in Europe – on 7 June 1962 on the ground floor of the 'Bärenhof' building at St.-Peter-Strasse 17 in Zurich.[617] This revolutionary new service for Switzerland responded to a genuine need, as demonstrated by the many customers, 'who, because of the lack of parking in Zurich's business district, have often expressed to us their wish to be able to do their banking business without leaving the car'. Once in the SKA Autobank, the cars would drive round the one-way system to one of the eight counters that were located in a staggered arrangement in the middle of the building. There were seven counters for left-hand drive cars and one for right-hand drive vehicles.

A week after the opening, the *Neue Zürcher Zeitung* described this new way of carrying out bank business to its readers: 'When it enters the bank the car triggers a sensor on the floor which switches on a trail of lights to show the driver how to get to a free counter. [...] A speaker system is used to allow the driver to talk to the person behind the counter. [...] A cassette box which slides out from the counter at the height of the car window is used to exchange documents and money. As an outpost of the bank, the Autobank naturally ... keeps in constant contact with the departments and service areas at head office.'[618]

To start with, the Autobank, located close to Paradeplatz in the center of Zurich's financial district, met with a great demand from the public: 'In its first year it was visited by nearly 20,000 drivers. It is estimated that 10% of counter customers now use the Autobank, though the facility's capacity is by no means being exhausted.'[619] However, changing consumer habits and the increasingly precarious traffic situation in central Zurich in the 1970s gradually ate into the success of the Autobank. It became unprofitable and finally in 1983 it was closed down as a result of the OVA (Overhead Value Analysis) efficiency program.

In 1962, SKA opened Switzerland's first Autobank on the St.-Peter-Strasse in Zurich. The facility set new standards for Europe; eight counters ensured that waiting times were kept to a minimum.

The site of the 'Forum St. Peter' communications center, which was opened on 3 January 1990, had previously housed SKA's Monetarium (1970–1978) and Autobank (1962–1983). Photo taken around 1975.

In 1968, SKA, SVB, Bank Leu and SBV jointly launched the first Bancomat ATMs. These allowed customers to withdraw cash at any time of day or night. Photo taken in 1980.

The first Bancomats were a joint venture by SKA, SVB, Bank Leu and SBV. On 21 March 1968, cash dispensers were put into operation in Zurich, Basel, Bern, Geneva, Lausanne and St. Gallen.[616] For the first time, cash transactions could be carried out without personal contact at the bank counter. This significantly changed the nature of customer relations. The benefits were compelling: 24-hour service had become a reality. The machines were available for use at any time of day or night. However, despite considerable initial success, it was clear that the new system would only live up to its full potential if it could be introduced throughout the whole of Switzerland and if it could function independently of the house bank. It was not long before other banks joined the four pioneers, and by 1981, 72 Swiss banks were participating in a network of 237 Bancomats. Every ten seconds, cash was being withdrawn from a machine somewhere in Switzerland[620] and the Bancomat soon became a 'second wallet' for many customers.

No competitive pressure on the banks: the effect of conventions

Structural changes in the banking sector left deep marks in the Switzerland of the 1990s.[621] By the end of 1998 there were only 376 independent financial institutions in the country, compared with 495 in 1990. Over the same period, the number of domestic bank branches fell from 4,161 to 3,199.[622] This clear-out within the Swiss banking industry had started in the 1980s, but the process was accelerated by three developments that occurred virtually simultaneously: the recession, the real estate crisis and the phased abolition of the conventions among the Swiss banks. The latter process began in 1989 when the anti-trust authorities demanded the immediate termination of major agreements between the banks. For the banks, this marked the start of a new era: 'Their world is no longer the same as it once was'[623], is how the *Tages-Anzeiger* newspaper described the change.

In the Swiss banking sector, as in other branches of the economy, free competition had been restricted for many decades by a dense web of regulation. The first convention governing bills of exchange transactions dates back to 1914. The primary aim of such conventions was to protect small providers and thus to ensure that Swiss banking would retain its diversity. Conventions were used to fix prices and conditions for services, thus removing margin pressure from the banks. Until the end of the 1980s, the key competitive criteria were closeness to customers, competence and service quality. Meanwhile, pricing – the level of interest rates and fees – was largely standardized across the industry by virtue of the agreements made amongst the market participants. As a result, there was a distinct absence of competition within the industry, and thus also a lack of creativity. The only area where competition was a factor was in the highly unquantifiable discipline of service quality.

By the time the Cartel Commission began its investigation into banking conventions in 1989, the Swiss banks had concluded numerous agreements, the most famous of which was the Courtage Convention on brokerage fees. The main forces behind the cartel agreements were the Swiss Bankers' Association and the local and regional banking associations. There were also accords made within individual banking groups. Finally, the Association of Swiss Securities Exchanges and the underwriting syndicates also promulgated important cartel agreements. The Swiss Bankers' Association had an array of instruments at its disposal for regulating the industry, including guidelines, circulars, conventions, and recommendations. The conventions themselves were made in the form of contracts among the banks that bound them all to behave in a certain way.[624]

Prices and conditions: detailed rules and regulations

By the mid-1980s there were 16 conventions sponsored by the Swiss Bankers' Association. A particularly important one was Convention III on customer acquisition and advertising, which included a crucial supplement restricting the use of advertisements in consumer credit business. This supplement, which evolved from various guidelines and came into force in 1980, drastically reduced the banks' advertising options. They were not allowed, for example, to give away gifts worth more than Sfr 5 at local events or during tours of bank premises.[625] Initial bonus payments on deposit accounts opened for new-born babies could not exceed Sfr 20; only two campaigns a year involving promotional gifts were permitted, and each bank could only hold one competition per year. Most of the conventions were concerned with detailed rules on the processes and conditions

The removal of conventions led to price competition and product differentiation.

Underwriting consortia and major bank syndicates

The banks were quick to realize that they could optimize the opportunities and risks involved in underwriting business by working together. In 1897, the Swiss major banks came together in an 'underwriting consortium', which from that point in time controlled the market as a cartel. Later on, this consortium was augmented by the Berner Kantonalbank and the 'Groupement des Banquiers Privés Genevois' to form the 'Emissionskonsortium Schweizerischer Banken' ('Swiss Banks' Underwriting Consortium'). The main aim of this grouping was to underwrite and issue all domestic public securities offerings by the federal government, cantons, towns and communities worth in excess of Sfr 6 million. In 1911, the consortium agreed with the 'Verband Schweizerischer Kantonalbanken' ('Association of Swiss Cantonal Banks') that public bond issues worth more than Sfr 12 million would be carried out by both organizations in partnership with each other. The 'Verband Schweizer Regionalbanken' ('Association of Swiss Regional Banks') also took part in this arrangement. These consortia also monopolized the market for private sector domestic and international issues, which became increasingly important in later years.

As well as the 'major bank syndicate' – which was formed by the major banks SBG, SBV, SKA, SVB and the cantonal banks especially to underwrite Swiss-franc bonds issued by foreign public-sector bodies and which was wound up at the start of the 1990s – there was also a 'major syndicate' for issues of domestic public sector bonds. This consisted of the 'Emissionskonsortium Schweizerischer Banken', the Swiss cantonal banks, the 'Verband Schweizer Regionalbanken' and the 'Gruppe deutschschweizerischer Privatbankiers' ('Group of Swiss-German Private Bankiers'). The banks concerned broke up the syndicate in 1989 on the recommendation of the Cartel Commission. The Commission had criticized the syndicate, 'for standing in the way of competition in the market for public sector bond issues over Sfr 20 million'.

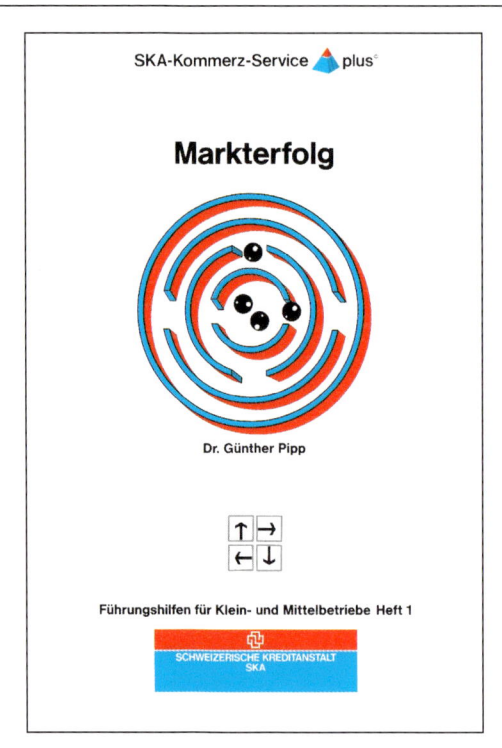

SKA has been publishing handbooks and manuals for different target groups for many years. Because these did not count as 'gifts' as defined by the Swiss Bankers' Association's Convention III, the bank could use such specialist information to advertise itself to broad groups of potential customers.

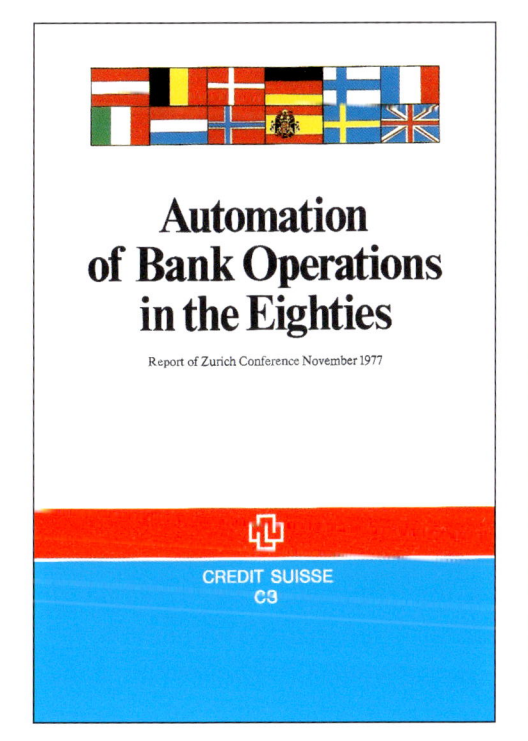

From agreements and protectionism to competition **363**

From the mid-1970s onwards, young people became an increasingly important customer segment. Advertisement for SKA's young people's salary account.

attached to banking services. Few agreements were made on interest rates under the aegis of the Swiss Bankers' Association; traditionally these were more the domain of local and regional accords, or 'Platzkonvenien'. However, the effect of these local agreements tended to extend beyond the immediate geographical area of influence and they were often harmonized with one another to become quasi-national in character.

For a long time, conventions exerted a substantial influence on the way the members of the Swiss Bankers' Association behaved, and the banks saw no contradiction between such compacts and the principles of a free market economy. The Swiss Bankers' Association regarded the conventions first and foremost as a way of preventing excessive competition between its members and thus making it easier for the weaker financial institutions to remain in existence. Seen from this point of view, the conventions offered a protective cloak to all financial services providers. In the 1980s, even the cartel commission still believed that the conventions helped to maintain a healthy diversity within the Swiss banking industry. Maintaining this diversity – and, in fact, the maintenance of existing structures in general – seemed to be a sacred duty that nobody dared challenge. Nevertheless, the conviction began to spread that the conventions were actually at the root of what had become an over-regulated system. By introducing and adhering to the conventions, the banks had bound themselves in chains. And the longer these chains held fast, the more their business operations suffered.

The end of the era of conventions

On 17 April 1989, the Cartel Commission published its report on 'Swiss-wide agreements in the banking industry'. Its investigations lead to 19 recommendations[626], ten of which were accepted by the banks without opposition. The Cartel Commission was prepared to make concessions on five of the contested conventions, but insisted that the other four be abolished. It immediately applied to the Federal Department of Economic Affairs (FDEA) to have the conventions quickly rescinded in stages. The banks, meanwhile, wanted to avoid a Swiss 'big bang' and campaigned for a more gradual implementation of the Cartel Commission's recommendations. In response to the idea that SKA should withdraw from all conventions, the bank noted that 'deregulation does not just have positive effects on a market'[627] and that the withdrawal of a major bank could 'set off a domino effect'. The SKA executive board stated that 'at the current time [1990], the withdrawal of SKA is not regarded as opportune'.[628] Despite such protests, the FDEA shortened the timetable for implementation of the recommendations. The banks now had to make some quick decisions, and the syndicate of major banks accepted the competition authorities decree. On 4 October 1990, the Association of Swiss Securities Exchanges followed suit and agreed to abolish the Courtage Convention by the end of the year. At the same time, the Swiss Bankers' Association decided not to contest the disputed convention on documentary credits any longer. However, it did

At the end of the 1960s, investment funds were introduced in Switzerland for the first time. From the start, SKA was one of the leading providers. In the 1980s and 1990s, the bank built up its funds business systematically and successfully.

decide to lodge an appeal against the FDEA's instruction to terminate the convention on custody account fees. This issue thus remained as the sole subject of the case brought before the supreme court.[629] Eventually, however, even this dispute was brought to an end when the board of directors of the Swiss Bankers' Association decided to terminate the custody account convention too. As a result, on 10 June 1993, the Cartel Commission announced that it regarded its investigation into the Swiss-wide agreements at work in the banking industry as ended.

With 'yourhome', a portal for information about home buying and home ownership, Credit Suisse is setting new standards for banking e-business. The service offers not only mortgage products, but also, thanks to partnerships with an initial 18 providers, everything else that could be of interest to the home-buyer or home owner: from finding apartments and houses, to planning, financing and construction, to moving house, furnishings and garden design.

'Pressure on earnings margins will increase, and the wheat will be separated from the chaff' (Rainer E. Gut in the *NZZ*, 13 April 1989).

Once the conventions had been abolished, competition between the banks intensified. Pressure on prices steadily increased, prompting the SKA executive board to state: 'The time of conventions is over; this means that we can no longer do everything and cross-subsidize services.'[630] Instead, the profitability of every product had to be measured individually; furthermore, the banks started to try and distinguish themselves from their competitors through deliberate product differentiation and product innovation.

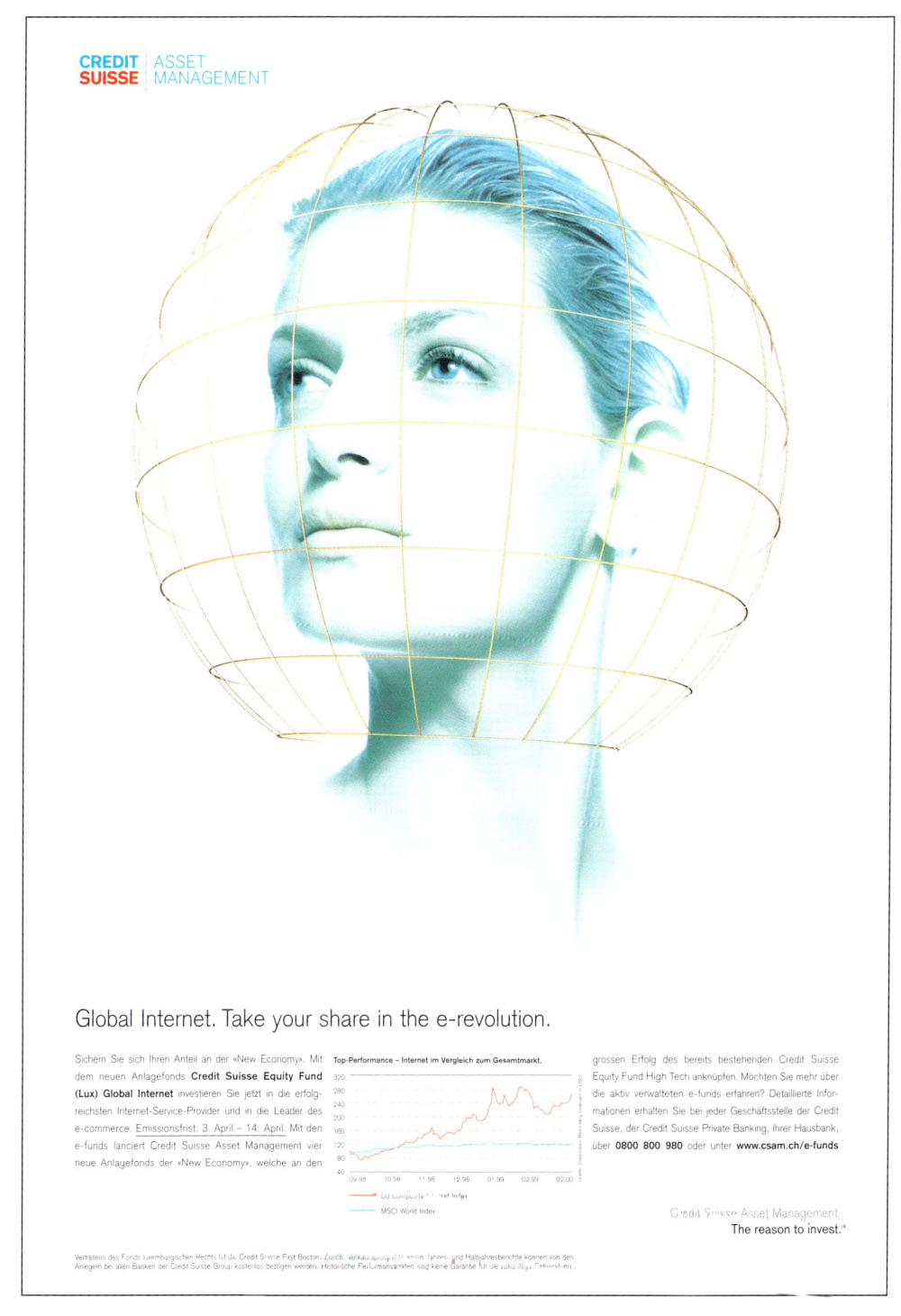

Part of the 2000 advertising campaign for Credit Suisse Asset Management's investment funds.

'youtrade' was developed jointly by the Credit Suisse and Credit Suisse Private Banking business units, and was launched in 1999. The new service offers customers access to the stock market via the Internet.

Financial institutions with favorable cost structures and/or substantial capital strength attempted to increase their market share by offering more attractive terms and conditions. In order to maintain revenue levels, as well as to expand market share, and thus make use of economies of scale, the stronger institutions began to absorb more and more of the weaker banks. SKA, for example, acquired Bank Leu, SVB and the NAB. Freed from the drastic restrictions imposed by the conventions, advertising became extremely important. The

In 1986, Telebanking was introduced as SKA's first Videotex product.

Cover of the 'CS Direct Invest' advertising brochure from 1996.

marketing methods that had already been employed by other industries, began to feature in the banking sector too. Free competition accelerated the pace of structural change.[631] It became a matter of the survival of the fittest, and the number of banks rapidly fell. Deregulation was the guiding principle of the time, and Switzerland could not escape its influence. The ability to compete on the international stage increasingly became the only benchmark that counted. Having been through this process of structural adjustment and concentration, the Swiss banking system and the Swiss financial center in general is today a model of flexibility and dynamism.

The benefits of modern communications technology

The introduction of Bancomat ATMs marked the start of a profound process of development that led to the creation of various information and communication channels, and ultimately to multi-channel management. One of SKA's strategies was to use the groundbreaking progress made in electronic data processing and information technology since the 1970s to optimize its internal processes and intensify customer relations.

SKA's computer-supported AIS investment information system, introduced in 1983, was an important new facility for customers, and the first service of its kind offered by any of the Swiss major banks. AIS was a modular system that allowed relationship managers to update customers on the latest details of their portfolios at any time. The advantage of AIS was that it could produce a wide variety of analyses and procure the required information extremely quickly. Parts of AIS were later made available to safekeeping account holders via Videotex.

Telebanking, first offered by SKA in March 1985 as part of its operational trials for Videotex, represented another step in the direction of unlimited access to banking products. Users now had independence not only with regard to opening hours, but also in terms of location. Videotex allowed them to use the available services from their homes or offices; they benefited from 24-hour access to financial information and could carry out banking transactions whenever they liked.

In 1986, the bank introduced SKA direct TEL, which provided customers with a 24-hour hotline. SKA believed that customers would value such a facility, 'especially in emergencies; for example if their ec-code were to be misused by an unauthorized party'.[632]

Another milestone in the evolution of what was eventually to become today's direct banking was achieved in 1993. On midnight on the night running into Sunday 15 May 1993, SKA opened Switzerland's first ever telephone bank with 32 staff in Horgen. The new bank offered a 24-hour service, 365 days a year. Customers could ring up for account and portfolio information, as well as carry out payment and securities transactions. Expert advisors gave out information about bank products in four languages.

The service, which went by the name of 'CS Firstphone', provided a complete banking solution for personal customers. Exactly one year later, CS Firstphone Business was launched. This allowed companies, too, to benefit from the advantages of round-the-clock access to their bank. In 1995, CS Direct Invest was introduced. This service allowed customers to execute investment transactions whenever they liked. Firstphone was a significant component of a new retail banking strategy that aimed to offer existing customers a greatly enhanced service, while at the same appealing to new potential client bases. In Firstphone's three-year trial phase, 30,000 new users were acquired as planned.[633]

With the Internet into a new millennium

In 1997, the banks of the Credit Suisse Group started to use the Internet as a communication and distribution channel. It was clear that the Internet would revolutionize banking, and Credit Suisse took a pioneering role, helping to shape the developments that were made. Indeed in 1999/2000 the Lafferty Group repeatedly praised the Credit Suisse website for being the best Internet service offered by any bank in Europe.

Credit Suisse was quick to recognize that the Internet was destined to be used to distribute bank services: being composed principally of data and with no physical components, such services were perfect for the new medium.[634] On 12 April 1999, Credit Suisse launched 'youtrade', thus becoming the first Swiss bank to offer a discount brokerage service on the Internet.[635] Initially, 'youtrade' offered the opportunity to trade in any security listed on the Swiss stock exchange. Credit Suisse's Swiss competitors were quick to follow its pioneering lead: speed of action had become vital to survival in the financial services markets. Because the products offered by different providers on the Internet began to resemble each other more and more, price started to play a decisive role too, and for a time Credit Suisse's online bank offered lower fees than any of its Swiss competitors.

By the end of 1999, 'youtrade' had attracted 12,000 users, 50% of whom were new customers. The fight for customers demanded that services be improved all the time, and Credit Suisse was soon expanding its Internet trading platform. The most important new features included access to other stock markets, first in the USA and then in Germany, and the option of receiving news, analyses and investment recommendations (either via e-mail or via 'short messaging' on a mobile phone). Real-time prices could be called up free of charge. Credit Suisse launched its news, stock recommendation and key data service in October 1999, followed by its interactive share trading service via mobile phone – in partnership with Swisscom – in the first quarter of 2000. The bank's strategic aim was to cover all the key stock markets as fast as possible, and to keep up with the latest technological developments.

Credit Suisse Private Banking also made sure that it was in the vanguard of Internet banking, launching Fund Lab in 1998. Fund Lab is an Internet site that supplies information on investment funds. Further Internet services followed in 1999, this time giving investors a comprehensive overview of new issues of all

When it was introduced in 1993, CS Firstphone was the only product of its kind in Switzerland.

types of security and of traded derivatives. As with Fund Lab, the information available from these services extended beyond Credit Suisse Private Banking's own products and services, with other leading international issuing houses being invited to publicize their products on the Credit Suisse Private Banking site.

Multi-channel management is the only way to succeed

Internet – or virtual – banking is not, however, intended to replace branch banking. Credit Suisse Group's strategy is based instead on integrated multi-channel management, which allows the customer to choose from a number of complementary channels – branches, ATMs, phone banking and Internet Banking – and to use the one which is most suitable on a case by case basis.

Just how attractive and important Internet banking is to Credit Suisse Group is reflected in the following statistics: if the cost of a banking transaction at a branch comes to 100%, the cost of the same transaction via phone banking is 22% and via the Internet only 8%.[636]

Credit Suisse as a first mover in Internet banking

'The Swiss banks are taking a leading role in Internet banking in Europe – especially Credit Suisse, which consistently tops the rankings in various ratings. Credit Suisse was quick to make the Internet a key strategic priority. Like others, the bank went through a number of phases, but has always been a first mover. It was Credit Suisse, for example, that in 1995 became the first Swiss major bank with its own web page on the Net. Shortly afterwards, its Internet presence was enhanced by interactive offerings. In April 1997 it became the first Swiss bank to offer a comprehensive Internet banking solution. In April 1999 it launched Switzerland's first online brokerage service. Credit Suisse is currently transforming itself from an Internet bank into an "electronic commerce bank" or "e-bank" for short' (René Louis *Schweizerische Informatikrevue*, 4/1999, p.24)

From agreements and protectionism to competition 371

> # Wie kommen Sie am schnellsten zu den Fonds unserer Konkurrenten?
>
> **FUND LAB** ist eine innovative Dienstleistung der Credit Suisse Private Banking. Diese interaktive Internet-Software ermöglicht es Ihnen, unsere eigenen wie auch fremde Anlagefonds unseres Angebots zu vergleichen, sich über Details zu informieren und so eine Auswahl zu treffen, die Ihren Bedürfnissen entspricht. Nehmen Sie mit uns Kontakt auf unter Telefon **+41 1 335 40 40** oder **www.cspb.com/fundlab**
>
> **CREDIT SUISSE | PRIVATE BANKING**   **FUND LAB. It's time for an expert.**

The 'Fund Lab' Internet site created by Credit Suisse Private Banking in 1998 gives customers an overview of investment funds. What was completely new was that a bank that had its own funds to sell also included funds provided by its competitors in the range shown to customers. The idea is that investors can buy the funds that best suit their needs, no matter who the provider is. This very open approach was warmly welcomed by the market.

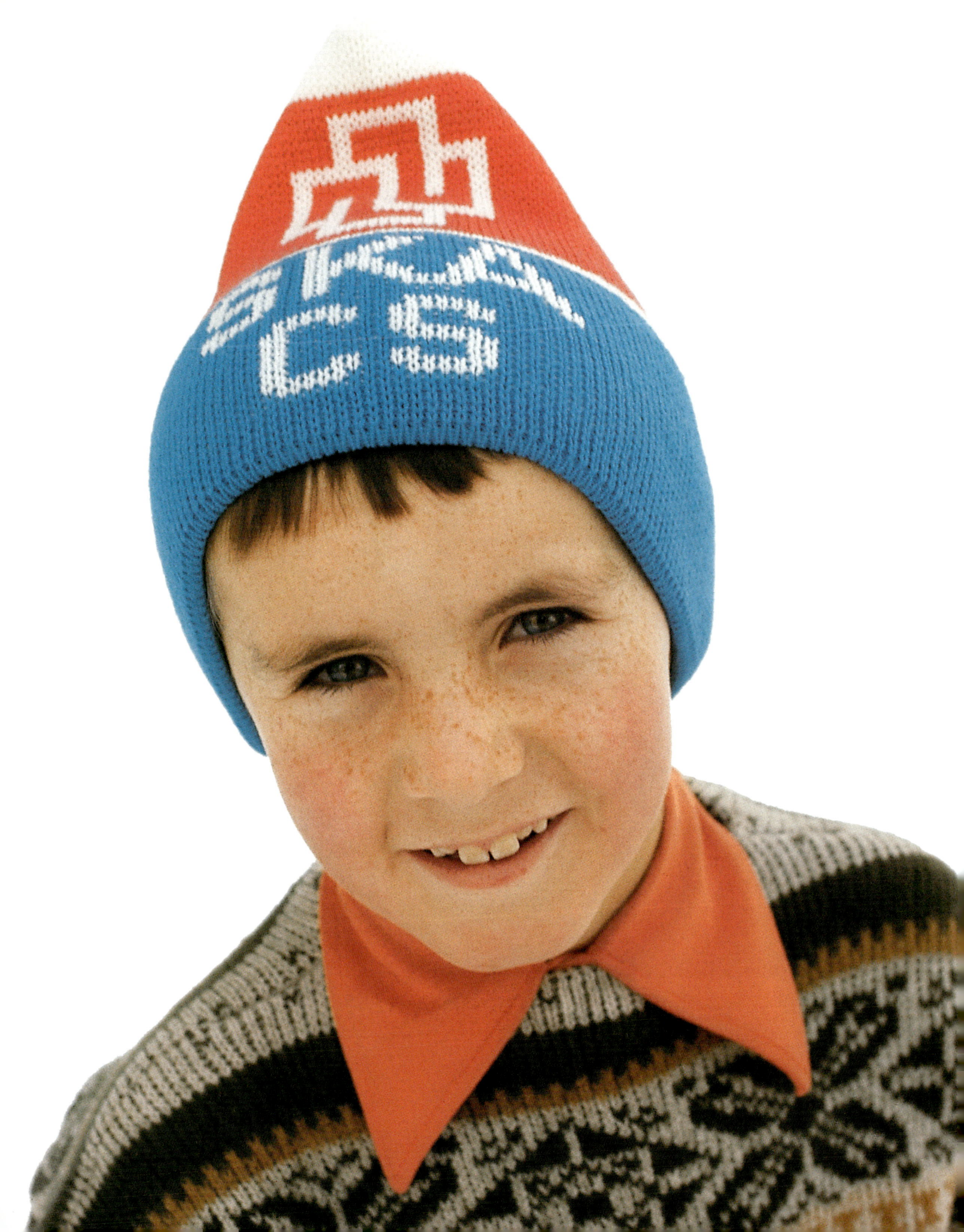

Marketing and communication

Unlike other branches of the economy, such as the consumer goods sector, the banking industry did not develop a serious interest in the tools of marketing until the 1960s. Until then, marketing had been of little significance to the banks because they were not compelled to go out and actively court customers or sell products: clients simply came to the banks of their own accord. The following section looks at the history of SKA's marketing and communications work, focusing particularly on the 'bulletin' magazine, advertising, sponsorship, art, and bank architecture. To start with, we take an overview of the key phases in this history.

The SKA ski hat was one of the most successful 'freebies' in advertising history: between 1976 and 1993, SKA gave away more than 800,000 of them. Photo taken around 1980.

Cartoonist Nico designed the 1969 advertising campaign for SKA's new salary accounts.

SKA started to court new groups of customers in the second half of the 1970s. In 1979, the desire to become a bank for the whole population was expressed in the slogans 'SKA – für alle da' ('SKA – there for everyone') and 'De père en fils au Crédit Suisse' ('From father to son: Credit Suisse'). Sticker for the launch of the new children's saving account, 1984.

SKA moves towards an explicit marketing strategy

The anniversary of 1956

Since 1895, SKA had maintained close contact with a specialist audience through its self-produced publications (*Effekten-Kursblatt*, *bulletin*). However, until the 1960s, the bank only really thought about communicating with the wider population when it came to its anniversaries. A good example of this approach is provided by the activity surrounding the bank's centenary in 1956, which SKA used as a welcome opportunity to draw attention to itself.

To celebrate the anniversary, wall calendars, New Year's cards, pocket diaries and note paper were produced that explicitly referred to the bank's 100 years of existence. The bank also commissioned a corporate history to be written[637], whole-page advertisements were placed in newspapers, and anniversary posters were designed for head office and the branches. At head office on Paradeplatz in Zurich, the display windows hosted an exhibition celebrating the key events in the bank's history. For the first time ever, a neon sign was erected on the main building, advertising the fact of the anniversary in large letters.[638] Staff parties were organized at head office and in the branches.

All the activities centered on image marketing; product marketing was only peripheral. Another feature of the marketing of that time was that there was absolutely no follow-up once the celebrations were over.[639]

Modernization and systemization of marketing activities

1965 was an important year in the development of SKA's marketing. Firstly, the bank's propaganda and public relations department was established that year; secondly, 1965 was also the year in which the bank started to work with external marketing specialists. In the words of the executive board, the aim of such cooperation was, 'to put our advertising and marketing on a new footing'.[640] The new approach was also intended to increase the volume of customer deposits.

In 1967, staff from various parts of the bank were brought together in a propaganda working group to discuss ways of further improving SKA's marketing. Two years later, the bank commissioned the Somafa market research institution to analyze advertisements put out by SKA, 'in order to discover whether the route taken thus far … was the right one, or whether the often-stated concern that too much money was being spent on advertising was true'.[641] The institution's findings were fundamentally positive, but certain deficiencies were identified, particularly with regard to the credibility of the advertisements amongst the younger generation.

The study also made it clear that though SKA's advertising and PR efforts were now better planned and more systematic, they were still compromised by the fact that they merely reacted to specific events and situations in piecemeal fashion rather than being bound into an overall marketing strategy. Marketing efforts came across as a colorful bouquet of isolated measures.

Having accepted that a service company like SKA could only implement its marketing activities efficiently if they were part of an overall strategy, in spring 1975 the bank created an internal interdisciplinary marketing commission, which concentrated primarily on defining SKA's business philosophy and target audience. The commission also promoted staff training and staff communications, as well as encouraging greater cooperation between different departments in order to exploit opportunities for cross-selling more effectively. The commission thoroughly analyzed SKA's current marketing activities and tried to correct the weaknesses it found.[642]

The turning point of 1978: from reaction to action

Hardly had the marketing commission begun its work, when the Chiasso Affair reared its head. SKA was forced to use all of its resources to embark on a course of uncompromising modernization; the bank had to grow, and it had to attract more customer deposits. Marketing was integrated into the bank's business strategy. This manifested itself very clearly in 1978 when all of SKA's communications tools were brought together into the newly created economics, public relations and sales promotion subdivision. This reorganization aimed 'to improve the co-ordination of the different instruments used for PR work, advertising and sales; to increase their effectiveness and to promote the distribution of our bank services'.[643]

The new subdivision, headed by Hans J. Mast, reported directly to the spokesman for the executive board Rainer E. Gut, underlining the importance that SKA's top management afforded to this area.

One of the key goals of the new marketing strategy was to go beyond mere organizational changes and to genuinely systematize the bank's various activities. In order to do this, the bank created a new tool: the marketing plan. This was a management and communications tool which allowed the bank to determine in minute detail who had to do what, where and when.

This approach was characteristic of SKA's new view of marketing: despite the attempts at co-ordination, the discipline was still regarded as a group of isolated measures. One activity should follow the next, one package of measures replace the last one. The bank's individual image-related or product-related objectives were implemented as part of an overall communications mix, but there was still no overriding marketing strategy.

The new central marketing plan centered on the twin aims of 'popularizing' and 'regionalizing' SKA. In order to achieve these goals, the bank attempted to extend its operations to regions in which it had previously hardly been present at all. At the same time, the bank was concentrating on gaining new customers. Marketing efforts were intended to support these two main aims. It made a lot of sense, therefore, when in 1978 SKA became the main sponsor of the Tour de Suisse cycle race, the largest mass sporting event in Switzerland. Sponsorship of the race also helped to popularize the new SKA logo: the bank had recently added red to the previously dominant blue to create a widely recognized visual image. Similar intentions lay behind another marketing activi-

'One major deficiency is that there is no motivation for staff at any level to adopt a market oriented approach.' Furthermore, 'only two thirds of staff at head office hold staff accounts with the bank' (Marketing commission, 1975).

In 1977, SKA held its first ever competition for the general public: 'Schöne Bräuche – schöne Preise' ('Attractive customs – attractive prizes'). Entrants had to correctly identify six Swiss customs from photographs. Pictured above is a New Year's doll from the Appenzell town of Urnäsch.

Features of the customer focus group

- Long-term analysis involving more than 1,000 respondents
- Monitors the same sample group's opinions, expectations and habits over time
- Written questionnaire on fixed and variable subjects three times a year
- Panel members provide a continuous description and evaluation of contacts with the bank (and with other banks)
- Basis for product innovations and monitoring of product range

The 'plus' strategy launched in 1982 raised great expectations amongst customers. SKA fulfilled these expectations by offering clear added value in comparison with rival products.

Employees of SKA are moving further and further away from the 'bank clerk' mentality. They are becoming customer and market-oriented.

ty: the production of a series of publications with suggestions for cycling tours. The promotion of popular participation sports was an ideal complement to the bank's sponsorship of elite cycling. SKA scored a massive hit with its promotional ski hats and sports bags, and with the pocket timetables it produced in cooperation with Swiss Federal Railways. The slogans 'SKA – für alle da' and 'De père en fils au Crédit Suisse' also helped to give the bank a more populist image.

Immediately after the marketing department was created, SKA also took on specialist staff to form a competence center for market research. There were two aims here: firstly, the bank wanted to see how effective its marketing activities were; secondly it wanted to collect information relevant to its strategy so that it could better assess its own position with regard to products and customer segments.

The market research department proved to be extremely useful, producing high quality work and, for instance, forming Switzerland's only customer focus group for long-term market analysis.[645]

The 1980s: the development of strategic marketing

SKA created bank marketing history in 1982 when it launched its multi-service 'plus' range of products onto the market. First of all came the 'SKA salary account plus', to be joined in later years by more and more 'plus' products, including a payments service, commercial banking service and a savings plan. The 'plus' concept greatly improved SKA's image and helped it to win market share at the expense of its competitor banks. The 'plus' range was part of a long-term concept that aimed to give customers added value – a 'plus' – by comparison with the ranges offered by other banks.

Regardless of the significance of the 'plus' strategy, it must be acknowledged that this 'multi-service' concept had a major flaw: it still paid too little attention to profitability. Because there was initially no proper control and monitoring of marketing in the 1980s, it was impossible to measure how successful the individual marketing measures were.

SKA's added value strategy was intended to impact not only on products but also on service quality. Two campaigns were thus launched with the aim of improving customer service.

Image studies indicated that there was plenty of potential for the bank to further develop its service quality. This prompted the executive board, which had declared the issue a matter of the utmost priority, to launch a campaign under the slogan 'Rasch, kompetent, freundlich' ('Fast, competent, friendly'), the idea being to make the bank's image more customer-friendly. The campaign was repeated in 1988 using a cloverleaf symbol. A market study in April of that year had shown that what customers wanted more than anything else was competent specialist advice. The campaign was also repeated because SKA's image had deteriorated again between 1986 and 1988, specifically with regard to the friendliness of its staff and speed of service. 'SKA service' was now barely any different from the service provided by other banks.

Corporate communication through the years

The tools used to build up and maintain relations between the bank and the social and political world around it have changed fundamentally over the course of SKA's history. Originally, managers took on a great number of management functions and political offices simultaneously, but as time went on, an increasing number of specialist staff units were set up in the stead of such accumulations of individual power. In the 19th century, members of the board of directors exercised operational management roles and often held important political mandates as National Councillors or members of the upper house of Switzerland's parliament. In the 20th century, a countervailing trend helped to bring an end to such dual roles. It became increasingly difficult to be member of the SKA executive board and a parliamentarian at the same time. 'The conservative parties are reluctant to adopt bankers onto their election lists', commented Adolf Jöhr in 1946. The then chairman of the SKA board of directors went on to say: 'It is harder for a banker than for a member of any other profession to act on the political stage without running the risk of putting his foot in it.'[644]

Meanwhile, SKA repeatedly appointed federal parliamentarians to sit on its board of directors in an effort to ensure that the bank could remain in touch with political developments. From the beginning of the 1970s onwards, SKA, initially in partnership with the other major banks, arranged regular meetings between leading bankers and parliamentarians to discuss economic, financial and social issues of concern to the banking industry. From 1976, SKA, now acting alone, organized several such meetings every year. To start with, representatives of all the conservative parties were invited together, though later on the meetings tended to be with each of the major parties separately.

SKA's commitment to Switzerland's political and social development also manifested itself in the late 1960s with the creation of a discussion forum for subjects of concern to the wider population. In 1968 in Zurich, for example, the bank organized a seminar on 'Switzerland and European Integration'. About a hundred business leaders and politicians from various parties took part in the event, debating Switzerland's relationship with the European Economic Community (EEC). The subject had become very topical in Switzerland after EFTA countries – including the United Kingdom – had mooted the possibility of entry into the EEC. Another example is the meeting about 'Financing the Economy', organized by SKA following the oil crisis of 1973. With events like these, SKA was breaking new ground.

Even before the 1960s SKA had kept the public informed about business and economic topics on a case by case basis, using various channels such as press releases, media conferences and articles in the bank's own customer magazine (*bulletin*). During the 1960s, it then began to professionalize its public relations work, bringing all the different strands together in newly created specialized staff units. This trend was accelerated in the late 1970s by the internationalization of the bank, the Chiasso Affair, and the subsequent referendum on the Social Democrat's banking initiative. An attempt to systematize media work had been made a few years before with the establishment of a dedicated public relations subdivision, which reported directly to the executive board. This subdivision brought together three previously separate areas: the press office, the propaganda bureau (later to become the advertising and marketing services department) and the central publications distribution office.

However, the real professionalization of the bank's PR work was triggered by the Chiasso Affair. Because until then, information given to the public had been more or less limited to sporadic reports about key events at the bank, SKA was completely unprepared for the crisis. In the immediate aftermath, the bank did not know which way to turn and as a result of the acute lack of information, SKA and its managers were pilloried unmercifully in the press. It was quite a while before at least some of the damage done to the bank's image was repaired through proactive corporate communication and the coordinated use of marketing communication. The lessons learnt during Chiasso formed the basis for a modern, active and transparent approach to PR work at the bank.

As one of the consequences of the Chiasso Affair, in 1978 the new economics, public relations and sales promotion subdivision was created. It reported directly to the spokesman for the executive board (president of the executive board from 1982) and for the first time brought all of the bank's communication activities together within a central unit.

The bank now also developed its first proper communications strategy. It included the adoption of groundbreaking new instruments such as an active 'issues management' program; this acted as an early warning system, letting the bank know in good time about important events and developments and ensuring that the appropriate communications measures were put in place. An 'ad hoc unit for unexpected events', headed by a member of the executive board, developed a set of responses to be used in crisis situations. Most important of all, however, the new, professional PR policy promoted regular, targeted contact with the media as well as discussions with politicians and the authorities at all levels – activities in which the president of the executive board himself was to take an active role.

In the wake of SKA's expansion and thorough rejuvenation in the 1980s and 1990s, the communications area underwent a series of restructurings. When the divisional organizational structure was introduced in 1987, the communications department was divided into two, with the economics subdivision on one side and the corporate secretariat, public relations, marketing services and advertising department on the other. The latter department's job was to develop and implement a targeted, image-focused communications and information strategy. In 1990, a further refinement of the different functions was made with the creation of an autonomous marketing, advertising and sponsorship subdivision. Following further realignments in 1994, public relations remained in the corporate secretariat and corporate communications subdivision, which also included the press office as well as the 'public affairs' staff unit that looked after the bank's political concerns.

There was also a steady improvement in the range of communications instruments used. The annual report, for example, was expanded so that it could be used not only as the bank's statutory financial report, but also as a flagship PR tool. The information it contained, as well as its design and appearance, were improved and adapted to match SKA's modern corporate identity.

In the 1980s, the bank began to expand its corporate communications in a targeted fashion to encompass the international arena too. With the USA being adopted as a new home market, the bank set up its first satellite communications department in New York. This new department dedicated itself to cultivating SKA's public image on the American continent.

In the meantime, Credit Suisse Group, as a globally active financial services company, has had to master the many responsibilities that have arisen as a result of the internationalization of communications work in a rapidly changing environment. Nowadays the Group runs separate departments for public relations, public affairs and investor relations. All of the business units also have their own PR and marketing departments. Communications work in a global environment requires expertise and sensitivity with regard to the bank's public image in different political systems and cultures, as well as a firm grasp of the workings of the international media. Personal contacts with political decision-makers remain important, and 'issues management' is also still a key factor in international communications work. The dormant accounts issue shows just how important it is for the bank to be able to deal with 'reputational risks'. In order to be able to anticipate possible problems more effectively, in March 1999 Credit Suisse Group established a Swiss and an international advisory board, each of which is made up of leading political and business figures. The job of these consultative committees is to provide support and advice for the bank's decision-making bodies.

The SKA name stood for top performance; this was symbolized by the pyramid.

Marketing budgets: SKA compared with SBG and SBV

'In 1991 we are putting Sfr 38 million into central marketing. In addition, Sfr 7.5 million is going to the PR subdivision; as well as press work, this will finance the *bulletin*, the annual report and our publications in particular. About 20% of the overall marketing budget will be available to the 17 regions and their 200 branches for local and regional activities. As far as the use of funds is concerned, it is worth drawing a comparison with our main competitors. We know that SBV and SBG each invest between 50% and 100% more money than us in marketing services. For instance, we spend about Sfr 2 million p.a. on youth marketing, while SBV and SBG have youth marketing budgets of about Sfr 5–6 million and of over Sfr 10 million respectively. These enormous sums are used to provide many discounts and prizes in an often irrational fight for promising customer segments.'[646]

The founding of the *Effekten-Kursblatt* (1895), and its transformation into the illustrated banking magazine *bulletin* (1970), are milestones in the history of banking publications.

Whereas the main aim of previous marketing campaigns had been to make up the ground lost to the other major banks, or at least to ensure that the gap did not grow any wider, in the 1980s, SKA's prime objective was to profile itself as the leading bank in Switzerland. The pyramid symbol introduced to its publicity material in 1985 was a visual expression of this aim to be at the top of the business.

The 1990s: from marketing as communication to integrated product and segment strategies

For a long time, SKA understood marketing merely as a mix of different communication instruments, but 1993 saw a structural change. The idea of marketing merely as a way of communicating evolved into a new concept incorporating products, prices and distribution. Building on the successful concepts of the 1980s, marketing is nowadays fully integrated into the bank's product and segment strategies. On top of this, SKA has consistently developed new products such as CS Firstphone, CS Direct TEL and CS Direct Invest, setting standards that have often been copied by competitors.

The success of SKA's marketing activities is all the more impressive when one recalls that the marketing budgets of the bank's main competitors, SBG and SBV, were much larger than SKA's. Aware of this situation, SKA dedicated itself to efficiency, integration and continuity in its marketing.

Finally, in the mid-1990s, the bank's marketing strategy was augmented by additional objectives.[647] In particular, these included the further development of customer care activities, greater attention to individual customer wishes (fewer standardized products, more tailor-made solutions) and the consolidation of the bank's position as a market leader in the provision of banking services via new distribution channels.

'bulletin' as a visiting card

From the 'Effekten-Kursblatt', to the 'Monats-Bulletin', to 'bulletin' magazine

In 1895 the bank launched the *Effekten-Kursblatt der Schweizerischen Kreditanstalt in Zürich* (Effekten-Kursblatt means 'list of stock prices') as a pioneering supplement to its annual report. Horst Pastuszek, in his book *Wirtschaftsordnung und Wirtschaftspublizistik*, described it as the world's first regular publication by a bank.[648] By the end of 1920, the publication was being produced monthly. Initially, it contained unadorned details of selected bonds and Swiss shares, the primary aim being simply to keep the bank's commercial and industrial customers informed about the latest investment opportunities. As early as 1896/97, however, the *Kursblatt* added detailed money market and stock exchange reports, as well as reports on the general economic situation. Then in 1904, it increased its value to customers greatly by publishing its first annual review of political and economic developments in Switzerland and abroad. The 'Financial notes' section added in 1907 marked a further improvement. Remarkably, SKA started publishing a French version of the *Kursblatt* as early as 1902, even though it would not open its first branch in French-speaking Western Switzerland – in Geneva – until four years later.

In 1921, SKA published the first edition of the *Monats-Bulletin* ('Monthly bulletin').[649] This switch to a bulletin in handy paperback form garnered a fair amount of praise. The old content was retained, but it was enhanced by new features such as a leading article. Each December issue contained an index for the previous year's editions – a tangible expression of the belief that the *Monats-Bulletin* would be collected as a working resource and as a valuable source of information. In December 1944, 50 years after it first came out, the publication was renamed *Bulletin*.

Over the course of the 1960s, the title page was redesigned several times: first of all, the blue bars were moved upwards, then the most important articles were trailed using headlines. In March 1968, the editors started using the white Wermelinger cross against a dark-blue background. The main movers behind the scenes at this point were Hans J. Mast, the great writer and internationally renowned economic and interest rate forecaster, and the young editor Victor Erne. These two were already planning a radical overhaul of the publication, for a time even considering producing a magazine that could be sold at newspaper stands.

An illustrated banking magazine as a medium for corporate communications

The first edition of the new *bulletin*, which appeared in July 1970, represented a quantum leap in publishing. The new concept was based on four basic ideas:

- Increase the amount of information for customers and staff
- Communicate customer information to employees as well (in the form of the staff *bulletin*)
- Integrate and periodically compile the individual editions to form a rich and informative resource for work
- Move over to a magazine format

An illustrated business magazine was a real innovation at this time. For SKA it represented a shift from information to communication, from a monologue to an exchange of ideas between the bank and its customers, its employees and the general public. The main focus continued to be on business and economic subjects, but new sections broadened the appeal of the magazine. Readers were also interested in current affairs, culture and sport. It also introduced a new women's page.

bulletin was also a milestone in the history of the bank's internal communications. 'Mitteilungen für das Personal der SKA' ('News for SKA staff') had been sent out three times a year since 1965, but in-depth information was not distributed until the publication of the staff *bulletin*, which was bound together with the customer *bulletin*.

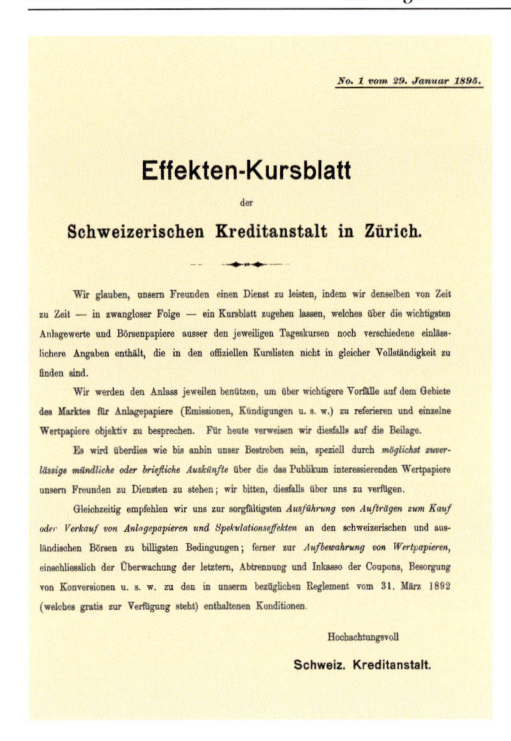

From the *Effekten-Kursblatt* (1895) to the *Monats-Bulletin* (1921) and the *Bulletin* quarterly report (1954) to the modern *bulletin* banking magazine (from 1970).

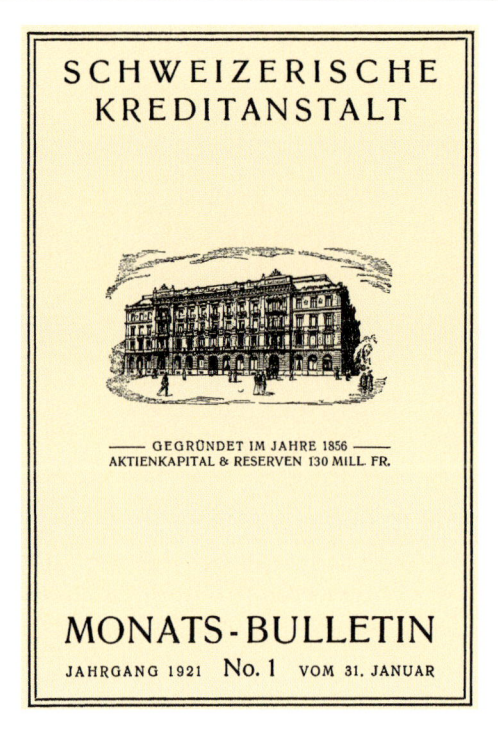

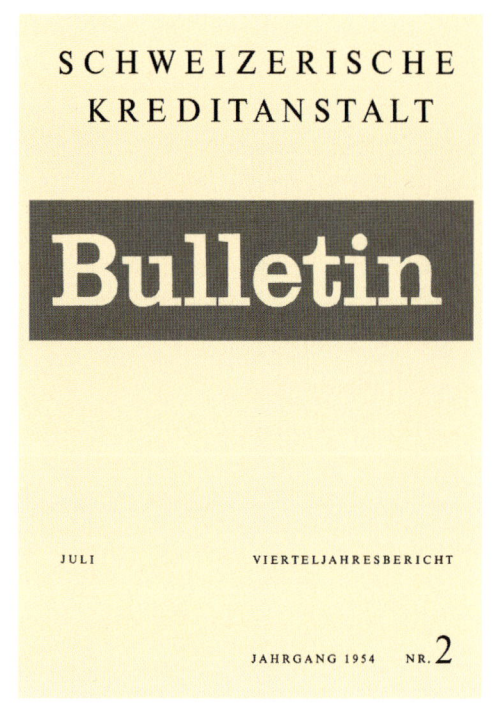

In order to pool the available editorial capacity and focus the interest of readers, right from the start the new publication incorporated the existing publications *Von den Börsen* ('From the stock markets'), *Kursliste, Devisen, Noten, Gold* ('Price lists for foreign exchange, banknotes, gold') and *Effektenkursliste* ('Securities price list'). Apart from contributions from members of the executive board and the board of directors, the magazine also published articles by well known figures from the worlds of business, academia and politics. Various newspapers, including the *Tages-Anzeiger* and the *Handelszeitung,* printed the *bulletin*'s economic forecasts verbatim and SKA's *bulletin* became an important planning tool for many companies.

In line with the bank's international activities and different customer groups, *bulletin* appeared between eight and nine times a year in German and French, as well as four times a year in English and Italian. A Spanish edition was also produced twice a year up to 1979 and special editions came out on an occasional basis in languages such as Arabic, Portuguese and Japanese. Within a short space of time, the combined print run for all languages rose from an initial 60,000 to 200,000 copies in 1974.

In 1987, the editors tackled another challenging new redesign. To take account of readers' changing habits, a more richly illustrated *bulletin* was now printed in four colors on glossy paper. The magazine was defined as a key component of the bank's corporate communications, and as such was employed in an increasingly targeted manner.

The reorganization of 1997 saw *bulletin* transformed into a customer magazine for the Credit Suisse business unit, which specialized in retail banking. Since the beginning of 1999, *bulletin* has been made accessible to even more readers via the Internet. Selected subjects are examined in more detail, adapt-

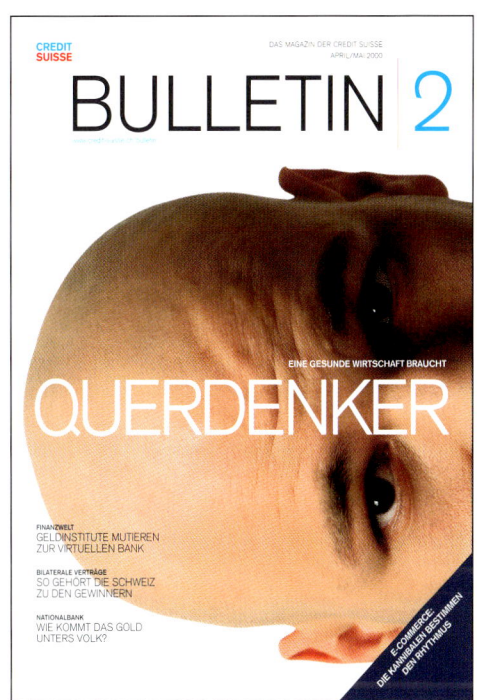

SKA's advertising

The mid-1960s: the dawn of professionalism

SKA set up an information office in 1906. In 1911 it created an 'advertisements office', which was renamed as the 'propaganda office' during the interwar years. Nevertheless, the bank maintained a very cautious attitude towards advertising for more than 100 years. This indifference reflected a mentality that prevailed amongst the banks in general, but which was particularly evident at SKA: SKA did not go out and look for customers, it could simply select the ones it wanted.

From the mid-1960s onwards, as SKA professionalized itself, it also overhauled its attitude to advertising.[650] In 1965 the propaganda and public relations department was mandated to put the bank's advertising on a new footing. There was now a clearly expressed desire for a systematic approach, and for control and standardization. The direction to be taken was derived initially from the first market research studies carried out in 1965.

Until this point, SKA had placed advertisements in the press in response to specific situations rather than following an overall strategy, but in April 1967 it launched its first systematic campaign. Guided by the long-term goal of increasing the volume of savings deposits, the propaganda office used three different series of advertisements aimed at the readers of specific newspapers.

By the end of the 1960s, the bank was directly addressing individual target groups, especially women and young people. In 1973 a successful campaign was launched with the slogan 's bluemete Trögli' (also the name of a popular Swiss

---

The 'Wermelinger Cross'

In the anniversary year of 1956, the executive board did not consider it necessary to create a logo. Ten years later, however, it took a very different view and decided that it wanted a distinctive and easily remembered logo. The first step towards this goal was taken with the directive of 11 November 1966, which defined the 'SKA blue' color. Then in 1967, in an attempt to secure a uniform outward appearance for the bank, all those responsible for marketing at the branches were invited to an inaugural marketing conference. Until this point, SKA had used various symbols to support its name on printed materials, including an anchor ('Anchored in trust') and a picture of the head office building on Paradeplatz, unlike the other major banks, however, it had failed to achieve consistency. In 1967 the bank launched a broad-based logo competition. In response, 124 graphic designers from all over Switzerland submitted 299 drafts, and in June 1967 these were assessed by a nine-person jury. The fact that the jury included three executive board members and two members of the board of directors alongside four respected designers underlined how important the project was to the bank. Finally, SKA decided to go with the cross logo designed by Willi Wermelinger. This was officially introduced at the start of 1968 and soon achieved widespread recognition as the 'Wermelinger-Kreuz' ('Wermelinger Cross').[651]

SKA logos:

The first logotype of 1856 was followed by the coin symbol with twenty stars representing the branches and head office (1930), the coin symbol with the abbreviation of the bank's name in German, French, Italian and English (1940), and the 'Verankert im Vertrauen' ('Anchored in trust') logo (1952).

The 'Wermelinger Cross' was the official SKA logo from 1968. Until 1976 it was shown against a dark blue background as a brand mark combined with the name. Thereafter – driven by the bank's popularization strategy and technical branding considerations – the cross on a red background was integrated with the bank's name on a blue background.

radio program). From 1969 to 1976 the bank consistently used the slogan 'SKA – der richtige Partner' ('SKA – the right partner') to build up trust and a sense of permanency.

From 1976/77: the blue, white and red conquers Switzerland

An analysis of the market carried out in 1975 showed that a third of the Swiss population spontaneously identified the 'Wermelinger Cross' as SKA's logo. This was quite an impressive result, but the levels of awareness were still nowhere near as great as for the logos used by SBG and SBV. Spurred on by these findings – but also out of concern about the lack of real distinction between the different banks' advertising – SKA created a new logo-block; this formed a key element of the bank's repositioning strategy. SKA still suffered from its image as a Zurich bank, even though three quarters of its branches were located outside the canton. The bank was now pursuing a strategy of openness to the outside world, and the fresh red color, representing Switzerland, was selected as the third house color in addition to the traditional Zurich colors of blue and white. This new combination helped to support the regionalization process. The 'Anstalt' ('institution') part of the bank's name, by contrast, proved rather a hindrance to the popularization of the bank, so the 'SKA' abbreviation was added to the new logo block alongside the full 'Schweizerische Kreditanstalt' name (the bank's international name 'Credit Suisse' was used with the abbreviation 'CS' on international publications and advertising material).

The advertising department was given the job of publicizing the logo, standardizing SKA's outward appearance and, at the product level, promoting retail banking in particular. In concrete terms, the bank's top management encouraged a more active, aggressive and populist form of advertising 'in bright colors'[652]; more than anything, however, the bank wanted to pursue a consistent overall, long-term advertising strategy. The advertising department – the old-fashioned name 'propaganda department' was dropped in 1977 – subsequently enjoyed a number of creative and innovative successes. SKA recognized that it needed to have its own unmistakable brand and started to pay a lot more attention to its public image. It issued its first 'Corporate Identity Manual' in autumn 1977.

In the summer of 1976 the advertising department took up an idea proposed by an employee in La Chaux-de-Fonds and designed a ski hat in the new SKA colors. To start with, the executive board withheld approval for the new promotional gift because it did not think that the hat was in keeping with the bank's style, but a few weeks later, the executive board discussed the issue again. In expectation of receiving the order from SKA, the supplier had already produced a large number of the hats in advance. Given this circumstance the executive board was willing to take on this initial production run at cost price. But then the success story started to take off. By winter 1976/77, the ski hats had become incredibly popular. In order to avoid problems with the Swiss Bankers' Association, SKA later stopped giving the hats away, instead distributing them by means of competitions. By the time this marketing legend was officially brought to a close in 1993, SKA had already distributed over 800,000 ski hats.[653]

Incredibly Swiss.

Matterhorn

Incredibly International.

Manhattan skyline

Consistent service quality and far-sighted strategic thinking are the foundations of Credit Suisse's international success. As the oldest of Switzerland's three big banks, we are totally committed to the solid traditional values for which Swiss banking is famous.

But our activities extend far beyond Switzerland. Credit Suisse, in partnership with CS First Boston Inc., is one of the world's premier financial services groups. We operate effectively in every market, offering expert service with a global horizon.

We do more to keep you at the top.

**CREDIT SUISSE
CS**

The 'Incredibly Swiss – Incredibly International' advertising campaign launched in 1989 linked Swiss quality with a worldwide presence. The campaign itself won several awards for quality.

Incredibly Swiss – Incredibly International

In Switzerland, SKA's pyramid symbol had become a widely regarded seal of quality and value. Outside Switzerland, however, there was no product-oriented advertising, and in 1989 the pyramid was replaced at the international level with the 'Incredibly' campaign. This enjoyed great success and was maintained right up until the formation of Credit Suisse Group in 1997.[654] The new international campaign linked a typically Swiss ('Incredibly Swiss') image with a typically international one ('Incredibly International'): the Matterhorn and the New York skyline, for example. It positioned SKA as a modern and efficient Swiss universal bank, which maintained a presence in all the world's key financial centers. Buoyed by the campaign's success, the bank added the 'Incredibly Global – Incredibly Private' series of advertisements in 1992. Interestingly these were also used within Switzerland, where the target group would have recognized the style from trips abroad.

Towards a new corporate identity

In 1991, the realization that optimum advertising could open up new channels of communication between the bank and its customers and the general public led to a change in values. SKA no longer talked about advertising, but about core communication and segment communication.

By 1997, the bank had developed from being a Swiss company with international activities into an international financial services provider with a head office and core operations in Switzerland. Consequently, Credit Suisse Group urgently required a new corporate identity. The creation and implementation of this identity, which cost about Sfr 70 million, gave the bank an ideal opportunity to make its groundbreaking new direction visible to all of its employees, customers and shareholders, as well as to the media. Because in legal terms SKA was being re-incorporated as Credit Suisse First Boston, and SVB was becoming Credit Suisse, there was also a need to terminate the old brands as of 1 January 1997. The new identity positioned the four new business units unmistakably beneath the common umbrella of Credit Suisse Group. Thanks to the modern logotype, as well as to the adoption of the familiar color combination of red and blue, and the well established name of 'Credit Suisse', the new corporate identity was able to lend the new structure the desired qualities of globality, competence and continuity.

SKA's commitment to sport and culture

In the beginning was the Tour de Suisse

'The onlookers by the side of the road particularly like the SKA people', wrote the *Schaffhauser Nachrichten* in June 1978 after the Tour de Suisse reached Schaffhausen. 'Especially during the rain of Saturday's stage, the caps and umbrellas were much appreciated.'[655] The 42nd Tour de Suisse, Switzerland's biggest sporting event, was won by the Belgian Paul Wellens, but the real winners were tour organizer Sepp Voegeli, always short of funds for the event, and marketing pioneer Victor Erne, who was far-sighted enough to arrange for SKA

Ever since it was founded, SKA has made donations to social and cultural causes. From the second half of the 1970s, more and more forms of social engagement were added: art at the bank, sports sponsorship, the Jubilee Foundation, and cultural sponsorship. With its trailblazing philosophy, SKA has played a pioneering role in sports sponsorship in Switzerland.

Tour de Suisse 1987. Millions of spectators followed the event from the roadside, or on the radio and television.

to be the Tour's headline sponsor, thus marking the bank's early entry into the world of sports sponsorship. It also marked the start of a close 22-year partnership based on mutual benefit.[656]

But to begin at the beginning: under enormous time pressure, the SKA team, which ultimately consisted of 36 members, seized the moment and organized an advertising coup for the bank at the Tour de Suisse that put everything that had gone before in the shade. In order to ensure that as many as possible of the 31 SKA branches on the Tour's route could get involved, the organizers dreamt up the 'Goldsprint', which subsequently proved to be a particularly popular part of the race. SKA staff were on hand at the event itself, and in the first year managed to hand out around 50,000 sun hats, 100,000 SKA 'Holiday Gazettes', 25,000 Tour de Suisse newspapers, 5,000 umbrellas as well as countless stickers, balloons and plastic bags. Banners and displays at the stage finishing lines clearly showed who had taken over – for Sfr 110,000 – as the main sponsor: 'SKA – Ihre Bank' ('SKA – Your Bank').

'Roughly speaking, SKA wants to counter the "marble halls" image of the major banks; instead it would like to establish itself as a provider of services to all sections of the population', commented the *Neue Zürcher Zeitung*. 'Nowadays, the banks' customers come from all sections of society, and business with the general public has become more important; from the marketing point of view, therefore, a popular event like the Tour de Suisse is certainly an excellent vehicle for the bank's advertising.'[657]

Working from thorough analysis of its impact, the bank's presence on the Tour was continuously expanded and improved using the full range of communication tools. Then, on 2 September 1999, Credit Suisse and Winterthur announced that they would not be renewing their contracts with the Tour de Suisse, the Tour de Romandie or the national cycling team. 'Every sponsorship commitment has its natural life cycle. [...] Companies often find that after five or six years, the partnership has passed its zenith and restructures its sponsorship accordingly. In this case, the partnership has lasted for over 20 years – not least because every year we were able to improve some aspect. Nevertheless, there have been signs that our involvement is becoming a little worn.'[658] The doping scandal at the 1998 Tour de France and the negative associations this created also compromised the objectives of the sponsorship. As a consequence, Credit Suisse decided to invest the funds now made available in its new core sports sponsorship areas: soccer and equestrian competitions.[659]

The 1980s: the expansion of sports sponsorship

SKA's commitment to the Tour de Suisse can be seen as a turning point in the bank's communications strategy; its great success provoked lively debate in the industry. The initial response from the Swiss Bankers' Association was to issue a convention limiting the definition of what constituted a legitimate competitive tool[660], but SKA's Tour de Suisse sponsorship was eventually to prove groundbreaking. In the 1980s, sponsorship established itself firmly in Switzerland, facilitating the organization of many high-quality events. Developments in Switzerland reflected the general trend in Europe, which was seeing a move away from pure sports advertising towards sports sponsorship.

Unlike other companies, however, SKA rarely sponsored individual sportspeople or teams, preferring instead to work together with event organizers and sports associations, not only to put on top-flight events but also to promote participation sports and encourage young sporting talent. Within SKA itself, this grass roots approach had long been a feature thanks to the bank's sports center in the Zurich suburb of Fluntern, which was built in 1927 and modernized in 1972. In 1981, SKA began to organize its 'Lauf-Träff' running events.[661] At around the same time it collaborated with a Swiss sports charity to create the SKA-Juniorenpreis (SKA Youth Prize); in its first year the prize was won by gymnast Sepp Zellweger.[662] SKA also supported cross country skiing, promoting the sport amongst the general population, and from 1985 organizing the 'Suisse-Loppet' race. Since 1997, Credit Suisse has sponsored the Engadine Skiing Marathon. Finally the bank has supported university sport since 1988, and has sponsored the Davos sports school since 1997.

Gradually, over the course of the 1980s, the bank began to prioritize new marketing goals. As part of its corporate strategy, the bank sought to secure a 'return on investment', meaning that sponsorship commitments had to create awareness of specific banking products and facilitate direct contact with the target groups concerned. 1986 marked another milestone in the history of SKA's sports sponsorship. Activities were put on an even more professional footing, with the introduction, for example, of the slogan 'Ein Sport-Engagement der SKA' ('Part of SKA's commitment to sport') on all publicity material. From this time on, the bank concentrated primarily on equestrianism, golf and chess, each of which offered good opportunities for contact with specific customer groups.

The monitoring carried out after every event confirmed that the new strategy was moving in the right direction, but also identified areas that could be

In the mid-1980s, golf – an attractive forum for customer contact – gained in significance.

SKA promoted popular participation sport for many years as the sponsor of the Suisse-Loppet cross-country skiing competition. Credit Suisse is continuing this tradition, having supported the Engadine Marathon – Switzerland's biggest winter sports event – since 1997. Photo taken in 1999.

improved in subsequent events. Collaborative support for equestrianism and golf has been further expanded in the intervening years, but the bank's twelve years of sponsoring chess tournaments was brought to a close at the end of 1997: the relationship between cost and return was no longer justifiable. Before this, however, SKA managed to organize the highest quality chess tournaments ever held in Switzerland with the 1994 and 1995 Credit Suisse Masters at the CS Communication Center in Horgen.

SKA has been associated with soccer for many years. In 1993, the rather piecemeal support for individual teams and for the Swiss Super Cup was transformed by the contract that made the bank the main sponsor of the Swiss national team – a contract that has since been extended to 2004.[663] Shortly after the contract was first signed, Switzerland, managed by Roy Hodgson, qualified for the 1994 World Cup held in the USA, and then for the 1996 European Championships in England. Systematic support for the national youth squad should ensure that the team can enjoy similar success in future.

Swiss soccer fever at the 1994 World Cup in the USA. Football is an important force for integration in Switzerland, with support cutting across all regional and linguistic barriers.

In a time of globalization and the blurring of national boundaries, the bank's involvement with soccer is particularly important. The sport is equally popular in all parts of Switzerland and is a more effective vehicle for creating a sense of national identity than virtually any other sport. In recent years Credit Suisse Group has also been involved in the construction of modern soccer stadiums such as the Stade de Genève, the Hardturm in Zurich and – via Winterthur – the St. Jakob in Basel, in each case providing a mixture of straight financing and sponsorship.

The 1990s: cultural sponsorship comes of age

SKA's Guiding Principles include a commitment for the bank to be a 'good citizen' in terms of its relationship with society at large. Since it was first established, the bank has fulfilled this commitment by, amongst other things, making donations to support social and cultural causes, and helping out in emergencies. In 1981, these efforts were complemented by the creation of SKA's Jubilee Foundation, which allowed the bank to make considerable sums available to promising projects.[664]

SKA's philosophical shift from encouraging culture to sponsoring culture was completed at the end of the 1980s. The fact that the bank was slower to move into cultural sponsorship than into sports sponsorship was reflected by the general trend in Europe. 'Customer care' became a key concept in cultural sponsorship too. As with sports sponsorship, earnings-oriented customer contact was the prime concern.

The first steps towards systematic sponsorship of cultural events were taken in 1981, when SKA began its 18-year association with the Swiss Young Musician of the Year competition. From 1985 onwards, SKA supported foreign tours by the Orchestre de la Suisse Romande, and facilitated concerts in Zurich and Geneva by the Berlin Philharmonic Orchestra under Herbert von Karajan.

The step-by-step progress of SKA's cultural sponsorship program is clearly reflected in the development of the 'le point' gallery at Paradeplatz. In 1983, following conversion work at the head office building, the free space created on the ground floor was adapted to accommodate art exhibitions. This was part of a deliberate strategy to remove any inhibitions about entering the building – i.e. to encourage non-customers to come into the bank, too. Visitors, the media and art professionals all showed great interest in the exhibitions, many of which subsequently went on tour around Switzerland and abroad. In 1987, the bank first started to produce brochures to accompany the exhibitions. These started off modestly, but later developed into highly informative and attractive catalogues, with print runs of up to 30,000. During the 1990s the 'le point' put on exhibitions that became real cultural magnets, attracting up to 60,000 visitors. 'le point' preview parties quickly became highlights of the social calendar. Important figures from the worlds of politics, economics and culture were attracted to such events, and in 1993 the launch of the 'Petra and the Incense Road' exhibition was attended by Queen Noor of Jordan. There was always at least one member of the bank's most senior management present, too, and relationship

'We support activities in the areas of politics, culture, charity and sport' (Guiding Principles 1976).

In 1981 SKA took over as main sponsor of the Swiss Young Musician of the Year competition. In 1990 the competition was given new impetus by Michael Haefliger's Davos music festival 'Young Artists in Concert', which provided talented young artists with an excellent opportunity to perform. Pictured is Ariane Haering of La Chaux-de-Fonds, prizewinner in 1989 and 1991.

'Engel sind überall' ('Angels are everywhere'). The last exhibition (27 October 1999 to 28 January 2000) in the 'le point' gallery at Paradeplatz before the renovation of the head office building.

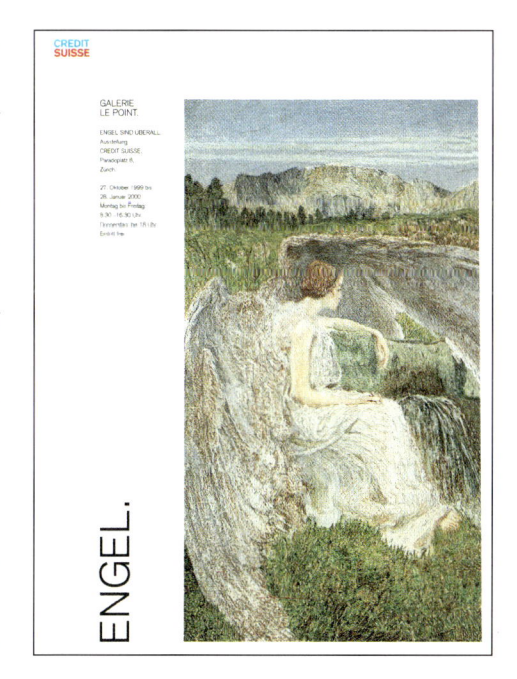

Schweizerische Kreditanstalt's Jubilee Foundation

In 1981, on the occasion of SKA's 125th anniversary, the annual general meeting of shareholders founded the bank's Jubilee Foundation (Jubiläumsstiftung der Schweizerischen Kreditanstalt), allocating Sfr 10 million as its foundation capital. In 1998, the Foundation was merged with Swiss Volksbank's Jubilee Foundation to form the Credit Suisse Group Jubilee Foundation, which today controls capital of about Sfr 65 million.

According to its articles of association, the purpose of the Jubilee Foundation is 'to promote social, charitable, cultural and scientific activities by donating money to institutions, organizations, individuals or groups'.

One of the Foundation's primary focuses is on charitable projects that combine various disciplines and take innovative approaches. It also fulfils a social role through its commitment to promoting young talent in cultural and scientific areas.

By concentrating on high-quality projects, either developed on its own initiative or selected from nearly a thousand applications each year, the Jubilee Foundation can grant substantial financial support, provide encouragement and help to get new ideas off the ground.

Thanks to the support of the Credit Suisse Group Jubilee Foundation, in autumn 1999 the International Red Cross and the International Red Crescent in Geneva were able to open their new exhibition space 'Espace 11 – Aujourd'hui / Raum 11 – Heute'. This new space is dedicated to the Red Cross's current activities.

Alberto Giacometti (1901–1966). Buste de Silvio. 1942–1945. Plaster. Bündner Kunstmuseum. The purchase of this sculpture was made possible by SKA's Jubilee Foundation.

Credit Suisse Group's Jubilee Foundation performs an important social role: at the beginning of 2000, it supported the Sixth Skiing World Championships for Disabled People. The event, held in the Valais, attracted wide interest and witnessed exemplary performances from sportsmen and women of many countries. The Championships also provided young people with an opportunity to meet contemporaries from other cultures and countries.

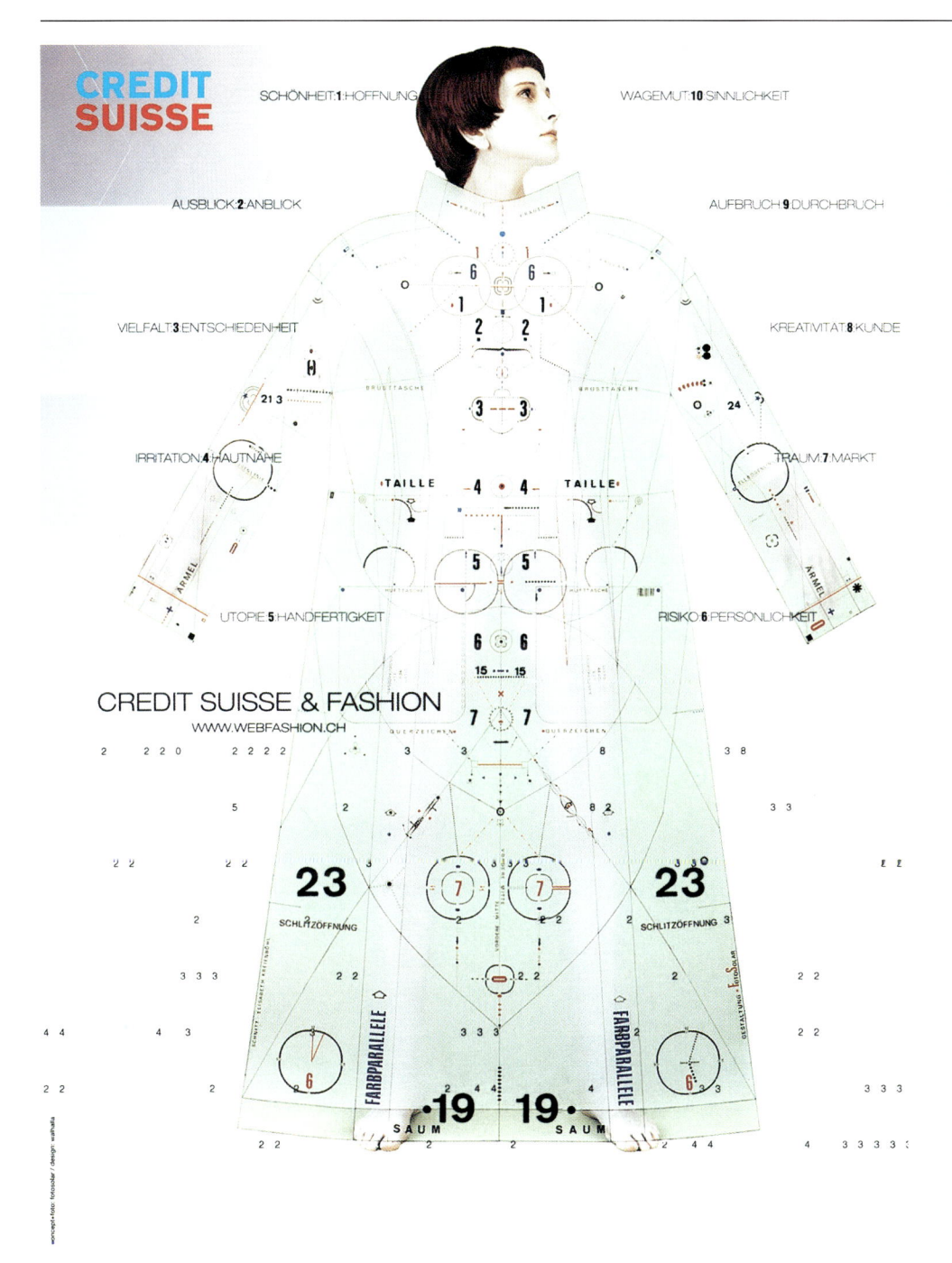

Cultural sponsorship today

The Credit Suisse Private Banking business unit is now responsible for the two main elements of the former SKA's cultural sponsorship program: classical music and exhibitions at major art museums.

The Credit Suisse business unit is breaking new ground by organizing its own events – jazz concerts, for example – and creating new forums, as it has in fashion.

Since 1998 Credit Suisse has supported creative young fashion designers by sponsoring the 'Gwand' fashion trade fair in Lucerne.

managers used the occasions as ideal opportunities for discussions with personally invited guests.

At the beginning of the 1990s, SKA began to sponsor one exhibition each year at one of the major Swiss museums. Highlights included the 'Giovanni Segantini' (1991), 'Gustav Klimt' (1992) and 'Joseph Beuys' (1993) shows at the Zurich Museum of Art. Here too, private previews and special guided tours provided ideal opportunities to meet selected customers and opinion leaders. The sponsorship team also organized very popular tours of the exhibitions for SKA staff.

Features of SKA's cultural and sports sponsorship

- Pioneering role in Switzerland: sports sponsorship since 1978, cultural sponsorship since the mid-1980s
- All sponsorship activities anchored in the bank's Guiding Principles, corporate strategy and marketing strategy
- Development from image advertising to customer platform and to event marketing
- Use of various communications tools and deliberate, proactive public relations work
- Catchy slogans: 'Credit Suisse: committed to sport' and 'Credit Suisse: committed to culture'
- Encouraging staff at all levels to identify with the bank
- Contractual agreements on what the bank expects in return for its support
- Work as partners, help with organization, image transfer
- Medium to long-term involvement; e.g.: Tour de Suisse 22 years, Swiss Young Musician of the Year 18 years
- Clear objectives, professional approach, monitor success
- Support for organizers and associations/ national teams rather than for club teams or individuals
- Support for top-level sport, participation sport and youth development
- Facilitate meaningful, creative events
- Maintain a personal presence at events – act as host
- Selective policy: find niches, occupy new ground
- Generous provision of funds (no half-measures)
- Identification with sponsorship partners
- Co-operate with other sponsors, but ensure SKA is the only bank involved

Building on its overall communications strategy, SKA's cultural sponsorship was aimed primarily at the middle and upper customer segments. Thematically, the bank concentrated mainly on classical music. It sponsored the Yehudi Menuhin Festival, which later became the Gstaad Saanenland Music Festival, for 13 years from 1986 onwards. In 1990 it added the Lucerne International Music Festival to its roster, SKA's support enabling the festival to host the Vienna Philharmonic in 1993. The most recent festivals supported by the bank are the Classic Open Air in Solothurn, the Festival d'Opéra in Avenches and the Zurich Festspiele at the city's Opera House, Tonhalle concert hall and Museum of Art.

Further highlights in SKA's program of classical music sponsorship since 1987 are the extra concerts put on by the Zurich Tonhalle, the Gala Concerts in Basel, Bern and Geneva, and the Rendez-vous concerts that toured various regional centers. These events, all of which brought international stars to Swiss venues, demonstrate the fact that SKA's support has made it possible to hold events in Switzerland that would not otherwise have been possible.

However, SKA's sponsorship sometimes went a step further, helping to get new creative projects off the ground. The best example of this was the 'Orchester zum Anfassen', or 'L'orchestre à cœur ouvert', tour of 1991. A professional orchestra was made available to communities in Central Switzerland and the Lower Valais for three days each. The events actually began weeks before the concerts themselves, with rehearsals in Engelberg, Stans, Sarnen, St-Maurice and Martigny. On the performance days, the professional musicians talked to children about their instruments, answered questions and played in schools, hospitals and old-peoples homes, before giving a concert together with talented young musicians and local musical societies. These events, memorable experiences for all involved, received extensive coverage in the local press[665]; *Schweizer Bank* summed them up as follows in an article entitled 'Gegen den kulturellen Holzboden!' (roughly translated as 'Against the cultural wasteland'): 'Urs Frauchiger, director of the Berner Konservatorium and designated director of the Pro Helvetia cultural foundation, is the father of the project, Sir Yehudi Menuhin and the Camerata Lysy the actors, and SKA – it goes without saying – the sponsor.'[666]

Credit Suisse Group's commitment to culture also manifested itself in support for outstanding infrastructure projects. The Culture and Congress Center in Lucerne, for example, designed by renowned French architect Jean Nouvel and opened in August 1998, benefited from a substantial contribution by Credit Suisse Group and its group companies.

Art at the bank

Up until the 1970s, SKA tended to decorate the walls of its buildings with engravings, though a few individual paintings were purchased for executive board members' offices. One of the most famous works bought by the bank was the 'Gotthardpost' by Rudolf Koller, which came into the possession of SKA in 1965.

Marketing and communication **393**

From Credit Suisse Group's art collection:

Alexandre Calame (1810–1864). 'Blick vom Rosenlaui auf Wellhorn und Wetterhorn'. 1840. Oil on canvas.

Cuno Amiet (1868–1961). 'Garten in Oschwand'. 1955. Oil on canvas.

Irene Thomet (*1958). Untitled. 1994. Egg tempera on canvas.

Karl Jakob Wegmann (1928–1997). 'Farbmeldung'. 1991. Oil on canvas.

Then in 1973, the bank bought Alexandre Calame's 'Blick aufs Wetterhorn' from the Viennese auction house Dorotheum.

SKA did not, however, follow a consistent purchasing strategy until the mid-1970s. Instead, paintings were bought every now and then as the occasion arose on the initiative of the executive board or individual managers. These tended to be interested primarily in the major artists of the 19th and 20th centuries.

In 1975, SKA set up its first art committee – rather late by comparison with the other Swiss major banks. The committee's purpose was to acquire works of art for the bank's premises on a continuous and systematic basis, thus building up a proper collection. It started off by buying twelve paintings by major Swiss artists, including works by Cuno Amiet, Eugen Früh, Giovanni Giacometti, Max Gubler and Ferdinand Hodler. The considerable sum of Sfr 200,000 was invested in such works each year.

After only two years, in 1977, the committee was disbanded as part of the fall-out of the Chiasso Affair. In this difficult time, SKA felt compelled to concentrate its resources on its core activities.

Art at the Üetlihof

However, 1977 did see the formation of the bank's first project-related art committee in association with the construction of the Üetlihof. This committee was charged with developing an integrated outward and internal visual identity for the new building, using art and architecture. Whereas the first art committee of 1975 had concentrated exclusively on established Swiss artists, the Üetlihof committee took the bold step of basing its strategy on the work of 14 young Swiss contemporary artists. The pieces installed in the corridors and rest areas were intended to improve the working atmosphere, stimulate debate, and introduce employees to modern art in general.

A new project group, 'Kunst am Üetlihof' ('Art at the Üetlihof') was formed in 1984 to perform a similar role during the expansion of the Üetlihof site. Six large walls were to be given over to artistic decoration. The committee, headed

Dieter Leuenberger (*1951). 'Lehmgrube'. 1984. Mural. The work shows the clay pit situated at the foot of the Üetliberg before the building of the Üetlihof. Leuenberger's work later had to be removed when the Üetlihof was extended.

by Roland Rasi, again invited Swiss artists to submit their ideas. One of them, Dieter Leuenberger, painted a view of the clay pit owned by the Zürcher Ziegeleien tile company as it would have looked before the construction of the Üetlihof. As well as organizing and selecting this type of integrated artwork, the committee also purchased a large number of smaller pieces for the meeting rooms and business floors. The 'Kunst am Üetlihof' project group's aim was to present staff with new perspectives on contemporary art and on their own working environment. It thus also devoted a lot of attention to the artistic adornment of working areas.

SKA's new self-image is reflected in its art collection

Since the construction of the Üetlihof, SKA has repeatedly linked its commitment to culture with the architectural design of its buildings. The project team responsible for any new building was always also in charge of the associated artistic concept, and for selecting the actual works to be displayed. Important 'Kunst am Bau' ('Art under Construction') projects were carried out in other locations apart from the city of Zurich, establishing significant milestones in the bank's effort to promote art. 'Integrated art' of this type has two purposes: to create a positive image, and to enrich the cultural life of the workplace. SKA's candid attempts to stimulate its employees' interest in contemporary art on its own premises were an unmistakable expression of the bank's new ideas about its own identity.[667] Counter halls became particularly important, because it was here that the bank could present its cultural commitment to the general public. At SKA's new Maghetti building in Lugano, the Ticinese artist Milo Cleis created a 24-meter-long stone relief to surround the entire customer hall. The work depicts a hedge, with an opening that acts as the entrance to the hall. Meanwhile, the glass wall at the back of the hall affords a view onto the water features and greenery of the building's inner courtyard.

It was not until the 1990s that the bank set up its first permanent art committee at head office. Chaired by Victor Erne, it reported directly to the executive board and followed a clearly defined strategy. The committee concerned itself mainly with new construction and renovation projects, where 1–2% of the budget was set aside for purchasing art. Because there was now a permanent committee responsible for the bank's art, rather than different construction committees or ad hoc art committees for each project, the bank could now choose works systematically. For each selected artist the committee published a brochure explaining the works concerned. These brochures would then be made available in client zones for the edification of interested customers.

One of the art committee's most important projects was the concept for the design of the CS Communication Center 'Bocken' in Horgen. Until that point, the bank had worked exclusively with Swiss artists, but now it set a new tone by inviting five respected international artists to create works for the public areas of the new building.

Alongside its work for particular projects, the art committee also continued to build up the bank's overall art collection, concentrating mainly on Swiss

'SKA has no art strategy; there is no clear policy on art' (Hans J. Halbheer, 1985).

artists under the age of forty. By recording information about all the works in the bank's possession electronically, the art committee created a clear overview of the collection, allowing the bank to follow a targeted acquisitions policy. However, the art committee never regarded the works of art as a capital investment. It saw itself first and foremost as an institution for the promotion of contemporary Swiss art, though the works it selected were also intended to enhance SKA's corporate culture. Its annual budget of Sfr 300,000 gave the committee greater resources than many museums.

When it took over SVB, SKA also came into possession of this bank's small but high-quality collection of Swiss art. SVB had set up an art committee ten years before SKA, and for more than 30 years it carefully built up a collection that represented all the different cultural regions and stylistic trends of 20th century Swiss art. The SVB collection is now run by Credit Suisse Group as an autonomous, self-contained collection.

When Credit Suisse Group was created, the art committee was reorganized in a way that clearly reflected the high priority given to art by the bank. Lukas Mühlemann chairs the committee, which also includes members of the executive boards of the individual business units.

The Credit Suisse Group art committee has continued in the same vein as the SKA committee, though it has developed new guidelines and set new priorities. 'Kunst am Bau' projects have been scaled back, and the art committee now tries to buy movable works of art that can be placed in different environments at different times. It focuses particularly on groups of work that reflect the latest developments in Swiss art, as well as pursuing the ambitious goal of adorning all of the bank's customer zones in Switzerland with high-quality works of contemporary art.

The changing face of bank architecture

In the early years, Swiss banks tended to operate from rented premises, often town halls and guildhalls, or from the private residences of the bankers themselves.

SKA's first offices were located in a few rooms in the 'Tiefenhöfe' buildings on Zurich's Paradeplatz. In April 1858, the bank moved into rented premises in the east wing of what was then the post office building on Poststrasse. Finally, from 1868 to 1876, it rented offices in the building at 'Im Hinteren Tiefenhof 1'.[668] Soon, however, growing staff numbers, the specific requirements of running a bank, and belief in the growth potential of banking business meant that SKA needed its own building.

Before the construction of SKA's head office, there were few examples of premises built especially for banks in Switzerland. The exceptions included the buildings of Bank in Glarus (1862), Eidgenössische Bank in Bern (1865–1867), Bank in Winterthur (1867–1869) and Bank in Zürich (1872/73). The first three of these leaned heavily on the style of urban residential property, while Bank in Zürich's building – constructed at the corner of Bahnhofstrasse and St.-Peter-

Strasse one year before SKA's head office – included architectural elements familiar from older bank and stock exchange buildings in other countries: columns on the first floor, great rectangular stone blocks on the ground floor. Such elements were intended to give an impression of solidity, demonstrating to customers that their money was being held securely.[669] This impression was often further reinforced by the use of barred arched windows.

SKA head office building on Paradeplatz

These architectural elements, typical for bank buildings of the time, were brought together in impressive form in SKA's building on Zurich's Paradeplatz (1873–1876). This was a new type of building for Switzerland, marking a significant development in Swiss architecture.[670] The façade of the second and third floors is divided into sections by a series of columns and pilasters, while the central part of the building is crowned by a top-floor frieze and sculpted groups of figures. The ground floor is fronted by great rectangular stone blocks and arched windows arranged in a strict rhythmical sequence. The external design of the first floor gives the impression that it could be a mezzanine, ranged as it is between the building's base and the colossal structure above. At the corners of the central section of the frontage, caryatids bear the wide bases of the three-part window arrangement above. The architectural combination of colossal order and traditional visual cues harks back simultaneously to temple buildings and castles. Secular and sacred forms are melded together to create a new image of monetary power. The cost of the building was budgeted at Sfr 2.5 million, though in the end it actually came to Sfr 3.4 million: about 15% of the bank's equity capital in 1873. This enormous sum reflected the optimism that ruled the still relatively young company. With the general economic situation so healthy, the bank was confident that its business would prosper.[671]

The monumental nature of the building on Paradeplatz generated an impression of inapproachability, a feeling that was originally intensified by the fact that there was no obvious entrance to the edifice. Access to the bank was through a door in the inner courtyard. Only at the end of the 19th century did SKA open a doorway straight out onto Paradeplatz. This change was made as part of the construction of the new counter hall in 1898/99, itself a response to the bank's growing client list, which now included a number of foreign customers too.

Branches

SKA's first branches were housed in existing bank buildings. The first purpose-built premises after the head office building on Paradeplatz was erected on Schwanenplatz in Lucerne in 1922 – an imposing edifice in the Neo-Renaissance style. Once again, the façade was decorated by great columns and pilasters in colossal order. Over the next few years, there was no need to design new buildings, because SKA's branch network remained so modest.

In the 1950s, the big Swiss banks embarked on a major expansion of their branch networks; rising incomes meant that more and more of the population were becoming eligible as bank customers. SKA, too, soon found that it needed more and more bank premises. It either built new buildings, or purchased existing office premises in central locations and adapted them to the requirements of a banking business.

From the 'Bärenhof' to the Üetlihof

As the bank grew, so the number of people it employed steadily increased. Towards the end of the 1930s, the space at head office on Paradeplatz was completely occupied, and plans were made to build the first extension to the main building on the site to the rear of Paradeplatz, which had been disused for some time. However, with the onset of the Second World War, the construction of this new building, the 'Bärenhof', was delayed on account of what was seen as the excessive costs involved and the lack of materials and labor. Finally, in 1946 the SKA board of directors gave the definitive green light to the site owner, Peterhof AG, for the execution of the project. It also provided a construction committee to help Peterhof AG. The committee put the proposed project costs at around Sfr 11 million, of which the pure construction costs accounted for Sfr 8.6 million. The new building – designed by architect Hermann Weideli as 'a solid construction, without the trappings of luxury but not completely undecorated'[672] – was completed after two years. It was ready for occupation in late autumn 1948; SKA and its associated companies moved into the upper floors, while Peterhof AG rented out the units on the ground floor to other users.[673]

Staff numbers at SKA continued to grow rapidly. The number of people employed at head office alone doubled over the course of the 1970s.[674] Head office operations departments were now scattered across more than 40 different locations in the vicinity of Paradeplatz, causing serious problems in terms

Adhering to ecological principals, SKA's Üetlihof administration center in Zurich attempts to achieve the greatest possible harmony between nature and architecture. Photo taken around 1990.

of communications and efficiency.[675] It was clear that the bank was going to have to build itself new premises. Thus it was that the Üetlihof came to be constructed under the aegis of Oswald Aeppli. Many head office employees moved out to this building, which was designed by the Stücheli architects' cooperative, Suter + Suter AG and H. Koella AG. The bank had initially acquired the 95,000 m² site – part of the former clay pit owned by the Zürcher Ziegeleien tile firm – in 1970.[676]

When planning first started, SKA decided that the new Üetlihof administration center would provide open-plan offices rather than individual office 'cells'.[677] This was because modern working methods increasingly required people to work in groups rather than alone. The honeycomb structure of the building, with its internal courtyards, was chosen because it allowed a greater number of desks to occupy window positions. This modular honeycomb structure gives the building its distinctive personality and also made it easier to accommodate the various extensions that have since been added.

In the 1950s, rationalization, mechanization and the adoption of organizational principles used in industry prompted the erection of office buildings which still contained individual offices, but which allowed companies to change the size of these offices to suit the function required. As organizational structures continued to develop and companies began to take account of workplace psychology, the concept of open plan office space emerged.

The development from town center office blocks with individual offices to administration buildings with open plan offices on the edge of town was in line with the general trend of the time.

One of the goals set for the construction of the Üetlihof was to surround the extensive complex with a wide variety of different native plants as well as various biotopes so that the building could blend in as much as possible with its environment. Existing habitats had to be maintained and new ones created; intervention was to be kept to a minimum. The planning authorities also demanded that roofs be covered in greenery and that the neighboring conservation area be respected and enlarged.[678] Today, about 55,000 m² of the entire site is given over to the natural world and in 1993 SKA won the 'Grünpreis der Stadt Zürich' for the Üetlihof. According to City Councillor Ruedi Aeschbacher, this prize for environmental friendliness was awarded in recognition of the bank's courage in sticking to its concept of comprehensive planting and greening for over ten years through all the various additional phases of building work up to 1993.[679] In 1998 the Üetlihof was selected by the Stiftung Natur und Wirtschaft (Institute for Nature and Economics) as one of its 'nature parks in the Swiss economy'.

The oil crisis of 1973 brought it home to people that oil was not going to be available in unlimited quantities. Efficient use of energy thus became a matter of great concern to the bank. Various measures were implemented at the Üetlihof to ensure such efficiency, including triple glazing for the windows, and the recycling of heat generated by the computer center to provide heating and warm water for other parts of the building.

Despite its unusual dimensions and all the technology it used, the bank also wanted the Üetlihof to have a positive feel – an atmosphere in which employees would be glad to work. Elements used to enhance the well-being of staff includ-

The new SKA Chiasso branch building, designed by architects Sergio Grassi and Sandro Cantoni, was ready for occupation in 1994. Photo taken around 1995.

ed the careful selection of colors and construction materials, artworks and views onto greenery.

The open plan concept presented new challenges for managers. In a conventional office set-up, the 'bosses' had their own offices; they often hid themselves away from staff and it was difficult to gain access to them. At the Üetlihof, by contrast, the physical walls between the various ranks have been dismantled. The boss sits in the same office as his or her staff, and anyone can speak to him or her. This way of working demands a great willingness to experiment and innovate on the part of the managers. It also requires a new way of thinking about prestige and self-importance.

When the Üetlihof was being planned, SKA could only guess at the future extent of office automation. It was, therefore, important that the architecture was flexible enough to accommodate new technologies when needed. Floor cavities and an innovative furniture system based on electronic desks meant that technical and organizational changes could be made without the need for major construction work.[680] Up to 3,000 workstations are changed around in some way every year at the Üetlihof in order to keep up with the bank's rapidly developing requirements. To start with, the Üetlihof housed 2,000 workstations, but by the end of 1999 this had risen to over 5,000. The building has long ceased to be purely a center for production and servicing, and it now hosts foreign exchange and stock market trading as well as other customer-focused departments.

Newer buildings

Another highlight of modern corporate architecture came in 1994 with the new building in Chiasso. This is one of the most impressive and expensive buildings to be built by SKA in recent times; an edifice made of granite, glass, wood and aluminum. Visitors are impressed by the building's open structures, large light-wells, the vertical flow of its lines and the generously designed customer hall. Offices are separated from internal courtyards by glass walls, and the counters on the first floor are reached by side stairs or futuristic elevators. The building's design takes account of the latest technological developments. Sophisticated technology is used to ensure that the different spaces, vertically open and linked by large windows, enjoy an ideal climate. However, the building's inefficient use of space means that the costs per workstation are excessively high. The building was built shortly before the bank's major restructuring. Planned and constructed as a sign of things to come, from today's perspective it actually marks the point before a turn towards a new era of banking architecture – one that was not predicted when the new Chiasso branch was built. This new era is marked by a much more cost-conscious and functional approach to building work.

The same can be said of the building designed by the internationally renowned New York architect Richard Meier on Viaduktstrasse in Basel. The building was intended to serve as SVB's main offices in the city. Cost was a secondary consideration to the prestige required of such a project. Before the planning phase was completed, however, SVB was taken over by CS Holding, meaning that SVB no longer needed a new branch in Basel. The executive board decided nevertheless to go ahead with construction, this being the best option from both the legal and the planning point of view. The architect amended the project by eliminating the customer hall and the strong room. The open, light-flooded building now houses offices and commercial operations.

The CS Communication Center in Horgen

In the early 1990s, SKA transformed the venerable old 'Bocken' estate in Horgen by Lake Zurich into the CS Communication Center.[681] Working with architect Egon Dachtler, the bank created an in-house facility to suit the changes occurring in the business world of the time. In re-designing the whole site, the main aim was to harmoniously combine the new with the old. The historical buildings – the mansion house, the stables and the playhouse – were sensitively restored. The modern Communication Center building itself provided a contrast, but was integrated into the overall feel of the place. Artistic installations and landscaping helped to bind the four buildings into a unified whole. The site now weaves together three different styles and eras: the baroque, the early Heimatstil (a traditional Swiss regional style), and the post modern.

Latest developments

Credit Suisse Group is currently involved in very few construction projects. The few new buildings it has commissioned in recent years have been lighter and more flexible than previously, and can be seen as a visual expression of the trend towards 'lean management'. Many buildings were sold, and when the branch network was downsized, the leases on many others were not renewed. Renting is gradually becoming a more attractive option once again, since it offers greater flexibility. Changing customer habits mean that individual advisory rooms, not to mention telephone services and Internet banking, are taking precedence over large customer halls.

A similar trend is occurring with administrative and office buildings. The 'Galleria' in Opfikon, the 'Murifeld' in Bern, the 'Cornavin' in Geneva and the Üetlihof in Zurich were all built as flagship administrative centers for SVB and SKA, and all of them have been through sometimes fundamental changes since they were first constructed. Even though fewer employees are required, the centralization of back-office activities in a small number of locations (Zurich, Bern, Geneva, Mendrisio) means that up to 30% more workstations had to be squeezed into the same space. Generous office arrangements have given way to more efficient uses of the available space.

Credit Suisse Group continues to take great care of its architecturally valuable buildings. The façades of the head office building on Paradeplatz and the neighboring 'Griederhaus' building, for example, were renovated at considerable expense and with great specialist expertise during the 1990s.

Beverly Pepper (*1924). 'Palingenesis'. 1993/94. CS Communication Center, Horgen. SKA's art committee invited five internationally famous artists to create works of art in the public spaces of the 'Bocken' estate. As well as American Beverly Pepper's iron sculpture, there are landscape installations by Israeli Dani Karavan, a video installation by Korean Nam June Paik, a stone sculpture by German Ulrich Rückriem and a mechanical work by German Rebecca Horn. All take very different views of the global themes of 'communication' and 'change'.

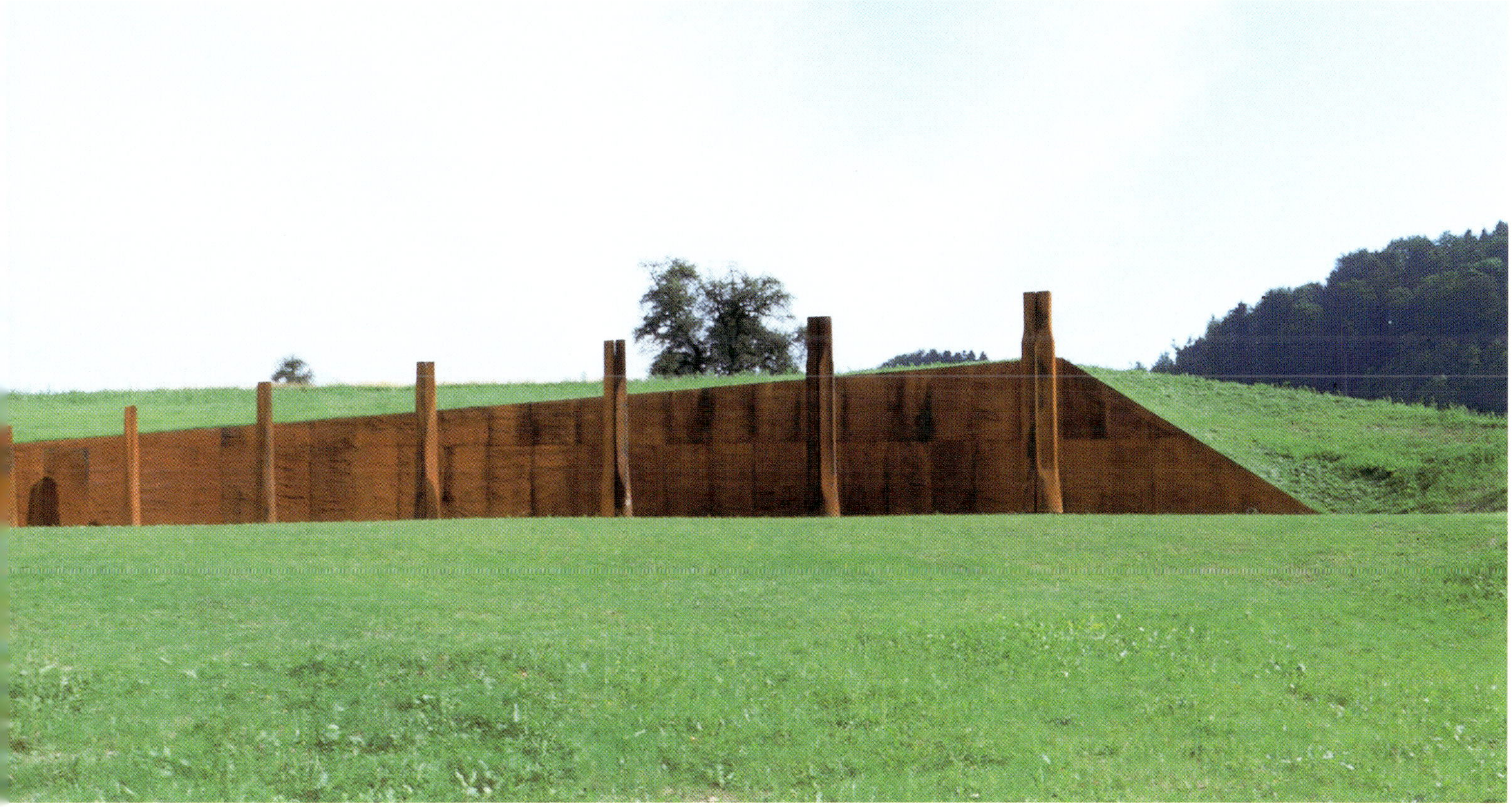

Outlook and review: the financial services industry in flux

By Lukas Mühlemann

At the beginning of 1997, our company announced a comprehensive reorganization and adopted a new group structure. CS Holding became Credit Suisse Group. The new organizational structure involved the creation of four autonomous business units, each concentrating on specific customer segments and markets: Credit Suisse focused on corporate and personal banking (retail banking) in Switzerland, Credit Suisse Private Banking on business with wealthy private customers, Credit Suisse First Boston on business with large companies and institutions (investment banking) and Credit Suisse Asset Management on business with institutional investors. This fundamental realignment, a crucial one for the future development of Credit Suisse Group, has created clear areas of responsibility and a greater transparency with regard to the objectives and the results of the individual business units and the Group as a whole.

About half a year later, Credit Suisse Group announced its merger with Winterthur Group, with which the bank had already established a successful partnership arrangement. By integrating the insurance operation with the banking group, we became one of the first companies to commit to the concept of Allfinanz, a trend that has since established itself within the financial services industry all over the world.

In Switzerland we were quick to take the action required for us to offer our customers comprehensive banking and insurance services. A whole series of initiatives was also launched internationally, most prominently the Personal Financial Services Europe strategy, which focuses on asset management for private clients in selected European markets. We aim to become one of the leading providers in this area of business, and the success of our pilot operation in Italy gives us great confidence for the future.

In order to strengthen our operations in the individual business areas, we have made a series of acquisitions over the past few years. In investment banking, we successfully acquired and integrated parts of BZW's European and Asian business in 1997. In 1998, we purchased Brazil's leading investment bank Garantia, and at the beginning of 2000 took over the Japanese equities business of Schroeders. Also in 1998, Credit Suisse Asset Management acquired the French Groupe Cristal. The acquisition in 1999 of Warburg Pincus Asset Management has considerably strengthened our position in US business. In 1997, Credit Suisse Private Banking took over France's Banque Hottinguer, followed in 1999 by Gestión Integral of Spain and the Spanish private banking arm of ABN Amro. In insurance business, we filled some strategic gaps in our operations in 1999 with the acquisition of Devitt and of the National Insurance and Guarantee Corporation, both based in the UK. At the beginning of 2000, we also acquired the Japanese insurance company Nicos Life. We plan to make further targeted acquisitions in future to strengthen our position.

The rapid development of e-commerce promises to alter the face of the financial services industry. Credit Suisse Group managed to position itself in this market at an early stage, and for various types of business it offers Internet-based services as an alternative to existing channels. At the same time, the Group is exploiting the opportunities afforded by innovative e-commerce applications to offer existing customers new products and to attract new customers. Furthermore, as part of the Personal Financial Services Europe strategy, we are launching new business models in which the Internet plays a pivotal role. With our strongly positioned brands Credit Suisse and Winterthur, an attractive product portfolio, a high quality of service, and a combination of traditional and new distribution channels, we have an excellent basis on which to build up our e-commerce activities.

The reorganization and realignment of Credit Suisse Group in 1997 created the preconditions for sustainable growth and high earning power. Between 1996 – before reorganization – and 1999, Group revenues increased by 19% per annum and assets under management rose 22% per annum. Working from 1996 Group operating results, net earnings per share have grown by 32% per year and return on equity has increased from 10% to 18%. We fully intend to maintain this momentum.

We view the market environment for financial service companies such as Credit Suisse Group over the coming years as extremely promising. On the one hand, the wealth of the world's population and the corresponding demand for suitable investment opportunities – especially for pension provision – will grow at an unprecedented rate. At the same time, companies and institutions worldwide will be using more and more of the products and services provided by professional, globally active financial service groups to help finance their operations and make more efficient use of their financial resources. Further consolidation is also expected in the global financial services sector, leaving the market to be contested by fewer, but stronger, corporations. Against this background, we have focused the Group's activities on two key disciplines. One of these is asset management (in the broadest sense), offering customers attractive savings, life insurance, pension and investment products, as well as other banking and insurance services. The other is investment banking, where we act as a financial market intermediary, servicing companies, countries and major institutions. We expect to achieve double-digit growth rates in both areas in forthcoming years.

In investment banking and in financial intermediation in general, few institutions remain that can keep pace with developments in today's highly competitive, global marketplace. Credit Suisse First Boston is one of the world's leading players in this sector.

With Credit Suisse, Credit Suisse Private Banking, Credit Suisse Asset Management and Winterthur we enjoy an excellent position in the savings, investment, and life insurance and pension markets.

To enable us to capitalize even more effectively on the great potential of the financial services market, at the beginning of April 2000, we realigned our organizational structure for the first time since the restructuring of 1997. As a result, Credit Suisse, Winterthur, and Personal Financial Services Europe have been incorporated into a new business area called Financial Services. The move allows us to more closely integrate our banking, insurance and e-commerce businesses and thus to develop new models for customer care as well as new and innovative products and services. This concentration of resources also facilitates the rapid development of our e-commerce activities, as well as the introduction of new business models in Switzerland and the exploitation of additional international business opportunities, notably in Europe.

These exciting prospects are, however, accompanied by ever more difficult challenges for providers of financial services: increasingly well-informed customers, growing difficulty in recruiting qualified staff, greater competition as other banks and insurance companies become more efficient, not to mention the competition from companies outside the industry. We aim to rise to these challenges.

The leader in technology investment banking.

The measure of leadership – 197 transactions valued at $114.6 billion in 1999

IPOs

Amount	Company	Type	Date
$2,160,000,000	Agilent Technologies	Initial Public Offering	November 1999
$1,024,650,000	TD Waterhouse	Initial Public Offering	June 1999
$450,500,000	Chartered Semiconductor	Initial Public Offering	October 1999
$425,500,000	Fairchild Semiconductor	Initial Public Offering	August 1999
$416,592,000	Freeserve	Initial Public Offering	July 1999
$414,000,000	NorthPoint	Initial Public Offering	May 1999
$383,500,000	mp3.com	Initial Public Offering	July 1999
$218,500,000	InterNAP	Initial Public Offering	September 1999
£145,000,000	Morse	Initial Public Offering	March 1999
$195,000,000	Kana	Initial Public Offering	November 1999
$187,680,000	Juniper Networks	Initial Public Offering	June 1999
$151,800,000	VA Linux	Initial Public Offering	December 1999
$144,900,000	USi	Initial Public Offering	April 1999
$134,550,000	InterTrust	Initial Public Offering	October 1999
$132,000,000	CacheFlow	Initial Public Offering	November 1999
$131,200,000	El Sitio	Initial Public Offering	December 1999
$126,000,000	1-800-flowers.com	Initial Public Offering	August 1999
$107,960,000	FreeNet	Initial Public Offering	December 1999
$107,217,000	Liberate	Initial Public Offering	July 1999
$103,500,000	Software.com	Initial Public Offering	June 1999
$100,740,000	iVillage	Initial Public Offering	March 1999
$98,670,000	TiVo	Initial Public Offering	September 1999
$95,480,000	tickets.com	Initial Public Offering	November 1999
$94,875,000	Retek	Initial Public Offering	November 1999
$92,000,000	marimba	Initial Public Offering	April 1999
$90,440,000	QXL.com	Initial Public Offering	October 1999
$89,160,000	Symyx	Initial Public Offering	November 1999
$88,000,000	miracle	Initial Public Offering	November 1999
$84,520,000	Andromeda	Initial Public Offering	July 1999
$80,500,000	autoweb.com	Initial Public Offering	March 1999
$80,500,000	Virata	Initial Public Offering	November 1999
$79,695,000	Commerce One	Initial Public Offering	July 1999
$77,630,000	Digital Impact	Initial Public Offering	November 1999
$76,500,000	ELMOS Semiconductor AG	Initial Public Offering	October 1999
$76,031,000	Netcentives	Initial Public Offering	October 1999
$73,600,000	Intraware	Initial Public Offering	February 1999
$73,600,000	phone.com	Initial Public Offering	June 1999
$72,000,000	AppNet	Initial Public Offering	June 1999
$72,000,000	Calipso	Initial Public Offering	December 1999
$69,000,000	bsquare	Initial Public Offering	October 1999
$69,000,000	Clarent	Initial Public Offering	June 1999
$69,000,000	Melita	Initial Public Offering	July 1999
$69,000,000	WF1	Initial Public Offering	November 1999
$67,275,000	careerbuilder	Initial Public Offering	May 1999
$66,400,000	E.piphany	Initial Public Offering	September 1999
$66,000,000	fogdog	Initial Public Offering	December 1999
$65,000,000	Destia	Initial Public Offering	May 1999
$64,664,000	Fanning	Initial Public Offering	July 1999
$64,400,000	Portal	Initial Public Offering	May 1999
$61,580,000	Interwoven	Initial Public Offering	October 1999
$60,000,000	greetings.com	Initial Public Offering	December 1999
$59,535,000	mortgage.com	Initial Public Offering	August 1999
$57,500,000	allaire	Initial Public Offering	January 1999
$55,200,000	Medscape	Initial Public Offering	September 1999
$55,200,000	Crossroads	Initial Public Offering	April 1999
$55,200,000	Viant	Initial Public Offering	June 1999
$55,200,000	Vitria	Initial Public Offering	September 1999
$53,800,000	Silicon Image	Initial Public Offering	October 1999
$53,130,000	pcorder	Initial Public Offering	February 1999
$53,130,000	Wavecom	Initial Public Offering	June 1999
$51,750,000	Silknet	Initial Public Offering	May 1999
$50,635,000	Tumbleweed	Initial Public Offering	August 1999
$48,000,000	Informatica	Initial Public Offering	April 1999
$46,346,000	Onyx	Initial Public Offering	February 1999
$45,700,000	parsytec	Initial Public Offering	June 1999
$44,850,000	NetIQ	Initial Public Offering	August 1999
$41,400,000	Audible	Initial Public Offering	July 1999
$37,500,000	Latitude	Initial Public Offering	May 1999
$35,000,000	the knot	Initial Public Offering	December 1999
€30,601,914	Dejo Team	Initial Public Offering	November 1999

Convertible Financings

Amount	Company	Type	Date
$1,250,000,000	amazon.com	Convertible Subordinated Debentures	January 1999
€350,000,000	Getronics	Convertible Bonds	March 1999
$450,000,000	bea	Convertible Subordinated Debentures	December 1999
$345,000,000	Veritas	Original Issue Discount Convertible Debentures	August 1999
$300,000,000	Citrix	Zero Coupon Convertible Subordinated Debentures	August 1999
$300,000,000	Conexant	Convertible Subordinated Notes	May 1999
$300,000,000	i2	Convertible Subordinated Debentures	December 1999
$200,000,000	Safeguard Scientifics, Inc.	Convertible Subordinated Notes	June 1999
$125,000,000	USi	Convertible Subordinated Debentures	October 1999
$300,000,000	Verio	Convertible Preferred	July 1999

This announcement is neither an offer to sell nor a solicitation of an offer to buy any of these securities. The offering is made only by the prospectus.
* As of December 20, 1999.

CREDIT SUISSE | FIRST BOSTON

Follow-on Common Stock Offerings

Amount	Company	Type	Date
$2,454,416,250	STMicroelectronics N.V.	Common Stock	September 1999
$1,024,650,000	phone.com	Common Stock	November 1999
$879,920,000	JDS Uniphase	Common Stock	July 1999
$464,260,000	VERITAS	Common Stock	June 1999
$352,750,000	CLARENT	Common Stock	November 1999
$327,750,000	COVAD	Common Stock	June 1999
$279,665,100	Sapient	Common Stock	November 1999
$248,800,000	VIANT	Common Stock	December 1999
$235,750,000	Xircom	Common Stock	December 1999
$230,470,000	MIPS	Common Stock	May 1999
$229,525,000	AppNet	Common Stock	November 1999
$218,500,000	PORTAL	Common Stock	September 1999
$209,760,000	EarthLink	Common Stock	January 1999
$187,500,000	NetIQ	Common Stock	November 1999
$167,400,000	CBSI	Common Stock	February 1999
$158,968,238	RF Micro Devices	Common Stock	January 1999
$148,800,000	allaire	Common Stock	September 1999
$141,740,000	DBT Online, Inc.	Common Stock	October 1999
$140,000,000	beyond.com	Common Stock	April 1999
$90,664,922	ACT	Common Stock	November 1999
$83,480,000	DuPont Photomasks, Inc.	Common Stock	March 1999
$80,681,900	ADVENT	Common Stock	June 1999
$78,057,400	KOPIN	Common Stock	November 1999
$75,600,000	iVillage	Common Stock	October 1999
$70,500,000	COM21	Common Stock	February 1999

Private Placements

Amount	Company	Type	Date
$500,000,000	ZHONE	Series A Convertible Preferred Stock	November 1999
$164,500,000	DATEK ONLINE	Series A Convertible Preferred Stock	June 1999
$155,000,000	emachines	Series B Convertible Preferred Stock	August 1999
$102,600,000	1-800-flowers.com	Series C Convertible Preferred Stock	May 1999
$67,375,000	Vyyo	Series C Convertible Preferred Stock	November 1999
$35,000,000	mortgage.com	Common Stock and Convertible Subordinated Debt	June 1999
$34,000,000	reciprocal	Series H Convertible Preferred Stock	November 1999
$32,800,000	qxl	Series D Convertible Preferred Stock	June 1999
$30,000,000	island	Common Stock	November 1999
$25,000,000	COMMERCE ONE	Series E Convertible Preferred Stock	April 1999
$23,620,000	greetings.com	Series G Convertible Preferred Stock	October 1999
$20,700,000	(Preferred Stock)	Series E Convertible Preferred Stock	October 1999
$19,200,000	INTERWOVEN	Series E Convertible Preferred Stock	June 1999
$17,800,000	phone.com	Series A Convertible Preferred Stock	March 1999
$16,500,000	INTERWORLD	Series A Convertible Preferred Stock	January 1999
$15,300,000	fogdog	Series D Convertible Preferred Stock	September 1999
$10,000,000	Lucent Digital Radio	Series A Convertible Preferred Stock	August 1999
$10,000,000		Series A Convertible Preferred Stock	July 1999

Debt Financings

Amount	Company	Type	Date
$4,500,000,000	Computer Associates	Senior Secured Credit Facility	June 1999
$500,000,000	GartnerGroup	Senior Credit Facility	July 1999
$410,000,000	FAIRCHILD SEMICONDUCTOR	Senior Secured Credit Facility	April 1999
$300,000,000	Gateway	Senior Secured Credit Facility	September 1999
$275,000,000	intersil	Senior Secured Credit Facility	August 1999
$220,000,000	ChipPAC	Senior Secured Credit Facility	August 1999
$180,000,000	Anteon	Senior Secured Credit Facility	June 1999
$100,000,000	RF Micro Devices	Senior Credit Facility	December 1999
$125,000,000	ZHONE	Senior Credit Facility	December 1999
$95,000,000	ICS	Senior Secured Credit Facility	May 1999
$45,000,000	DATEK ONLINE	Senior Credit Facility	April 1999
$32,000,000	Western Multiplex	Senior Secured Credit Facility	November 1999
£3,500,000	interactive investor international	Senior Secured Credit Facility	September 1999

Investment Grade and High-Yield Offerings

Amount	Company	Type	Date
$1,500,000,000	EDS	Senior Notes	October 1999
$300,000,000	FAIRCHILD SEMICONDUCTOR	Senior Subordinated Notes	March 1999
$200,000,000	intersil	Senior Subordinated Notes	August 1999
$160,000,000	ChipPAC	Senior Subordinated Notes	July 1999
$100,000,000	ICS	Senior Subordinated Notes	May 1999
$100,000,000	Anteon	Senior Subordinated Notes	April 1999
$100,000,000	Cherokee International	Senior Subordinated Notes	April 1999

Credit Suisse First Boston

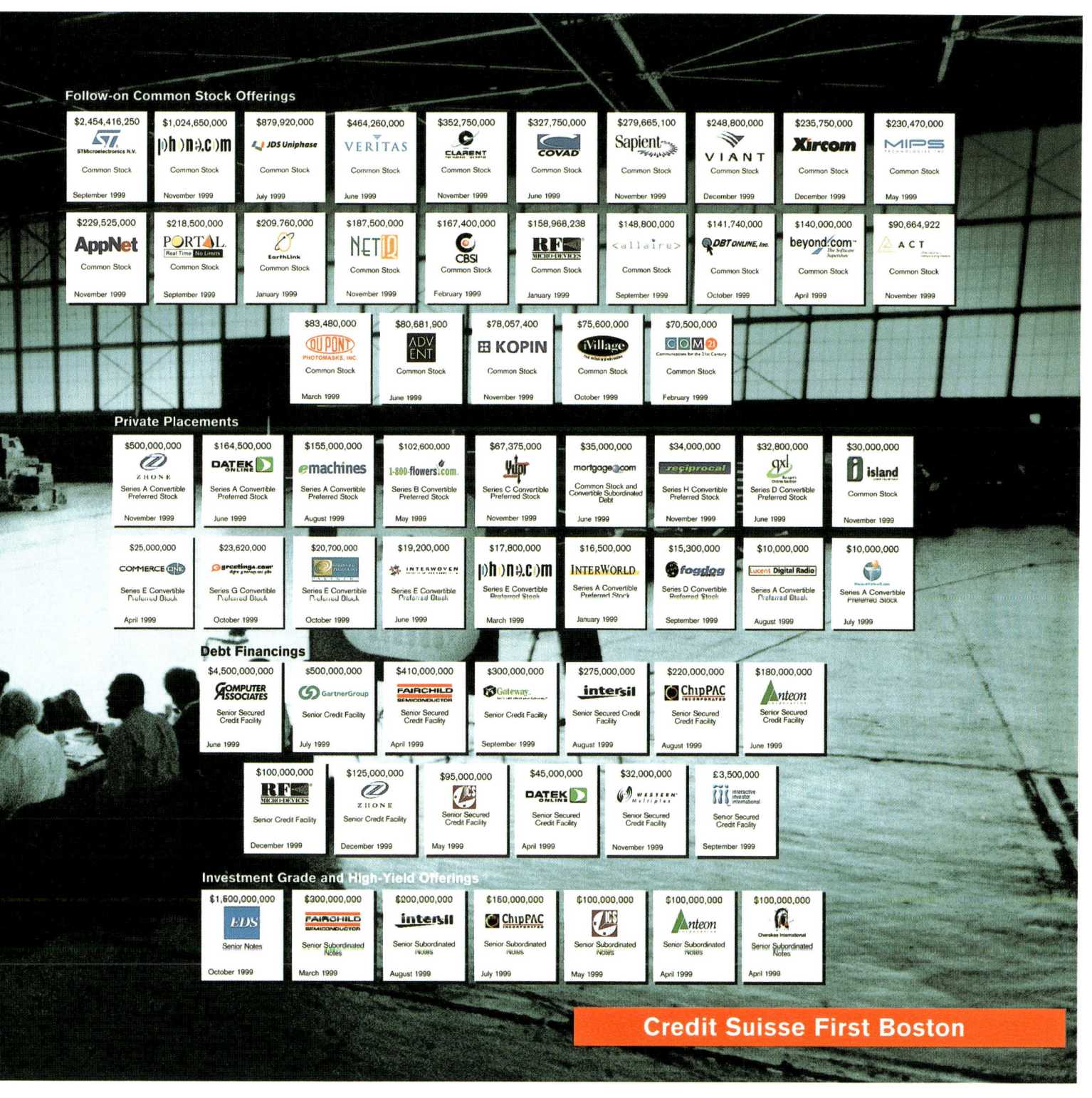

The most influential technology investment bank in 1999
- #1 in technology IPO transactions
- #1 in lead-managed Internet IPO volume
- #1 in technology equity private placement volume
- #1 in aftermarket performance
- Leader in industry-defining landmark transactions
  - largest software debt financing in history (Computer Associates)
  - largest Internet IPO (TD Waterhouse)
  - largest technology follow-on offering (ST Microelectronics)

www.tech.csfb.com

Appendices

|1950 |1960 |1970 |1980 |1990 |1996

The time chart shows all the *banks* in Switzerland taken over by SKA (CS Holding) in the period between 1856 and 1996.

Details of the individual banks do not always take account of changes in company name or ownership structure.

Financial, fiduciary and leasing companies taken over by SKA are not included; nor are subsidiaries founded by SKA.

kredit-Anstalt, ♦ 1976 SKA

ed Bank in Luzern (Centralschweizerische Hypothekenbank), ♦ 1925 SKA

e Aargauische Ersparniskasse (✶1812), ♦ Neue Aargauer Bank, ♦ 1994 CS Holding

e de Crédit, Geneva, ✶1927, ♦ 1971 SKA

✶1928, ♦ 1961 SKA

✶1934, ♦ 1974 SKA

Citybank, Zurich, ✶1954, ♦ 1981 SKA

White, Weld & Co., Zurich, ✶1955, ♦ 1962 SKA, 1973 renamed Clariden Bank

Krefina Bank, St. Gallen, ✶1955, ♦ 1981 SKA, 1993 wound up

Bank für Handel und Effekten, Zurich, ✶1958, ♦ 1981 SKA

SKA and its banks in Switzerland

	up to 1850	1860	1870	1880	1890	1900	1910	1920	1930	1940

- Bank Marcuard & Co., Bern, ✱1745, ◆ 1919 SKA
- Bank Leu & Co., Zurich, ✱1755, 1854 converted into a state-controlled joint stock company, 1869 privatized, ◆ 1990 CS Holding
- Bank Necker, Lachenmeyer & Co., Geneva, ◆ 1905 SKA
- Ersparniskasse Olten (EKO Bank), ✱1829, ◆ 1992 SKA
- Bank in Zürich, ✱1836, ◆ 1907 SKA, 1982 wound up
- Bank in St. Gallen, ✱1837, ◆ 1906 SKA
- Sparkassa Zug, ✱1840, 1906 renamed Bank in Zug, ◆ 1937 SKA
- Bank in Glarus, ✱1852, ◆ 1912 SKA
- **Schweizerische Kreditanstalt (SKA), Zurich, ✱1856**
- Bank in Luzern, ✱1856, ◆ 1912 SKA
- Bankhaus Wilhelm Köster & Co., Mannheim, ✱1856, 1896 renamed Oberrheinische Bank, ◆ 1904 SKA's Basel branch
- Bank Neumünster, Zurich, ✱1860, ◆ 1978 SKA, 1994 Bank Leu
- Bank Wädenswil, ✱1863, ◆ 1968 SKA, 1978 wound up
- Bank in Horgen, ✱1863, ◆ 1912 SKA
- Gewerbebank Baden, ✱1864, ◆ 1992 SKA, ◆ 1995 Neue Aargauer Bank
- St. Gallische Hypothekarkasse, ✱1864, ◆ 1907 SKA
- Bank Gebrüder Oechslin & Co., Schaffhausen, ✱1866, ◆ 1962 SKA
- Volksbank in Bern, ✱1869, 1881 renamed Schweizerische Volksbank, ◆ 1993 CS Holding/SKA
- Sparkasse Neumünster, Zurich, ✱1888, ◆ 1910 SKA
- Spar- und Leihkasse Aussersihl-Wiedikon, ✱1890, ◆ 1911 SKA
- Zürcher Hypothekarbank, ✱1896, 1903 SKA participation, 1906 renamed Schweizerische Boden
- Rhätische Bank, Davos, ✱1896, ◆ 1930 SKA
- Bank Hofmann & Co., Zurich, ✱1897, ◆ 1972 SKA, renamed Bank Hofmann AG
- St. Galler Handelsbank, ✱1901, ◆ 1906 SKA
- Obwaldner Gewerbebank, Sarnen, ✱1908, ◆ 1968 SKA
- Société de Banque et de Dépôts, Lausanne, ✱1909, ◆ 1921 SKA
- Centralschweizerische Hypothekenbank, Lucerne, ✱1909, 1916 renam
- Aargauische Hypotheken- und Handelsbank, ✱1909, ◆ 1989 Allgemei
- Banque Industrielle et Commercia
- Banque Populaire de Martigny,
- Affida Bank, Zurich

✱ Year of foundation
◆ Takeover/merger

Members of the executive board of Schweizerische Kreditanstalt (1856–1996)

1 Heinrich Abegg (1856–1857)
2 Johann Heinrich Fierz (1857–1859)
3 Caspar Huber (1859–1867) [not pictured]
4 Gottlieb Julius Martin (1867–1870)
5 Georg Stoll (1873–1885)
6 Theodor Spühler (1885–1900)
7 Wilhelm Caspar Escher (1900–1916)
8 Julius Frey (1900–1911)
9 Hermann Kurz (1905–1920)
10 Ernst Gross (1911–1920)
11 Emil Walch (1911–1918)
12 Adolf Jöhr (1918–1939)
13 Rudolph Gottfried Bindschedler (1919–1936)
14 Fritz Autenrieth (1920–1931)
15 Walter Fessler (1920–1944)
16 Heinrich Blass (1931–1946)
17 Henri Grandjean (1931–1948)

18 Joseph Straessle (1931–1941)
19 Wilhelm S. Merian (1937–1945)
20 Peter Vieli (1937–1951)
21 Ernst Gamper (1941–1953)

22 Heinrich Wegmann (1941–1948)
23 Theodor Frey (1945–1950)
24 Albert Linder (1945–1959)
25 Eberhard Reinhardt (1948–1973)

26 Felix W. Schulthess (1951–1963)
27 Edgar R. Zurlinden (1951–1960)
28 Jacques Jenny (1953–1967)
29 Jean-Jacques Kurz (1959–1965)

30 Robert Lang (1959–1975)
31 Hans Konrad Escher (1960–1977)
32 Robert H. Lutz (1963–1974)
33 Mario Singer (1963–1967)

34 Heinz R. Wuffli (1967–1977)
35 Oswald Aeppli (1969–1977)
36 C. Walter Fessler (1973–1980)
37 Rainer E. Gut (1973–1983)
38 Sergio Demiéville (1976/77)
39 Hans H. Hartung (1976–1981)
40 Robert A. Jeker (1976–1993)
41 Hans R. Frey (1977–1987)
42 Hugo von der Crone (1977–1990)
43 William Wirth (1977–1994)
44 Ernst Schneider (1979–1990)
45 Max P. Kopp (1981–1992)
46 Hans-Ulrich Doerig (1982–1993, 1996)
47 Kurt Widmer (1983–1993)
48 Hans Geiger (1987–1996)
49 Rudolf W. Hug (1987–1996)

50 Klaus Jenny (1987–1996)
51 Roland C. Rasi (1987–1990)
52 Hans-Jörg Rudloff (1987–1989)
53 Hans Peter Sorg (1987–1996)

54 Ruedi Stalder (1989/90)
55 Josef Ackermann (1990–1996)
56 Victor Erne (1990–1996)
57 Oswald J. Grübel (1991–1996)

58 Beat M. Fenner (1993–1996)
59 Alfred Gremli (1993–1996)
60 Paul Meier (1993–1996)
61 Franz von Meyenburg (1993–1996)

62 Martin Wetter (1993–1996)
63 Manfred J. Adami (1994/95)
64 Christopher W. Roberts (1996)

List of tables

Development of European major banks compared to SKA (1900–1990)	33
The chairmen of the board of directors of Schweizerische Kreditanstalt/ Credit Suisse Group (1856–2000)	58
Comparison between the major commercial banks (1880/1913)	69
Independent Commission of Experts Switzerland – Second World War: Gold deliveries by the Reichsbank to the Swiss commercial banks (1939–1945)	86
Comparison of SKA, SBV, SBG and SVB (1946/1956/1966/1976)	91
SKA securities safekeeping accounts (1945–1970)	93
SKA savings products (1970–1990)	118
Price performance of Leu Holding AG bearer shares (Sfr 100 nom.)	135
Price performance of CS Holding bearer shares (Sfr 500 nom.)	135
Effect of SKA/SVB merger on Swiss market share	140
SKA, SBV and SBG: number of branches and representative offices outside Switzerland (1959–1996)	167
Number of employees in non-Swiss branches and representative offices relative to number of employees at SKA head office (1959–1996)	167
White Weld's rank, volume and market share of global equity and debt capital transactions (1970–1977)	175
Rank, volume and market share of the main banks in Eurobond business (1963–1977)	179
Rank, volume and market share of Dillon Read and First Boston in global equity and debt capital transactions (1970–1977)	183
Global business with high-yield US securities: CS First Boston and the other major investment banks (1983–1990)	196
Members of the executive board of Schweizerische Kreditanstalt (1856–1996)	414

Appendices 419

List of charts

Chart	Page
Contribution made by banks to GDP (1998)	17
Development of the major Swiss banks (1755–1998)	24
Number of each different type of bank (1800–1945)	32
Cantonal banks and major banks: total assets (1914–1945)	35
Proportion of total assets accounted for by each type of bank (1800–1945)	36
Proportion of total assets accounted for by each type of bank (1945–1998)	39
SKA's total assets and foreign assets (1925–1950)	75
SKA's foreign assets in Germany, France and the USA (1933–1950)	76
From SKA to CS Holding (1989)	100
CS Holding group (as at April 1994)	103
Break-up of Elektrowatt (1997/98)	106
Project 'Focus' (1996/97)	107
Organizational structure of Credit Suisse Group (1 January 1997 to 31 March 2000)	108
Organizational structure of Credit Suisse Group (from 1 April 2000)	108
Customer deposits: SKA, SBV, SBG and SVB (1970–1990)	116
Savings deposits: SKA, SBV, SBG and SVB (1970–1990)	118
Mortgages: SKA, SBV, SBG and SVB (1970–1990)	119
Customer deposits in the form of savings and investments, in relation to mortgage loans issued by SKA, SBV, SBG and SVB (1970–1990)	120
Number of branches: SKA, SBV, SBG and SVB (1960–1990)	122
Customer deposits in the form of savings and investments, per branch: SKA, SBV, SBG and SVB (1970–1990)	124
Lead management (by volume) in underwriting business for domestic issuers: SKA, SBV and SBG (1970–1990)	127
SKA, SBV and SBG: position in Swiss core market (1990/1996)	145
From White Weld (Zurich) to CS First Boston (New York)	185
Transaction volumes in global underwriting business: Credit Suisse First Boston compared with non-US banks (1987–1999)	193
Transaction volumes in global underwriting business: Credit Suisse First Boston compared with the world's other major investment banks (1984–1999)	193
Transaction volumes in global M&A business: Credit Suisse First Boston compared with non-US banks (1987–1999)	194
Transaction volumes in global underwriting business: Credit Suisse First Boston compared with the world's other major investment banks (1984–1999)	194
Global M&A business: comparison between the major investment banks (1980–1999)	200
Global underwriting business: comparison between the major investment banks (1980–1999)	201
SKA's involvement in the establishment of insurance companies	216
Sales of life insurance and pension products: banks' share of premium volumes (1997)	219
Domestic business done by Swiss banks and life insurance companies	220
Assets held by Swiss investment fund companies in Switzerland and abroad (1990–1999)	221
CS Life: premium volumes (1992–1996)	226
CS Life: growth rates in Swiss direct single-life business (1992–1996)	227
CS Life: capital investments (1992–1996)	227
Bearer share price (indexed): SKA, SBV and SBG (31 March 1977 to 30 June 1977)	260
Texon's financial structure	269
Age of executive board members (1945–1996)	302
Graduates/non-graduates on the executive board (1945–1996)	304
Universities from which graduate executive board members earned their degrees (1945–1996)	305
Appointments to executive board (1945–1996)	306
Departures from executive board (1945–1996)	307
Origin of executive board members (1945–1996)	308
Rank of executive board members in the Swiss army (1945–1996)	310
Executive board membership of guilds and service clubs (1945–1996)	311
Management responsibilities at SKA: organization chart as at 1 January 1906	330
Development of SKA's organizational and management structure	332
Management responsibilities at SKA: organization chart as at 1 January 1987	335
Introduction of technology at SKA	349
IT staff (departments Oa/Os) as a proportion of head office personnel (1983–1995)	352
IT investment at SKA (1981–1996)	352
IT expenditure at Credit Suisse Group (1998/99)	353
IT staff at Credit Suisse Group (1998/99)	353
Development of communications and information technology from c. 1950 (SKA/Credit Suisse Group)	355
SKA and its banks in Switzerland	412

Glossary of abbreviations

Notes

Department names refer to SKA departments unless otherwise indicated.

Political parties and government departments are Swiss unless otherwise indicated.

The original German forms of Swiss company names (full and abbreviated) have been used throughout this book, e.g. SKA, SBV, SBG, Rentenanstalt. This is primarly to avoid confusion with regard to the structural and name changes undergone by some of these companies over the course of their history.

ABECOR	Associated Banks of Europe Corporation
AC	Assessment Center
AEG	Allgemeine Elektricitäts-Gesellschaft
AGB	Allgemeine Geschäftsbedingungen (General Conditions)
AIS	Anlage-Informations-System (Investment Information System)
Ap	SKA's Corporate planning and development department (subsequently Up)
ATAG	Allgemeine Treuhand AG
ATM	Automated teller machine
BAG	Bayernwerk AG
BAR	Schweizerisches Bundesarchiv (Swiss Federal Archives, Bern)
BBC	Brown Boveri & Cie. AG
BEKO	Betriebskostenrechnung (SKA's operational cost accounting system)
BG	Bundesgesetz (Swiss federal law)
BHB	Basler Handelsbank
BiW	Bank in Winterthur
BNP	Banque Nationale de Paris
BRB	Bundesratsbeschluss (decree by the Swiss Federal Council)
BT	Bankers Trust
BU	Business unit
BZW	Barclays De Zoete Wedd
CA	Creditanstalt-Bankverein, Vienna
Cb	Central bureau (SKA's accounting and controlling department, nowadays department CFA at Credit Suisse)
Cbu	Part of department Cb
CEO	Chief Executive Officer
CFA	Business unit Credit Suisse's accounting department (formerly Cb)
CIC	Planning/controlling/reporting subdivision (part of Credit Suisse's IT and operations division)
CIF	Customer Information File
CIS	Community of Independent States
CKW	Centralschweizerische Kraftwerke
CRAPA	Customer Relations and Profitability Analysis
CRM	Credit and Risk Management
CS	Credit Suisse
CSAM	Credit Suisse Asset Management
CSFB	Credit Suisse First Boston
CSFP	Credit Suisse Financial Products
CSPB	Credit Suisse Private Banking
CSG	Credit Suisse Group
CSH	CS Holding
CSWW	Credit Suisse White Weld Ltd., London
CS & WW	Société anonyme financière du Crédit Suisse et de White Weld, Zug
CTC	Custodian Trust Company
CVP	Christlichdemokratische Volkspartei (Christian Democratic People's Party)
DBV-Winterthur	Deutsche Beamtenversicherung Winterthur
DIS	Depot Information System (portfolio information system)
EBIC	European Banks International Corporation
EBRD	European Bank for Reconstruction and Development
EDP	Electronic data processing
EEC	European Economic Community
EFIC	European Financial Institutions Center (McKinsey)
EGL	Elektrizitäts-Gesellschaft Laufenburg
EIBA	Eidgenössische Bank
EKO Bank	EKO Hypothekar- und Handelsbank, Olten (formerly Ersparniskasse Olten)
ELG	Elektrizitäts-Lieferungsgesellschaft
EMA	Effekten-Maatschappij Amsterdam
EnBW	Energie Baden-Württemberg AG
ETH	Eidgenössische Technische Hochschule (Swiss Federal Institute of Technology)
EU	European Union
fasc.	Fascicle
FATF	Financial Action Task Force on Money Laundering
FBC	Federal Banking Commission
FCSFB	Financière Crédit Suisse – First Boston, Zug
FDEA	Federal Department of Economic Affairs
FDP	Freisinnig-Demokratische Partei (Radical Democratic Party)
FDPA	Federal Department of Political Affairs (now Federal Department of Foreign Affairs)
Fed	US Federal Reserve Board
Fides	Fides Treuhand-Vereinigung, Zurich
FISKA	Führungsinformationssystem SKA (Credit Suisse management information system)
FITS	Foreign Exchange Information and Trading System
FNCB	First National City Bank
'Focus'	Project for the restructuring of SKA / CS Holding into Credit Suisse Group with its four business units CS, CSPB, CSAM and CSFB, and the realignment of the bank's Swiss infrastructure
FTA	Federal Tax Administration
GBR	Gesellschaft für Bankrevisionen
GDP	Gross domestic product
GFI	Credit Suisse Group's IT office
GfS	Schweizerische Gesellschaft für praktische Sozialforschung
GHF	Credit Suisse Group's foundations, corporate history and archives department
GSK	Gesellschaft für Schweizerische Kunstgeschichte
Gss	SKA's corporate secretariat
GwG	Geldwäschereigesetz (Swiss law on money laundering)
HLS	Historisches Lexikon der Schweiz
HTL	Höhere Technische Lehranstalt (Swiss Technical College)
IAB	International Acceptance Bank
IBA	International Banking Act
IBM	International Business Machines
ICE	Independent Commission of Experts Switzerland – Second World War
ICEP	Independent Committee of Eminent Persons (Volcker Committee)
IFC	International Finance Corporation
IFR	International Financial Review
IMS	Information Management System
ING	Internationale Nederlanden Groep
IPO	Initial public offering
IT	Information technology
KOREAG	Kontroll & Revisions AG, Basel
KOSKA	Kostenstellenrechnung SKA (SKA's cost center accounting system)
KWL	Kraftwerk Laufenburg
KWR	Kraftübertragungswerke Rheinfelden
LAN	Local area network
LBO	Leveraged buyout

M&A	Mergers and acquisitions	vol.	Volume
'Match'	Synergy project between SKA, SVB and NAB	VSB	Vereinbarung über die Standesregeln zur Sorgfaltspflicht der Banken (Agreement on the Swiss Banks' Code of Conduct with Regard to the Exercise of Due Diligence)
MFO	Maschinenfabrik Oerlikon		
MIS	Management information system		
MIT	Massachusetts Institute of Technology	WAN	Wide area network
MVS	IBM mainframe operating system	'Winterthur'	Winterthur-Versicherungen (known internationally as Winterthur Insurance)
n.a.	Not available		
NAB	Neue Aargauer Bank	WW	White Weld
NOB	Nordostbahn	ZKB	Zürcher Kantonalbank
NOK	Nordostschweizerische Kraftwerke	'Zürich'	'Zürich' Versicherungs-Gesellschaft (now Zurich Financial Services Group)
NSDAP	Nationalsozialistische Deutsche Arbeiterpartei (Germany's National Socialist Workers' Party)		
NZZ	Neue Zürcher Zeitung		

Currencies

Oa	SKA's organization and automation department (later organization and applications development department)
OECD	Organization for Economic Co-operation and Development
OGR	Organizational Guidelines and Regulations
OPEC	Organization of Petroleum Exporting Countries
OVA	Overhead Value Analysis
Part. cert.	Participation certificate
PAT	PC-aided teaching
PdA	Partei der Arbeit (Swiss Communist party)
PFS	Personal Financial Services
PIAS	Personnel Information and Administration System
PKI	'Individual customers' segment in retail business
PKU	'Universal customers' segment in retail business
PR	Public relations
Publ.	Publisher
Rm	Marketing services department
RoA	Return on assets
RoE	Return on equity
Rück	Schweizerische Rückversicherungs-Gesellschaft (now Swiss Re)
SASI	Swiss American Securities Inc., New York
SBG	Schweizerische Bankgesellschaft (known internationally as Union Bank of Switzerland, or UBS; merged with SBV to form today's UBS AG)
SBKA	Schweizerische Bodenkredit-Anstalt
SBV	Schweizerischer Bankverein (known internationally as Swiss Bank Corporation, or SBC; merged with SBG to form today's UBS AG)
SBA	Swiss Bankers' Association
'Schweiz'	'Schweiz' Allgemeine Versicherungs-Aktien-Gesellschaft
SCO	Swiss Compensation Office
SDA	Schweizerische Depeschenagentur
SE-Banken	Svenska Enskilda Banken
SEC	Securities and Exchange Commission
SIC	Swiss Interbank Clearing
SIP	Société Internationale de Placements
SKA	Schweizerische Kreditanstalt (known internationally as Credit Suisse; in 1989, SKA was integrated into CS Holding, which in 1997 restructured to form today's Credit Suisse Group)
SLS	Schweizerischer Landesverband für Sport
SLV	Schweizerischer Leichtathletikverband
SMEs	Small and medium-sized enterprises
SNB	Swiss National Bank
SP	Sozialdemokratische Partei der Schweiz (Social Democratic Party of Switzerland)
StGB	Strafgesetzbuch (Swiss Penal Code)
SVB	Schweizerische Volksbank (known internationally as Swiss Volksbank)
SVP	Schweizerische Volkspartei (Swiss People's Party)
SWIFT	Society for Worldwide Interbank Financial Telecommunication
Swissam	Swiss American Corporation, New York
TdS	Tour de Suisse
UH	Üetlihof
Up	Corporate planning and development department (formerly Ap)

DM	German mark
Esc	Escudo
Ffr	French franc
Sch	Austrian schilling
Sfr	Swiss franc
£	British pound sterling
$	US dollar
Can$	Canadian dollar

Numbers

m	million (1,000,000)
bn	billion (1,000,000,000)

Notes

NB: Dates in the Notes are written in American format: month/day/year.

Part One: Events

1. Cf. Cassis, Financiers, p. 310.
2. The chart 'Contribution made by banks to GDP (1998)' is based on information from Credit Suisse's Economic Research Department.
3. The seminal text on the history of banking in Zurich in the 16th and 17th century is: Peyer, Handel und Bank.
4. Cf. Körner, HLS.
5. Cf. Iklé, Finanzplatz, p. 17ff.
6. Cf. Iklé, Finanzplatz, p. 25.
7. Cf. Bauer, Swiss Banking, p. 58. For the history of Bank Leu cf. also Keller, Leu; Landmann, Leu.
8. For savings banks cf. e.g. Ritzmann, Schweizer Banken, p. 23ff. Sparkasse der Stadt Zürich was taken over by Zurich Kantonalbank in 1990.
9. Cf. Cassis, Banking in Switzerland, p. 1015.
10. Cf. Körner, Schweiz, p. 279.
11. Über Banken in der Schweiz 1835, p. 2, p. 31.
12. Cf. Ritzmann, Schweizer Banken, p. 38.
13. Cf. Cassis, Financiers, p. 294f.
14. Alongside Kantonalbank von Bern and Banque Cantonale Vaudoise, these were the two state mortgage banks in Bern (Hypothekarkasse des Kantons Bern) and Geneva (Caisse Hypothécaire du Canton de Genève) and the cantonal savings bank in Geneva (Banque de Genève). Cf. Ritzmann, Schweizer Banken, p. 46, p. 313ff.
15. Zimmermann, Escher 1994, p. 14.
16. Cf. Körner, Schweiz, p. 281.
17. For the history of Geneva as a financial center see e.g. the relevant sections of: Iklé, Finanzplatz; Mottet, Schweizer Banken. Cf. also Bulletin 7/1981, p. 14f.
18. E.g. 1849 the company 'Omnium, Société Civile Genevoise d'emploi de fonds'; Cf. Iklé, Finanzplatz, p. 16; Mottet, Schweizer Banken, p. 74.
19. Cf. Iklé, Finanzplatz, p. 16. Later merged with Comptoir d'Escompte.
20. Cf. Wetter, Lokal- und Mittelbanken, p. 19. The 'property loan crisis' ('Bodenkreditkrise'): During the 1850s and 1860s there was a profound change in attitudes on the Swiss credit market. Unsecured, high-interest loans, especially in the form of equities and bonds, increasingly became the preferred instruments, while low-interest loans became less and less popular with the banks. At the same time the general level of interest rates began to rise. This phenomenon could be seen particularly strongly in 1863, a booming year for company start-ups, and led to a property loan crisis.
21. The number of joint-stock banks went up from eight in 1850 to 48 by the end of 1873. Cf. Pfau, Bankwesen, p. 66.
22. Jöhr, Notenbanken, p. 90. Cf. Martin Vollenwyder, Das Bankwesen in Europa zwischen 1830 und 1890, 11.3.1998 (lecture).
23. Cf. Ritzmann, Schweizer Banken, p. 92.
24. Cf. Bauer, Swiss Banking, p. 139.
25. Cf. Reichesberg, Handwörterbuch, vol. I, p. 409f.
26. These and other examples are from Ritzmann, Schweizer Banken, p. 106.
27. Cf. Bauer, Swiss Banking, p. 152; Cf. also Mottet, Schweizer Banken, p. 162.
28. Cf. Reichesberg, Handwörterbuch, vol. III/1, p. 364.
29. Cf. Bänziger, Bankengesetz, p. 8.
30. Cf. Bänziger, Bankengesetz, p. 10. Owing to the large number of bank collapses, some cantons introduced an overall cantonal regulator for savings banks: 1885 Canton Aargau and 1890 Canton St. Gallen.
31. Cf. Ritzmann, Schweizer Banken, p. 105.
32. Roesle, SKA, p. 7.
33. Cf. Pohl, Bankgeschäfte, p. 209.
34. Cf. Iklé, Finanzplatz, p. 26.
35. The four mixed institutions were Pestalozzi im Thalhof, Sal. Pestalozzi zum Steinbock, Hans Conrad Schulthess Erben (subsequently Rahn & Bodmer) and Hans Caspar Schulthess & Co. (liquidated in 1862). The company Tobler-Stadler can be described as a pure bank. The Ragionenbuch of 1837 does not list Bank in Zürich, founded in 1836. Cf. Wetter, Lokal- und Mittelbanken, p. 9.
36. Cf. Iklé, Finanzplatz, p. 28.
37. Cf. Körner, Schweiz, p. 285.
38. Cf. Ritzmann-Blickenstorfer, Historische Statistik der Schweiz. The figure of 454 banking institutions does not include private banks, foreign banks, finance companies or Raiffeisenkassen (rural credit banks). There were already 453 banking institutions in Switzerland by 1884. The figures quoted in Historische Statistik differ, sometimes significantly, from those that appear in other sources. This can be explained by the different definitions and methods of counting used by different researchers.
39. Cf. Ungerer, Finanzplatz Schweiz, p. 49.
40. For Ticino as a financial center, cf. Allenbach, Tessin.
41. Cf. Ungerer, Finanzplatz Schweiz, p. 45.
42. Cf. Pohl, Bankensysteme, p. 228.
43. Wetter, Lokal- und Mittelbanken, p. 92.
44. Cf. Cassis, Evolution of Financial Institutions, p. 67.
45. All data on Barclays Bank, Crédit Lyonnais and Deutsche Bank come from theses banks' annual reports and internal statistics. It should be noted that total assets and headcount shown for Barclays comprise the consolidated figures for Barclays Bank and Barclays Bank DCO (Dominion, Colonial & Overseas), despite the fact that these two organizations were not brought together under the same roof (Barclays Plc.) until 1985.
46. Cf. Bänziger, Bankengesetz, p. 25f.; Cassis, Evolution of Financial Institutions, p. 67.
47. Cf. Ungerer, Finanzplatz Schweiz, p. 48f. The USA's great wave of mergers at the end of the 1920s came some time after Europe's. Cf. Bulletin 1929.

48 Cf. Ungerer, Finanzplatz Schweiz, p. 58 (no exact annual figures).
49 Cf. Ritzmann-Blickenstorfer, Historische Statistik der Schweiz.
50 Cf. Albisetti, Handbuch 1964; Wetter, Lokal- und Mittelbanken, p. 8.
51 The terms used in the text and charts for the different groups of banks, the figures for the cantonal banks' and the major banks' total assets and the figures for the performance of the different types of banks are based for *the period up to 1945* on: Ritzmann-Blickenstorfer, Historische Statistik der Schweiz.
52 For the history of Basel as a financial center, see e.g. the relevant sections of Bauer, Swiss Banking, p. 77ff. Cf. also Mottet, Schweizer Banken, p. 151ff.
53 Cf. Ungerer, Finanzplatz Schweiz, p. 58.
54 Mast, Entwicklungstendenzen 1973.
55 Cf. Iklé, Finanzplatz, p. 97.
56 Cf. Lusser, Bankenstruktur, p. 33. The major banks' share of retail business rose from about 20% (1946) to about 40% (1970).
57 Cf. Zur Bankenkonzentration, Bulletin special publication (P), February 1974, p. 1f.; SBA, Kompendium 2000, p. 57.
58 Cf. Kilgus, Grossbanken, p. 53f.; Schweizerisches Bankwesen im Jahre 1946.
59 Cf. Schweizerisches Bankwesen im Jahre 1946.
60 Cf. Ungerer, Finanzplatz Schweiz, p. 66.
61 The terms used in the text and charts for the different groups of banks, and the figures for the total assets of the different types of banks are based *for the period after 1945* on the Swiss National Bank's statistical publications: Schweizerisches Bankwesen im Jahre 1945ff., Die Banken in der Schweiz 1996ff. Because as late as the early 20th century the figures for total assets were sometimes based on estimates, and because survey methods and the criteria for categorizing bank types have repeatedly changed over the years, there are small discrepancies between the figures from Historische Statistik der Schweiz (which form the basis of the chart that details the proportion of total assets by type of bank 1800–1945) and those from the SNB's statistical publications (which form the basis of the chart that details the proportion of total assets by type of bank 1945–1998).
62 For information about the figures used in this section, cf. Kilgus, Grossbanken, p. 53f.; Schweizerisches Bankwesen im Jahre 1950, 1977, 1990. At the end of 1998, 16 private banks remained in Switzerland.
63 Cf. Allenbach, Tessin, p. 175, p. 178.
64 Cf. Die Banken in der Schweiz 1998, p. 20. For the period prior to 1995, there are differences between the SNB's figures and those obtained from the SBA Kompendium.
65 Cf. SBA, Kompendium February 2000, p. 12.
66 Cf. Die Banken in der Schweiz 1997; Bulletin 5/1999, p. 11.
67 Cf. SBA, Kompendium 2000, p. 57.
68 Cf. Bergier, Wirtschaftsgeschichte, p. 336.
69 For the history of SKA, cf. the main texts produced on the occasion of the bank's 100-year and 50-year anniversaries: Jöhr, SKA; Esslinger, SKA. Cf. also Roesle, SKA.
70 Cf. Baumann, SKA und NOB, p. 153f.
71 In 1919, Ernst Gagliardi published a monumental work on the life and works of Alfred Escher: Gagliardi, Escher. No later comprehensive study of Escher exists, and despite various brief portraits and examinations of individual aspects, there is no real tradition of Alfred Escher research. For an overview, cf. Jung, Gottfried Keller-Stiftung, p. 60ff.; Zimmermann, Escher 1982; SKA, Escher 1994. For Escher and liberal Zurich, cf. Craig, Geld und Geist. For the young Alfred Escher, cf. Schmid, Der junge Escher.
72 Cf. Bauer, Swiss Banking, p. 75.
73 Gründerstatuten (founding articles) 1856, § 12c.
74 Cf. Bauer, Swiss Banking, p. 106f.; Ritzmann, Schweizer Banken, p. 63.
75 Cf. Jöhr, SKA, p. 44. For details of the corporate objectives, cf. SKA annual report 1857; minutes of the SKA board of directors 12. 24. 1856; 9. 28. 1857; 3. 20. 1858.
76 SKA annual report 1860.
77 Cf. e.g. Esslinger, SKA, p. 151.
78 SKA annual report 1867. In 1996, the annual accounts of SKA (parent company) showed a technical loss, partly because of the cost of restructuring activities (extraordinary provisions and write-downs, changes to credit risk management).
79 Cf. Jöhr, SKA, p. 214 .
80 According to its articles of association, the NOB had equity capital of Sfr 50 million, of which only Sfr 39 million was issued as shares. Cf. Baumann, SKA and NOB, p. 142.
81 Cf. Baumann, SKA und NOB, p. 158 (note 31). The personal equity portfolios of the SKA board members are not included in the figure.
82 SKA annual report 1871. SKA's participation in the consortium initially came to Sfr 2.25 million for its own account. At this point in time, the Swiss members of the consortium had to raise a total of Sfr 29 million. Cf. Häsler, Gotthard, p. 113. SKA made another financial commitment to the Gotthard project at the end of 1871 when it helped the NOB to raise the money it would need to build the Gotthard line. This consisted of Sfr 3.5 million in write-offs and a Sfr 9 million syndicate stake.
83 The total cost of the construction of the Gotthard railway (1872–1880) finally came to Sfr 228 million. Despite a drastic reduction in the building program, this was still Sfr 40 million over budget. Italy committed the most money with Sfr 58 million; Switzerland came next with Sfr 31 million, followed by Germany with Sfr 30 million. The remainder was provided by banks and private investors by means of bond and equity issues. Cf. Bergier, Wirtschaftsgeschichte, p. 313. For details of how the costs were divided up, cf. e.g. Lüönd, Gotthard, p. 83; Häsler, Gotthard, p. 113.
84 The initiative to set up the Nationalbahn came from National Councillors Johann Jakob Sulzer

and Theodor Ziegler-Bühler, both of whom were also directors of Bank in Winterthur. The City of Winterthur was also involved. Cf. Strehle, Ganz oben, p. 35.
85 Cf. Baumann, SKA und NOB, p. 149.
86 Conrad Widmer first contacted Bank Leu, which had recently (1854) been converted into a joint-stock company (Aktiengesellschaft) with help from the government, to found the company 'free from self-interest from any side'. Cf. Rentenanstalt 1857–1957, p. 27.
87 Cf. statement by Moritz Ignaz Grossmann. In an official report for SKA he recommended participating in the establishment of Rückversicherung ('Gutachten zu Handen der Tit. Schweizerischen Creditanstalt in Zürich über eine von derselben unter Mitwirkung der Allgemeinen Versicherungs-Gesellschaft "Helvetia" in St. Gallen zu gründende Rückversicherungsgesellschaft').
88 Cf. Jöhr, SKA, p. 118.
89 Cf. Esslinger, SKA, p. 181.
90 For information on the economic crisis at the Maggi company and on the federal government's original participation, cf. Jung, Gottfried Keller-Stiftung, p. 120ff.
91 Cf. Roesle, SKA, p. 70.
92 Cf. Jöhr, SKA, p. 180f.
93 Cf. Esslinger, SKA, p. 136f.
94 SKA annual report 1897.
95 In 1955, Hypothekenbank was transformed into an investment and management company for the property held by the bank at that time. It was finally wound up in 1960.
96 For further information on unsecured credits and current account business, cf. Jöhr, SKA, p. 109.
97 The 1863–1873 annual reports only distinguished – without further details – between three categories: 'Borrowers from Canton Zurich', 'Borrowers from Switzerland outside Canton Zurich' and 'Foreign borrowers'.
98 Cf. Bergier, Wirtschaftsgeschichte, p. 214, p. 218.
99 Jöhr, SKA, p. 173.
100 SKA annual report 1906.
101 Cf. Esslinger, SKA, p. 139.
102 SKA annual report 1900.
103 Cf. minutes of the SKA board of directors, 6. 29. 1911.
104 Roesle, SKA, p. 43.
105 Cf. SKA Gründerstatuten (founding articles) 1856, § 12 g.
106 Cf. Eidgenössische Bank 1863–1913, p. 31.
107 Cf. Duperrex, SVB, p. 156.
108 Cf. Jöhr, SKA, p. 130.
109 In 1900 SKA, together with Deutsche Bank, took a stake in Oberrheinische Bank in Mannheim. SKA participated out of a desire to have an influence over the branch that Oberrheinische Bank already planned to open in Basel. Cf. Esslinger, SKA, p. 124.
110 Jöhr, SKA, p. 216.
111 Minutes of the SKA board of directors, 8. 24. 1882; for details of the failure of this plan, cf. minutes of the SKA board of directors, 11. 30. 1882.
112 Cf. minutes of the SKA board of directors, 2. 13. 1897.
113 Cf. Wetter, Bank in Winterthur, p. 113.
114 Cf. minutes of the SKA board of directors, 2. 2 . 1911.
115 For the table 'Comparison between the major commercial banks (1880/1913)', cf. the annual reports of the banks concerned. For the Volksbank in Bern, the co-operative capital is given under the 'Share capital' column. Shareholders' equity includes the share capital, plus the reserves and profits carried forward; in the case of Volksbank in Bern it comprises the co-operative capital, plus the reserves and profits carried forward.
116 Minutes of the SKA board of directors, 7. 30. 1914.
117 Minutes of the SKA board of directors, 9. 3. 1914.
118 Cf. minutes of the SKA board of directors, 9. 4. 1914.
119 Cf. Jöhr, SKA, p. 289.
120 Cf. minutes of the SKA board of directors, 3. 21. 1935.
121 Cf. Jöhr, SKA, p. 391.
122 For these figures and the subsequent information about SKA's securities portfolio, cf. Jöhr, SKA, p. 278, p. 387, p. 473.
123 Cf. Jöhr, SKA, p. 303.
124 Cf. Cassis, Evolution of Financial Institutions, p. 68.
125 Cf. Jöhr, SKA, p. 299ff.
126 Cf. minutes of the SKA board of directors, 1. 5. 1939.
127 Cf. minutes of the SKA board of directors, 5. 19. 1930.
128 Cf. minutes of SKA finance committee, 2. 12. 1925, 1. 10. 1929.
129 Cf. Wilkins, Swiss investments, p. 124.
130 For the quotations, cf. minutes of SKA's finance committee, 12. 12. 1938. By April 1941, Swiss American Corporation and New York Agency had to move to a neighboring building at Pine Street 30 because space was already becoming tight at the former Speyer offices.
131 Letter from the chairman of the SBA's 'Schutzkomitee Deutschland' (Protection Committee, Germany), Adolf Jöhr, to the FDEA's trade department, 1. 8. 1937.
132 Memorandum from SKA's legal department, 12. 14. 1945.
133 Letter from Colonel Müller to Eberhard Reinhardt, Director of the Swiss Federal Finance Administration, 2. 16. 1945. Printed in facsimile in: NZZ, 1. 27. 1998.
134 SCO's audit report on SBKA, 10. 15. 1945, p. 29. BAR, E 7160-07 (-) 1968/54, Spezialfall 4/SBKA.
135 SCO's report to the FPD, 2. 1. 1946, p. 3. BAR, E 7160-07 (-) 1968/54, Spezialfall 4/SBKA.
136 SCO's report on investigations into the Société de Gestion Rodopia, 1. 10. 1946, p. 1. BAR, E 7160-07 (-) 1968/54, Spezialfall 4/SBKA; Report on the visit to the intelligence service of the Zurich Cantonal Police of 7. 13. 1945, p. 6. BAR, E 7160-07 (-) 1968/54, Spezialfall 4/SBKA.

137 SCO's report to the FPD, 2. 1. 1946, p. 9.
138 Separate minutes of the Bank Leu board committee, 1. 20. 1943.
139 Cf. ICE, Gold Transactions, p. 60.
140 Letter from Federal Councillor Ernst Nobs to former Federal Councillor Ernst Wetter, 5. 10. 1946. BAR, 6100 (A) 25/2326.
141 ICEP, Dormant Accounts, p. 10f.
142 ICEP, Dormant Accounts, p. 13f.
143 CSG Annual Report 1996/97, p. 21.
144 Minutes of the SKA board of directors, 10. 21. 1945.
145 The tables for 1946–1976 are based on the annual reports of the banks concerned.
146 Annual profit in relation to average equity capital.
147 Costs in relation to income. The cost-income ratio is a measure of the efficiency of the earning performance.
148 Cf. minutes of the SKA board of directors, 4. 25. 1968.
149 Cf. Jöhr, SKA, p. 495.
150 Jöhr, SKA, p. 492.
151 Cf. Felix W. Schulthess, Strukturwandlungen im Kreditgeschäft der Schweizer Banken (1960), p. 4, Schulthess Archive.
152 Cf. minutes of the SKA board of directors, 12. 11. 1952.
153 Cf. SKA annual report 1970, p. 27.
154 Felix W. Schulthess, Zins und Kredit in der Schweiz, 3. 12. 1974, p. 9, Schulthess Archive.
155 Cf. Valcambi SA, Chiasso (company brochure, 1995).
156 Cf. minutes of the SKA board of directors, 6. 2. 1949.
157 Minutes of the SKA board of directors, 8. 23. 1951, p. 270.
158 Minutes of the SKA board of directors, 7. 5. 1951.
159 Cf. minutes of the SKA board of directors, 10. 20. 1955.
160 The Euromarkets are international money, credit and capital markets on which bank deposits, bank loans and securities denominated in national currencies – but invested outside the national territory concerned – are granted and traded. Cf. Albisetti, Handbuch, p. 268.
161 Cf. minutes of the SKA board of directors, 8. 20. 1970.
162 Cf. minutes of the SKA board of directors, 4. 25. 1972, p. 91f.; minutes of SKA's finance committee, 4. 25. 1972, 11. 16. 1972.
163 Cf. SKA annual report 1973, p. 30.
164 Interview with Felix W. Schulthess, 1. 18. 1975, p. 4, Schulthess Archive.
165 SKA annual report 1976, p. 33.
166 Cf. minutes of the SKA board of directors, 5. 7. 1981.
167 Bulletin 4/1989, p. 6.
168 Cf. Bulletin 4/1989, p. 6 (Speech by Rainer E. Gut to the annual meeting of shareholders of 12 April 1989).
169 Cf. Bulletin 6/1996, p. 5.
170 Rainer E. Gut at the CSH annual meeting of shareholders of 5. 31. 1996 (manuscript).
171 For media reporting of the sale of Elektrowatt AG, cf. e.g. NZZ, 12. 30. 1996; NZZ, 4. 1. 1998; Börsen-Zeitung, 5. 24. 1997.
172 NZZ, 8. 17. 1996.

Part Two: Strategic Pillars

173 Felix W. Schulthess, Die Bank als Dienstleistungsbetrieb, 3. 16. 1971, p. 10, Schulthess Archive.
174 Cf. letter from Karl Reichmuth, manager of the Schwyz branch, to Heinz R. Wuffli, member of the executive board, 11. 18. 1975.
175 Werner Flückiger, Passivgeschäft/Privatkundschaft, 1. 5. 1978, p. 1 [Flückiger, Passivgeschäft].
176 Cf. Flückiger, Passivgeschäft, p. 3.
177 SKA, Directive W-1065, 3. 5. 1982.
178 Klaus Jenny, address to commercial banking division, 9. 19. 1991, p. 88 [commercial banking division address]. Mortgage claims comprise direct mortgages (called 'mortgage investments' in the balance sheet) and indirect mortgages (called 'fixed advances and mortgage-backed loans').
179 Cf. commercial banking division address, p. 82ff.
180 Cf. minutes of the SKA board of directors, 2. 15. 1962, p. 68.
181 Cf. minutes of the SKA board of directors, 3. 3. 1977, p. 349.
182 Minutes of the SKA board of directors, 5. 11. 1978, p. 77.
183 Cf. Handelszeitung, 5. 11. 1978.
184 Minutes of the SKA board of directors, 3. 3. 1977, p. 349.
185 Cf. Albisetti, Handbuch 1977 (under entry for 'Bankstelle').
186 Cf. minutes of SKA senior managers' conference, 11. 17. 1978.
187 Cf. Bulletin (P) 11·12/1988, p. 56.
188 When it was first established, the cartel's members were SKA, Union Financière (Association of Genevan Private Bankers) and Schweizerischer Bankverein. By 1905 Eidgenössische Bank, Kantonalbank von Bern, Basler Handelsbank and the Basel private bank Speyer & Co. had joined; Bank in Winterthur, Bank in Luzern and Leu & Co. joined in 1908, and finally SVB joined in 1911. Kantonalbank von Bern chaired the cartel.
189 The standing consortium for the underwriting of bonds issued by foreign borrowers consisted of SKA, SBV, SBG, Leu, SVB, the Association of Genevan Private Bankers, A. Sarasin & Cie., Basel, Privatbank & Verwaltungsgesellschaft, Zurich, the Zurich Private Bankers Group (Julius Bär & Co., Rahn & Bodmer, J. Vontobel & Co.), and Switzerland's oldest private bank, Wegelin & Co., St. Gallen.
190 Steigmeier, Elektrowatt, p. 146.
191 The figures shown in the chart 'Lead management (by volume) in underwriting business for domestic issuers: SKA, SBV and SBG (1970–1990)' include transactions involving public bonds, mortgage bonds, convertible

bonds and subordinate bonds of domestic issuers and of their foreign subsidiaries guaranteed by the Swiss parent company. The chart does not include either issues of shares, participation certificates and other equity paper, or private placements; however the figures shown account for the greater part of Swiss-franc underwriting business conducted with domestic borrowers.

192 Between 1957 and 1964 the major banks abided by a voluntary code on underwriting. This was then replaced by statutory underwriting controls when the federal government decided to fight against the inflow of capital from abroad and the resulting high level of inflation by restricting lending and by intervening on the money and capital markets. Between 1967 and 1972, new voluntary restrictions on the part of the banks replaced the legal system of control. Then state controls on underwriting business were reintroduced as a result of interest rate and inflation policy; these lasted till 1975. However, controls became less and less justifiable as the Swiss capital market relaxed in the wake of recession.
193 Cf. Ernst Kilgus, Wir werden keine Elefantenhochzeiten haben ('No giant mergers for us'). Interview, in: Sonntags-Zeitung, 4. 29. 1990 [Kilgus, Elefantenhochzeiten].
194 Cf. Thiemann, Zukunft, p. 13ff.
195 The term 'retail business' (according to the American definition) refers to all corporate business except business with multinationals, plus all personal banking business, except private banking. Cf. Invest, Magazin der Finanz und Wirtschaft, no. 11, 1996, p. 22.
196 Cf. Josef Ackermann, Experiences from the union of two major banks, speech of 1. 20. 1994, p. 6.
197 Cf. Kilgus, Elefantenhochzeiten.
198 Cf. e.g. Commercial banking division address; SVB annual report 1991.
199 Finanz und Wirtschaft, 4. 11. 1990, p. 13.
200 Handelszeitung, 4. 12. 1990, p. 15.
201 Cf. Tages-Anzeiger, 4. 11. 1990, p. 1.
202 Cf. Exchange offer and listing prospectus, 5. 17. 1990.
203 Cash, 12. 21. 1990.
204 Cf. NZZ, 7. 10. 1991, p. 35.
205 Cash, 12. 21. 1990.
206 Basler Zeitung, 4. 30. 1992.
207 Wall Street Journal, 4. 30. 1992.
208 Cf. Public exchange offer by CS Holding to the bearer shareholders of Leu Holding AG, Zug, November 1993.
209 Cf. e.g. Basler Zeitung, 4. 30. 1992.
210 Cf. Commercial banking division address, p. 85.
211 For information on EKO Bank cf.: Tages-Anzeiger, 10. 24. 1992; Oltner Tagblatt, 10. 24. 1992 (quote from Silvio de Capitani); NZZ, 10. 27. 1992; KPMG Fides, Kurzbericht über die Bonitätsprüfungen der Ausleihungen, Basel, 10. 26. 1992; reports by the Revisionsgesellschaft der Regionalbanken (Reba) and by KPMG.
212 Tages-Anzeiger, 11. 4. 1992.
213 Article 6 of the takeover agreement restricted the guarantee to Sfr 40 million.
214 NZZ, 10. 24. 1992.
215 Sonntags-Zeitung, 10. 25. 1992. For Ackermann's statement to the Olten municipal council, cf. Oltner Tagblatt, 10. 27. 1992.
216 Oltner Tagblatt, 10. 27. 1992 (editorial). EKO Bank had been subject to FBC regulation since 1935. See list of companies subject to FBC regulation according to the Federal Law on Banks and Savings Banks of 11. 8. 1934, 5. 1. 1966.
217 Oltner Tagblatt, 10. 27. 1992 (editorial).
218 Quote by the chief councillor of Olten to EKO Bank's board of directors, in: minutes of the SKA board committee, 1. 7. 1992.
219 NZZ, 1. 9/10. 1993.
220 NZZ, 1. 9/10. 1993.
221 Cf. manuscript of the CSH analysts' conference, 1. 14. 1993. When the SKA/SVB union was announced, SKA was working with the market share figures for 1991.
222 For the various comments by Markus Lusser, SBG and others: NZZ, 1. 7. 1993.
223 Cf. the report entitled: Reorientation of the SVB and integration into CS Holding, 1. 5. 1993 to 6. 30. 1995, p. 30 [SVB/CSH report].
224 Kurt Widmer, SVB management conference, closing speech, 6. 4. 1994.
225 Cf. SVB/CSH report, p. 39.
226 For more on this subject, cf. Invest, Magazin der Finanz und Wirtschaft, no. 11, 1996, p. 85.
227 Unlike the chart 'Lead management (by volume) in underwriting business for domestic issuers: SKA, SBV and SBG (1970–1990)' the underwriting business in the chart 'SKA, SBV and SBG: position in core Swiss market (1990/1996)' covers public and private placements for domestic and foreign borrowers on the Swiss capital market.
228 This was a semi-serious piece of advice from Felix W. Schulthess to foreign customers, suggesting that they invest their assets in Switzerland. Cf. interview with Felix W. Schulthess, 'What does bank secrecy mean?', March 1975, Schulthess Archive.
229 Minutes of the SKA board of directors, 6. 20. 1991.
230 Cf. Invest, Magazin der Finanz und Wirtschaft, no. 11, 1996, p. 85. For the theoretical background to asset management, cf. Blattner, Vermögensverwaltungsgeschäft.
231 NZZ, 1. 5. 1993.
232 For SBG in the 1990s and for the SBG/SBV merger, cf. Schütz, UBS.
233 Tages-Anzeiger, interview with Robert Studer, 12. 9. 1997.
234 Esslinger, SKA, p. 69.
235 Minutes of the SKA board of directors, 8. 1. 1878.
236 Jöhr, SKA, p. 118.
237 Cf. minutes of the SKA board of directors, 6. 29. 1911; Jöhr, SKA, p. 220.
238 Minutes of the SKA board of directors, 5. 11. 1939.
239 No approval was required from the New York Banking Department to set up such a business corporation.

240 Cf. minutes of the SKA board of directors, 5. 11. 1939.
241 Minutes of the SKA board of directors, 2. 15. 1940.
242 Cf. Jöhr, SKA, p. 523.
243 Cf. minutes of the SKA board of directors, 6. 10. 1954.
244 Cf. minutes of the SKA board of directors, 4. 11. 1957.
245 For information on engagements in the Middle East, cf. minutes of the SKA board of directors, 2. 16. 1961, p. 403; 9. 21. 1967, p. 406; 4. 26. 1973, p. 75f.; 8. 23. 1973, p. 159; 6. 13. 1974, p. 434.
246 Cf. minutes of the SKA board of directors, 8. 17. 1972, p. 168.
247 For information on expansion in the USA, cf. minutes of the SKA board of directors, 8. 22. 1968, p. 170f.; 4. 25. 1972, p. 97f.
248 Minutes of the SKA board of directors, 4. 25. 1972.
249 Cf. minutes of the SKA board of directors, 8. 26. 1976, p. 163.
250 Business became more international, and traditional lending business was increasingly replaced by equity/bond issues, with the banks acting as brokers.
251 Cf. Speck, Auslandgeschäft, p. 41ff.; Schweizer Bank, no. 12, 1987, p. 22ff.; speech by Robert Lang to the Schweizerischer Bankpersonalverband, 11. 21. 1974.
252 The so-called '50:50 rule' requires that a balance is kept between domestic and international activities in both asset and liability business.
253 Cf. minutes of the SKA board of directors, 9. 13. 1984, p. 99.
254 Felix W. Schulthess, Zur Bankpolitik unserer Zeit, 3. 3. 1970, p. 5, Schulthess Archive.
255 Cf. minutes of SKA senior management conference 1971, p. 1ff.
256 'Internationale Geschäftstätigkeit der SKA', Büro Ap/SKA, 10. 29. 1971, p. 18 ['International business activities' study].
257 'International business activities' study, p. 13.
258 'International business activities' study, p. 15.
259 'International business activities' study, p. 17.
260 Cf. Bulletin (P) 3/1976, p. 46; minutes of the SKA board of directors, 9. 13. 1984, p. 96f. Wholesale banking comprises national and international commercial and investment banking business for corporations and large-scale customers. Commercial banking includes interbank business and business with commercial customers – bank accounts, payment transactions, money market, currency and banknote trading, as well as lending and documentary credits business. Investment banking includes securities business (underwriting and trading), advisory business (mergers & acquisitions), as well as financial analysis. As a full-service bank, SKA aimed to provide a comprehensive, worldwide wholesale banking service by building up a comprehensive international operation and later through cooperation with other CSH group companies.
261 Cf. speech by Robert Lang to the Schweizerischer Bankpersonalverband, 11. 21. 1974.
262 Cf. SKA Guiding Principles (Leitbild), Kommission Y, 7. 1. 1976, p. 8f.; Schweizerische Kreditanstalt, Leitbild-Weissbuch (results of a survey of all members of senior management at SKA), Zurich, April 1976, p. 22ff.
263 Cf. minutes of the SKA board of directors, 6. 30. 1977, p. 431f.
264 Cf. SKA Guiding Principles (Leitbild) 1981, p. 14f.
265 Cf. minutes of the SKA senior management conference 1979, p. 11.
266 Cf. minutes of the SKA board of directors, 11. 15. 1979.
267 E.g. 1982: New York, Hong Kong, Mexico, Brazil, South Africa; Cf. Bulletin 8·9/1982, p. 14ff.
268 Cf. minutes of the SKA board of directors, 5. 24. 1984, p. 36ff.
269 Cf. minutes of SKA senior management conference 1976, p. 3f.
270 Cf. minutes of the SKA board of directors, 9. 13. 1984, p. 102.
271 Cf. minutes of the SKA board of directors, 2. 15. 1940; 50 years of CS New York, in: Bulletin 8·9/1990, p. 9f.; Directory of CS New York Branch, 2. 4. 1988.
272 Cf. minutes of the SKA board of directors, 9. 13. 1984, p. 102.
273 Cf. documents for the SKA executive board seminar week 1984, 12. 20. 1983, p. 1ff.
274 Cf. Bulletin 4/1985, p. 10ff.
275 Cf. minutes of the SKA board of directors, 1. 17. 1985.
276 Cf. SKA-Strategie 1990, 9. 27. 1983, p. 29; minutes of the SKA board of directors, 1. 17. 1985, p. 3f.
277 Cf. Bankenrevolution in Amerika, in: Tages-Anzeiger, 10. 25. 1999; US Clears Way for Banking Revolution, in: Financial Times, 10. 23. 1999; Die US-Bankenreform unter Dach und Fach, in: NZZ, 11. 6. 1999; Der lange Schatten von Glass-Steagall, in: NZZ, 11. 13/14. 1999.
278 Cf. 'Adler-Papier' (SKA's strategy for Germany), 6. 21. 1985.
279 Cf. Bulletin 1·2/1985, p. 37; Bulletin (P) 7/1986, p. 45; Robert A. Jeker, SKA senior management conference, speech, 1989, p. 39.
280 Cf. Rudolf Hug, SKA senior management conference, speech, 1996, p. 1.
281 Cf. 50 Jahre CS New York, in: Bulletin 8·9/1990, p. 9f.; minutes of SKA senior management conference 1972, p. 10f.; SKA-Strategie 1990, 9. 27. 1983, p. 30.
282 Cf. Bulletin (P) 7/1990, p. 54.
283 Cf. Robert A. Jeker, Visionen für die SKA, in: Bulletin 3/1990, p. 7ff.
284 Cf. Interview with Robert A. Jeker, in: Badener Tagblatt, 7. 25. 1992, p. 10f.
285 Cf. Cassis, Place financière suisse, p. 345f.
286 Cf. annual reports of banks concerned.
287 Cf. Bulletin 11·12/1994, p. 17f.; Ecotass, 12. 16. 1991; SKA eröffnet Filiale in Moskau, in: NZZ, 9. 9. 1994.
288 SKA annual report 1996, p. 15.

289 For information on the creation of the CS First Boston subsidiary cf. Bulletin 11·12/1994, p. 17; minutes of the SKA board of directors, 9. 23. 1993, p. 135f.

290 Cf. CSG, Fakten und Zahlen 1998/99, p. 3, p. 13.

291 CS Holding strategic sketches, 3. 18. 1994.

292 Minutes of the SKA board of directors, 5. 17. 1962.

293 Schweizerisches Handelsamtsblatt, 8. 9. 1962.

294 Numerous instruments are available to issuers for the purpose of raising funds. A company can obtain long-term debt capital by issuing bonds – i.e. by offering the public long-term, interest-bearing IOUs in the form of securities. Alternatively, a company can obtain risk-bearing equity capital by issuing new shares or participation certificates. There are also hybrid forms – convertible bonds and warrants – which allow firms to obtain both debt and equity capital. These are bonds that also carry an entitlement to acquire equity paper (which is why they are called 'equity-linked issues'), and are thus counted as equity capital transactions. For the data used in the table 'White Weld's rank, volume and market share of global equity and debt capital transactions (1970–1977)', cf. note 306.

295 Cf. memorandum from Rainer E. Gut, 1. 24. 1972.

296 Cf. minutes of the SKA board of directors, 2. 21. 1974.

297 Schweizerisches Handelsamtsblatt, 5. 13. 1974.

298 For a description of CSWW's pioneering role in the Eurobond market, cf. Kerr, Eurobond Market and IFR Awards, 1999.

299 The directors owned 32%, with the remaining 38.4% held by previous partners and directors; the biggest shareholder owned 4.1% of the outstanding shares.

300 Institutional Investor, no. 5, 1987, p. 43.

301 Examples of business contacts with large multinational companies: Honeywell, Monsanto, St. Regis Paper, Time Inc., Quaker Oats, Tenneco, Control Data.

302 SBG, SKA and SBV declaration of intent, appendix P, SBG minutes, 4. 7. 1972, para. 2.4.

303 Baring's and Northern Trust 20%, Chemical Bank and SKA 30% of the founding capital (cf. minutes of the SKA board of directors, 2. 12. 1970).

304 Minutes of the SKA board of directors, 4. 27. 1972.

305 SKA, Société Générale (with Société Alsacienne de Banque as minority participant), Société Générale de Banque (with Sofina as minority participant) and Amro-Bank had equal stakes in the capital of $ 11 million. The structure of the voting shares meant that SKA could exercise control and appoint six of the thirteen members of the board of directors.

306 The charts and tables on pages 175 to 201 are based on the database maintained by Thomson Financial Securities Data Inc., New York (TFSD). The TFSD database was used between September 1999 and February 2000, but the statistics gathered then had to be further processed to satisfy the demands of this study's historical approach. The disadvantage of the method TFSD used to build the database is that figures for financial institutions that merge are added together with retrospective effect – i.e. even for the period before the merger took place. Consequently, the ranking lists given by the database do not provide an accurate picture of the historical situation prior to the merger. For example: the figures for Morgan Stanley and Dean Witter are not given separately even for the period before the 1997 merger between the two companies, but are added together retrospectively.

Working together with Professor Gayle DeLong (Baruch College, City University of New York), the following approach was developed: Instead of the usual method of recording the data for the parent company, data for the 'top 150' subsidiaries was collected for the period concerned. Taking account of all the mergers between financial institutions since 1970, the figures for the various subsidiaries could then be allocated to the historical parent companies (98–100% accuracy).

307 Cf. minutes of the SKA board of directors, 9. 7. 1978.

308 Proxy Statement First Boston; Special meeting of stockholders to be held December 22, 1988, 12. 2. 1988, p. 67f.

309 Consent and Proxy Solicitation Statement, CS First Boston, 11. 21. 1990, p. 17.

310 'M&A' (mergers and acquisitions) consists of providing strategic advice prior to a possible transaction, searching for a suitable partner, giving support and advice during negotiations, providing advice on the actual purchase/sale, and processing the transaction. Cf. Krumnow, Gabler Bank Lexikon, p. 916f.

311 Cf. Kerr, Eurobond Market, p. 59.

312 Cf. Hayes, Investment Banking, p. 351.

313 Cf. minutes of the SKA board of directors, 8. 20. 1988.

314 Cf. e.g. Economist, 4. 23. 1988; Fortune, 3. 14. 1988; Los Angeles Times, 2. 3. 1988; New York Times, 2. 3. 1988 and 2. 28. 1988; Pension and Investment Age, 1. 11. 1988.

315 Approximately 300 members of management with a max. 0.5% shareholding each.

316 Cf. minutes of the SKA board of directors, 6. 16. 1988.

317 Notes on the charts and tables on global M&A business and global underwriting business:

Company names: The current names of the banks/financial institutions are used, except in the case of UBS prior to 1998, where the (German) names of the two predecessor banks, SBV und SBG, are used.

Company figures: For the period 1980–1987 we have used the figures from SKA combined with those of Société anonyme financière Credit Suisse – First Boston and the First Boston Corp. to produce figures for Credit Suisse First Boston; for the period 1988–1996 SKA figures are combined with CS First Boston's. The Morgan Stanley Dean Witter and Salomon Smith Barney figures up to 1997 are produced from data from the predecessor firms Morgan Stanley and Salomon Brothers. For Lehman Brothers the figures from the following predecessor firms were used: for the period 1980–1983 Lehman Brothers Kuhn Loeb, for the period 1984–1987 Shearson Lehman Brothers, for the period 1988–1993 Shearson Lehman Hutton und from 1994 Lehman Brothers.

Basis of data for global M&A business: For M&A business, pending, partially pending, completed and unconditional transactions are included. Transactions involving equity swaps are excluded.

Method of calculation for global M&A business (volume and number of transactions): We have used the standard methods for calculating this type of business, whereby the transactions for the domestic and international target companies (from the point of view of the USA) are attributed to both the buyer and the seller.

Basis of data for global underwriting business: In underwriting business, a distinction has to be made between equity and debt transactions. The equity transaction data include transactions involving European and international ordinary shares, European and international convertible debt paper, European and international preference shares, US ordinary shares, US convertible debt paper, US preference shares, US ordinary shares under Rule 144A (Rule 144A of the Securities Exchange Act regulates, amongst other things, the public sale of non-registered stocks), convertible US debt paper under Rule 144A, as well as US preference shares under Rule 144A. We have excluded debt paper redeemable/recallable within a year, issues which do not qualify for classification, unsubscribed issues, swaps and US subscription rights issues. Data on debt capital transactions include transactions involving European and international debt paper, European and international preference paper, mortgage-backed securities, US debt paper, US preference paper, 'R144D' bonds under Rule 144A, 'R144P' preference paper under Rule 144A, and taxable debt paper issued by a municipality for private-sector projects. We have excluded debt paper redeemable/recallable within a year, issues which do not qualify for classification, unsubscribed issues, swaps and US subscription rights issues, European debt paper and European preference paper from private placements and transactions where an issuer offers securities in another local market (outside the US market).

Calculation method for underwriting business: As is usual for this type of business, the volume of equity and debt transactions is allocated in full to the lead-managing bank (in the event of joint consortium management: 100% for each consortium bank).

Currency: All transaction volumes are given in US dollars.

318 Junk bonds (high-yield bonds) are bonds with a high risk of default and, therefore, a lower rating (BBB or lower) or even no rating at all.
Notes on the tables of high-yield US securities:
Company names: The historically relevant company names are used. E.g.: CS First Boston (and not Credit Suisse First Boston).
Company figures: The First Boston Corp. figures are used for CS First Boston; for Shearson Lehman Hutton up to 1987, the figures for the predecessor firm Shearson Lehman Brothers are used.
Basis for data: The high-yield bond data are based on mortgage-backed securities, US debt paper, US preference paper, 'R144D' bonds under Rule 144A, 'R144P' preference paper under Rule 144A, and taxable communal debt paper issued for private-sector projects. We have excluded debt paper redeemable/recallable within a year, issues which do not qualify for classification, unsubscribed issues, swaps, US subscription rights issues, securities backed by mortgages or claims under Rule 144A, bonds with less than 18 months to maturity, high-yield bond splits and transactions by agents acting as issuers.
Method of calculation: As is usual for this type of business, the volume of transactions is allocated in full to the lead-managing bank (in the event of joint consortium management: 100% for each consortium bank).
Currency: All transaction volumes are given in US dollars.

319 'Chapter 11' contains the rules on settlement and rehabilitation detailed in the US bankruptcy and settlement law: the 'Bankruptcy Reform Act' of 1978. This federal law contains the statutory regulations on all types of bankruptcy in the United States. According to 'Chapter 11' one of the options open to the bankrupt company is to produce a plan to rehabilitate the debts from the bankrupt estate. This requires an estate contract agreed by the creditors and the bankruptcy court. Although 'Chapter 11' is tailored to the needs of companies, it also applies to private individuals.

320 Cf. minutes of the CSH board of directors, 11. 8. 1990.

321 Euromoney, 5. 13. 1994.

322 Return on equity 1993: CS First Boston 36.8%, J. P. Morgan 31.8%, Morgan Stanley 30.4%, Salomon Brothers 29.7% und Lehman Brothers 9.8%.

323 Equity capital 1994: CS First Boston $ 1.784 billion, Salomon Brothers $ 4.492 billion, Morgan Stanley $ 4.555 billion, Goldman Sachs $ 4.771 billion, Merrill Lynch $ 5.199 billion and J. P. Morgan $ 9.568 billion.

324 For information on the development of the global financial markets, the global challenges facing financial service providers, and other topics: Doerig, Universalbank.

325 Herald Tribune, 1. 6. 2000.

326 These combinations include Travelers/Citicorp; Salomon Brothers/Smith Barney; SBV/Dillon Read/SBG; Morgan Stanley/Dean Witter;

BankAmerica/Nationsbank; Bankers Trust/Alex. Brown/Deutsche Bank; Banca Commerciale Italiana/Banca Intesa; San Paolo di Torino/IMI; Industrial Bank of Japan/Dai-Ichi Kangyo Bank/Fuji Bank; Sumitomo Bank/ Sakura Bank; and BNP/Paribas.

There were also many mergers and acquisitions in the 1980s, but these were more modest than those seen in the 1990s, partly because there were many difficulties involved in creating large, diversified financial institutions. Examples: merger between Prudential Insurance and Bache Halsey Stuart; American Express's acquisition of Shearson, Lehman Brothers and E. T. Hutton. For attempts at cross-disciplinary diversification, cf. the acquisition of Dean Witter by Sears Roebuck or of Kidder Peabody by General Electric.

327 Title of an article in: Fortune, 7. 26. 1999.
328 Title of an article in: The Economist, 4. 17. 1999.
329 For an up-to-date overview of the Allfinanz business, cf. Economic Briefings no. 12: Allfinanz. Nicht neu, aber mit Zukunft. Cf. also Matthias Haller, Allfinanz – eine Revolution in Raten, in: NZZ, Allfinanz, B 3, 9. 4. 1997.
330 Roesle, SKA, p. 151. While SKA created the Rentenanstalt – its own company dedicated to life insurance – entry into the life insurance business remained a pipe dream for another of the Swiss banks based on the Crédit Mobilier model. The articles of association of Banque Générale Suisse de Crédit foncier et mobilier, founded in Geneva in 1853 and wound up in 1869, foresaw the creation of a banking department that would, amongst other things, conclude contracts for life insurance and pensions. Cf. Ritzmann, Schweizer Banken, p. 62.
331 Roesle, SKA, p. 154.
332 Cf. Rentenanstalt 1857–1957, p. 38; Rentenanstalt's letter to the SKA, 2. 21. 1862.
333 Cf. Schweizerische Rentenanstalt's annual accounts for 1873, p. 3.
334 Quote from the Governing Council cited in Roesle, SKA, p. 156.
335 Cf. minutes of the SKA board of directors, 2. 13. 1879; 2. 27. 1879; 9. 13. 1878.
336 Roesle, SKA, p. 158.
337 Cf. minutes of the SKA board of directors, 2. 16. 1886; 7. 5. 1900; 8. 4. 1910.
338 Cf. letter from SKA to Conrad Widmer, director of Rentenanstalt, 11. 22. 1857.
339 Letter from Conrad Widmer to SKA, 5. 10. 1872.
340 Cf. letter from SKA to Rentenanstalt, 5. 25. 1872.
341 Letter from SKA to Rentenanstalt, 3. 20. 1874.
342 Minutes of the SKA board of directors, 2. 14. 1880; for detailed information cf. minutes of the SKA board of directors, 4. 15. 1880.
343 Cf. letter from the accountant Fellenberg to SKA, 5. 23. 1884; letter from vice president Hagenbuch to Carl Abegg-Arter, 9. 30. 1884; letter from SKA to Conrad Widmer, 10. 9. 1884.
344 Cf. Art. 3 Para. 2 of the 'Bundesgesetz betreffend die Beaufsichtigung von Privatunternehmungen im Gebiete des Versicherungswesens' (Federal Law on the Supervision of Private Companies in the Insurance Sector) of 1885.
345 Art. 13 Para. 1 of the 'Bundesgesetz betreffend die Aufsicht über die privaten Versicherungseinrichtungen' (Federal Law on the Supervision of Private Insurance Organizations) of 1978 (VAG), version of 6. 18. 1993.
346 Cf. Maurer, Privatversicherungsrecht, p. 111 (note 180).
347 Cf. Hauser, Zürcher Kantonalbank, p. 24.
348 'Non-insurance business' has long been prohibited to insurance companies that do not have the proper license. Nowadays this rule is enshrined in Art. 12 Para. 1 VAG. 'Non-insurance business' refers primarily to banking business.
349 Cf. Zuberbühler, Allfinanz, p. 41.
350 For information on 'Financial Services' in the USA, the United Kingdom and Japan, cf. e.g. Kirsch, Financial Services Revolution; Moran, Financial Services Revolution. To give an example of the acquisition activity in the financial services sector, we have listed the major acquisitions made by the American Express Companies in the 1980s:
1981 Shearson Loeb Rhoades
1983 Investors Diversified Services
1983 Trade Development Bank
1984 Lehman Brothers
1984 The Columbian Group Inc.
1985 L. Messel & Co.
1988 E. F. Hutton & Co.
351 Data for the chart 'Sales of life insurance and pension products: banks' share of premium volumes' come from McKinsey EFIC.
352 Data for the chart 'Domestic business done by Swiss banks and life insurance companies' come from the Swiss National Bank and the Federal Office of Private Insurance.
353 For information on assets held by Swiss investment fund companies in Switzerland and abroad (chart), cf. Bopp, Fondsführer.
354 For CS Life, cf. Peter Küpfer, Ein Jahr CS Life, in: Bulletin 6/1991, p. 12.
355 Cf. Mit der Allfinanzstrategie über die Grenzen – Lancierung von Personal Financial Services Europe in Italien, in: Group News, July 1999, p. 4ff.; Das ABC von PFS, in: Group News, December 1999, p. 3ff.

Part Three: A New Paradigm

356 Cf. Jöhr, Nachkriegsdeflation.
357 Felix W. Schulthess, Die Bank als Dienstleistungsbetrieb, 3. 16. 1971, p. 15, Schulthess Archive.
358 'Credit Suisse was run like a country club': adapted from David Packard, 'Stanford University was run like a country club'.
359 Felix W. Schulthess, minutes of the SKA board of directors, 8. 22. 1968, p. 145.
360 Subsequent quotations are from Wolfgang Farbstein, Banken und Kunden – Schlussbericht

einer psychologischen Marktuntersuchung, Zurich 1965, p. 62ff.
361 Subsequent quotations are from Farner (advertising agency), SKA – Public Relations und Werbung, Zurich 1965, p. 12 and p. 15.
362 Subsequent quotations are from Explora AG, Bericht über eine Marktanalyse im Sektor Spareinlagen, Zurich 1975, p. 78, p. 81, p. 85, p. 88.
363 The 'White Book' ('Weissbuch') resulted from an anonymous survey of all SKA senior managers carried out in 1975. The respondents were asked to give a subjective description of the mood within the modern SKA. The information thus collected was categorized in accordance with specific criteria in April 1976. Amongst other things, the 'White Book' served as a basis for the production of SKA's first Guiding Principles.
364 Cf. Bulletin (P) 2/1977, p. 65.
365 Subsequent quotations are from Slogan Competition, List of Winners, April 1977.
366 Stauffer, Public Relations bei Banken, p. 80.
367 Minutes of the SKA board of directors, 9. 10. 1981, p. 157.
368 Cf. file on the foundation of Texon from 1961; report of the special commission of the board of directors on the Chiasso branch/Texon Finanzanstalt, Vaduz, 5. 31. 1977, p. 11ff. [Report of the Special Commission].
369 Ernst Kuhrmeier, Geschichte der Texon Finanzanstalt, 4. 24. 1977, p. 1f. [Kuhrmeier, Geschichte Texon].
370 Kuhrmeier, Geschichte Texon, p. 2.
371 Kuhrmeier, Geschichte Texon, p. 4f.
372 Cf. interrogation of Ugo Primavesi, 5. 7. 1977, p. 2. All records of interrogations/questioning from the investigation files of the SKA board of directors' special commission are referred to in the notes as follows: Interrogation of X, date, page.
373 Memorandum by Hans-Ulrich Frey, 2. 17. 1969, in: Special commission's investigation files.
374 Memorandum by Hans-Ulrich Frey, 2. 17. 1969, in: Special commission's investigation files.
375 Memorandum by Hans-Ulrich Frey, 2. 17. 1969, in: Special commission's investigation files.
376 Cf. Memorandum by Julius Weibel, 9. 16. 1969, in: Special commission's investigation files.
377 Letter to Ernst Kuhrmeier, 9. 19. 1969, in: Special commission's investigation files.
378 Letter from Ernst Kuhrmeier to Hans Escher, 9. 25. 1969, in: Special commission's investigation files [Ernst Kuhrmeier to Hans Escher].
379 Ernst Kuhrmeier to Hans Escher, 9. 25. 1969.
380 Ernst Kuhrmeier to Hans Escher, 9. 25. 1969.
381 Ernst Kuhrmeier to Hans Escher, 9. 25. 1969.
382 Cf. Memorandum by Julius Weibel, 9. 19. 1969, in: Special commission's investigation files.
383 Memorandum by Hans-Ulrich Frey, 10. 16. 1969, in: Special commission's investigation files.
384 Letter from Büro N, 10. 20. 1969, in: Special commission's investigation files.
385 Answer from Chiasso branch, 10. 23. 1969, in: Special commission's investigation files.
386 Memorandum by Gerhard Stuker, 2. 20. 1970, in: Special commission's investigation files.
387 Cf. minutes of SKA Chiasso management meeting ('Verbale Riunione Direzione'), 2. 26. 1975.
388 Cf. interrogation of Heinz R. Wuffli, 5. 6. 1977, part 1, p. 6.
389 Cf. interrogation of Felix W. Schulthess, 5. 7. 1977, p. 10.
390 Cf. Paolo Bernasconi, Lehren aus den Strafverfahren in den Fällen Texon, Weisscredit und Ähnlichen. Special supplement of the Schweizerische Zeitschrift für Strafrecht, vol. 98, Bern 1981, fasc. 4.
391 Cf. legal department's files on a possible takeover of Weisscredit, in: Special commission's investigation files.
392 Cf. interrogation of Robert A. Jeker, 5. 5. 1977, p. 2ff.
393 Cf. 'In fede' declaration (declaration of good faith) accompanying Texon balance sheet as per March 1976, 3. 23. 1977.
394 Minutes of SKA general meeting of shareholders, 3. 29. 1977.
395 For Ernst Kuhrmeier's confession, cf. interrogation of Oswald Aeppli, 5. 16. 1977, p. 4.
396 Cf. Texon balance sheet as at 31 March 1977, 4. 6. 1977.
397 Cf. 'Datenmässiger Ablauf der Angelegenheit T', p. 4; appendix to interrogation of Josef Müller, 5. 5. 1977.
398 Cf. SKA press release, 4. 14. 1977.
399 Cf. NZZ, 4. 15. 1977; Tages-Anzeiger, 4. 15. 1977.
400 Tat, 4. 15. 1977.
401 Cf. Tages-Anzeiger, 4. 16. 1977; Tat, 4. 16. 1977; NZZ, 4. 16/17. 1977; editorial in Tages-Anzeiger, 4. 16. 1977; editorial in Basler Zeitung, 4. 16. 1977; Tages-Anzeiger, 4. 19. 1977; NZZ, 4. 20. 1977; Tat, 4. 18. 1977.
402 SKA press release, 4. 25. 1977.
403 Agreement between Texon-Finanzanstalt, Vaduz, and Schweizerische Kreditanstalt, Zurich, 4. 18. 1977.
404 Subsequently referred to simply as Albarella; not to be confused with the Albarella-Neve project in San Bernardino GR, which also ran into difficulties at this time but which had nothing to do with Texon.
405 Cf. correspondence between SKA and district attorney Paolo Bernasconi, 4. 28./5. 3. 1977.
406 Cf. report by Heinz R. Wuffli to the SKA board of directors, 4. 19/28. 1977.
407 SKA press release, 4. 25. 1977.
408 SKA press release, 4. 25. 1977.
409 Rumors in the Ticino about the possibility of the people involved fleeing or colluding with each other had reached such a point by this time that district attorney Paolo Bernasconi had no choice but to make the arrests.
410 Cf. Tat, 4. 26. 1977.
411 Cf. Avviso per i Signori Clienti, 4. 25. 1977.
412 Cf. NZZ, 4. 26. 1977.
413 Cf. SDA report, 4. 25. 1977.
414 Two examples of many: Finanz und Wirtschaft, 4. 27. 1977: 'Does SKA Need a Sfr 3 Billion Loan?' and 'The Sfr 3 Billion Misunderstand-

ing'; Tat, 4. 27. 1977: 'Huge Furor About the Sfr 3 Billion Offer Made by the National Bank and Two Major Banks to Help their Scandal-Hit Sister, the Kreditanstalt: SKA "Doesn't Need It"!'
415 Press release from the Federal Chancellery, 4. 27. 1977.
416 Cf. report by Heinz R. Wuffli to SKA board of directors, 4. 19/28. 1977.
417 Press release from the SKA board of directors, 5. 2. 1977.
418 Tat, 7. 19. 1977.
419 Schweizer Illustrierte, 5. 2. 1977.
420 Cf. Amtliches Bulletin der Bundesversammlung (Official Bulletin of the Federal Parliament) [Amtl. Bull.] Nationalrat (lower chamber), 1977, p. 504ff.; Ständerat (upper chamber), p. 201f.
421 Nationalrat Richard Müller (SP Bern), Amtl. Bull. Nationalrat, 1977, p. 505.
422 Cf. Basler Zeitung, 5. 6. 1977; Tages-Anzeiger, 5. 7. 1977.
423 'Der Verwaltungsrat der Schweizerischen Kreditanstalt teilt mit' (Information from the SKA board of directors), 5. 6. 1977.
424 Cf. interrogation of Heinz R. Wuffli, 5. 6. 1977, part 2.
425 Max E. Eisenring, Interrogation of Heinz R. Wuffli, 5. 6. 1977, part 2, p. 5.
426 Eberhard Reinhardt, Interrogation of Heinz R. Wuffli, 5. 6. 1977, part 2, p. 10f.
427 Interrogation of Heinz R. Wuffli, 5. 6. 1977, part 2, p. 3.
428 Eberhard Reinhardt, Interrogation of Heinz R. Wuffli, 5. 6. 1977, part 2, p. 13.
429 Eberhard Reinhardt, Interrogation of Heinz R. Wuffli, 5. 6. 1977, part 2, p. 14.
430 Cf. Tages-Anzeiger, 5. 7. 1977: 'SKA has cleared chairman Aeppli of any blame … The fact that he [Wuffli] has not also been named, indicates that SKA … has already made some decisions about implications for its personnel…'; Finanz und Wirtschaft, 5. 7. 1977: 'It is interesting that the report only mentions Dr. Aeppli'; Tat, 5. 9. 1977: 'SKA boss Wuffli hits back. SKA boss Heinz Wuffli has broken his week of silence, He is defending his head and his honor.'
431 Cf. press release from the SKA board of directors, 5. 10. 1977; Wuffli's resignation letter quoted verbatim in an internal press review (SKA), 5. 11. 1977.
432 Tages-Anzeiger, 5. 11. 1977.
433 Cf. Basler Zeitung, 5. 11. 1977; 24 heures, 5. 11. 1977; La Suisse, 5. 11. 1977; NZZ, 5. 12. 1977; Tat, 5. 11. 1977.
434 Press release from SKA board of directors, 5. 10. 1977. The allusion here was to the warning that Felix W. Schulthess had received from his SBG counterpart Alfred Schaefer in spring 1976.
435 Sergio Demiéville had exceeded his authority in the case of Molini Certosa, which was also widely reported in the press. A recorded guarantee credit of Sfr 17 million had grown into an exposure of more than Sfr 70 million for SKA. Molini Certosa did not have anything to do with the Chiasso Affair, though the fact that the two affairs happened at the same time and that the Molini Certosa problem was cleared up together with the Texon issues may have led the public to think that it was connected.
436 SKA shareholders letter, 5. 12. 1977.
437 At the end of 1978, when it was first possible to access the criminal investigation files, it became apparent that Ernst Kuhrmeier and Claudio Laffranchi had mentioned under questioning that Eberhard Reinhardt had talked to them in 1966/67 after being told about risky business at the Chiasso branch by his SBG counterpart Alfred Schaefer. At that time, Ernst Kuhrmeier had been able to set Eberhard Reinhardt's mind at rest by dismissing the allegations as competitive envy.
This supposed warning was not covered by the special commission's investigation; Reinhardt himself could not comment because he died on 10. 10. 1977.
438 Statement by Heinz R. Wuffli, 6. 18. 1979, from the witness box during the criminal trial against Ernst Kuhrmeier and accomplices.
439 Statement by Heinz R. Wuffli, 6. 18. 1979, from the witness box during the criminal trial against Ernst Kuhrmeier and accomplices.
440 Interrogation of Heinz R. Wuffli, 5. 6. 1977, part 2, p. 12.
441 Cf. statement to the FBC's annual press conference in Bern, 5. 12. 1977; NZZ, 5. 13. 1977; Tat, 5. 13. 1977.
442 Letter from Nello Celio to Oswald Aeppli, 5. 3. 1977.
443 Cf. exclusive interview with Meinrad Perler, in: Schweizer Illustrierte, 5. 9. 1977. SKA had an ambiguous relationship with Meinrad Perler. His rapid release from custody disturbed Zurich. While Ernst Kuhrmeier and Claudio Laffranchi were sacked without notice, Meinrad Perler continued to be only suspended, though his signature was deleted from the bank's official record of signing authorities. His employment contract was not actually terminated until the end of October 1977 after the statutory notice period of three months.
444 Cf. minutes of the SKA board of directors, 5. 18. 1977. 'During the 1977 Chiasso crisis I was catapulted overnight to the top of SKA'; comment by Rainer E. Gut in an interview with the Tages-Anzeiger magazine, no. 41, 10. 16–22. 1999.
445 Amongst the accounts receivable were many risk exposures to which head office (department N) had objected over the years. Ernst Kuhrmeier had written these items off through Texon's 'Stralcio' account, thus avoiding any loss for SKA.
446 Cf. directive of the executive board/SKA, 5. 20. 1977.
447 These statements are taken from a working paper by the Farner PR agency of 5. 10. 1977 that looked at the reconstruction of SKA's image. Farner believed that Chiasso had damaged the bank's image so much that over the long term it ought to consider changing its name to Credit Suisse in Switzerland, too.
448 Cf. Tat, 6. 20. 1977.

449 Cf. FBC decree, 5. 27. 1977. KOREAG's mandate was later extended further to include assessing the requirement for write-downs and provisions submitted by SKA as per 12. 31. 1977 as well as the presentation of the Texon affair in SKA's 1977 accounts.
450 Tat, 6. 20. 1977.
451 This led to an accusation by Tat that SKA was manipulating the meeting: 'SKAndal AGM Has Been Rehearsed Four Times, and Today Is the Premiere!'; Tat, 6. 24. 1977.
452 Cf. minutes of SKA extraordinary general meeting of shareholders, 6. 24. 1977; Tages-Anzeiger, 6. 25. 1977.
453 Cf. Extract from the chairman's address, minutes of SKA extraordinary general meeting of shareholders, 6. 24. 1977 [Chairman's address (extract)].
454 Cf. Report of the Special Commission. This report was presented to the SKA board of directors at its extraordinary meeting of 6. 3. 1977 and approved.
455 Report of the Special Commission, p. 18.
456 Report of the Special Commission, p. 50.
457 Cf. Report of the Special Commission, p. 52ff.
458 Cf. Report of the Special Commission, p. 59.
459 Report of the Special Commission, p. 59.
460 Chairman's address (extract), p. 13.
461 Chairman's address (extract), p. 16.
462 Chairman's address (extract), p. 16.
463 Chairman's address (extract), p. 18.
464 Chairman's address (extract), p. 19.
465 In the run-up to the extraordinary general meeting of shareholders, Jürg Meister had tried to form a lobby group of SKA shareholders. However, the votes he represented were not sufficient to force a separate proposal onto the meeting's agenda (according to the bank's articles of association at that time, Sfr 5 million of shares had to be lodged before a proposal could be made). In 1978, Jürg Meister initiated proceedings of personal liability against ex-chairman Felix W. Schulthess. These civil proceedings, in which SKA itself did not take part, ended in 1979 with a settlement about which the parties agreed to remain silent.
466 Shareholder Ghisletta, minutes of SKA extraordinary general meeting of shareholders, 6. 24. 1977, p. 5.
467 Zürichsee-Zeitung, 6. 25. 1977; for 'L'Eddy Merckx de la banque' cf. also Mabillard/de Weck, Scandale, p. 87ff.
468 Cf. NZZ, 6. 25/26. 1977; Finanz und Wirtschaft, 6. 29. 1977, Schweizerische Finanz-Zeitung, 6. 29. 1977; Bund, 6. 25. 1977; Gazetta Ticinese, 6. 25. 1977; Tat, 6. 25. 1977.
469 Cf. minutes of the SKA board of directors, 8. 25. 1977. The total exposure also included additional direct loans of Sfr 82 million, 'which were needed urgently to rescue the threatened companies' (Hugo von der Crone, minutes of the SKA board of directors, p. 477); Max Schmidheiny 'found it difficult to approve the proposed global limit of around Sfr 2.182 billion. One could at best take note of the existing, as yet unregistered limits, but not register them in retrospect. He was reluctant simply to say yes to the new commitment' (Max Schmidheiny, minutes of the SKA board of directors, p. 476); 'The additional new funds are necessary if we are to take on the assets pledged to us from the Texon empire' (Oswald Aeppli, minutes of the SKA board of directors, p. 476). In the end, the board of directors approved the recording of the overall limit.
470 Cf. Texon special unit's credit register.
471 Cf. e.g. Cary Reich, Credit Suisse after Chiasso, in: Institutional Investor, November 1977, p. 147ff.
472 Tat, 12. 7. 1977.
473 For information on the outcome of the proceedings, cf. e.g. NZZ, 1. 11. 1980, 5. 16. 1980.
474 Hugo von der Crone, minutes of the SKA board of directors, 12. 17. 1977, p. 561.
475 The Jelmoli sale was on the agenda of the meeting of the SKA board of directors called by circular letter for 12. 1. 1977. The sale was universally welcomed. 'It is regrettable … that much of the large profits that we will make from this investment will have to be used to cover the losses from the Chiasso/Texon affair' (Oswald Aeppli, minutes of the SKA board of directors, p. 565). 'After all that has happened in Chiasso … the sale is to be warmly welcomed' (Max Schmidheiny, minutes of the SKA board of directors, p. 567). 'As far as press reaction is concerned, we fear that that we will be accused of having had to sell Jelmoli because of Chiasso. On the other hand, such press comment may help finally to impress upon the national government that the Chiasso Affair really does represent a very serious blow for our bank' (Robert A. Jeker, minutes of the SKA board of directors, p. 568). 'We should not be deflected by any negative reaction from the press' (E. Luk Keller, minutes of the SKA board of directors, p. 570).
476 Cf. minutes of the SKA board of directors, 12. 1. 1977, p. 561.
477 Cf. NZZ, 12. 2. 1977; Basler Zeitung, 12. 2. 1977.
478 Cf. minutes of the SKA board of directors, 12. 17. 1977, p. 603f.
479 Cf. contract between SKA and Texon: acquisition of Texon's assets by SKA, 12. 28. 1977.
480 Cf. KOREAG's report of 1. 5. 1978 to the FBC on its assessment of the need for write-downs and provisions determined by SKA as per 12. 31. 1977, plus supplements of 1. 12. 1978. KOREAG's report to the FBC of 2. 3. 1977 on its assessment of SKA's plans for the presentation of the Texon affair in its 1977 accounts. Cf. also minutes of the SKA board of directors, 3. 1. 1978, p. 18.
481 Cf. SKA annual report 1977, p. 27.
482 Cf. job description and list of duties for the Texon press office (Jörg Neef, 'Texo 11'), 1. 24. 1978.
483 Bulletin 1·2/1978, p. 8ff.
484 SKA's 1977 financial statement was widely covered by the press: cf. Basler Zeitung, 3. 2. 1978; Luzerner Neuste Nachrichten, 3. 2. 1978; Tat, 3. 2. 1978.
485 'Address by Dr. O. Aeppli, chairman of the

board of directors to SKA's extraordinary general meeting of shareholders', SKA special publication, 4. 4. 1978.

486 In order to produce a gross profit of Sfr 689.9 million in this unusual year (as opposed to Sfr 288.8 million in the previous year) the bank had to use hidden reserves. Only then was it possible to pay a dividend.

487 Unlike his predecessor Felix W. Schulthess, Oswald Aeppli took part in executive board meetings from the moment he assumed office.

488 The Federal Tax Administration also claimed interest on arrears of Sfr 23 million, which Texon and SKA appealed against. However the appeal was withdrawn in February 1978 when it became apparent that it would not succeed; SKA paid the interest (charged against Texon).

489 The federal government was forced into this action by members of parliament. According to a report in Tat of 3. 2. 1978, Andreas Gerwig (SP, Basel) demanded that 'in view of the great political significance and financial implications' the Federal Council should appeal against the SNB decree.

490 Following extensive correspondence (as well as the federal government and SKA, numerous former Texon investors also lodged appeals) the Supreme Court rejected the government's appeal in a judgment of 10. 25. 1979 (Tages-Anzeiger, 10. 26. 1979: 'Supreme Court Rebuffs Government') and upheld part of SKA's appeal with reference to the calculation of negative interest on account transfers. This led to a substantial reduction in the sum originally calculated by the SNB: from Sfr 81.7 million to Sfr 59.5 million. The basic obligation to pay negative interest was, however, confirmed by the Supreme Court, which is why all the individual appeals lodged by Texon investors were rejected (except in the case of account transfers as defined by the Supreme Court).

491 File on creditors/former Texon investors.

492 Cf. SKA press release, 4. 14. 1977.

493 Cf. responses by KOREAG, named as legal expert, to the questions and supplementary questions posed by the investigating judge on 6. 12. and 11. 29. 1978.

494 Cf. Atto d'acusa N. 15/79, Lugano, 2. 8. 1979.

495 Cf. NZZ, 5. 25. 1979; Basler Zeitung, 5. 25. 1979; Vaterland, 5. 26. 1979; Stuttgarter Zeitung, 5. 26. 1979; Blick 5. 27. 1979; Tribune de Genève, 5. 26/27. 1979; Corriere del Ticino, 5. 28. 1979.

496 Cf. Berner Zeitung, 5. 29. 1979; Tribune de Genève, 5. 29. 1979.

497 According to statements by Elbio Gada 'there was sufficient evidence to suggest that Zurich knew about the matter, so I saw no reason not to get involved with Texon'; cf. NZZ, 5. 29. 1979. Alfredo Noseda defended himself in particular against the charge of seeking profit through disloyal business practices.

498 Cf. Corriere del Ticino, 5. 30. 1979: 'Kuhrmeier: la Texon non è mai stata insolvente'; Neue Zürcher Nachrichten, 5. 30. 1979: 'Kuhrmeier: Much Lower Damages'.

499 Cf. NZZ, 6. 20. 1979; Basler Zeitung, 6. 20. 1979; Tages-Anzeiger, 6. 20. 1979.

500 The partial claim for Sfr 20 million was made for tactical reasons. Firstly, the total amount of damages suffered by SKA was not yet clear even in 1979; secondly, SKA wanted to avoid a discussion in court about possible reasons to minimize damages or even a referral to the civil courts. The sum of Sfr 20 million was chosen because it was small enough to be approved even in the criminal court without lengthy wrangling. Finally, it was clear that the financial circumstances of the accused would not allow them to meet even this demand for partial compensation.

501 Judgment by the Corte delle Assise criminali of 7. 3. 1977.

502 Cf. NZZ, 4. 7. 1979; Tages-Anzeiger, 7. 4. 1979; Finanz und Wirtschaft, 7. 4. 1979; La Liberté, 7. 4. 1979; Basler Zeitung, 7. 4. 1979.

503 Ernst Kuhrmeier's death also became a topic of interest for the media. Cf. Tages-Anzeiger, 7. 11. 1979; Basler Zeitung, 7. 12. 1979.

504 Cf. judgement by the Ticino Court of Appeals, 1. 25. 1980; judgement by the Federal Court of Apepals, 11. 7. 1980; second judgement by the Ticino Court of Cassation, 4. 9. 1981.

505 Cf. judgement by the Ticino Court of Appeal, 11. 21. 1981.

506 Cf. press trip to Winefood of 10. 3/5. 1978.

507 Cf. press trip to Albarella of 8. 27/28. 1979.

508 Special publication 'Streamlined Italian Investments', in: Bulletin 3/1979, p. 20.

509 SKA annual report 1978, p. 23f.

510 Ulrich Albers, minutes of the SKA board of directors, 9. 16. 1979, p. 138.

511 Report of the board of directors' control committee, minutes of the SKA board of directors, 2. 26. 1981, p. 48ff.

512 Minutes of the SKA board of directors, 6. 25. 1981, p. 119.

513 Cf. minutes of the SKA board of directors, 2. 25. 1982, p. 37ff.

514 Report of the board of directors' control committee, minutes of the SKA board of directors, 2. 24. 1983, p. 51f.

515 Minutes of the SKA board of directors, 2. 28. 1984, p. 11.

516 Cf. minutes of the SKA board of directors, 2. 21. 1985, p. 21.

517 Report of the board of directors' control committee on the 1987 financial statement, 2. 24. 1988, p. 3f. (appendix to the minutes of the SKA board of directors, 2. 25. 1988).

518 Schweizer Illustrierte, 7. 10. 1979; extract from the editorial by editor-in-chief Jürg Deutsch.

519 The VSB's full title in 1977 was: Vereinbarung über die Sorgfaltspflicht bei der Entgegennahme von Geldern und die Handhabung des Bankgeheimnisses (Agreement on the Swiss banks' code of conduct with regard to the exercise of due diligence in the acceptance of moneys and the application of banking secrecy). For information on self-regulation cf. e.g.: Nobel, Überblick, p. 15. The quote is from: Nobel, Finanzmarktrecht, p. 551, § 11, no. I.

520 Fritz Leutwiler, Die Schweiz als Internationaler Finanzplatz – Wachstum in Grenzen, speech to the 107th ordinary general meeting of the Schweizerischer Handels- und Industrie-Verein, 9. 16. 1977, p. 5.
521 Schürmann, Sorgfaltspflichtvereinbarung, p. 137.
522 Twelve of the parliamentary motions were submitted after the Chiasso Affair was exposed on 4. 14. 1977. Cf. Amtl. Bull. Nationalrat, June Session 1977; Amtl. Bull. Ständerat, Spring Session 1977.
523 Schürmann, Sorgfaltspflichtvereinbarung, p. 137.
524 VSB 1998, Preamble.
525 Nobel, Selbstregulierung, p. 128.
526 SBA, annual report 1977/78, p. 70.
527 Schürmann, Sorgfaltspflichtvereinbarung, p. 140f.
528 Cf. Amtl. Bull. Nationalrat, 6. 20. 1977, p. 790ff.
529 Helmut Hubacher, Amtl. Bull. Nationalrat, 6. 20. 1977, p. 795ff.
530 Cf. Amtl. Bull. Nationalrat, 6. 20. 1977, p. 797ff.
531 Lilian Uchtenhagen, Amtl. Bull. Nationalrat, 6. 21. 1977, p. 805ff.
532 Cf. Georges-André Chevallaz, Amtl. Bull. Nationalrat, 6. 22. 1977, p. 839ff.
533 Felix Auer, Amtl. Bull. Nationalrat, 6. 22. 1977, p. 853.
534 Cf. Amtl. Bull. Nationalrat, 6. 22. 1977, p. 845ff.
535 Cf. Georges-André Chevallaz, Amtl. Bull. Ständerat, 6. 23. 1977, p. 441ff.
536 Cf. NZZ, 6. 23. 1977: 'Chiasso as political issue'.
537 Tages-Anzeiger, 6. 23. 1977: 'Chiasso: Exception or Systemic Failure?'
538 Editorial in Tages-Anzeiger, 6. 23. 1977: 'On Wednesday there was a harsh confrontation between the parties in the National Council. The lively dispute was caused once again by the events at the Schweizerische Kreditanstalt (SKA). […] Party chairman Hubacher showed a tactical naivety on Monday when he called 'Chiasso' the rule rather than the exception in banking, thus putting the entire conservative bloc in the dock – since the conservatives represented the system that had made Chiasso possible. […] The conservatives should be grateful for Hubacher's sweeping generalization. It was easier to counter and there was barely any need for objective argument. 'Anti-banker' Jean Ziegler came under particularly heavy fire, and the conservatives could sneer at the attempt to criminalize 70,000 largely upstanding bank employees.'
539 Schürmann, Sorgfaltspflichtvereinbarung, p. 138.
540 de Capitani, GwG, chapter 3.2.3.
541 Schürmann, Sorgfaltspflichtvereinbarung, p. 138.
542 FBC annual report 1991, p. 36.
543 Cf. NZZ, 1. 4. 2000: 'Self-Regulation for Non-Banks – Less Danger of Compulsory Enforcement'.
544 Money Laundering Guidelines (FBC Circular no. 98/1, Para. 3).
545 Nobel, Überblick, p. 15.
546 CSPB's Directive W-1152, 7. 1. 1998; cf. also the older Directive W-1113 issued by SKA on 8. 20. 1992.
547 The observations made in this section are based on the following sources: SKA personnel files; SKA and CS Holding annual reports; editions of Bulletin from the years concerned. Some of the details could only be discovered through personal interviews. The statistical evaluations are based on the total number of 47 executive board members. Key date for the charts on p. 302–311 is 31 December of the year concerned.
548 The age structure can be determined by either the median or the mean average of the age data collected for each year. The median average – half the ages collected lie above this value, half below – is the middle value where there are an uneven number of values, or the average of the two middle values where there are an even number of values. Isolated data that diverge sharply from the norm produce less of a distortion if the median is taken rather than the mean average of the age data for each year.
549 The chart 'Universities from which graduate executive board members earned their degrees (1945–1996)' is concerned only with first degrees.
550 The chart 'Appointments to executive board (1945–1996)' also takes account of executive board members who joined the board before 1 January 1945, but who were still in office after this date. In the text, by contrast, we have only taken account of the executive board members who actually joined the board on 1 January 1945 or later.
551 In the chart 'Departures from executive board (1945–1996)' the ten members of the executive board who left to sit on the executive boards of CSG's newly created business units as a result of the restructuring of 1 January 1997 are shown as non-leavers. The total number of executive board members given for each year refers to the number on 31 December of the year concerned. However, the columns in the chart also show the changes that took place over the course of the year concerned.
552 Only Christian faiths were ever represented on the board.
553 The chart 'Origin of executive board members (1945–1996)' also takes account of executive board members who joined the board before 1 January 1945, but who were still in office after this date.
554 For information on SKA's public image: p. 239ff.
555 The data on religious confession refer to the time when the person joined the executive board. One executive board member had no religious affiliation.
556 The analysis of military careers refers exclusively to the Swiss army. Military careers of non-Swiss executive board members in the armies of their home countries are not accounted for.

557 The Gesellschaft zur Constaffel is counted as a guild for the purposes of this analysis.
558 The Rotary Club has had its own section in Switzerland since 1924, the Lions Club since 1947.
559 SBG's image as a 'military bank' comes not least from its Wolfsberg training center, which provided a decidedly uniform training of a type familiar from the army.
560 Bulletin, September 1970, p. 21.
561 Bulletin, September 1970, p. 21.
562 SKA personnel department (publ.), Das Schulungszentrum der Schweizerischen Kreditanstalt in Zürich, 1968, p. 18.
563 Minutes of the SKA board of directors, 12. 15. 1977, p. 591.
564 Cf. Bulletin (P) 3/1983, p. 57.
565 For the proportion of staff working in the personnel area, cf. internal statistics (up till 1966: Head office headcount as at 31 December per department; from 1982: SKA resources management: Budget/actual comparison, head office as at December).
566 Cf. Victor Erne, Human Resources, Vision 2000, undated.
567 Cf. SKA Pension Fund (publ.), Sozialversicherung in der SKA, 1. 1. 1994 [Sozialversicherung SKA].
568 Sozialversicherung SKA, § 8. 1.
569 Cf. Personal-Etat 1876; minutes of the SKA board of directors, 2. 10. 1881, p. 191.
570 Cf. Bulletin (P) 7/1981, p. 51f.
571 Cf. Bulletin (P) 4/1987, p. 49.
572 Bulletin (P) 4/1987, p. 50.
573 Cf. Bulletin (P) 4/1987, p. 50.
574 Bulletin (P) 8·9/1988, p. 60.
575 Kay Mitusch, Organisations- und Anreizstrukturen in Banken aus theoretischer Sicht, Arbeitskreis für Bankgeschichte, working paper no. 3/1998, p. 1.
576 Cf. Roesle, SKA, p. 41.
577 Cf. Esslinger, SKA, p. 14.
578 Cf. minutes of the SKA board of directors, 4. 30. 1877; Esslinger, SKA, p. 38.
579 Cf. Roesle, SKA, p. 43f.
580 Jöhr, p. 127.
581 Cf. first regulations issued by SKA central bureau, 1905.
582 Cf. instructions for the managers of SKA branches, 9. 30. 1912.
583 Cf. minutes of the SKA board of directors, 7. 5. 1928, p. 216; 10. 26. 1928, p. 259.
584 Cf. minutes of the SKA board of directors, 7. 5. 1928, p. 216; 10. 26. 1928, p. 259; Jöhr, SKA, p. 215f., p. 322f., p. 560.
585 Cf. Federal Law on Banks and Savings Institutions, 11. 8. 1934 (version of 1. 14. 1997), Art. 1, p. 1.
586 Cf. minutes of the SKA board of directors, 7. 9. 1953, p. 244.
587 Cf. Auswertung der Geschäftsverteilung der GD der SKA 1953–1996, CSG/GHF, 1999.
588 Cf. Gedanken zur Leistungsfähigkeit der Kreditanstalt, SKA/Ap, 6. 14. 1967, p. 10ff.
589 Cf. Studie Führung und Organisation der SKA, 7. 22. 1976.
590 Cf. SKA audit regulations, 1. 1. 1979; SKA annual report 1975, p. 8; 1976, p. 8f.; 1977, p. 8f., p. 45; Leitfaden für die Kontrollkommission des Verwaltungsrates SKA, 12. 13. 1977.
591 Cf. Bulletin 5·6/1977, p. 3.
592 Cf. Organisationsstruktur SKA, Cb, 4. 18. 1979.
593 Cf. Thesen zu Struktur und Arbeitsweise GD, Oa, 12. 21. 1981; material for the debate on the organizational structure, Cbu, 12. 8. 1981.
594 Cf. ETH Zurich/BWI, SKA – Prognosen und Beziehungen, August 1968.
595 Cf. 'Zentrale Unternehmensplanung', executive board decree, 9. 23. 1968; minutes of the SKA board of directors, 8. 22. 1968, p. 145.
596 Systemansatz der SKA-Unternehmensplanung, Ap, March 1971; Planungszyklus SKA, Ap, 4. 14. 1978.
597 Cf. minutes of SKA senior management conference, 12. 17. 1976.
598 Cf. Up archives (formerly Ap).
599 For more information on divisional structures cf. Thommen, Betriebswirtschaftslehre, p. 179ff.; Kilgus, Bank-Management, p. 137ff.
600 The four divisions more or less matched the structure used by SBV, but not the organizational structure favored by SBG. Cf. Finanz und Wirtschaft, 9. 20. 1986.
601 Cf. Entwicklung Anzahl MGD und DU (HS + ZN), SKA/Gss, 6. 17. 1992.
602 Cf. OGR SKA, 1. 1. 1987, paragraph 31.
603 Cf. SKA annual report 1993, p. 4, p. 9; SKA annual report 1995, p. 9.
604 Cf. SKA annual report 1996, p. 4f.; CSG annual reports 1997/98, 1998/99.
605 Cf. department Oa's report on the control mechanisms that had previously been in place at the Chiasso branch, 1. 6. 1978.
606 The 'Administrative Rationalization' project had also been carried out with similar success in the branches. Cf. interview with Oswald Aeppli, in: Bulletin (P), March 1974, p. 3ff.
607 Cf. Das Rechnungswesen und Controlling in der SKA, Zürich (SKA, Cb), April 1995, p. 27ff., p. 65.
608 Seventeen centers: seven SKA management units with seventeen regions. Each region operated its own logistics center. Fourteen centers (after the 'Match' project): eleven regional service centers and three joint production centers.
609 The details concerning information technology come mainly from the following sources (SKA, CS Holding and Credit Suisse Group): Elektronische Daten-Verarbeitung im Dienste unserer Kunden (1959 brochure); Technische und organisatorische Fortschritte im Dienste unserer Kunden (1963 brochure); Dieter Marti, Optisches Lesezentrum für schweizerisches Bankenclearing, speech on 3. 23. 1972; investment figures from subdivision CFA; SKA's EDP strategy 1983/1990; EDP introductory program 1981–1986; EDP development plans 1984–1987; IT strategy 1988; IT plans 1988–1992, 1990–1993, 1991–1994, 1992–1994; Credit Suisse's IT strategy 1998; Key Metrics CIC; GFI

Reporting 1998/99; Match News (1993–1995).

610 Information for the charts 'IT staff (departments Oa/Os) as a proportion of head office personnel (1983–1995)' and 'IT investment at SKA (1981–1996)' is based on the following sources: EDP plans (up to 1992); CIC Key Metrics (1993–1996); official figures (1981–1996) from FIBU report by former department Cb. In the case of the chart on IT investment, the value of these items also forms the basis for the calculation of write-downs.

'IT investment at SKA (1981–1996)': 'IT investment' includes investment in IT equipment at the computer centers (hardware/ infrastructure), investment in telecommunications and decentralized systems (e.g. PCs, printers) in Switzerland and in international branches. For these purposes, hardware consists only of purchases that are carried as assets and written off over a specific period of time. Other major investments, such as computer center real estate, software licenses and IT staff costs are not included in these figures. The marked rise in investment in 1994 was caused by the large amount of equipment that had to be installed for the trading center at the Üetlihof. In 1996, by contrast, the 'Focus' restructuring project led to a reduction in project activity and thus to lower investment spending.

611 'IT staff at Credit Suisse Group (1998/99)': the chart covers all IT staff at Credit Suisse Group, but not employees of other firms.

'IT expenditure at Credit Suisse Group (1998/99)': By contrast with the figures for SKA's IT investments between 1981–1996, Credit Suisse Group's IT expenditure figures reflect all costs relating to information technology (taking account of internal cost accounting). These include: staff cost of IT employees, hardware and software costs, IT premises costs, IT work done by external contractors, telecommunications costs, market data (Bloomberg and Reuters for example) and depreciation, etc. Extraordinary costs and income (IT work required for Y2K and the introduction of the euro) are not included. Total IT spending by Credit Suisse Group (consolidated) for 1998: Sfr 3,099 million; for 1999: Sfr 3,705 million.

612 For details of the latest developments cf.: Hans Peter Kurzmeyer, Multichannel-Strategie, in: Bulletin 6/1997, p. 14f. For comparison: Dieter Marti, Informatik – Lebensnerv einer modernen Grossbank, in: Die Schweizer Industrie, no. 3, 1988.

613 Cf. Bulletin 1·2/1977, p. 10f. SKA was the second Swiss bank after the SVB to provide this service over the counter.

614 Cf. Bulletin 4/1989, p. 41.
615 Heinz R. Wuffli, Zum Marketing der Banken, speech of 5. 2. 1963, p. 13f.
616 Cf. Bulletin 8·9/1979, p. 17.
617 Cf. Bulletin 2/1962, p. 91f.
618 NZZ, 6. 13. 1962.
619 Cf. NZZ, 3. 21. 1968.
620 Cf. Bulletin 1·2/1982, p. 20.
621 Cf. Niklaus Blattner, Die Schweizer Banken im verordneten Wettbewerb. Konzept und Praxis der schweizerischen Wettbewerbspolitik im Bankensektor, in: Der Schweizer Treuhänder, no. 3, 1991, p. 95 [Blattner, Schweizer Banken].
622 Cf. Bulletin 5/1999, p. 10.
623 Tages-Anzeiger, 4 . 18. 1989.
624 Cf. Albisetti, Handbuch 1987, p. 406ff.
625 Cf. Convention III, Art. 7 Para. 1 a–g.
626 Cf. Blattner, Schweizer Banken, p. 95ff.
627 Minutes of the SKA executive board, no. 1, 1989.
628 Minutes of the SKA executive board, no. 1, 1990.
629 Cf. SBA annual report 1992/93, p. 64.
630 Minutes of the SKA executive board, no. 1, 1991.
631 Cf. Bulletin 11·12/1996, p. 32.
632 Bulletin (P) 11·12/1986, p. 59.
633 Information on CS Firstphone users: Users tended to be graduates or self-employed people; they were more likely to live in towns than in rural areas. Most of the firms that used CS Firstphone were SMEs.
634 Cf. Invest, Magazin der Finanz und Wirtschaft, 12. 1. 1999.
635 Cf. Handelszeitung, 3. 19. 1999, p. 7.
636 Cf. Handelszeitung, 10. 22. 1999.
637 Cf. Jöhr, SKA.
638 Cf. Schweizerische Kreditanstalt's Anniversary, proposal by the anniversary committee to the executive board, 1. 7. 1956.
639 For more on marketing, cf. amongst others: Victor Erne, Der Beitrag des Marketing-Service zum Erfolg der SKA, speech of 11. 21. 1991; Karl Völk, Das Schweizer Bankmarketing heute, in: Bank und Markt, November 1975; Hergiswil marketing seminar, SKA documentation, March 1990; directive no. 9 (creation of an economics, public relations and sales promotion subdivision), 11. 15. 1977.
640 Letter from the SKA executive board, 4. 24. 1967.
641 Minutes of the propaganda working group's meeting, 5. 7. 1969, p. 1f.
642 Minutes of the SKA marketing commission, 5. 14. 1975, p. 1. For the remarks on staff accounts, cf. memorandum to Pers on staff accounts, 6. 30. 1975.
643 Directive no. 9, 11. 15. 1977.
644 Minutes of the SKA board of directors, 3. 28. 1946.
645 Minutes of the SKA executive board, 11. 21. 1991, p. 113.
646 Minutes of the SKA executive board, 11. 21. 1991, p. 112.
647 Cf. Victor Erne, Erfolgsgrundsätze für die SKA-Marktbearbeitung, 6. 30. 1993.
648 Cf. Pastuszek, Wirtschaftsordnung, p. 168ff.
649 For information on the history of the Bulletin, cf. in particular Bulletin 1·2/1974, p. 16 ('80 Jahre: Eine Bankpublikation im Wandel der Zeit'); Bulletin (P) 7/1975, p. 58 ('Seit 5 Jahren: 'bulletin', das schweizerische Bankmagazin'); Bulletin 1·2/1987, p. 1 ('Zum 'bulletin' in neuer Form'); Bulletin 1·2/1994, p. 16 ('100 Jahre 'bulletin'. Von der Information zur Kommunika-

tion'). Cf. also Victor Erne, speech on the 20th anniversary of bulletin, 5. 8. 1990.

650 For the history of SKA advertising cf. in particular the 'White Book' [Weissbuch SKA 1976]; documents, minutes and memoranda on advertising strategies, advertising campaigns, competitions, corporate identity, corporate design and market research; Corporate Identity Manual 1977; 'Amwi 1978–1985' documents (Amwi = Ausschuss für Marketing, Werbung und Information = Committee for Marketing, Advertising and Information); Corporate Design Manual 1989; Corporate Design Manual 1997; 1985–1994: 10 Jahre Partnerschaft (documents partnership between SKA and the Euro RSCG advertising agency).

651 Cf. minutes of the meeting of SKA logo competition jury of 6. 21/22. 1967; Bulletin (P) 6/1976, p. 61; Bulletin (P) 6/1979, p. 46f.; Bulletin (P) 5/1991, p. 60; Finanz und Wirtschaft, 3. 31. 1979.

652 Weissbuch SKA 1976, p. 38.

653 Cf. Team 4/1993, p. 24f.

654 The slogan 'Incredibly Swiss' had been used previously and was intended to show that SKA was 'more Swiss' than other banks – i.e. more secure, reliable, creative and dynamic. Cf. Bulletin (P) 4/1981, p. 50f.

655 Schaffhauser Nachrichten, 6. 20. 1978.

656 For information on the Tour de Suisse and sports sponsorship, cf. Victor Erne, Zum Sponsoring der SKA, speech on 10. 15. 1987; Victor Erne, SKA und Sport: Warum Sponsoring durch die SKA?, in: Bulletin (P) 3/1981, p. 51; Gerry Heller, Zum Sponsoring der SKA, speech at the 'Marketing im Sport' seminar held by the Stiftung Schweizer Sporthilfe, 3. 2. 1990; Keller, Sponsoring-Erfolgskontrolle.

657 NZZ, 6. 22. 1978.

658 Bulletin 5/1999, p. 46.

659 Cf. Tages-Anzeiger, 9. 3. 1999.

660 Had SKA contravened the Swiss Bankers' Association's rules? Hans J. Mast talked about a 'Lex Anti-SKA' (Tages-Anzeiger, 7. 31. 1979). However, SBG (t-shirts) and SBV (windcheaters) were also criticized for giving away excessively expensive promotional gifts.

661 In partnership with the Schweizerischer Leichtathletikverband (SLV) and the Schweizerischer Landesverband für Sport (SLS).

662 In 1983 SKA together with Schweizer Sporthilfe launched the 'Millionenspiel' campaign. Since 1997 all presentations honoring Swiss sportsmen and women have been made at the Credit Suisse Sport Gala.

663 Cf. 'Der Sport', no. 10, 1993.

664 For SKA's support for cultural activities cf. Victor Erne, Zum Sponsoring der SKA, Bulletin 8·9/1986, p. 38; Jörg Neef, Zur Kulturförderung der SKA, speech, 6. 23/24. 1988; Rasi, Kulturförderung; Joseph Jung, Kultursponsoring der Schweizerischen Kreditanstalt, speech, 6. 29. 1989; Keller/Rosenbaum, Sponsoring-Erfolgskontrolle.

665 Cf. amongst others Gazette de Martigny, 7. 11. 1991, Nouvelliste, 8. 28. 1991, Obwaldner Wochenblatt, 8. 30./9. 6. 1991, Luzerner Neuste Nachrichten, 9. 5. 1991, Vaterland, Schwyzer Zeitung, Nidwaldner Volksblatt, Zuger Zeitung, each 8. 23./9. 6. 1991.

666 Schweizer Bank, no. 8, 1991, p. 37.

667 In 1985, Hans J. Halbheer maintained that SKA did not have a clear strategy for art. Cf. memorandum by Hans Halbheer, 2. 1. 1985.

668 Cf. Diethelm Fretz, Die Geschäftssitze der Schweizerischen Kreditanstalt, 1856–1876, Zollikon 1945, p. 1.

669 Cf. Hans Jörg Rieger, Das Bankgebäude – eine neue Bauaufgabe des 19. Jahrhunderts, in: archithese, no. 2, 1981, p. 32ff.

670 Cf. Nievergelt, Credit Suisse am Paradeplatz, p. 7ff.

671 Cf. Jöhr, SKA, p. 128f.

672 Minutes of the SKA board of directors, 9. 26. 1946, p. 358.

673 Cf. Jöhr, SKA, p. 518.

674 Cf. Bulletin 5·6/1980, p. 16.

675 Cf. Bulletin (P) 11/1979, p. 46; interview with Hugo von der Crone.

676 Cf. Bulletin (P) 3/1971, p. 1ff.

677 Cf. Bulletin 5·6/1980, p. 16.

678 Cf. Hans Zaugg, Naturnahes Gartenkonzept zum SKA-Verwaltungsgebäude Üetlihof, Zürich, in: Der Gartenbau, no. 1, 1984, p. 1f.

679 Cf. Team 10/1993, p. 24.

680 Cf. Bulletin 5·6/1980, p. 16.

681 For information on the history of 'Bocken', cf. Jung/Renfer, Bocken.

Sources and bibliography

Preamble

The list of sources includes the most important internal and external sources used in the writing of this book. Sources are shown in the notes in abbreviated form. A list of all the newspapers and magazines used is also given.

Basic sources, such as the minutes of the board of directors and SKA annual reports, were systematically reviewed for the period between 1856 (establishment of SKA) and 1996 (reorganization into Credit Suisse Group). Work on other sources was limited to the periods relevant to the individual chapters concerned. Internal sources come from Credit Suisse Group's Central Corporate Archive. The Swiss Federal Archive in Bern, as well as UBS's Historical Archive, Swiss Life's Historical Archive and Swiss Re's Corporate Archive (all in Zurich) were used to clear up specific issues.

We have not included a list of the individual documents taken from internal sources, such as memoranda, reports of individual events, letters, loose notes, etc. These, like articles quoted from newspapers and magazines, are shown in the relevant notes.

The tables and charts are based on extensive data collected from a variety of internal and external sources and complied in a database. These sources are given at the appropriate point in the text or shown in the individual chapters. Credit Suisse Group's subdivision GHF (Foundations, Corporate History and Archives) would be happy to allow any interested specialists to view the data it has collected. The bibliography includes all of the works quoted in this book as well as other selected background titles. All of the titles are given in abbreviated form in the notes. For reference purposes, the abbreviated forms are also given in the bibliography at the end of the full titles [in square brackets]. If no abbreviated form is given in the bibliography, the work has not been quoted in the book.

Sources

a) Internal sources

Minutes

Schweizerischen Kreditanstalt (SKA) minutes: board of directors [minutes of the SKA board of directors], board of directors committee [minutes of the committee of the SKA board of directors], senior management conference [minutes of SKA senior management conference], finance committee [minutes of SKA's finance committee], executive board [minutes of the SKA executive board], Marketing-Kommission [minutes of SKA's marketing commission].

CS Holding (CSH) minutes: board of directors [minutes of the CSH board of directors].

Credit Suisse Group (CSG) minutes: board of directors [minutes of the CSG board of directors].

Bank Leu minutes: separate minutes of the committee of the board of directors [separate minutes of the committee of the Bank Leu board of directors].

Publications

Bulletin – Das Magazin der Credit Suisse, 1996ff. (predecessors: Effekten-Kursblatt der Schweizerischen Kreditanstalt in Zürich, 1895ff.; Monats-Bulletin, 1921ff.; Bulletin, 1944ff.; bulletin, 1970ff.) [Bulletin] [Bulletin (P) = personnel edition].

Economic Briefings, CS Economic Research (publ.) [Economic Briefings].

Annual reports: Bank Leu & Co., Clariden Bank, Credit Suisse First Boston [CSFB], Credit Suisse Group [CSG], Schweizerische Kreditanstalt [SKA], Schweizerische Volksbank [SVB], Winterthur Insurance and Winterthur Accident, Winterthur Life [… annual report].

Group News, 1997ff. [Group News].

Team (Credit Suisse staff magazine), 1992ff. [Team].

b) External sources

Annual reports

Schweizerische Bankgesellschaft [SBG], Schweizerischer Bankverein [SBV], Schweizerische Nordostbahn [NOB], Schweizerische Rückversicherung [… annual report].

Newspapers and magazines (individual issues)

i) Switzerland

Badener Tagblatt, Basler Zeitung, Der Beobachter, Blick, Der Bund, Cash, Corriere del Ticino, Finanz und Wirtschaft, Gazetta Ticinese, Gazette de Martigny, The Geneva Papers on Risk and Insurance, Finanz-Revue, Handelszeitung, 24 heures, Invest (Magazin der Finanz und Wirtschaft), La Liberté, Luzerner Neuste Nachrichten, Neue Zürcher Nachrichten, Neue Zürcher Zeitung (NZZ), Nidwaldner Volksblatt, Nouvelliste (Sion), Obwaldner Wochenblatt, Oltener Tagblatt, Schaffhauser Nachrichten, Schweizer Bank, Schweizer Illustrierte, Schweizerische Finanz-Zeitung, Schweizerische Zeitschrift für Strafrecht, Schweizerisches Handelsamtsblatt, Schwyzer Zeitung, Solothurner AZ, Sonntags-Zeitung, Sport, La Suisse, Tages-Anzeiger, Die Tat, Tribune de Genève, Vaterland, Zürichsee-Zeitung, Zuger Zeitung.

ii) International

Bank und Markt, Die Börsen-Zeitung, Business Week, The Economist, Euromoney, Financial Times, Fortune, Frankfurter Allgemeine Zeitung (FAZ), IFR Awards 1974–1999, IFR 25th Anniversary, Institutional Investor, International Herald Tribune, Los Angeles Times, Moody's Investors Service, New York Times, Pariser Tageblatt, Pension and Investment Age, La Repubblica, Stuttgarter Zeitung, Wall Street Journal.

Bibliography

Albisetti Emilio et al., Handbuch des Bank-, Geld- und Börsenwesens der Schweiz, Thun 1964 (2nd edition), 1977 (3rd edition), 1987 (4th edition) [Albisetti, Handbuch 1964, 1977, 1987].

Allenbach Beat, Tessin. Bilder eines Lebensraumes, Zurich 1999 [Allenbach, Tessin].

Bachmann Gottlieb, Die Schweiz als internationales Finanzzentrum, in: Die Schweiz 1931. Ein Nationales Jahrbuch. Published by the Neue Helvetische Gesellschaft, Zurich 1930, p. 29–38.

Bänziger Hugo, Die Entwicklung der Bankaufsicht in der Schweiz seit dem 19. Jahrhundert (Bankwirtschaftliche Forschungen, vol. 95), Bern/Stuttgart/Vienna 1986.

Bänziger Hugo, Vom Sparerschutz zum Gläubigerschutz – Die Entstehung des Bankengesetzes im Jahre 1934, in: 50 Jahre eidgenössische Bankenaufsicht, published by the Federal Banking Commission, Zurich 1985, p. 3–82 [Bänziger, Bankengesetz].

Bauer Hans, Blackman Warren J., Swiss Banking. An Analytical History, London/New York 1998 [Bauer, Swiss Banking].

Baumann Jan-Henning, Auf dem Weg zur Universalbank. Die Schweizerische Kreditanstalt in der Zeit der Nordostbahnkrise 1876–1879, in: Cassis Youssef, Tanner Jakob (publ.), Banken und Kredit in der Schweiz (1850–1939), Zurich 1993 [Baumann, SKA und NOB].

Bergier Jean-François, Alfred Escher und die 'Revolution im Bankenbereich', in: Schweizerische Kreditanstalt, Alfred Escher. Ausstellung in der Galerie 'le point' am Hauptsitz der Schweizerischen Kreditanstalt, Zurich 1994, p. 30–40 [Bergier, Escher].

Bergier Jean-François, Wirtschaftsgeschichte der Schweiz. Von den Anfängen bis zur Gegenwart, Zurich 1990 [Bergier, Wirtschaftsgeschichte].

Bernet Beat, Haller Matthias, Maas Peter (publ.), Allfinanz oder Financial Services? Aktuelle Trends im Finanzdienstleistungs-Bereich, St. Gallen 1999.

Bierbaum Detlef, Feinen Klaus (publ.), Bank und Finanzwirtschaft – Strategien im Wandel, Wiesbaden 1997.

Birchler Urs W., Rich Georg, Bank structure in Switzerland, in: Kaufmann George G. (publ.), Banking structures in major countries, Boston 1992, p. 389–427.

Blattner Niklaus, Gratzl Benedikt, Kaufmann Tilo, Das Vermögensverwaltungsgeschäft der Banken in der Schweiz, Bern/Stuttgart/Vienna 1996 [Blattner, Vermögensverwaltungsgeschäft].

Briner Carl, Hundert Jahre 'Schweiz' Allgemeine Versicherungs-Aktien-Gesellschaft Zürich 1869–1969, Zurich 1969.

Bruhn Manfred, Sponsoring. Unternehmen als Mäzene und Sponsoren, Frankfurt am Main 1987.

Bruhn Manfred, Sport-Sponsoring. Strategische Verklammerung in die Unternehmenskommunikation, Bonn 1988.

Bruhn Manfred, Dahlhoff Hans-Dieter (publ.), Kulturförderung – Kultursponsoring. Zukunftsaufgaben für die Unternehmenskommunikation, Frankfurt am Main 1989.

Cassis Youssef, Banks and banking in Switzerland in the nineteenth and twentieth centuries, in: European Association for Banking History E. V. / Pohl Manfred (publ.), Handbook on the History of European Banks, Aldershot (England)/ Brookfield (USA) 1994, p. 1015–1133 [Cassis, Banking in Switzerland].

Cassis Youssef, La place financière suisse et la City de Londres, 1890–1990, in: Bairoch Paul, Körner Martin (publ.), Die Schweiz in der Weltwirtschaft (15.–20. Jh.) – La Suisse dans l'économie mondiale (15e–20e s.), Zurich 1990, p. 339–352 [Cassis, Place financière suisse].

Cassis Youssef, Debrunner Fabienne, Les élites bancaires suisses 1880–1960, in: Schweizerische Zeitschrift für Geschichte, no. 40/1990, Basel 1990, p. 259–273.

Cassis Youssef, Feldman Gerald D., Olsson Ulf (publ.), The Evolution of Financial Institutions and Markets in Twentieth-century Europe, Hants (UK) 1995 [Cassis, Evolution of Financial Institutions].

Cassis Youssef, Tanner Jakob, Finance and financiers in Switzerland, 1880–1960, in: Cassis Youssef (publ.), Finance and Financiers in European History 1880–1960, Cambridge et al. 1992, p. 293–316 [Cassis, Financiers].

Craig Gordon A., Geld und Geist. Zürich im Zeitalter des Liberalismus 1830–1869, Darmstadt 1988 [Craig, Geld und Geist].

de Capitani Werner, Kommentar zum Geldwäschereigesetz (GwG), Zurich [in press] [de Capitani, GwG].

Doerig Hans-Ulrich, Am Ball oder im Abseits? Der Finanzmarkt Schweiz im internationalen Konkurrenzkampf. Fakten, Facetten und Fallstricke rund um das Risiko, Zurich 1993.

Doerig Hans-Ulrich, Der Finanzmarkt Schweiz auf dem Weg zur internationalen Konkurrenzfähigkeit. Themen, Thesen, Trends für die 90er Jahre, Zurich 1991.

Doerig Hans-Ulrich, Universalbank. Banktypus der Zukunft. Vorwärts- und Überlebensstrategien für Europas Finanzdienstleister, Bern 1996 [Doerig, Universalbank].

Duperrex Emile, 100 Jahre Schweizerische Volksbank, 1869–1969, Bern 1969 [Duperrex, SVB].

Dupont Chandler Alfred, Strategy and structure: chapters in the history of the industrial enterprise, Cambridge/Massachusetts 1962 [Dupont, Strategy and structure].

Eidgenössische Bank (Aktiengesellschaft), 1863–1913, Zurich 1914 [Eidgenössische Bank 1863–1913].

Eidgenössische Bankenkommission (Federal Banking Commission, FBC), annual reports 1970–1999 [FBC annual report 19..].

Emmenegger Urs, Das schweizerische Bankwesen im Wandel der Zeit. Unter besonderer Berücksichtigung der Finanzplätze Genf, Basel und Zürich, Bern 1992.

Ermatinger Gerold, Kapital und Ethos …, Zurich 1936 [Ermatinger, Kapital].

Esslinger Martin, Geschichte der Schweizerischen Kreditanstalt während der ersten 50 Jahre ihres Bestehens, Zurich 1907 [Esslinger, SKA].

Gagliardi Ernst, Alfred Escher. Vier Jahrzehnte neuerer Schweizer Geschichte, Frauenfeld 1919 [Gagliardi, Escher].

Gall Lothar, Feldmann Gerald D., James Harold, Holtfrerich Carl-Ludwig, Büschgen Hans E. (publ.), Die Deutsche Bank 1870–1995, Munich 1995.

Geering Walter, Kunert Karsten K. K., Intercultural Bank Management in Switzerland, in: Schuster Leo (publ.), Banking Cultures of the World, Frankfurt am Main 1996, p. 563–578.

Geiger Hans et al., Schweizerisches Bankwesen im Umbruch (Bank- und Finanzwirtschaftliche Forschungen, vol. 228), Bern/Stuttgart/Vienna 1996 [Geiger, Bankwesen].

Gruner Heinz, Neuer Raum für neue Ideen, Zurich 1996 [Gruner, Neuer Raum].

Guex Sébastien (publ.), La Suisse et les Grandes puissances 1914–1945. Relations économiques avec les Etats-Unis, la Grande-Bretagne, l'Allemagne et la France / Switzerland and the Great Powers 1914–1945. Economic Relations with the United States, Great Britain, Germany and France, Geneva 1999.

Halbheer Hans J., Kilgus Ernst (publ.), Der Finanzplatz Schweiz und seine Bedeutung aus nationaler und internationaler Sicht. Festgabe zum 65. Geburtstag von Dr. Hans J. Mast (Bankwirtschaftliche Forschungen, vol. 91), Bern/Stuttgart/ Vienna 1985.

Häsler Alfred A., Gotthard. Als die Technik Weltgeschichte schrieb, Zurich 1983 [Häsler, Gotthard].

Hasler Georg, Schweizerische Unfallversicherungs-Gesellschaft in Winterthur 1875–1950, Winterthur 1950.

Hauser Paul, 100 Jahre Zürcher Kantonalbank 1870–1970, Zurich 1969 [Hauser, Zürcher Kantonalbank].

Hayes Samuel L., Hubbard Philip M., Investment Banking. A Tale of Three Cities, Boston 1989 [Hayes, Investment Banking].

Huber Rudolf, Gemeinkosten-Wertanalyse – Methode der GWA als Element einer Führungsstrategie für die Unternehmensverwaltung, Bern 1987.

Iklé Hans, Die Schweiz als internationaler Finanzplatz, Zurich 1970 [Iklé, Finanzplatz].

Independent Commission of Experts Switzerland – Second World War, Switzerland and Gold Transactions in the Second World War: Interim Report, Bern 1998 [ICE, Gold Transactions].

Independent Committee of Eminent Persons (ICEP), Bericht über nachrichtenlose Konten von Opfern des Nationalsozialismus bei Schweizer Banken / Report on Dormant Accounts of Victims of Nazi Persecution in Swiss Banks, December 1999 [ICEP, Dormant Accounts].

Jenne Willy, Die Spar- und Leihkassen der Schweiz, 1914.

Jöhr Adolf, Die schweizerischen Notenbanken 1826–1913, Zurich 1915 [Jöhr, Notenbanken].

Jöhr Walter Adolf, Die Nachkriegsdeflation. Konjunkturtendenzen der Nachkriegszeit und die Aufgaben der schweizerischen Beschäftigungs- und Währungspolitik, St.Gallen 1945 [Jöhr, Nachkriegsdeflation].

Jöhr Walter Adolf, Schweizerische Kreditanstalt 1856–1956. Hundert Jahre im Dienste der schweizerischen Volkswirtschaft, Zurich 1956 [Jöhr, SKA].

Jung Joseph, Das imaginäre Museum. Privates Kunstengagement und staatliche Kulturpolitik in der Schweiz. Die Gottfried Keller-Stiftung 1890–1922, Zurich 1998 [Jung, Gottfried Keller-Stiftung].

Jung Joseph, Renfer Christian, Der Landsitz Bocken am Zürichsee (Schweizerische Kunstführer GSK), Bern 1994 [Jung/Renfer, Bocken].

Keller Hans-Ulrich, Rosenbaum Isidor, Sponsoring-Erfolgskontrolle. Das Beispiel der Schweizerischen Kreditanstalt, in: Schoch Rolf B., Zollinger Hans (publ.), Sponsoring – Modetrend oder Wissenschaft? Ergebnisse neuer marktpsychologischer und -soziologischer Forschungen über Sponsoren und Sponsoring, Zurich 1990, p. 197–239 [Keller/Rosenbaum, Sponsoring-Erfolgskontrolle].

Keller Theo, Leu & Co. 1755–1955. Denkschrift zum zweihundertjährigen Bestehen der Aktiengesellschaft Leu & Co., Zurich 1955 [Keller, Leu].

Keller Urs, Die wirtschaftliche Bedeutung von Allfinanz, in: Zobl Dieter (publ.), Rechtsprobleme der Allfinanz, Zurich 1997, p. 85–96.

Kerr Ian M., A History of the Eurobond Market. The first 21 years, London 1984 [Kerr, Eurobond Market].

Kilgus Ernst, Die Grossbanken (Bankwirtschaftliche Forschungen, vol. 53), Bern/Stuttgart/Vienna 1979 [Kilgus, Grossbanken].

Kilgus Ernst, Strategisches Bank-Management (Bank- und Finanzwirtschaftliche Forschungen, vol. 188), Bern/Stuttgart/Vienna 1994 [Kilgus, Bank-Management].

Kindleberger Charles P., A Financial History of Western Europe, New York / Oxford 1993 (2nd edition).

Kirsch Clifford E. (publ.), The Financial Services Revolution: Understanding the Changing Role of Banks, Mutual Funds and Insurance Companies, Chicago 1996 [Kirsch, Financial Services Revolution].

Körner Martin, Banken, in: Historisches Lexikon der Schweiz (HLS), Online-Version, Bern 1999 [Körner, HLS].

Körner Martin, Schweiz, in: Pohl Hans, Jachmich Gabriele (publ.), Europäische Bankengeschichte, Frankfurt am Main 1993, p. 279–285 [Körner, Schweiz].

Krumnow Jürgen, Gramlich Ludwig (publ.), Gabler Bank Lexikon: Bank – Börse – Finanzierung, Wiesbaden 1999 (12th, fully revised and updated edition) [Krumnow, Gabler Bank Lexikon].

Kuhn Moritz, Allfinanz – Ein Konzept für die Zukunft?, in: Zobl Dieter (publ.), Rechtsprobleme der Allfinanz, Zurich 1997, p. 5–36.

Kuntze Wolfgang, Möglichkeiten und Grenzen von Allfinanzkonzepten aus Sicht des Kreditaufsichtsrechts, in: Gies Helmut, Müller Helmut, Kuntze Wolfgang, Möglichkeiten und Grenzen von Allfinanzkonzepten (Münsteraner Reihe, fasc. 5), Karlsruhe 1990.

Landmann Julius, Leu & Co. 1755–1905. Jubiläumsschrift. Hrsg. zum einhundertfünfzigjährigen Geschäftsjubiläum, Zurich 1905 [Landmann, Leu].

Lehmann Axel, Ruf Sabine, Allfinanzvertrieb – zwischen Vision und Wirklichkeit. Tagungsband zur 24. Schwerpunkttagung der I. VW-Management-Information vom 3. Nov. 1993 in St. Gallen, St. Gallen 1993.

Lindemann Heinrich, Grundlagen der Kosten- und Erlösrechnung im Bankbetrieb, Zurich 1974.

Lüönd Karl, Neugierig auf morgen: 125 Jahre Zürich, Geschichte und Vision eines Weltkonzerns, Zurich 1998 [Lüönd, Zürich].

Lüönd Karl, Iten Karl, Das grosse Buch vom Gotthard, Zurich 1980 [Lüönd, Gotthard].

Lusser Markus, Die Entwicklung der schweizerischen Bankenstruktur, in: Geiger Hans et al., Schweizerisches Bankwesen im Umbruch, p. 31–45 [Lusser, Bankenstruktur].

Mabillard Max, de Weck Roger, Scandale au Crédit Suisse, Geneva 1977 [Mabillard/de Weck, Scandale].

Marguerat Philippe, Banque et industrie en Suisse, fin 19e–1945: considérations préliminaires, in: Cassis Youssef, Tanner Jakob (publ.), Banken und Kredit in der Schweiz – Banques et crédit en Suisse (1850–1930), Zurich 1993, p. 201–208.

Mast Hans J., Die Euromärkte unter neuen Umweltverhältnissen (Schriftenreihe der Schweizerischen Kreditanstalt, fasc. 32), Bern/Stuttgart 1975.

Mast Hans J., Entwicklungstendenzen der europäischen Finanzmärkte und ihrer Institutionen, in: NZZ, 7 Jan. 1973 [Mast, Entwicklungstendenzen 1973].

Mast Hans J., Geldpolitik und Schweizer Banken, in: Schweizer Zeitschrift für Volkswirtschaft und Statistik, 1971.

Maurer Alfred, Schweizerisches Privatversicherungsrecht, Bern 1995 (3rd edition) [Maurer, Privatversicherungsrecht].

Mazbouri Malik, Place financière suisse et crédits aux belligérants durant la Première Guerre mondiale, in: Guex Sébastien (publ.), La Suisse et les Grandes puissances 1914–1945, Geneva 1999, p. 59–90 [Mazbouri, Place financière].

Meier Christian, Lehren aus Verlusten im Kreditgeschäft Schweiz (Bank- und Finanzwirtschaftliche Forschungen, vol. 219), Bern /Stuttgart/Vienna 1996.

Meier-Schatz Christian J., Spezielle aufsichtsrechtliche Probleme, insbesondere Risikokontrolle und Grossbankenaufsicht, in: Aktuelle Rechtsprobleme des Finanz- und Börsenplatzes Schweiz, Bern 1999, p. 61–86 [Meier-Schatz, Risikokontrolle].

Meyen Hans G., 120 Jahre Dresdner Bank. Unternehmens-Chronik 1872 bis 1992, Frankfurt 1992.

Moran Michael, The Politics of the Financial Services Revolution. The USA, UK and Japan, London 1991 [Moran, Financial Services Revolution].

Mottet Louis H. (publ.), Geschichte der Schweizer Banken: Bankier-Persönlichkeiten aus fünf Jahrhunderten, Zurich 1987 [Mottet, Schweizer Banken].

Nievergelt Dieter, Die Credit Suisse am Paradeplatz in Zürich (Schweizerische Kunstführer GSK), Bern 1998 (2nd edition) [Nievergelt, Credit Suisse am Paradeplatz].

Nobel Peter, Schweizerisches Finanzmarktrecht: Einführung und Überblick, Bern 1997 [Nobel, Finanzmarktrecht].

Nobel Peter, Selbstregulierung, in: Freiheit und Ordnung im Kapitalmarktrecht – Festgabe für Jean-Paul Chapuis, Zurich 1998, p. 119–134 [Nobel, Selbstregulierung].

Nobel Peter, Überblick über die Entwicklung des Finanzmarktrechts, in: Nobel Peter (publ.), Aktuelle Rechtsprobleme des Finanz- und Börsenplatzes Schweiz, Bern 1999, p. 9–24 [Nobel, Überblick].

Paquier Serge, Banques, sociétés financières, industrie électrique de 1895 à 1914, in: Cassis Youssef, Tanner Jakob (publ.), Banken und Kredit in der Schweiz – Banques et crédit en Suisse (1850–1930), Zurich 1993, p. 201–208.

Pastuszek Horst, Wirtschaftsordnung und Wirtschaftspublizistik, Cologne 1957 [Pastuszek, Wirschaftsordnung].

Peyer Hans Conrad, Von Handel und Bank im alten Zürich, Zurich 1968 [Peyer, Handel und Bank].

Pfau J. J., Das Bankwesen der Schweiz und des Auslandes. Nebst Anregungen zur Gründung eines schweizerischen Clearing House, Zurich 1875 [Pfau, Bankwesen].

Pfund Peter, Allfinanz aus versicherungsaufsichtsrechtlicher Sicht, in: Zobl Dieter (publ.), Rechtsprobleme der Allfinanz, Zurich 1997, p. 67–84.

Pohl Hans, Banken und Bankgeschäfte bis zur Mitte des 19. Jahrhunderts, in: Pohl Hans, Jachmich Gabriele (publ.), Europäische Bankengeschichte, Frankfurt am Main 1993, p. 196–217 [Pohl, Bankgeschäfte].

Pohl Hans, Jachmich Gabriele (publ.), Europäische Bankengeschichte, Frankfurt am Main 1993.

Pohl Manfred, Bankensysteme und Bankenkonzentration von den 1850er Jahren bis 1918, in: Pohl Hans, Jachmich Gabriele (publ.), Europäische Bankengeschichte, Frankfurt am Main 1993, p. 218–233 [Pohl, Bankensysteme].

Popp Werner, Zimmermann Theo (publ.), Strategie und Innovation in Universalbanken. Erfahrungen und

Perspektiven (Bank- und Finanzwirtschaftliche Forschungen, vol. 273), Bern/Stuttgart/Vienna 1998.

Praxmarer Marc A., Allfinanzstrategien aus der Sicht der Banken. Rahmenbedingungen und Gestaltungsansätze unter besonderer Berücksichtigung der Universalbanken in der Schweiz (Bank- und Finanzwirtschaftliche Forschungen, vol. 177), Bern/Stuttgart/Vienna 1993.

Rasi Roland, Unternehmenskultur und Kulturförderung am Beispiel der Schweizerischen Kreditanstalt, in: Kunst als Ausdruck der Unternehmenskultur? Innovation und Integration (Basler Beiträge zu Kunst und Wirtschaft, vol. 1), Basel [1989], p. 77–85 [Rasi, Kulturförderung].

Reichesberg N. (publ.), Handwörterbuch der schweizerischen Volkswirtschaft, Sozialpolitik und Verwaltung, 3 vol., Bern 1903–1911 [Reichesberg, Handwörterbuch].

Reinle Adolf, Kunstgeschichte der Schweiz, vol. 4: Die Kunst des 19. Jahrhunderts. Architektur/Malerei/Plastik, Frauenfeld 1962 [Reinle, Kunstgeschichte].

Ritzmann Franz, Die Schweizer Banken. Geschichte - Theorie – Statistik, Zurich 1973 [Ritzmann, Schweizer Banken].

Ritzmann-Blickenstorfer Heiner (publ.), Siegenthaler Hansjörg et al., Historische Statistik der Schweiz, Zurich 1996 [Ritzmann-Blickenstorfer, Historische Statistik der Schweiz].

Roesle Alexander, Die Entwicklung der Schweizerischen Kreditanstalt (A.G.) in Zürich (Zürcher volkswirtschaftliche Studien, fasc. no. 7), Zurich 1905 [Roesle, SKA].

Saunders Anthony, Walter Ingo, Universal Banking in the United States: What could we gain? What could we lose?, New York 1994.

Scheele Martin, Zusammenschluss von Banken und Versicherungen. Analyse des Privatkundengeschäfts anhand industrieökonomischer Modelle (Schriftenreihe neue betriebswirtschaftliche Forschung 'nfb', vol. 125), Wiesbaden 1994.

Schmid Christian, Varnholt Burkard (publ.), Finanzplatz Schweiz – Probleme und Zukunftsperspektiven, Zurich 1997.

Schmid Walter P., Der junge Alfred Escher. Sein Herkommen und seine Welt. Mitteilungen der Antiquarischen Gesellschaft in Zürich. vol. 55, Zurich 1988 [Schmid, Der junge Escher].

Schürmann Leo, Die Sorgfaltspflichtvereinbarung der Banken in rechtspolitischer Sicht, in: Freiheit und Ordnung im Kapitalmarktrecht – Festgabe für Jean-Paul Chapuis, Zurich 1998, p. 135–142 [Schürmann, Sorgfaltspflichtvereinbarung].

Schütz Dirk, Der Fall der UBS. Warum die Schweizerische Bankgesellschaft unterging, Zurich 1998 [Schütz, UBS].

Schweizerische Bankgesellschaft, Schweizerische Bankgesellschaft 1862/1912/ 1962, Zurich 1962.

Schweizerische Bankiervereinigung (Swiss Bankers' Association, SBA), Der schweizerische Bankensektor: Entwicklung, Struktur und internationale Position. Kompendium Ausgabe 1999, Basel 1999 [SBA, Kompendium 1999].

Schweizerische Bankiervereinigung (Swiss Bankers' Association, SBA), Der schweizerische Bankensektor in Zahlen. Februar 2000, Basel 2000 [SBA, Kompendium Februar 2000].

Schweizerische Bankiervereinigung (Swiss Bankers' Association, SBA), Der schweizerische Bankensektor. Kompendium Ausgabe 2000, Basel 2000 [SBA, Kompendium 2000].

Schweizerische Bankiervereinigung (Swiss Bankers' Association, SBA), Jahresberichte 1970–1999 [SBA, annual report 19..].

Schweizerische Kreditanstalt, Alfred Escher. Ausstellung in der Galerie 'le point' am Hauptsitz der Schweizerischen Kreditanstalt, Zurich 1994 [SKA, Escher 1994].

Schweizerische Lebensversicherungs- und Rentenanstalt 1857–1957, Zurich 1957 [Rentenanstalt 1857–1957].

Schweizerische Nationalbank (Swiss National Bank), Das schweizerische Bankwesen im Jahre 1945ff., Zurich 1944ff. [Schweizerisches Bankwesen 19..].

Schweizerische Nationalbank (Swiss National Bank), Die Banken in der Schweiz 1996ff., Zurich 1995ff. [Die Banken in der Schweiz 19..].

Schweizerische Rückversicherungs-Gesellschaft, Schweizerische Rückversicherungs-Gesellschaft Zürich, 1863–1963, Zurich 1963.

Smith Roy C., Walter Ingo, Global Banking, New York 1997.

Speck Kurt, Strukturwandlungen und Entwicklungstendenzen im Auslandgeschäft der Schweizer Banken, Zurich 1974 [Speck, Auslandgeschäft].

Staehelin Max, Schweizer Banken und Schweizer Wirtschaft im Wandel der Zeit, Zurich 1984.

Stauffer Peter D. et al., Öffentlichkeitsarbeit für Dienstleistungen: Konzept und Praxis der Public Relations bei Banken, Versicherungen und Treuhandunternehmungen, Zurich 1979 [Stauffer, Public Relations bei Banken].

Steigmeier Andreas, Power on. Elektrowatt 1895–1995, Zurich 1995 [Steigmeier, Elektrowatt].

Strehle Res, Trepp Gian, Weyermann Barbara, Ganz oben – 125 Jahre Schweizerische Bankgesellschaft, Zurich 1987 [Strehle, Ganz oben].

Tanner Jakob, Banken und Franken: Zur Geschichte des schweizerischen Finanzplatzes im 19. und 20. Jahrhundert, in: 1291–1991. Die schweizerische Wirtschaft. Geschichte in drei Akten. St-Sulpice 1991, p. 168–171.

Tanner Jakob, Die Entwicklung des schweizerischen Finanzplatzes: Fragestellungen und Problemfelder, in: Cassis Youssef, Tanner Jakob (publ.), Banken und Kredit in der Schweiz – Banques et crédit en Suisse (1850–1930), Zurich 1993, p. 20–28.

Thiemann Hugo, Mut, Motiviertheit und Vision – Schlüssel zur Gestaltung unserer Zukunft, speech to the ETH Zurich (printed version), Zurich, 26 Jan. 1989 [Thiemann, Zukunft].

Thommen Jean-Paul, Betriebswirtschaftslehre, 3 vol., Zurich 1989 [Thommen, Betriebswirtschaftslehre].

Über Banken und deren Anwendung in der Schweiz, Zurich (Broschüre Orell Füssli) 1835 [Über Banken in der Schweiz 1835].

Ungerer Martin, Finanzplatz Schweiz. Seine Geschichte, Bedeutung und Zukunft, Vienna/Düsseldorf 1979 [Ungerer, Finanzplatz Schweiz].

Walter Ingo, Smith Roy C., Investment Banking in Europe. Restructuring for the 1990s, Cambridge 1989.

Weisz Leo, Studien zur Handels- und Industriegeschichte der Schweiz, vol. 1, Zurich 1938.

Wetter Ernst, Die Bank in Winterthur 1862–1912, Winterthur 1914 [Wetter, Bank in Winterthur].

Wetter Ernst, Die Lokal- und Mittelbanken der Schweiz, Zurich 1914 [Wetter, Lokal- und Mittelbanken].

Wilkins Mira, Swiss Investments in the United States 1914–1945, in: Guex Sébastien (publ.), La Suisse et les Grandes puissances 1914–1945, Geneva 1999, p. 91–139 [Wilkins, Swiss Investments].

Ziegler Jean, Une Suisse au-dessus de tout soupçon, Paris 1976.

Zimmermann Werner G., Alfred Escher – Leben und Werk, in: Schweizerische Kreditanstalt, Alfred Escher. Ausstellung in der Galerie 'le point' am Hauptsitz der Schweizerischen Kreditanstalt, Zurich 1994, p. 4–29 [Zimmermann, Escher 1994].

Zimmermann Werner G. (ed.), Alfred Escher. 20. Februar 1819 bis 6. Dezember 1882. Zum Gedenken an seinen hundertsten Todestag, Zurich 1982 [Zimmermann, Escher 1982].

Zobl Dieter (publ.), Rechtsprobleme der Allfinanz, Zurich 1997.

Zuberbühler Daniel, Allfinanz aus bankaufsichtsrechtlicher Sicht, in: Zobl Dieter (publ.), Rechtsprobleme der Allfinanz, Zurich 1997, p. 37–66 [Zuberbühler, Allfinanz].

Picture credits

Private archives/institutions

Bündner Kunstmuseum, Chur	390
Familie Fierz-Etzweiler	58
Familie Straessle (Frau Giselle Irwin)	415
Familie Vieli	415
Gonet & Cie, Geneva	25
Lombard Odier & Cie, Geneva	25
Musée international de la Croix-Rouge et du Croissant-Rouge, Geneva	390
Pictet & Cie, Geneva	25
Robert L. Genillard	178

Publications

Basler Handelsbank (publ.), Die Basler Handelsbank 1862–1912. Festschrift um 50jährigen Jubiläum, Basel 1912.	37
Briner Carl, Hundert Jahre 'Schweiz' Allgemeine Versicherungs-Aktien-Gesellschaft Zürich 1869–1969, Zurich 1969.	211
Gambee Robert, Wall Street – Financial Capital, London 1999.	182, 202, 207
'Helvetia' Schweiz. Unfall- und Haftpflicht-Versicherungsanstalt (publ.), 60 Jahre 'Helvetia', Schweiz. Unfall- und Haftpflicht-Versicherungsanstalt in Zürich. 1894–1954, Zurich 1954.	211
Kleine vermischte Schriften von J. J. Rüttimann, publ. by A. Schneider, Zurich 1876.	212
Lüönd Karl, Neugierig auf morgen. 125 Jahre Zürich. Geschichte und Vision eines Weltkonzerns, Zurich 1998.	211
Mottet Louis H. (publ.), Geschichte der Schweizer Banken. Bankier-Persönlichkeiten aus fünf Jahrhunderten, Zurich 1987.	37
Rieger Hans Jörg, Die Schweizerische Kreditanstalt am Paradeplatz 1876–1976 – Eine Baugeschichte, Zurich 1976.	31
Schmid Hans Rudolf / Meier Richard T., Die Geschichte der Zürcher Börse. Zum hundertjährigen Bestehen der Zürcher Börse herausgegeben vom Effektenbörsenverein Zürich, Zurich 1977.	414
Schweiz. Rückversicherungs-Gesellschaft (publ.), Schweizerische Rückversicherungs-Gesellschaft in Zürich. Gegründet 1863, Zurich (no year)	211
Schweizerische Lebensversicherungs-und Rentenanstalt (publ.), 75 Jahre Schweiz. Lebensversicherungs- und Rentenanstalt Zürich. 1857–1932, Zurich 1932.	211
Schweizerische Lebensversicherungs- und Rentenanstalt 1857–1957, Zurich 1957.	212

Other

Kurt Aeberli ('TRUK'), cartoonist	286
Franziska Bodmer, Bruno Mancia, photographers	148, 149
Jean-Paul Bovée ('BOVÉE'), cartoonist	294
COMET aerial photograph	14
Keystone	176, 390
Silvia Luckner, photographer	146
Peter Morf, photographer	42
Johann Sonderegger ('Joheiso'), cartoonist	223

All pictures not mentioned on this page were sourced from the Credit Suisse Group's Central Corporate Archive, or were provided by the documentation offices of the individual Credit Suisse Group business units.

Acknowledgements

This book could not have been written without the conversations the author had with former and active managers of SKA and Credit Suisse Group, with specialists from different areas of the financial industry and with academics from various disciplines. First and foremost, I would like to thank Rainer E. Gut, Chairman of the Board of Directors of Credit Suisse Group.

For copious advice and constructive criticism of the text, I would like to thank: Christoph Ammann, Member of the Executive Board, CSPB; Alois Bischofberger, Head of Economic Research, CS; Dr. Hugo von der Crone, former Vice Chairman of the Board of Directors, CS Holding; Dr. Gustav Däniker, Kilchberg; Dr. Peter Derendinger, Member of the Executive Board, CSPB; Dr. Hans-Ulrich Doerig, Vice Chairman of the Executive Board and Chief Risk Officer, CSG; Dr. Rolf Dörig, Chief Executive Officer, CS; Dr. Victor Erne, former Member of the Executive Board, SKA; Philip Hess, Chief of Staff, CSG; Dr. Hans Ueli Keller, Member of the Executive Board, CS; Urs Lauffer, Vice Chairman of the Swiss Advisory Board, CSG; Lukas Mühlemann, Chief Executive Officer, CSG; Richard E. Thornburgh, Vice Chairman of the Executive Board, CSFB; Charles G. Ward III, President and Co-Head of Investment Banking and Equities, CSFB; Dr. Thomas Wellauer, Head Financial Services, CSG, and Chief Executive Officer of the Winterthur Group.

For more detailed discussions about specific periods and about individual aspects of and events in the history of the SKA, I am very grateful to: Dr. Oswald Aeppli, former Chairman of the Board of Directors, SKA; Peter Angehrn, Member of the Executive Board, Winterthur Life; Bruno Bonati, Member of the Executive Board, CS; Peter Dubs, Customer Segment Management Private Customers, CS; Hans Rudolf Erzberger, former Head Swiss IT and Operations, CSFB; Dr. Beat M. Fenner, Member of the Executive Board, CS; Reinhard Giger, Head of Construction and Real Estate, CS; Dr. Hans J. Halbheer, former Head of Public Affairs, SKA; Hans Häsli, former Head of Human Resources, SKA; Matthew L. Hickerson, Marketing and Communications Group, CSFB; Robert A. Jeker, former President of the Executive Board, SKA; Robert H. Lutz, former Member of the Executive Board, SKA; Dietrich Marti, former Head of Organization and Applications Development, SKA; Dr. Hans J. Mast, former Head of Economics, Public Relations and Sales Promotion, SKA; Dr. Alfred Schaufelberger, Head of Human Resources, CS; Ernst Schneider, former Vice Chairman of the Board of Directors, SKA; Felix W. Schweizer, former Head of Eastern Europe and CIS Region, SKA; Jennifer E. Serban, Investment Banking Management, CSFB; Hans Peter Sorg, former Member of the Executive Board, SKA; Fritz Stahel, Economic Research, CS; David P. Walker, Head Strategic Planning, CSFB; Dr. Kurt Widmer, former President of the Executive Board, SVB; Dr. William Wirth, former Member of the Executive Board, SKA.

I was also given useful information by: Dr. Peter Affolter, Investment Banking Switzerland, CSFB; Dr. Raimund Birri, Assessment Center, CS; Werner Blum, Head of Dormant Accounts, CSG; Professor Gayle DeLong, Baruch College and City University, New York; Dr. Markus Dennler, Member of the Group Executive Board, Winterthur Insurance; Heinz Detzel, former Head of Resources Management, SKA; Dr. Rudolf Diggelmann, former First Vice President, SKA; Thomas Enzler, Regional Manager, CSPB; Arthur Eugster, former Partner, Bank Wegelin & Co., St. Gallen; Otto Flückiger, Supply Management/Investment, CS; Werner E. Flückiger, former Head of Bank Neumünster; Dora Frey, Art Department, CS; David P. Frick, Head of Legal Department, CSG; Robert L. Genillard, former Vice Chairman of the Board of Directors, CSG, and Honorary Chairman of the Board of Directors, Clariden Bank; Josef Giger, formerly of Corporate Finance, CSFB; Dr. Felix P. Graber, Head of Legal Services, CSPB; Dr. Heinz Gruner, Credit Suisse Communication Center; Christian Gut, Head of Trade Finance/Traders, CS; Felix Hagenbuch, IT Operations, CS; Gerry Heller, Marketing Services, CS; Urs Hofmann, Head of Human Resources, CSPB; Karl Hörsch, Accounts Department, CS; Andreas Hubschmid, Member of the Executive Board, Swiss Bankers' Association; Franz Indergand, Human Resources, CSPB; Alfred Jud, Accounts Department, CS; Robert Jung, former Regional Head Lucerne, SKA; Hans A. Keller, Head Fixed Income and Derivatives, CSFB; Harry Keller, Dormant Accounts, CSG; Fritz Klein, former Head of Global Operational Banking, CSFB; Rolf Krummenacher, Head of Supply Management, CS; Christian Lubicz, Head of Equity Capital Markets Switzerland, CSFB; Dr. Jörg Neef, former Head of PR/Communications, CSFB; Lucie E. de Oude, Human Resources, CSG; Ulrich Pfister, Head Public Affairs, CSG; Gottlieb Plankensteiner, former Associate, Human Resources, SKA; Karin Rhomberg, Head Group Communications, CSG; Dr. Richard Roberts, London; Karl P. Ruoss, Human Resources, CS; Thomas Schärer, Information Management, CSAM; Dr. Christian Schmid, Legal Department, CSG; John Schoch, Corporate Design, CS; Marcel Steinauer, Group IT Office, CSG; Stefan Süess, Construction and Real Estate, CS; Christoph Strasser, Head of Business Process Management and Services, CSPB; Pierre Tschopp, Legal Services, CSPB; Dora Tschumi, former Head of Advertising, SKA; Dr. Conrad Ulrich, Zurich; Dr. Barbara Unger, Legal Services, CSPB; Dr. Robert U. Vogler, Head of Group Historical Research and Archives, UBS; Professor Ingo Walter, Stern School of Business/University of New York, New York; Rochus Weber, former Member of Senior Management in IT and Operations, CS; Rudolf Weber, Staff Training/Computer Based Training, CS; Roger Wichser, Special Finance, CS; Dr. Jürg Wille, Feldmeilen; Dr. Heinz R. Wuffli, former President of the Executive Board, SKA; Urs Wyss, Sponsorship, CS.

The archives, libraries and documentation offices of the following institutions kindly made material available: ABN Amro, Amsterdam (Ton de Graaf); Barclays Bank, London (Jessie Campell); Construction and Real Estate, CS (Paul Müntener); Clariden Bank, Zurich (Peter Gysel); Clariden Heusser, Basel (Ernst Mutschler); Crédit Lyonnais, Paris (Roger Nougaret); CSAM, Zurich (Martin Somogyi); CSFB, New York/London (Ian Anderson, Laura M. Finch, Libby Hills, Robert Lord, Tracy Norris, Gavin Sullivan, Denise Weber-Mishkel); Corporate Services, CSFB; Deutsche Bank, Frankfurt am Main (Dr. Martin Müller); Economic Research, CS; *Euromoney*, London (Rosalyn Hempton); *Finanz und Wirtschaft*, Zurich; 'le point' gallery, Zurich; Marketing Services, CS; *Neue Zürcher Zeitung*, Zurich; SASI, New York (Kenneth Barbalato); Swiss Bankers' Association, Basel; Swiss National Library, Berne; Swiss National Bank, Zurich (Dr. Patrick Halbeisen / Livio Lugano); Swiss Life, Zurich (Augusto Capozzi); Stadtarchiv Ebersbach/D (Eberhard Haussmann); Swiss Re, Zurich (Peter Joos); UBS, Basel (Dr. Urs A. Mueller-Lhotska); Winterthur Insurance, Winterthur (Alfred Stamm); Zurich Central Library, Zurich.

I owe a special thanks to my colleagues in the Foundations, Corporate History and Archives subdivision of Credit Suisse Group. The project would have been impossible to contemplate without their extensive research and systematic review of the sources used. These colleagues are, for Part One and Part Two as well as for various detailed studies: Urban Kaufmann and Dr. Mark De Snaijer; for the chapter on Allfinanz: Fritz Bodenmann, former Head of the Europe Staff Unit at Winterthur Insurance, and Martin Trachsler; for Part Three: Peter Allemann, Martin Fricker, Alexandra Locher, Dr. Brigitte Marti, Adrian Meyer, Dr. Judith Raeber, Barbara Schuler; for preparing the illustrations: Angela Hartmann; for preparing the documents from the Central Corporate Archive and for numerous clarifications: Jürg Hagmann; for the very demanding logistics and IT management: Dominik Pfoster; for various tasks: Marianne Erb; for research connected with many of the key figures: Bernhard Henggeler, former Member of Senior Management at Central Credit Management, CS. I would also like to thank Markus Geel, former Legal Counselor at SKA, who looked after the Texon file from 1977, and who analyzed and prepared the file for this book; Andreas Schiendorfer and Dr. Franz Xaver von Weber for academic analysis and editing. For all his support I would like to thank my deputy as subdivision head, Kurt Egger, who as the former head of the CS Legal Department was also able to contribute much important banking and legal expertise. Finally, I would like to thank Edgar Haberthür for his meticulous proofreading, Roger Turin for producing the charts, and Heinz Egli, of the Buchverlag NZZ, for all his help.

I would like to thank James Knight very much for the translation of this book into English. Many thanks also to Martin Trachsler, Alison Lopez and Alfred Schaufelberger for proofreading the text. Bret A. Cohen's input was also much appreciated.

Joseph Jung